YOUR
WORKING LIFE

EDWIN L. HERR, Consulting Editor

KNOWING YOUR SELF **Will M. Kidwell**
Professor of Psychology
San Diego State University
Vernon A. Wallace
Director, Placement Center
San Francisco State University

MAKING DECISIONS WORK **Patrick J. Weagraff**
Consultant and Program Director
Sierra Media Systems
Sacramento, California
James J. Lynn
Director, Psychological Services and Career Education
Hollister School District
Hollister, California

SCHOOLS AND CAREERS **Edwin L. Herr**
Professor and Head, Department of Counselor Education
The Pennsylvania State University

GETTING THE JOB **Richard L. Lynch**
Program Leader, Distributive Education
Virginia Polytechnic Institute and State University

COMMUNICATION AT WORK **Patrick J. Weagraff**
Consultant and Program Director
Sierra Media Systems
Sacramento, California
James J. Lynn
Director, Psychological Services and Career Education
Hollister School District
Hollister, California

WORKING AT HUMAN RELATIONS **Rosemary T. Fruehling**
Teacher Education Specialist
Minnesota State Department of Education

GROWING ON THE JOB **Maurice E. Wilson**
Director, Department of Manpower Development and
  Training
Dade County Public Schools
Miami, Florida

Your Working Life is an adaptation of the *Career Core Competencies* program. It is also available as seven student text-workbooks. Audiovisual material is also available for each text-workbook.

YOUR WORKING LIFE

A Guide to
Getting and Holding a Job

Gregg Division
McGraw-Hill Book Company

New York	*Düsseldorf*	*Panama*
Atlanta	*Johannesburg*	*Paris*
Dallas	*London*	*São Paulo*
St. Louis	*Madrid*	*Singapore*
San Francisco	*Mexico*	*Sydney*
Auckland	*Montreal*	*Tokyo*
Bogotá	*New Delhi*	*Toronto*

Design Supervisor: Eileen Kramer

Cover Designer: Jackie Merri Meyer
Cover Illustrator: Denman Hampson

Library of Congress Cataloging in Publication Data
Main entry under title:
Your working life.
    "An adaptation of the Career core competencies
program."
    Includes index.
    1. Vocational guidance.   I. Herr, Edwin, L.
II. Career core competencies: a cooperative work-
experience program. [Filmstrip]
HF5381.Y68   650.1'4   79-28360
ISBN 0-07-028342-7

Your Working Life: A Guide to Getting and Holding a Job

    4 5 6 7 8 9 0   SMBP   8 7 6 5 4 3 2 1

CONTENTS

PREFACE

Work? Who needs it? The answer is "just about all of us"—if not for the work itself, then for what it will earn. Most people work for money. They use money to buy the things they need—food, shelter, and clothing. And they use money to buy the things they want—a new car, a vacation, and better food, shelter, and clothing.

People also work because work broadens their sense of identity. "I'm not just Jane Doe; I'm Jane Doe, the carpenter" or "I'm John Doe, the mechanic." People identify with their careers, and their careers give them a sense of belonging or importance. To a certain extent, what people choose to do in their working lives determines how they spend their spare time, who their friends are, and where they live.

Today, people want and expect different things from work, such as personal satisfaction and a means of expressing themselves. Work can be interesting. In fact, more and more people are now saying that their work *should* be interesting. Sure, there are many boring jobs, and every job has its less exciting and more routine aspects. But today, there are many different types of jobs from which to choose. And if you begin your planning early and plan well, you can work at a number of jobs, learn and grow from the experience of each job, and build a successful and satisfying career.

So far, you have read the words "work," "job," and "career." These terms refer to the activities you do to earn a living. Remember that work can take place in school, in an office or factory, at home, or outdoors. It can be done for money or experience on a volunteer, part-time, or full-time basis. The word "job," however, generally refers to an activity performed for pay. The word "career" also relates to work done for pay, but "career" means more than just a particular job. It is the pattern of work a person chooses to do during a lifetime.

Your Working Life is intended to help you develop specific skills for choosing a career, getting a job, and adjusting to work. These are skills that you will learn in each part of the text.

Part 1: Knowing Your Self

You will acquire and develop self-awareness by discovering and analyzing your feelings, aptitudes, traits, interests, abilities, and needs. This self-awareness will form the basis for your career choice.

Part 2: Making Decisions Work

You will develop skills in career decision making by understanding that decision making is not a static event. It is a process involving thought, input from various sources, and a systematic series of steps. You will also learn how to reevaluate your decisions as new information becomes available.

Part 3: Schools and Careers

You will become aware of how technological changes and work and education are related. You will also learn about educational opportunities and their relationship to career options. This will help you develop skills that will enable you to plan your education.

Part 4: Getting the Job

You will learn how to locate jobs, prepare a résumé, and complete job application forms. You will also become familiar with forms such as social security applications and tax forms. You'll learn about the laws involved in the world of work and the procedures important to the job interview and its follow-up.

vii

Part 5: Communication at Work

You will develop your communication skills—listening, speaking, reading, and writing—and learn how they relate to effective job performance.

Part 6: Working at Human Relations

You will understand the importance of good human relations skills as a key to success. Communication skills are the basis for human relations and for developing an awareness of the human relations needs of different groups of people. By understanding this, you will learn how to cope with some of the human relations problems that you may encounter on the job.

Part 7: Growing on the Job

You will learn how to get off to a good start on your first job, how to understand the deductions made from your paycheck, and how to plan for advancement. You will also become familiar with safety standards, working conditions, and the legal rights of workers.

The order of the parts of this book suggests a process. The process begins with learning about yourself—your interests, your aptitudes, your abilities, your needs, your values, and your goals. Once you have some knowledge of careers and of yourself, you begin to make decisions and to use school to help you prepare for your career. Then you are ready to go out and get a job. When you get a job, your skills at communicating and getting along with other people will be crucial to your success. The growth process on the job continues as you understand your work environment and plan for advancement.

YOUR
WORKING LIFE

KNOWING YOUR SELF

LEARNING ABOUT YOUR SELF

Your goals in this unit are given in the following list:

To recognize the following parts of your self—the body self, the social self, the knowing self, and the consistent self

To use the various parts of your self to begin defining your self-identity

To begin recognizing some identity problems that can occur and to begin resolving some of your own identity problems

To begin using your knowledge of self to set career goals

Have you ever heard the statement, "You have to know your self before you can decide what to do with your life"? You might think, "Well, how do I know my self if I don't know what my self is? How do I find my self? How do I look for my self?" Some people feel silly asking such questions. But these are not silly questions. They are very real and difficult questions that everyone has, and even a lifetime of searching does not completely answer them.

You have been trying to find out about your self all your life—first as a child, then as a fast-changing adolescent, and now as a young adult moving toward maturity and independence. Part of developing your *self-awareness*, or knowing who you are, comes from dealing with change in your life. Change is often a part of your life long before you are aware of it. Growing is a type of change. From the time you were an infant, you grew physically, mentally, and emotionally. As you grew, you changed in your appearance, in the things you liked and disliked, and in the things that were important to you. You will probably continue to change and to grow as an individual. Change will not suddenly stop, and it is not something to fear. You can understand change, and you can look forward to it. But you need a systematic way of keeping track of who you are. Right now is a good time to begin discovering some ways to do that.

Your self is everything that makes you who you are. Your self includes your body, which gives you the strength to do heavy work, or the dexterity for fine-detail work, or the steadiness to do routine work. The self includes how you think other people see you and how you see yourself. Your self also includes your mind and its ability to remember things in the past, to learn things in the present, and to think about things in the future. Another part of your self is an ability to remain steady from day to day in your beliefs and in the way you act.

Your *self-identity* is what makes you the person you are. You are unique in this world. There is not another person like you. You have a special set of characteristics that make you different from everyone else. It is these characteristics that make you, you—a one-of-a-kind human being.

Knowing your self-identity comes from being aware of the ways in which you are different from everyone else. It is the knowledge that causes you to say, "This is the kind of person I am. These are the things about my self that make me different." It is what makes you say, "This is me." You can begin to gain this knowledge about your self and to build a good self-identity by taking a closer look at the different parts of your self that combine together to form the unique whole self.

CHAPTER 1

THE BODY SELF

Suppose you wanted to tell a friend about a new person who just moved into the neighborhood. How would you start? More than likely you would begin with how the person looks—tall, brown eyes and hair, a nice smile, and so on. In fact, isn't this description—these physical characteristics—one of the first things you notice when you meet someone?

Your physical makeup is the most obvious part of your self. It includes your bones and muscles, nerves, senses, and all the organs that give you strength and sensitivity. Your body has the ability to grow and heal and to adapt to change. For example, if your vision is poor, your body will try to *compensate*, or make up, for poor eyesight with better hearing. Or perhaps you will be able to recognize things with fewer visual cues. If your muscles are not very strong, your body self may compensate with an ability to do fine, exacting work with your hands.

Each part of your self that combines to form your uniqueness is yours and yours alone. You have a combination of bodily strengths and weaknesses that is different from anyone else's. Other people may be good truck drivers or bricklayers, while you might become a fine watchmaker or mechanic. Or perhaps it is the other way around. Every person's body self is good at some things and poor at others. The trick is to know your body self so that you can make the best choices in planning your life.

KNOWING YOUR BODY SELF

It is important to learn as much as you can about the strengths and weaknesses of your body self. For example, just how good are your eyes? Could a visit to an eye clinic help answer this question? If your eyes are less than perfect, how does your body self compensate? Does the career you are thinking of require perfect vision? If it does, is there a job in the same area that does not require excellent eyesight? Your career plans, in fact all plans you make, should include alternative plans or possibilities for change.

Perhaps you have your heart set on a career as an airplane pilot. But, after an eye checkup, you find that your vision does not meet that job's requirements. Since you like being around planes, you might decide on a closely related job, such as scheduling flights or being a traffic director.

This is just one instance of many, many examples of knowing and using your knowledge of your body self to make realistic career plans. But it does show the kinds of questions, and answers, you must deal with as you explore your body self.

MAKING USE OF YOUR BODY SELF

"I'm just too short," you complain to your friend; "and I'm too tall," your friend groans. All of us have feelings that something is wrong with our bodies, that our bodies are not perfect. Well, little can be done about, say, changing your height from 5 feet, 2 inches, to 6 feet. Yet a great deal can be done about how you look at your body self. It's hard to believe right now, when you think about your shortness or tallness or your beauty or plainness or your hairiness or smoothness, but whatever it is that bothers you about your appearance may make little difference in what you do with your life.

Let's take Martin Luther King as an example. He was a little heavy. Eleanor Roosevelt's teeth were far from perfect. Abraham Lincoln spoke in a squeaky voice. Helen Keller was blind and deaf. But Martin Luther King's voice enabled him to become a great preacher and civil rights leader. Eleanor Roosevelt's vigor and activity

3

made her an international statesperson. Abraham Lincoln had a perceptive mind, and his speeches are still being read and quoted from today. And without sight and hearing, Helen Keller wrote many books.

The point is that it is not what is wrong with your body that counts. It is what you do with what you have that is important. You have to build up your strengths and play down your weaknesses. Most important, you have to accept those things about your body self that you cannot change and find a way to compensate. To make the best use of your body, take the time to explore your strengths and weaknesses. Avoid wasting valuable time and effort trying to be someone you are not. Be aware of your body self.

BODY IMAGE AND SELF-IDENTITY

Your *body image* is your view of the strengths and weaknesses of your body self. Body image plays a big role in the lives of young people because adolescence is a time of rapid physical development. Your self-identity changes as you develop different physical strengths and abilities. A strong, well-coordinated young person who has a black belt in karate feels a certain way about herself or himself. And someone who has received a certificate in music feels another way.

Weight, posture, figure or build, and skin blemishes can be problems to you. Some people think they are all arms and legs, while others feel too big or too small. Some people wish their ears did not stick out, some wish their feet were smaller, and some wish for still other things. Well, we could go on and on, and the list would never end. The important idea is that body image has a strong and direct effect on self-identity. Some people accept this and do not try to do much to adapt to their body images. Often they are unhappy in their lives, and feel that somehow they have missed something important. But many people—such as Martin Luther King, Eleanor Roosevelt, Abraham Lincoln, and Helen Keller—made adjustments for their body images. They adapted their self-identities to their body images in important ways.

Adjusting Your Self-Identity

Many young people are able to adjust their self-identities to their body images. They have decided to take an active role in making good

Ray Charles (top) overcame the handicap of blindness to become a famous musician and entertainer. Marjorie Lawrence (bottom) became a successful opera singer despite the effects of a crippling childhood illness. (Top, Retna, Inc.; bottom, courtesy Metropolitan Opera Archives)

Wilma Rudolph (center), the first American woman to win three gold medals in track at the Olympic Games, set an outstanding example of taking positive action about body image. (Keystone Photo)

things happen to their lives. Consider the case of Wilma Rudolph:

Wilma Rudolph was a 1960 Olympic champion, winning two races and anchoring a victorious relay team. She was the first American woman to win three gold medals for track. The miracle, though, was not so much her winning but the fact that she could run at all.

Born into a large, rural, southern family in 1940, Wilma was a sickly child, fighting many bouts of illness. At the age of 4, double pneumonia and scarlet fever left her with the use of only her right leg. Her family, after consulting a specialist, made sure she received therapeutic treatment, and, at 8, Wilma began to walk with the aid of a special shoe for her left foot.

Evidently, though, her disability didn't make Wilma mope and feel sorry for herself. Her mother says that it didn't make her cross and she tried to play with other children.

By the time she was 11, Wilma no longer needed the shoe, and within three years she became an outstanding basketball player on her high school team. After high school, she went on to Tennessee State University, practicing her running and listening to the advice of her coach. Then another siege of illnesses occurred. She became ill during the 1958 season and couldn't run at all, and in 1959 she pulled a muscle in a meet between the United States and the USSR. In 1960, she became very ill after her tonsils were removed.

Despite it all, Wilma was ready for the 1960 Olympic Games in Rome, winning her three gold medals and setting new world records.

From this example, you can see that you can do something about body image if you try. You may have heard the term *body language*. This is the way your body communicates, without using words, with you and with other people. Sometimes your body tries to tell you the direction you ought to take in planning your life. You must stop and listen to all parts of your body self.

CHAPTER 2

THE SOCIAL SELF

Because the physical, or body self, is the easiest to recognize, it is often the easiest to know. But there are other parts of your self-identity that are important too. To know these parts of your self, you might have to explore in different ways.

You've probably heard the popular song about "people who need people are the luckiest people in the world." But have you really thought about what that means? You spend a lot of time with other people—your parents, brothers and sisters, neighbors, teachers, and friends. Because these people spend time with you and know you, they see you in a certain way. How you think these people see you is another way to learn about your self and to develop a good self-identity. For example, if people find it easy to become friends with you, your idea of your self might be that you are outgoing and easy to get along with. This is part of your social self.

Your *social self* is made up of all the things you can learn about your self from the reactions of people around you. You watch and listen for the reactions of others in the same way that you wait for an echo after shouting down an empty corridor. You also watch and listen for the reactions of others in the same way that you glimpse your reflection while passing a mirror. The echoes and reflections you get about your self from all the people around you help you to learn more about your self-identity.

THE MANY VIEWS OF YOUR SOCIAL SELF

Naturally, because people are different, you get different signals about your self from others. A friend may see you as outgoing, fun-loving, and dependable—someone to confide in. A person you are meeting for the first time, though, may see you as shy and as someone he or she may or may not want to know better. Your math teacher may

see you as a hard worker and a cooperative student, but your shop instructor may feel you waste too much time. Most irritating of all, sometimes your parents seem to like you just the way you are, and at other times they seem to want to change you completely.

All of these different reactions are confusing—right? Well, let's try to get some order into this confusion. First of all, when you focus on your social self and try to know more about your self, be careful not to be too quick in deciding how other people see you. There are no shortcuts to exploring this view of your self. You need to see your self through the eyes of others. And your hardest task will be to make sure that your social self is giving you a realistic image.

ARE YOU WRONG ABOUT OTHERS' THOUGHTS?

Usually, the way others see you is a reasonably accurate picture of your self. This is especially true if the people who are close to you very nearly agree. But sometimes your own view of how others see you— your social self—does not accurately reflect the view that others have of you. Perhaps you clown around a lot to make people laugh at you most of the time. That could mean that they think you have a good sense of humor. Or it could mean that they think you are never serious about anything. Suppose they see you as never being serious, and you think they see you as just having a good sense of humor. Then you have an inaccurate self-identity, and you might have a problem making decisions that are best for your self.

Take the case of Phil, for example:

Phil needed attention. He found that others took notice of him when he acted like a clown. So he joked and fooled around most of the time during his sophomore and junior years of high school. In fact, about the only way that he got along with people was as the class clown.

Phil liked the attention he got, but he did not think of himself just as a clown. He also had his serious side, and he felt that everyone he knew could see that side of him too. When Phil decided to run for class president, he didn't have any trouble getting the signatures he needed on his petition. He thought he had a good chance to win. After all, he was popular, and he never had any problem talking to groups of people.

Phil worked hard on his speech for the nominating assembly. Standing before the assembly, he began, "My friends, I want to be your class president in order . . ." But that was as far as he got. There was an uproar of laughter from the audience. When the noise died down a bit, Phil started again, "But I'm really serious about . . ." Again, he got no farther. This time the laughter was joined by stomping feet and the rhythm of clapping hands. Everyone thought he was a riot and that this was the greatest put-on he had ever come up with.

Phil saw that there was no way the audience was going to take him seriously. So he yelled into the microphone, "Now that we have your attention, I'd like to let the serious candidates take over." He sat down quickly to hide his disappointment and embarrassment.

Phil had a false view of how other people saw him. He had been using only one way of getting along with the people around him. He had

Having a realistic view of your social self will help you to be successful in choosing a career. If you enjoyed helping others as a child, you could satisfy this characteristic in your career choice. (Philip Teuscher)

not thought very carefully about the impression he made. He thought that people could see a lot of things about him—more serious things that would make him a good choice for class president.

In order to get a better view of how others see him, Phil needs to take a long, hard look at his social self. Then he will probably want to begin acting in a way that is more true to the way he wants others to see him.

YOU CAN IMPROVE YOUR SOCIAL SELF

Sometimes you may not be satisfied with your social self. You may see others expecting certain things from you that do not agree with your inner view of your self. Have you been in a situation where your friends expected you to act in one way, but your respect for your self, or your *self-esteem*, made you want to act differently? Phil had this problem.

Everyone expected Phil to be a clown, but he wanted to be serious about running for office. In the end, he just decided to act the way people expected him to act. Even though his self-esteem was hurt, Phil pretended to be clowning all along.

When there is a large difference between your social self and your inner view of your self, you should give this careful thought. Perhaps you are the kind of person who enjoys doing things alone. But, to please other people, you may act in a way that gives the false impression that you prefer always to be doing things in a group. If this is so, then there is a good bit of difference between your inner view of your self and your social self. There may come a time when you may have to say, "Look, that's just not me. I have a different idea of who I am. According to my self-identity—how I feel about my self—I like being with people, but I also like to do some

things alone too. So from now on, I'm going to start acting like I really am inside."

USING YOUR SOCIAL SELF

Understanding the difference between your social self and your inner view of your self can also help you select a job. Careers can be separated into three categories: those that deal with people, those that deal with data (information), and those that deal with things. Suppose you are trying to decide between working with people, such as a teacher, or working with things, such as an automobile mechanic. Having choices is good, although making the decision is often difficult. But if you have a good self-identity, you can choose without too much trouble. For example, if you know that you enjoy dealing with people and you don't like working alone for a long period of time, you can easily choose the right category of careers. You would probably train for a career working with people—a teacher, perhaps—rather than one dealing with things—a mechanic.

Take a close look at your social self and see if it agrees with your self-esteem. Just as it is helpful to listen to the messages from your body self, it is a good idea to pay attention to the reactions you get from people around you.

You can't please other people all the time, but if others often disapprove of things you are doing, usually it is not wise to ignore them. Naturally, you will want to examine carefully the reactions of other people. You will not always change your behavior, but sometimes you will find that some change will be for the better. The important thing to remember is that some change should be good for you. This type of change is all part of knowing more about your self and of keeping your self alive, well, and growing.

CHAPTER 3

THE KNOWING SELF

Imagine you have just come home from school, and you decide to have a snack. As you are eating, your mind starts to wander. "Let's see, what do I have to do tonight? Well, there's homework, of course. I want to go see Bob's new puppy. And Jane has a new·LP she wants me to hear. I've got to prepare for my meeting with my counselor, Mrs. Paulett. I wonder if Phil has finished that book he said I could borrow. Maybe I'll give him a call later." And on and on your mind goes, jumping from one thing to another.

This is an example of another way of exploring your self. It is called your knowing self. Your *knowing self* is that part of your mind that thinks about your self and its world. Your mind remembers the past, thinks in the present, and imagines the future. Your mind is like a screen. Ideas and images of people, things, and places are always flowing across it. This is called the *stream of consciousness.*

THE KNOWING SELF COLLECTS
AND SELECTS INFORMATION

You and a friend may be sitting in a room in an apartment in a busy city. In the room, the radio is playing. In another room, someone is talking on the telephone. The windows in the apartment are open, and you can hear the traffic from the streets. There are many things going on both inside and outside that room. Your mind is aware of most of these things. Yet, you are able to carry on a serious conversation with your friend in the midst of all the activity. How is this possible?

It is possible because the mind filters out some of what flows through it. This is how we understand a situation, or remember a face, or think of a way to solve a problem. Your mind knows that you are in a room in your friend's apartment. Your mind knows all the faces you see in the apartment. Your mind also knows that you can solve the problem of getting home from that apartment, even though you live across the city. In a way, the mind is like a fish filtering water through its gills. The fish takes the oxygen it needs out of the water. The mind takes what it needs out of the stream of consciousness and adds that to the knowing self.

THE KNOWING SELF USES INFORMATION

Suppose somebody says to you, "Decide what career you want to prepare for. Decide how you want to spend much of your working life." You can agree to begin the process of making this decision or you can decide not to worry about this problem right now. Each of these choices requires thought and causes certain consequences. Making either decision is your option, and yours alone to take.

If you agree to decide on a future career, you will use your knowing self. A great deal of information goes into the stream of consciousness. This information includes ideas about how people do their work, the skills they need, where they work, how much money they earn, whether their work is easy or hard, whether it makes them happy, and much more. Your knowing self will draw from all this information you have gathered about the world of work. Even though you cannot know about all the possibilities open to you in the working world, you may have to make a decision. At least, you may select something that is not completely worked out in your mind.

Throughout your life, your knowing self will continue to collect more information about your self and your world. You can see this from the way your knowing self has worked so far. There are always new things to learn, new people to meet, new ideas to try, and so forth. There will always be something more to know.

No decision is ever absolutely final, because new knowledge may force you to change your mind. There is nothing wrong with changing your plan. For example, you may want to become a truck driver and then realize that you don't enjoy being away from home for long periods of time. Or you may take a job that you consider to be

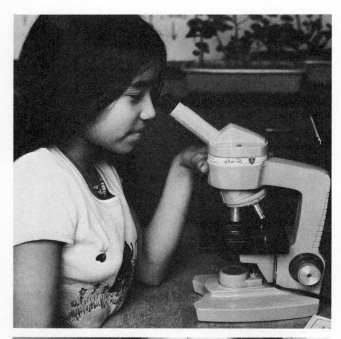

The knowing self keeps on learning as you grow and mature. (Top, Philip Teuscher; bottom, courtesy United Nations/Nagata/jr)

only temporary and learn that there are great opportunities for you in that type of work.

There is a lot of truth in that tired old phrase about "a rapidly changing world." New technology is being developed every day, and these advancements cause changes in many job areas. For example, many farmers had to learn about and use new methods of pest control when DDT was banned by the federal government as a pesticide. The world of work is always changing. And you are always changing. These changes are part of growing, and they make it necessary for your knowing self to be constantly gaining and using new knowledge.

THE KNOWING SELF GROWS

Your knowing self continually grows and develops. Think of the people you have known and have tried to be like at different times in your life. All of us have people whom we look up to as models. It is natural to try to identify with someone you admire. When you were young, you probably imitated one of your parents. Or you tried very hard to be like an older brother or sister. A little later you may have admired a more glamorous person, such as a movie star, a popular singer, or a sports figure.

As you mature, you look for the best qualities of all the people you think highly of. And you try hard to make their qualities your own. Finally, you will find some of your own qualities that you can also admire. As you add them to your total self, you will develop a good self-identity.

The Knowing Self and Experiences

It is both natural and helpful for young people to use models in the development of their self-identity. But there comes a time when you have to leave your models and let your own experiences form your knowing self.

The following story of Henry Ford illustrates what the knowing self means:

> Henry's parents did not earn much money, and they were not well educated. Young Henry went to school in the country district of Greenfield, Michigan. He did well in school, but he liked most to tinker with things. Henry's parents did not always like the way he spent his time, but Henry was naturally curious.
>
> When Henry was 16, he became an apprentice machinist. He worked hard at his job and at

trying to understand himself. At work one day, he thought of the strange idea that a horse-drawn buggy could be made to move by itself with the power of a piston engine.

There was no sense talking about this strange idea, because people would only laugh. So Henry decided to make an engine-driven buggy in the small house where he lived. In his spare time, he put together what he called a "quadricycle." "Quad" means four in Latin, and Henry's horseless carriage had four wheels. It also ran by its own power. But this early "car" also had a problem. Henry had been so busy making his quadricycle that he forgot he would someday have to get it out of his room. So he had to tear down a wall in the house to get the quadricycle outside for a ride.

Henry was proud of his quadricycle. He invited a friend to ride along and to show off the new invention. His parents were not interested in taking a ride. Henry's parents were farmers who depended on horses to do much of their work. They did not care for a horseless carriage.

The Knowing Self and Conflicts

Many young people, especially in the days of Henry Ford, identified with their parents when it came to choosing a vocation. Henry's knowing self was beginning to understand that he did not want to farm like his parents. He wanted to make buggies that pulled themselves. Henry Ford knew that he was becoming mature, because his knowing self was making him aware, but his parents did not see him as a mature and serious young man. Henry had a problem. His knowing self told him to do certain things, and his social self told him that doing these things would displease his parents. A problem such as this is known as a *conflict*, or a battle, between the different parts of your self. Finding a solution to a conflict takes courage. But, and this is even more important, it takes a strong sense of self-identity. Henry Ford knew himself. He had a well-developed self-identity.

Today, young men and women have choices that were not available to their parents. But having choices involves making decisions, and making decisions involves a strong and well-developed self-identity.

THE KNOWING SELF ADJUSTS

The knowing self adjusts to handle different situations in different ways. You are not *static.* That is, you don't always act the same way—unchanging, regardless of the circumstances. For example, when you are with your parents, you act in one way. With a teacher, you act still differently, perhaps being a little more formal than with your parents. And when you're with a friend, you act in still a third way. The point is that people shift gears to meet a particular situation. There is nothing dishonest or phoney about shifting gears. This is all part of getting along with others and with your self. Henry Ford shifted gears in that he followed his own opinions, not his parents'. If he had been static, he could not have made his quadricycle.

THE KNOWING SELF SHOULD BE USED TO STAY ALERT

To achieve some of your dreams in life, it is important to make the best possible use of your knowing self. It is never wise to pass up a chance to learn something new—whether about new people, new places, new situations, or new parts of our selves. Because so much of your life will be spent at work, you should seek as much knowledge as you can about the kinds of work you can do and want to do and the things you need to know to do them. You can gain knowledge by using the knowing self almost anywhere—at home, in school, with friends, at the library, on television, on the job, and in many other kinds of situations.

The knowing self has to be used and kept alert at all times. Or, like a body without exercise or a talent without practice, it will get out of shape and won't be able to serve when needed.

Your future plans, whatever they are, require that all parts of your self be strong, healthy, and well developed. You will always need the abilities of your knowing self. And, like the messages of the body self and the social self, the knowing self keeps on working in an effort to help you develop a good self-identity.

CHAPTER 4

THE CONSISTENT SELF

Mary is excited as she and her brothers help their parents in the kitchen. They are preparing food for the family reunion. "I can hardly wait to see Bob, and Uncle Ed, and Aunt Alice," Mary says. "It's been so long since they moved away. I wonder if Uncle Ed is still a big teaser, or if he's changed."

"I'm sure, Mary, that he's changed," her mother says.

"Oh, I don't know about that," Mary's father says as he picks up a box of food to put in the car. "I remember him when we were boys growing up. I bet, Mary, that you will find that he's changed but that he hasn't changed."

As they ride to the lake where the reunion is being held, Mary puzzles over what her father had said. "How can Uncle Ed change, but not change?" she wonders.

They finally arrive at the lake. Uncle Ed and his family are already there. "Uncle Ed," Mary yells as she gets out of the car. Uncle Ed hugs her and then stands back to look at her. "Well, Mary, you certainly have changed," he says. "You've grown so."

Mary looks at him and says, "You have too." Uncle Ed has gotten just a little bit stouter and has a little less hair.

Then Uncle Ed breaks into a laugh and says, "Tell me, Mary, are you still collecting all the stray cats in the neighborhood?"

Mary grins back at him, realizing what her father meant. "Yes, Uncle Ed, and a few dogs too. In fact, next fall after I graduate I'm going to State University. I'm really thinking about being a veterinarian."

Surely this same situation has happened to you—someone whom you haven't seen in a long time commenting on the changes in you. Yes, you have changed. And most of that change is physical. You've grown taller, perhaps, or slimmer or put on some weight. Maybe even the color of your hair has changed, but in some ways you have not changed. Because, although you change as you grow and mature, you do remain basically true to the ways you have acted and thought in your past. This steady and constant quality of your life is called the *consistent self.* The consistent self makes all the parts of your self-identity fit together as the whole self. If you did not have a consistent self, your friends, parents, and teachers would not recognize you from day to day. It would even be difficult for you to recognize yourself.

Your knowing self and social self adjust to handle different situations in a variety of ways. For example, when you are at home, in school, with your friends, or on a part-time job, you probably play a different role, or a different part, in each situation. While the parts of your self are changing to handle these different roles, you are still the same person. It is your consistent self that keeps you basically the same from day to day. For example, perhaps you are a friendly, easygoing person. It could be that you and a friend have an argument, and both of you are really angry about whatever happened. Your friend seems to stay angry, though, and barely nods when you meet. But you, being you, decide to be the first to break the ice. You speak first, and soon the two of you are good friends again.

Sometimes there may be conflict, or a battle, between the different roles you play. Sometimes your self will have to adjust, or make some changes, in order to handle these conflicts. For example, if you enjoy the freedom to move around in the outdoors, you might find it difficult to adapt to a job that keeps you in an office all day. To solve this conflict, you might decide to get an outside job. Or you might adjust your consistent self by learning to enjoy the challenge of the inside job and getting in your outdoor activities during weekends and other spare time.

THE CONSISTENT SELF IS A DEVELOPING SELF

You started to become your self from the time you were born, perhaps even before you were born. When you were a child, you first learned about lasting relationships in your family. You learned about what things you were able to do and what things you couldn't do, about what belonged to you and what you couldn't take. Probably when you were about 2 years old, you started to say no to the people around you— especially to your parents. You were beginning to develop a sense of your own self and how it was separate from the wishes of your family.

As you went through school, you gradually developed likes and dislikes in terms of subjects, people, and activities. Perhaps you liked sports, art, and music more than you liked science, reading, and math. Or maybe it was the other way around. You probably began regularly to choose activities in the areas you liked more than in the areas you didn't like. You may even have developed a pattern of grades in school that reflected this growing consistency in your self. Possibly you began to get poor grades in some subject areas you didn't like, and your consistent self prompted you to try to get better grades in every subject in school. You weren't happy with good grades in some areas and poor grades in other areas.

Being consistent does not mean that you are static. The consistent self grows just as the self grows. The self is always developing because there is always some change, some growth, and some conflict in your self and your life. Just as you began saying no as a toddler, you probably began disagreeing with your parents quite frequently during your junior high school years. That is because you were entering a new period of developing an awareness of your special abilities and needs. You were also developing your self-identity.

Such periods can be uncomfortable, or even frightening. But over a period of time, your consistent self carries you through. You work out some balance between the safety and comfort of a family and the need to strike out on your own. You fight to gain your independence but recognize that you still need the help and support that your home and family can give. You may argue a lot with your parents, but you can still find ways to show your love and to accept theirs. Getting your independence can often be a difficult and confusing time for you and everyone around you. But something good is also happening. From this period of change and conflict, a consistent "you" is coming into being.

Although conflict can be a problem, some conflicts can help you decide what is most important to you. For example, you might be the kind of person who doesn't like to travel on buses,

If enjoyment of outdoor activity is part of your consistent self, you might be most satisfied in a career that focuses on appreciation of the outdoors. As Robert Frost said, "My object in living is to unite/My avocation and my vocation/As my two eyes make one in sight. . . ." (Courtesy United Nations/Y. Nagata/ARA)

trains, or planes. But, at the same time, you might find it exciting and interesting to visit new places. The conflict here, of course, is how can you get to see new places if you don't like to travel? You probably will work out this conflict as you become aware of what is more important to you. Is your desire to visit new places more important than your not wanting to travel? Or is your not wanting to travel more important than your desire to see new places? You'll find out when you have to make that decision.

HOW CONSISTENT CAN YOU BE?

Everybody has a lot of different things to do, believe, and try in a lifetime. And everyone is a complex person, playing many roles, who grows and changes. At the same time, the consistent self is also at work.

The late President Lyndon B. Johnson once described himself as "a free man, an American, a United States Senator, a Democrat, a liberal, a conservative, a Texan, a taxpayer, a rancher, and not as young as I used to be nor as old as I expect to be." Although LBJ acted all these roles and others during his lifetime, his family and friends were probably able to recognize him. They recognized him because his consistent self always came through in each role he played.

At one time or another, someone has said to you, "Why did you do that? That certainly isn't like you." That person didn't recognize you in your actions. Your consistent self wasn't at work then. Your consistent self should always come through in each role you play. Your consistent self keeps all your roles in tune with your self-identity, whether you are with your friends or family, at school, or on the job. Your consistent self makes all the people in your life able to recognize you. And your consistent self keeps you the basic person that you are.

Awareness of the consistent self helps set career goals. What clues can you learn from your consistent self? (Top, Philip Teuscher; bottom, Martha Swope/Dance Theater of Harlem)

Getting It All Together

1. Why is it important to explore your self now?

2. Describe at least one way you can improve your body self, your social self, your knowing self, and your consistent self.

3. How will knowing your self help you select a career?

4. How does your concept of your self today differ from your self-concept of five years ago?

5. In what ways do your relationships with other people affect the development of your self-image?

EXPLORING THE DIMENSIONS OF YOUR SELF

Your goals in this unit are given in the following list:

To recognize some of the many dimensions of your self—aptitudes, traits, interests, abilities, and needs

To begin using some of the many dimensions of your self—aptitudes, traits, interests, abilities, needs—to develop your self-identity

To recognize roadblocks to discovering the dimensions of your self

To begin using some of the dimensions of your self—aptitudes, traits, interests, abilities, needs—to understand your career goals

In the nineteenth century, when Elizabeth Blackwell decided to become a doctor, no medical college would accept her. Most of the men felt they would be embarrassed to have a woman in their classes. But Elizabeth was definitely set on finding her own identity. No matter what other people thought, Elizabeth knew that she wanted to work in medicine. So she applied to 22 medical schools before one finally accepted her—almost as a joke. In 1849, she graduated at the top of her class.

When Elizabeth went to New York City to begin her work as a physician, she discovered that none of the hospitals there would let a woman doctor practice medicine. Elizabeth knew what she had to do. She opened her own hospital and started a medical school so that other women would finally have the chance to become doctors. The New York Infirmary, which Elizabeth Blackwell founded, is still in operation today.

Not only did Elizabeth Blackwell stretch her own abilities but she also helped others find their identities. She trained other doctors and nurses in her hospital to go into poor neighborhoods to help heal people who could not afford hospital care. All this happened because Elizabeth Blackwell was determined to find her own identity.

Today women are no longer faced with the problem Elizabeth Blackwell had. But, like Elizabeth Blackwell, many of you—both men and women—may have doubts and troubles about where you are going. To grow from the person you are to the kind of person you want to become, you will need more than the basic tools of self-awareness discussed in Unit 1.

Your feelings and emotions are two dimensions of your self that affect not only your body self and your social self but also your knowing self and your consistent self too. You will need ways to recognize them and methods of dealing with them. There are certain aptitudes and traits that will help you recognize and develop your consistent self. Your knowing self can help you recognize your interests and abilities and lead you to develop new ones. After developing these parts of your self, there are certain needs that must either be filled or changed.

Becoming aware of the dimensions of your self can help you avoid many disappointments and hurts. This awareness can help you widen your horizons and become better at new and different things. It can help you to find the things at which you are most likely to succeed and to build personal strengths.

CHAPTER 5

YOUR APTITUDES AND TRAITS

Josie entered the classroom where her math class was being held. She felt a little nervous. "I wonder what this is going to be like," she said to Grace as she took a seat next to her. "I'm a little scared."

"Why?" said Grace. "You always get good marks in math. I'm the one who should be scared. I always struggle through every math course."

"From what I've heard," said Josie, "this is different from anything we've had."

Mr. Ortiz explained that he wanted to get an idea about everyone's math background. He started questioning the class and asked for volunteers to answer. The questions were easy at first, but, as they became harder, fewer and fewer hands went up.

At one point, Mr. Ortiz asked a very difficult question, especially for a class with no geometry background. Josie sat and thought and suddenly her hand popped up. Then she answered the question correctly.

She and Mr. Ortiz looked at each other with surprised expressions on their faces. "Well, Josie, very good!" he said. "How did you figure that out?"

"I really don't know, Mr. Ortiz. It just came to me. I remembered a problem we had in last year's class, and I just sort of put the two together."

"You should do well in this class, Josie," Mr. Ortiz said. "Perhaps, you should think about taking advanced courses later. You certainly have an aptitude for math."

WHAT ARE APTITUDES?

Aptitudes are seemingly natural tendencies to do well in some areas. An aptitude is not a skill or an ability. An aptitude only makes it a little easier for you to acquire a skill or ability. For example, you may have an aptitude—or bent, as it is sometimes called—in math, as Josie did, or perhaps in sports, or in writing, or whatever.

What you have to remember, though, is that, although you may have an aptitude in some particular area, you will not be able to develop a skill or ability in that area without work and practice. For example, no one can be a great musician without musical aptitude, but aptitude alone does not make a great musician. It also takes years of study and practice.

The same is true of all careers. If you want to be good at what you do, you have to find something for which you have an aptitude and then work hard to acquire the necessary skills and background for your chosen career. You probably have many aptitudes, but you will be able to develop good skills in only a few of your aptitude areas.

Different People Have Different Aptitudes

Different people seem to be born with different natural gifts. Or, if they were not born with these gifts, something about their experience makes them good in certain areas. Some people seem to have a gift for language. For instance, they learn to read easily, they are natural storytellers, they find it easy to write interesting letters, or they do particularly well in word games. In short, they have an aptitude for language. This is often called verbal aptitude.

If you have a verbal aptitude, that means it will be possible for you to learn rather quickly the skills needed, for instance, to do newspaper reporting, or writing, or editing books or magazines. You will have to work hard to develop your skills, but you will be able to succeed if you do work at it. If you don't have a verbal aptitude, you probably will not be able to succeed at these kinds of jobs. You would have to work too long and too hard to develop the needed skills. Therefore, you would try to find and develop some other aptitude that will make it easier for you to succeed in another occupational area.

Aptitudes range over all the areas of human activity. Some people are good at learning about shapes, space, and proportions—the sort of thing that might make them good drafting technicians, architects, artists, or landscapers, for example. Some people have an aptitude for learning how to think logically and solve problems. These abilities may make them good mathematicians, or scientists, or computer programmers, or actuaries. People who have a mechanical aptitude understand how machines work. They can develop skills at putting things together or taking them apart. Such people can become mechanics or electronics technicians, for example.

The Parts of the Self Have Different Aptitudes

Some aptitudes are associated mainly with the body self. Perhaps you can easily become skilled at sports, typing, dancing, driving, or some other activity that depends mainly on coordination, reflexes, senses, or another part of the body self. You might already be exploring a dancing career.

Some aptitudes are linked with the social self. Perhaps it is very easy for you to size up a person within a short time after first meeting. Or you may find it very easy to know just what a friend needs to get out of a bad mood. You might already be developing your abilities in a sales or a counseling career.

Some aptitudes are associated with the knowing self. You might find it easy to learn things that require careful thought. Or perhaps you can think of a lot of ways to solve a problem with little effort. You might have the skills needed to become a lawyer or a researcher.

Some aptitudes are linked with the consistent self. It may be easy for you to remain calm in a crisis, or to keep an even outlook when people about you seem to swing from one side to another. Perhaps you are able to keep friends out of trouble when they have the impulse to pull off some dangerous prank. If such things come easily for you, you may be able to develop the skills needed to become a manager, or social worker, or law enforcement official. You might be suited for any job that requires someone who can be steady in difficult, changing situations.

People who have aptitudes for learning shape, space, and proportion might be suited for careers in architecture or art. Aptitudes are developed through study and practice.

WHAT ARE TRAITS?

"Pete is just naturally even-tempered and good-natured. He smiles all the time, and always has a good word for everybody. He's been like that since the day he was born." Surely you've heard something like that before—either about your self or about someone else. The person is saying that Pete—and everybody—has certain traits. And it seems that everyone is born with these traits.

Whether or not we are born with traits is not clear. Psychologists can't agree on how much of our heredity and how much of our environment influence the development of traits. Traits result from a combination of both, but the exact percentage of each is not known.

A *trait* is a distinguishing mark of one's personality. Although some traits seem to be built-in parts of the self, many are habits that have been learned and developed over a period of several years.

How Traits Develop

It is dangerous, though, to think that we are born with all of our traits. If so, this would mean that we can't change, and we certainly do change. For example, people are not born biting their nails or disliking certain foods. Rather, certain characteristics of our personalities or patterns of behavior are built up over the years. These characteristics or patterns of behavior are called "habits." A *habit* is any behavior a person learns and then shows consistently and automatically. A habit then becomes a recognizable part of the self, and in that way becomes a learned trait. A habit can be more easily changed and improved than a trait. You can stop biting your nails or smoking and learn to like certain foods. No habit is easy to change. It depends on how important the change is to you.

If you develop the trait of not thinking things through for your self, you will probably also develop the trait of depending on others to make your decisions. If you carry out these traits for a few years, gradually people will get to think that you aren't very independent. And they will think you are just naturally helpless.

And they are partly right. You are helpless because that's the easiest way for you to act, and it is hard to change. With some time and effort, you can change. You could begin to get into habits that will make you more independent.

Independence is a good trait to develop. Independence is a good trait to acquire, but what is it? Independence is freedom from control by others. It is made of *competence*, or being able to do things well. It is made of *self-sufficiency*, or knowing how to take care of yourself. It is made of *self-discipline*, or being able to make yourself do certain things when they should be done.

A sense of individuality is also important to independence. *Individuality* means developing your own abilities, being your self, not being an imitation of somebody else. If you always try to please other people, you are bound to fail. To be independent, you must develop your own ideals. Real independence cannot belong to you unless you understand and respect the individuality and feelings of others.

Children usually adopt the ideals of their parents. Older children look to community leaders, athletes, writers, performers, or other glamorous persons for their ideals. Adolescents may admire their parents and people they read about or see on TV, but they need people in their own lives to model themselves on, such as coaches, teachers, bosses, youth workers, or counselors. In adolescence you get the skills you need to be independent as an adult. Your upbringing at home shapes you, of course, but your own ideals are taking shape too.

Your social self probably helps to develop independence more than any other part of you. Your social life is launched in babyhood when you first relate to your family and goes into orbit in high school and the later years. Meeting people, getting along with them, and deciding who and who not to be with all help you to develop independence. You are making decisions about people. You see if your decisions are good ones. If they are bad ones, you can change them. All this gives you the feeling that you can handle your self and that you can handle your life—that is what independence is all about.

Organization is a good trait to develop. As a young adult, you start to fit all the pieces of your self-identity together. It is a little like a jigsaw puzzle. You must find the proper place for each piece to fit. And if a piece is missing, it certainly shows. *Organization* is the process of putting these pieces together. If you succeed at developing the trait of independence, then you can better organize your self. Someone will probably tell you, "You know, you've really gotten yourself together."

Traits, such as the ability to show kindness, are parts of the self that are developed over the years. (Courtesy United Nations/Jerry Frank)

What sort of pieces are you trying to get together? Your interests, your abilities, your needs, getting along with people, what you think and feel about marriage, where you want to live—all these pieces must fit together if your self-identity is going to be organized so that you can use it. The pieces must not only fit, they must get along with each other.

What does organization mean? Read the case of Jeanne that follows:

Jeanne started to organize herself early in high school. She liked schoolwork, and she was active in out-of-class projects. Jeanne grew up in a large family, and her parents encouraged her to be active in making decisions.

In her junior year, Jeanne decided that she would like to be an architect. She talked her decision over with her parents, her counselor, and her mechanical drawing teacher. All the feedback she got from them and from others supported her opinion that she might be a good architect and that she might like it.

Jeanne laid out a plan. First, she had to succeed in high school, particularly in mechanical drawing and mathematics courses. Second, she had to get into a college architectural program. Third, she had to find part-time jobs, preferably in architectural firms, to pay her way through college. Fourth, she had to look for opportunities to master a variety of architectural skills beyond college because architectural firms hire only the best people available.

Jeanne had made a good plan. It would take independence and hard work. But her self-esteem told her she could do it. She had an organized self-identity. She knew her traits and aptitudes, and she decided they would help her become a good architect. Jeanne knew her abilities, and she believed they could be satisfied by her plans. Jeanne also had a sense of purpose, and that is why she was able to think up such a plan and follow it. Jeanne had consistency—she was able, day after day, to keep on working toward her career goals.

Becoming independent and well organized does not mean choosing a definite career at an early age. It does mean, however, that you know what direction you are going in and you are able to make appropriate plans. Jeanne, for some reason or other, may decide later that architecture is not for her. However, with an independent and organized self-identity, she will be able to adjust her plans and make use of her experiences in whatever she does.

Jeanne was successful because she organized her self-identity early in life. And now is the time for you to learn about your aptitudes and to develop them. When you do this, you are also on the way toward developing your independence. This trait of independence, in turn, leads to the organization of your self-identity. You will then be able to use all parts of your self toward exploring a suitable career. Some people need more time than others to pull themselves together. With patience and effort, everyone can be independent and organized, and able to make competent decisions about his or her own career goals.

6

YOUR INTERESTS AND ABILITIES

How do you spend most of your time? Do you like to read or do creative writing? Do you take part in sports or play a musical instrument? Do you like working with plants or repairing cars? Do you enjoy dancing? Or do you prefer doing things with your hands? Whatever you like to do and spend much of your time doing are considered your *interests*. Your interests include all the activities you enjoy doing, think about doing, or dream of doing.

Like most people, you probably have a lot of interests. But are you really good in each of your interest areas? Or do you have ability in only a few of your interest areas? Your abilities are limited to the few areas of interest that you have taken the time and effort to develop. You might find all sports interesting, but have the time and aptitude to develop your ability in only swimming or basketball. You might be interested in spaceflight, but have only the opportunity and aptitude to become involved in learning about electronic communications systems involved in spaceflight.

HOW MANY ARE TOO MANY?

It is almost impossible for a person to have too many interests. Part of the joy of life is the almost endless variety of interesting things to do. You may find that nearly everything appeals to you and that you easily become involved in most things you read or hear about. That's fine—you probably get a lot out of life. But problems can arise if you let your interest in everything prevent you from becoming good at a few things. In other words, you must learn to develop your abilities in those areas that interest you most.

It Takes Time and Money to Pursue Interests

It is a basic law of economics that your human and physical resources are limited. Your *human resources* are things like your knowledge, aptitudes, time, and energy. Your *physical resources* are your earnings, your ability to get credit, your savings, and the things you own. If you use your time or your money to do one thing, that may prevent you from doing something else.

When a resource is limited in quantity, you must choose how to use it. You have to focus on only certain interests and abilities. You have to choose how best to spend your limited time and money to develop your interests and abilities. You must concentrate your resources on the areas in which you are likely to succeed.

It Takes Concentration to Focus Interests

One way to teach yourself how to focus on your interests and abilities is to concentrate on one thing at a time. This takes discipline. At the beginning, you may have to cut out whatever calls for your attention outside the task you are trying to do.

Here's an example of how you can concentrate your energies to develop an ability. Suppose your task is to improve your reading ability. You may want to follow this advice:

> Select a room that is as free of noise as possible. Leave your radio, tapes, or phonograph somewhere else. However, sometimes a little soft background music can help drown outside noises. Sit in a straight-backed chair, because softer chairs may encourage you to doze. Pick something

21

to read that promises to keep your interest. And select something that is slightly below your reading level. Put a time limit on how long you read, so that you stop while you still want to read more. Do this at the same time each day or night. Increase the time you spend reading every few days, but never read long enough so that you will become bored.

By taking these simple steps, you can develop the ability to concentrate while you read. This method works not only for reading but for other abilities as well. The feeling of accomplishment you will get will build up your self-confidence. And developing an ability also builds up self-confidence.

CAREERS SHOULD REFLECT INTERESTS AND APTITUDES

No matter how talented we might think we are, none of us can develop ability in every area of

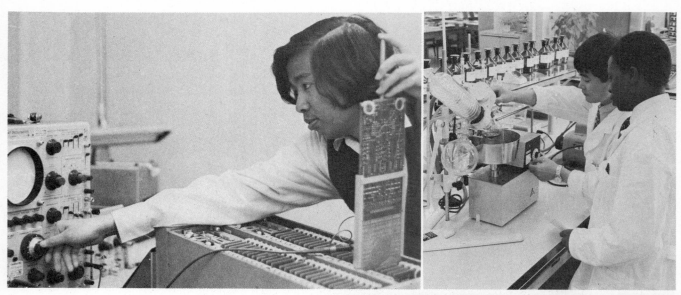

To develop your abilities, select areas of interest that you have the time and aptitude to pursue. Get involved in activities that develop your skills. (Top left, courtesy Kaiser Aerospace and Electronics; top right, courtesy United Nations/PAS; bottom right, courtesy NASA.)

interest. You should learn to select the interest areas for which you have the aptitude, time, and money to follow. This is true of leisure-time activity, as well as in the world of work. Since an important part of your life will be spent working, you should try to select a career that matches both your interests and your abilities.

One of the signs of maturity is when you are able to recognize that you cannot be all things. One way of narrowing down your career interest areas is to be aware of your aptitudes. You might, for example, like films and the theater and think that acting would be an exciting career possibility. But, if your performance in class skits and school plays shows that you have no aptitude for acting, you might want to reexamine your career plans.

Rechanneling Your Interests

In trying to find a career that will satisfy one of your major areas of interest, you may have to drop or rechannel those interests that do not match your aptitudes. For example, if you discover that you have no aptitude for acting, you might be able to rechannel your interest into the hundreds of other careers involved with films and theater. If you have a strong verbal aptitude, you might become a film editor or script writer. If you have an aptitude for understanding space, shapes, and proportions, you might become a stage set designer or a costume designer.

Developing New Interests

We talked about having many interests and learning to focus and rechanneling your interests to match your aptitudes. But what if you have only a few interests to start with, and most of your interests turn into dead ends? You are in the sort of position as someone who has been best friends with one person for a long time and is lost when that person moves away. You might feel that it's no use trying to build such a close friendship with anyone else. Or you might find ways to make new friends. Well, there are always ways to develop new interests too.

Stay alert.   It is easy to think of only one kind of career, and say you're not interested in any others. Many people have always dreamed of being a doctor, or plumber, or pilot, and have believed that this is the only career for them in

life. Then they found out that they couldn't afford medical school, or they couldn't qualify for an apprenticeship program, or they developed vision problems, or something else came up that prevented them from pursuing their dreams.

It is at times such as these that you must make an effort to stay alert and look for new interests to develop. In fact, such problem times can turn out to be quite exciting. They offer an opportunity to take a fresh look at things. Many people who might have been deeply depressed when they were laid off or fired from a job instead used that chance to look at their lives and decide that they weren't happy in their chosen careers. It's never too late to make a change. An open mind can mean a new start in the right direction.

Explore different careers. It is easy to be passive or lazy about looking for new ideas about your self. Perhaps you feel that you've been through the whole business of exploring various career opportunities. Perhaps you don't feel that past sessions with school counselors have gotten you anywhere. But if you decide on a new approach of openness and enthusiasm, you should be able to find some new ideas that are interesting to you.

Everyone has pursued some interests and has some abilities in a few areas. But, since the knowing self never stops learning, there are always new abilities to develop, no matter how able or skilled you are.

One thing to keep in mind as you renew your efforts at career exploration is that, assuming aptitude and interest, you can develop abilities in an area where you lack ability right now.

WAYS TO TURN INTERESTS INTO ABILITIES

Take a new look at your self and know your strengths. Once you know your strengths, or your aptitudes, the next step is to decide how to develop and improve them so that you turn interests into abilities. Two important ways to develop your abilities are training and education.

Training Programs

If you are interested in developing an ability in stenography, you learn the basic symbols and then practice your shorthand as a teacher or a record gives dictation. You are training to be a stenographer or a secretary. Any act you repeat over and over involves training. *Training* means learning how to do something. Training is more concentrated than general education, although it can be a part of general education. You may be in a general high school program but have one class that involves training in agricultural mechanics. In this training class, you would develop your abilities to work with farm machinery.

Here are some other examples of training: you train to become an athlete, pianist, plumber, teacher, or gardener. You train to do something. You train in certain places. And in these places, you follow certain requirements to make sure that the training you receive is the type you need. You can receive training in public and private schools, apprenticeship programs, on the job, colleges and community colleges, vocational programs, and government-sponsored training programs. You can also train by taking correspondence courses.

General Education Programs

General education is less specialized than training. It usually takes more time, and it deals more with answering the question of "why" than with learning the "how to." In a way, it deals more with the mind than with the hands. General education seeks to help you to learn your interests, become flexible, and adapt to new situations. It prepares you to learn many things, rather than to develop your ability to do a specific task.

General education is sometimes called academic education or liberal arts education. Public and private schools, colleges, universities, community colleges, and correspondence courses provide general education. Some vocational schools provide general education in limited amounts. General education can give you the requirements needed for certain careers, such as journalism, where most of the training is done on the job. It can prepare you to enter one of the professions, such as medicine or law. It can also help you to appreciate life and become a more knowledgeable citizen.

Other Helpful Opportunities

As long as you have the interest and the aptitude, you will find many opportunities to develop your abilities. Teachers and counselors can be helpful in pointing out opportunities to develop your abilities. They may help you with special projects or let you know about special courses in the interest area you wish to pursue.

If your interest area draws you away from school right now, your counselor may help you locate a special training program to prepare you for a job you like. Newspaper want-ads often post notices of training positions or part-time jobs in an area you might like to explore. And there is always the public library. Books are not just for fun or for class assignments. Most librarians can help you locate books that discuss your interest area—be it higher mathematics, or crafts, or sailing, or interior decorating.

ABILITIES ARE ASSETS

Abilities that have been developed and used are assets. They represent talents. Knowing your abilities will help you to make career choices that are satisfying to you. Knowing your abilities will help you become more valuable to yourself, to the person or company you are working for, and to the people who are depending on the goods and services you produce.

Just as you need all the parts of your self to develop a good self-identity, you need aptitudes and interests to develop the abilities that make you a strong, well-rounded, and valuable person. Developing your abilities will take some effort and work.

No matter how skilled you are in one area, there are always some new abilities that you can develop. For example, Pearl Bailey, a successful entertainer, has also served as a United States delegate to the General Assembly of the United Nations. (Courtesy United Nations/T. Chen)

CHAPTER 7

YOUR NEEDS

I need ten dollars! I need a new couch! I need to see that movie! I need a vacation! I need to pass that test! I need a job! What is a need? A *need* is something that you cannot get along without. Psychologists have found that everyone has five basic needs. These five basic needs are as follows:

1. *Keeping alive*—These needs satisfy your physical wants. They are food, water, air, exercise, and rest.
2. *Being free of fear and anxiety*—These needs satisfy your desire to feel safe. They are safety from bodily harm, freedom from fear and anxiety, and security from financial want.
3. *Being loved*—These needs satisfy your desire for love. They are acceptance by other people, the ability to give and receive love, and the satisfaction of belonging.
4. *Being admired and respected*—These are the needs for self-worth. They grow out of confidence in your abilities and an awareness of being accepted by those around you.
5. *Realizing your potential*—These are the needs to express your self creatively in your world. They grow out of the ability to satisfy your curiosities about your surroundings.

According to psychologists, these five basic needs also fall into an order of importance. They are listed above in the order of their importance. When the first group of needs is satisfied, the second group of needs can be met. For example, when a person is well fed and feels secure and free from harm, the energies of that person are released so that he or she can work on giving and receiving affection and fulfilling a sense of belonging.

YOUR MANY NEEDS

All the parts of your self have needs. Your physical needs for food, water, and rest are most easily recognized. And all of these are needs that satisfy the body self. Your social self needs the friendship of some of your classmates and the concern your parents show for you. Your knowing self needs the stimulation of using and learning facts and ideas. And your consistent self needs some sameness to give order and stability to your life. Everyone needs these things because no one can get along without them.

You will never lose the need for such basic things as food and water, other people, mental activity, and some stability in your life. Your other needs will change and develop as you grow and mature, however.

YOUR CHANGING NEEDS

When you were a baby, you needed nearly total acceptance from your parents, or from someone else who was responsible for taking care of you. Your basic physical needs had to be satisfied often when you were an infant. You probably had to be fed about every 3 or 4 hours. When you were just a few weeks old, you could smile at your parents or guardians when you were picked up and given food. As you became more aware of the world around you, you began to explore the world, and you were curious about it. And your needs changed as you grew and developed.

When you became a toddler, you needed to be told "no" sometimes. Complete acceptance of your actions would have been dangerous for you. Your parents or guardians had to watch out for your safety, and you learned some of the first rules of how to get along with other people.

| Keeping Alive |
| Being Free of Fear |
| Being Loved |
| Being Admired and Respected |
| Realizing Your Potential |

The five basic needs are shown in the order of their importance. You have to satisfy one need before moving on to the next.

You needed a structured life when you started school. You still had physical needs, of course, but they could be met less often. You could go for a longer time without food. You knew your physical needs were being satisfied, so you could turn your attention to other activities. You were learning the basic skills of reading, writing, and arithmetic. You were also adding more knowledge to what you knew about getting along with others. As you went through junior high and high school, you needed more freedom. You began to choose certain courses and to set your own learning patterns. Your world was also growing in terms of friends and you were beginning to develop special interests.

At this period in your life, you might need the excitement of competitive sports, music concerts, group activities, or a wide circle of friends. As you grow and develop, your needs will continue to change. For example, you may lose the need to be so competitive. Or you may grow to need more privacy and quiet activities more often than you did in the past.

My Needs for Me; Your Needs for You

The five basic groups of needs are essential for survival, and they are common to all people. But we all have other needs in addition to these

basics. And just as the different parts of your self have different needs, different people also have different needs.

There are people who need to feel physically attractive, so they do all the grooming that they think will make them look just perfect. Other people are quite satisfied if they look presentable and feel comfortable. Some people need the attention of a lot of friends, while others are happy with a few close friends.

These are needs that *some* people *can* get along without but *others cannot.* They are not essential to survival, but they are important to happy, well-rounded individuals.

KNOW YOUR REAL NEEDS

"But I N-E-E-D it," you say. Just how many times have those words passed through your lips? There are N*E*E*D*S, and there are real needs.

It is important for you to know your *real needs.* These are the needs beyond the physical ones that are necessary for you. If you are to make the proper career choice for your future, these real needs must be met. In order to know your real needs, you must know all the parts of your self. If you know your self, you will take the steps to satisfy your real needs.

Every need, if it's to be met, will cost you something. As long as you believe something is a real need, you will be spending a part of your self to fill it. And since your physical and human resources are limited, you must concentrate on satisfying your most important real needs first and foremost.

If you are spending your time on things that are not real needs, you will also be less free than you could be. So you must make sure that your needs are real needs. You must decide what you really want. On the other hand, it is dangerous to ignore your real needs and try to act as if they don't exist. If you really need the security of a regular routine, for example, it could be damaging to your self to try and function in a traveling sales job that requires rapid adjustments to new conditions.

Needs Can Be Tested, Modified, or Delayed

Remember that a basic law of economics is that all resources are limited. You probably will not be able to fill everything that you consider a need right away. Learning to sort out, test, modify, and delay your needs will help you make the best use of all your resources. As you prepare for your future, take a close look at the things you have been considering your needs. Are the material possessions you want right now really needs, or are they wants, desires, or dreams? Getting the money for school usually requires some sacrifices. Becoming a journeyman in a trade requires some lean years of apprenticeship.

What could you get along without right now? Perhaps your need for material comfort is not so basic that you couldn't delay a year or two in taking a steady paying job to gain some valuable experience in a volunteer organization. Perhaps your need for the security of a regular routine isn't as real as it seems. Perhaps it could be tested by trying, at least for a few months, to get started on that career as a free-lance writer. You might discover that you can survive quite well on an irregular income and a more challenging routine. Or, on the other hand, you might discover that, indeed, your original needs were real needs.

Needs also can be influenced by experience. Your need to be free of close supervision may be the result of an unpleasant experience on a part-time job. You might find, by trying, that a good supervisor will quickly help you attain the feelings of success and independence that you need so much.

Needs Can Be Short- and Long-Term

Most of us feel that fulfilling our every need is a matter of immediate urgency and importance. But isn't it sometimes worth delaying a need as an investment in your future? Needs can be divided into two categories. There are *short-term needs* that can be met almost immediately. A need to be a leader and to dominate others may be satisfied as a short-term need in class or with brothers and sisters in a home situation. There are also *long-term needs*, which require more effort, planning, and a longer time frame to be satisfied. That need for leadership may have to be a long-term need as you start and learn your first job.

As a child, you really needed the protection and comfort of a secure home to be able to deal with the world. That was an immediate, short-term need. But as you grew older, you probably decided to strike out on your own more often. In the future, you may want to be completely independent of your parents. This is a long-term need. To work toward filling this need, you should begin developing some independence before leaving home.

Right now, you may be exploring career possibilities in an effort to plan for your future. You will be satisfying both short-term and long-term needs, but you may often feel that you are taking short steps to meet long-term needs.

SHORT STEPS FOR LONG-TERM CAREER GOALS

Nearly everyone wants to feel successful. But how soon does success come? If you let a strong need for success prevent you from starting a career, you are closing off a lot of possibilities in your life.

Your career goals can be recognized as long-term rather than short-term needs. At first, you will gain far greater rewards if you set short-term goals for your self. You will be able to reach greater success if you progress toward your long-range career goals in shorter steps. You will need education and experience in order to meet your goals. Each one of these short-term goals must be something that is within your reach.

Suppose that you would like to get started on a career as a free-lance photographer. Quite naturally, you will need some training in the use of the camera as well as darkroom techniques.

You will need some experience in using the camera so that you will know the lens settings and types of film that work best for you. Camera equipment is expensive, so you will probably find your self doing without other things in order to buy what you need to develop your abilities in photography. In other words, you will be setting these and probably other short-term goals to meet your long-range goals. You might discover that you can survive quite well on the irregular income of a beginning free-lance photographer. You might find that you just cannot make it totally on your own, but that you can manage very well by taking part-time special assignments from commercial photographers. You will adjust your needs to the situation that fits you best.

YOUR EMOTIONS HELP YOU DISCOVER YOUR NEEDS

Your needs and your emotions are related. Remember that emotions are your feelings that are stirred up by a person, a situation, an idea, or a thing. And your emotions can be pleasant or unpleasant, depending on whether or not your needs are being met.

When babies need food, they show their need by crying. In other words, they are expressing their need by showing an emotion. When babies need to be picked up and comforted, they also cry or become fussy. They stop crying and show happy feelings when their needs are met.

As you grow and develop, your emotions and needs become more complex. After infancy, you soon learn to show certain emotions in order to satisfy certain needs. You later begin to learn that you must combine words and actions in order to satisfy your needs because you cannot simply cry when you need something. And some of your needs have to be adjusted in order to respect the needs of others.

The case that follows is about a girl named Susan who finally became aware of a need. Notice how her needs and emotions are related to one another and how her emotions helped her discover a basic need in her life.

Susan's parents were a highly successful dance team. After she was born, they dreamed of her learning to dance and the three of them becoming a family act. At the proper age, they applied for her acceptance at the Dance Academy, but the dance school rejected her application. After her audition for acceptance, the school informed her parents that she had little aptitude for dance. They applied to other, less-known schools, but the answer was always the same—Susan had no aptitude for dance.

Susan's parents, especially her mother, became increasingly frustrated. She could think of nothing but the fact that now there would be no family act and of Susan's disappointing her. She completely ignored the fact that Susan certainly had aptitudes in other areas. And, although she didn't realize it, Susan's mother's disappointment showed itself to Susan.

At first, Susan had no feelings about her mother's attitude. She was content with her warmth—with the security it gave her. But, as time went by, Susan felt her mother's disappointment in her.

Susan felt anxiety and alienation. Her mother's disappointment made her feel as though something were wrong with her. As she became an adolescent, she asked herself, "What am I like?" She looked in her mirror and saw her body

If you feel that a regular 9-to-5 job might not be for you, test this feeling by working on a free-lance basis. (Courtesy Bethlehem Steel)

image. It satisfied her, and it seemed to please others. She could not understand what was wrong.

She noticed some other things. Her mother was giving her more freedom, about as much as her friends had. She was doing well in school, and she was getting along with her classmates. But she felt anxious, and she still felt alienated from her mother.

One day in class, the students were asked to write about their self-identities. Susan had to do a great deal of thinking and remembering. Sometimes she found it hard to remember things that are unpleasant. She found she would rather forget about them. When Susan came to the question, "What do you need most?" she was surprised by what she wrote, because she wrote it almost automatically. "Acceptance" she wrote.

Susan had uncovered a need. She had discovered something important deep inside her. It was a discovery that helped her set her direction in life. From then on, Susan decided to reject decisions that did not fit her need for acceptance.

POSITIVE STEPS
TOWARD SATISFYING A NEED

Suppose you realize that you lack the security of having one of your basic needs satisfied. Suppose you feel the unsatisfied need for acceptance, like Susan. All of your energies will be directed toward meeting this need before you can continue on your path to "conquering the world." But, like all goals, there are right and wrong directions to take. Some people in such a situation would withdraw from family and friends. They would have a difficult time achieving success in life, because they would lack self-confidence and self-esteem. Their unsatisfied need would get in the way of their gaining independence and making plans.

But there are some positive steps you can take to gain confidence and fulfill a need:

- Find and make friends
- Do what you know you can do well
- Develop enjoyable hobbies
- Set short-range goals
- Volunteer for jobs and chores at home and in your community that you know you can do

These steps will start you on the road to developing some security. You will begin to feel safe enough to explore your self and to take chances. You will begin to gain confidence and independence.

Support from Family, Friends, and Others Helps the Setbacks

When you explore and take chances, you often suffer setbacks. You may take on a job that is too difficult for you. You may try to please everyone and end up pleasing no one. Setbacks are natural. They are a part of growing. The trick to handling them is to be flexible, or to stay loose. When setbacks threaten your security, it helps to have a concerned family and friends for support.

Family support is possible when the home is happy and peaceful. But some homes have conflict in them. When they do, it is hard to get a feeling of security from them.

If this is the situation in your home, take comfort in the fact that you are not alone. Studies have shown that there is some conflict in the homes of about one third of all young people. This conflict centers around three issues: (1) disputes over money, such as the size of allowance, part-time jobs, or support while in school; (2) disputes over social matters, such as selecting friends, attending social events, appearance, selecting clothes, or accounting for time away from home; and (3) personal problems, such as temper.

When family support is not available, you must find security from friends, teachers, counselors, members of the clergy, or other adults whom you trust and admire.

Suppose that, instead of feeling insecure, you feel too much security. The person who has been smothered with attention often stays at home well past adolescence. What can this person do? The same positive steps suggested for persons who lack security can help persons who think they have too much security. The goals are the same: gain independence, recognize and satisfy your needs, explore your options, and make decisions that are best for you.

INDEPENDENCE IS NOT A LONELY TERM

We have talked about gaining independence as a goal of knowing your self. Independence does not mean being alone. Remember the song about "people who need people." Independence is an attitude of self-reliance. You will always need other people, but you don't have to be controlled by other people. You can and should ask help and advice from others when you decide about your future, but the decisions should be yours. After all, it is your future. Gaining independence and developing a strong self-identity involve taking steps toward satisfying your needs.

CHAPTER 8

GETTING A PERSPECTIVE ON YOUR SELF

As Lisa bicycles toward the grocery store, she thinks she sees a familiar face. Getting closer, she recognizes Pete and calls out, "Hi, Pete. How've you been?"

"Just fine," Pete answers. Stopping near the curb, Lisa says, "I guess it's been nearly a year since I saw you last. What have you been doing lately?"

"Well, right now I'm busy filling out application forms," Pete says. "I graduate from Northwest High in June and after that I want to study electronics."

"Oh? You were so good on bass in that rock group when I heard you play last year. I'm surprised you're not planning to go to City Conservatory of Music."

"I'm still into music, Lisa. And it'll always be one of my interests but not my job."

"What happened?" asks Lisa.

"Not any one thing especially," answers Pete. "About six months ago I had a chance to do a lot of thinking about my self when I went out West to visit my oldest brother. Not long before that I had sprained my wrist in a bike accident. And during the time that I had to rest my wrist, I realized I missed working with the band's sound equipment a lot more than I missed playing bass! Since then, I've really gotten into my electricity and electronics courses in the work-experience program. After graduation, I plan to go to a technical institute so I can become an electronics technician."

"That's great, Pete. Sounds like you've got it all together these days."

Now that you have started to explore and understand some of the many dimensions of your self—your aptitudes and traits, your interests and abilities, and your needs—it's time to put all these qualities together to fill out your self-identity. If you explore your self as Pete did, you can find out how to put your self's many dimensions to work for you.

WAYS TO IDENTIFY YOUR SELF

When you get busy understanding your self, you win a big prize. You find out what you are worth as a person, and it's always a safe bet that you are worth more than you supposed. But how do you do this? Ask yourself the following questions:

- What are your special abilities?
- What do you need?
- What do you want?
- What makes you the special person you are?

How will you know when you are on the right track to self-understanding? You should find that you are asking yourself some questions that are hard to answer. These tough questions will make you dig deep to find answers. When you dig deep, you become aware of your self, and you will become curious about your self and others.

Concentrate on Reality

If you want to become aware of your self, keep your mind's eye on the way things really are in life—not on images and shadows. You don't want to wear a mask or play a role that is not really you. In other words, don't pretend to be what you aren't. An example of playing a role that is not really you would be to put on a show when you apply for a job—pretending to be what you think the employer wants you to be instead of being your self. Of course, you should try to make a good impression and do your best, but be your self. Otherwise, you could end up in the wrong job and become miserable.

Learn Your Strengths and Weaknesses

Like everyone else, you want to be comfortable, to be secure, to help others, to be recognized, and to create things. If you use your inner strengths and know your weaknesses, you can reach your goals.

You have weaknesses as well as strengths, and your weaknesses can limit you. But, at the same time, your strengths overcome your weaknesses. You will understand your weaknesses and strengths as you begin to know your self. You will find some hidden strengths and some hidden weaknesses. However, do not be afraid of weaknesses. If you face them and don't cover them up with a mask, you can deal with them. Recognize your interests, abilities, and aptitudes because these are your strengths. By knowing your self and understanding your strengths and weaknesses, you can decide what to do and what to be. If you understand how much you really want to do something or to be someone and if you know your real needs, you will develop your strengths so that you can achieve your goals. In other words, you will have *motivation*, or the strong desire to take action to fill your needs.

If you want to become aware of your self, don't hide behind a mask and pretend to be someone else.

Know Your Background

What is your background? Your *background* is where you come from and what you have gotten from your parents and their parents and so on. You are a product of your parents. You are a product of their culture with its customs and traditions and their attitudes or ideas about the way to think and act.

Who were your grandparents? Where did they come from? Are you different from your parents? Look at your brothers and sisters, and ask the same question about them. Doing this seems so simple that you might not think about it at all. Many people never ask themselves these questions. As a result, they often do not know who they are, yet they may act as if they do.

Heredity and environment are parts of your background that make you what you are. *Heredity* is the part of your background that your parents pass on to you. *Environment* refers to the physical surroundings where you grow up or live. If both your parents are broad shouldered, you will probably be broad shouldered because of your heredity. If you grew up in a family that does not talk much at mealtimes, you will probably be quiet at meals because of the influence of your environment.

Although you are born with a certain amount of intelligence and a special set of aptitudes, environment plays an important part in shaping you as an individual. Your environment, rather than heredity, influences your attitudes, your values and beliefs, and the way you use your intelligence and develop your aptitudes. For example, you may have the inborn aptitudes to be a great musician. If you aren't around musical instruments to learn how to play them, you will not develop your aptitudes.

Of course, you cannot become something for which you have no aptitude or background of experience. In general, you can become what you try to be. Look at the story of Louis Armstrong, for example:

> Louis Armstrong grew up in New Orleans, Louisiana. He loved the music he heard at parades and in the streets of the city, but he could not buy a musical instrument. When he was about 10 years old, a teacher in a training school gave him a trumpet and taught him how to play it. Because of Louis' natural talents and developing abilities, he quickly became an important member of the school band. After his school years, Louis joined other popular jazz bands that traveled around the United States. As Louis traveled with these

bands, he was learning more and more about trumpet playing, and he was becoming a famous musician in cities like Chicago and New York. Eventually, he was known worldwide by music lovers for his special style of jazz that influenced many other musicians.

SOME ROADBLOCKS TO SELF-IDENTITY

Some people think that the process of finding their self-identities and following their career goals will move along in a straight line without any problems. That is wrong. People generally do meet some problems along the way. These problems usually arise when people have unclear information about themselves.

Some problems can become roadblocks that get in the way of developing a strong self-identity and setting career goals. If you know some of the roadblocks, you will be better prepared to handle them. Some of these roadblocks will be discussed below.

Don't Confuse Your Aptitudes, Interests, and Abilities

An aptitude is a talent that is undeveloped and untrained. An interest is liking one thing more than another. Trouble can arise if you think that an interest in a certain type of job means that you are automatically able to do that job. This trouble can arise the other way around too. Just because you have an aptitude for a certain job does not mean that you have an interest in it.

Watch out for this roadblock. It can cause problems in finding your self-identity and the job that fits it.

Don't Get Stuck in a Groove

Do you feel just fine doing what you are doing? Are you satisfied with staying where you are? If that's the case, watch out for another roadblock. It can cause you to not recognize your own potential. If you are content with being static, you are stuck in a groove. You might ignore your potential even when it is pointed out to you clearly by other people. This can trip you up later, and you may become bored or unhappy because you may not be able to get the things you want. If you are able to think about your weaknesses and your strengths—whether or not they are pointed

out to you—you will avoid this roadblock. A sure sign of maturity is being able to accept your strengths and weaknesses.

Don't Wear Masks

Sometimes you wear masks—not real ones, of course—to hide your real feelings and thoughts from others. You are not the only one who wears masks. This is something that everybody does for one reason or another. There are many masks and many ways to wear them. For example, you may pretend to be calm and easygoing, but you may really be impatient and worried. Or you may seem to be pleasant to someone when you may really want to be with another person. In both cases, you are masking your real self.

If you wear a mask often, it can become part of you. You may forget that you are wearing a mask and lose track of your real feelings and thoughts. This can cause a great deal of trouble—another roadblock. People may say that you are out of touch with yourself or that you haven't gotten your self together. The older you get, the better able you will probably be to hide your real self. If this happens, it will be harder to get to know your self. Cover-ups, or masks, help save face. This can lead you to try to shift the responsibility for your self and the way things happen to other people.

Training programs are an effective way to develop your strengths. (Courtesy Board of Education, City of New York)

Don't Fail in Career Knowledge

You can have a self-identity problem if you do not know enough about the world of work. But this roadblock is a little easier to avoid. If you know how many different types of careers there are, you will know what you can be expected to do. The best way to find out, of course, is to work with people on a job, but that takes time. Life is too short to try out all the jobs you might be interested in doing. So what can you do? You can do the following:

- Take a careful look at books and pamphlets that describe occupations. There are plenty of them, and your counselor can help you find them.
- Make a list of the occupations that suit you best and talk about it with your counselor.

Find out about the career possibilities that fit your aptitudes and interests. Suppose you have a great imagination, that is a trait or quality that could make you very successful in certain jobs.

DON'T LET PROBLEMS GET YOU DOWN

You have learned about some possible problems, or roadblocks, that can get in the way of your becoming what you most want to be. These problems can happen to anyone, including you. The important thing is to not let them throw up permanent roadblocks in your path. And you can do this if you are honest with your self. If you are honest with your self, you will be able to recognize your problems and work them out so that they do not hold you back.

For example, if you know your limitations and problems, you can avoid getting into programs that will prepare you for a career that does not suit you. If you realize your weaknesses, you can choose training or education programs that will develop your strengths.

As you have seen, Louis Armstrong met some problems as he was growing up. After he discovered his strengths and developed them, he overcame his problems. You may not become world-famous, but if you work from your strengths you can overcome your problems and become a self-fulfilling person.

Identify Your Problems and Turn Them Into Assets

If you have a weakness, don't be afraid to admit it. Do you have a limited ability in some areas? Have you found some personal trait that stands in your way? Are your attitudes about your schoolwork forming obstacles? Do you have some urgent need that is not being satisfied? Are you worried about an emotional problem? Does some desire seem completely out of reach for you?

The following story of Laura shows how a disadvantage can be overcome when it is faced. Laura actually turned her disadvantage into an advantage.

Laura was a college graduate who had a difficult time getting a job because she suffered muscle spasms. She walked with a slight limp, and nobody would hire her. Employers feared that her appearance would put customers off and they would lose sales. Laura thought over her problem and finally convinced a life insurance company that she could sell life insurance policies by making appointments over the telephone. She got a chance to do this. Laura became one of the company's best salespeople by interesting people in buying insurance policies over the telephone.

Laura had a physical limitation. What about a personal trait that is limiting? A "loner," a person who liked working alone, was interested in police work. But the loner knew that being on a police force means working with many people. After special training at a police institute and working with a "private eye," the loner became a private detective.

If you are honest with your self, you will know your weaknesses. If you know you have them, you can turn them into real advantages. By recognizing them, you can do something about them. If you refuse to recognize them, they will stay with you and put up roadblocks.

Getting It All Together

1. How are aptitudes different from abilities?

2. How are traits and habits similar? How are they different?

3. How are interests and abilities the same? How are they different?

4. Why do some needs prevent you from ever considering certain careers?

5. Why might some needs prevent you from considering certain careers at one time but allow you to consider those same careers at another time?

6. Why is it important to look at more than one dimension of your self when setting career goals?

YOUR VALUES
AND YOUR IDENTITY

Your goals in this unit are given in the following list:

To understand the concept of value

To recognize how you express your values

To recognize some effects of clear and unclear values

To recognize and understand various sources of your values

To recognize how values affect your choice of career

What is most important in your life now? What things, people, or ideas are most important to you? What do you want to have in the future that you do not have now? These questions, which will cause you to stop and think, have to do with your values.

A *value* is an idea that you have about what is most important, desirable, and worthwhile in your life. Different people have different values, and values are determined by personal feelings. A stamp collector might prize an old envelope for its stamp, whereas an historian might prefer the letter inside the envelope because of its information. Both the stamp collector and the historian would spend a lot of time, energy, and money searching out old letters, but each would have different reasons for wanting them. What you think is important guides your judgment about what is of value, not what someone else considers to be important.

The ancient Greeks used to tell a story about King Midas. When Midas saved the life of one of the gods' favorite subjects, he was told that he could have whatever he wished. Midas, who was already a very rich king, wanted to become richer, so he wished for everything that he touched to be turned to gold. Parts of his palace became gold, as well as his clothing, but his magic touch became a real problem when food and drink turned to gold on his lips, and he was always hungry and thirsty as a result. After

touching his beautiful daughter, even she turned to a golden statue, and this made King Midas very sad. He learned that his love for his daughter was more important to him than all his gold and riches. In other words, King Midas had to face up to his true values. And Midas decided that he preferred having his daughter as she had been rather than all the gold he had gained.

Your values act as guideposts to the decisions you make. Your values determine how you spend your time, energy, and money. Your values also determine whether you will take risks and make sacrifices to reach your goals. How you use your life and how you make it count will be guided by your values. And your values will probably change as you grow and mature.

This brings up an important point about values. As you know, almost everyone has to work in order to live. But how do you decide which career area is right for you? This is when your work values will help you decide. Do you like to be creative in your work? Do you want to work in comfortable surroundings? Do you want a job that gives you status or doesn't status matter to you? Do you eventually want to work with many people or mostly alone?

All these questions have to do with your work values. You'll find that being able to ask and answer questions like these will help you in deciding on a career that's right for you.

CHAPTER 9

HOW YOU EXPRESS YOUR VALUES

"We only do what we want to do," the speaker told an audience.

"You're dead wrong to say that," someone in the audience said angrily.

The speaker calmly replied, "Give me an example."

"All right, I will," the person answered. "I'm a lawyer. I never wanted to go to law school, but I was forced to go there by my parents."

"How did they force you to go to law school against your will?" the speaker asked.

"That's simple," came the reply. "My parents said they would disinherit me if I didn't go into law and carry on the family tradition of practicing law. They meant what they said."

"You have just answered yourself," the speaker said. "Being part of your family and sharing your parents' money was of more value to you than anything else. You certainly did what you wanted to do."

Your values are your ideas about what you think is most important, desirable, and worthwhile. Just as values determined the action of the lawyer, your values act as guideposts in your own decisions. You show your values in the many ways you act them out.

YOU ACT OUT YOUR VALUES

When you spend your time, energy, and money on someone or something, you are acting out your values. And your values determine the times you take risks and make sacrifices. There are other ways of showing your values. You act out your values in your attitudes and by the way you live, or your *lifestyle*. Look more closely at the various ways you can act out your values.

Values and Time

Most people try to do something useful with their time, because time is important and they do not want to waste it. Benjamin Franklin once said, "Do not squander [waste] time, for that is the stuff life is made of."

What do you do in your spare time? Think about how you spend it. Do you try to do at least one useful thing each day? Do you put off getting necessary things done?

As a young man, Albert Einstein, the physicist, had a dull office job. Instead of passing the time with idle talk with other people in his office, he spent his spare time working on and thinking out his first scientific paper. This paper later developed into the theory of relativity that changed people's understanding about nature.

Louis Agassiz, the famous naturalist, once turned down an invitation to lecture before an important public society. Agassiz did not want to take time away from his work. The person who invited the naturalist to talk had a different set of values and asked him again, saying, "We are ready to pay you well for your services." The naturalist was not convinced, and he replied, "I can't afford to waste my time making money." Knowledge was more important to Louis Agassiz than money.

If you know your values, as Einstein and Agassiz did, you will spend your time in what you think are useful ways.

Values and Energy

Since people do not have unlimited amounts of energy, they must decide how they will use their

36

Your values are reflected in the ways you behave. What values are each of these people acting out?

energies to reach their goals. Everyone needs to balance the busy times with some quiet times. Energy is an ingredient that is not to be wasted.

There is a story about a man who boasted that he would retire after he had made a million dollars and then he would "really live." The man worked day after day, year after year. After making a million dollars, he quit work. When he started to "really live," he found that something inside himself had died. He had never learned to enjoy life, so he did not know what to do. The man had not arranged his values to help him get what he really wanted. He thought he knew what he wanted, but his life was empty and sad. He had used all of his energy to make a million dollars and had not learned to enjoy life. Also he had cheated himself because he had not paid any attention to the way values shape our lives.

Like this man, many people think they cannot reach their goals until they are older. People who know what they want use their energies to the best advantage, and age does not matter.

When you know your values, you can concentrate your energies on working at them. You will not waste your time and energy on other things that, in the long run, will mean little to you.

Values and Material Possessions

Everyone needs a certain amount of money to get along, and money also buys a lot of extra things. How people use their money shows where their values lie. People need some *material possessions*, or those things that they can buy and own. These include cars, homes, furniture, clothing, tools, equipment, and gadgets. Different people have different sets of values about their material possessions.

If you have some extra money, how do you spend it? Do you buy a new LP? Do you add to your savings? Perhaps you may buy a new outfit. Or do you give to your favorite charity or religious group? Your decisions about spending money tell what you value.

There is another side of people's ideas about having money and owning things. When people spend money, they like to feel that they are getting something rather than they are losing something. Consider this example:

"Why," the manager of a candy store asked herself, "did Tobi always have more customers than any of the other salespeople?" Finally she asked about it.

"That's easy," Tobi told her. "When the others weigh the candy, they scoop up more than a pound and then start taking some away. I don't do that. I scoop up less than a pound, and then I add to that."

Still another side of looking at the subject of money is this: Do you enjoy the time and effort you spend making money? Or is making money, no matter how you do it, just a way for you to be able to buy what you want? After you have answered these questions, think about how much you need. How much you think you need is another way of telling your self what you think is worthwhile. The idea of values and possessions and how they relate to one another is important to consider.

Values—Risks and Sacrifices

Are you familiar with the expression "let it all hang out"? This expression means that people should let their feelings show in what they are doing. When people "let it all hang out," they also show their values.

People especially show what their values are by the way they act in the times that call for important decision making. These times are usually during an emergency or when large amounts of money are spent. In either situation, some risk may have to be taken or a sacrifice may have to be made. For example, if you have ever been seriously ill or in trouble, your parents probably had to spend a larger amount of money than usual or make an unusually difficult decision. In other words, they may have had to take a risk or make a sacrifice—if not both—to help you. Such difficult situations happen to everyone at some time or other. And it is usually in such stressful situations that people show their true values in the ways they act.

Values and Lifestyles

As you know, a lifestyle is shown by the way a person lives and in the ideas he or she values. A lifestyle also determines the way a person thinks and feels about things. People who have similar lifestyles generally belong to the same social class and do things together. However, people with the same lifestyle will differ in some of the details of their everyday lives.

Your lifestyle includes your career, the way you spend money, the make of car you buy, the books you read and the music you listen to, the kind of clothes you wear, the way you spend your vacation and your spare time, and the type of hairstyle you choose. These are just some of the ways you express your lifestyle. Your parents, relatives, classmates, and friends reflect the values that are important to them in their lifestyles also. A lifestyle is an expression of values that you can examine every day—at home, at school, or on the job.

Values and Attitudes

An *attitude* is a feeling or idea that can lead to action. Attitudes strongly reflect values. But how? Look at the attitude of an elderly Irishman who was seeing his oldest child off to America:

"Now, Shannon, my lass," he said. "Remember the three bones, and ye'll always get along all right over there."

A stranger who overheard this remark was interested and puzzled by it. When the daughter had left, the stranger asked the father what he had meant by the three bones.

"Sure, now, ye don't know about the three bones?" the old man asked with a smile. He answered, "And wouldn't it be the wishbone that keeps you going after things? And it's the jawbone that helps you find out how to go after them when there's something you don't know. And it's the backbone, for sure, that keeps you at it 'til you get there."

Actually, there are several values shown in the old man's advice. Think about them. They can lead to an interesting classroom discussion.

Your attitude is one way in which you act out your values. (Courtesy Action Vista)

CHAPTER 10

HOW VALUES AFFECT PEOPLE

"Hi, Lou," Marie says. "I just called to remind you that I'm going to pick up the tickets tomorrow for the dance concert. I can hardly wait to see Foster and Adale dance. We should really learn a lot just by watching them."

"Gee, Marie," Lou moans. "I don't have the money for the tickets anymore. I just bought that new LP that everyone is talking about."

"But, Lou, how can we ever be a dance team if you keep doing these things? Last week, you didn't show up for practice because you got involved in a TV program, and you know we are supposed to audition for the county talent show next month. We need all the practice we can get. And now, you don't have money for the concert. Isn't it important to you anymore? Do you just want to quit and forget about it?"

"Oh, no, Marie. I don't want to quit. I really think we have a good chance at that audition. It is important to me. It's just that I seem to get sidetracked by other things. I don't know what the matter is, and the LP's not all that good, either."

What is the difference between people who have a clear set of values and people who have unclear values? People with clear values know how to get along with other people. There is purpose and enthusiasm in their lives. They find consistent ways to deal with the many changes in their lives. They do not often feel bored. They know what they want out of life, like Marie, and they know how to work to get it. In other words they have motivation. They have a clear self-identity. They arrange their values in order of importance.

People who have unclear values are confused, just as Lou seemed confused about what he wanted. They get bored easily. What they do does not make sense sometimes. They have no purpose or enthusiasm. In other words, they have no motivation. Such people are often insecure, scared, or edgy. They lack a sense of self-identity. These people often wear masks. Frequently they wind up in jobs without really knowing why. They did not pick their jobs because of their values—they just fell into them, as if by accident.

You might be squirming a bit now, thinking that some of your values aren't too clear. Most young adults are unclear about their values, but this isn't necessarily bad—if they do something about it. The point is that once you recognize the fact, you can then go on, through work and time, to develop and clear up your values.

THE EFFECTS OF CLEAR VALUES

How are values developed? Why are values important? What do values do for you? If you look at some effects of clear and unclear values, you can better understand how your values help you deal with life. First, examine some of the effects of having a clear set of values.

Values Can Give Purpose

People who have a strong set of values usually know what they want. They have a sense of purpose and therefore can act purposefully in setting their goals and achieving them. Consider this example of how a sense of purpose can result in successful action:

Maria Tallchief, a ballerina famous throughout the world, was born in Fairfax, Oklahoma, the daughter of an Osage Indian father and a

39

Scottish-Irish mother. From her life on the reservation, she remembers as a child watching Indian tribal dances. During that time, she also took dance and music lessons. Her family moved to Los Angeles when she was about 7, where she continued her music and dance lessons.

At first, she intended to be a concert pianist, but her interests increased in ballet. In one of her recitals she devoted half the program to piano and the other to dance. Finally, during her late teens, she decided in favor of ballet as a career and concentrated her studies in that area. She continued her work, and after graduating from high school, at the age of 17, made her debut with the Ballet Russe de Monte Carlo in Canada. Later, she went on to be a guest artist at the Paris Opera Ballet and then became associated with the Ballet Society, from which the New York City Ballet Company evolved. One of her most widely acclaimed performances was that in Igor Stravinsky's "Firebird."

Maria Tallchief knew what was and what was not important to her. That is, she had a clear set of values. Thus she had a purpose and was able to carry out her plans to become a ballerina. If you have a clear set of values, you will know what you want, and you will be able to carry out your plans. You will be able to act purposefully because your values will guide you.

Values Can Build Confidence

People who have a clear set of values feel certain about themselves. They are *confident*, or they feel that they can succeed. In other words, they have faith in themselves.

You may ask how you go about finding confidence. When you develop and begin to follow your value system, you build confidence in your self. One of the best ways to build your own self-confidence is to win a series of little achievements toward the goal you have set using your values as guideposts. By doing this, your skills for whatever goal you have in mind increase. And with this increase in skills, your confidence grows.

Look at this example of how one person's values increased his self-confidence:

To Dave, creativity—especially as it relates to photography—is a value he'd put at the top of a list of values he wants to satisfy in his career. He had just accepted a part-time job in a small photography supply store, and he was even considering the possibility of a career in photography. So far, though, he hadn't used a camera much—only family snapshots. Mostly, he had just read about photographers and their work, and he

Values build confidence and give purpose so that goals can be set and achieved. What do you think this person wants to accomplish?

wasn't confident that he would be able to succeed in this profession. To find out, Dave decided to take a photography course that the local Y offered. During the course, he learned some of the techniques of picture taking and how to develop film. He learned about shots and angles, the right kind of light, composition, and so on. Little by little, Dave's pictures improved and little by little so did his skills and confidence. Dave decided that maybe, just maybe, his work was good enough to enter a photography competition sponsored by a local civic group. He didn't win first prize, but the recognition that his work received encouraged Dave to continue, and it built up his self-confidence in his ability as a photographer.

As you see, values and self-confidence go together. And, once again, you see the power of knowing what you want. Having a clear set of values builds confidence in reaching your goals.

SOME EFFECTS OF UNCLEAR VALUES

People who are unclear about their values are confused. They have little self-confidence and often feel unworthy. Sometimes they are bullies. Sometimes they depend too much on others. Such people easily follow others. They may drop names, put things off, or put down others. They may try to be so perfect that they never really get much done.

People who are unclear about their values lack confidence and purpose. They may live their lives through others, such as heroes or their friends. They sometimes think of themselves as losers, which makes them not want to have much to do with other people. In general, they have not discovered how to like themselves. Look at some special problems that can occur when people are unclear about their values.

The Dissenters

People who nearly always disagree with everyone and everything are called *dissenters.* There are many ways to express your disagreement with something or someone. Being a positive dissenter is one way to find your self and to clarify your values. By pointing out the weakest parts in an argument or in a situation, trying to find out what is or is not true and what is or is not important, you can try to determine whether or not you agree with something or with someone. This kind of positive dissent is helpful, although, like anything else, it can be carried too far.

Extreme dissension is represented by those who want to destroy just for the sake of destroying. These kinds of dissenters have no interest in finding out about themselves or clarifying their own sets of values. They have no other goal than destruction. In a sense, they are running away from their need of finding values. They are "copping out." Some people even consider them lazy—too lazy to find out what is really worthwhile in life.

Moderate positive dissent is important for your development as a person. It is an aid in finding your self, in developing your self-confidence, and in clarifying your values. Positive dissent builds a healthier, better you.

The Over-Conformists

People who are about as opposite from a dissenter as they can get are called over-conformists. *Over-conformists* are those people who are always trying to please everybody. Over-conformists may be lazy too. These people do not get into the trouble that awaits the violent dissenter. They get into serious trouble with themselves.

People with unclear values often lack self-confidence, feel confused, and think of themselves as losers. (Magnum Photo/Alex Webb)

To understand over-conformists, examine what conforming means. Everyone needs to conform somewhat to get along with family, a religious group, school, and friends. These groups determine some of the values of society. People need to conform to these values in order to get the comfort and approval that go with them.

When you were younger, you probably accepted the values of older people as a matter of course. But, as you became older, you started questioning some of those values, and you felt the need to have your own set of values. Fulfilling this need, that is, developing a set of values for your self, is a major part of being mature.

Inconsistent People

The blades of a windmill will spin around, depending on whichever way the wind blows—one way and another. *Inconsistent people* are like windmills—attracted to one thing and then another, one person and then another. They flit around without a steady purpose. Inconsistent people seem to be always changing because they have no clear idea about their values.

Ray, who told different stories about his parents to different people, was inconsistent. Read the following story, and you will see why:

> Ray, whose parents were divorced, wanted to be a plumber. But Ray wanted to make a good impression on the union apprentice committee that was deciding whether or not to accept him, so he told them that his parents were together. Later, when he applied for a driver's license, he told the truth because the form he filled out warned that all statements must be true. Still later, when he was talking to his best friend, he was honest about his parents' divorce. But when he was with his girlfriend, he lied about his parents again. To impress her, he boasted about how close his family was.

Ray was inconsistent, and he was confused about the value of being honest. He did not understand that truthfulness is the best way to accomplish a purpose. Ray was unclear about his values. He had not developed his values so that they could act as guideposts for him. If you have developed your values, you will be able to avoid the type of problem that Ray had.

YOUR VALUES AND YOUR FUTURE

What do you want to do? What do you want to be? Do you want to work in your home community? Or do you want to go away to college before getting a job? You may be unclear about some of your values. This is normal when you are a young adult. You are experimenting with life. During this time, you are probably often ambivalent. To be *ambivalent* means that you are attracted by an object, an activity, or a person at the same time that you are not attracted to one of them. You are ambivalent when you want to be loved and then do not want to be loved, want to go to a dance and then want to stay home, or want to feel hurt and then do not want to feel hurt.

The ambivalent person has not yet established strong values and does not know what is personally most important in life. Some ambivalence is normal throughout life, but it can be harmful if it becomes a major part of the way you act or feel.

It takes time and effort to develop your values. But it is important that you do work at developing them. For a clear set of values builds greater self-confidence and purpose. With clear values, you know where you are going. You can set your goals—whether in a school, home, or work setting—and act purposefully in attaining them. You will continue to grow as a healthy, mature person.

11

WHERE DO YOU LEARN YOUR VALUES?

Bill Russell, the former Boston Celtics basketball star, was making a TV commercial for a telephone company. He was supposed to miss a tough shot at a hoop over his fireplace, and remark, "I can miss, but you can't miss with long-distance."

It seemed a good idea, but on the first rehearsal Russell sank the ball into the basket without even touching the hoop. He tried to miss several more times, but the pro just could not bring himself to shoot poorly. Finally, the maker of the commercial gave up and rewrote the script showing Russell dropping one in and saying, "You can't miss with long-distance."

Bill Russell hits baskets like some people miss them—every time. But why? He has always been shooting to sink them, and this has become so much a part of him that he cannot change.

Achievement, or shooting to sink baskets, is one of Bill Russell's values. This value is so much a part of him that he is not conscious of it. But he was not born with that value or any other value. No one is born with a sense of values. Your values are developed through your experience. You clarify your values as you form and shape them into a system so that they work together.

Your value system comes from many influences in your environment. Social scientists call these influences *primary sources*, or influences in the first rank of importance, and *secondary sources*, or influences in the second area of importance. Thus, the primary sources for your values are your family, close friends, and other persons your own age. The secondary sources of your values are schools, people who are well known by the public, religious groups, community sources, and the mass media. The *mass media* include books, newspapers, magazines, television, radio, records, movies, and labels on things you buy.

Some of the secondary sources of values are more important than others, depending on your own feelings and your primary sources.

Usually between the ages of 14 and 18 years is when you begin to question your values. Perhaps you have already begun this process of questioning. The values you have at these ages are difficult to recognize because you have not noticed yourself acquiring them. Therefore you are usually not aware that you are questioning them, but your actions show it. Look at some sources of your values. First, examine the following primary sources.

YOUR FAMILY

You are a product of your family, with its customs, traditions, and attitudes. Your family's values are passed on to you, sometimes so slowly and quietly that you are not aware of it. These values are often *ingrained*, that is, they are a part of you in much the same way that the grain, or the lines, in a piece of wood are part of the wood. Sometimes parents never put their values into words, but you can tell from their actions what they prize most. For example, when you see your parents show concern with a kiss, a pat, or a smile you know that they value things such as kindness and concern. Sometimes, too, a sharp look or a swat on the behind lets you know this. Your family's lifestyle is pretty much your lifestyle as you are growing up. Perhaps your parents value togetherness, and family outings are a tradition in your home. But as you grow up and become aware of other values and other lifestyles, you may decide to choose new ones that are different from your family's.

The customs and traditions of your family will play an important part in influencing your values. (Magnum Photo/Elliot Erwitt)

To a certain extent, the United States has been a country where people are not bound by their backgrounds. For example, Abraham Lincoln—the president, Henry Ford—the automobile manufacturer, A. Philip Randolph—the labor leader, and George Washington Carver—the agricultural chemist and educator, are just a few of the people who rose from poor backgrounds to positions of importance.

Society, today, is not static. It continually changes, often very quickly. Many people are able and do choose to live quite differently from their families because they find other values and lifestyles more satisfying. In the maturing process, you test your parents' values and lifestyle. If they satisfy you, then more than likely you will keep them for your own. If not, you will continue to look for others that do.

YOUR FRIENDS AND CLASSMATES

Being accepted by people and making friends is an important part of your life. At a certain age, you start to seek acceptance outside your family. You want acceptance from other people as well, especially from friends. But wanting to be accepted is not the only reason young people need friends. You also need to express your deepest thoughts and feelings to people your own age because you are looking for help in forming your own values.

Young people want to be accepted by the crowd so much that sometimes they reflect the crowd's values instead of their own. The pressure to do this is very strong in high school. What is at work here is *social conformity*, that is, going along with the crowd's values in order to be liked.

Your social self develops and grows throughout your life. And your social values and skills are learned in many different ways. Your friends and other people your age play a big part in the way you think about and select your values. But you must be careful to consider what really is important. It is one thing, for example, to wear a plaid shirt or blouse every Tuesday and Thursday because that is the crowd's "in" thing to do. It is quite another to get bad marks through lack of study because the "in" thing is to stay out late on school nights.

There are many secondary sources of values, and they vary greatly. Look at how two of them, schools and the mass media, can influence and form values.

SCHOOLS

A school's values are likely to be the values of the students who attend it. Schools try to stress the best values of society, but these values are not always agreed on easily. One reason for this is that there are many groups of people with different values involved in running schools. Still, schools do affect your values to a certain degree. Certain teachers, for example, will contribute to shaping the values of some of their students.

You may have seen the recent film, *Conrack*, about a teacher who had a strong influence on his students. He taught in a one-room schoolhouse on an island off the coast of Georgia. Through his caring, for the first time in their lives most of the students learned about the wider world around them. Because Conrack valued learning and helping others to learn, he was able to show his students the value of education.

True democracy—one person, one vote—in a large society such as ours can become slow-moving and complex. That is why we in the United States use a representative form of democracy, with elected persons voting on issues for us. Sometimes, though, small groups, such as the population of a school, are able to practice democracy in a creative way. One school did experiment with democracy, teaching students values they otherwise may have overlooked.

Mrs. Fontaine, the principal, solved old problems in new ways. She didn't believe that rules should be presented and enforced just for the sake of having them. But she did believe in democracy, and she believed the best way for her students to learn democracy was to practice it. She permitted the students to vote on issues facing the school. In other words, she took democracy out of the civic and social studies classrooms and put it to work in the daily life of the school. Students soon learned the reasons for rules and regulations and what was really important about the running of a school and about their education. The school earned a reputation for practicing what it preached, and students from all over the city began trying to enroll there.

All in all, schools can strengthen the values that students bring with them to school, but rarely can schools directly change those values. Thus, one of the duties of a school is to help students search for new values or to reexamine the values they already have.

THE MASS MEDIA

Perhaps no society has been as strongly and constantly influenced by mass media as ours in this latter part of the twentieth century. Mass media may not only influence the brand of cat food or deodorant you buy but also some of your basic values as well. You are influenced by both what the mass media print or broadcast and by what they choose to leave out. Editorials in newspapers, magazines, on the radio, or on TV try to shape your opinions about issues at home and around the world. For example, consider the arguments for and against air and water pollution. Some editorials emphasize the need for cleaner air and waterways, pointing to human diseases and the loss of plant and animal life caused by pollution. Other editorials stress the need for cheaper sources of fuels and the need for profit, which is part of our economy. Both editorials are trying to influence your thinking about the pollution issue. How will you vote—yes or no—for an atomic energy plant, for instance? That depends on your values.

The mass media cannot be discussed without dealing with two important factors—the speed with which life is changing and the fact that there is no longer broad agreement about goals and purpose. The mass media, especially TV, keep us posted about changes, and this increases the speed of change. As a result, values are being changed to adjust to a changing world.

The mass media also influence your values and keep you posted on changes in the world. (© Jim Anderson 1979)

VALUES IN A CHANGING WORLD

In the past, certain values were held in common by most people. It was pretty much agreed on that this thing was better or more important than that thing. One reason for this was that new ideas were not known so widely and quickly as they are now because of the slowness of communication. Today, however, the mass media play a major role in introducing people to many different ideas and lifestyles. The wide publicity of the passage of the Civil Rights Act in 1964 certainly made people aware of a new way of living. Equal pay for equal work and equal opportunity to work for all have introduced the possibility of new value systems and new lifestyles to everyone.

You have probably heard the phrase, "the generation gap." That means that you and your parents have difficulty in understanding each other and you may disagree about certain things. What may be important to you may not be important to them, and vice versa. You may prefer to lead a different lifestyle, for example. Not every young person challenges the values of the family, but it happens often these days.

If you make a comparison between the values of your generation and your parents', you may see a difference between the generations. The following list gives some possible examples of the generation gap. Look them over and think about them. You, and your parents, may not necessarily agree with all of those listed under "Younger Generation" nor disagree with those under "Older Generation."

Although older and younger generations often have differ-
ent values, sometimes there are values common to both. In
recent years, both generations have demonstrated actively to
ensure the quality of life for the future. (Left, Marsha Cohen;
right, courtesy Sun City)

Older Generation	*Younger Generation*
If you work hard enough, you will be rewarded and get ahead.	Self-fulfillment counts in work. Work is something you want to do, not necessarily what you have to do.
Be glad you have a job. Self-satisfaction can come later, during your leisure time.	I have a right to self-satisfaction as part of my work. If I can't get it on the job, then I'll quit.
A woman's place is in the home. A woman isn't equipped biologically or emotionally for responsible jobs.	Men and women are equally able and should have the same opportunities for all jobs.
Law and order is very important. Centers of power must continue to be respected.	You should be permitted to do whatever you wish as long as it does not harm others. When centers of power no longer command respect, they should be challenged.
The man is the breadwinner in the family.	My wife earns more money than I do. I have the right to take paternal leave when our baby is born so that she can get back to her job.
Men with long hair are dirty, lazy, and irresponsible.	Wearing long hair is just part of a different lifestyle. It has nothing to do with a person's habits or characteristics.
Go to college so that you'll have plenty of money and be happy and successful.	If you prefer, go to a trade school. Happiness and success don't always depend on how much money you earn.

Just as your values are changing and developing as you grow and mature, the sources of some of society's values are also changing and being challenged. One value that has become an important issue concerns the place of women in society. In turn, this issue affects the family.

As you grow and mature, you choose the values that are best for you and fit your self-identity. You rank your values to suit your time as well as your self. All people in your generation are doing the same, and the values of your generation will form the base for the future and your world. In this way, you and your generation will be prepared for the challenges of the future. "Life is not only what it is but what it may become" a philosopher once wrote. And, when writing on values, John Dewey once said, "What one person and one group accomplish becomes the standing ground and starting point of those who succeed them."

Getting It All Together

1. In your own words, explain what values are.

2. In what ways do you act out your values?

3. Why are young people frequently ambivalent?

4. What are some of the effects of having a clear set of values?

5. Name some of the sources of values.

6. How do values guide you in the goals you set for your self?

7. How do your values affect your career decision?

8. Why do people of the same age and from the same background often have very different values?

9. How do you think your values have changed in the last three years?

10. How are your values different from those of your parents? How are they the same?

GETTING ORGANIZED ABOUT YOUR SELF

Your goals in this unit are given in the following list:

To identify your self further through some resources in your school

To think about choosing your career goals

To understand the meaning of "success"

"Hi, Pete," Maria says in the hall. "Did you see the notice on the bulletin board? Mr. James is giving a series of self-inventories next week. I think I'll take them, because I'm really not too sure about what I want to do. If I take them, I can get some ideas about my future."

"I'm not about to waste a free period taking tests that I don't have to take," Pete answers. "Besides, I know what I'm going to be doing. I'm going to trade school and take the auto mechanics training course. Mechanics make good money, the work's steady, and the hours are good."

"I've never heard you talk about automobiles before, Pete," Maria says. "Remember how hard it was for you to get through shop class? Are you sure that's what you want to do?"

"Well, why not?" Pete asks.

The purpose of this last unit is to point out the "why not" of Pete's remark. Certainly there is nothing wrong with Pete's decision to be an auto mechanic. There would be nothing wrong if he had decided to be an astronaut, a baker, or anything else. But there is something basically wrong with the way he arrived at his decision.

You have already learned about some factors that are involved in making a decision in terms of your career. But there are other factors that can be used, such as the career resources available in your school.

Maria is being smart by considering taking self-inventories to determine her career interests. Self-inventories are one example of a resource that is available to you in making a career choice. Various other resources are also discussed in Chapter 12. Through the use of these resources you can determine your aptitudes, abilities, values, and needs. Some of these resources can also show where your interests lie. Counseling, both individual and group, is another resource that is discussed. Using these resources can get you off to a good start.

Work values—what is important to you, what will satisfy you in the world of work—are guideposts in your career planning. There are two questions that you may be asking your self: What kind of job will I be happy with? What kind of job will I be successful at? If you have an idea of what kind of lifestyle you wish to have, you can make a wise career selection.

Now is the time to choose your career goals. These goals can be short-range or long-range. Your short-range goals tend to require training, while your long-range goals require general education, followed by some special training. Chapter 13 gives you some guidance for choosing your goals.

Chapter 13 also discusses the meaning of success in terms of career and some popular standards of success. Success is unique to each person.

12

USING CAREER IDENTITY RESOURCES

"Hi, Rose. Did you find out the results of the standardized test we took a few weeks ago?" Bobby asks.

"Yes, I did, Bobby" Rose answers. "It was pretty interesting, but I'm not sure about how I did on it."

"What do you mean?" Bobby asks. "You're not supposed to get a grade, Rose. Didn't you get an idea of how you would do in some career areas?"

"Yes, I did. As a matter of fact, the results seem to back up my decision to enter the urban planning program at City College next year."

"That's how I felt about my results too. I'm going to State University to study mining. You know, there was something about the scoring. Didn't Mr. Lopez say that we are compared with people who took the test all over the country? I don't understand exactly what that means."

"You know, Bobby, Mr. Lopez is holding a group counseling session Thursday afternoon. It's supposed to help us in decision making about our jobs and in planning our educational goals. Maybe we can learn more about the scoring too. How about going?"

"OK," says Bobby. "I think I will."

Bobby and Rose are taking advantage of different programs their school offers to help them in making their career decisions. They are using some of their school's resources, or sources of support and information, to help them plan for and explore their career choices. Most schools use some, if not all these resources, depending on their size and location. If some resources are not available in the school, they are made available within the community or school district.

You have explored your self by understanding your self-identity and by examining some of the many dimensions of your self. You have begun to discover your system of values. By exploring the parts of the whole self and establishing some clear ideas about your values, you are preparing for the career decisions that you will be making. Planning and achieving your career goals will go more smoothly also. You can further explore your self and your career possibilities through the resources that may be available to you through your school. There are many of these resources. Look at some of them and consider how you may use them.

EVALUATIVE INSTRUMENTS

Evaluative instruments are resources that can be used for understanding your career interests, aptitudes, and abilities. They can help you sort through all the career areas that possibly appeal to you so that you can center on the one area, or the few areas, that fit you best. Consider two types of these instruments, or systems.

Self-Inventories

Self-inventories are not tests, and they have no right or wrong answers. They are a series of questions through which you rate your self. In answering the questions, you develop information about your self and show your preferences. The results of these self-inventories will develop into a pattern that indicates your preferences. This pattern of preferences can guide you in planning your career goals. Self-inventories do not measure intelligence, aptitude, or skill. However, they do establish your attitudes, feelings, needs, types of experience, wishes, and values.

Self-inventories point out the career areas where your interests lie. They can be used to guide the development of your major career areas. For example, if after taking a self-inventory you find that your interests are similar to those of others who are actually working in mathematics and the sciences, you would take some more courses to determine which area fits you best in terms of a future career.

Standardized Tests

A *standardized test* attempts to reveal some of your qualities by having you do certain assignments using questions, tasks, and situations. Your responses are scored, and the results show how far above or below average you are in performing certain tasks. These tests indicate aptitude, intelligence, achievement, readiness, creativity, and other traits. Sometimes you take them in a group; sometimes you take them separately. Sometimes how fast you do them is an element in scoring them.

Standardized tests are often scored by a machine, but it takes a qualified person to interpret them. Your score is compared to a standard that has been developed in giving the same test around the country. Standardized testing enables you to understand how you compare with others in your age group. By taking standardized tests, you can further understand your self.

School and community resources can help you explore your self-identity. (Courtesy Adelphi University)

You have probably noticed that there are separate categories for interests and values in self-inventories and standardized tests. Remember that your values determine what you consider most important, desirable, and worthwhile in your life. On the other hand, your interests express your preferences for the activities that you like and spend most of your time doing. These self-inventories and standardized tests can give you a good start in determining your values and interests. If you are interested in taking a self-inventory or a standardized test and have not done so, talk to your school counselor.

COUNSELING

In order to use self-inventories and standardized testing to their best advantage, the results of your performance on these evaluative instruments can be interpreted through discussion with the counseling resources that are available at or through your school. By using these resources, you can gain further guidance and insight for your career planning. There are two types of counseling, individual and group.

Counseling involves talking. Talking is a useful way to get at some of your deepest thoughts and feelings. Somebody once said that "Language is the dress of thought." That means that every time you talk, your mind shows itself to others as well as to your self. You think out loud in counseling, and this enables you to gain a better insight into your self-identity and values.

Individual Counseling

Individual counseling is done on a one-to-one basis. It should be done with somebody who has been trained to counsel others—usually the school guidance counselor. Since counseling cannot be accomplished in one day, it may take a great deal of time. In talking with someone, you are able to discover important things about your self.

Individual counseling can help you find out what career information you need and where you can get it. Through counseling, you think about your values and goals. You are helped to clarify them. Counseling can help you develop and strengthen your self-identity, and it can help you make plans to choose a career that suits your self-identity. You are able to decide whether the career areas you are considering suit your values and interests by talking to your counselor. If you are confused or uncertain about the lifestyle you want to follow, your counselor can help you.

Individual counseling works best when you have thought out what you want from it before you start. But if you are uncertain or uneasy about your self and your future, individual counseling may help you to clear up your feelings and to put aside your uneasiness. You can also clear up your feelings by taking part in a group.

Group Counseling

Group counseling involves more than two people, usually 5 to 10 persons or 15 at the most. The leader of a group is someone trained to counsel others and creates trust and helpfulness in the group. This type of counseling can also help you clarify your self-identity and your values. Sometimes counseling of this type is organized to solve a certain problem or group of problems that are common to a selected group.

In group counseling, you begin by telling the others who you are. Telling who you are means much more than giving your name, age, and address. You describe what you think your self-identity is and how you feel about your self. Why is it necessary to tell people these things about your self? You do this because you need feedback from others. You need their responses and reactions to who you think you are.

Group counseling can help you overcome shyness if you are reluctant about talking in a group situation. In group counseling situations, you can learn to feel more comfortable with other people your age. You begin to understand that others have problems like your own. When you see how others solve their problems, you are able to solve your own problems.

Sometimes group counseling sessions are called "truth sessions." Each person in the group has the right and the duty to talk back. By talking in a group, each person sees that his or her problem is not unique. Since most people often feel less threatened in a group, group counseling can also give you encouragement. Through group counseling, you can feel that you are in charge of your search for your self-identity and values.

Confidants

In an individual or a group counseling situation, a counselor can help you tackle tough decisions by providing facts and by helping you to relate the facts to your problem. Sometimes you can solve your problems by asking a person's opinion and sharing your thoughts with that person. This person may also be able to help you when you are trying to make a decision. Such a person is called a confidant. A *confidant* is somebody to whom you confide something, such as your deepest thoughts. Confidants can be parents, a trusted teacher, a relative whom you admire, or a close friend your own age or older. You can have more than one confidant.

A word of caution about confidants: Sometimes your confidant may not be able to help you. And he or she may not have the necessary training or experience to help you solve more serious problems. In this case you should speak to your counselor at school.

USING THESE RESOURCES

Self-inventories, standardized tests, and counseling are some important resources that can be used for understanding your self. They can help you gain further insights into your self and your career possibilities. By using a combination of these resources, you can make the best advantage of them in planning your career.

Although these inventories, tests, and counseling are not the final say in what you will be doing later on in life, they should not stop you from further pursuit of a particular goal.

Group counseling can help you to overcome shyness. (Courtesy Union Carbide Corp.)

CHAPTER 13

CHOOSING YOUR CAREER GOALS

As you think about the careers that appeal to you and as you sort out your work values and career goals, keep in mind that being a doctor or lawyer is not better than being a mechanic or salesperson. Jobs in the professions are not better than industrial or service work; they are merely different. Also keep in mind that making a lot of money is not better than making less money. Doing what satisfies you, whether that requires you to set short-range or long-range goals, is better than doing what others expect of you or what seems easiest to do.

EXPLORE YOUR SELF

A review of the preceding chapters and your answers to the questions at the end of each unit will help you determine your career goals. For example, you explored your self-identity and the many parts of your self in Unit 1. In Unit 2, you discovered some further dimensions of your self. In Unit 3, you explored your values, and in Chapter 12, you learned about some resources that you can use to determine your career goals. Now you can unify your career goals by summing up what you have learned about your self.

HOW ARE CAREER GOALS DEVELOPED?

Career goals begin in your wishful thinking. You never lose this ability to daydream. Daydreaming helps you to understand what you really want to do and be.

In childhood your daydreams often involve people and things around you. As you grow older, you push your daydreams farther into the future. They begin to form a picture of what you would like to become. In adolescence, you start to put your daydreams in order and begin to realize which ones are most important. You also start to try out your daydreams in real life. This is called *reality-testing*. Adults do this too.

Now apply this process to choosing a career. At first you daydream about the many career areas in which you are interested. For example, you may consider the field of entertainment. You dance pretty well, and people say you have a good voice. Being an entertainer is a possibility. But then there is the whole area of science. New developments are always happening in that area, and the idea of doing something new and exciting intrigues you. On and on you daydream. Then comes another level of daydreaming. After considering all of the many career areas, you finally decide upon science, for example. The number of careers in science is endless, however. You may picture your self walking on another planet, collecting samples of its crust for future study. Maybe you see your self being another Marie Curie and making a breakthrough in scientific research.

As you mature and become more realistic, you narrow your choices down to one career area. Let's suppose that your main interest is in biology. What kind of job do you want in biology? Do you want to teach? Or do you prefer doing research? Depending upon your abilities, time and money, values, interests, and other factors in your life, you make your decision about a career.

BELIEVE IN YOUR SELF

What influences your chance of reaching your career goals? You already know that your values guide your choice of goals. For instance, in the above example, if you prefer working independently, you'd probably choose research. On the other hand, if you prefer helping people and working with them, you'd decide to teach.

Certainly your economic condition influences your chance of reaching your career goals. For example, you may not have enough money to complete the training or education needed for getting the job you want. If that is the case, you may have to make some compromises. However, if you value education and training, you will find a way to get what is necessary for the job you want even though this may cause some sacrifices on your part.

Your talents and abilities are important influences in reaching your career goals too. But the most important influence is your self-identity. You must believe in your self before you can put your talents and abilities to work for your self. You also need a clear set of values. Remember, values build self-confidence. And self-confidence enables you to reach your goals.

The story of Thomas Edison's success is well known. He had self-confidence, curiosity, and determination. All of these things led to his success. But what was the key to Edison's self-confidence, this most important influence on reaching goals?

One possible key to Edison's self-confidence may be what he thought about failure. Many people think that failure is a terrible thing, but Edison thought failure was an opportunity to succeed in a better way. He once said that his efforts to develop a new storage battery had 50,000 failures. One of his assistants voiced some discouragement about the failures, but Edison told him, "Why, I've gotten a lot of results—I know 50,000 things that won't work!" He knew 50,000 things not to try again and to Edison that was progress.

WHAT IS SUCCESS?

"I want to teach." "I want to earn a million dollars before I'm 40." "I want to be a help to people throughout my life." "I want to raise a family." What is success? To different people success means different things.

Being kind, caring for children, or making others comfortable can mean success in life for some. Another measure of success is to determine how well one does in a job. But what is success in terms of a career? People are unique, and so they have different definitions of success. For some it may be doing a job well, for others it may be supervising a few people, and still others will not be satisfied until they are running the whole show.

Here are some popular standards for determining success in a career:

- Amount of monthly salary
- Total amount of lifetime earnings
- Position and status in society
- Amount of security in a job
- Size of organization—whether a business, agency, or service
- Personal achievement
- Amount of independence
- Ability to carry out the aims of a company, agency, or profession
- Ability to do a job well
- Ability to please others
- Opportunity to serve society

Although success itself is difficult to define, *overall success* can probably be defined. It is the feeling that more and more each day you are reaching the worthwhile goals you have set for your self. For example, it may come from the successful completion of a course needed for a promotion on your job.

You can be a success and have a sense of achievement if you choose a career that uses your full potential. If you work in an area that fits you and your capabilities, you will be able to realize your potential. John Wooden, one of the most successful coaches in college basketball history, did not coach his players to win. Instead, he coached his players to be a success. For Coach Wooden, success meant playing as well as possible, and finding and using one's full potential. Coach Wooden's idea can be applied as a useful guide to success in a career.

Researchers have found that people try hardest when their chances of success or failure are about even. In such a situation, understanding your self can make the difference between success and failure. If you understand your self, you can match your abilities and interests with your career goals.

Getting It All Together

1. How can standardized tests and self-inventories be used for making decisions about your career goals?

2. How can counseling be used for making decisions about your career goals? What types of counseling are there?

3. Describe what "being a success" means to you.

4. Why is self-confidence so important in succeeding in what you want to do?

5. Discuss what is meant by this statement: The first step in finding a job is finding your self.

MAKING DECISIONS WORK

THE IMPORTANCE OF DECISION MAKING

Your goals in this unit are given in the following list:

To recognize the importance of making decisions

To recognize why you must be responsible for your decisions

To understand how your values help you to establish goals and make decisions

To identify work values and realize their importance to career decision making

"So, what's to decide? Get up. Go to school. Graduate. Get a job. Whatever's available."

It's true. Some people approach their lives like that. They just take what is available when it is time to go to work. Some are lucky. They manage to land in a lifelong job that is somewhat interesting to them. The majority are less lucky. They spend their lives toiling at something they do not particularly care for. They took a job because it was there, or because it was like what their parents had, or it was what their friends were doing.

It doesn't have to be like that. Did you know, for example, that there are more than 21,700 separate jobs in this country? Sure, some jobs are hard to get. They take a lot of time and expensive formal education or special training. The main point you should keep in mind now, though, is that you have a variety of jobs to choose from. You can make your own decisions about your career. To do this well, however, you need to know three things:

- You need to know yourself.
- You need to know what careers exist.
- You need to know how to make effective decisions.

Effective decisions are workable or practical choices for action. And making effective decisions is what this book is all about. Specifically, it is about making decisions for a satisfying career. Note the word "satisfying." Making effective decisions is no guarantee that you will become rich or famous or powerful. However, if you do make effective decisions about what you want to be, your chances of having a satisfying career—doing what you like to do—(and maybe some of those other things also) are very good indeed.

Making an effective career decision does not mean taking the first job that comes along. Effective career decision making is a process. It is beginning early to think about what you are like, what your values are, and about your career goals. It means exploring available opportunities and finding out what jobs and careers are best for you. Making career decisions is not a one-shot process. Rather, it is continuous, and it changes as you change and the world of work changes.

You may wonder, "How could I not decide what's best for me? Won't I do what I want to do?" Well, the answer to both those questions is, unfortunately, "Not always."

Making the best decisions for yourself is not always easy, but it is within your power to shape your future. You can learn how to make effective career decisions. In this first unit, you will learn why it is important to make effective decisions and how your values and goals affect your decision making.

14

WHAT IS DECISION MAKING?

"It's raining. What shall I wear today?" "Will I have eggs or cereal for breakfast?" "Which television program shall I watch?" These are examples of everyday situations in which you make a decision. Simply put, *decision making* is choosing between two or more possibilities.

If there is only one action you can take, then you do not have to make a decision. If you have only one raincoat, that is what you will wear in the rain. You may be running late one morning, and cereal is faster to prepare than eggs—so cereal it is for breakfast. Your area only carries one TV channel, so you will settle down to watch Channel X. More often, though, you will have choices, and therefore you must make decisions. And the results of those decisions are more important than what you wear, or eat, or watch on TV.

EFFECTIVE DECISION MAKING

At this point, you may be thinking, "Well, since I make decisions all the time, what's the point of studying about decision making? What's the big deal? A person just decides, and that's that." The reply to that is, yes, anyone can make a decision. But what about effective decision making?

Surely you can remember one or two decisions you have made that didn't turn out well for you. If you think back, maybe, just maybe, there might have been something that could have helped you to make better decisions. For example, you may know someone who decided to leave school at age 16. That's a decision, but how effective is it? What were the results for that person a month after leaving school? Did the person find a job? Is the person happy, bored, or

scared? More important, what will be the results for that person 5 years from now, 10 years from now, 20 years from now?

What's in the Future?

In making decisions, you must know what you are doing and why you are doing it. You must have a good idea of what will happen as a result of your decisions. In other words, decision making is similar to making a guess about the future. It's like walking around a dark room, trying not to stumble into furniture. Effective decision making, though, is similar to making an educated guess about the future. You have some light to help you find your way.

To take a simple example, suppose you are driving to your friend's house. You decide to take one route rather than another because you expect it to be the faster way to get there. Through this action, you are making a guess about the future. It so happens that the street you chose is being repaired. You now have to use another street to get to your friend's house, and the delay makes you late. Your guess about the future— that you will arrive on time—is wrong, and you will have to live with the results of your decision. Thinking you weren't coming, your friend made other plans and isn't home.

Decisions of this kind are simple. They require little thought, and their results are not lasting. Arriving at your friend's house late may upset your plans for the day, but that is all. There is no permanent effect on your life. When decisions involve important matters, such as your career or where you will live, or whether or not you will marry, it becomes more difficult to know

```
     9:30          11 Hazel; Shirley Booth.        7 News, Sports, Weather.      berg, Ron Palillo,
Collins Show.             2:30                     9 The Avengers.              Dan,  John Ford
centration; Jack Narz.  2, 3 Guiding Light.       11 Star Trek.                Angela Bacari, R
n Acres; Eddie Albert.   4 The Doctors.           13 VILLA ALEGRE.             Dangerfield.
ypoint on Nutrition.    7, 8 One Life to Live.    41 News, Sports, Weather.    13 Wall Street Week.
Addams Family.          11 Joya's Fun School.     68 Uncle Floyd's Show.       41 Barata de Primaver
    10:00               13 Lilias, Yoga and You.            6:30               68 Yankees-Mets High
he Price is Right.               3:00              5 Partridge Family.                  9:00
ord and Son.            2, 3 All in the Family.   13 ELECTRIC COMPANY.         2, 3 Movie· "The S
Girl; Marlo Thomas.      4 Another World.         41 Lo Imperdonable.          Connection,"  Barr
IE; "MARRIAGE-GO-        5 Casper Cartoons.       47 Sacrificio de Mujer.      man.  International
ND." Susan Hayward,      9 Lucy Show; Lucille Ball. 68 Journey to the Center of spy thriller fizzles.
n e s Mason. Amusing    11 Felix the Cat Cartoon.     the Earth.               4 ROCKFORD FILES
  about an American     13 Inner Tennis.                   7:00               Garner, John Saxo
is attracted to a free- 68 Stock Market Reports.  2, 3 News; Walter Cronkite.  hires Rockford to
oriented S w e d i s h           3:15             4 News; Chancellor-Brinkley.  gate her sauve ge
an (1961)              7, 8 General Hospital.      5 Andy Griffith Show.        friend from the Ea
per Room.                        3:30              7 News; Harry Reasoner.      13 U.S.A.:   PEOPLE
gan's Island            2 Match Game              9 FIRING LINE WITH WIL-       POLITICS;   James
CTRIC COMPANY.         3, 5 MICKEY MOUSE CLUB.      LIAM F. BUCKLEY; Leo        Barber. A profile
    10:30                9 Lassie.                  Pfeffer, Allard Lowenstein.  Republican    pres
rity Sweepstakes.       11 Magilla Gorilla Cartoons. "State Aid to Sectarian   candidate.
Griffith Show.         13 Hodgepodge Lodge.         Schools."                  47 La Otra. Novela.
ly Affair.                       4:00             11 Dick Van Dyke Show.        68 Jack Bilby's Talent
h. Children's series.    2 DINAH SHORE SHOW;      13 FLASH GORDON'S TRIP                9:30
    11:00                Bert Convy, George Ken-    TO MARS; "The Black        41 Las Mascaras. Nove
mbit.                    nedy. Lendon Smith, Max-   Sapphire of Kalu" (R)               9:45
el of Fortune.           ine Nightingale, Allan Rich, (Part 8).               9 QUARTERFINAL S
tched.                   Billy Braver.            41 Chespirito.                GAME; COSMOS-RO
ght Talk.                4 Family Doctor.         68 Peyton Place.              (Tape delay).
tship of Eddie's Father. 5 Porky, Huck and Yogi.           7:30                      10:00
mily at War             7                         2 $25,000 Pyramid            4 POLICE STORY
```

Every day you make a lot of decisions about your routine activities, such as what you are going to eat and what you are going to do in your free time.

what will happen. At the same time, it is more important to be aware of the possibilities and alternatives available to you so that you can choose what is best for you.

Growing Up

Effective decision making is difficult. But in spite of the difficulty, most of us prefer to make our own decisions and to determine our own future. Your parents and other adults made most decisions for you when you were a child. As you grew older, you wanted more control over your own life. More control meant making more of your own decisions. This is only natural and good. Making your own decisions is part of the process of maturing and growing up.

However, as with most good things in life, there is also a catch. Along with making your own decisions comes responsibility. For as you gain more control over your own life and make more of your own decisions, you become more responsible for what you do. You must take the credit, or discredit, for your actions.

DECISION MAKING AND RESPONSIBILITY

To be responsible means that you take the credit or the blame for whatever happens as a result of your decisions. *Responsibility*, the act of taking the credit or blame for your decisions, goes along with the freedom to decide. Just as you would

blame your parents if their decisions created unwanted results for you, so you must blame yourself for decisions that bring unwanted results. For example, if you failed an examination because you did not study, it is unreasonable, not to say pointless, to blame your teacher for your failure. After all, when you pass an examination, you do not give the teacher credit, do you?

Outside Factors

You are responsible for the results of your decisions, but that does not mean you must blame yourself whenever something does not work out right. Sometimes things go wrong. For example, you plan a picnic, but it rains all day. You decide to save your money for a vacation, but an unexpected medical expense comes up. You are to pick up a friend at 8 o'clock, but a flat tire makes you late. None of these failures is your fault.

Sometimes your decisions are affected by factors beyond your control. No person is in complete control of events and situations. This is why it's important to consider as many things as possible before making a decision. What can go wrong? If things go wrong, what can be done? Ask questions to make effective decisions.

Don't Blame Me

You probably have heard someone say, "Don't blame me. I had nothing to do with it." "If only

Sue had done her job, everything would have turned out all right." "It's Joe's fault. I did the best I could." Such statements are common. Sometimes these excuses are true, but sometimes they are only remarks people use to rid themselves of responsibility.

If you want to make your own decisions and have some say in your life, you must be careful not to fall back on such excuses. Most of the time, you are responsible for the results of your actions. Excuses may allow you to "save face" when things go wrong, but they may also keep you from accepting your responsibility for your decisions and keep you from having the freedom to control your life as best you can.

Consider the two cases of Kathy and Ted:

In her sophomore year in high school, Kathy decided to take a business program. She had been the class secretary for 2 years and enjoyed her duties in that position. She liked to type reports of the class meetings, and she had very good writing skills. Everyone agreed that Kathy was the best choice for class secretary, and she worked hard to do the job well.

In her junior year, Kathy began to work in an office on weekends. She was surprised to realize that she was enjoying the work less and less. She also found that she didn't like to type for long periods of time. Kathy decided to reconsider her plans about continuing further in the business program.

She talked with her parents, teachers, and the school counselor. Kathy decided to take some occupational interest and aptitude measures, and in doing so, she rediscovered a strong interest and talent in drawing. She thought that she might like to teach art to young children, and so she decided to take some college preparatory work as well as the business courses. Thus, Kathy thought, she would be in a good position to make a decision later on that she could live with.

Kathy had a mature attitude. She realized that only she could make decisions about a career, and that she alone was responsible for whatever decision she made. She did not blame her teachers, parents, or friends for her first decision to follow a business program. Instead, Kathy took the responsibility for making that decision by getting all the information she could about other interests. Instead of locking herself into only one area, she gave herself other careers to choose from when the time came to make a final decision.

Ted was just the opposite of Kathy:

Ted usually found some person or some thing to blame for his poor decisions. He made excuses. When he failed algebra, Ted blamed it on the teacher, rather than admitting that he hadn't done his homework or had not asked the teacher to explain what he didn't understand.

Ted also had problems outside school. He had either quit or been fired from three part-time

Who, do you think, is responsible if this worker's papers are damaged as a result of the situation shown here?

You can start being responsible by deciding what to wear when you go out. (Courtesy Zion Benton News)

jobs. He never realized that his failure to hold a job was partly his own fault. He always blamed the working conditions or his supervisor. Ted never even thought that maybe part of the problem was within himself. Instead, he excused himself by saying, and believing, that what happened was beyond his control.

Ted did not have a mature attitude. Rather than being responsible for making his own decisions, he would let things "happen" to him. That way he could blame others for his problems. It never occurred to him that if he continued to blame others he would always have problems.

Take a tip from Kathy. Consider the alternatives, or choices. Don't just settle for something that sounds good. Try to get information to help you in your effective decision making. Make the best decision you can and accept the responsibility for it. By not making your own decisions and by not being responsible for them, like Ted, you will be letting others determine your life and your future.

AVOIDING DECISIONS IS NOT THE SOLUTION

Some people have trouble making any decisions. Consider Lou's case:

Lou decided that the safe way to avoid unwanted results was to let other people decide for him. Gradually, Lou's attitude became one of, "I'll let the other person decide. Then I won't get blamed

if something goes wrong." Lou was happy to have his parents make decisions for him. He much preferred his teachers and guidance counselor to make course choices for him.

However, when Lou got his first job, his attitude started to get him in trouble. By always avoiding decisions and waiting for the other person to decide, his work production was low. His supervisor felt he really didn't want a job and his co-workers thought he was trying to push all the work onto them. After a while, Lou was fired.

Lou thought he was playing it safe and avoiding responsibility by not making decisions. Well, he may have avoided responsibility, but not the consequences. Actually, he was making one decision all the time—not to make decisions. His basic decision was not a good one. In the end, he was forced to accept the responsibility for that poor basic decision. He was fired.

All of us must accept the results of our decisions, as well as the results of our indecisions. It is impossible to avoid responsibility.

DECISION MAKING AND YOU

You may be thinking: "It sounds as though being responsible is a trait of a person. And a trait is not easy to change, is it? Can a person decide to become more responsible and then go ahead and do it? And how can I tell whether I'm responsible or not?"

Most experts on human behavior will agree that some people are more responsible than others. Some are completely responsible, while others are completely irresponsible. Most of us fall somewhere between the two extremes.

You can judge how responsible you are. Honestly try to answer the following questions about yourself. You will only be fooling yourself if you try to gloss over your weak points.

If something goes wrong as a result of one of your decisions, do you take responsibility for it? Or do you tend to blame others or look for excuses? Do you feel that generally you control your life? Or do you feel that others always make decisions for you? Do you think you can affect your future? Or do you feel that you must just sit tight and see what happens?

If you want to make your own decisions and shape your own future, you can do it. But you cannot expect to put off being responsible until some magic day when other people and outside events will leave you alone. Right now, you can start being responsible in little ways—in deciding how to dress, when to eat, with whom to go out, and where to go.

Try to be aware of the connection between the decisions you make now and the results you get later. When you find yourself making excuses, ask yourself whether they are true or whether they are excuses to keep you from accepting responsibility. If you want to have control over your life, you have to take control.

15

DECISION MAKING AND YOUR VALUES

One of the most important things in making a decision is to know what you want. To make a decision, you need to know what your *goals*, or the things that you want to achieve, are. And to set your goals, you have to know your *values*, or what is important to you. Only when you know your values can you set a goal and make effective decisions to reach that goal.

IDENTIFYING YOUR VALUES

Your values are an important factor in making effective decisions about a job or career, but first you have to know what your values are. Knowing his values, Barry made effective decisions to set his goal:

> Barry's father is a successful building contractor. He takes pride in his work, and he likes making a lot of money and being his own boss—two things that are important to him in work. Barry has different ideas about what he wants to do with his life. Barry wants to work with people, not things. Therefore, Barry has decided on a career in social work. To reach that goal, he has enrolled in the social work program at college and works part time at a local public health agency.

Barry's decision was based on his values. He knew that he cared more about helping people than about running a business. If he cared about the same things his father did—independence and material rewards—he might have joined his father's firm. But Barry had different values and, therefore, a different goal.

Barry knows what is important to him, and he has started working to obtain his goal. To find out your values, consider the different ways that

are described below. The results you get about yourself may not be definite, but they can act as guides toward a career or job that is best for you.

Either-Or Situations

One way to identify your values—to find out what is important to you—is to imagine some "either-or" situations. For example, would you rather take a part-time job to earn extra money or have more free time and less money? Would you rather live in the country or the city? Would you rather have many friends or have just a few? Would you rather go to a large school or go to a small school?

These questions may be easy to answer. But if you stop to think about your answers, you will find that they give you a clue to your general values and that they can have an influence on the goals that you set for yourself.

Talking to Others

Talking to others is a good way to learn about your values. Through the give-and-take of discussion, not only do you get to know yourself better but you also understand others better. You will understand why people behave as they do and why they make the decisions they do.

Choose a subject that means a lot in your group. If you discuss controversial issues, such as pollution, drug use, or social welfare, you are likely to find several different sets of values expressed. For example, some of your friends may be definitely for the use of public funds to aid people, some may be definitely against using

Identifying your values will give you clues to what you really want. You can make effective decisions when you know your values. (Marsha Cohen)

public money this way, and others may fall between these two extremes.

You may wonder how friends who seem to have so much in common can think so differently about one subject. The answer is simple: Their values are different. In regard to social welfare, for example, you may believe hard work is the answer and that only lazy people want public assistance. On the other hand, one of your friends may believe that helping others is very important and that some people are not as fortunate as others, regardless of how hard they work.

These differences in values cause you to disagree. Neither you nor your friend can be proved "right" in your opinions. You can only feel sure of your own decisions, which are based on your values.

The point is that in order to set your goals—whether or not to leave school, whether or not to take that business course, whether or not to do whatever—your decision should reflect your values. What is important to you should aid you in setting your goals and achieving them.

USING VALUES TO SET GOALS

To make meaningful, effective decisions that will help you to grow and realize your potential, you must have goals. Clearly defined values will help you set goals. Unclear values lead to a lack of goals and ineffective decisions. *Ineffective decisions* are impractical or unworkable choices.

For example, if you value independence, you will make decisions about work and personal relationships that keep you free from being tied down too much. If you value friendship, sharing things with your friends and helping them will be important to you. If you value your health, you will spend time, energy, and money to maintain or improve it. You will exercise often and form good eating and sleeping habits. Your values do affect how you live your life.

Goals and values are closely related. Values refer to how you feel about something and are expressed in words such as independence, honesty, and self-control. Goals are your values translated into action or plans for action. Suppose you value independence. You then might have goals like earning enough money to pay all your own bills and getting your own apartment.

Here is the story of Wanda, whose values and goals are clearly related:

Wanda, the senior class president, has been named "most likely to succeed" by her classmates. She seems always to be trying to get ahead. Right now, Wanda is trying to make a decision between two very good job offers.

One job is with a local department store where she has worked part time. The pay is pretty good, and she could continue to live at home until she saved enough money to get an apartment. The second job is with a new oil exploration company that employs her uncle. This job pays less to start, but Wanda thinks it would be more exciting. The job involves travel, and she might even get a chance to work in Asia after she has had a year or so of experience.

Wanda's uncle is encouraging her to take the job with the oil company. "If you join us, the rewards can be great. If our oil exploration is successful, the company will grow, and you would have the opportunity for advancement. However, there are some risks. If we don't discover oil, the business will fail. That would mean that you would have worked long, hard hours for little pay."

Wanda thinks about both jobs and about her goals. She wants an exciting life and a certain amount of recognition. Security is not a primary concern for her right now. Wanda decides to work for her uncle's oil company.

Why did Wanda make this decision? She values an exciting life, and she is ambitious. She has shown already that she has a strong desire for recognition. Security is not important to her, at least now, so she is willing to take a risk because she wants the excitement and possible benefits that the job offers.

WHEN VALUES CLASH

Once you identify your values, you are on the way toward effective decision making. However, there still will be some stumbling blocks, and one of those stumbling blocks is conflict in values. This conflict can come about when your values and those of your parents clash, and it can come about within yourself when you try to satisfy two or more equally important values at the same time.

Join group activities in your community. Talking to other people in your age group will help you to identify some of your own values. (Courtesy United Nations/T. Chen/JMcG)

You and Your Parents

Your parents have their own values, and these values were also yours as you were growing up. But as you mature, you may start to question some of their values. Through your own experiences, you may keep some of their values, reject others, and add other ones.

Consider the story about Barry, and how he had different values and a different goal from those of his father. If Barry's father had wanted him to continue the family business and if Barry had wanted to satisfy his father, his choice would have been difficult to make. He would have had to choose between two sets of values—his and his father's.

But Barry knew his values, and he knew what he wanted to do with his life. Naturally, you will want to consider other people's values in making decisions, because it is good to have other opinions. But the final decision is yours, and it is your values and your goals that are important in making that decision.

You and Yourself

Values help you make choices, but since several things can be important to you at the same time, now and then you will face conflict and have to make a choice. Thus, making decisions can be difficult. You may also find yourself in a situation where the most desirable choice is also the most difficult to obtain.

Suppose you are an advertising copywriter, for example. You like working at home, setting your own hours, and creating your own material for advertisements. Eventually, you hope to have your own advertising agency. But assignments are slowly coming in, and you don't have much money. You certainly would like to earn a good wage, for you have to pay rent and buy food, not to mention the supplies that you will need for carrying out your work.

You are offered a permanent job in an advertising agency. The pay is excellent and you would have a steady income. However, your hours are 9 to 5, you must work in the agency's offices, and you have to write what you are told. Now you will have to decide what is more important—a good income or the opportunity to work as you please. And will you ever be able to have your own agency?

When making decisions, sometimes the immediate results of a choice clash with the results that come later. Consider this example:

Adrian, a senior, works three evenings a week in a local bookstore. He is allowed to study his schoolwork in the store when there are no customers.

One week Adrian had an exam in English on Friday. Throughout the week, he put off reading his assignment, saying to himself, "I'll be able to do my reading at work on Thursday." But on Thursday evening, although business at the bookstore was slow, Adrian still did not read his assignment. Instead, he talked to his friends on the telephone awhile and then read a magazine.

Friday morning, while Adrian was struggling with his English exam, he promised himself to study the next time.

Adrian made decisions according to what he most wanted to do at the time. First, he decided to put off reading the assignment until Thursday night, which was his last chance. Then he decided to make phone calls and read a magazine. The immediate results of both decisions were pleasant. But the later results were not so pleasant. He failed the exam and got a low final grade in English.

It is especially important to know what you value most when you are faced with choices. Immediate satisfaction sometimes can stop you from reaching a goal. For example, the next time Adrian faces conflicting choices, he will probably give up immediate satisfaction in order to achieve a satisfactory result in the future.

CHANGING VALUES AND GOALS

As you mature, you will find that your values and your goals will change throughout your life. What may seem important to you now may become less important later on. Sometimes this change happens after you have reached a goal that you have set. For instance, if independence is very important to you now, you will make decisions to be independent. After you become independent, you set other goals, depending upon other values.

Recognize that this kind of change means growth. Do not be afraid of it, thinking that you may be a wishy-washy person with no backbone. This kind of change is not the kind where you have no clear goals and you go however the winds blow. This change comes from knowing where you want to go and trying to get there. It is the result of growth, achievement, and other changing conditions.

If you think about it, you will find that you already have changed your values and goals

Stumbling blocks in decision making and disagreements are more likely to arise in situations when people have different values that clash. What do you think is happening here?

many times. An example is that perhaps, as a child, you may have wanted to be a firefighter. Now that you are older, you are considering being a marine biologist. This is all part of developing your potential. The process of change will, and should, continue throughout your life.

Some of your basic values will never change much. Only the goals you set or the decisions you make that are based on these values will change. These basic values include honesty, helping others, and reliability. You can probably think of many others. If you value honesty now, you are not likely to do a turnabout later on and begin to be dishonest.

These values are the basis upon which your decisions are made. They help make up the consistent you that you present to the world, as well as affect how you see yourself.

Whatever occupation you decide on, remember that it cannot satisfy all of your values. Therefore, you should examine your values closely. Suppose you want to be a teacher, but the pay is only average. What is more important—helping people or a high salary?

Perhaps you want to be a musician. Are you willing to study and work hard and to wait, possibly for many years, before you receive recognition? Think about those values you cherish the most and match them with the job or career in which you are interested. You may have to rearrange your values so that you can make effective decisions and reach your goal.

16

YOUR VALUES AT WORK

Your personal values directly affect your day-to-day life. These values help you to set goals and to make decisions. Naturally, values are also reflected on the job. This is important to remember in your decision making about a job. Because so much of your life will be spent on the job, your work should satisfy as many of your values as possible. These values will determine how you perform on the job, how you view your work, and how you cooperate with co-workers.

WHAT IS IMPORTANT TO YOU?

Values that apply in the world of work are often called *work values.* Work values include independence, getting along with others, security, money, creativity, supervision, and many more. If a quiet and orderly atmosphere is important to you, you will not like working in a job that must be done in a noisy, hectic atmosphere. If you want creativity in your work, you certainly won't be happy in a job that is routine.

A person who wants security above all else will work in a different way from one who doesn't mind taking a chance. Someone who wants to work independently will work differently from a person who likes to work in a group. Each of these people will select the jobs that satisfy their individual values.

You should stop to think about your work values and try to match them to a suitable job or career. Try to find out what is really important to you in a job. Remember that you will spend a great deal of your life working. Your job shouldn't be just a means of marking time. Rather, your working life should give you many years of enjoyment and satisfaction.

WORK VALUES ON THE JOB

Your work values not only guide you toward the job that is best for you. Work values also help you make decisions about work, and they help you set work-related goals. For instance, authority and status may be important to you on the job. Therefore, you will not be satisfied working, for example, as a teller in a bank. More than likely, you will study and work hard to become head teller and eventually an officer of the bank. On the other hand, if you like to be supervised and don't want the worries that supervisory people have, you may be perfectly satisfied with your job as teller.

The goals that you set can be short term or long term. For example, suppose you want to buy a ten-speed bicycle. In order to buy one, you will have to save money. Therefore you set yourself the short-term goal of saving a certain amount of money each week toward the long-term goal of owning the bicycle. Setting goals on the job works the same way. To go back to the example of a teller, your earning a certificate in banking procedures would be a short-term goal toward becoming head teller or a cashier, your long-term goal.

See if you can tell what work values lie behind Betty's behavior in this example:

"You have another hour until quitting time and the end of the year, Betty. Even if you aren't able to break the annual sales record, you certainly deserve congratulations for the job you've done so far. You really are a good salesperson."

"Thank you, Mr. Miller," Betty replied. "I'm going to do the best I can. There's no point in easing up with only an hour to go."

Fifteen minutes before closing time, Mr. Jackson came into the store and asked about the price of tires.

"What kind of tires do you have in mind?" Betty asked.

"Oh, I don't know really," Mr. Jackson answered. "Aren't all tires pretty much the same?"

"No, sir!" replied Betty. "There's a big difference in tires. We have some that sell for as little as $25 each and others that sell for $75 each."

"I see," said Mr. Jackson. "Well, I planned to spend only about $100 for all four tires."

"What kind of driving do you do?" asked Betty. "Do you drive mostly around town, or do you do a lot of freeway and long-distance driving? Do you go on long trips?"

"I drive mostly around town," Mr. Jackson said. "I rarely use the freeway or go on long trips."

Wanting to make the sale, Betty said, "I see. Well, I think I've got just the tire for you. It's a steel-belted radial tire, and they are very safe. They cost $60 each, but I can let you have all four for only $220."

"But I have only $100 to spend on tires," Mr. Jackson objected.

"No problem," Betty answered quickly. "You can put the $100 down and pay the rest on our easy credit plan. And we'll rotate your tires free of charge so that you'll get longer life and even wear out of them. Shall I put them on your car now? We're going to close soon."

As you can guess, Betty's decision to sell Mr. Jackson the expensive set of tires was based on her desire to break the annual sales record.

Betty's work values of economic rewards and competition are more important to her than the work value of helping people. If she had been interested in helping Mr. Jackson to get the most suitable tires for the least amount of money, she would have told him more about all the types of tires. And she would not have rushed Mr. Jackson just because the store was about to close. Her behavior and her feelings about customers reflect her work values.

Consider Betty's goals on the job. She just might reach her short-term goal of breaking the sales record. But what about her long-term goal of being an excellent salesperson? If Betty does not change her work values somewhat, customers will begin to realize that she does not care about helping them, but cares more about making a sale. They will stop coming to her. Then she won't achieve any of her goals, and she just might lose her job.

In setting your goals and making decisions, do not let a strong desire to reach an immediate goal blind you to the long-run consequences.

MANY WORK VALUES

There are many different work values that people show through their behavior and attitudes on the job. Some workers feel that they need only enough money to live comfortably. Others want to make lots of money in order to be wealthy. Some people value their special abilities and want to develop them on the job. Others do not care whether or not they develop their talents. People

Since work values guide job decisions and help set work-related goals, it is important to match your choice of a career with your work values. (Woodfin Camp & Associates/Ian Yeomans)

who value achievement will work hard and long to finish a job. Others may value their time off the job so much that they will refuse to put in any extra effort. Even work surroundings are important, as in Jackie's case:

> Jackie's most important work value is her surroundings. She wants to work under pleasant conditions, which means working outdoors. Since childhood, Jackie has loved forests and wide-open spaces. She always had the aptitude for doing physical tasks—especially outside. Jackie was interested in hiking and studying and observing nature.
>
> Jackie's interests, abilities, and values led her to decide to take courses in natural resources and recreation. Today she is a ranger with the U.S. Forest Service. Her job is an ideal match for her abilities, interests, and work values. She loves her surroundings and doesn't mind the physical work involved in wildlife management. Working as a forest ranger, Jackie is doing what she likes most because her job matches her work values with her interests, aptitudes, and abilities.

Interests, Aptitudes, and Abilities

Not everyone is as lucky as Jackie. She was able to identify her work values, set goals, and make decisions that brought the results she wanted. In Jackie's case, her work values went hand-in-hand with her interests, aptitudes, and abilities.

Sometimes, though, work values do not match interests, aptitudes, and abilities so closely. You may be an enthusiastic shortstop on your school's baseball team, but unless you have outstanding ability and an interest in the sport, the chances are slight that you will make the major leagues.

You may play a musical instrument and enjoy doing it very much, but unless your musical abilities are outstanding and your musical aptitudes are high, you may not be able to earn your living through music. It is not enough, then, to know just your work values. You must also know what your interests, abilities, and aptitudes are. And you must work to develop your natural abilities and aptitudes. You generally develop those aptitudes and abilities in which you have an interest. You learn about your interests, abilities, and aptitudes in school, by taking special measures, by talking with counselors, and by trying out various activities in which you are interested. In other words, you work at developing your strengths.

Success

Whatever your interests, aptitudes, and abilities are and whatever job you plan to pursue, your work values will greatly affect your success in what you do. Remember that success is not always judged on how much money you earn. There is more to job success than money. Money may be one of your work values, but other values will affect your life too. Remember, in making any decisions, your values sometimes may clash. For example, you may want to make a lot of money, but also want lots of free time. Therefore, you will have to decide which value is more important.

You will find that your work values change as you grow and develop. Perhaps money may be very important when you are starting out but less so later on. After you accomplish some of your goals at work, other values and goals may develop and become more important to you.

CAREER DECISIONS AND WORK VALUES

A career is the course or progress of your entire working life. Your career may be made up of several different jobs. Your career will develop throughout your life as you grow and mature. There was a time when people thought that making a decision about a career was a once-in-a-lifetime thing. All the events that happened to a person before a career decision was made were thought to have had some effect on that decision. The rest of a person's life didn't seem to have much effect on that career decision.

Actually, you do not usually make a single lifelong decision about a career. *Career goals* are what you want to achieve in your career. And you set career goals based on your work values. Throughout your life, you will make many decisions to reach your career goals. Even your goals and your values will change as conditions and you change. Many decisions affect a career. Here is an example:

> As a child, Carlotta became aware of the kinds of work her parents did. She also came in contact with people in different occupations. At an early age, Carlotta started to become aware of her own abilities and interests. Carlotta's first years of school began to prepare her for her career. She acquired basic skills such as reading and writing. She learned to discipline herself to follow necessary rules.

Carlotta's career development continued as she moved into the upper elementary grades. At this point, she started to compare herself to people working in different jobs. How was she similar to or different from a hairdresser, a secretary, a flight steward, a plumber? Her self-discipline continued to develop, and she began to value work as a useful activity. During this period, Carlotta's knowledge about and interest in workers in various jobs grew. Seeing various life patterns and discovering the changing roles of women in the world of work, Carlotta developed an awareness of herself and learned better how to get along with others.

When Carlotta entered junior high school, she became aware of her values and their relationship to jobs. She realized that she was a unique, independent individual. The *lifestyles*, or patterns of life, of people in the business world seemed attractive to her. Carlotta decided to take business courses in senior high school.

As Carlotta's career development continued, she began to test herself as a person working in the business world. She tried several part-time and temporary jobs. After graduation, she decided to attend a local business college for a year to get further training.

During her year at business college, Carlotta decided she wanted to work in accounting. Her first job, as an accounting clerk, gave her a chance to test her interest in business. At this point, Carlotta's career development might appear complete. She was working in business and seemed to be happy. However, as Carlotta gained additional working experience, she continued to grow.

As her view of herself and her work values changed, Carlotta reexamined her career. She decided to obtain additional training and to become an accountant. Later she married and decided that, for a while, she would spend time at home raising her children. After a few years, she began working outside her home again and eventually became a management consultant.

Carlotta's career developed throughout her life. It did not depend upon a single decision, educational course, or job. As Carlotta grew and matured, her interests became better focused and her work values changed. She was able to develop all aspects of her life and find self-satisfaction at home and on the job.

Your career development, like Carlotta's, will be a continuous process. It will go through stages as you grow and mature. Each person has different aptitudes, abilities, interests, and values. To make effective career decisions, know yours so that you can have many satisfying years in the world of work.

Career development is a process that continues throughout one's entire working life. A career can consist of several different jobs that are interrelated.

Getting It All Together

1. Why must everyone take responsibility for his or her own decisions?

2. How do your values affect your decisions?

3. How are values and goals related?

4. Do values and goals change? Why?

5. What happens when your values clash?

6. What are some values that are related to work?

7. You are working as an usher in a movie theater. One night, while sweeping under the seats, you find a wallet with $50 in it. What would you do? What values affect your decision?

UNIT

6

THE NATURE
OF DECISIONS

Your goals in this unit are given in the following list:

To recognize that your self-identity and your career identity are closely related and affect your decisions

To recognize how aptitudes and interests affect your career decisions

To identify three kinds of decisions

To recognize four stages of decision making

To understand why some decisions fail

Knowing your values and having goals will help you make decisions. If life were simple, you could say: "This is what I value. This is my goal. This is what I will do." Decision making would be as easy as A B C. Life, of course, is not that simple. There are many other factors that will affect your decisions.

How you see yourself—your *self-identity*—will affect your decisions. If you have a poor opinion of yourself, you will probably set low goals for yourself. On the other hand, if you think too highly of yourself, you may set goals that are too high. If you have a realistic and positive opinion of yourself, you will make effective decisions.

When making decisions, you should also be aware of what you are able to do and what you are interested in doing. Having the potential to do something does not mean that you will have an interest in it as well. Neither does the fact that you are interested in something mean that you will be able to do it well. Making career decisions without being aware of these factors can cause problems for you.

Part of being an effective decision-maker is in knowing that there are three kinds of decisions. These kinds of decisions are feeling, automatic, and thinking. *Feeling decisions* are those choices that are based on emotions. *Automatic decisions* are those choices that are based on reflexes, or set ideas and habits. *Thinking decisions* are those

choices that are based on reasoning.

Decision making goes through four stages: initial, exploratory, tentative, and realistic. This is all part of the process of reality-testing. *Reality-testing* is when you try out your daydreams in real-life.

Initial decisions are those daydreams you have about what you want to be. For example, lots of careers may sound interesting, but you have little information about them or about how well they may fit you. *Exploratory decisions* are made when you find out more about the career that interests you and start to discover your own interests and work values. *Tentative decisions* help you clear up your goals and work values. You may still be uncertain about your final choice, but you are able to do some experimentation. *Realistic decisions* are when you make a choice and begin to work in a particular field. You have tested various careers and have found the one that best suits you.

Because it is impossible to foretell the future, and decisions have to do with future results, there can be no guarantee that your decision will succeed. The effective decision-maker reduces the chances of failure by finding out everything possible about the results of a decision before making it. If the decision turns out to be ineffective, an effective decision-maker is able to take the necessary steps to improve it or to change it.

CHAPTER 17

SELF-IDENTITY AFFECTS DECISIONS

Your self-identity is your picture of yourself. It is how you feel about yourself. Your self-identity reflects your values. Your self-identity involves not only how you feel about yourself but how you think other people feel about you.

Many factors in your life affect the picture you have of yourself. Your relations with your family and friends influence your self-identity. School affects it. Your talents, attitudes, and values all contribute to your self-identity.

Your self-identity, like your physical appearance, changes as you grow and mature. Just as you no longer look like a 4-year-old or a 12-year-old, you no longer have a 4-year-old's or a 12-year-old's self-identity. Just as your values and goals change as you grow and have new experiences, your self-identity passes through many different stages also. Throughout your life, your self-identity will continue to grow and develop. As experiences cause you to change or form new attitudes and values, your self-identity will reflect the changes.

A REALISTIC SELF-IDENTITY AIDS EFFECTIVE DECISION MAKING

Basically, there are three different kinds of self-identities. One is a negative, or poor, self-identity. A negative view of yourself can lead you to set low goals. You don't use all of your capabilities, and you will never attain your potential. Another kind of self-identity is being overconfident. Overconfidence leads you to set too-high goals—again never accomplishing anything. Both of these self-identities are unrealistic, and they both lead to poor decision making.

The third, and most desirable, is a positive self-identity. It strikes a balance between the two extremes of negativism and overconfidence. With a positive self-identity, you set goals that are neither too low nor too high. You will be able to accomplish many things that you set out to do. This third self-identity is realistic, and having a realistic attitude toward yourself can help you in your effective decision making.

Let's look at these three self-identities and how each influences decision making.

Negative Self-Identity

A negative self-identity shows itself in all areas of a person's life. Read about Donald and his poor view of himself:

Donald doesn't like himself very much. He feels other people are better than he is. Donald has a hard time getting along with his classmates. They call him stupid, and think he is sloppy. Their attitudes toward him strengthen the negative self-identity Donald holds of himself.

In school, Donald seems to invite his teachers' criticism. He turns in assignments late, if he bothers to turn them in at all. When an examination comes up, Donald's attitude is, "Well, here comes another failure. I'll never pass this test. Why bother to study? Nothing that I can do will make any difference." And, of course, Donald rarely passes his examinations.

A new student, Terry, has moved to town, and Donald has noticed that she seems lonely too. However, he is afraid even to approach her and say hello. "She'll probably laugh at me," Donald decides. "People always laugh at me," he says to himself.

72

Because of his negative self-identity, Donald gives up before he even tries. He doesn't value his own abilities. He doesn't even know what they are. Donald certainly has a poor attitude toward himself. But how did his self-identity develop in this way?

While there is no simple answer, it is fair to assume that past experiences have played a large part. As a child, Donald most likely was told that he could not do this or that very well. After hearing over and over, "You can't do anything" and "Look what a mess you've made" and "Jan can do that better," Donald came to believe that such statements were true.

When he failed, Donald's failures strengthened his negative attitude toward himself. Sometimes he succeeded, but Donald did not give his successes as much thought as his failures. And now he has come to expect failure all the time.

As a result, Donald does not try to do much of anything anymore. He decided not to study and not to be friendly to Terry. He has given up, rather than face the possibility of another failure.

Overconfident Self-Identity

Being overconfident is just as bad as being negative. Rose is an example:

> Rose feels she can do no wrong. Her feeling toward herself is, "I'm the greatest, the smartest, and the most beautiful." For some reason, Rose feels she is better than everybody else. Therefore, when she does poorly on an exam, she blames the teacher for her bad grade. Rose has lost two part-time jobs during the past year, but, in her opinion, this was not her fault. Rose thinks, "If only my supervisor had left me alone, I could have done a great job." Rose does not bother to be social. She says, "Those stupid high school kids aren't worth my time." She has few friends, and most people do not like to be around her. They feel Rose does not like them, and so they move on.

Like Donald, Rose makes decisions on the basis of her self-identity. She has an attitude toward herself that leads her to make excuses and to give other people less credit than they deserve.

At first, it may seem that Donald's negative self-identity is a worse handicap than Rose's overconfidence. If the only factor that matters is how a person views himself or herself, this would be the case. But one's view of the self is not the full picture. How the self views other people is also a factor.

Self-identity, after all, is a comparison between yourself and other people. You hold an attitude toward yourself on the basis of the attitudes you hold toward others. If you think everyone is better than you are, you will put yourself down. But if you think you are better than everyone else, you will put other people down.

Both Donald and Rose have a long way to go toward developing realistic self-identities—identities that allow them to deal effectively with others and to make effective decisions for themselves. In future, they may change.

Effective decision makers have a positive self-identity which can strike a balance between negativism and overconfidence. What's missing in this situation?

Positive Self-Identity

To be an effective decision-maker, you want to be certain that your self-identity is realistic. Otherwise, you will make decisions that work against you. You need a clear picture of yourself to make decisions that bring the results that you want.

If you like yourself, you have a positive self-identity. And this does not mean that you are being selfish. In order to develop a positive self-identity, you must recognize your strengths as well as your weaknesses. And, in doing so, you develop your strengths so that they work for you. At the same time, you are aware of your weaknesses and try to compensate for them or eliminate them altogether.

If you feel that your self-identity is unrealistic, such as Donald's or Rose's, don't think that you have to be like this for the rest of your life. This is not true. You can work toward and develop a more positive self-identity by being honest with yourself.

Donald and Rose can change their self-identities. If they come to understand that their attitudes toward themselves affect their decision making, and if they see that their decisions are not effective, they will be taking the first step toward a more realistic view of themselves. Donald, for instance, can discover that all human beings sometimes fail and sometimes succeed. He will see that he is no worse and no better than anyone else. Then his decisions will reflect a more positive self-identity. When he comes to like himself better, Donald will give himself a chance and his decision making will reflect this change.

Rose, too, will learn a few things by looking at life realistically. There is nothing wrong with having a good opinion of yourself. But Rose's problem is that she considers all other people to be less good than she is. And her decisions are affected by this view of herself and others. When Rose comes to value other people's feelings and opinions, she will find that her relationships with others will improve. She will start to take responsibility for her decisions and give herself an even break.

The best self-identity is one that is positive both toward oneself and toward others. If you think that you are worthwhile and that others are also worthwhile, you can make decisions that are responsible. Such a self-identity will help you achieve your goals and will contribute to your growth and development. You will find satisfaction in all the areas of your life also—on the job, at school, at home, or with your friends.

DEVELOPING YOUR CAREER IDENTITY

Your *career identity* is the part of your self-identity that has to do with your career. Your values and the attitudes you have toward work make up your career identity. Your career identity greatly affects decisions having to do with your work.

Early in your life, your self-identity is influenced mostly by your immediate surroundings. As you grow and gain experience, your self-identity begins to change, and you also begin to develop your career identity. Here's how one person's changing self-identity affected his decisions and eventually his career identity:

Joe grew up in a rundown section of town. Both his parents worked. His mother cleaned offices in the evening, and his father worked at odd jobs as he could find them. Joe grew up knowing very well that he was from a low-income family.

In grade school, he often went without lunch. The other children had better clothes than Joe, and he was amazed by their stories about their toys or about family trips. During this period in his life, Joe did not think much about his future or about what he wanted to be when he grew up. Joe was kept busy just getting by each day. His decisions were affected by his environment.

In junior high school, Joe met new teachers and classmates. They went on many fieldtrips, and Joe began to learn more about the world as his environment became larger. And he started to explore and discover his world and his part in that world. Joe thought about what he liked to do and what was important to him. He began to identify his values. He made several visits to the career center at school to learn about the many kinds of jobs that were available. Joe imagined himself as a banker, a carpenter, a machinist, and, finally, a lawyer. Joe decided to become a lawyer.

Thinking he would go to college and then to law school, Joe took college preparatory courses in high school. Because he had to work, he could not study as much as he should and his grades were poor. He also realized it would take a lot of money to go to college and law school. He decided to change his goal and decided to take business courses instead of college preparatory work.

But after a year of business courses, Joe still was not satisfied. He finished high school after taking general courses. Although Joe still felt he would like to be a lawyer when he graduated, he realized that he was not prepared for that career. His goal seemed out of reach because of the amount of money and training needed. His self-identity made him decide to give up that goal.

Jobs were few, and since he did not know what he really wanted, Joe decided to join the U.S. Army. In the army, Joe was assigned to the military police force. To his surprise, Joe enjoyed his work as a military police officer. When he left the army, Joe decided to return to his hometown and get a job as a police officer.

Today, much of his work involves helping people in trouble. Joe is doing many of the things he dreamed about when he wanted to become a lawyer. He enjoys these things very much. He has found that he is good at it, and this has made him believe that he could do well in law school. Because of this and the fact he has a full-time job to support himself, Joe has decided to take evening courses in law and psychology at a local college to begin working toward a law degree.

This picture of Joe includes only a few of the many factors that affected his development over the years. Yet, we can see a pattern in his life. In junior high school, Joe began to realize that he could explore himself and make decisions about what kind of life he wanted. This period of self-discovery changed Joe's self-identity. He decided to become a lawyer, and this decision led him to take college preparatory courses. After doing poorly in his first year in high school and doing little better as a business student, Joe decided he could not be a lawyer. His self-identity made him feel that his goal was out of his reach.

Not knowing what else to do, Joe joined the army. Then he discovered that he enjoyed his work in the military police. His self-identity changed enough so that he could now see himself as a police officer. When he left the army and joined his hometown police force, Joe's self-identity changed once more because he did well in the job and enjoyed it. He could now see himself as a lawyer, so he enrolled in college. Notice that each time Joe changed his self-identity, his decisions changed.

Sometimes a person is able to develop a realistic career identity fairly early in life. Consider Nora's experience:

Nora walked briskly toward the tall office building. It was a warm, sunny day, and she felt that something good was going to happen. Under her arm, she carried a large portfolio of illustrations she had drawn during the past year in art school. Nora was on her way to be interviewed for a job as an illustrator. Her interest and excitement in the work showed during her interview, and she was offered the job. She accepted at once.

Nora's decision was an important one. It will affect how she lives in the future, even though this is her first job. How and why did Nora decide something so important so easily? Joe, remember, had more trouble establishing a career identity. Let's look at Nora's life more closely:

Ever since she was a young girl and first began to draw, Nora has dreamed of being an artist. She has been forming that career identity for a long time. In grade school, Nora loved to sketch and work with clay. Her family, friends, and teachers all praised her talent for drawing, and Nora came to value her talent highly.

In high school, she developed her artistic abilities because she started to imagine what it would be like to live an artist's life. She felt that she was creative and artistic, and her self-identity slowly turned into her career identity—to become an illustrator. After high school, Nora decided to go to art school. She knew that when she finished her training at the school, she probably would be able to get a job in which she could use her artistic talent and training.

Some people are able to develop a realistic career identity somewhat early in life. For example, many performing artists such as musicians begin their careers at an early age. (Philip Teuscher)

Nora was fortunate that she was able to know her career identity and work toward it so early. Not everyone is able to do this. Joe, for instance, took a long time before he was able to establish his career identity and work toward it.

This is the case with most people. Circumstances, often beyond their control, force them to change plans and delay reaching their goals. This is how life is. The important thing for you to remember is to try to develop your career identity and know what your work goals are. You may be delayed on the way, but with this important knowledge to help you, more than likely you will succeed. And with a clear career identity, your work experiences will be more satisfying. This will lead to your own fulfillment.

CAREER IDENTITY CAN CHANGE

In this discussion of developing your career identity, it is important for you to know that you don't have to decide now exactly what you want to do. This is not the case, nor should it be. Everybody and everything changes over time, including career identity.

A career identity is not set in cement. It changes and develops. These changes will affect the decisions you make. Furthermore, your self-identity and your career identity are closely interrelated. Thus, changes in one will affect the other.

The example of how Nora's self-identity came to be her career identity shows how closely related self-identity and career identity are. It is important to keep this in mind.

Hank's Changing Career Identity

The way you feel about yourself and the way you feel about your work do affect each other. As your self-identity changes, so can your career identity. In the following case, Hank's self-identity was improved by a change that affected his career identity:

Hank started to work 2 years ago on the assembly line at a manufacturing company. He was unhappy at his work, though, because he was bored with working on the assembly line. He did not feel good about his work or about himself. Hank felt that he could handle more responsibility than his job gave him, and he wanted to develop his skills as a worker.

Although Hank did not like his job, he had a good attitude toward the company. He decided to learn as much as he could about other operations on the assembly line, as well as about other aspects of the company's business. His willingness to learn was soon noticed by his supervisors. In time, he was offered the opportunity to take special training and become an inspector of the assembly line.

Hank's new job was more interesting to him. He had greater responsibility, and he earned more money. These two changes made Hank feel better about his self-identity. He had greater confidence in himself, and he was happy to be challenged to use all his skills. Being able to take pride in his work, Hank became more satisfied with his self-identity.

Delia's Self-Discovery

In Hank's case, a change in career identity resulted in an improved self-identity. But the relationship between career identity and self-identity can work the other way too. In the following example, an improved self-identity results in a changed career identity:

Delia had worked as a telephone operator for the Mid-South Telephone Company for almost 2 years. At first, she was shy and had little confidence. In time, however, she became more comfortable on the job. Her self-identity began to improve as she developed her abilities.

Delia decided that she wanted to learn more about telephone communications. Whenever she got a chance to visit other company offices, she would volunteer to go, even though she had to do it on her own time. Her self-confidence continued to improve as she learned about the company's operations.

One day, Delia went with Dan Kane, a communications consultant, as he visited several businesses. Dan's job was to study how the employees of a company were using their telephones and to make suggestions about how to improve the telephone communications system. Delia thought this kind of work was very interesting, and she began to imagine herself doing it. Slowly her career identity began to change, and she decided she wanted to become a communications consultant.

Delia visited the personnel office of her company and learned that the company was looking for people to train as communications consultants. She applied for the training and was accepted. After several months of training, Delia reached her goal. She had a new career identity as a communications consultant.

Delia's process of self-discovery resulted in an improved self-identity. As a beginning telephone operator, she had been shy and lacked confidence. But as she grew and developed, she became more sure of herself and her abilities. This self-confidence caused her to see herself in a better light. As a result, Delia saw that she could develop her talents, and her career identity started to change. She came to see herself as a communications consultant rather than as an operator. And once she had this new career identity and was more confident of herself, she was able to make the decision to change her career goals—and to get what she wanted in a career area.

SUMMING UP

You can see, then, that your career identity and your self-identity affect each other a great deal. A change in one will be reflected by a change in the other. Notice, too, that decisions are made on the basis of self-identity and career identity, and that decisions change as the picture of yourself changes. This is to be expected, since decisions reflect your values, and they are made in order to achieve your goals. As self-identity and career identity develop, your goals will often change.

The important thing to remember is that you alone are responsible for discovering what your values and goals are. This process is continuous.

CHAPTER 18

APTITUDES AND INTERESTS AFFECT DECISIONS

You already have learned about some of the factors that influence your decision making. For example, you know that your values and goals are closely related and that your decisions about careers are based on them. You have found out that self-identity and career identity are also related, and that they, too, will influence you. So what else of importance do you need to know about yourself to be able to make effective career decisions? The following sections tell you the other important things about yourself you need to know.

YOUR APTITUDES

You need to know what your aptitudes are. An *aptitude* is being able to do something well. It is a natural talent. An aptitude is not the same thing as an ability or a skill. However, an aptitude can make it easier for you to develop an ability or a skill. For example, some people have the aptitude to write well, while others have an aptitude for fixing mechanical things. Some people might be able to do both well.

Some aptitudes are easier to know about than others. For example, you can tell rather easily if you have a talent for singing or playing a musical instrument. On the other hand, whether you have an aptitude to sell, or to manage people, or to do repair work may not be so easy to find out.

Watch repairing, for example, requires a combination of physical and mental skills. You must be able to use your hands easily and quickly. If you are all thumbs, then you probably do not have much of an aptitude for repairing watches.

Besides using your hands, you must use your mind when repairing watches. You must be able to figure out what is wrong and then find a way to fix it. Many careers require this combination of mechanical and mental aptitudes. Therefore, you should make an effort to find out all that you can about the mechanical and mental aptitudes that you have.

Measurements of Aptitudes

Do you have artistic or musical aptitude? Are your strongest aptitudes in mathematics or science? Maybe you have an aptitude for mechanical reasoning. A good way to find out what your talents are is to measure your aptitudes. A school counselor can help you with this, as can various counseling centers and psychological clinics.

Consider how Andy decided to find out more about his aptitudes:

Andy, a ninth grader, wanted to be a doctor. He went to a counseling service operated by his religious group and had his aptitudes measured. Although Andy scored above average on verbal abilities, his numerical and abstract reasoning aptitudes both were below average. Andy's counselor explained to him that both numerical and abstract reasoning aptitudes are important requirements for doctors.

Andy found that his real strengths were in language use, spelling, and verbal reasoning. Occupations such as writing, editing, and reporting more closely matched Andy's aptitudes. The counselor suggested that Andy explore occupations in journalism, a field for which he had natural tendencies.

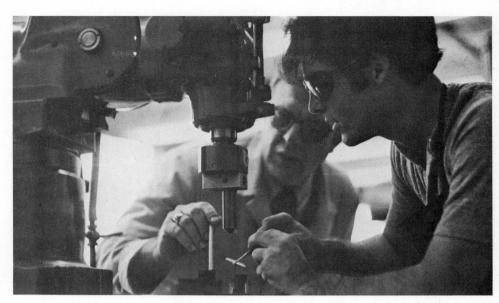

Effective career decisions can be made when you know your aptitudes. (Courtesy National Tool, Die & Precision Machining Assn.)

Aptitude measurements, by no means, are the final answer to a career choice. Perhaps Andy did not particularly enjoy writing and had no desire to go into journalism. But the results that he got about his abilities certainly will help him in his decision making about a job or career.

Finding out about your aptitudes will help you also. When you examine the results of your aptitude measurements, you will be better able to decide about courses you wish to take in school and eventually a career that suits you.

A good way to find out if you have an aptitude for a particular field is to compare yourself with someone who is already working in the field. Being experienced, of course, they will be able to do the work better than you. But if your aptitudes compare well with theirs, you probably have an aptitude in this field.

Aptitude measures are only one way to discover your aptitudes. There are others. Consider the following ways:

Grades.   School grades, for example, can often indicate aptitudes. If you do well in your mechanical drawing classes, this is an indication about some of your aptitudes. More than likely, you have a talent for drawing, you can do precise work, and have high abstract reasoning skill. You probably also get good grades in your math and science courses.

Talking to others.   You can also find out about your aptitudes by talking to others. Your parents sometimes can help you find out if you have a particular aptitude. Friends are helpful too. It is

always a good idea to consult your school counselor, who is especially trained to help you in this area.

Doing things.   Actually, doing things is an excellent way to discover your aptitudes. For example, if you take a part-time job at a soda fountain and have trouble getting the orders right, you will have found out something about your aptitudes. The same is true if you work in a clothing store and find you are just too shy to wait on people. Naturally, you may also find out that you are just right at doing these things.

Having an aptitude for a particular career does not mean that you will automatically be able to do the work successfully. Even persons with a lot of talent for singing must practice all the time. It is the same with any aptitude. You may have an aptitude, but unless you work to develop it, you will never acquire the necessary abilities to use it in a career situation. The more you work, the more successful you will be, especially if your career decisions have led you into a career for which you have an aptitude.

YOUR INTERESTS

When you know that you have an aptitude for a particular occupation, you are well along in your efforts to know yourself so that you can make the best career decisions. You have not, however, finished your self-examination. There is one more important thing that you must know about yourself—your interests. What do you like to do?

After aptitudes have been identified, they may be developed in training programs. (Courtesy National Tool, Die & Precision Machining Assn.)

What appeals to you? What do you enjoy doing? The answers to all of these questions are your *interests*.

At first, you may think that anything you have an aptitude for will appeal to you. That is true to some extent—but not completely. Sometimes you will find that you have talent for doing something that does not interest you in the least.

Interests Lead to Abilities

It is worth knowing as many of your aptitudes as you can. Even if you do not like working with your hands, for example, it is still worth knowing whether or not you have this aptitude. If working with your hands is one of your aptitudes, you may build a satisfying hobby around it. Such an aptitude comes in handy for doing necessary repairs around home—even if that is not one of your most outstanding aptitudes.

Of course, a major reason for discovering what aptitudes you have is to explore the possibility of doing something with them. By discovering your aptitudes, you can try things out. If you never discover what your aptitudes are, you may not think of trying some things that you may be able to do very well and that you may like to do.

Knowing your aptitudes can help you discover your interests. It can work the other way also. If you know your interests, you may be able to discover abilities that you didn't know you had. Consider how Claire found out about some abilities through her interests:

Claire, a junior in high school, was discouraged. She did pretty well in her secretarial courses, but she was bored with the class work. What was discouraging was that she had planned to be a secretary when she finished high school. But now she didn't know what she wanted to become. One day she went to see the guidance counselor.

"I really don't like the secretarial courses I'm taking," she said. "I wonder what else I could do after I graduate."

"Maybe you just don't like those classes in school," Ms. Morris, the counselor, said. "When you are actually working in an office, you may find that you like secretarial tasks."

"I have a part-time job in an office now," Claire said. "I don't like it at all. It bores me silly."

"Well," Ms. Morris asked, "what other things do you think you might like?"

"I really don't know," Claire said. "Other than school work, all I've ever done is secretarial office work. There must be something else."

"I'm sure there is," Ms. Morris agreed. "Tell me, have you ever taken an interest inventory?"

"I don't think so. At least I don't remember it if I did," Claire answered.

"Well, here is what we'll do. I'll give you a series of these inventories. Maybe we will find something out about you that you do not know."

Ms. Morris explained how the interest inventories were designed to show a person what kind of work he or she would probably be interested in doing. She stressed that they looked like tests, but they were not. One answered the questions according to what he or she liked best.

Claire took the inventories. She was surprised when Ms. Morris told her that they indicated she enjoyed working with her hands and building things.

"What do you mean?" Claire asked. "I never did anything like that in my life."

"Well, I think it means that you should consider some career that would require you to work with your hands and build things," Ms. Morris told her.

"But I don't know if I can do that type of work," Claire said.

"That's true," Ms. Morris said. "And it is a very important point to keep in mind. Just because you have an interest in something does not mean you have the aptitude to do it, just as having an aptitude does not mean you are interested in something."

"I know that much anyway," Claire said with a laugh. "I'm a good secretary, but I don't like the work. What should I do now?"

Ms. Morris said, "I'll give you a series of measurements to see what your aptitudes are."

Claire's results showed she would be a good secretary, as she knew. They also showed that she did indeed have an aptitude for working with her hands. Claire began to read about different careers in which she could develop her aptitudes and satisfy her interests.

"Woodworking," she said one day to Ms. Morris.

"Sounds good to me," Ms. Morris said. "The thing now is to get some training and experience in woodworking to find out if it really is what you want. We have some excellent woodworking courses here. I will enroll you in one for this coming semester."

Claire took the course, did very well in it, and decided that she wanted to be a cabinetmaker and make fine furniture.

Many people do not discover what their interests and aptitudes are. Often they settle into work that's boring to them without finding out that there are other things that they can do and enjoy doing as well. You don't have to settle. Find out more about yourself by finding out about your aptitudes and interests.

Talent Is Not Enough

Claire had some talent for being a secretary, but she did not like the work. She was unaware of her other aptitudes and did not find out about them until she took some inventories to discover her interests. Using the results as guidelines, Claire discovered other aptitudes.

Things worked out well for Claire because she took steps to find out about herself before making decisions. Sometimes people do not do this. Some think that having a strong talent is all

that is needed to be successful and happy in a career. Read what happened to Clifford:

Clifford had unusual musical talent. He started playing the piano at the age of 5. At 9 years of age, Clifford was performing difficult musical scores with ease.

His childhood was different from that of most children. Clifford's parents insisted that he practice the piano several hours every day. But his musical activities kept him from relationships with other people in his age group.

Because he had an unusual musical talent, Clifford thought music would be his whole life. So he never explored other career possibilities.

By the time Clifford reached high school, he was an accomplished pianist. But he was also becoming unhappy. He began to feel that there were other things to do beside playing the piano. Yet he never made any effort to find out what else might be interesting to him. To please his parents, he continued with his music.

Clifford entered college as a music major, but, after a year, he dropped out. By this time he had no interest in playing the piano. He drifted around and changed jobs frequently. Clifford was never able to get along with other people comfortably, and he remained uncertain about his future and his goals.

Clifford's problem highlights the importance of interests in personal and career success. In Clifford's case, he lost interest in playing the piano. And having no particular interest in or knowledge of any other field, Clifford drifted along with no goals or ambitions.

You may already be developing your aptitudes and interests in a particular area. Eventually, you may even make your career in this area. This is fine and worthwhile. But don't box yourself in and shut out other interests and other areas. Know about other things. Having a variety of interests makes you a well-rounded person.

SURVEY YOUR INTERESTS

You have to survey your interests. What are your interests? Would you rather work outdoors or indoors? Do you prefer to work with machines or with people? How about your artistic, musical, or literary interests? Perhaps you would be interested in things that you have not experienced or about which you know little. Just as counselors can help you to identify your aptitudes, they can also help you discover your interests.

By exploring your interests, you can discover your full potential. (Top, Woodfin Camp & Associates/Timothy Eagan; center, courtesy U.S. Department of Agriculture; bottom, courtesy Pratt Institute)

You may think that it is silly to take an inventory to find out what your interests are. You probably feel that everybody automatically knows what he or she finds interesting. Well, take a moment to write down several things that you like to do. On a separate sheet of paper, make the list as long as you can. Look it over when you are done. It may be very long, but as long as it is, the list only reflects what you have experienced. That is, it can only indicate those things which you already know.

A list, though, based on an interest inventory that you have taken, will indicate things with which you are not necessarily familiar. That is the point about inventories. You cannot tell until you try something whether it will interest you, and it is not possible to try everything.

Measurements and inventories are a way of finding out about things without actually experiencing the work or task. They provide a way of making an orderly search of what you may find enjoyable. For example, if you want to find out what kind of ice cream you like the most, the best way is simply to try out all the flavors. That's a fun kind of inventory. But when you want to find out what career you will like best, it is not possible to try them all out. So, your best bets are measurements and inventories.

CHAPTER 19

THREE KINDS OF DECISIONS

It was the week of final examinations, and four friends met in front of the school. "Let's all go to see the war picture at Cinema City," Nancy suggested. "I need to get away from the books for a while."

"Great!" Pete agreed. "I don't feel like studying anyway. I'd like to get lost in a film."

"Count me out," Sharon declined. "War pictures turn me off."

"I'd better not go, either," Frank said. "I need to put in some extra time on my job. I need more money for my vacation."

This conversation illustrates the three kinds of decisions that people generally make: feeling decisions (Pete), automatic decisions (Sharon), and thinking decisions (Frank). Understanding these three kinds of decisions will help you become a responsible decision-maker. Each kind of decision works well in some situations but poorly in other situations. As you read about these three kinds of decisions, think about how you make your decisions. Which kind of decision do you usually make?

FEELING DECISIONS

"No," replied Mindy, "you go ahead. I don't feel like swimming today. Maybe some other time."

Dave's eyes sparkled. "I just got a great idea," he said. "Why don't we work on our electrical circuit diagrams together and turn in the same assignment? We don't have the same teacher, we'd never get caught."

"I want to do something that's fun. Let's go play miniature golf," Gordon urged. "Study later."

These are some examples of feeling decisions. Feeling decisions are based on emotions or hunches. Outside circumstances don't have much affect on these kinds of decisions. The most important factor concerns how the decision-maker feels inside.

Mindy's decision not to go swimming was based on how she felt, for example. She didn't give any particular reason for not going. She just didn't feel like going swimming. Dave's decision was made on the spur of the moment. He got an idea and jumped into it without thinking things through. Gordon's decision was based on his feelings also. He did not want to study, and he wanted someone else to join him in playing miniature golf.

Remember Emotional Decisions

You have already read about one of the most common forms of feeling decisions. These feeling decisions are made when you are being influenced by your emotions. As you remember, it is not a good idea to make a decision when your emotions are out of control, or your emotions are controlling you. This is true whether the emotion is anger or happiness.

All of us sometime make feeling decisions. Such decisions are normal and are part of human nature. The point is, you should try to control your emotions, rather than let your emotions control you. If the matter you are dealing with is unimportant, the results are probably not too important. When you are dealing with important matters, such as whether or not to study for an exam, you do not want your emotions to interfere with your decision making. Your emotions might cause you to make feeling decisions. And feeling decisions aren't always in your best interests.

Remember Your Responsibility

Feeling decisions are a common kind of decision making. In feeling decisions the decision-maker gets an idea or has a mood and then acts on it with little thought. Often, this kind of decision is made to avoid something—usually responsibility. Usually no planning or follow-through is involved. At the time, the decision may sound good because it feels right.

Betty and Bruce offer two examples of feeling decisions:

> Betty liked to think of herself as a rebel. If someone told her to do something, she would do just the opposite. At school, she seemed to enjoy going against her teachers' instructions. She didn't care if her grades suffered.
> Betty's attitude was, "I'm my own boss. I do what I want to do." Her decisions usually were based on angry feelings, and she didn't think things through.

If Betty had considered her decision to act rebelliously, she would have realized that she was hurting herself more than others. For example, her poor grades, which didn't bother her, might prevent her from doing something she would want to do later.

> Bruce was just the opposite of Betty. He always did exactly as he was told. He never disagreed with his parents, and, in grade school, he always followed his teachers' instructions carefully and promptly.
> In high school, things started to change. Teachers gave the students more freedom, and Bruce found that he was expected to do things on his own. This confused and frightened him because Bruce always had based his decisions on what others expected. Now he found it difficult to make decisions, because he didn't always know what was wanted. Since Bruce was afraid to make a wrong decision, he was afraid others wouldn't like him if he acted on his own.

Betty and Bruce illustrate two extremes of decisions that are based on feelings. Betty's decisions resulted from her rebelliousness. Bruce's decisions resulted from his need to be liked. In both cases, feeling decisions were ineffective.

Control Your Feeling Decisions

Feeling decisions are common, but they should not become a way of life. No one can rebel all the time or obey all the time. Decisions should accomplish the decision-maker's goals, and they should satisfy his or her needs. If you always make decisions in the same way, they will not always be effective. Because situations differ, you must take the particular situation into consideration when making your decisions. Otherwise, you are not being free or being responsible.

Think about the decisions you made today or during the past week. Were some of them based on feelings? Most of them? If so, it will be worthwhile to consider whether or not such decisions have paid off. Have the results of such decisions helped you achieve your long-range goals? Even though they may have seemed right at the time, were they actually working against your purposes? Did you find yourself doing things you didn't really want to do? If so, you may want to change.

Keep feeling decisions in mind as you read about two other kinds of decisions. First, consider automatic decisions.

AUTOMATIC DECISIONS

> "Remember how helpful that group was when we needed help," Jane said sternly. "We must return their favors now. After all, what are friends to do?"

> "You shouldn't talk like that, Harry," Sue cautioned. "It isn't nice."

> "I know it's the best car on the market," Chris announced, "and I'm going to get one. I don't have to bother about looking at others."

These statements are examples of automatic decisions. Automatic decisions are based on reflexes, set ideas, and habits, or previously learned rules. Like feeling decisions, automatic decisions do not involve thinking about the possible results of such decisions. They usually are made in haste, and they rarely take feelings into account.

Jane's decision to help the group was based on her reflex to be the kind of friend on which people could count. Sue's warning to Harry also was based on a set idea. The word "shouldn't," or "should," is a clue that her decision was automatic. Such decisions are really based on rules. Sue's decision was based on a rule that came from her

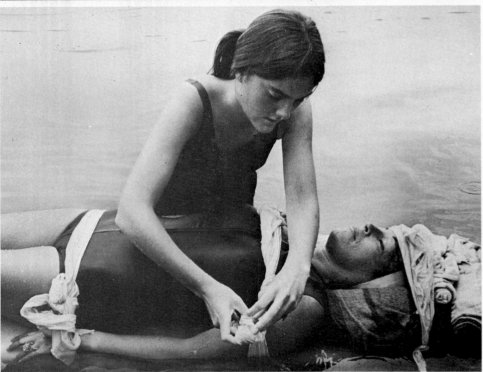

Firefighters and lifeguards often make automatic decisions in on-the-job emergencies. (Top, courtesy F.D.N.Y. Photo; bottom, American Red Cross/Ted Carland)

parents. The same applies to Chris's decision. He didn't think about the features that each kind of car offered. Instead, he based his decision on what he thought he already knew.

The Role of Past Experience

Automatic decisions grow out of past information, and sometimes they produce effective re-sults. For instance, if your car goes into a skid on an icy road, you may avoid an accident by remembering a warning to steer into the skid and to slowly pump rather than to quickly slam on the brakes.

Similarly, if you have had good service from a particular auto dealer, it might make sense to automatically go back to that same dealer for your next car. In other words, when past experiences have resulted in goals that satisfy you, it's helpful to consider them when making decisions in similar situations.

Problems may arise in making automatic decisions on the basis of unexamined or out-of-date information. You may have been lucky in a past experience. Can you be sure that the same actions will produce the same results again?

People who always base their decisions on past rules and information are not interested in thinking about other solutions or results. Some people use this pattern of decision making all the time. They usually consider themselves right in all situations, regardless of the facts. They seldom admit past mistakes, and they make many excuses. As with feeling decisions, people who make automatic decisions don't accept responsibility for their actions. Consider the following situation involving an automatic decision:

"Go to summer school? Are you crazy?" Randy said.

"Wait a minute before you decide," John remarked. "If we take these special computer courses, we definitely will be able to get those jobs with the civil service this fall."

"Oh, I'll get one anyway," Randy said.

"Not necessarily," John argued. "People who take these courses will be given extra credit toward those jobs. If there are only a few openings, you could lose out—even if you did well on the exams."

"I did fine on the exams. I'm going to enjoy the summer," Randy said.

"Listen, it's worth a few weeks of school to be sure," said John.

"I don't want any part of it," Randy insisted. "If you want to waste a beautiful summer in school, go ahead. I'm going to enjoy myself until it is time to go to work."

John spent the summer taking computer courses while Randy relaxed. By fall, there were more than enough applicants for the jobs. Only those who had taken the computer courses were accepted. John got a civil service job, and Randy had to look for other work.

When school was mentioned to Randy, he reacted automatically. He was not about to "waste" his summer in a classroom. Randy ignored the facts of his situation. As a result, he failed to get the job he wanted because he acted automatically.

Effective and Ineffective Automatic Decisions

In many work situations, you will find that making an automatic decision is best. For example, if you have been told to perform a task in a certain way, you probably should do it automatically. In such situations, however, it is a good idea to be aware of any new facts that may make it necessary to do things a little bit differently from time to time. Wayne failed to do this and ran into difficulty on his job. Consider what happened when he was unaware of new information:

Wayne was a receptionist in a small company. His instructions were never to let people past the reception area without having the person they were visiting come to meet them. Wayne had not been on the job very long when an elderly man came in. The older man said, "Good morning" pleasantly and started to walk into the office area.

"Just a minute, please," Wayne said, jumping up from his desk. "You can't go in there until someone comes out here to meet you. Whom do you want to see?"

"Oh, you must be new on the job," the man said. "Good work. But my name is Jacques Conti. I am the father of Tom Conti, one of the owners. Here is my identification."

"Well, I still don't think I can let you go back to the office area. Let me call your son's secretary. The rule is that no visitors can go in without an escort."

"Very well," Mr. Conti said. He waited patiently until Wayne contacted the secretary. The secretary came out to the reception area and met Mr. Conti.

Several days later, Mr. Conti came again and started to walk back to the office area. "I'm sorry, but you can't go back there," Wayne said.

"Now wait a minute," Mr. Conti said. "You know who I am. I don't have time to wait here for you to call my son's secretary. I've got to see him, and I'm in a hurry."

"You may not. The rule says no visitors can go back to the office area without an escort," Wayne said. "I'll call your son and let him know you are here."

Although he was following company policy, Wayne did not last very long on the job. Sometimes policies must be changed to fit the circumstances of a situation. Because Wayne made an automatic decision, he lost his job.

Think about some decisions you have made recently. Were they automatic? Did you consider the situation? Or did you decide things on the basis of what had worked or hadn't worked in the past? If most of your decisions were automatic, you might want to consider whether they turned out as you expected or wanted. Did you get the results you got in the past? Or did something go wrong?

The four-step-decision-making process helps when you are reasoning out a thinking decision. Use it.

You might want to add some feelings to your automatic decisions, because sometimes feelings will reflect the facts of a situation. Even better, you might want to add a little thought to your decisions. If you make all decisions on the basis of slogans (such as, "Better safe than sorry") or rules (such as, "Never lend nor borrow money"), you may find yourself in an unfortunate position. You may not expect the results of your decisions. Keep these disadvantages in mind as you read about another kind of decision. Consider how it may be used.

THINKING DECISIONS

"After a careful examination of the facts, I've decided to. . . ."

"When I weighed the pros and cons, it seemed best to. . . ."

"We discovered what the real problem was, and then we were able to. . . ."

These statements are signals that each person made a thinking decision. Thinking decisions are based on reasoning. Thinking decisions involve four steps. Thinking decisions utilize the following four-step-decision-making process:

1.   Analyze the situation
2.   Identify the alternatives, or possible choices
3.   Consider the results of each alternative
4.   Make a choice

These steps make the difference between thinking decisions and feeling or automatic decisions because they cannot be taken hastily and they cannot be made on the basis of emotions. Consider this example:

In his senior year in high school, Ed became depressed. He hardly ever smiled or enjoyed anything. He spent more and more time sleeping. Ed seemed to be hiding from life.

Ed realized that something was wrong. He hadn't always acted this way, and he wasn't happy with the results of his behavior. Ed decided to do something about his problem. He realized that all the sleep and his sad moods were symptoms of something wrong.

He thought about his best friends, Karen and Steve. Karen had decided to join the U.S. Navy after graduation, and Steve planned to work for a trucking company. Both were happy and excited when they talked about their plans.

Ed began to realize that, unlike Karen and Steve, he had no goals. Whenever his friends asked him what he was going to do after graduation, Ed made a joke and passed it off, saying, "I think I'll be a ski bum." For the first time, he began to realize that his situation wasn't funny at all. When he realized he had no personal goals, he became worried. Then he realized he should do something.

Ed considered some solutions. He thought about joining the navy, like Karen. He also considered working at the trucking company with Steve. Neither plan appealed to Ed. Then he thought about what sort of person he was and what he wanted from life. He considered his abilities and realized that he was very good at repairing things.

Ed's world opened up. He had alternatives. He could learn about mechanical repair work in military service, or he could attend a nearby college, or he could go to evening classes for adults at the high school. In his community, there also was a technical school that taught courses in air-conditioning and refrigeration repair. After learning about his alternatives, Ed decided to join the adult classes in mechanical repair work at the high school. He would be able to work part time during the day and attend classes in the evening.

Ed made a thinking decision. He followed the four-step-decision-making process. In step one, Ed analyzed his situation. After looking for possible alternatives—step two, Ed went on to step three. He considered the results of each alternative. Finally, Ed took step four by making his choice. Through the decision-making process, Ed found out what he wanted to do. He set a goal and worked effectively toward that goal.

Think about some of your recent decisions. Did you follow a process like Ed's? Did you use this four-step process? When you use this process, you can find out what you want and start moving in the right direction. However, if you make all your decisions on the basis of a reasoning process, you may be working too hard.

Let's look at the three types of decisions together. Consider how each type of decision can be used.

WHICH KIND OF DECISION PAYS OFF?

At this point, you may be asking: "Are thinking decisions the only kind I should make?" "Are thinking decisions the only decisions that pay off?" As you may know, the answer is "No." It would be slow and impossible to make all decisions on the basis of the four-step process. However, most important decisions could be improved by carefully considering your alternatives.

Sometimes a feeling decision or an automatic decision is more appropriate. For instance, if you use the four-step process to decide what to wear, you probably would never get dressed. In some situations, it's impossible to know everything that might happen. If you relied entirely on thinking decisions, you might make no decisions at all.

Sometimes automatic decisions work more effectively than thinking decisions. Consider what would happen if a firefighter took time to consider the outcome of every possible action? At times, it's more important to act than to think

because emergency situations call for immediate action. Automatic decisions are quick and effective in such cases. They can save trouble and time when something has to be done fast.

YOUR BEST BET: A COMBINATION

In making decisions, the most useful approach is to combine your feelings, automatic responses,

Sometimes a combination of several kinds of decisions leads to the best career choice. What combination of decisions perhaps entered into this health aide's choice of a career? (Courtesy Visiting Nurse Service of New York)

and reasoning abilities. If you know what you hope to accomplish—what goal you seek, you can take a moment to decide the best course of action. Often, just a moment's thought will make it clear that you can follow your feelings or that you can act automatically. At other times, it becomes clear that the best thing for you to do can be achieved by following the four-step-decision-making process.

Decisions often involve a mixture of feelings, automatic responses, and reasoning abilities. How much you rely on each of these factors is determined by your past experience with similar situations and the facts of the situation at hand. Also, keep in mind that it is important to know your goals. After you have your goals in mind, you can move toward them by acting on your feelings, automatic responses, and reasoning.

20

THE STAGES OF CAREER DECISION MAKING

When you were a child, you probably had many ideas about what you wanted to "be" when you grew up. Perhaps you wanted to be an explorer, or an astronaut, or a firefighter. These are exciting and adventurous jobs. It's a safe bet, though, that the job decisions you are considering now are far removed from what you wanted to be when you were a child.

Sometimes people do become what they dreamed of as children. More often than not, most people change their ideas about possible jobs and careers. As they change and mature and have new experiences, so do their values and goals change. Eventually, through reality-testing, they make realistic choices. Reality-testing is trying out daydreams in a real-life situation. Through reality-testing, people find out what is best for them.

REALITY-TESTING A DECISION

To reach reality-testing, you usually pass through four stages of decision making: initial, exploratory, tentative, and realistic. These four stages are not connected with any specific age. However, when you are young, you tend to be at the initial and exploratory stages, while you tend to be at the tentative and realistic stages when you get older.

Regardless of your age or maturity, a decision about a career will always involve all four stages. Studies have shown that, on the average, people change jobs at least three or four times during their working lives. Therefore, you should expect to make many decisions about your career throughout your life.

Read the following story about Roxanne. Throughout this chapter, you will see how Roxanne goes through the four stages of decision making as she tries to make a decision about her career:

When Roxanne was 7 years old, she wanted to be a nurse. She liked nurses' uniforms. By the time Roxanne was 10, she had changed her mind about her career at least three times. At one point, she decided to be a waitress in a restaurant because "They get tips." Then she thought she wanted to be an artist because "They have fun painting." Next, Roxanne thought she wanted to be an airplane pilot because "It's exciting."

Throughout high school, Roxanne continued to explore and think about different careers. However, when she graduated, she was still interested in flying. She worked as an office clerk at the county airport. And on Saturdays, she took flying lessons.

Initial Stage of Decision Making

The initial stage of decision making contains an element of fantasy, or imagination. For example, you may not know much about a particular career, but it may certainly sound enjoyable.

Roxanne's decision at the age of 7 to become a nurse is an example of the initial stage of a career decision. In several ways, her decision was a fantasy or unrealistic choice. Even though she was impressed by nurses' uniforms, Roxanne did not really know what is involved in the work of being a nurse.

At the age of 7, Roxanne was not sure about her aptitudes and interests. More than likely, she

The initial stage of deciding on a career often begins in childhood daydreams or fantasies. (Magnum Photo)

didn't even know what they were and how important they would be to her. Because her self-identity was not well defined as a young girl, she made several different initial career decisions. She wanted to be a waitress, an artist, and an airplane pilot. At this point, Roxanne really wasn't serious about any of these decisions.

When Roxanne said, "I want to be a nurse," there was no real *commitment*, or pledge on her part, to become one. She was not ready to realistically consider her aptitude for nursing, her interest in caring for others, or her work values in the health-care field.

Roxanne was young when she made these initial decisions. Now consider Frank, who is older:

> Frank had been working for 3 years in a science laboratory as a technician. One Sunday afternoon, while reading the newspaper, he happened to glance through the "help wanted" section. A local television studio was advertising for a TV announcer. The ad caught his eye. "I wonder," Frank said to himself, "if I could be a TV announcer? I've got a pretty good voice, and I bet I would look great on television."
>
> That night Frank dreamed about making announcements and doing the sports segment of the evening news as a TV personality. The next morning Frank decided to apply for the job.

Like Roxanne's decision to be a nurse, Frank's decision to try for the TV announcer's job was the initial stage of a decision. This type of deci-

sion is not always made by young people. It is also sometimes made by older people, like Frank, who are thinking about a change in careers. The wishful thinking, or fantasy quality, of the choice is what makes it an initial decision.

An initial decision can be the first step in making a career decision, or it may go no further than the wishing, or daydreaming, stage. What if your initial decision seriously interests you? Then you're ready to move on to the second stage of your career development—exploratory decision making.

Exploratory Stage of Decision Making

Exploratory decisions help you find out more about careers in which you initially have shown interest. They also help you discover your own interests and work values. At this stage, your questions might include: "Can I see myself in this career? Do I like the lifestyle of workers in this field? What kind of education or experience do I need to enter this career? Can I satisfy my personal and occupational goals in this career?" You may have other considerations.

Roxanne's initial decision was to become an airplane pilot. When she was in high school, she explored the airline transportation field. She talked to a vocational counselor about careers in aviation. Her work at the county airport revealed that there were many different careers in aviation other than being a pilot.

When exploring a particular career area, it is wise to consider a number of possible jobs in that area. In Roxanne's case, her work at the airport resulted in her enrolling in a work-experience program. This program allowed her to work 12 hours a week at the airport for credit towards her graduation from high school.

Both initial and exploratory decisions can be the beginning of well-thought-out career decisions. This process of identifying career choices and finding out about them can be the groundwork for making career decisions in the future.

As a result of exploring a career area, you may decide that it's not for you. However, after you make initial and exploratory decisions, you may still be interested in a particular career. Then you are ready to try it out. You are then ready to make a tentative, or possible but uncertain, career decision.

Tentative Stage of Decision Making

After Roxanne spent part of her senior year in high school working at the county airport, she learned that it would take some time for her to become an airplane pilot. She adjusted her career goals, or compromised, by getting a clerical job at the airport. Then she took flying lessons. After 6 months as an office clerk, she became an airport guard and continued her flying lessons.

Roxanne's decision to become an airport clerk was a tentative decision. It was made at the tentative stage of her career decision making. Tentative career choices are temporary. There is no firm commitment to a career at this point. However, Roxanne was reality-testing her tentative choice. Her job at the airport would give her an opportunity to see how she liked working in a transportation career. The job allowed her to test both her self-identity and her career identity.

Tentative choices help you clarify your career goals and work values. Roxanne was no longer just exploring an aviation career; she was actually working in it. She was still uncertain about what she would eventually decide on for a career. But her tentative decision allowed her to experiment with a job in aviation and, at the same time, to get advanced training.

Exploring and identifying career possibilities takes place in the exploratory stage of career decisions. (Courtesy Danskin)

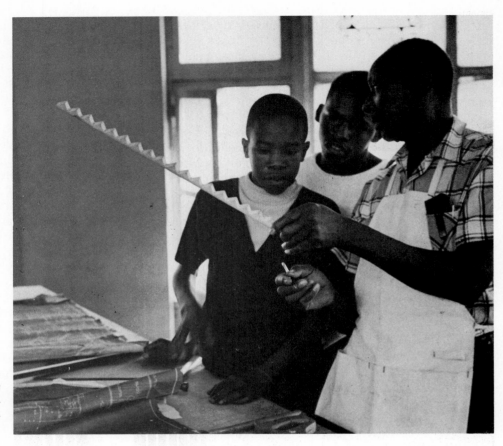

In the tentative stage of making a career decision, training programs can help clarify a decision. (Magnum Photo)

You make tentative career decisions when you decide to major in specific programs. Taking a part-time or summer job are other examples of tentative career decisions. During the period that you are making tentative decisions, you are able to clarify your self-identity and your career identity.

Questions you might ask during this stage of vocational decision making include: "Am I satisfied with doing this kind of work? Do I enjoy this lifestyle? Are my work values similar to the values of other people in this career?" If the answer to most of these questions is "No," you should consider other careers. However, if the answer to most is "Yes," your career development has matured. You are ready to enter the realistic stage of decision making.

Realistic Stage of Decision Making

The major difference between a realistic career decision and a tentative decision is a commitment based on knowledge and experience. A realistic decision means that you actually begin working in a particular career. Roxanne's decision to become an airport guard was a realistic career decision. And Roxanne was now at the realistic stage of decision making. Remember that this is the fourth and final stage in the process of making a career decision.

Roxanne had to reach a certain stage of career maturity before she could make a realistic decision. She had to examine her aptitudes, interests, and work values. She had to make initial, exploratory, and tentative decisions about the world of work before she could make a realistic decision. In Roxanne's case, as a result of self- and career exploration, her self-identity and her career identity matched.

Often, making a realistic decision involves a compromise. Becoming a security guard was a compromise for Roxanne. Although she was not a pilot, she worked at an airport. Her job provided occasional excitement, and she was working in aviation. Setting realistic career goals for yourself often involves making a compromise rather than hoping or wishing for a dream career that is removed from reality.

The realistic stage of career decision making begins on the job. (Top, courtesy Metropolitan Life; bottom left, courtesy Adelphi University; bottom right, courtesy Western Electric)

SUMMING UP

The four stages of career decision making—initial, exploratory, tentative, and realistic—are progressively more mature. Mature here does not mean mature in the sense of age, but mature in the sense of being realistic and responsible. For example, an 18-year-old can make a realistic career decision, whereas a 30-year-old may make an initial career decision.

All four stages of career decision making are important to your career development. The initial decision is the fantasy choice—anything is possible at this stage. Career exploration helps you discover whether or not you are seriously interested in a career. Your knowledge of the experience and educational requirements involved in your choice plays an important part now. You are ready to make tentative, or trial, career decisions. A summer job or part-time work permits you to see if a possible career matches your needs and work values. At this point, you are ready to make a realistic career decision. Then you are able to decide about a career because you know who you are and where you want to go. This will lead to satisfaction in your chosen career.

21

DO ALL DECISIONS WORK?

When you decide on some frames for your eyeglasses, are you sure another style would not have looked better? When you decide to read one book for a research report, are you sure another book would not have been better? When you decide to go to one job interview but not to another, are you sure you have chosen wisely? In other words, is it possible to decide things with absolute certainty? Is it possible to be dead sure that your choice will produce the results you want? Of course, the answer is "No."

UNCERTAIN DECISIONS

Even after going through all the stages of making a decision, you cannot always be certain that your final decision will produce the results you want. Almost all decisions include a degree of uncertainty.

Consider the following examples of two high school seniors who think their decisions will produce certain results:

Michelle wants to go to a technical school after high school and specialize in electronics. To be sure that she gets accepted, she has applied to three different technical schools. Michelle has decided that she'll get into at least one of the three schools, so she is not looking for any others.

Vince has decided that he needs to work full time when he graduates. He now has a part-time job as usher at the Bijou Theater, and he feels certain that his application for a full-time job there will be accepted. He has decided not to bother looking anywhere else.

Have Michelle and Vince decided with certainty? Can Michelle be certain that she will get into a

technical school? Can Vince be certain that he will get a full-time job?

Actually, many factors are involved in both cases. All three technical schools may turn Michelle down. For example, this probably will depend on her grades, her achievement test scores, and whether or not any of the schools have an opening. Nor can Vince be certain to get a full-time job. Does he have a good work record? Does he get along well with the manager of the theater? Who else might want the job, if there is one? Until such factors are considered, Michelle and Vince cannot be certain that their decisions will produce the goals they want.

People who think they are deciding with certainty often are fooling themselves. Some decisions may seem to be sure things, but there is always the chance that something may go wrong. Effective decision-makers try to take a degree of uncertainty into account, but some decisions can never be as certain as others.

Lessen the Uncertainty

Just about all decisions have a degree of uncertainty. There is usually less uncertainty with simple decisions. If you decide that wearing a particular outfit will please you and is the best for the weather that day, chances are the results will prove the decision to be a good one. Chances are that if the weather changes or something unexpected comes up, you may regret your choice.

Effective decision-makers try to lessen the amount of uncertainty in their decisions. To lessen uncertainty often involves making a thinking decision and using the following four-step-decision-making process:

Remember that all decisions contain some element of uncertainty. Do you consider this when buying a used car? (Helena Frost)

1. Analyze the situation
2. Identify the alternatives, or possible choices
3. Consider the results of each alternative
4. Make a choice

To lessen the uncertainty of a decision, first you must identify your goal. Then consider possible approaches to your goal and how likely they are to be successful. Finally, pick the approach that has the most certain outcome. Consider this example of Florence and the decision that she is weighing:

Florence has been offered two jobs during spring vacation. One job involves yardwork and pays $3.75 an hour. This work will take about 40 hours. The second job involves working as an assistant to a veterinarian. This job pays only $3.10 an hour, but there is a chance that the job will be available for 15 hours a week for the rest of the semester.

Florence is uncertain about which job to take. If she takes the yard job, she knows she'll make more money at first. And money is an important consideration to Florence. However, if she takes the job as veterinary assistant, she might be able to work more hours and earn more money in the long run.

No matter which job Florence takes, there will be some uncertainty. To lessen the uncertainty, Florence should gather all the facts, consider her alternatives, and try to guess the results of each alternative. Then, depending on her needs, her values, and her knowledge about her choices, Florence would make a decision. She would base her decision on the four-step process.

Consider the Degree of Uncertainty

In circumstances such as these, the decision-maker has to consider the degree of uncertainty involved with each alternative. It is helpful to remember, though, that there is always some uncertainty in trying to determine the future. Some people always try to decide with absolute certainty. Others make decisions only on the basis of hunches and feelings, even when the results are uncertain. These people are not thinking through in their decisions.

You can prepare yourself for unwanted results by considering the amount of uncertainty in each possible solution to a problem. By doing so, you will become a more capable decision-maker. By thinking about what might happen if a solution goes wrong, you will be able to decide whether or not to try that solution. Sometimes the uncertainty is too great. On the other hand, you may discover that even the worst that could happen would not be so bad. In this way, you accept your responsibility for the results of your decisions.

RISKY DECISIONS

Some decisions are more uncertain than others. The situation may be such that you cannot possibly know what will happen. Or the chances of the results being something other than what you want may be very great. Or you may have a lot to lose if you make the wrong decision. In such situations, you are faced with the need to make a risky decision. A *risky decision* is one in which the uncertainty is great, the chances of something going wrong are many, or you have much to lose.

If it has rained for the past 3 days and more rain is expected, it would be risky to plan a picnic on the fourth day. If your team has failed several attempts to complete a pass in football, it would be risky for the team to try another pass play. If your supervisor has warned you often about being late for work, it would be risky to be late again.

Some decisions involve a greater degree of risk than others. Sometimes the amount of risk is determined by how much a particular result is wanted. In an emergency, for instance, you might take a great risk in order to save someone's life. Police officers, firefighters, and rescue teams face such risks every day. The risk seems worth it to them, because lives might be lost if they do not act. Consider how Etta decided that an outcome was more important than a risk:

> Etta was a lifeguard for the summer. One morning, she decided the ocean was too rough for swimming, and she posted "No Swimming" signs along the beach. As she finished placing the signs, she heard a cry for help. A young boy, who had not seen the signs and had gone swimming, was having trouble fighting the waves. Etta immediately ran into the water and swam to rescue him. Fortunately, they both got out of the water safely.

Etta valued the life of the young swimmer enough to risk her own life in saving him. Of course, when she decided to take a job as a lifeguard, she realized the time might come when she would have to risk her own life. As is often the case, one decision lead to another. If Etta were not prepared to do this or if she did not value the lives of others, she would not be a lifeguard.

When a lot of risk is involved, it is often better to decide to take the course of action in which the least amount of risk is involved. Sometimes, as is the case of firefighters, emergency medical technicians, surgeons, or police officers, for example, it is impossible to avoid a risky choice.

Notice that the three types of decisions—thinking, automatic, and feeling—were involved in Etta's case. Seeing the rough water, Etta made a thinking decision and put up the "No Swimming" signs. Later, when the boy called for help, Etta had to make an automatic decision. The boy just saw the water, decided he wanted to swim, and made a feeling decision.

Etta's thinking decision to post the signs did not involve any risk at all. It was an effective decision. Both the boy's feeling decision and Etta's automatic decision involved a great deal of risk. While the boy's decision must be judged to have been ineffective, Etta's decision, based on experience and training, was effective.

Ordinarily, you would not be involved in such life and death situations on a daily basis. You may face risky situations in which you must make a decision. Risk is involved whenever you decide to change jobs, for example. The other job may appear to offer greater advantages, but you cannot be sure until you are actually working in it. If you take it, you must give up the security of a familiar job.

IMPROVING POOR DECISIONS

Because of uncertainty and risk, you will make a wrong decision occasionally. Effective decision-makers usually make the right decisions and learn from their occasional poor decisions.

> Bertha works as a cook's assistant at Le Francais, a French restaurant. One Saturday morning while the cook, Mr. de Lay, is busy talking to the manager, the meat delivery truck arrives.
>
> "Is Mr. de Lay here?" the driver asks Bertha.
>
> "Yes. He's talking with the manager in the office. Can I help?" she says.
>
> "Well, yes," replies the driver. "How about signing this receipt so I can deliver the meat?"
>
> Bertha thinks about it for a second and then answers, "Sure, give me your pen."
>
> When Mr. de Lay returns to the kitchen, he notices the meat delivery. "Bertha, what's this? How did we get this meat?" he asks.
>
> "I signed for it," Bertha answers.
>
> "Don't ever do that again!" yells Mr. de Lay. "I am the only person who signs for food deliveries! Is that clear?"
>
> Bertha, realizing she had made the wrong decision, replies "Yes, I'm sorry, Mr. de Lay."

Effective decision-makers learn from their poor decisions and try to avoid unfortunate situations in the future. What decision could have been made to prevent the situation shown here?

You may be sure that Bertha will not sign for any food deliveries at Le Francais again.

You may make poor decisions sometimes. However, even a poor decision can show that you are able and willing to take some action. Remember, you can learn something from poor decisions. When you do make a poor decision, admit your error, find out what caused it, and learn all you can from it.

DECISION MAKING IS AN ONGOING PROCESS

Decision making is an ongoing, or a continuous, process. First, you use past experiences to arrive at decisions. Second, you are involved with the results long after you have made decisions.

When you get results from a decision, you may want to improve, or change, the results in some way. The results don't go away just because you do not like them. But you can determine whether or not you made the best decision, and you can take steps to improve it if necessary. Ben did that:

> Ben liked what he knew of the medical field. He enjoyed the thought of helping other people. And his parents wanted him to be a doctor.
>
> Ben decided to take some premedical courses when he entered college. During his freshman

year, he did not do very well. He had a strong interest in medicine, but his aptitude for science was poor. After almost failing his chemistry course, Ben began to question his career choice.

> He decided to discuss his goals with a counselor. In the discussion, Ben realized that he may have chosen the premedical program more to please his parents than to please himself. His counselor pointed out that there were other careers in the medical field that he might consider.
>
> Ben thought this over. He remembered a part-time job in a community hospital he had held the previous summer. He had worked in a ward for physically handicapped children. While working there, Ben had had an opportunity to learn about several health-related careers. One particularly stuck in his mind—physical therapy. At the hospital, he had observed Jessica Whitty. Jessica was a physical therapist who helped children to overcome their handicaps. She also helped the children's parents adjust to their problems. Ben admired Jessica's work and thought it was very important.
>
> He decided to work for a bachelor's degree in physical therapy rather than staying in the premedical program. Later on, Ben was pleased with his decision.

Ben's first decision—to become a doctor—was a poor one because he did not have the aptitudes to be a doctor. Fortunately, Ben realized he could improve his decision, and he set out to do so. As a result, his entire outlook at college changed. His grades improved, and he found he was genuinely interested in his courses.

Things worked out well for Ben. But what would have happened if he had been the kind of person who thinks decisions can never be changed? He probably would have struggled through college, wasting at least 4 years, before getting a probable rejection from medical school. Instead, Ben was able to turn his life around by keeping an open mind and being responsible for his decisions. He knew that one decision often leads to another, and he decided to make decisions that would lead to the results he wanted.

An important part of decision making is in evaluating the results. If you do not get what you expect, ask yourself, "What went wrong?" Was there a problem with how you acted on your decision? Or was the decision ineffective? Be flexible. If one course of action did not work, analyze why it did not work. Then look for a more effective approach.

ONE DECISION OFTEN LEADS TO ANOTHER

Decisions at any stage can lead to further decisions. They often are related, just as small decisions can lead to big ones. Sue's small decision led to a much bigger one:

> Sue wanted some money for guitar lessons. She decided to get a job for the summer. This decision led her to the school counseling office where she discussed possible summer jobs with Ms. Thorndike and investigated careers.
>
> Sue wrote letters to several large hotels and motels at Clear Lake, a recreational community near her hometown. She spent the summer working as a waitress and water-skiing instructor. As a result, Sue decided to get a full-time job in the recreation field after graduation. Sue's little decision to take guitar lessons and get a summer job led to the bigger decision of working toward a career in recreation and tourism.

This process can work the other way too. Sometimes a big decision can lead to a lot of small decisions. You can be making a number of small decisions and, at the same time, be thinking about one or two big decisions that you have to make. Decisions are not always made one at a time. You do not often say "Well, that decision is made. Now I'll start on the next decision." In actual practice, you make many decisions at the same time. Consider Martina's case:

> After visiting a local newspaper office when she was in junior high school, Martina became interested in being a reporter. Martina always liked to write. She was curious about current events and read the newspaper every day.
>
> Martina is now in senior high school. She is taking college preparatory courses. Her favorite classes are English and creative writing. She also takes typing. Martina recently joined the staff of her high school newspaper, and she expects to be a full-fledged reporter next semester. Martina hopes to go to college before trying to get a job on a newspaper. At times, she dreams about her future job.

Martina made a number of decisions that contribute to her self-identity. Martina likes to write. Because she is interested in what's going on in the world, she reads the newspaper regularly. By the time Martina entered senior high school, she had decided to become a newspaper reporter.

More decisions had to be made at this point. What courses should she take? Martina chose three subjects related to the field of newspaper reporting—English, creative writing, and typing. Her decision to take college preparatory courses reflected her desire to study journalism in college. Martina further identified herself as a reporter by joining the school's newspaper staff.

These decisions were part of a continuous process, and they are related. One decision led to another. The sum of Martina's decision equaled a major career decision: "I'm going to become a newspaper reporter."

Just as Martina's decisions were part of a continuous process, your decisions are also related. The decisions you make now will lead to other decisions. Try to be aware of how your decisions will add up.

Getting It All Together

1. What are some of the factors that affect your self-identity?

2. What is the relationship between your self-identity and your career identity?

3. What are some reasons why feeling decisions can be ineffective?

4. How are feeling decisions and automatic decisions similar?

5. Why should you not make thinking decisions all the time?

6. Describe a situation for each of the three kinds of decisions in which that kind of decision is most suitable.

7. Describe briefly how the four stages of decision making are related.

8. Describe how one decision often leads to another. Give some examples from your own life.

9. You are working part time at a local department store. Kathy, a friend of yours, is having trouble keeping up with her schoolwork and her chores at the store. You have often covered or filled in for Kathy to help her keep her job. Kathy really needs the extra money.

   A promotion has just become available, and your supervisor, Ms. Stevens, gives it to Kathy. Ms. Stevens told you, "Kathy has been doing very good work. I feel she deserves this promotion."

   What would your reaction be: *(a)* Tell Ms. Stevens that you often did Kathy's work for her; *(b)* tell Kathy to tell Ms. Stevens that she doesn't deserve the promotion; *(c)* quit the store in protest; or *(d)* do nothing, but don't help Kathy anymore.

USING THE DECISION-MAKING PROCESS

Your goals in this unit are given in the following list:

To identify the four steps in the decision-making process and to apply them in reaching your career goals

To recognize three major sources of career information

To be able to evaluate your decisions

As you read in Chapter 19, you can make an effective decision by using the following four steps:

- Analyze the situation
- Identify your alternatives, or possible choices
- Consider the results of each alternative
- Make a choice

These steps are essential when you are making decisions about almost anything—from choosing a winter coat to planning a summer vacation. With simple, routine decisions, you might move through the process very quickly. When making a decision that will have a major effect on your life, you will take more time going through the process. Then this process may become more complex and take a longer time.

When you are making major decisions, every step is important. Each step is related to the next step, just as the links in a chain are connected. If one link is weak, the entire chain may become weak. For example, if you do not analyze the situation correctly and completely (step 1), you will not be able to complete step 2 effectively. That is, you may not discover alternative solutions. Then the solutions you would discover may be inappropriate. For example, they would probably not relate to the real problem.

It is also possible to complete steps 1 and 2 accurately, yet fail in step 3—by misinterpreting the results. If your judgment of the results in step 3 is faulty, you would not be able to make the best choice—step 4.

If you go through the four-step-decision-making process every time you make a choice, you are being unrealistic. Human beings just do not make decisions in such a mechanical way. As you know, people make feeling decisions and automatic decisions with very little thought or study.

According to the circumstances and luck of a situation, feeling and automatic decisions may be effective or ineffective. Sometimes they are essential, as in an emergency. When you must make a quick decision, your knowledge of yourself, your values, and your goals will pay off. Clear values and realistic goals will increase the possibility of your decision's being effective—even if it is a feeling or automatic decision.

For those times when you must think through a decision carefully, learn to use the four-step-decision-making process. If you follow this process when you are making major decisions in your life—such as those related to careers, you will generally be effective. However, since there is an element of uncertainty in nearly all decisions, you should also be able to evaluate the results of your decisions and to make changes when they are necessary. In this unit, you will examine each of the steps in the decision-making process and consider how to evaluate the results of your decisions.

22

PREPARING FOR A CAREER DECISION

A decision that is made without clearly understanding the situation can lead to unwanted results. Consider Harry's case:

> Five evenings a week, Harry works at a service station. One evening, a car that had no headlights on pulled into the station. The driver of the car said, "My headlights just went out. Can you fix them for me?"
>
> "Sure," Harry said, quickly deciding that the customer's lights had burned out. "I'll change these headlights right away." Harry started to remove one of the headlights when the station manager, Mr. Sinclair, came over to him.
>
> "What seems to be the problem, Harry?" Mr. Sinclair asked.
>
> "Oh, just some burned-out headlights."
>
> "Did you check the headlight fuse?" Mr. Sinclair asked.
>
> "Oh, no. I didn't."

When Harry checked the headlight fuse, he discovered that it had burned out. The headlights did not have to be changed at all. Harry had made a hasty decision. He had not taken the time to think about the real problem—a burned-out fuse. Harry's decision to remove the headlight before he clearly understood the car's problem led to some unwanted results—and some extra repair work for him.

STEP 1: ANALYZE THE SITUATION

When you are making a decision, your first step is to analyze the situation. Basically, analyzing the situation means finding out who you are, where you are, and where you want to go. This also means that you must learn as much as you can about your circumstances. And you must dis-

cover how your circumstances may affect your decision.

Finding out who you are, where you are, and where you want to go probably sound familiar. Finding out about yourself involves identifying your values so that you can set realistic goals. It also involves learning your abilities and interests.

Your abilities and interests are major factors in future job satisfaction. By comparing your abilities to the careers that appeal to you, you can eliminate those that do not fit your abilities. By trying out careers, or reading about them, or talking to people in them, you can find out if they interest you.

Use Your Knowledge

As you know, you can determine your abilities and interests through measures, such as self-inventories and standardized tests. Once you have this knowledge, you then can apply it in different situations. And that is the other part of analyzing a situation. You determine the facts in each situation and relate them to what you know about yourself and your goals.

In most daily situations, this can be a simple process. For example, if someone suggests going for a swim and you know that you have neither the interest nor the ability for swimming, you can very quickly decide against it. You can easily relate your interests and ability to what you know about swimming.

However, when you are preparing for a career, things get more complicated. But again, your decision rests firmly on being able to know yourself. It is also important to know exactly what you want when making a decision.

Right now, you may be making some general decisions about a career, for example. These decisions would involve what courses to take in school or what part-time jobs you may want. If you are considering a part-time job, you usually would decide whether or not you want it. You may or may not want it because of the money involved or because it would or would not give you experience and training in a field that may interest you. Furthermore, your choice of the kind of part-time job you want would be limited by what is available.

Decisions are not made because of one reason alone. Many factors affect all of your decisions. You must analyze the situation so that you can identify as many of these factors as possible.

Be Aware

When you are analyzing a situation, it is important to realize that a decision must be made. Decisions are often pushed on you. There is usually no need to "realize" that a decision must be made. It is suddenly there, so you must act.

In most cases, this is true. For example, you may know that you must decide what courses to take next semester. Or you must decide what you will be doing during your summer vacation. What will you do next weekend, for example?

However, some people are not aware that they have the ability to make choices about their careers. They tend to believe that their choices are determined by their parents' careers or by what careers are available in their communities. Furthermore, many people do not realize that they can begin making career decisions while they are in high school. In fact, if you recognize that the high school period is the time to make some career decisions, you have begun an important step in analyzing your situation.

By knowing that what you do now will affect your future, you can make realistic and effective decisions. However, you may not be able to get the part-time job that you want to further your career goals. You must realize that other factors may interfere. This does mean that you can relate your present decisions to your future career goals as closely as possible. If you are not aware that this is a time to decide on a future career, you may not make effective decisions.

Know the Problem

Once you recognize that a decision must be made, know the real need, or the problem, in a situation. If you misunderstand the situation, you will not make an effective decision. So therefore, explore your needs at this time.

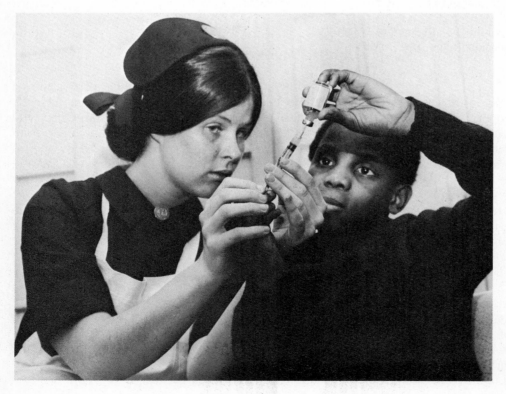

Discover your career possibilities by meeting and talking with people in the career areas that interest you. (Courtesy Visiting Nurses Service of New York)

In a sense, you must separate the symptoms from the problem. A *symptom* is a sign that there is a problem. However, the symptom is not the problem. When you are making a decision, be sure that you are focusing on the problem and not the symptom. Look at this example of how Jake separated a problem from its symptoms:

A junior in high school, Jake works one evening a week at an ice cream store. Returning home from school one day, Jake found a telephone message his father had taken for him. It said: "Your supervisor, Ms. St. John, called. Frank is sick, and she needs a cashier for the store. Could you work this evening from 5 to 9? Please call and let her know."

Jake had to make a decision. Should he work this extra night or stay home? His first reaction was, "Ugh! Work again." He thought about all the homework he had to do. Then he said to himself, "I feel pretty tired tonight. I don't think I should go in to work." He remembered that his favorite TV program would be on at 8:30.

Thinking about all these reasons for not working made Jake realize something. "You know," Jake thought, "I've got to face it. I'm sick and tired of being a cashier. I'm bored, and I don't get paid enough."

At first, this seemed to be a small decision— deciding whether or not to put in an extra evening's work. As Jake thought about his situation, he kept thinking about his reasons for not working—his homework, his tiredness, and his favorite TV show. Suddenly, Jake realized that these "reasons" were really only excuses. They were symptoms of a problem. When he thought about it, he realized that his job was boring. His problem wasn't homework or any of the other excuses. Jake's real problem was that he was not happy with his job.

Of course, Jake will still have to make the minor decision about whether to work tonight. But he will also have to begin looking for solutions to his real problem—finding another job.

If Jake hadn't thought carefully about the reasons why he did not want to work, he might have based his decision on a symptom, not on the problem. He might have decided not to work because he did not want to miss his TV program. This decision by itself would not have solved his problem.

When you are having trouble making a decision, remember that you may not be aware of the problem. You may be reacting to symptoms. In such cases, you may not make the most effective decision because you may base your decision on a symptom rather than a cause.

Learning to look beyond symptoms is not easy. Symptoms are usually the first things you notice, but they also can be the most troublesome information you have. Your emotions are involved, and how you feel can affect the rest of the decision-making process.

If you look into why the symptoms are there, you can discover the basic problem. Of course, all decisions do not involve big problems. But if you don't have the information you need, making any decision can be a problem. However, when you recognize the symptoms and identify the real problem, you are taking an essential step in making a thinking decision.

Get the Facts

When you know more about a situation, it is easier to evaluate the situation and make a good decision. How much fact-finding should you do? This depends on the type of situation and on the complexity of the situation. Two other considerations are: How much time is available? Is it an emergency situation?

How are the facts gathered for making most decisions? Sometimes you may already know the necessary information. But when you don't, newspapers, magazines, journals, government agencies, counselors, and other knowledgeable people can provide information. The sources are almost unlimited. But remember that it is up to you—the decision-maker—to uncover them and to use them.

Once the facts have been collected, arrange them in a way so that you can interpret them. For example, it helps to group similar ideas together. This way, you can separate important facts from less important ones. By organizing your information, you will think of more alternatives.

STEP 2: IDENTIFY YOUR ALTERNATIVES

Step 1 leads into step 2. When you are gathering information and analyzing your situation, you are also discovering possible alternatives, or choices of action. There is this difference, though. When you are analyzing the situation in step 1, you are finding out as much as you can about everything that might be involved. This begins with information about yourself, your values and goals, and your interests and abilities. This includes recognizing the need for making a decision and knowing about the situation. As you know, you must separate the symptoms from the basic problems. When you begin doing step 2—looking for alternatives—find out what your possible decisions, or choices, are.

There are many ways to identify alternative courses of action. First, get more information. When you are making decisions about your career, take some related courses. This is a good way to discover your alternatives. Outside school, there are at least three ways in which you can explore careers so that you can develop possible courses of action. They are:

- Through work experience
- Through interviewing workers
- Through reading occupational literature

Each one of these courses of action can be very helpful in determining your career alternatives.

Work Experience

A direct way to find out about a career is by taking a part-time job in a possible career area or in a related one. For instance, if you are interested in mechanical repair work, working at a part-time job in a service station might be helpful. This firsthand experience would give you some information about a possible career area that you would not be able to get from any other source. You would find out whether or not this career area would fit your interests, needs, and abilities. You would also find out something about the lifestyle of a career in this area.

Interview Workers

Find out about career areas by talking to people who work in them. When you talk to a person who is employed in a career that appeals to you, try to remember the following three basic points: (1) The person may tend to overrate or underrate the career and, therefore, won't be able to answer all your questions. (2) The person may not be aware of the present or future demand for workers in the career area. (3) The person may know only about a particular department and may not know about other important aspects of that career area.

In spite of all these difficulties, workers are often a good source of information about a possible career area. If there is no printed material about some particular career area, workers in

that career area may be your best source of information.

Read Occupational Literature

A popular way to find out about career areas is by browsing through occupational literature. A wide variety of occupational literature is available. Newspapers, books, magazines, and pamphlets are some sources.

When you are seeking career information, do not limit yourself to the obvious sources. You can find much information. For example, consider the following list:

Fiction about people in actual jobs. Stories, novels, television programs, and movies contain useful information about careers. From these sources, you might learn about qualifications, duties, job requirements, conditions of work, chances of advancement, and the lifestyles of people in some careers. A word

Explore your career alternatives by taking a part-time job in a career area that interests you. In this way, you may discover the career that fits you best. (Courtesy Camp Fire Girls, Inc./Martha Blevins)

of caution when you are using these sources: they may overemphasize conditions in a career area by making them very glamorous or very undesirable.

Biographies and autobiographies of people in careers that interest you. These stories, written about or by people and their careers, will often provide useful information. Such stories can tell about the problems and successes a person had when preparing for or working in a career.

Recruitment literature published by companies. Such information will usually inform you about job conditions, pay, benefits, requirements, and chances of promotion in a career area. When you are reading such literature, remember that the company has a purpose in publishing it. The company is trying to get people interested in working for it. Therefore, the literature may put a career in its most favorable light and may gloss over things that are unfavorable.

Posters and charts. Posters and charts in state employment offices or in school vocational guidance centers, on community bulletin boards, and in company offices often provide usable information in a brief, highlighted fashion. Therefore, the information you want may be quickly sought out.

The federal government publishes a great deal of career information. Among the federal agencies that publish career information are: U.S. Department of Agriculture; U.S. Department of Commerce; U.S. Department of Health and Human Services; U.S. Department of Education; and the U.S. Department of Labor. Some state agencies also print career information.

Professional associations, unions, and industrial organizations are some other excellent sources of information about careers. All should be investigated when you are gathering information about possible careers.

Two of the most useful printed sources of information about careers are published by the U.S. Department of Labor. One is the *Dictionary of Occupational Titles* (often called the DOT) and the other is the *Occupational Outlook Handbook* (frequently called the OOH). Both these publications may be available in your school or public library. They are important tools when you are trying to discover alternative choices for a career decision. Learn how to use them.

The *Dictionary of Occupational Titles* is in two volumes. The first volume lists some 30,000 jobs alphabetically by title, with a brief description of each. Just leafing through it, you will get an idea of the wide variety of careers. The second volume arranges jobs into occupational clusters. This volume also contains descriptions of worker traits for different groups of occupations. You can begin to match your abilities and interests with those described.

The *Occupational Outlook Handbook* covers occupations in 13 career cluster groups:

- Industrial production and related occupations
- Office occupations
- Service occupations
- Education and related occupations
- Sales occupations
- Construction occupations
- Occupations in transportation activities
- Scientific and technical occupations
- Mechanics and repair persons
- Health occupations
- Social science occupations
- Social service occupations
- Art, design, and communications-related occupations

The OOH gives you important information about each occupation, such as areas of employment throughout the country and the employment outlook—that is, whether or not jobs in a particular field are likely to be available in the near future. It also gives facts about the nature of the work, training and other qualifications required, potential salary, and working conditions. The OOH also lists other sources of information about careers, so it is a good source of information about career alternatives.

The OOH is updated every year. Make sure that you use the latest issue so that your information will be accurate. As you know, accurate information is very important.

DON'T STOP WITH THE OBVIOUS

When you are searching for possible alternatives, or choices, do not stop after determining one or two obvious ones. If you identify possible choices that aren't obvious, your decision will be better.

In doing the obvious, Jason found out about the not-so-obvious and was able to make a satisfying career choice:

Jason had a strong mechanical ability, and he enjoyed working with his hands. The obvious career for him seemed to be in automobile repair. He thought of a job in an automobile repair shop or with an auto dealer. However, Jason was not very excited about working on cars because that was not his major interest.

Still, he could do repair work, and he liked it well enough. So he worked part time in a garage, thinking that some day he would probably own one himself. But that idea did not completely satisfy him.

Jason began thinking that there must be other places where a good mechanic could work. His counselor at school suggested that he read the *Occupational Outlook Handbook.* Jason went to the library and looked up mechanics in the index. He was surprised to see 16 different kinds of mechanics listed.

"Boat motor mechanics" caught his eye. Jason did not live near an ocean or a large lake, so he had not thought of working on boat motors. When he saw the job listed in the OOH, he knew it would be more interesting and exciting than repairing automobiles. Having such a career would mean living on or near the water, something that Jason had always wanted to do. Soon Jason was devoting all his energy toward a career in an area that he had never known of before reading about it in the OOH.

Jason's obvious career choice was working in a local garage as an automobile mechanic. His decision to work on boat motors was a creative decision. Therefore, Jason went beyond an obvious decision.

Brainstorm

When you are thinking about possible careers, try to go beyond the obvious. This may mean doing more research, as Jason did. It may mean playing hunches or checking out guesses. You can develop creative alternatives by brainstorming. *Brainstorming* is a process in which new ideas are developed, but the ideas are not evaluated or criticized. This technique is used in many businesses. Brainstorming can be done in small groups or when you are alone.

When you brainstorm in a small group, everyone in the group is free to offer an idea or solution. When you brainstorm alone, try to come up with as many ideas or solutions as possible, keeping them all. The time for evaluating these new ideas comes later.

In brainstorming, all ideas are considered uncritically. Research has shown that creative thinking and evaluation, especially criticism, do not seem to work well together. Decision-makers at almost all brainstorming sessions postpone an evaluation of their ideas until after the creative period ends.

Go beyond obvious career choices by looking into creative alternatives. For example, if you are artistically inclined, you might consider a career in art restoration. (Courtesy United Nations/ RC/DB)

Let Ideas Incubate

After you have thought of a number of ideas, let them incubate. Just as parent birds take turns sitting on their eggs until they develop and hatch, give your ideas time to develop, or *incubate.* Think about something else for a while. Some possible solutions will come to mind. You can make new relationships between your thoughts, and better ideas may surface during the incubation period.

How long should you let your ideas incubate? There is no answer to this question. Some decisions may cause you to incubate alternative solutions for only a few minutes. Other decisions, may cause you to let your ideas incubate for weeks or months.

Some choices may have been incubating inside you for years—your career choice, for example. After a period of incubation, evaluate your alternatives. Then think about the probable results of each alternative.

23

MAKING A DECISION

At this point, you are about ready to make a decision as you follow the four-step-decision-making process. After taking steps 1 and 2, you have gathered all the information you need to make a decision. You could pick one of the many choices that you developed in step 2 and decide, "That's what I'll do."

If the information about yourself was thorough and the information about your choice was accurate, you probably would make a fairly effective decision if you did so. However, there is one more step you should take before actually making a decision.

STEP 3: CONSIDER POSSIBLE RESULTS

At step 3, you compare the information you developed in step 1 with the alternatives you discovered in step 2. You will carefully consider each of your possible career choices in terms of your values, goals, abilities, and interests. At this point, ask yourself the following key questions:

1. *Does the work described interest me?* Most publications describe the work performed and the equipment used. Keep an open mind, because work that does not appeal to you now may seem more interesting after you have read about it.
2. *What is the demand for workers?* Most publications will describe expected employment trends for the next 5 to 20 years in your possible career areas.
3. *What is required to enter and succeed in the occupation?* Look for the education and training and abilities and interests needed to

enter and succeed in your possible career areas.
4. *Is there any financial or other kind of assistance available for the training needed for entering the career area?* Publications usually mention any kinds of assistance that are offered by unions, professional organizations, employers, school or college placement offices, and the like.
5. *Is advancement likely?* Watch for any mention of the usual lines of promotion within a career area or after transferring to a related career area. Generally, advancement occurs with increased experience or further education in your career area.
6. *What are the earnings?* Take careful note of beginning earnings and average earnings. Is there a big difference between them? *Beginning earnings* refer to the income when beginning a career area; *average earnings* refer to the average income of all people working in a career area. Also notice typical fringe benefits, such as vacation time, insurance coverage, and retirement plans. You may want to compare the financial benefits of one career with those of another.

Sort Out Your Alternatives

If you have a number of possible alternatives, it may be difficult to sort them out. Do not let this stop you from developing as many choices as possible. It is worth the trouble to be able to make a final choice from many alternatives. The more choices you have, the more likely your decision will be an effective one.

A useful way to sort out your choices before making a career decision is by drawing up a chart. On the chart, you can compare the knowledge you have about yourself with the information you gathered about possible careers.

Maryjane wanted to get an idea of what the results of each of her choices would be. Here is how she went about sorting out her alternatives:

Maryjane was interested in the career cluster called office occupations. She read the *Occupational Outlook Handbook* to get an idea of what kinds of careers were available in that cluster. She was not interested in clerical work, bookkeeping, filing, or typing, so she skipped over that group. Computers appealed to her, so she put down computer operator as one possible choice. She also liked the idea of working for an insurance company. A claims adjuster sounded exciting; that career would be somewhat like that of a private detective. So she put that career area down also. In the office occupations cluster, she also found administrative and related careers. This was a large grouping. In the administrative grouping, she found city managers and personnel workers with entering positions as administrative assistants. She listed these career areas as possible choices also.

These were the options she felt were open to her among office occupations. Maryjane wanted to examine each one more closely. To do so, she prepared the chart on page 112. Across the top, Maryjane listed her major skills, interests, and goals, which reflected her values. On the right side, she listed the four occupations that most appealed to her. She could consider others later if none of these seemed suitable after comparing them with what she knew about herself.

Maryjane colored in the squares opposite the occupation if its skills and aptitudes, interests, or goals and values applied to her. She did not color in the square under a high school diploma after city manager because a college degree was required for that job. Her chart told Maryjane that she had the most skills to be successful as a computer operator or as a claims adjuster. Although the career of a city manager fit most of her goals, she had no skills for it and only slight interest in it. She had few personnel skills.

Of the two careers for which she had the most skills and aptitudes, the one of claims adjuster met most of her interests as well as fulfilling most of her goals and values. On the basis of what her chart told her, Maryjane decided to try for a career in the insurance business, with the intent of being a claims adjuster to start. She knew that she could change her career later if it did not work out, but she wanted to make an effective choice at the start. On the basis of all the evidence she had, the possible outcome of her decision—to become a claims adjuster—would be favorable for her.

Since experience and education can lead to advancement in all areas, employees who show the potential to become managers are often given the chance to participate in company-sponsored training sessions. (Courtesy Sheraton Hotels and Inns)

		Computer Operator	Claims Adjuster	City Manager	Personnel Worker
GOALS, VALUES	INDEPENDENCE	white	dark	dark	white
	EXCITING, VARIED ROUTINE	white	dark	dark	white
	ADMINISTRATIVE POSITION	white	white	dark	dark
	REASONABLE SECURITY	dark	dark	white	dark
	GOOD INCOME	white	dark	dark	dark
INTERESTS	SOLVING PROBLEMS	dark	dark	dark	dark
	WORKING WITH FIGURES	dark	dark	light	white
	WORKING WITH PEOPLE	white	dark	dark	dark
SKILLS, APTITUDES	ABILITY IN MATH	dark	dark	light	white
	TYPING SKILL	white	dark	white	light
	HIGH SCHOOL DIPLOMA	dark	dark	white	dark

Maryjane matched her characteristics to four careers. Dark squares are definite matches; light ones are possibilities.

Conflicts Can Occur

Of course, Maryjane's chart did not cover all the factors that can influence career decisions. As you have read, sometimes your needs and values can clash. Therefore, you must make a compromise, and compromises cannot be shown on a chart. For example, consider Carl's situation:

> Carl, a high school sophomore, works part time as a community aide at Self-Help, a local agency that helps get better jobs for people with low incomes. Although Carl is not making as much as he would like, he enjoys his work. Because he enjoys working with people and feels that what he is doing is worthwhile, Carl has been thinking about a career in social services.
>
> One evening, Carl's father told him that a friend of the family's called that day to offer Carl a job at a tomato cannery. The job would pay more money than Carl was making at the agency.
>
> "Mrs. Belardi says you could work 15 hours a week for the next 2 months, Carl. What do you say?"
>
> Carl thought about how he could use the money, and replied, "I guess I'm lucky to have a chance to earn more money. I'll take the job."
>
> The 2 months at the cannery passed quickly, and Carl had managed to save a little money. However, his friends and family noticed that he did not seem quite as happy anymore. Carl just did not have the same enthusiasm. He did not feel as useful as he did when he was working at Self-Help.

Carl felt that he needed more money. So he gave up a job that he liked and would perhaps lead to a satisfying career for a job he liked less. Because he became unhappy in the higher paying job, he is relieved that it's over. More than likely, he will decide not to go back to it.

Carl may not, however, be able to ignore the need to earn money. Very few of us can do that. But it is foolish to make a career decision based on money considerations alone. Doing so can lead to unhappiness. At the same time, it is not possible to ignore money altogether, as Carl learned.

Money is important not only in terms of potential income but also in terms of the cost of an education required for a given career area. Not everyone can afford the many years of schooling or training needed to enter some of the professions. A person with a strong drive and the necessary talents can usually find money through scholarships, grants or loans or by part-time work. However, money must be considered in your career decision. But money should not be the end-all or the be-all of your career decision. Although money is often an important factor, it is not the only one. The most important factors are your abilities, goals, and values. If you have clearly identified them in step 1, you are likely to make effective career decisions regardless of other factors. Making an effective career decision does not, however, mean that you can instantly achieve your goals. There are other factors to be considered, as you will learn. Even though some results can be known immediately, others are often delayed.

Immediate Outcomes

The outcomes of many decisions are known immediately. Consider Randy's case for an example of how this can occur:

> Randy, a quality control inspector on a bakery assembly line, looks for defects in baked goods as they move along a conveyor belt. When Randy decides to tag a loaf of bread or a cake because it is imperfect, the result of that decision is known immediately. The imperfect product is taken off the conveyor belt and either discarded or given away. If the fault is rather small, Randy may decide to let it pass. However, he may hear about this later if a customer complains.
>
> In the case of a minor defect, Randy's decision to pass the product has no immediate effect. However, it can have a delayed effect. If Randy fails to consider both the immediate and delayed results of his decisions, he will be a poor quality control inspector.

Delayed Outcomes

People usually consider the most obvious and immediate results of a decision. You should also consider delayed results. Read about John, and think about his decision:

> John heard that the U.S. Army is offering a cash bonus for enlisting in that military service. He could use the money, so he decided to enlist when he graduates from high school. The immediate outcome of this decision would be that John will get some extra money. Unless John has considered the delayed outcomes of his decision, he may be unhappy about how he spends the next few years of his life. He should ask himself if he will like military life and if a military career will satisfy other values that he may have.

Careful decision-makers consider the possible outcomes of their decisions. How, do you think, this person could have avoided the situation shown here?

Effective decision-makers say to themselves, "This is probably what will happen if I make this decision." They also ask themselves, "What else could happen, or what might happen later, if I choose this course of action?" Consider Dorine's case:

> Dorine's parents are going on a ski trip during the holidays. She has just been offered a part-time job at a local day-care center. The director of the day-care center asked Dorine to begin work during the holidays.
>
> If Dorine considers the immediate outcome, she may choose to go on a ski trip with her family. However, if she also considers the possible delayed effect of going skiing now, she may decide not to go. The center director would probably hire someone else if Dorine doesn't take the job when it is offered.

Effective decision-makers carefully consider both the immediate and delayed results of their decisions. When you are making career decisions, the delayed results are especially important. Most of the time, delayed results will be more important than immediate results. In fact, sometimes you will have to accept some unwanted immediate results in order to reach more desired results later. If you know your goals, you will realize this and make decisions that will pay off for you throughout your career.

STEP 4: MAKE YOUR CHOICE

This is the final step. If you have followed the first three steps, this one should be the easiest to take. When you make the best choice, you make your decision. By the time you take this step, you have considered all your possible choices and the possible results of each choice. The best choice is easier to make now, although you still may have to deal with conflicts and the influence of outside factors.

"I'll take the blue one instead of the green." "Coffee, please—black and no sugar." "I'm not going this weekend." All of these statements reflect decisions, step 4 in the decision-making process. In these cases, you took step 4 without bothering much about the previous three. This is fine in these kinds of everyday decisions. But, when you are making an important decision, such as deciding what career to follow, be sure to go through the four-step process.

SUMMING UP

You will not always need to go through the steps in such great detail, of course. Once you have found out about your abilities and interests, you do not need to bother seeking this information again when another decision has to be made. You already have this information. The same applies to your values and goals. Once you have identified them, they will serve you in making many decisions about your career and other matters.

When you are identifying your career goals and values, ask yourself the key questions mentioned in this chapter. They are:

- Does the work interest me?
- What is the demand?
- What financial assistance is available for training me?
- Is advancement likely?

- What are the earnings?

The answers to these questions will help you identify your career goals and values. If you substitute the appropriate words to fit these key questions in other decisions, you can use them as a guideline to identify goals and values in other situations. Remember, goals and values may change as you change. But, since you are aware of this, you will take this into account when you are making a decision.

CHAPTER 24

EVALUATING A DECISION

Decisions are made for the future. Even though you make decisions in the present, they affect your future. That future may be 5 minutes from the time you make the decision, or it may be 1 or more years away. If you could predict the future, you would always make the right decisions. Since you cannot predict the future, you follow the four-step-decision-making process and make the best decision possible. After making a decision, you must evaluate it and judge the results of your choice.

HOW TO EVALUATE A DECISION

If a decision helps you to reach a goal, it is effective. If not, it is ineffective. Evaluating decisions is not always easy. It may help to ask yourself some questions, such as, "How did the decision affect me?" "How did my decision affect others?" "Did it help me reach my goal?" "Could I have done something else that would have been better?" "What would have been the results of a different decision?"

Wiley Makes a Decision

Look at a series of decisions that Wiley made, examine their results, and evaluate his decisions:

"Wiley, I'd like to see you for a minute," said Mrs. Kuder, the English teacher.

"Yes, Mrs. Kuder," Wiley answered, thinking to himself, "I'll bet I know what she wants."

"Have a seat, Wiley," Mrs. Kuder said, gesturing to the chair by her desk. "How is your part-time job at the post office working out?"

"My job? Oh, it's fine, Mrs. Kuder."

"That's good. Wiley, I want to talk to you about your term paper. Have you finished it?"

Shifting nervously in his seat, Wiley replied, "No. I just haven't had time to do it."

"I realize that working and going to school keep you busy, Wiley. I don't like to say this. But if you don't turn in that term paper, you will fail this course. The semester ends next week, Wiley. I'll give you until next Friday to complete it."

"Thanks, Mrs. Kuder. I'll get it done," Wiley replied.

"You've already had more time than the other students. I'll be expecting your paper next Friday."

Walking out of Mrs. Kuder's room, Wiley thought to himself, "That was close. I thought she was going to tell me I had not passed. I'd better get busy on that paper. Let's see now, the only real free time I'm going to have is this weekend. I'll write the paper then and turn it in Monday morning."

As the rest of the week went by, Wiley put the term paper out of his thoughts. After classes on Friday, Wiley met his best friend, Wayne. "Hey, Wiley, only one more week of school before graduation. Let's drive over to my parents' cabin on the lake this weekend and celebrate."

"That sounds great, Wayne. No, wait a minute. I can't."

"What do you mean, you can't? You took all your exams this week, didn't you?"

"Yeah, but I still have to do a term paper for English."

"Listen, Wiley, don't worry about the term paper. We'll be back by Sunday afternoon. You'll have plenty of time to write it then."

"I don't know, Wayne."

"Look, Wiley, how would you like to spend your weekend, writing a term paper or having a good time at the lake?"

"Well, I heard the weather is going to be great this weekend. OK, let's go. But remember, we have to get back here on Sunday so I can write that paper."

Wiley and Wayne did have a great weekend. They arrived home late Sunday afternoon. After supper, Wiley went upstairs to work on the paper. But he just could not get started. "I hate English," Wiley thought. "I especially hate term papers." After struggling with an outline for an hour, Wiley gave up. "There's a good movie on TV, and I'm going to watch it. I can write the paper sometime later this week," Wiley told himself.

Of course, the last week of school was a very busy one for Wiley. When Friday arrived, he still had not completed the term paper. He managed to avoid seeing Mrs. Kuder on the last day of classes. "Everything will be OK," he said to himself. "I'm just glad that school's over. Next month I'm going to take that examination for a full-time job with the post office."

A week later Wiley found out that he had not passed English, and, as a result, he would not be graduating. Later in the week, he received a letter from the post office saying that he could not take the exam for full-time employment. Wiley was just 17. The letter said that he would have to be either a high school graduate or 18 years old to take the exam.

Evaluate Wiley's Decision

Let's evaluate Wiley's decision. What were the results of his decision not to complete the term paper? The most immediate effect was that he did not pass English. This also meant that he did not graduate from high school. Unfortunately, when he decided not to write the term paper, Wiley did not realize all the future consequences. He was not aware that he had to be either a high school graduate or at least 18 before he could take the post office exam.

If Wiley evaluates his decision by asking himself, "What else could I have done? What would have happened if I had done that?" he will realize that he should have completed the term paper. If he had done so, he would have passed English, would have graduated from high school, and would have been able to take the post office exam. As it was, his decision not to turn in the paper delayed his reaching a goal—employment as a postal clerk.

Insofar as your career is concerned, you are the one who must make the final judgment about whether or not a decision of yours is effective. An effective decision is one that helps you reach your goal. That is, you have made a choice that could result in the best possible outcome. An ineffective decision, of course, can keep you from reaching your goal. Your choice, for example, may have brought about unwanted results.

OTHER PEOPLE ARE OFTEN INVOLVED

Although you are the final judge of your decisions, especially those about your career, other

After making a decision, it is important to evaluate and judge the results. Do you think this team is pleased with its decisions? (Woodfin Camp & Associates/Marvin E. Newman)

people are often involved. These other people may be affected by your decision, just as you may be affected by theirs. Consider the situation in which Ken and his mother found themselves:

Ken planned to go away to Barton Business School in September. Costs for the 1-year course are about $4,000 for tuition and living expenses. He has been looking forward to this experience.

Ken's mother, Joan Upton, is a contract manager at Lockton Aerospace Company. She makes $18,000 a year, but she dislikes her job. Mrs. Upton had an offer from the county government to work as a juvenile probation officer. Despite the fact that the job starts at only $14,000 a year, Mrs. Upton considered it because she really would like to do that kind of work. During the last 3 years, she has spent her evenings working towards a master's degree in psychology at the university.

Ken knows that his mother has had to work especially hard since his father's death 9 years ago. He also knows that she has been eager to change to a more satisfying career. Ken knows that the family has only a small savings fund—for emergencies. He realizes that if he goes to the Barton School, he would put a financial burden on his mother. What should Ken do?

A number of factors affect Ken's decision, as well as his mother's. The financial factor is an important one. Ken has only $500 saved for school. He has been counting on his mother to pay for most of the tuition and to send him a check every month for room and board. Mrs. Upton would be able to afford to do this with her present job at the Lockton Aerospace Company.

However, if she becomes a juvenile probation officer, she won't be able to afford to send Ken to school for a year. To drop from $18,000 a year to $14,000 a year in salary would require the family to change its lifestyle. There are also two younger children in the family, and their needs must be taken into consideration.

Personal values are very much involved in this decision. Ken has been planning on going away to school and has his hopes set on doing that. He knows that when he graduates he will be able to get a good job, and this will give him a good start on his career.

Mrs. Upton wants Ken to have the opportunity to go away to school. But she also has been planning on changing careers and doing the kind of work she really wants. She has to weigh the risks involved in making this decision. What if she doesn't like being a probation officer? Will she have difficulty getting another job?

She considers the fact that if she decides to accept this job, she may start a chain of decisions in the family. Ken could go to a local community college. In any case, the younger children would have to get along with less money or find part-time jobs.

The decisions that Ken and his mother have to make are difficult ones. The economic and personal considerations of their choices clash, and both Ken and his mother must consider the effect of their decisions on each other.

Others May Evaluate Your Decision

You need to consider other people when you are making decisions. Even if you have no concern about others who may be affected by what you decide, it is often not practical to ignore them. Other people involved will evaluate your decisions. "You did the right thing," they may say. Or they may ask, "Why did you do that?" And some may say, "Do it this way."

When someone questions or criticizes one of your decisions, you will realize that it is time to evaluate—if you have not already done so. Your evaluation may convince you to change or it may convince you that you were right regardless of the reaction.

Decisions on the Job Affect Others

When you make career decisions, remember that other people are often involved. Other decisions, such as those you make on the job, will almost always affect other people. For example, when you decide not to go to work, your co-workers are affected. Perhaps they will have to do some of your work or be unable to complete a project as planned. Your supervisor will be affected. He or she may need to find a substitute for you or just accept the fact that some work will not get done that day. If you are in a service industry, customers are affected.

If you are considerate of others, you will ask yourself some questions before making a decision, such as, "Will my decision help get the job done?" "Will my decision cause someone else to do extra work?" "What are my co-workers' feelings?" "Will my decision contribute to good morale or will it cause resentment?" Considering what effect your decision will have on others is important most of the time and in all situations, not just on the job.

On-the-job decisions nearly always affect many people. Take this into account and consider your associates at work. (Courtesy Metropolitan Life)

"I DON'T KNOW"

Remember that avoiding a decision is no solution. This is particularly true when you are thinking about your future. In such cases, not deciding is just drifting. You will find yourself in situations now and then, however, when the best decision is to say, "I don't know." This can be an effective decision if it is based on a realistic idea of your abilities or capabilities. Some people think that saying "I don't know" is the same as not making a decision, but this is not so.

Consider the following situation:

Ed worked in a chemical laboratory. A co-worker asked him, "Ed, should I put more acid in this mixture?"

"I don't know," Ed answered. "Let's check it out."

Ed's decision was a good one. He did not know what the best mixture was, and he was honest about it. If Ed had thought that "smart people always know the answers and make decisions," he might have decided to make a guess and tell his co-worker to add more acid. If the guess had been wrong, the result could have been costly in terms of wasted supplies and time. It may also have resulted in an accidental injury to Ed or his co-worker.

Being an effective decision-maker does not mean that you know all the answers. It does mean that you know enough to realize you do not know everything, and that you are not afraid to say so.

DECISIONS AND YOUR LIFE

The emphasis here has been on making decisions about your career and on the job. You do, of course, have to make many decisions in other areas of your life. Some of these decisions, though, may have an indirect influence on your career. For example, deciding where you want to live can be very important. Some people let their jobs decide where they will live. Others decide where they want to live and then look for work in that area.

Either method is a useful way to approach this situation. Whatever way you approach it, follow the four-step-decision-making process. Your choice will be determined by your values. If you care more about the area in which you live, you will pick a place to live and then find your work. If you think your career is a more important consideration, you will find work and live where it is necessary. Know what is important to you before you begin considering your alternatives. Of course, that is part of step 1—analyzing the situation.

Getting It All Together

1. Why is it necessary to understand a situation before making a decision?

2. What does step 1, analyzing the situation, involve?

3. What are some ways of looking for alternatives in step 2?

4. What kinds of information can you find in published sources?

5. What are some questions you should ask yourself when considering possible results, step 3?

6. Why is it necessary to evaluate your decisions?

7. What was the hardest decision you had to make during the past year? Did you follow the four-step decision process? Are you satisfied with your decision?

SCHOOLS AND
CAREERS

SCHOOL AND THE REAL WORLD

Your goals in this unit are given in the following list:

To become aware of how a changing world affects careers

To begin doing some things that will help you to cope with the changing world of careers

To get some ideas as to how to use your school years to your best advantage

To begin to know the difference between the way the world outside school seems and the way it really is

What good is school?

There must be a catch to a question like that. After all, your school bought this book, so whoever wrote the book is going to try to sell you on how great school is. Right?

Wrong!

It would be pretty silly to try to tell someone who has been a student for many years what school is all about. If you are in school, then you know what it's all about and what it can do for you. But maybe you don't. Maybe you think you're in school just because you have to be. Maybe you've never asked yourself how school is going to help you later on.

When you are in school, you sometimes wonder whether you are in the real world. You wonder if the real world is "out there" where there are no teachers, no homework, no rules, and no routines—just a big chance to make money and have fun.

Well, nobody is going to try to persuade you that such an idea is wrong. You'll have to decide for yourself. School is part of the real world, but just a part of it. If school does not help you to live the best possible life when you get "out there," then school is no good at all—for you. And sometimes—not always—you can help your school to do a better job.

You can decide why you are there, explore how you fit in, and determine what you want to get out of the experience. In other words, school is supposed to lead to the world "out there" and teach you how to learn, even when you're not in school. In fact, if schools do their jobs, you will want to continue to learn once you leave school. Learning is something you should always do. The world changes and moves quickly, and learning can help you to keep up.

Think about what "out there" means, and then get back to the question "What good is school?" "Out there" can mean working full-time when you quit school, or when you finish high school or college. It can also mean working part-time while you are going to school. You can get "out there" in a hurry, or you can take one step at a time. You can end up "out there" prepared for the challenges, or you can decide that "whatever happens, happens." It's up to you, and school may help you to decide.

One of the biggest problems with getting "out there" is that it is very tough to know what it's really like. Learning about the outside world while you're in school is like trying to find out how cold the water is before you jump in. Go slowly, so that by the time you're in the water there will be few surprises.

25

THE REAL WORLD IS A CHANGING WORLD

The whole world is changing so fast that nobody can keep up with it.

It seems that people are always saying that these days. But why? Why should you try to keep up with it? Maybe the answer has to do with your future. This is the world in which you are going to live and work. The more you understand about it, the better things will be for you.

At one time you could have expected to live pretty much as your great-great-grandparents did. You would have been educated by your parents and gone on to earn a living just as your parents had done.

Today, you have chances and opportunities that your parents did not have. But you will also have more difficult decisions to make about what to do with your life.

The world is very different from the way it was when your parents or grandparents were in high school. And the future you face is very different from the future your parents and grandparents faced when they were young. The world is not as simple as it used to be, and the world did not always change so quickly.

HOW CHANGE AFFECTS THE JOB WORLD

Change can be good, and it can be bad. Machines are built to make our lives easier. With each new machine, the world changes and becomes more complicated. Machines make new jobs, but they also end old jobs.

For example, newspapers used to be tied with string into bundles of fifty. The bundles were trucked to delivery people and to newsstands. People used to count and tie the bundles of newspapers. Now a machine counts the bundles and ties them with wire, and another machine, a conveyor belt, shoots the bundles into trucks. This is technology at work. In this case, technology ended jobs for some people, but it provided new jobs for people who could repair and run the machines.

The kinds of jobs available and the nature of the jobs are the result of supply and demand. And a changing world is always affecting the balance between supply and demand. *Supply* means the amount of a product or service available at a specific price. The amount of a product or service that the public is willing to buy is called *demand*. When a new invention—like the tape cassette—comes on the market, the demand for the older type of product—the record—decreases. The available supply of the older product is probably far greater than the demand for a while. So what happens? An industry either closes down or adapts to fit the new situation. Such changes mean new skills to be learned and new jobs for some. But such changes can also mean the loss of jobs for others.

What is going to happen when change affects your job? You are going to have to learn the new way to do the job. You might have to learn how to run a new machine. In your lifetime, the world is going to change even faster than it is changing now. The most important requirements for a job will be knowledge and an ability and willingness to learn and to change with the times.

123

HOW TO HANDLE CHANGE

Change has made a big difference in the lives of many people. It can make a difference in your life. What can you do about it? You can learn to understand change and to prepare for it.

Understand It

The first thing you can do about change is to understand it. Change rolls along like a snowball, getting bigger and bigger and going faster and faster. Each new thing you learn shows you that there is something else new you must learn. Each new thing that is discovered leads to another discovery. New industries make other industries to serve them.

You must understand that this is the way the world is going to be for the rest of your life, and the only way you can get along in such a changing world is to keep on learning. You have the capacity. The human mind is like a box that can never be filled up. Understanding change can tell you a lot about the kind of future you can expect. Because of change you can probably forecast the following:

- There will be fewer jobs for unskilled workers and workers with only a little skill.
- There will be more jobs for skilled workers, especially workers with special training.
- There will be a bigger need for learning more about the work you do as you go along in life and a bigger need for different kinds of training.
- There will be more choices to consider and more decisions to make.
- There will be a need to learn more about yourself.

Prepare for It

That is just a small picture of the future. But what can you do to prepare for it? Ask yourself these questions:

- What careers seem to be growing, and what opportunities do they offer?
- What education or training is needed for these careers?
- How much competition from other workers can you expect?
- How will it feel to work in the careers that interest you?

New machinery means new jobs. (Courtesy A. T. & T.)

By asking, exploring, and eventually answering these questions, you will find that you can do something about your future. But you will need much more information. Schools have this kind of information. They can help you to look ahead, because they buy information for you from people who study jobs and the way jobs change.

A good way to prepare for change is to think in terms of a job versus a career. The terms "position," "job," "occupation," and "career" are often used interchangeably in conversation, but they mean different things. It is useful to think about what they mean.

A set of tasks performed by one person is a *position.* There are as many positions as there are workers in a place of employment. A position with Blair Shoe Company might include answering phones, greeting visitors, typing, filing, and many other duties performed during the course of a day. A position with Cinder Foods Corporation might involve keeping track of inventory, recording purchase orders, and billing.

Similar positions in one workplace are all known as *jobs.* Several people can be employed doing the same job. In Lancaster Memorial Hospital, two hundred men and women might be employed in the job of pediatric nurse. The tasks performed by these people are similar.

Similar jobs in different places are called *occupations.* An illustrator at General Publications, Inc., and a designer at Cranlow's Jewelers would both have occupations as artists.

The sequence of occupations a person holds during a lifetime is called a *career.* Usually this term also includes information about one's lifestyle, life goals, and educational aims. It might include the many different jobs a person has held in the past as well as the person's goals for the future.

Sometimes the word "career" refers to several occupations that have common characteristics. The person holding the previously mentioned position at Blair Shoe Company could have a career in the secretarial sciences. The one filling the position at Cinder Foods could have a career in bookkeeping. The pediatric nurses at Lancaster Memorial all have careers in nursing. And the illustrator at General Publications and the jewelry designer at Cranlow's Jewelers both have a career in art.

Until fairly recently most workers thought only about getting a job. They usually were not concerned about how their choice would affect later career opportunities. They did not think about how such a choice would help them to reach their total career goals. In fact, they may not have had planned career goals at all. They did not consider what would happen if the job or occupation they chose were suddenly to change or come to an end. Today, more people are not only planning for finding a job; they are also considering how a choice of a job can be fitted into a career.

Just finding a job is all right if you can be confident that the job will last a lifetime. But because the world changes, people often shift their occupations four, five, and more times during their working life. Some of these shifts occur because jobs are replaced by improved machinery, new inventions, or the changing needs of society. Other shifts occur because people want to advance toward long-range career goals. In either case, it is worth looking at the whole picture of possible choices and goals if planning is to be most effective.

Have you ever thought of your school years as a time for effective planning?

Technology means more jobs for skilled workers. Shown here are people working in marine biology, climatology, and geology—all fields which require highly specialized training. (Top, courtesy U.S. Navy; middle, National Oceanic and Atmospheric Administration; bottom, United Nations/Jerry Frank)

26

MAKING THE MOST OF YOUR SCHOOL YEARS

Your school years are important. Are you making the best use of them?

Stop for a minute and check up on yourself. Your frame of mind is important. Do you know what you want out of life? Is school helping you to get what you want? Are you aware of all the things you are learning in school? Are you thinking realistically about what the world will be like when you get out of school? These are all good questions to ask yourself if you want to be sure you're using these years to get all the help you will need to keep pace with the world of the future.

DISCOVER WHAT YOU WANT

Psychologists say that people learn best when what they are learning helps them to do something they want to do. Of course, you cannot know if what you are learning is helping you to do something you want unless you first know what it is you want.

People Want Different Things

Individuals have different desires and wants. The basic needs of human beings—including keeping

In making your career plans, remember to be realistic about the world of work. (Courtesy Metropolitan Life)

alive and being free of fear and anxiety—are the same for everyone, but after that, people differ. Some people want money and material goods—a nice house, a sharp car, plenty of clothes. Others want to be free to travel. Still others want to have lots of leisure time, or time for hobbies.

What you want usually develops—directly and indirectly—from what you value. Your values—what you consider important or useful—are learned and shaped from many sources. They come from the beliefs of your family and your community, the things that television and magazines show as important, and what your friends think about different things.

Values are of many types. You may value ideas and enjoy thinking, reading, and figuring out how things work. You may value making things work. Perhaps it means a great deal to you to master a machine and make it perform as well as it can. You may value serving other people—whether or not they can do you any personal good. Or you may value people for what they can do for you. You may value material gains and see making money as your major life purpose. You may value influencing others through the expression of ideas. If so, you may further value literature, music, or art as ways of expressing ideas. Other things you may value include security, independence, advancement, or esteem from others.

People Work for Different Reasons

People who work full-time spend most of each working day on the job. What they do often determines their lifestyles and influences their choice of friends. In addition, people work to satisfy values. And since people have different values, they work for different reasons.

Material gain. Is it true that most people work to earn a living—that is, for money? This is certainly the most obvious reason for working. Suppose you do not have enough money to afford food, shelter, and clothing—to satisfy your most basic "survival needs." You are likely to be so tied up in solving this problem that other values will not seem so important.

Earning enough money to meet your basic survival needs tends to satisfy you if you value security—freedom from anxiety and fear. This kind of freedom is another basic need. If you are

laid off or fired and your earnings stop, you will no longer feel secure. Earnings you can depend on and security go hand in hand. But once you feel that your basic needs have been filled, other values are likely to become important to you.

People don't stop wanting money just because their basic needs are satisfied, or just because their most important desires are fulfilled. People have continuing wants. People value continuing material gain. They want the latest-model car or a longer vacation, for example. Teachers may enjoy their careers partly because they can get long periods of time off for travel and vacations.

Some people who are financially independent still have a desire to work. It is not necessary for them to earn money, but they have attached a value to working for things they want.

Work activity. Many people want work that is interesting to them. They value the work itself. The work of these people must be filled with new ideas and things to be learned. It must constantly challenge their understanding.

Work may be valued because it gives an opportunity for self-expression. It allows people to satisfy a basic need to realize their potential. In such cases, work must provide a chance for people to make use of their abilities and interests.

To value work for the work itself—rather than for the material gain it brings—usually means that a person wants the opportunity to use his or her skills and knowledge. Some people place a high value on work that has variety. This can mean an opportunity to travel or to perform different kinds of duties. A person in a health services career has plenty of opportunities to help people in a variety of ways.

Human relations. Work, to many people, is the best way to achieve satisfying relationships with other people. Many people need to belong to a group, and work can provide this opportunity. People who become flight attendants, for example, know that they are part of a group working closely together to promote the safety and comfort of passengers. Through serving on a team of workers, a person can identify with others in a common cause. Or by making a contribution to a product, a worker can gain the esteem of others. These goals are difficult to achieve in many other areas of life.

People work for many reasons. Among them are the gratifi-cation that comes from the work itself and the opportunity to achieve a satisfying relationship with people. (Left, courtesy Smith, Hinchman, & Grylls Associates Inc.; right, Magnum Photos Inc/Bruce Davidson)

Some people's choice of work is influenced by the desire to have as much prestige as possible. *Prestige* means standing or rank in the eyes of others. It has to do with a basic need to be admired and respected. It comes from how others see you and how you see yourself. It also comes from the other workers you associate with and the place you fill in society. Titles, badges, uniforms, and special language can all make a difference in how workers feel about their *status* or standing.

Work then can fulfill needs and satisfy many values. Because people have needs to fulfill and values to satisfy, they find that work is natural. They want to work. Not all careers satisfy the same values. Do you know what your values are? Do you know what it is you really want? Many people think they know what they want to do when they get out of school. But when they honestly check their career plans against their values—against what is important to them—they find the life they have been planning for would not make them happy at all.

After you have a pretty good idea of what you want, you might go on to another question. Is what you are doing now helping you to get whatever it is that you want? In other words, you should decide where you are going and then

check to see if you are using the right road to get there.

THINK ABOUT WHAT YOU ARE LEARNING

No matter what subjects you are taking, there are many things happening in school that help you to explore careers and decide which may be the right one for you. School can also help you to find and keep the right job. These things go on every day, and you hardly ever think about them. In other words, you are probably learning much more than you realize.

Learning About Yourself

First of all, although you may not know it, these are years when you are probably learning a lot about yourself. This is important. To know what kind of life you want, whether this kind of life is the best one for you, and how to prepare for it, you have to know a great deal about yourself. The following list shows some of the things you may be learning about yourself or doing for yourself during your school years. Try to think about each item on the list. Give each one the

Your school years are a time for learning about yourself and about the world.

same amount of time and attention that you would give to someone you were meeting for the first time.

- Finding ways to talk about yourself and understand yourself
- Connecting the interests you have with your abilities
- Setting standards—which means rules for you to live up to
- Finding out what your ideals are—the ultimate goals you want to achieve
- Being able to approve of yourself
- Solving problems in the world around you instead of getting lost in your own head
- Developing independence
- Finding out what your strengths are and using them to understand what you like and what you dislike
- Learning how to shoot for good things in the future instead of using all your energy to get the little things you want right now
- Setting priorities—which means deciding what is the most important thing you want, and then the next important thing, and so on
- Figuring out what you are going to have to do to get what you want
- Looking ahead to see what might change or stand in the way of what you want to do
- Deciding what really interests you and what you think is really important in your life
- Understanding how you get along with others and how you can get along better

- Understanding how what you are doing now affects the future
- Accepting the consequences—the results—of what you do and how you act
- Being aware of what you do best and the good things you have done
- Learning how to make decisions
- Knowing how much you can change
- Knowing what gives you the most pleasure

These are not exactly things you learn from books, are they? But if you think about it awhile, you will understand that you are learning these things every day—in class, at recreation, in sports, in clubs, in work-experience programs, and just about everywhere you go. The reason that school plays such a big part in all this is simply that you spend a lot of time there, meeting many people and getting many ideas.

Learning About Others

School gives you your first big chance to live and work and play with many other people. In fact, learning about others is one of the most important things that goes on in school. Following are just a few of the things you are doing when you go to school with other people:

- Accepting others the way they are
- Learning how to follow some of the time and to lead at other times

- Understanding that an important part of life is helping others and paying attention to what they need and want
- Learning how and why people are different
- Cooperating with others and competing with them
- Sharing
- Planning with others

Learning to Work

This book is about learning to work, and so the next list is also important. It shows what you may be doing now in order to prepare yourself for future jobs.

- Developing the language you need to do certain jobs (Have you noticed that each job, each sport, and each activity has its own language?)
- Figuring out how school and the jobs you get when you leave school are all tied up with each other
- Learning to use your time and energy to do certain things when they have to be done
- Solving problems
- Developing good study habits
- Understanding that you are going to keep on learning all your life and that the more you learn, the better your life will be
- Picking up the basic skills you need
- Learning how jobs change
- Finding out which jobs are dying and which ones offer the best chances for a good career

Learning About the World

Last of all, this is a time for preparing yourself for the world "out there." What sort of things are you doing now to get ready for the larger world, of which school is just a part? Check yourself against the following list:

- Accepting the way the world is and realizing that you can help to change it only when you understand it
- Realizing that life means dealing with bosses, earning enough money, getting along with people who do not know you, putting up with doing the same thing often, handling disagreements, knowing how to get around, and recognizing when and if you should move
- Learning the difference between what you want and what you have to do to get it

- Learning where to get information and how to use it
- Getting along outside your family
- Making decisions as part of a group
- Understanding your duties to the rest of the world
- Using spare time well
- Deciding how much you want to earn, how much you want to buy, and where you want to live
- Learning how and where you can get the education or training you need now and in the future
- Learning how people work together to deal with problems that affect them all

Sure, you are aware of many of these things. But when they are listed like this, they paint a pretty big picture of what is going on in school and in your life. Another of those questions you should ask yourself right now is this: How well are you handling all this learning? Your school years are like the time you spend getting ready for a camping trip. Are you packing in what you need?

When you plan what you'll take on a camping trip, you don't do a very good job unless you have a realistic idea of what you're getting ready for. It's the same when you use your school years to get ready for the outside world.

BE REALISTIC

"Hey, that's unreal!" You have probably heard a friend say this when something is hard to figure out. Part-time and vacation work can be a little "unreal." You still live at home. Your parents still pay most of the bills. You are still in school. You are not dealing with the real world of work full-time, just part of the time. You have to make sure that you are not confusing your feelings about part-time work with the way you would feel about full-time work.

Some students enjoy their part-time jobs so much that they quit school thinking everything is going to be a ball. They enjoy having their own money. But after a while they learn that working for a living is not the way it looked when they were still in school. They learn that they do not know enough to make a good living.

What can you do about this difference between the way work looks when you are working part-time and the way it really is when you are working for a living? This is a question that concerns schools. More and more school officials are beginning to realize that the home and the community must play bigger parts in helping young people understand how it feels to work full time. This is the idea behind the work-experience programs that many schools offer. Some schools are arranging with watchmakers, dental technicians, optical mechanics, garages, and factories for students to be trained on the job. In this way, skilled workers teach the students job skills. The schools teach them what they need to know to learn the skills—reading, writing, and mathematics—and what they need to know to live in the world—social studies, science, and history.

What can you do to make sure you are not fooling yourself about how real your part-time job is? What can you do to make sure it is the kind of work you want to do when you leave school? There is one simple answer. Ask questions. Ask your supervisors, the people who work with you, your teachers, your counselors, and your parents and friends as many questions about what they are doing as pop into your head. People like to talk about themselves and what they are doing. Ask them about their jobs.

If you are being trained by a skilled worker in a work-experience program, ask that worker what he or she feels about work and life, about making a living, about training and school.

SUM IT ALL UP

In order to be sure you are getting the most out of your school years, what should you do? It all boils down to a way of thinking. You should know what it is you want and where you want to go. You should be sure that school is helping you to get what you want and guiding you toward wherever you want to go. You should appreciate what you are learning—you may be underrating school and not fully realizing all the things you are finding out about yourself, about other people and what makes them tick, about work and work habits, and about the world in general.

A final word of caution. Be realistic. Be sure that any vacation jobs or part-time jobs that you have while you are still in school are not giving you a false picture. Avoid confusing your feelings about part-time work with the way full-time work would feel.

Getting It All Together

1. Why is school a better source of information about career possibilities than a particular employer?

2. Why is it generally not a good idea to drop out of school before you are sure what career you want to enter?

3. How will learning about yourself in school help you fit into the right job? How will learning about others help?

4. What are the three courses you've taken over the last few years that you liked best? Describe something you have learned in each course that will help you in the outside world.

5. What is the difference between a job and a career?

CURRICULA AND CAREERS

Your goals in this unit are given in the following list:

To know how many different kinds of jobs there are and how much education and training it takes to do them

To learn how to find out more about jobs that interest you

To develop ways to decide which career is right for you

To be able to match courses that interest you with careers that interest you

The world is filled with careers you may never have heard of. One of those careers may be exactly right for you. But how do you find out which one? If you pick a career, how much do you have to know in order to get off to a good start in it? In other words, how can you use your curriculum to prepare yourself for a career?

As you begin to identify your own personal goals, some sources will emerge as more useful than others in achieving those goals. You know already that you will not have total freedom in choosing your courses. There are always courses you have to take—like English and basic math. However, you still have quite a lot of choice in what you study. The choices you make should depend strongly on the goals you want to achieve.

There are so many different kinds of jobs for people with different kinds of skills and different amounts of schooling. You are going to take a look at hundreds of jobs. And you are going to learn how picking the right courses in school can prepare you for work. Many courses that you take in school are required courses. They are important because from them you get basic skills and knowledge that will help

you in the career you choose. You also take elective courses, and these may give you ideas about different careers and help you gain skills and knowledge.

This unit contains some pretty long lists of occupations. Lists usually look dull. Often students are tempted to skip them. But these lists may help you to plan a better life. Consider them very carefully. When you spot an interesting occupation on one of the lists, daydream about it a little. Try to put yourself in the place of someone in that occupation. Figure out whether your favorite courses and your interests suit that occupation. Start to discover some ways to learn just where you are and what you can do next to get ready for the world "out there."

In this unit you are going to take a look at many real jobs. You are going to get a lot of ideas about how jobs are related and how they differ in terms of the amount of education and responsibility they require. What you learn should start you thinking about what really suits you. By understanding what suits you, you can find out even more what you can get out of school. With a little careful thinking and looking ahead, your daydreams can start to come true.

27

CURRICULA, CAREER CLUSTERS, CAREER LATTICES, AND THE DOT

A house is only as good as its foundation. Every builder knows that. The cracks in the walls that begin to appear too early in the life of the house are more than likely caused by a shaky foundation. And the house that stands for centuries always turns out to be the one that was built on a solid base.

But foundations are not just for buildings. A foundation can be the basis or groundwork for anything—even your life.

Have you stopped to think that your school years are the years in which you lay the foundation for the rest of your life? In order to lay as firm a foundation as possible, you should be familiar with all the tools you have at your disposal.

The school curriculum you choose will be instrumental in forming an important part of that foundation. And there are terms like "career cluster" and "career lattice" that you should be familiar with. Understanding these terms can help you to see ideas that can serve as important building tools. Another important tool that you should be familiar with is a book: the *Dictionary of Occupational Titles*, usually called the DOT. This book can give you a good idea of just how many jobs are available. When you know how to use it, it can provide valuable information about all these jobs.

WHAT IS A CURRICULUM?

The word *curriculum* is a Latin word that means a plan of study. Subjects and courses are parts of a curriculum. A curriculum prepares you to do something or to study something further, such as nursing.

A *course* is a group of subjects that have something in common. For example, a mathematics course might include arithmetic, geometry, algebra, and calculus. They are subjects in a course. When mathematical subjects and courses are put together in a curriculum, they may prepare you for a job, a trade school, or a college curriculum that requires a background in mathematics. Two or more plans of study are called *curricula*.

It seems that some people decide very early just what they want to do with their lives. They can decide in middle school which curriculum to follow. Others decide in high school. Still others never decide and drift out of high school or on to college without having any career or plan for life in mind. It is never too late to do something about this and make a decision. You can always change your curriculum if you have made a mistake. It will be worth the trouble—even though you may have to take additional courses in summer school or night school. It is always the right time to make plans or a new decision. So keep your mind open as you read on.

How Curricula Differ

There is a curriculum for students who wish to learn a trade. There is a curriculum for students who wish to go into business. There is a curriculum for students who are going to college. In

What curriculum would be helpful preparation for the job shown here? (Courtesy Metropolitan Life)

short, there are all kinds of curricula, depending on what you want to learn or do.

Since learning in many areas is important for living a well-rounded life, you can be in one curriculum and take courses that are part of another curriculum. For example, the fact that a student is in a curriculum that prepares her or him to learn a trade doesn't mean that studying typing—a business education curriculum subject—wouldn't be helpful. And English courses will be a necessary part of any curriculum you choose.

A curriculum to prepare you for college stresses reading, because you do a great deal of reading in college. A trade school or vocational curriculum includes reading, but it also stresses the way your hands do what your mind wants them to do, because learning a trade calls for a great deal of work with your hands. Other curricula prepare you for careers by stressing skills needed in those careers. All curricula should help you to live a productive life, doing what best suits you.

The goal of any curriculum is to prepare you to get more training or education—in a trade school, an apprenticeship program, or a college, for example. After you have moved to the next step, you will have a new curriculum to follow. In fact, for most people in most jobs preparation and learning never stop. Thousands of people in thousands of jobs are studying to do their work

better and to get better jobs, even though many of them have been out of school and at work for many years.

The Right Curriculum for You

"How do I choose a curriculum, or how do I know if I'm in the right one when I don't know what I want to do?"

Does that question sum up your situation? If so, you're not alone.

It's certainly a fact that it can be difficult to decide which is the right curriculum for you if you have not picked a goal. Having to decide without a goal is a *dilemma*, a problem that does not seem to have any answer, no matter which way you turn. But there is one way to handle this dilemma. Find out what sort of person you are, and choose the curriculum that seems to go with this person.

How can you find out what sort of person you are? You start with your likes, dislikes, interests, and abilities. But that is only a beginning. Learning about yourself involves a great deal of time and effort, but it is an interesting assignment because the result is getting acquainted with yourself. You are now learning about many kinds of careers, and as soon as you learn about yourself a little, you will be able to start matching up the kind of person you are with learning and with career goals. It will be like putting together an interesting puzzle.

CAREER CLUSTERS

A good way to begin learning about all the different kinds of careers is to start with career clusters. A *career cluster* is a family of occupations that have something in common with each other. You know that occupations are made up of similar jobs. Jobs in general may be divided into two big groups—jobs for making goods and jobs for providing services. If you work in a factory that makes television sets, you have a job that fits in the first group. If you are a firefighter, you provide a service—protecting people and buildings—and your job belongs in the second group. These two groups are the biggest career clusters.

The 15 Career Clusters

These two groups are, however, too big to help you make decisions about a career. So the federal

These people have jobs that are different, but all of the jobs belong to the same cluster. (Top, Courtesy Greyhound Bus; center and bottom, American Airlines)

government—the government in Washington, D.C.—has divided jobs into the 15 career clusters listed below:

- Agribusiness and natural resources
- Business and office
- Health
- Public service
- Environment
- Communications and media
- Hospitality and recreation
- Fine arts and humanities
- Manufacturing
- Marketing and distribution
- Marine science
- Personal services
- Construction
- Transportation
- Consumer and homemaking education

Two people can have jobs that are different but belong to the same career cluster. For example, a farmer and a scientist who studies soil (an agronomist) have jobs in the same career cluster, since they are both interested in soil and growing things.

"Cluster" is just a word that means a number of things of the same kind. There will be more of these clusters in your lifetime because technology is always making new careers. Each cluster has many jobs that are connected to each other and to the name of the cluster. For example, both a surgeon and a general-duty nurse have jobs in the health cluster. An able seaman and an oceanographer (someone who studies the oceans) both have jobs in the marine science cluster.

A Closer Look at a Cluster

Nurses and doctors are not the only workers whose jobs are in the health cluster. Researchers, therapists, chemists, biologists, psychiatrists, psychologists, dentists, dental hygienists, laboratory technicians, X-ray technicians, secretaries, maintenance people, receptionists, nursing aides, laundry workers, cooks, dietitians, and many more workers may all have jobs in the health cluster.

These workers may specialize in mental health, mental illness, mental retardation, finding cures for diseases, running hospitals and clinics, operating equipment, teaching, dentistry, and so on. To *specialize* means to get particular training and develop skills to do certain things.

In the health cluster there are *administrators*, or people who specialize in running organizations. There are people who sell medical insurance. There are artists who draw the diagrams and illustrations doctors use. There are librarians who run medical libraries. There are auditors and accountants who supervise the ways hospitals and clinics earn and spend money. There are even lawyers who represent hospitals and doctors or patients. There are ambulance drivers, clerks, and writers. This whole chapter could be filled with the names of jobs in the health cluster.

Some of the other clusters have even more jobs than the health cluster. For this reason a career lattice is useful. It can provide a way of looking at the jobs within a cluster to see how they are related to each other in terms of the amount of education and responsibility required.

WHAT IS A CAREER LATTICE?

A lattice is a set of wooden or metal strips that cross each other to form something that looks like ladders standing next to each other. The strips form a pattern. A *career lattice* is a pattern of jobs within a career cluster. Each level or strip means a different level of responsibility, training, and education.

Each of the 15 career clusters has a large number of jobs. Some of the jobs are very complex, like those of nurses, doctors, or researchers. You need many years of education and training to do them. Some of the jobs are less complex—like ambulance driving, maintenance, or laundry work. You do not need as much training to do them. But each job has an important place on the career lattice. You build a career lattice by deciding how much education and responsibility each job requires and then arranging the jobs in a pattern. The jobs at the top of the lattice call for the most education and training. The jobs at the bottom do not call for as much.

Before you go further you had better examine a word that you will meet again and again—responsibility. *Responsibility* means being expected to do certain things in a job. When a job carries a lot of responsibility, you have to do many things, and some of these things may be pretty difficult. You may be responsible for large sums of money or for training other workers. You have to make many decisions, and you must answer for whatever happens as a result of your decisions.

Using a Career Lattice

It is important to know the different steps on a career lattice. You may be interested in the health cluster and think of becoming a doctor, or a nurse, or a dentist, but you may realize that you are not a good enough student to get the education and training these jobs call for, or you may not want to spend all the time required to prepare for these jobs. Does that mean you have to throw out your dream of doing health care work? Certainly not. Look over the career lattice in the health cluster. One of the jobs on that lattice may just suit the kind of person you are and the amount of education you want. This type of exploration of jobs on a lattice may be done for any of the 15 career clusters.

One of the saddest ideas people often get into their heads is that there are only a handful of jobs in a career cluster and if they cannot train for them they are out of luck. In fact there are hundreds of different jobs in each cluster—and many new ones are being created each year. If a career cluster interests you, the chances are very good that you can find just the right job in it.

THE DOT—A HELPFUL WAY TO EXPLORE CAREERS

Finding out about all the different jobs in our country might be an impossible task without

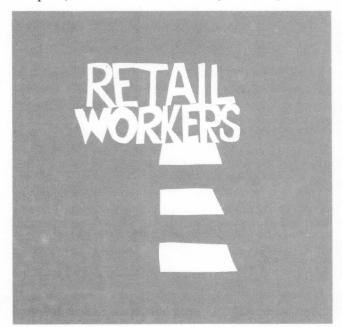

A career lattice shows how jobs can be compared with one another in terms of the education needed to do them as well as the responsibility they involve.

another helpful tool, the *Dictionary of Occupational Titles*—the DOT for short. This book is published by the U.S. Employment Service, a division of the Department of Labor. It tries to give every kind of job a name. Here is how the DOT works.

The DOT Code

Each job named in the book is given a nine-number code to show you what you need in order to do the job.

The first three digits identify a particular occupational group. The first digit represents one of the nine broad categories into which all occupations are clustered.

0 and 1 Professional, technical, and managerial occupations
2 Clerical and sales occupations
3 Service occupations
4 Farming, fishery, forestry, and related occupations
5 Processing occupations
6 Machine trades occupations
7 Bench work occupations
8 Structural work occupations
9 Miscellaneous occupations

The second number stands for a division within the category. The number of divisions vary among categories.

The third number in the code stands for the occupational group within the division. Adding the third digit gives us what is known as the "three-digit-group." (That is, the three numbers to the left of the decimal point.) All occupations having the same three-digit-group belong to the same job family and are listed together in the DOT. All jobs within the same job family have some fundamental similarity.

Data, People, Things

The middle three numbers, called the worker functions code, begin to tell you what the job is like. They tell you how much the person doing the job has to work with data, or information, people, and things. This is measured on a scale from 0 to 8. The closer to zero a number is, the more responsibility or education the person doing the job needs.

The table that follows shows what these middle three code numbers stand for.

Data		People		Things	
0	Synthesizing	0	Mentoring	0	Setting up
1	Coordinating	1	Negotiating	1	Precision working
2	Analyzing	2	Instructing	2	Operating-controlling
3	Compiling	3	Supervising	3	Driving-operating
4	Computing	4	Diverting	4	Manipulating
5	Copying	5	Persuading	5	Tending
6	Comparing	6	Speaking-signaling	6	Feeding-off-bearing
7	No significant relationship	7	Serving	7	Handling
8	No significant relationship	8	No significant relationship	8	No significant relationship

Be sure you know what some of these words mean.

Synthesizing means making something out of different parts.
Coordinating means making different parts or people work well together.
Analyzing means separating something into parts to find out what makes it work.
Compiling means putting things together for some purpose.
Computing means figuring something out.
Mentoring means teaching.
Negotiating means getting people to agree on something.
Diverting means heading something off and sending it in a new direction.
Manipulating means handling with skills.
Tending means taking care of something.

Are there any other words in the lists that you do not know? Look them up in your dictionary—it is a good way to build your vocabulary. Every job has its own vocabulary. The words in these lists can be used in many ways. Here they are used in special ways to tell you what a job is all about.

The last three digits of the occupational code number serve to differentiate a particular occupation from all others. A number of occupations may have the same first six digits, but no two can have the same nine digits. If a 6-digit code is applicable to only one occupational title, the final three digits assigned are always 010.

ATTENDANT, CHILDREN'S INSTITUTION (any ind.) **359.677-010 child-care attendant; house parent.** Cares for group of children housed in city, county, private, or other similar institution, under supervision of superintendant of home: Awakens children each morning and insures children are dressed, fed, and ready for school or other activity. Gives instructions to children regarding desirable health and personal habits. Plans and leads recreational activities and participates or instructs children in games. Disciplines children and recommends or initiates other measures to control behavior. May make minor repairs to clothing. May supervise housekeeping activities or other workers in assigned sections of institution. May counsel or provide similar diagnostic or therapeutic services to mentally disturbed, delinquent, or handicapped children.

The DOT lists many jobs and tells how much the jobholder works with data, people, and things. (George W. Gardener)

Practice Using the DOT Code

Here is a code number: 195.107-022, SOCIAL GROUP WORKER (social ser.). The middle three digits tell how much the social worker deals with data, people, and things. You can use the lists to understand this. The social worker's "data" number is 1, meaning that the social worker has to coordinate information. The "people" number is 0, meaning that the social worker teaches skills to people. Also, the social worker's "things" number is 7, meaning that things (objects) are handled but are not very important in the work of a social worker.

Here is another code: 311.137-014. It belongs to the job of head waiter. Do you think you can figure it out by using the lists? Here is the answer in a nutshell: the head waiter coordinates data, supervises people, and handles things.

By examining just these two codes you have learned about two kinds of careers. You can easily see that the DOT is a very useful tool for helping you learn how many different kinds of careers there are in the world and what they ask of the people who follow them. The DOT is fun. It gives you a chance to unlock the secrets behind a code. If you learn to use it, you can save a great deal of time and work trying to find out about careers that interest you.

But here is something to remember. The DOT does not tell you what courses you must take to prepare for the careers it names. Also, the DOT does not list every single job there is. New jobs are being created so fast that it is impossible to keep the book perfectly up to date. But the DOT can give you a lot of helpful information.

28

MATCHING COURSES AND CAREERS

Courses and careers go together like a key and ignition. The right courses, the right key, turn the ignition on and get you going toward the right career.

But how do you know which courses are the right ones? Which courses will start you toward the right career?

There are many ways to choose your courses and many people, like parents, teachers, and counselors, who can help you decide.

There is one way not to choose your courses. Never choose a course just because a friend has chosen it. If you do, your friend may be the only one who is happy about your decision.

The right courses can get you started toward the right career.

The table on page 141 matches the 15 career clusters you learned about in the last chapter with the courses that are the most useful in helping you to prepare for a career in each cluster. There are many courses that are useful in preparing you for many careers. Only the most important and the most basic courses are included in the table. Remember, too, that a course can include many subjects. A business education course might include typing, shorthand, bookkeeping, and accounting.

HOW TO USE THIS MATCHUP

How can you use the matchup of career clusters and useful courses shown on the table on page 141? Suppose you think that you would like to go to sea with the Merchant Marine. That would put you in the Marine Science cluster. Look across from "Marine Science" in the matchup and you will see "natural sciences" and "mathematics" as two of the most important courses. These are the courses that will best help you prepare for your career at sea. But that is as far as you can go without making some decisions. What sort of decisions? Do you want to be a seaman or an officer? If you want to be a seaman, do you want to specialize in cleaning, painting, and keeping up equipment, or do you want to learn how to run the radar, sonar, and other electronic equipment? If you want to be an officer, do you want to specialize in running the ship, navigating, or buying supplies? Some of these jobs call for a little basic science and mathematics—the kind of fundamentals you get in high school. Others call for a great deal of science, or a great deal of

Career Cluster	Useful Courses
Agribusiness and natural resources	Natural sciences, mathematics, agriculture, business education
Health	Natural sciences, mathematics
Business and office	Business education, English, social sciences
Public service	Social sciences, foreign languages
Environment	Natural sciences, mathematics, agriculture
Communications and media	English, social sciences, art
Hospitality and recreation	English, social sciences, home economics, music, physical and health education
Manufacturing	Mathematics, vocational trade and industrial education, industrial arts
Marketing and distribution	Business education, mathematics, social sciences, distributive education
Marine science	Natural sciences, mathematics
Personal services	Social sciences, home economics, vocational trade and industrial education, industrial arts, physical and health education
Construction	Vocational trade and industrial education, mathematics, industrial arts
Transportation	Natural sciences, mathematics, vocational trade and industrial education
Consumer and homemaking education	Social sciences, home economics, English, mathematics, business education
Fine arts and humanities	Art, music, social sciences, foreign languages, English

mathematics, or a great deal of both—the kind you get in college or graduate school.

Sit down with your counselor, and map out a plan for getting the information you need. One of the things you would do is write to the Merchant Marine Academy at Kings Point, New York. People there will tell you how you can become an officer and what an officer's life is like. They will tell you what officers may specialize in doing. Then you would write to the Seafarers' Union for information about their schools and what the life of a seaman is like—and what seamen may specialize in doing. You can find all the addresses you need for your letters of inquiry at your school or community library.

But that is only a start. Your library may have books or pamphlets about the Merchant Marine. Try to get the most recent publications to be sure your information is up to date. One recent change in the Merchant Marine, for example, is that women now are becoming seamen and officers.

The U.S. Government Printing Office has information about the Merchant Marine, too. And if you live near the sea, you might talk to some seamen and officers and listen to their ideas.

Your teacher can help you to know which courses are important to which career. (Philip Teuscher)

A few letters to the right people will almost always turn up the information you need to make decisions about a career.

No matter which career cluster interests you, there will be hundreds of people and places with information about careers in that cluster. The information you collect will help you to decide if the career you are thinking about is the right one for you.

HOW TO MAKE A CLOSER MATCH

The matchup of career clusters and courses that you examined in the preceding section is careful and direct, but the courses listed are not the only ones you need to prepare for a career in each cluster. A curriculum—whether it is the one you have been following or one that you are going to follow—must include other courses, too.

For example, almost any career calls for a knowledge of the fundamentals of English and mathematics. What additional skills in English and mathematics are required depends on the career cluster and the job in the cluster. This is true whether you begin a career right after high school or go to trade school or college. Studies have shown that one of the biggest problems many students face in their first year at college is poor preparation in English. Because their English is poor, many students do not understand test instructions and do poorly when their answers must be written out.

A *technical writer*—somebody who explains how equipment and programs work—a scientist, and a secretary all need to know English and mathematics, but each of them needs to know different amounts of English and mathematics.

The idea that different jobs require different amounts of knowledge of a subject is illustrated in a survey made of vocational education specialists. The specialists were asked to rank a series of job areas from different career clusters according to how much knowledge of mathematics was important to the jobs. The results are given below. The job areas at the top of the list, with the lower numbers, require more knowledge of mathematics than the job areas at the bottom of the list.

Job Area	Rank
Drafting	1
Machine shop	2
Carpentry	3
Sheet metal	4
Electricity	5
Environmental studies	6
Electronics	7
Welding	8
Masonry	9
Distributive education	10
Data processing	11
Printing	12
Auto mechanics	13
Auto body	14
Foods	15
Medical and dental assisting	16
Cosmetology (applying cosmetics)	17

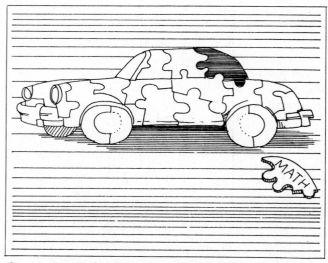

Career preparation is never complete without some mathematics—but just how much depends on the cluster and the job in the cluster.

What does this survey mean to you? If you are thinking about a drafting job, or a machine shop or carpentry job, it is important that you have a good understanding of mathematics. But if you are interested in auto body work, a job in the food industry, or cosmetology, you will need only a basic understanding of mathematics.

All jobs can be ranked in a similar way. Once you know you are interested in a job, you will have to find out which subjects are important for preparing you to do the job. Then you will have to find out how well you will have to know these subjects. All this is not difficult to do. You go about it in a way similar to the one you would use to find out about a job in the Merchant Marine.

WHAT SHOULD A COURSE DO FOR YOU?

The name of a curriculum or a course or the subjects in a course does not tell you enough. You need to know what is taught in your courses. The vocational education specialists who studied how important mathematics is to certain jobs decided that the following mathematics skills are the most important for the jobs they listed:

- Addition, subtraction, multiplication, and division of **whole numbers**
- Addition, subtraction, multiplication, and division of **fractions**
- Reading, writing, rounding off, addition, subtraction, and multiplication of **decimals**
- Understanding **percentages**
- Changing **fractions to decimals**
- **Reducing fractions** to common terms

These skills were mentioned most often by the people surveyed. There were also 50 other basic mathematics skills mentioned, such as reading a rule, measuring angles, and figuring the area of a circle. The skill that students most often lacked, according to the survey, was finding the square root of a number.

You may have the chance to choose some of the courses you take in high school. But you do not have much choice about what goes into the courses—the subject content. The subject content depends on what goals your teachers set up for these courses—what they hope you will learn.

So it makes sense that the best way to figure out what you should learn from a course is to ask the teacher of that course.

WHEN IS IT TOO LATE?

It is never too late to change to courses that match careers that are beginning to interest you. Suppose you are in the eleventh or twelfth grade and the courses you have been taking do not seem to match the careers that are beginning to interest you. The first question to ask yourself is, "Would the courses that do fit in with the careers I'm interested in interest me?" If not, then you are probably thinking about the wrong careers.

But if you have been drifting through your courses without thinking about a career, there is always time to switch courses. "Even if I'm going to graduate this year?" Sure! You can go to night school while you are working. You can go to a community college to take courses you need. You can go to college and make sure you take the courses you need. You can go to trade school, or you can work and study at the same time. There are many ways to study what you need once you pick a career and make sure that what it calls for is what really interests you.

Keep testing your decisions. Keep asking yourself the following questions:

- Would I be happy doing a job that calls for a lot of math? Or history? Or science?
- Would I prefer to work alone or with other people?
- Which people do I admire? Why? What do I like about them? Do I want to be like them? Could I learn to be like them?
- Where do I want to work?
- Do I want to move around a lot or stay in one place?
- Would I like a quiet job or a job with lots of excitement?
- Would I like to be famous, or am I the kind of person who would be happy to just quietly earn a good living?

All these questions may be summed up by one big question: "What do I really want?"

29

MATCHING REQUIRED COURSES WITH JOBS

What is your favorite course? English? Mathematics? And are there any courses or subjects you would just as soon do without? Just be careful, though, when you make these judgments. Sometimes you think you dislike a subject because you do not like the teacher who teaches it or because it is taught in a boring way. You might, however, like the same subject very much if it were taught by somebody else in a more exciting way. Always give a subject a second chance.

Some of our best writers hated English when it was taught to them in high school, but later in life they found that they liked it very much. Albert Einstein, probably the greatest mathematician of our century, not only disliked mathematics when he was in school; he also actually flunked it in one of his courses!

Whatever your favorite courses or subjects are, there are hundreds of jobs where they can be put to good use. But what are these jobs? How can you find out what jobs call for what courses? And how can you find out how much understanding of a course a job calls for?

These are very important questions, but the answers are not hard to find. The Minnesota State Department of Education has given a great deal of thought to questions like these and has prepared a number of interesting charts that show how much knowledge is required by a large number of jobs.

The information from the Minnesota study has been reorganized and made into the tables shown on the pages that follow. The purpose of these tables is to show the wide variety of jobs in which the knowledge you can gain from your high school courses is important.

Often, when you like or do well in a certain course in school, you are only aware of the occupations that are most obviously associated with that course. Of course, there is no way to list all the jobs in which knowledge of certain course areas is important. But the tables in this chapter will give you an idea of a wide variety of jobs that

Always give a course a second chance. Albert Einstein, probably the greatest mathematician of our century, not only disliked mathematics when he was in school, but actually failed one of his math courses. (UPI Photo)

might not ordinarily come to mind when thinking of a certain course of study.

This chapter is about required courses, those courses you must take in high school. These are the courses that will help you get the skills and knowledge you need for many different jobs and for everyday living. English is an example of a required course. Throughout your life you will need good reading and writing skills, and there probably isn't a job you could mention in which English skills are not important. In fact a person starting out in adult life without good English skills is like a bird beginning a flight with a broken wing. The person will be handicapped from the start.

Although English and the other required courses are important for most jobs, we have tried to list examples of the different types of jobs that specifically require English skills. In some jobs English skills are more important than they are in other jobs, and in some jobs you need a more in-depth knowledge of English than you do in other jobs. Also, in some jobs you will need more years of formal schooling than in other jobs.

It is difficult to divide jobs by educational requirements. Consider the job of salesworker, for example. The main function of a salesworker is to communicate with customers in order to sell a product or a service. Without good skills in English, communication is difficult if not impossible. This can be said with certainty. But how much education does a person need in order to become a salesworker? This is a question without an easy answer. Some companies require their salesworkers to have a high school diploma. Some companies say that 2 years of formal training after high school is needed to sell their products. Some companies require their salesworkers to have 4 years of college. And, in order to sell specialized products, a masters' degree is often needed.

This is the idea of the career lattice. If you are interested in a certain career or a certain cluster of jobs, there are places on the lattice for people with different skills and different educational backgrounds. Salary and opportunities for additional responsibility and promotion also fit into the picture. A salesperson with more years of education, more years of experience, and more highly developed skills will earn more money and have better opportunities for responsibility and promotion than a salesperson with fewer years of education and experience and less developed skills.

When you think of training and educational levels, however, keep in mind that there are many roads to education and training. Education and training beyond high school may mean community college, college, graduate school, a technical institute, on-the-job training, an apprenticeship, military school, a trade, industrial, or business school, independent study, or a correspondence course. It's up to you, as an individual, to decide on your field of interest, the job you would like, and the level of education you want to achieve. Whatever your decisions, there are many opportunities open to you.

The tables in this chapter and in Chapter 30 should help you to become aware of your many opportunities. Each one of the courses you are required to take in high school will teach you something that could be valuable in many jobs.

MATHEMATICS

Mathematics is a required course. A knowledge of mathematics is needed for many jobs. This is especially true now that technology plays such a large role in today's world. A wide variety of jobs in which a knowledge of mathematics is helpful is shown in Table 1.

You may not know what all these jobs mean. You can usually find out by looking up the words in a dictionary, but it is also a good idea to ask your teacher or counselor.

NATURAL SCIENCES

Technology changes jobs and makes new jobs, and most of the technical jobs call for some knowledge of mathematics. But many of these jobs also call for some knowledge of the natural sciences. Science is used to find out why and how different processes happen. It is also used to solve problems. Curing diseases, saving our natural resources, and understanding how the human mind works all call for science.

Table 2, on page 147, shows jobs in which a knowledge of the natural sciences is important.

Did you notice that some jobs appear to be related, at least in the way they sound? This has to do, once again, with the concept of the career lattice and of different educational levels. For example, a person may begin a career in photography by working as a photographic technician. Further study or training, however, could open the way for the same person to become a photographer. It is true of many jobs that the more you know about a job, the more responsibility you have, the more you are paid, and the better your chances of promotion become.

ENGLISH

"Why do I have to keep studying English?" some students ask. Their argument goes like this: "English is my native language. I learned it when I was a baby. I learned to read and write it in

With technology playing such a large part in today's world, a knowledge of mathematics is needed in many jobs. (Courtesy Smith, Hinchman & Grylls Associates)

Table 1: Jobs in Which Mathematics Is Important

Accountant	Cost clerk	Optometrist
Actuarial assistant	Drafting technician	Patternmaker
Actuary	Econometrician	Payroll clerk
Airplane inspector	Economist	Personal secretary
Airplane mechanic	Electrical engineer	Pharmacist
Airplane pilot	Electrician	Physicist
Appraiser	Farmer	Psychometrist
Architect	Farm manager	Purchaser
Assessor	Financial-aid officer	Radio operator
Astronomer	Floorlayer	Roofer
Auditor	Forester	Salesclerk
Banker	Garage mechanic	Sales manager
Bank examiner	Geologist	Salesperson
Bank teller	Insurance clerk	Secretary to accountant
Billing clerk	Investment advisor	Sociometrician
Bookkeeper	Lab technician	Statistical clerk
Buyer	Machine designer	Statistician
Card punch operator	Machinist	Stockbroker
Carpenter	Marine engineer	Surveyor
Cartographer	Market-research analyst	Systems analyst
Cashier	Mason	Tax attorney
Chemist	Mathematician	Tax collector
Civil engineer	Mathematics teacher	Ticket agent
Computer operator	Merchandise manager	Tile setter
Computer programmer	Meteorologist	Tool designer
Construction worker	Office manager	Tool maker
Contractor	Optician	Well driller

Table 2: Jobs in Which Natural Sciences Are Important

Agronomist	Forest ranger	Physical therapist
Airplane pilot	Gardener	Physician
Animal trainer	Gas station attendant	Physicist
Anthropologist	Geologist	Police scientist
Apiarist	Glass blower	Pollution control engineer
Astronautic engineer	Gymnast	Poultry farmer
Audiologist	Horticulturist county agent	Practical nurse
Biological research aide	Laboratory technician	Psychiatrist
Biologist	Landscape architect	Psychologist
Botanical artist	Landscape gardener	Range management specialist
Chemist	Lumber inspector	Sales engineer
Chiropractor	Manufacturer, electronic equipment	Salesworker, scientific supplies and equipment
Coal miner	Mathematician	Science illustrator
Conservationist	Medical illustrator	Science teacher
Construction engineer	Medical secretary	Secretary to chemist, physicist
Cook	Medical technician	Ship builder
County agent	Metallurgist	Soil conservationist
Curator	Meteorologist	Speech and hearing therapist
Dairy farm worker	Mortician	Surveyor
Dental hygienist	Nurse	Taxidermist
Dental technician	Nursery worker	Textile technician
Dentist	Nurse's aide	Trapper
Dietitian	Occupational therapist	Tree surgeon
Dry cleaner	Optometrist	Truck gardener
Embalmer	Pharmacist	Veterinarian
Engineer	Pharmaceutical salesworker	Veterinary hospital attendant
Firefighter	Photographer	Weather observer
Fish culturist	Photographer technician	Wildlife specialist
Floriculturist	Physical education teacher	Zoo caretaker

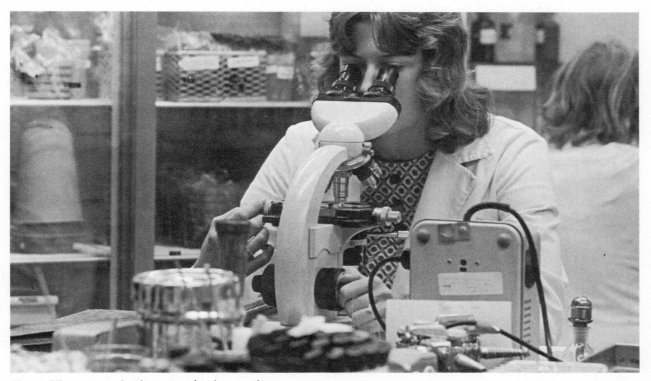

If you like courses in the natural sciences, then you may want to consider a job in the health cluster. (Courtesy Good Samaritan Health Services)

elementary school. So why am I forced to take courses in English?"

It is easy to learn enough English to get by with, but it is difficult to master the language. And yet every job depends on a certain amount of English. Suppose you are good at mathematics, and you decide to follow a career that calls for a great deal of mathematics. How are you going to understand complicated mathematics problems if you do not understand complicated English? The fact is that many students fail high school and college examinations simply because they do not understand the questions. Their English is not good enough.

But there are other reasons for learning English well. Many jobs depend on your ability to speak and write well. Not only writing and teaching jobs but engineering and other technological jobs as well require such communication skills. In many jobs, especially the more important ones to which you may be promoted, you must write reports and instructions, and you must speak at business and work meetings.

Today's world is filled with sophisticated forms of communication—television, billboards, radio, movies, newspapers, bulletins, charts, instructions, letters, forms, speeches, tapes, records, telephones, videotapes, and recently even videotelephones. Whatever job you get is going to require that you use one or more of these methods of communication.

Here is one good example of the importance of learning English well. Not only will you have to communicate on the job; you will also have to communicate to get a job. There is the initial letter or telephone call. There are applications, résumés, and interviews. Many companies will not hire employees who do not use English well.

Almost every job requires a knowledge of English. Some examples of specific jobs in which English is especially important are given in Table 3.

FOREIGN LANGUAGES

Foreign languages are not required courses in every curriculum. However, their importance should not be underestimated. People are traveling to other countries more and more today. Businesses in our country run many businesses in foreign countries, and many foreign businesses run businesses here. This means that more and more Americans are traveling and working in other countries. Even when they do not live and

Table 3: Jobs in Which English Is Important

Actor	Foreign correspondent	Public relations advisor
Airplane pilot	Foreign-exchange clerk	Radio announcer
Advertising manager	Guidance counselor	Reading specialist
Air traffic controller	Hotel manager	Real estate salesworker
Art critic	Hostess	Receptionist
Art director	Immigration inspector	Reporter
Auctioneer	Insurance agent	Retail manager
Author	Interior designer	Sales engineer
Bus driver	Interpreter	Salesperson
Buyer	Interviewer	Scriptwriter
Camp counselor	Journalist	Secretary
Child care aide	Judge	Security guard
Clergy member	Lawyer	Speech therapist
Clerk-typist	Librarian	Sportswriter
Compositor	Lifeguard	Stenographer
Cryptographer	News commentator	Tailor
Customer service representative	Newspaper columnist	Teacher
Dental hygienist	Notary public	Teacher's aide
Dietitian	Nurse	Technical writer
Drama critic	Occupational therapist	Telephone operator
Editor	Office manager	Traffic manager
Educational administrator	Pharmacist	Translator
Emergency medical technician	Phone operator	Tour guide
Fashion writer	Physical therapist	Usher
Firefighter	Police officer	Veterinarian
Flight attendant	Proofreader	

work in another country, their jobs here often call for reading foreign magazines, books, reports, and instructions.

Many students choose to study French in high school. German has always been important to anyone interested in science and technology. Spanish is a very popular language, especially because there are large numbers of Spanish-speaking persons in the United States. There is a growing interest in Russian, Arabic, and Japanese because the nations whose peoples speak these languages are very active in world affairs.

Table 4 shows a variety of jobs in which a knowledge of a foreign language is important.

SOCIAL SCIENCES

Service careers make up the fastest-growing group of careers in the nation. They call for providing services to other people—hundreds of different kinds of services, such as police protection and psychiatric treatment.

Service jobs call for different levels of knowledge of social studies, history, geography, economics—all the subjects that fit a social sci-

Communication skills are important. Many jobs depend on your ability to speak and write well. (Magnum Photos)

A future in which people have more time for exercise and recreation could mean more jobs in which knowledge of and skills in physical and health education are important. In this picture, a demonstration is being given to show how a surfboard can be used to remove a "victim" of a suspected neck (or back) injury from the water. (Courtesy Ted Carland/American Red Cross)

Table 4: Jobs in Which Foreign Languages Are Important

Actor	Flight attendant	Opera singer
Archeologist	Foreign-exchange clerk	Pharmacist
Armed forces	Foreign language teacher	Physician
Art collector	Foreign service officer	Police officer
Art historian	Geologist	Receptionist
Branch manager, airways	Hotel reservations clerk	Researcher
Broadcaster	Hotel worker	Secretary, bilingual
College language teacher	Interpreter	Taxi driver
Critic	Immigration inspector	Tour conductor
Curator	Importer	Translator
Customs inspector	Language librarian	Travel agent
Dealer, foreign books and newspapers	Master chef	Travel bureau manager
Diplomat	Merchant marine	Traveling companion
Engineer	Missionary	Wireless operator
Exporter	News analyst	Writer
Fashion buyer	Nurse	

Table 5: Jobs in Which Social Sciences Are Important

Anthropologist	Government service worker	Philologist
Archeologist	Health inspector	Police officer (city, county,
Assessor	Historian	state, national)
Bailiff	House canvasser and agent	Political scientist
Bank teller	Human relations worker	Private investigator
Bellhop	Industrial economist	Professional athlete
Building inspector	Industrial executive	Psychologist (industrial, clinical,
Bus driver	Interviewer	school, social)
Buyer	Judge	Radio or TV announcer
Cartoonist	Justice of the Peace	Radio or TV production
Chamber of Commerce	Labor arbitrator	or performing worker
educational director	Labor economist	Religious worker
City planner-designer	Law clerk	Reporter
Community relations worker	Lawyer	Salesperson
Conservationist	Librarian	Secretary
Counselor (school, employment,	Library assistant	Social-civic services
vocational)	Market analyst	Sociologist
Court worker	Museum curator	Social worker
Criminologist	Museum guide	Taxi driver
Economist	National and state parks guide	Teacher
Editor	Newspaper columnist	Tour conductor
Employment interviewer	News commentator	Train porter
Firefighter	Paleontologist	Travel bureau manager
Foreign service officer	Park ranger	Truck driver
Geographer	Personnel coordinator	Union official
		Youth group coordinator

ences curriculum. These are subjects that help you to understand people, the ways people run their affairs, the ways countries do things, the ways business shapes people's lives, and the problems people and countries have with each other. Careers that demand a knowledge of these matters are increasing in the fields of government work, social work, teaching, law, writing, medicine, conservation, and travel.

Table 5, given above, shows a variety of jobs in which an understanding of the social

sciences is valuable and important.

PHYSICAL AND HEALTH EDUCATION

You must be healthy to do a job. This means that physical exercise and recreation are important to your whole life. Today people have more leisure time than ever before, and they probably will have more free time in the future—more time for exercise and recreation.

Table 6: Jobs in Which Physical and Health Education Is Important

Athletic manager	Health education leader	Recreation therapist
Athletic trainer	High school athletic coach	Referee
Caddie	Hospital rehabilitation therapist	Research physiologist attendant
Camp counselor	Hunting and fishing guide	Sanitation engineer
Camp director	Lifeguard	School nurse
Choreographer	Masseur or masseuse	Sporting goods store manager or salesperson
Circus aerialist	Occupational therapist	Sports announcer
College athletic coach	Parks and recreation program director	Sports cartoonist
Community center worker	Park supervisor	Sports columnist
Community recreation leader	Physical education teacher	Sports editor
Dancing master	Physical therapist	Sports writer
Fishing warden	Playground director	Swimming pool attendant
Golf club attendant	Playground worker	Tennis court attendant
Golf club maker	Professional athlete	Timekeeper (athletics)
Greenskeeper	Recreation facility attendant	Umpire

There will be more jobs in physical and health education as people find more ways to use their free time. There are already many more physical education and recreation jobs than there were when your parents were your age.

A variety of jobs in which knowledge and skills in physical and health education are important are shown in Table 6.

One of the tables in this chapter must have told you about the required course in which you are most interested. Did you read the lists carefully? It wouldn't hurt you to go back to at least that one most important table and to read it a second time. It may include some jobs you never knew or thought about before. And one of these could be the right job for you.

30

MATCHING ELECTIVE COURSES WITH JOBS

In addition to the basic courses that everyone takes in school, there are other types of courses—elective courses. These are courses you choose to take because they interest you or help you to prepare for a job or for further training or education.

Your school offers electives for many reasons. Elective courses give you the opportunity to learn more about subjects—like music, art, and typing—that can help you to lead a fuller, happier life. Many people who never became artists or musicians can thank an art or music course for hours of pleasure they later experienced touring an art museum or listening to records. And many who have never become secretaries or stenographers have, for very practical reasons, been grateful for the high school typing course.

Electives also give you a wider range of choices in terms of a future career. An agricultural education subject, such as animal science, may not be for everyone, and not everyone is required to take it. But studying animal science is a boon to anyone who is sure that his or her place is on the farm.

And such a subject is also valuable to those who think they want to make farming a full-time career. They may need to find out more about the field while it is still early enough to change their mind if they have made the wrong decision. There may be, for example, people who love the outdoors and think that working on a farm will bring them happiness. After studying plant or animal sciences they may conclude that they were absolutely right. The reverse may be true, too—they may find that there is more to farming than fresh air!

There are those who may enjoy studying animal science but would prefer the advantages of life in a large city. The kind of tables given in Chapter 29 could be helpful in giving such people ideas about jobs that might satisfy both interests. For this reason, the same kind of matchup will be done in this chapter. Once again, these tables show the variety of jobs in which knowledge you can gain from your high school courses is important. Remember the concept of the career lattice and keep in mind the different educational levels that need to be reached for success in different jobs. The big difference between the matchup in this chapter and the tables in the last chapter is that this time jobs will be matched with elective courses, such as art education, instead of required courses.

Elective courses, such as art education, are courses you may choose to take because they interest you or help you to prepare for a job or for future training or education. These students are learning silk screening. (Courtesy Pratt Institute)

Table 1: Jobs in Which Art Is Important

Advertising designer	Ceramicist	Hand etcher
Advertising manager	Commercial artist	Hand grainer
Animator artist	Craftworker	Histological illustrator
Anthropologist	Curator	Interior decorator
Archeologist	Delineator	Jeweler
Architect	Designer:	Jewelry store manager
Architectural modeler	Advertising	Landscape architect
Art appraiser	Clothing	Layout artist
Art dealer	Costume	Lithographer
Art director	Fashion	Medical illustrator
Art editor	Jewelry	Photoengraver
Art gallery guard	Millinery	Photographer
Art historian	Stage	Photographic technician
Artist	Textile	Political cartoonist
Art librarian	Die designer	Sculptor
Art teacher	Display specialist	Show card writer
Arts and crafts director	Drafting technician	Sign painter
Auto designer	Draper	Stagehand
Bookbinder	Floral designer	Stone carver
Buyer of art goods	Glass blower	Wardrobe director
Cartoonist illustrator	Greeting card illustrator	Wood engraver

Table 2: Jobs in Which Music Is Important

Accompanist	Music arranger	Piano repairer
Arranger	Music critic	Piano stringer
Choirmaster	Music librarian	Piano tuner
Chorus master	Music store manager	Salesclerk, music store
College music teacher	Music teacher, private	Salesperson of music and
Composer	Musical instrument repairer	musical instruments
Concertmaster	Opera singer	Stagehand
Conductor	Orchestrator	Violin maker
High school music teacher	Organ tuner	Violin repairer
Impressario	Organist	Violinist
Instrumental musician	Pianist	Vocalist

ART

For some people, art is a hobby. For other people, art is a career. There are jobs that call for training and skill in art in distribution, marketing, business, production, construction, medicine, research, journalism, publishing, advertising, and many other fields. The ability to present ideas in attractive colors, shapes, forms, and lines can lead to many interesting careers. An interest in art, even when you are not artistically talented yourself, can lead to just as many careers.

Table 1 lists some of the many jobs for which a knowledge of art is important. Remember to ask about jobs that are not familiar to you.

MUSIC

Like art, music for some people is a hobby. For other people it is a way of life. A knowledge of music can lead to many careers.

Examples of jobs in which musical knowledge and skill are important are given in Table 2.

HOME ECONOMICS

Have you ever heard the phrase "quality of life"? It is used these days in connection with air and water pollution, adequate nutrition, medical care, mass transportation—all the things that make our lives either better or worse.

People used to be concerned mainly with how many goods and services a way of life or an economic system could provide. But now they are paying more attention to how good these services and goods are, or how poor. Home economics is important to many jobs concerned with trying to improve the quality of life. Such jobs have to do with child care, family life, nutrition, homemaking, sanitation, interior decorating and designing, recreation, and similar matters.

Table 3 shows some of those jobs in which a knowledge of home economics is important.

DISTRIBUTIVE EDUCATION

This country produces great amounts of goods and services. It also imports and exports goods and services. That is, it buys them from other countries or sells them to other countries. All this calls for many different kinds of jobs. Persons doing these jobs must know about warehousing, transportation, display, selling, advertising, bookkeeping, research, personnel management, and even a little psychology.

Some of the jobs in which knowledge gained from your distributive education course might be helpful are given in Table 4.

VOCATIONAL TRADE AND INDUSTRIAL EDUCATION

Everyone who does technical work—from the designer of a machine to the machine operator—needs some industrial and vocational training.

Table 3: Jobs in Which Home Economics Is Important

Alteration seamstress	Extension home economist	Meat cutter
Apartment caretaker	Family service worker	Merchandising display assistant
Apparel specialist	Fashion designer	Nutritionist
Baker	Fashion merchandising worker	Public health nurse
Building inspector	Food chemist	Recreational therapist
Camping staff member	Food processing technician	Recreation worker
Caterer	Food salesworker	Resort manager
Chef or cook	Food service technologist	Sanitation consultant
Child care aide	Home economics teacher	School food services worker
Clothing care service worker	Homemaker-home health aide	Social worker
Comparison shopper	Homemaking consultant	Supermarket manager
Consumer affairs specialist	Hospital orderly	Tailor
Custodial service worker	Hotel aide	Teacher's aide
Decorator assistant	Hotel housekeeper	Textile chemist
Dietitian	Hotel manager	Textile designer
Dressmaker	Interior decorator	TV product demonstrator
Dry cleaner assistant	Journalist	Upholsterer
Dry cleaning manager	Laundry worker	Waiter/Waitress
Executive housekeeper	Meat and dairy inspector	

Table 4: Jobs in Which Distributive Education Is Important

Accountant	DE teacher-coordinator	Parts/service manager
Advertising account executive	Deliveryperson	Product demonstrator
Advertising copy proofreader	Display specialist	Program manager TV station
Advertising layout artist	District sales manager	Public relations worker
Advertising manager	Door to door salesworker	Purchasing agent
Agricultural broker	Estate planner	Radio-TV serviceperson
Agricultural business manager	Estimator	Reservations clerk
Apartment house manager	Factory manager	Resort owner-manager
Appraiser	Farm real estate appraiser	Retail and wholesale dealer
Auctioneer	Fashion coordinator	Salesclerk
Banker	Floral designer	Sales manager
Bell captain	Freight agent	Sales representative
Broker	Freight dispatcher	Service department manager
Bulk plant manager	Hotel-motel manager	Service representative
Business manager	Industrial relations manager	Service station manager or owner
Buyer	Interior decorator	Stock clerk
Cashier	Loan or credit company manager	Stockkeeper
Checker	Manufacturing or sales representative	Store manager
Comptroller	Marina operator	Systems or market analyst
Copywriter	Market-research analyst	Travel consultant
Credit manager	Office manager	Wedding consultant
Credit sales payroll clerk		

Those who are considering a career as a chef would find home economics a helpful elective course to take in high school. (Courtesy Stouffer's Restaurant)

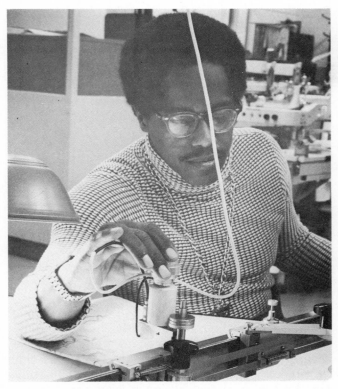

Everyone who does technical work—from the designer of a machine to its operator—needs some trade and industrial education. (Courtesy U.S. Department of the Interior)

How much training depends on the job. Job requirements vary from simply being able to use a tool to knowing how to design complex equipment or how to monitor equipment that controls systems of machines automatically.

Trade and industrial education is important in engineering, construction, communications, transportation, and maintenance. Many jobs in these fields call for a knowledge of electricity, chemistry, physics, and mechanics.

Some of these jobs that require a knowledge of vocational trade and industrial education are given in Table 5.

BUSINESS EDUCATION

Thousands of big and small businesses provide all the jobs you are exploring, except the jobs provided by different levels of government. Both businesses and government agencies and departments need people to manage, supervise and coordinate them. These people must know how to hire other people and to train them, schedule workers and their work, keep books, meet deadlines, run offices, prepare letters and reports, and find new business. These skills are usually taught in business education courses.

A number of jobs that call for some sort of business education are given in Table 6.

VOCATIONAL AGRICULTURE

Vocational agriculture is a field that is changing rapidly with the times. Today there are fewer farms, and the farms are larger than the farms of 50 years ago. Small farms are being combined into big farms. Big farms are facing the problems and challenges of big businesses. The people involved in agricultural production today need more technical skills than the farm workers of other generations. They need technical knowledge in order to work with farm equipment, seed, feed, fertilizers, herbicides, and bulk petroleum products. They need recordkeeping skills in order to keep track of supplies and expenses.

These people also need a great deal of agricultural education. Agricultural education is also important for many new agriculturally related fields such as conservation, wildlife management, forestry, landscape gardening, and floriculture.

Some of the many jobs that call for vocational agriculture knowledge are shown in Table 7 on page 157.

Table 5: Jobs in Which Vocational Trade and Industrial Education Are Important

Aeronautical engineer	Diesel mechanic	Operating engineer
Air-conditioning engineer	Drafting technician	Optician
Airplane pilot	Drill press operator	Photoengraver
Appliance repairer	Editor of industrial publications	Photographer
Architect	Electrical engineer	Plasterer
Auto assembly worker	Electronics assembler	Plumber
Auto body repairer	Fluid power technician	Printer
Auto-diesel mechanic	Foundry worker	Radio and TV repairer
Automotive engineer	Gas appliance servicer	Railroad track worker
Automatic welder operator	Gas station attendant	Recreation therapist's aide
Aviation mechanic	Graphic arts technician	Refrigeration mechanic
Blueprint machine operator	Heavy-equipment operator	Riveter
Boiler inspector	Industrial chemist	Roofer
Brake adjuster	Jeweler	Sales engineer
Building trades contractor	Leather worker	Sawmill worker
Bulldozer operator	Lineman, telephone and telegraph	Sheet-metal worker
Business machine servicer	Linotype operator	Small-engine mechanic
Cabinetmaker	Longshoreman	Stationary engineer
Cable splicer	Machine operator	Stonecutter
Carpenter	Maintenance person	Teacher of industrial arts
Ceramic engineer	Mechanic	Telephone lineperson
Civil engineer	Mechanical engineer	Tinsmith
Compositor	Meteorologist	Tool design technician
Construction worker	Metallurgist	Truck driver
Crane operator	Multigraph operator	Wastewater treatment specialist
Custodian	Oil well driller	Welder

Table 6: Jobs in Which Business Education Is Important

Accountant	Credit manager	Personnel clerk, (insurance
Accounting clerk	Data processing systems analyst	hospitalization, workmen's
Actuarial clerk	Employment manager	compensation)
Airline reservationist	File clerk	Personnel manager
Auditor	Game farm manager	Personnel training director
Bank teller	Hospital administrator	Police reporter
Banker	Hotel-motel manager	Postal worker-sorter
Bookkeeper	Hotel-motel reservation clerk	Receptionist
Business manager	Journalist	Salesworker (auto, bond, insurance, real estate)
Buyer	Keypunch operator	Secretary
Cashier	Law clerk	Small-business manager
Census taker	Law librarian	Statistician
Certified public accountant	Manager of golf club	Stenographer
Clerk	Medical records librarian	Stockbroker
College or high school teacher	Messenger	Stock clerk
of business education	MTST operator	Tabulating machine operator
Computer and console operator	Multigraph operator	Tape librarian
Computer programmer	Office machine operator	Technical writer
Construction estimator	Office manager	Telephone operator
Comptroller	Park manager	Typist
	Payroll clerk	Warehouse supervisor

USING JOB AND LEARNING-LEVEL INFORMATION

Did you just skip over those long tables? If you did, you made a big mistake. They can help you to pinpoint jobs that might fit your interests and talents. Many of these jobs may never have crossed your mind. Thousands of people would be working in different jobs and would be much happier with their work if only they had known how many different jobs there were when they were young. You have a chance to avoid their problem by thinking about these lists carefully.

When your parents were your age, lists like the ones you have just read would have said "salesman" and "foreman" and "repairman," but

Agricultural education subjects, such as Animal Science, are important to anyone who wants a future on a farm, or on a ranch, or in the many agriculture-related businesses.
(Courtesy United Nations GR/VMB)

Table 7: Jobs in Which Vocational Agriculture Is Important

Agribusiness teacher	Farm insurance adjuster	Livestock grader
Agricultural broker	Farm loan operator	Logger
Agricultural chemical plant manager	Farm machinery manager	Meat inspector
Agricultural economist	Farm real estate appraiser	Meat plant manager
Agricultural engineer	Farm supply salesclerk	Milking machine servicer
Agricultural journalist	Feed plant clerk	Milk processor
Agricultural metallurgist	Floriculturist	Milk sanitarian
Agronomist	Florist	Nursery manager
Animal scientist	Food process buyer	Nursery salesperson
Apiarist	Forest entomologist	Park superintendent
Bulk feed truck driver	Forester	Plant pathologist
Bulk fertilizer spreader operator	Forest fire warden	Poultry buyer
Butcher	Forest ranger	Poultry products inspector
Chain saw service operator	Frozen food processor	Produce grader
Construction engineer	Game warden	Recreation forestry aide
County agent	Golf course superintendent	Seed technologist
Credit supervisor	Herbicide salesworker	Soil conservationist
Dairy plant manager	Horticulturist	Tree sprayer
Dairy plant technologist	Insecticide salesperson	Tree surgeon
Dairy products salesworker	Landscape architect	Veterinarian
Ecologist	Landscape gardener	Wildlife biologist
Farm equipment designer	Livestock auctioneer	Wildlife conservation officer

now they say "salesperson" and "supervisor" and "repairer" because today women have a chance to do jobs that used to be limited to men. Today a young woman who wants to be a forest ranger or a truck driver or a doctor or lawyer or farmer has a better chance to do these jobs than her mother had. Today women are employed as truck drivers, farmers, lawyers, and doctors.

What should you do next? Decide which school courses interest you most. They will probably be the courses in which you get good marks. Then check these lists to see the wide variety of jobs that call for a knowledge of courses that you like best. Pick some of the jobs that interest you. Think about the amount of education and training you need to handle them. Also think about the length of time this education and training is going to take.

Now that you have read this unit you have some valuable tools to help you make good decisions about your future. You know about many jobs. You are aware of the subject areas you will need to know to do them. You also know what school can do for you.

Getting It All Together

1. Why do different curricula have differences in the kinds and levels of skills the students are expected to develop?

2. How can you use your understanding of career clusters and career lattices to help you choose a job goal?

3. Although you have little or nothing to say about the subject content of courses, why is subject content important to you, and how should it influence your schoolwork?

4. Why are students in school required to take certain courses? Give two examples of a required course.

5. What are two reasons why your school offers elective courses?

6. How does planning a career goal help you make the most of your school years?

7. What are two reasons for learning English well?

AFTER SCHOOL: WHAT NEXT?

Your goals in this unit are given in the following list:

To become aware of the many ways you can continue to learn and to grow after high school

To learn where you can get information about educational programs for after high school

To learn the kinds of things you should know about any educational program before entering it

To learn of various ways of paying for your education and training after high school

To begin deciding which educational and training program is best for you after high school

You are building a good life. Like anything else, it must be built one stage at a time. You are in the school stage now. The next stage comes after high school. Open your toolbox, and see if you have the right tools to build this stage.

- You know how fast the world is changing and why
- You know that there are many different and interesting kinds of jobs
- You know what it takes to do many of these jobs
- You know what you have been getting out of school and if you are in the right curriculum

You also know that learning never stops. You know that because you know the world is not waiting for anyone to catch up with it. So the next question is "What do you do after high school?"

You may choose to keep on going to school. There are many types of schools you can choose from. There are schools that take less than 4 years—vocational schools, technical institutes, or community and junior colleges. And there are schools for those who choose to spend a longer time in school—4-year colleges, universities, and professional schools.

Or you may decide on a system of working and learning at the same time. There are many possibilities. You may, for example, decide to learn on the job.

Another way to combine working and learning is to combine a job with formal schooling. In a nursing program, for example, there are curricula and courses and subjects, but there is also practical on-the-job training in a hospital. This kind of learning is becoming more common because so many jobs that used to call for on-the-job training alone now call for an understanding of certain school subjects, too. Knowing these subjects helps you do the work better and helps you to grow in your job. And there is always value in having the opportunity to give a practical application to whatever it is you have learned in school.

Learning at home is also becoming popular. This allows people to keep on doing what they need to do at home or to hold on to jobs while they learn. Possible ways to learn at home include correspondence courses and educational television.

Once you decide what you want to learn, start shopping around to find the best place to learn it. Make comparisons. Ask questions. Determine costs. And read. Such research is important.

31

FORMAL SCHOOLING AFTER HIGH SCHOOL: LESS THAN 4 YEARS

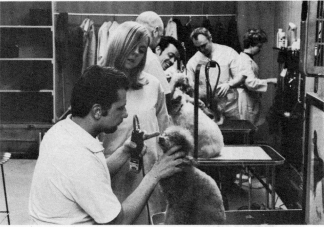

There are many different ways to learn after high school and many different programs available. These students are learning a marketable skill at a vocational training school. (Top, courtesy Oberlin College Conservatory; bottom, New York School of Dog Grooming)

Who are the most interesting people you know?

Ask anyone who has been out of school for a few years, and you'll probably find that the answers given will all name people who have one thing in common. They will always be people who have continued to learn and grow after high school.

There are many different ways to learn after high school and many different kinds of programs available. Each program has its own particular merit. The best way to tell which one is the right one for you is to look them all over carefully—one at a time.

Some learning programs can take a long time—as long as 8 to 10 years. But there are many others that don't require such lengthy training or schooling. Many programs require less—sometimes considerably less—than 4 years of formal schooling after high school.

VOCATIONAL TRAINING SCHOOLS

Vocational training schools seldom require more than 2 years of formal schooling. There are three major kinds of vocational training schools: business schools, beauty and barber schools, and trade schools.

Business schools teach bookkeeping and accounting, secretarial skills, business machine operation, and electronic data processing. Some business schools teach only computer operation and programming—they specialize in those skills. Business schools usually offer 1- or 2-year courses in which apprenticeship programs and state licenses are not required.

Beauty and barber schools teach hair styling, scalp and facial treatment, shampooing, shaving, and sanitary procedures. Their programs usually take 6 months to a year, and they prepare students to take the state examinations required for licenses to work as barbers and beauticians.

Trade schools teach drafting, radio and TV repair, auto mechanics, refrigeration and air-conditioning maintenance, watchmaking, electrical technology, carpentry, camera repair, heavy-equipment maintenance and operation, small-appliance repair, masonry, machine shop work, plumbing, tool and die technology, and surveying. Trade school courses run from 6 months to 2 years. Sometimes they are combined with apprentice shop work, cooperative education, and work-experience programs. State examinations are required for the licenses needed to do many of the jobs learned in trade schools.

Vocational schools also teach other skills—many more than can be listed here. Some of these include health and dental assistance, environmental control technology, food service, linotype operation, practical nursing, printing, small-engine repair, warehousing, and welding.

In addition, vocational schools teach subjects that some people learn as a hobby and others pursue as a career—cartooning, sign painting, portrait painting, commercial art, flying, dance, drama, music, fashion modeling, landscape design, gardening, clothes designing, photography, and interior decorating. The time you spend on such subjects depends on what you want.

Flight schools, for example, prepare you to get different types of licenses to fly—private, commercial, instrument, and instructor. There are also courses, such as airport management, aviation mechanics, and air traffic control, that prepare you for occupations connected with fly-ing. Flight schools are closely supervised by the Federal Aviation Administration. How long you spend in one depends on the license you want.

How Vocational Schools Operate

Some vocational schools are privately owned and run to make money. Others are run by the state or community or by a union. The privately owned are likely to cost more to attend. Union schools may be tied to apprenticeship programs.

Vocational schools are very flexible about entrance requirements. Generally high school graduates are accepted, and sometimes those with less than a high school education can enter.

Vocational training schools usually do not grant degrees. They award certificates or diplomas, and they prepare you for licensing examinations whenever such examinations are required.

Most vocational training schools offer evening and Saturday classes as well as classes during weekdays. This makes it possible for you to attend them full-time or part-time. When the school is run by the state or county or community, night-time classes are usually held in high schools or area vocational technical schools.

How to Get More Information

Your school guidance office, the state employment service office, and your teachers and parents are the best sources of information about the ways to keep on learning after high school. Your city or school library has publications about vocational training schools. When a library does not have the publication you want, you can usually get it by writing to the organization that published it. Here is a list of sources of information about different kinds of vocational education. Ask your counselor or librarian to help you find any publications on this list that interest you.

Accredited Institutions of Postsecondary Education, 1979-1980, American Council on Education, One Dupont Circle, Washington, D.C. 20036.

Bennett, Robert L., *Careers Through Cooperative Work Experience,* Wiley, New York, 1977.

Directory of Hotel and Restaurant Schools, Council on Hotel, Restaurant, and Institutional Education, Suite 534, 1522 K Street, N.W., Washington, D.C. 20005.

Directory of National Trade and Professional Associations of the United States, U.S. Department of Commerce, Room 300, 917 15th Street, N.W., Washington, D.C. 20005.

Hecht, Miriam, and Lillian Traub, *Alternatives to College,* Macmillan, New York, 1974.

Lederer, Muriel, *The Guide to Career Education,* Quadrangle, New York, 1974.

Lovejoy, Clarence E., *Lovejoy's Career and Vocational School Guide,* Simon and Schuster, New York, 1973.

Russell, Max M. (ed.) *The Blue Book of Occupational Education,* CCM Information Corporation, New York, 1971.

Splaver, Sarah, *Your Career—If You're Not Going to College,* Messner, New York, 1971.

TECHNICAL INSTITUTES

Another type of school that requires less than 4 years of formal schooling and that you should know about is the technical institute. Technical institutes train *technicians*—persons who are specialists in the practical details of a scientific or mechanical subject.

Vocational training schools and technical institutes are alike in that the career areas in which they train people may be similar. But the training in technical institutes tends to be more intense, more technical, more specialized, and sometimes longer. Technicians are usually semiprofessionals, meaning that they often directly assist such professionals as engineers, architects, doctors, and scientists. Most vocational training school graduates, on the other hand, have a level of responsibility that is somewhat lower than that of technicians.

Technical institutes are often part of larger institutions, such as hospitals. This makes it possible for them to offer their students on-the-job training.

You usually study at a technical institute for 1 to 3 years, depending on the skill you learn.

The U.S. Department of Education and the National Industrial Conference Board have identified areas that are most likely to offer good jobs for technicians in the future. Skills needed in order to work in these areas can be learned in 2 years or less. The career areas suitable for technicians are the following:

- Aeronautics and aerospace
- Agriculture
- Air conditioning and refrigeration
- Architecture and construction
- Automation
- Chemistry

Technical schools train people to be specialists in the practical details of a scientific or mechanical subject. (Courtesy American Institute of Architecture)

- Civil engineering technology
- Commercial aviation
- Electricity
- Electrochemistry
- Electronic data processing
- Electronics
- Fire protection
- Forestry
- Health service
- Industrial protection
- Instrumentation
- Marine life and ocean fishing
- Mechanical design
- Metallurgy
- Nuclear and radiological technology
- Oceanography
- Office specialization
- Police science
- Sanitation and environmental control

Here are some of the organizations and publications that offer more information.

Allied Medical Education Directory 1974, American Medical Association, 535 North Dearborn Street, Chicago, Illinois 60610.

Directory of Accredited Private Trade and Technical Schools, revised annually, National Association of Trade and Technical Schools, 2021 L Street N.W., Washington, D.C. 20036.

Employment Outlook for Technicians, U.S. Government Printing Office, Washington, D.C. 20402.

Engineers Council for Professional Development, 345 East 47 Street, New York, New York 10017.

Ferguson Guide to Two-Year College Programs for Technicians and Specialists, J. G. Ferguson, Chicago, 1971.

Hecht, Miriam, and Lillian Traub, *Alternatives to College*, Macmillan, New York, 1974.

Industrial Designers Society of America, 1750 Old Meadow Road, McLean, Virginia 22101.

Lederer, Muriel, *The Guide to Career Education*, Quadrangle, New York, 1974.

National Council of Technical Schools, 1835 K Street, N.W., Washington, D.C., 20006.

Prakken, Laurence W., and Jerome C. Patterson (eds.), *Technician Education Yearbook*, 1969–1970, Prakken, Ann Arbor, 1969.

NURSES' TRAINING

Training to be a nurse may take 4 years, or it may take less time. Some community and 4-year colleges and all schools of nursing train men and women for careers in nursing. One might choose to train to be a licensed practical nurse or a registered nurse. Nursing aides are generally trained after they are hired.

Training to become a licensed practical nurse usually takes 1 year of study in a vocational school, community college, hospital, or clinic.

Registered nurses may receive their training in any one of three available programs—a diploma program, a baccalaureate program, or an associate degree program.

Diploma programs usually require 3 years of study, compared with 2-year programs in community colleges and 4-year programs in 4-year colleges. The diploma programs are usually offered in hospitals. Students receive intensive training as student nurses but receive no associate degree or baccalaureate.

A 4-year college program for nurses offers a baccalaureate in science and combines nursing training with arts and sciences studies. Students in this type of program must serve as student nurses in a hospital under the supervision of the college nursing staff.

Some community colleges offer 2-year programs and an associate degree in nursing. They offer practical on-the-job training in hospitals and prepare you for state examinations.

Remember that many men are nurses. Remember also that the armed services offer a number of programs that prepare young people for careers as registered nurses, practical nurses, and nursing aides.

The following three organizations offer more on careers in nursing:

National Association for Practical Nurse Education and Service, 122 East 42 Street, New York, New York 10035.

National Federation of Licensed Practical Nurses, Inc., 250 West 57 Street, New York, New York 10019.

National League for Nursing, 10 Columbus Circle, New York, New York 10019.

JUNIOR AND COMMUNITY COLLEGES

Junior colleges offer two types of programs. They offer the first 2 years of a 4-year college program. Students enrolled in such a program may finish their education with an associate of arts or science degree, or they may transfer to a 4-year college to earn a baccalaureate degree. Junior colleges also offer 2-year programs in career education. Students enrolled in such programs are prepared for careers in secretarial studies, retailing, hotel management, medical technology, interior design, and other specialities.

Community colleges are junior colleges paid for by cities, counties, and states. In many states they add up to grades 13 and 14 of the public school system. They are likely to offer a broader range of curricula and programs than many junior colleges or technical institutes. Their programs are geared to the needs of the community in which they are located.

You may transfer to a 4-year college from a community college or train for a technical skill depending upon the curriculum you choose. Don't make the mistake of assuming that any curriculum you choose will be equal to the first 2 years in a 4-year college. Some curricula lead to a technician's degree and this degree will not permit you to transfer later to the third year of a baccalaureate program.

Because community colleges are paid for with tax money, they usually try to offer courses that prepare students for jobs that are offered in the area they serve. If the area has many farms, then the community college usually will offer many courses that deal with agricultural skills. If a large chemical industry is near the college, the college will try to teach skills that help students get jobs in the chemical industry.

Programs Offered by Community Colleges

The Commonwealth of Pennsylvania has 15 community colleges. They offer programs to meet the needs of the Pennsylvania job market. A list of these programs will give you a good idea of what community colleges in most states offer:

- Accounting
- Advertising design
- Apparel management
- Applied fine arts
- Architectural drafting technology
- Aviation
- Banking

- Biological science
- Broadcasting
- Business administration
- Business data processing
- Carpentry and construction technology
- Chemistry
- Child care technician training
- Commercial art
- Computer technology
- Correctional administration
- Dental assistant training
- Diesel technology
- Early childhood education
- Economics
- Electrical technology
- Electromechanical technology
- Electronic administration
- Engineering
- Executive secretarial skills
- Fire science
- Food service or dietary technology
- Forestry technology
- Health and physical education
- Horticulture
- Hotel, motel, and restaurant management
- Industrial design and art
- Industrial photography
- Inhalation therapy
- Journalism
- Laboratory technology
- Labor management
- Language arts and social science
- Law enforcement
- Legal secretarial skills
- Liberal arts and humanities
- Liberal arts and theater
- Library science
- Market management
- Mass media
- Mathematics
- Medical assistant training
- Medical records technology
- Medical secretarial skills

- Mental health
- Metallurgical engineering technology
- Music
- Nursing
- Office machine technology
- Ophthalmic dispensing technology
- Park management
- Physical therapy assistant training
- Physics
- Police administration
- Political science
- Postal technology
- Predental training
- Prelaw training
- Premedical training
- Preveterinary training
- Professional piloting
- Public health technology
- Real estate
- Retail management and merchandising
- Small-engine and small-appliance repair
- Social work technician training
- Sociology
- Teaching assistant training
- Technical illustration
- Telecommunications
- Transportation technology
- Urban affairs
- Welding engineering technology

Each of the programs listed offers one of these degrees: associate in applied science, associate in career studies, associate in arts, associate in science. The first two degrees are technicians' degrees. The last two are offered to students transferring to 4-year colleges, and they equal 2 years in college.

There are also many certificate and diploma programs that call for 1 year or less of training. Not all the programs are offered by each community college, however.

Publications with more information about junior and community colleges are the following:

Accredited Institutions of Higher Education, annual new ed., American Council on Education, 1 Dupont Circle, Washington, D.C. 20036.

Cass, James, and Max Birnbaum, *Comparative Guide to Two-Year Colleges and Four-Year Specialized Schools and Programs*, Harper & Row, New York, 1975.

Gleazer, Edmund J., Jr. (ed.), *American Junior Colleges*, American Council on Education, 1 Dupont Circle, Washington, D.C. 20036, 1971.

Proia, Nicholas C., *Barron's Handbook of College Transfer Information*, Barron's Educational Series, Woodbury, New York, 1975.

While reading in this chapter about the different kinds of schools, you may have noticed that many skills can be learned in more than one kind of school. You might learn electronics, for example in a technical institute, a vocational training school, and a community college.

It is best, therefore, to check all possible schools in your area.

32

FORMAL SCHOOLING AFTER HIGH SCHOOL: 4 OR MORE YEARS

Everyone should at least consider the possibility of at least 4 more years of school after high school.

Just because a way of learning takes longer is no reason for dismissing it. The last chapter introduced learning possibilities requiring less than 4 years of formal schooling. Such programs have many merits. But the long-range programs have advantages as well. Additional time spent learning is always time well spent. Occupations with more responsibility often open up to people who have advanced degrees. And sometimes these degrees can open the way to higher salaries as well.

At any rate, every possibility should be carefully investigated. This includes traditional college baccalaureate programs, college work-experience programs, and professional and graduate schools.

There are more than 2,000 colleges and universities in the United States. Some have only a few hundred students. Others have as many as 50,000 students—sometimes even more.

Some colleges and universities are financed by the state. These are known as state schools. State schools often have additional branches in cities other than the ones in which the main campuses are located. Some colleges are financed by large cities. These are known as city colleges. Other colleges and universities are financed by private groups. These are known as private schools.

Some of these schools offer many curricula, while others offer only a few. Some may offer associate degrees, but the main purpose of all of them is to offer *baccalaureates,* or bachelor's degrees, and graduate or professional degrees.

People who have received advanced degrees find that jobs involving greater responsibility are open to them.

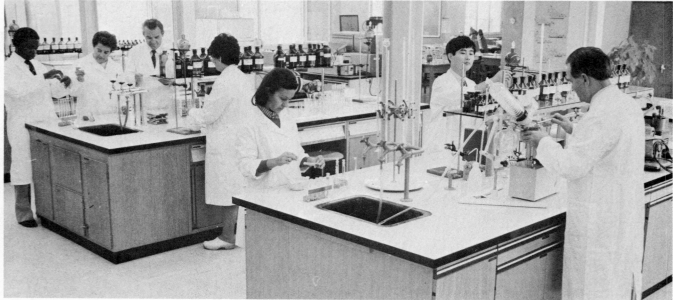

In baccalaureate programs, the first 2 years are usually spent learning general subjects. The last 2 years are spent specializing in a particular field. (Top, courtesy Adelphi University; bottom, United Nations/PAS)

BACCALAUREATE PROGRAMS

Most baccalaureate programs take 4 years to complete, but a few take 5 years. These programs offer a more general education than the programs of the schools described in Chapter 31. They also offer more opportunities to specialize. How can they do both of those things? The first 2 years of college are usually spent learning general sub-jects. The last 2 years are spent specializing in a specific field. The field a student specializes in is called his or her *major*. There are many majors in college. The following list gives some examples:

Agriculture: agribusiness, agricultural education, agricultural engineering, agronomy, animal science, floriculture, food science, forest science, horticulture, and wood science

Arts: architecture, art history, fine arts, music, and theater

Business administration: accounting, finance, insurance and real estate, logistics, management, and marketing

Earth and mineral science: ceramic science, geography, geology, material sciences, metallurgy, meteorology, mine engineering, petroleum and natural gas engineering, and polymer or plastic science.

Education: administration, research, and teacher training

Engineering: aerospace, architectural, chemical, civil, electrical, environmental, industrial, mechanical, and nuclear

Human development: city planning, food service, health planning and sciences, housing, individual and family planning, law enforcement and corrections, nursing, and nutrition

Liberal arts: anthropology, economics, foreign languages, history, journalism, literature, philosophy, political science, psychology, and sociology

Science: astronomy, biological sciences, chemistry, computer science, mathematics, microbiology, physics, and premedicine

There are many other curricula in 4-year colleges. Most of the curricula differ in emphasis from curricula in junior and community colleges and technical institutes. In 4-year colleges, there is usually more time to explore and focus on "why" things happen rather than having to learn in a brief period of time "how" things happen.

Most people do not think that 4-year colleges offer vocational education and training, but many of them do. In fact, most of the occupations that are called "professional" are not open to you unless you have a degree from a 4-year college. Here are some examples: engineer, architect, linguist, physicist, and teacher.

The following list of publications may help you to decide whether a 4-year college program is for you. Ask your counselor or librarian to help you find the publications on this list.

Accredited Institutions of Higher Education, 1973–74, American Council on Education, 1 Dupont Circle, Washington, D.C. 20036.

College Blue Book, revised annually, Macmillan, New York.

The College Guide for Students With Disabilities, Abt Publications, Cambridge, Massachusetts, 1976.

College Handbook, revised periodically, College Entrance Examination Board, P.O. Box 592, Princeton, New Jersey 08540.

Furniss, W. Todd (ed.), *American Universities and Colleges,* American Council on Education, 1 Dupont Circle, Washington, D.C. 20036, 1973.

Lovejoy, Clarence E., *Lovejoy's College Guide,* Simon and Schuster, New York, 1974.

The Official Guide to Catholic Educational Institutions, revised annually, Official Guide, 200 Sunrise Highway, Rockville Centre, New York 13118.

Splaver, Sarah, *Non-Traditional College Routes to Careers,* Messner, New York, 1975.

Willingham, Warren, *The Source Book for Higher Education,* College Entrance Examination Board, New York, 1973.

WORK-EXPERIENCE PROGRAMS IN COLLEGE

Many colleges provide work-experience or cooperative education programs. Such programs make it possible for you to test what you have learned in class in a job situation. The programs are a mixture of classroom learning and on-the-job study. They are called "cooperative" because schools and employers cooperate to make it possible for you to try out on the job what you are learning in college.

These programs are becoming increasingly popular because they provide an excellent way for you to obtain experience and to apply what you are learning to real-life situations.

PROFESSIONAL AND GRADUATE SCHOOLS

Colleges sometimes operate inside universities. When this happens, the college students are called *undergraduates.* The university students are called *graduates.* The graduates almost always have baccalaureate degrees, and they usually study the fields in which they majored in college. They are seeking master's and doctoral degrees. It is possible to major in one field in college and then switch to another field in graduate school, but this often means taking extra courses to get ready for the graduate program. In some ways graduate schools form grades 17 through 20 of your education.

Professional schools usually require you to have a baccalaureate degree before they will accept you. They prepare you for work that requires more education and training than you can get in 4 years at college. They train you to be a physician, for example, or a lawyer, or a dentist.

The names of the degrees offered by professional and graduate schools differ depending on your specialty. A professional school might award you an M.D. (Doctor of Medicine), an LL.B (Bachelor of Laws), A D.D. (Doctor of Divinity), or a D.D.S. (Doctor of Dental Surgery).

From graduate school you might receive an M.S. (Master of Science), an M.Ed. (Master of Education), a D.Ed. (Doctor of Education), a Ph.D. (Doctor of Philosophy), or a D.Bus.Ad. (Doctor of Business Administration).

There are also many other degrees you might receive from graduate schools and professional schools.

Whatever it might be—whether baccalaureate, graduate, or professional—an advanced degree may lead you to a prestigious and responsible job. It may lead to a considerably high salary, particularly if it is a professional degree. It should greatly increase the likelihood of your becoming a leader in your community and making a substantial contribution to it. And it will lead to a fuller and more developed appreciation of many of the more interesting sides of life.

For all these reasons and more you should give the matter a lot of serious thought before ruling out the possibility of at least 4 more years of school after high school.

WORKING, EARNING, AND LEARNING

School or work?

Are you finding it hard to make a decision? It doesn't always have to be either one or the other, you know. It's also possible to enjoy the best of both worlds. There are many available systems of working and learning at the same time. You might, for example, want to be an apprentice.

APPRENTICESHIPS

Teaching skills to young people by having them work under master tradespecple is as old as recorded history, and probably much older. Before the Industrial Age began, apprentices usually lived with the artisans who taught them. They did chores, ran errands, cleaned shops, and learned a craft by helping the artisans.

Today apprentices are paid while they learn, and their apprenticeships are regulated by unions, or state or federal governments.

The Bureau of Apprenticeship and Training of the U.S. Department of Labor defines an *apprentice* as a worker who learns a skilled trade that calls for 2 or more years of on-the-job experience and instruction. An apprenticeship program is usually based on a written agreement between the apprentice and the experienced workers who teach the apprentice a skill.

Young women should keep in mind that it may be difficult for them to win acceptance as apprentices in many trades. Only about 60 trades admit women as apprentices. However, the law says that it is illegal for publically funded training programs to discriminate against women.

About 350 occupations are registered with the Bureau of Apprenticeship and Training. Most

Before the Industrial Age, apprentices usually lived with the artisans who taught them. They did chores, ran errands, cleaned shops, and helped the artisans in order to learn a craft. (Woodfin Camp & Associates)

of them are in the construction, manufacturing, transportation, and service industries. The list that follows includes the 90 basic trades throughout which the 350 apprenticeable occupations are distributed.

- Aircraft fabricator
- Airplane mechanic
- Arborist
- Asbestos worker
- Automotive body repairer

169

- Automotive mechanic
- Baker
- Barber-stylist
- Blacksmith
- Boilermaker
- Bookbinder
- Brewer
- Bricklayer
- Butcher-meatcutter
- Cabinetmaker-millwright
- Candymaker
- Canvas worker
- Carpenter
- Car worker (factory, railroad)
- Cement mason
- Cook
- Cooper
- Cosmetician
- Dairy products maker
- Draftsperson-designer
- Dry cleaner
- Electrical worker
- Electroplater
- Electrotyper
- Engraver
- Fabric cutter
- Farm equipment mechanic
- Floor covering installer
- Foundry worker
- Furrier
- Glazier-glassworker
- Heat-treater
- Ironworker
- Jeweler
- Lather
- Lead burner
- Leatherworker
- Lithographer
- Machine operator
- Mailer
- Maintenance machine repairer
- Marking device maker
- Mattress maker, custom
- Metal polisher and buffer
- Miller
- Millwright
- Modelmaker
- Musical instrument mechanic
- Operating engineer
- Optical technician
- Orthopedic-prosthetic technician
- Painter and decorator
- Paint maker
- Patternmaker
- Photoengraver
- Photographer

- Plasterer
- Plate printer
- Plumber–pipe fitter
- Pottery worker
- Printing press operator
- Rigger
- River pilot
- Roofer
- Rotogravure engraver
- Sheet-metal worker
- Sign painter
- Silversmith
- Spotter-presser
- Stereotyper
- Stonemason
- Stone mounter
- Stoneworker
- Tailor
- Telephone worker
- Terrazzo worker
- Textile technician-mechanic
- Tile setter
- Tool and die maker
- Upholsterer
- Wallpaper craftsperson
- Wire weaver
- Wood-carver

Apprenticeship Standards

Apprenticeship programs registered with the Bureau of Apprenticeship and Training must meet the following basic standards:

- An apprentice must be at least 16 years old.
- Everyone must be given a fair opportunity to apply for an apprenticeship.
- An apprentice may be selected only on the basis of qualifications necessary to do the job.
- All training and on-the-job experience must follow a prescribed schedule.
- Each program must include instruction in the technical subjects that relate to the trade.
- One hundred forty-four hours of instruction a year is usually necessary.
- There must be a schedule of pay raises.
- Each program must provide supervised on-the-job training.
- Each apprentice's work on the job and in class must be reviewed from time to time, and records must be kept of these reviews.
- There must be cooperation between employers and employees.

- When an apprentice successfully completes an apprenticeship program, it must be properly recognized.
- There must be no discrimination on the basis of race, religion, or national origin in either the employment or training of apprentices.

After training an apprentice is called a journeyman and receives a certificate that shows that he or she can do a certain kind of work. The salary a beginning apprentice earns is half that which a journeyman earns. An apprentice gets a pay raise every 6 months.

For more information about apprenticeships, you may write to the Bureau of Apprenticeship and Training, U.S. Department of Labor, Washington, D.C. 20202. The publications in the following list also tell you more about apprenticeships:

Apprenticeship—Past and Present, Manpower Administration, U.S. Department of Labor, Washington, D.C. 20202.
Jobs for Which Apprenticeship Training Is Available, Bureau of Labor Statistics, U.S. Department of Labor, Washington, D.C. 20212.
The National Apprenticeship Program, Manpower Administration, U.S. Department of Labor, Washington, D.C. 20202.

ON-THE-JOB TRAINING

Only a small percentage of workers can get into apprenticeship programs. Many more workers have to depend on on-the-job training as a means of learning a skill.

On-the-job training means learning a job after being hired. Training may take a long time. This kind of training is different from apprenticeship training because there is no written agreement between you and your employer. There are usually no classes, and there are no federal or state standards.

Learning on the job takes effort and hard work because you are not always guaranteed instruction. Sometimes you have to move from job to job to learn the skills you need.

Some companies offer training programs. Retail stores, factories, government agencies, insurance companies, sales organizations, banks, and almost all types of offices use on-the-job-training to prepare their employees for their jobs. Almost all supervisory or management training is done on the job in these organizations.

Part-time or vacation work may provide opportunities to learn on the job. Work in school shops and laboratories is another possibility.

Here are two publications that tell you more about on-the-job training.

If you would like to read either of these publications, ask your librarian or counselor to tell you how to obtain a copy.

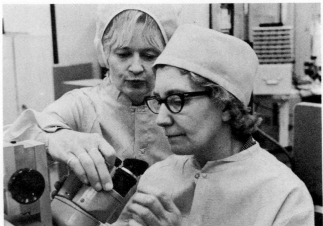

On-the-job training means that you learn your job after you are hired. (Top, courtesy United Nations/W. Watriss; bottom, Western Electric)

Liston, Robert A., *On the Job Training and Where to Get It*, Messner, New York, 1973.
Transferring Military Experience to Civilian Jobs, Manpower Administration, U.S. Department of Labor, Washington, D.C. 20210.

HOME STUDY AND CORRESPONDENCE COURSES

Another way of learning while you work is through home study—correspondence courses, educational television, or tape recordings. You can keep your job and work at your own pace when you study at home. It sounds easy, but it takes self-discipline and a strong desire to complete your courses.

The National Home Study Council says that in 1979 there were between 3 and 4 million persons taking correspondence courses. These courses may lead to college credits, certificates of performance, or just plain personal improvement. Here's how correspondence courses work.

You get your lessons in the mail. You do your assignments and then return them by mail. You take examinations under your own supervision and send each test back to the school that directs the course. An instructor grades each test and then tells you how to improve.

More than 200 institutions accredited by the National Home Study Council offer correspondence courses or independent study courses for credit, certification, or personal improvement. Many colleges and universities offer some academic subjects through correspondence or independent study courses.

Here are five publications from which you may learn more about home study and correspondence courses:

Directory of Accredited Private Home Study Schools, National Home Study Council, 1601 18th Street, N.W., Washington, D.C. 20009.
Guide to Independent Study Through Correspondence Instruction, National University Extension Association, 1 Dupont Circle, Suite 360, Washington, D.C. 20036.
Looking at Private Trade and Correspondence Schools, American Personnel and Guidance Association, Inc., 1607 New Hampshire Avenue, N.W., Washington, D.C. 20009, 1972.
Thomson, Frances Coombs (ed.), *The New York Times Guide to Continuing Education in America*, Quadrangle, New York, 1973.
Wellman, Henry, *Teenager and Home Study*, Rosen Press, New York, 1971.

MANPOWER DEVELOPMENT TRAINING PROGRAMS

With so many ways of learning, it might surprise you to learn that millions of Americans have no jobs, no skills, and few chances to take advantage of one of the programs you have been exploring. The federal government tries to help these Americans find useful work through a number of manpower development training programs. The Job Corps, the Concentrated Employment Program, Public Service Employment, the NAB Program, the Work Incentive Program, and Comprehensive Employment Training Act (CETA) programs are some of the federal efforts to help jobless people.

These programs provide basic education, classroom instruction, preapprenticeship training, or on-the-job training. Whenever jobs are provided, these are temporary in nature. The government hopes they will prepare people for other jobs in private business and industry. Your local CETA sponsor or your state employment service office is the best source of information about such programs. Ask your counselor for help in locating one of these sources.

LEARNING WITH MILITARY HELP

The military services offer many opportunities for working and learning at the same time. Through the military you might learn a trade or a skill, complete high school, or obtain a college education.

Skills and Trades

Most of the skills that you can learn in a vocational school, a technical institute, or a community or junior college may be learned in the military.

You can become an apprentice and get business and technical on-the-job training while you are in one of the military services.

The Army, Navy, Air Force, Marine Corps, and Coast Guard use complex equipment. Many of the jobs they offer call for a great deal of training and skill. And many of these jobs are similar to jobs in civilian life. The chance to learn one of these jobs is an important reason why many young people join one of the military services. In fact, much of the armed forces recruiting information now relates military and civilian jobs.

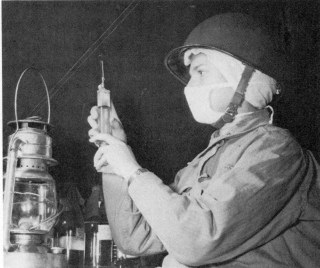

The military services offer many opportunities for working and learning at the same time. (Top, courtesy United States Navy; center, U.S. Army Photograph; bottom, Army News Features)

One way the military services try to interest you in joining them is to guarantee you the job and the training you want before you join. The Air Force is an example. Among the jobs it is willing to guarantee are the following:

- Aircraft electrical repairer
- Air traffic control radar repairer
- Carpentry specialist
- Construction equipment operator
- Dental specialist
- Electrician
- Electronic computer systems repairer
- Helicopter mechanic
- Jet engine mechanic
- Medical laboratory specialist
- Medical service specialist
- Operating room specialist
- Precision measuring equipment specialist
- Radiology specialist
- Radio relay equipment repairer
- Reciprocating engine mechanic
- Refrigeration and air-conditioning specialist
- Telecommunications control specialist

The Air Force guarantees training for more than 100 skills. The Community College of the Air Force offers training and on-the-job experience in seven schools of applied aerospace sciences. Students may use their records from such a program to get college credits, or they may use their training in the program to equal apprenticeship experience. They may also use their records to show employers that they have the skills needed to do certain jobs.

The Army, Navy, Marine Corps, and Coast Guard have similar training programs.

If you join a military service and sign up for one of the training programs, you will receive pay while you are studying. You will also qualify for an educational benefits program to which you and the Armed Forces can contribute money which you can use to continue your education when you leave the military service.

Off-Duty Study

You can use your off-duty time to study by correspondence or in classes on your base or ship. The United States Armed Forces Institute (USAFI) offers courses at the elementary, high school, technical, vocational, and college and university levels. Advanced courses are often offered to students by colleges and universities through the USAFI. There are more than 800 USAFI courses, including courses in communications, humanities, mathematics, science, social science, and technical and vocational training.

Taking a USAFI course is like studying at home. You study in your spare time and take examinations when you are ready. Most colleges and technical training programs will accept the credits you earn from USAFI courses. This gives you a head start when you transfer from the USAFI to a nonmilitary school. Most USAFI courses are taken by one person alone, but some military bases conduct USAFI courses in classes.

Many military bases have education centers and officers who specialize in helping people to take courses in nearby civilian schools that will lead to high school and college diplomas. If a person in a military service decides to attend classes at a local civilian school during off-duty hours, the government may pay up to 75 percent of the tuition.

A Word of Caution

Even when a military service guarantees a certain kind of training, you must remember that the guarantee is good only if you pass an aptitude test and other tests for that training after you join. If you fail these tests, the service may assign you to some other job.

Military services are not allowed to refuse to train women for certain jobs, but it is still very difficult for women to get training in many jobs that are usually held by men. Young women who are interested in joining a military service in order to learn a job skill should find out what kind of tests they must take. They should also find out how many women are doing the job that interests them in the service they are thinking about joining. Once they do that, they should talk to some of these women to find out how they got the training they wanted.

Military Scholarships and Academies

Young men and women who are willing to promise to serve 2 years in active military duty and 4 years in a reserve unit may apply for scholarships from the Reserve Officer Training Corps (ROTC). These scholarships are for 4, 3, or 2 years. Students must compete for them. Once a student wins an ROTC scholarship, the scholarship money will cover tuition, laboratory fees, books, certain other costs, and an allowance.

ROTC students must attend military science classes in college. They must also twice attend summer camps supervised by military personnel. When they graduate from college, they are commissioned as officers.

Instead of going to civilian colleges, a large number of people compete for the few carefully selected opportunities for admission to one of the military academies—the U.S. Military Academy at West Point, New York; the U.S. Naval Academy at Annapolis, Maryland; the U.S. Air Force Academy at Colorado Springs, Colorado; and the U.S. Coast Guard Academy at New London, Connecticut.

Standards for admission to these academies are high. You must be in good health and have good grades in mathematics and science. The academies offer courses similar to those in 4-year colleges. When students graduate, they receive baccalaureates in science in addition to military commissions. The graduates of the academies must then serve for at least 5 years in full-time duty in the service in which they have been commissioned.

For More Information

You may find out more about military schools from these publications:

Occupations, Military-Civilian Occupational Source Book, July 1975, U.S. Department of Defense, Washington, D.C. 20305.

United States Air Force Occupational Handbook, Air Force Recruiting Service, Randolph Air Force Base, Texas 78148.

United States Navy Occupational Handbook, Bureau of Naval Personnel, Washington, D.C. 20370.

The U.S. Army Career and Education Guide, Adjutant General, Department of the Army, Washington, D.C. 20325.

USAFI Catalogue and Correspondence Courses Offered by Colleges and Universities Through the United States Armed Forces Institute, Department of Defense, United States Armed Forces Institute, Madison, Wisconsin 53713.

Woman Marine, U.S. Marine Corps, Washington, D.C. 20380.

A Woman's World of Exciting Jobs, Army Recruiting Command, Hampton, Virginia 23369.

Your Life Plans and the Armed Forces, American Council on Education, 1 Dupont Circle, Washington, D.C. 20036.

34

DECIDING WHAT TO DO AND HOW TO PAY FOR IT

When you buy a new car, you usually start by deciding just what it is you want—sports car, compact, station wagon, 4-door, 2-door. You pin down exactly what type of car you are looking for. Then you shop carefully to be sure you find the best car available, the car that can give you the most value for whatever amount you are able to pay.

Next you get to the hard part—paying for what you have selected. This often requires careful planning and sometimes many sacrifices. Whether the sacrifices are worthwhile depends on whether you have done a good job with the first two steps. If you have made a wise choice as to the type of car you want to buy, and if you have carefully shopped for the best the market has to offer for your particular needs, then this last step—although sometimes difficult—is one you seldom regret.

BUYING A WAY TO LEARN

You should follow much the same procedure when you decide to "buy" a way to learn a skill or profession. First of all, you need to have a pretty good idea of what you want. Then it is very important to shop around carefully.

Make Comparisons

A good shopper always makes comparisons. In order to compare ways to learn a skill or profession, look over the catalogs or bulletins in your school library or counselor's office. Carefully study each school and each program. Talk to students attending the schools that interest you. Talk to workers who have learned their jobs in the programs you are considering. Talk to admissions officers of the schools that interest you. Talk to military service recruiters. Try to visit schools and programs, union offices, or employment offices. Compare what people say to you.

Ask Questions

Another thing a careful shopper does is ask plenty of questions. You should never worry about your questions sounding dumb. If you have questions, then they are important to you and should be answered.

The following 16-point checklist will help you to be sure you are asking all the right questions and taking everything into consideration.

1. Education after high school costs money and time. Make sure you have all the information you need about how to learn the job that interests you.
2. Make sure your abilities and talents, as well as your interests, match the job you choose.
3. Always investigate a school before you enroll in it. Your school counselor, your state's Department of Education, your local Chamber of Commerce, and your local Better Business Bureau can help you.
4. Try to visit schools that interest you. Are the classrooms, shops, and laboratories well lighted, properly ventilated, and fully equipped? Do the schools have demonstra-

There is almost always a way to pay for education and training, but it means asking questions and going to the library to do some research. (William E. Frost)

tion and teaching aids? Are the courses explained completely? Are you told which books, tools, and equipment you will need?

5. Compare the costs at one school with the costs at other schools. Make sure you include special fees and the cost of supplies, tools, and equipment in your comparison.

6. Check living arrangements. Do students live in dormitories, rooming houses, or apartments? Are meals provided? How?

7. What are the admission standards? Is a high school diploma required? Which courses are required? Is a high school equivalence certificate accepted?

8. Will the school give you credit for courses you have taken elsewhere or for knowledge or skills you have already acquired?

9. Never let anybody talk you into enrolling in a school or program. Ask your own questions. Make your own decisions. A good school or program will never try to talk you into enrolling.

10. Are there plenty of jobs for people trained in the skill that interests you? Will it be easy or hard to switch from this career to another one? To which careers can you switch? The *Occupational Outlook Handbook* published by the U.S. Department of Labor can help you answer some of these questions. It is probably available in your guidance office or school library.

11. Ask officials of the schools and programs that interest you how many students they have

helped place in jobs. Where are these students working? What are they being paid?

12. Never sign a blank enrollment contract or any other contract if you do not understand it. Ask your counselor to help you understand it first.

13. Is financial help available? What kind—scholarships, grants, loans, part-time work?

14. Do you understand the enrollment fee and the tuition and payment plan? Will the school or program refund part of your money if you do not finish the course or if you sign up and then do not attend? For example, many schools that teach truck driving and heavy equipment operation will not refund the flat fee you must pay in advance if you drop out after the first day.

15. Which unions, professional organizations, or accreditation agencies recognize the school or program in which you are interested? Always find out if the school or program is approved by your state's Department of Education or listed in one of the publications named in this chapter. If the school offers correspondence courses, find out if it is listed with the National Home Study Council, 1601 18th Street, N.W., Washington, D.C. 20009.

16. If you are thinking about colleges, go to your guidance office and get a copy of *How to Visit Colleges*, published by the National Vocational Guidance Association. This booklet tells you how to plan visits to colleges and other institutions in order to check them out.

PAYING YOUR WAY

Now comes the next step—paying for whatever it is you have selected as a way of learning.

There is almost always a way to pay for education and training. But you have to ask questions, read booklets, and fill out forms. You must put in time and effort, the same kind of time and effort you put into picking the right career.

Some people work part-time to pay for school and training. They find time to work during evenings, weekends, and vacations.

Some people borrow money from banks, from their families, or from special loan programs. The National Student Loan Fund is an example of a special loan program. It is run by the loan or student aid offices of colleges and other types of schools.

The Independent Order of Odd Fellows Education Foundation, P.O. Box 214, Connersville, Indiana 47331, lends money to high school graduates who want to attend technical institutes, business schools, barber and beauty schools, and other schools and courses. Students repay their loan little by little as they earn money.

Most states encourage banks to make loans to students at low rates by guaranteeing to repay the banks if they cannot get their money back.

Special scholarships and loans are available to physically handicapped persons. State vocational rehabilitation agencies will be able to supply information about these opportunities.

Special industry programs sometimes pay for the education of promising young employees.

Grants, awards, and scholarships are also offered by religious and professional organizations and national or local service groups.

The list that follows names organizations and publications that can tell you who may help you pay for your career education and training.

College Entrance Examination Board, 888 Seventh Avenue, New York, New York 10019.

Division of Student Financial Aid, U.S. Office of Education, Washington, D.C. 20202.

Feingold, S. Norman (ed.), *Scholarships, Fellowships, and Loans*, Vol. 5, Bellman Publishing, Cambridge, Mass., 1972.

Financial Aid for Higher Education, Superintendent of Documents, U.S. Government Printing Office, Washington, D.C. 20402.

National Commission for Cooperative Education, 52 Vanderbilt Avenue, New York, New York 10017.

The National Merit Scholarship Corporation, 990 Grove Street, Evanston, Illinois 60201.

National Scholarship Service and Fund for Negro Students, 1776 Broadway, New York, New York 10019.

Need a Lift, revised annually, American Legion, Americanism Division, 700 North Pennsylvania Street, Indianapolis, Indiana 46206.

The Student Assistance Handbook, Superintendent of Documents, U.S. Government Printing Office, Washington, D.C. 20402.

Getting It All Together

1. List all the examples of formal schooling after high school that you can think of.

2. List all the ways you can think of for learning and working at the same time.

3. What two basic programs are open to students who enroll in junior or community colleges?

4. In what industries is apprenticeship training most commonly found? Describe apprenticeship regulations about minimum age, basis for selection, amount of time needed for training, and wages.

5. What are some of the advantages and disadvantages of correspondence courses?

6. What are some ways to meet the financial cost of postsecondary training?

7. Agree or disagree: Everyone needs a college education. Why?

GETTING THE JOB

UNIT

GETTING YOUR RECORDS TOGETHER

Your goals in this unit are given in the following list:

To understand why money will be deducted from your paycheck for social security insurance

To understand federal regulations about the employment of minors and the need for an employment certificate (student work permit)

To understand why income taxes will be deducted from your paycheck and the use of a federal W-4 or W-4E form

To understand the need for individuals who are willing to serve as references for you when you apply for a job

You have examined various methods of determining the type of career that you might wish to enter. You have spent much time thinking about things that you like to do. You have completed and discussed the results of various interest inventories and aptitude tests with your teachers, guidance counselor, family, and friends. You have examined various occupations of interest to you. Your next step in finding a job is to get all your records together before going on job interviews or making formal job applications.

You will need to provide a good deal of information to potential employers. Much of this you already have, but you may have to get some of it. Here are some examples:

Sara recently applied for a job at the Day Drugstore. Mrs. Day asked Sara for a copy of her driver's license because part of the job is to deliver prescriptions to customers. But Sara did not have a driver's license, and so Mrs. Day could not hire her at this time.

Kevin recently applied to be an aide at the local hospital. Before he could be hired, Kevin had to show the supervisor his birth certificate. The hospital needed proof that Kevin was 16 years old. Kevin was unable to supply his birth certificate and didn't know where to get one.

When Molly applied for a job as cashier in a cafeteria, she was told to supply three personal references. But Molly didn't know what the manager of the cafeteria was talking about. She was unaware that this meant she needed to give the manager the names, addresses, and telephone numbers of three persons who would recommend her for employment.

This unit is concerned with the many records and forms you need to understand in order to obtain a job. You need to know about the social security system, including how to get a social security number. In addition, you must understand federal regulations about the employment of teenagers and how to get a student work permit. You also need to know about various forms: those used for income taxes, birth certificates, physical examinations, health certificates, special licenses or diplomas, and drivers' licenses. Finally, before applying for a job, you need to obtain personal references.

35

YOUR SOCIAL SECURITY CARD

When you start to work, you most likely will have to give part of your earnings to the social security system. Nearly 90 percent of all people employed in this country must pay a portion of their salary to this system. By law, the amount you are required to pay into the social security system must be deducted from your paycheck. Thus, part of your earnings automatically goes into social security. Your paycheck is reduced by that amount.

Many workers complain because social security is deducted from their paychecks. They do not understand the system, and they do not like being forced to pay for somebody else's retirement. But social security includes other benefits, too. It is important that you understand the reasons for the social security system. You may need to claim social security benefits even before you retire.

THE PURPOSE OF SOCIAL SECURITY

The social security system in the United States was first developed by the federal government and passed into law in 1935. Since then, many changes have been made in the law. No doubt, more changes will be made in the future.

The basic idea of the social security plan is quite simple. Employees and their employers each contribute to the social security system. This money is placed in three trust funds. One is for retirement and survivors' insurance. Another is for disability insurance. The third trust fund is for hospital insurance. This system is basically a plan to purchase insurance, except that you don't have a choice. You must contribute part of your earnings to the social security system.

If certain things happen in your life, you may be entitled to draw money from the social security system. You may retire from your job. You may become injured and be unable to work. You may lose a parent who has been supporting you.

Money from the three trust funds is used for six major purposes of the Social Security Act:

1. To provide unemployment insurance for people who have been laid off from their jobs so that they can continue to feed and support themselves and their families
2. To provide income upon retirement
3. To provide income for workers who become physically disabled and are unable to work
4. To provide income for children whose working parent dies while they are still dependent upon that parent for food, clothing, shelter, and education
5. To provide income to widows or widowers of workers when they reach the age of 65 (or, in some situations, the age of 62)
6. To provide health insurance for persons 65 or older

THE COST OF SOCIAL SECURITY

The amount you contribute into the social security system is based upon how much you earn. In 1980, those persons covered by social security contributed 6.13 percent of their earnings up to $25,900. Thus, once you earned $25,900, you stopped paying into the social security system. But, for most people, the 6.13 percent was paid on all of their earnings. If you worked 20 hours a week and were paid $3.10 per hour, your total earnings for the week were $62.00. Your contribution to the system was \$3.80 (6.13 percent times \$62.00). In 1981, the percentage contribution will be 6.65 percent on all earnings up to \$29,700. The percentage rate and the amount of earnings upon which the rate is computed is determined by the U.S. Congress and changes periodically. Employers, too, must pay an equal amount into the social security system. Thus, whatever you pay into the system must be matched by your employer.

An employee's earnings and contributions are reported to the federal government, and a record is kept by the Social Security Administration. When an individual's earnings stop because of disability, retirement, or death, cash payments are paid regularly to the worker or to the worker's family. When the worker dies, an amount is paid to the surviving spouse or to the person who paid the burial expenses. A more recent aspect of social security provides money for medical care to persons over 65. This part of social security is called Medicare.

UNEMPLOYMENT INSURANCE

Besides providing for a worker's old age, survivors, and disability, social security also provides for unemployment insurance. Today, this part of social security is handled mostly by the state governments, which get federal financial help.

Other aspects of social security are handled by the Social Security Administration of the federal Department of Health and Human Services.

Unemployment insurance is now administered by state governments. In most states, the cost of unemployment insurance is paid by the employer. The rate the employer pays is based upon his or her length of time in business and on the number and amount of claims of unemployment against the employer's business. If the employer has had to lay off a lot of employees or cut back permanently on the number of persons employed, the rate charged by the state government is considerably higher.

For example, most new firms are charged 1.4 percent of their taxable payroll for unemployment insurance. If there are few claims in the next two years, the rate may be lowered to a minimum of .07 percent of the employer's payroll. If there are many unemployment claims against the employer or if the state is experiencing unusually high unemployment, the rate may be assessed as high as 4.48 percent of the employer's taxable payroll. Some states also require employees to contribute a small percentage of their salaries for unemployment insurance.

Unemployment insurance provides some financial help to workers so that they can continue to support themselves and their families while

Figure 1 (Courtesy Social Security Administration)

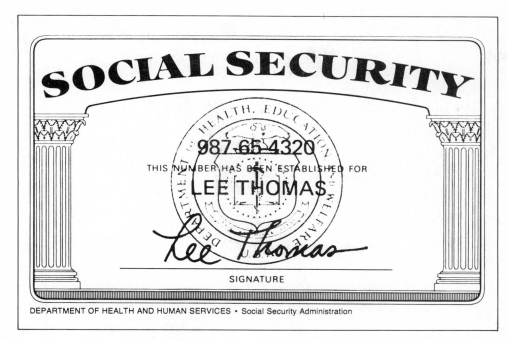

SOCIAL SECURITY

987-65-4320

THIS NUMBER HAS BEEN ESTABLISHED FOR

LEE THOMAS

SIGNATURE

DEPARTMENT OF HEALTH AND HUMAN SERVICES • Social Security Administration

Figure 2 (Courtesy Social Security Administration)

looking for other jobs. If you are laid off by your employer, you may qualify for unemployment. You need to contact the local office of your state's employment commission if you are laid off by your employer.

YOUR SOCIAL SECURITY CARD AND NUMBER

Every worker must have a social security card and number. Sometimes parents may get a social security card for their children while they are still young. In any event, you will need a social security card and number before you can be paid for any work you do. Nearly all job application forms require you to state your social security number. If you do not have a social security card, you should get one as soon as possible.

You can apply for a social security card at any social security office. The address and phone number for the social security office are listed in the phone book under the major heading, "United States Government." Application forms can often be obtained at post offices, banks, some large companies, state employment offices, selective service offices, and public welfare agencies. If there is no nearby social security office, you might apply at one of the other offices.

Figure 1 is a sample application form (Form SS-5) for a social security number that has been completed by Jennifer Mary Jackson. Be sure to print all information in dark blue or black ink. If possible, you should type the information.

Note that the application form has 14 numbers on it. Each number refers to important information needed by the Social Security Administration. The following guidelines should be helpful to you in completing your application form for a social security number. They are numbered to match the numbers on the form.

1. The first line asks you to print the full name you plan to use in your work. Be sure to print your first name, then your middle name or initial (or draw a line if you do not have a middle name), and then your last name. This is the name that will be used on your social security card.
2. Line 2 asks you to print the full name given to you at birth. You should check your birth certificate to identify the exact name that your parents gave you. They should have a copy of your birth certificate. If not, you can get a copy from the records office in the city or county where you were born.
3. On line 3, print the city, county, and state in which you were born. If you were born outside the United States, print the name of the country in which you were born.
4. Line 4 asks for your mother's full name at her birth. This refers to your natural mother.

*Contact any social security office
immediately if you:*

► lose your card—to get a duplicate card.

► change your name—to get a card in your new name.

► are unable to work because of a severe disability
expected to last a year or more.

► are 62 or older—to ask about retirement checks.

► are within 2 or 3 months of age 65, even if you
don't plan to retire—to sign up for Medicare.

U.S. Department of Health and Human Services
Social Security Administration
Form OA-702.1 (6-74)

Figure 3

If you were adopted, print your adopted mother's full name at her birth and print the word "adopted" after her name.

5. On line 5, print your father's full name. Include his first name, middle name, and last name. If your father is an adopted father, foster father, or stepfather, indicate this after his name, for example, "Jonas Michael Jackson, stepfather."

6. Print your date of birth. You may use numbers to identify this. For example, if you were born April 27, 1952, you may print "4/27/52."

7. Print your present age as of your last birthday. Even if you will be 16 next week, you should still indicate 15, since you are sending the form before your sixteenth birthday.

8. Place an X in the box that indicates your sex.

9. Place an X in the box that indicates your race.

10. This line asks you to indicate if you have ever applied for or had a social security, railroad, or tax account number. For most of you, the response will be no. But if you have ever filled out an application for a social security number, railroad number, or tax account number, you should check yes, even if you never received your card. If you check yes, give the name of the state and the approximate date on which you applied. If you did receive the card, enter the appropriate number here.

11. On this line, print your mailing address.

Provide the complete address, including number and street, city, state, and zip code. If you get your mail in the country and have no street address, show your rural route number and/or box number. If you get your mail at the post office, show your post office box number. If you are in a small town without street addresses or box numbers, simply indicate the town, state, and zip code. If you do not normally receive mail at the address you show, use an "in care of" address on this line.

12. Print the date on which you are mailing this application.

13. Print your telephone number, including area code, for example, 614–283-7129. If you do not have a telephone number, print the word "none." If you can use a neighbor's number, print the number with the word "neighbor" after it.

14. Write your name. Note that you do not print in this space. Write your name as you normally sign checks or the signature you use on school work or other forms.

Your final step is to mail the completed form to the nearest Social Security Administration office.

Some time later, you will receive two copies of your printed social security card. A sample card for Lee Thomas is shown in Figure 2. Note that the front of the card includes Lee's social security number and her name. There is also space for Lee to sign her name. On the back of the card, Figure

Department of Health and Human Services – Social Security Administration		DO		Form Approved OMB No. 72-R121

REQUEST FOR CHANGE IN SOCIAL SECURITY RECORDS
Read Instructions On Back Before Filling In Form. Print in dark ink or use typewriter.

SOCIAL SECURITY NUMBER
123-45-6789

1 IF REQUESTING NAME CHANGE *Print* NEW NAME HERE EXACTLY AS YOU WILL USE IT AT WORK
(First Name) JENNIFER *(Middle Name or Initial—if none, draw line –)* JACKSON *(Last Name)* JONES

DO NOT WRITE IN THIS SPACE

2 *Print* YOUR NAME AS SHOWN ON YOUR LAST CARD
(First Name) JENNIFER *(Middle Name or Initial—if none, draw line–)* MARY JACKSON *(Last Name)*

☐ DUP. ISSUED

3 DATE OF BIRTH *(Month)* *(Day)* *(Year)* 7/24/--

4 BIRTH DATE PREVIOUSLY REPORTED *(If different from Item 3)*

5 PLACE OF BIRTH *(City)* NASHUA *(County)* CHICKASAW *(State)* IOWA

6 SEX: MALE ☐ FEMALE ☒

7 MOTHER'S FULL NAME AT HER BIRTH *(Her maiden name)* KATHERINE JANE MOORE

8 FATHER'S FULL NAME *(Regardless of whether living or dead)* BERNARD JAMES JACKSON

9 DO YOU HAVE YOUR CARD? YES ☐ → IF "YES," ATTACH CARD ON BACK OF THIS FORM. IF "NO," ENTER YOUR NUMBER, IF KNOWN, IN NO ☐ → UPPER RIGHT CORNER AND COMPLETE ITEM 10.

10 WHERE AND WHEN DID YOU GET YOUR FIRST CARD? *(State)* IOWA *(Year)* 19--

11 YOUR MAILING ADDRESS *(Number and Street, Apt. No., P.O. Box, or Rural Route)* 117 FIFTH STREET, APT. 2B *(City)* WATERLOO *(State)* IOWA *(ZIP Code)* 50617

12 TODAY'S DATE 3/12/--

14 NOTICE: Whoever, with intent to falsify his or someone else's true identity, willfully furnishes or causes to be furnished false information in applying for a social security number, is subject to a fine of not more than $1,000 or imprisonment for up to 1 year, or both.
Sign YOUR NAME HERE *(Do Not Print)* *Jennifer Jackson Jones*

13 TELEPHONE NO. 515-773-2112

FORM OAAN-7003 (2-73)

Return completed application to nearest SOCIAL SECURITY OFFICE

Figure 4 (Courtesy Social Security Administration)

3, there are instructions that tell Lee all the reasons why she should contact any social security office.

The information on the back of the card, for example, indicates that you should contact a social security office if you are unable to work because of a severe disability expected to last a year or more, are 62 years of age or older, or are within 2 or 3 months of 65 years of age. If you lose your card, you should apply for a copy of it, not a new number. If you change your name, you should notify the social security office at once.

Figure 4 is an example of Social Security Form OAAN-7003. You should complete this form if you change your name or if you need to correct any information on your original card.

Since most of you will be applying for your first card, you do not need directions on how to fill out this form. If you do need to send this form to your social security office, provide all the information requested. Ask a teacher or someone at the social security office to help you.

Obviously, your social security number is very important. It is the major link between you, your employer, and your government. It is the key to any benefits you may be entitled to. You keep it for life and use it for many things: job applications, college examinations, insurance applications, military identification, marriage licenses, and even library cards. It is also your tax number and must be shown to anyone who pays you interest, salary, dividends, or wages.

You should memorize your social security number so that you can write it whenever asked without having to check your card. Place one copy of the card in a safety deposit box at the bank, in a safe at home, or someplace where it will not be lost or destroyed. Carry the other copy with you always. Your social security card is one of your most important possessions. Make every effort not to lose it.

36

UNDERSTANDING FEDERAL LAW AND EMPLOYMENT UNDER 18 YEARS OF AGE

This chapter will give you information that will help you determine whether or not you are legally allowed to work. Federal and state governments have passed laws that limit the types of work and the hours of work in which young people may be employed. It is important that you and your potential employer understand these laws and obey them in order to avoid possibly paying a fine. The laws discussed in this chapter must be followed in all parts of the country. In addition, many states have even stricter laws. In such cases, the stricter laws must be obeyed. You may wish to discuss your state's laws with your teacher or guidance counselor.

OCCUPATIONS IN WHICH AN EMPLOYEE MUST BE AT LEAST 18 YEARS OF AGE

The federal law referred to as the Child Labor Provisions of the Fair Labor Standards Act establishes 16 years as the minimum age of employment. A 16- or 17-year-old person may work in any occupation that is not considered hazardous by the federal government. A hazardous occupation is one that the government considers dangerous. If a job is considered hazardous, all employees in that occupation must be 18 years old or older. The only exceptions are agricultural occupations. Thus, persons under 18 may drive tractors and operate machinery on a farm.

At present, the federal government has declared 17 nonagricultural occupational areas as hazardous. In the following occupational areas, employees must be at least 18 years of age:

- Occupations in or about companies that manufacture or store explosives, such as shotgun shells, small-arms ammunition, blasting caps, or other such materials.
- Occupations in which one would be employed as an operator or outside helper of a motor vehicle, including such jobs as commercial bus driver, truck driver, and taxicab driver. There are some exceptions, such as driving a school bus. Of course, the 16- or 17-year-old must have a driver's license. Employment in other occupations in which one drives a motor vehicle only on occasion is permitted.
- Occupations in or about a coal mine. The following are exceptions: office work, repair work, groundskeeping, and other jobs located above the coal mine itself.
- Occupations in logging and all occupations in the operation of any sawmill, lath mill, shingle mill, or cooperage-stock mill. Exceptions include office work, repair and maintenance, and cleanup work.
- Occupations that involve the operation of power-driven woodworking machines, unless the person is enrolled in a school-approved apprenticeship or student-learner program.
- Occupations involving exposure to radioactive materials and to ionizing radiations.
- Occupations that involve the operation of freight elevators, cranes, hoists, high-lift trucks, and other kinds of power-driven lifting machinery.
- Occupations that involve the operation of power-driven metal forming, punching, and shearing machines (such as punch presses,

apron brakes, hammering machines, and guillotine shears). Exceptions may be made for apprentices and student-learners enrolled in school-approved work programs.

- Occupations in mining, other than coal, with similar exceptions as applied to coal mining, for example, office work and maintenance work.
- Occupations that involve the slaughtering, meat-packing, processing, or rendering of animals. Exceptions may be made for apprentices and student-learners.
- Occupations that involve the operation of power-driven bakery machines. This includes dough mixers, batter mixers, bread-cutting machines, dough-brake machines, and bakery-band saws.
- Occupations that involve the operation of power-driven paper-products machines. This includes wire stickers, band saws, die-cutting presses, and guillotine paper cutters. Exceptions may be made for apprentices and student-learners.
- Occupations that involve the manufacture of brick, tile, and such products.

- Occupations that involve the operation of circular saws, band saws, and guillotine shears. Exceptions may be made for apprentices and student-learners.
- Occupations that involve wrecking, demolition, and ship-breaking operations.
- Occupations in roofing operations. This includes installation of roofs, shingling, repair of roofs, installation of television antennas and ventilating equipment. Exceptions may be made for apprentices and student-learners.
- Occupations that involve excavation operations, such as digging trenches, office buildings, and tunnels. Exceptions may be made for apprentices and student-learners.

OCCUPATIONS IN WHICH 16- AND 17-YEAR-OLDS MAY WORK

Sixteen- and 17-year-olds may work in any occupation that is not included in the hazardous occupations listed above. According to federal laws, these persons may work at any time of the

All employees in jobs that are hazardous must be 18 years old. Can you name other jobs that are hazardous? (Courtesy A.T.&T.)

day or night. They may work as many hours a week as they or their employers wish.

All 16- and 17-year-olds must be paid the same wages as other employees working in companies covered by the Fair Labor Standards Act. The 16- and 17-year-olds must also be paid one and one-half times their regular pay for all hours worked over 40 hours a week. Any work over 40 hours is considered overtime. Thus, the government has determined that employers will pay one and one-half times the workers' salary for any overtime hours.

Regardless of age, each employee must be paid a minimum wage in companies covered by the act. A *minimum wage* is the least amount of money an employer is obligated to pay his or her employees. For example, if the minimum wage is $3.10 an hour, it is illegal for an employer to pay you $3.00 an hour. All employees working in companies covered by the act must be paid a minimum of $3.10 per hour for the first 40 hours in a week. They must be paid $4.65 for any time over 40 hours (overtime) in the regular workweek.

Thus, suppose you are working for a chain department store. Your wage rate is $3.10 per hour. Because of a sale, you were asked to work 8 hours a day for 6 days last week. You, therefore, worked 48 hours. Your pay would be determined by figuring 40 hours at $3.10 per hour, for a total of $124.00. The 8 hours of overtime would be figured at $4.65 per hour, for a total of $37.20. Thus, your total pay would be $161.20 ($124.00 plus $37.20).

Generally, companies that are covered by the Fair Labor Standards Act include:
- Retail or service establishments that have an annual volume of sales or business of at least $325,000 (including restaurants, hotels, and motels)
- Laundry and dry-cleaning establishments
- Construction establishments
- Federal, state, local, and interstate governments and agencies; hospitals; nursing homes; and public and private preschools, schools, and colleges
- Homes or institutions employing full-time domestic-service workers
- Other establishments with an annual volume of sales or business of at least $325,000

Sixteen- and 17-year olds may work in any job that is not included in the hazardous occupations. (Courtesy Good Samaritan Health Services)

There are instances where employers may pay less than the minimum wage. For example, many people are employed in jobs where tips are included as part of their pay. A special provision has been made for employees who receive tips of more than $30 a month on a regular basis. In such cases, the law provides that tips which are actually received may be credited up to 40 percent of the minimum wage. Therefore, employees who are entitled to $3.10 an hour and receive an average of $1.24 or more an hour in tips must be paid $1.86 per hour by the employer. Even if the employee averages $5 an hour in tips, the employer must pay him or her $1.86 (60 percent times minimum wage of $3.10). If the employee averages less than $1.24 an hour in tips—say $1 an hour—then the employer must pay him or her $2.10 an hour so that the employee's earnings always equal at least the current minimum wage. If the employer plans to take advantage of the provision in the law to pay less than minimum wage, the employee must be so notified in advance and must be allowed to keep all tips.

There are other instances in which companies in these categories may pay less than the minimum wage of $3.10 per hour. Full-time students may be employed on a part-time basis in retail and service establishments, agriculture, and institutions of higher education at 85 percent of the minimum wage of $3.10 per hour. Full-time students you may only be paid $2.64 per hour. Also, full-time students who are employed as part of a school-sponsored educational program may be paid 75 percent of the minimum wage. This includes students who are enrolled in cooperative education, work-study, and work-experience programs. Thus, if you are enrolled in one of these programs; you may only be paid $2.33 per hour. Special certificates to permit this lower pay are issued through the Wage and Hour Division of the United States Department of Labor. Such certificates may be issued only to lower the pay for full-time students. They cannot be used to reduce the federally determined minimum pay rate for 16- and 17-year-olds who are not full-time students.

Failure to pay the minimum wage rate and overtime pay may result in civil or criminal actions against employers. If so, employees may receive back pay and have full wages restored.

OCCUPATIONS IN WHICH 14- AND 15-YEAR-OLDS MAY WORK

In recent years, federal laws have been relaxed to permit the employment of 14- and 15-year-olds in certain occupations. Thus, if you are 14 or 15, you may be employed under certain conditions in the following types of occupations:

- Office and clerical work, including the operation of office machines.
- Cashiering, selling, modeling, art work, work in advertising departments, window trimming, and comparative shopping.
- Price marking and tagging by hand or by machine, assembling orders, packing, and shelving.
- Bagging and carrying customers' groceries or other merchandise.
- Cleanup work, including the use of vacuum cleaners and floor waxers and ground maintenance. This does not include the use of power-driven mowers or cutters.
- Kitchen work and other work involved in preparing and serving food and beverages, including the operation of such machines as dishwashers, toasters, dumbwaiters, popcorn poppers, blenders, and coffee grinders.
- Service-station work and other work on cars and trucks involved with dispensing gasoline and oil, cleaning and polishing cars, and courtesy service. However, 14- and 15-year-olds may not work with pits, racks, or lifting machinery.
- Cleaning vegetables and fruits and wrapping, sealing, labeling, weighing, pricing, and stocking goods when performed in areas that are not near where meat is prepared and that are outside freezers or meat coolers.

In order to be employed in any of these occupations, however, it must be shown that the employment will not interfere with your schooling, health, or well-being.

The federal government has put some limits on the employment of 14- and 15-year-olds. If you are 14 or 15, you may not be employed:

- During school hours, unless there is a written agreement signed by the federal administrator of the Bureau of Work Programs and filed at the place of employment. Your principal also must sign the form, saying that such work will not interfere with your schooling, health, or well-being.
- Before 7 a.m. or after 7 p.m. from Labor Day through May 31. From June 1 through Labor Day, you may be employed between the hours of 7 a.m. and 9 p.m.
- More than 3 hours a day on school days.

- More than 18 hours a week during weeks when school is in session.
- More than 8 hours a day on nonschool days.
- More than 40 hours a week during weeks when school is not in session.

Of course, 14- and 15-year-olds cannot work in any of the occupational areas listed earlier in which 16- and 17-year-olds could not work. In addition, 14- and 15-year-olds may not work in manufacturing, mining, processing, operating, cleaning, or repairing power-driven machinery, or as public messengers. In work connected with warehousing, storage, transportation, communications, public utilities, or construction, 14- and 15-year-olds may work only in sales or office jobs.

Fourteen- and 15-year-olds must also be paid the minimum wage established by federal law. If they are full-time students, they may be employed at 85 percent of the minimum wage if the employer has an authorized certificate to do so. A 14- or 15-year-old who is enrolled in a school-approved work-study, work-experience, or cooperative education program may be employed at 75 percent of the minimum wage. Again, the employer must have an authorized certificate to do so.

OCCUPATIONS IN WHICH PERSONS UNDER AGE 14 MAY WORK

Under federal law, persons 13 years of age and younger may work in certain kinds of employment. These persons may perform the following types of employment for wages:

- Deliver newspapers to consumers
- Baby-sit
- Act or perform in motion pictures, theaters, and radio and television productions
- Work for parents in jobs other than manufacturing, mining, or nonagricultural hazardous occupations

Federal law permits children 13 years of age and younger to work as actors in television productions. In what other jobs may children this age be employed? (© 1980, Children's Television Workshop)

• Agricultural work outside school hours, unless the work is hazardous. In that case, the person must be 16 years old.

The federal minimum wage law does not cover persons under 14 years of age. In some states, there are laws about the wages to be paid to persons under 14 who are employed on farms or in entertainment. Anyone under 14 who plans to work in one of these areas should contact the State Employment Commission to get information about minimum wages.

THE EMPLOYMENT CERTIFICATE

In most states, anyone under 18 years of age has to get an employment certificate before being employed. The name of this document is not the same in every state. Some states call it a work permit, an age certificate, or working paper. In some states, only those under 16 need an employment certificate. This certificate is usually a one-page document that is issued and signed by a public official. It certifies the person's age and is proof that the employee is old enough to work. It also alerts the employer that the person cannot be asked to do jobs that have been declared hazardous by the federal government. Therefore, it protects both employees and employers.

The procedure for getting this form differs from state to state. In some states, a minor must have a written promise of a job, in which the employer describes the hours and the type of work. This letter and proof of age are then taken to a public official who issues a certificate. In some states, the school principal (or a representative) also must supply proof that the student is in good standing at school before the person can get an employment certificate. This usually means that the student has a good attendance record and passing grades. In other states, the minor can receive an employment certificate and then look for a job. A job is not needed before a certificate will be issued. Talk with your guidance counselor, teacher, or principal about the procedures that apply in your state.

In nearly all states, you will need to show the certifying officer your birth certificate. This is to prove that you are old enough to work. If you do not have a birth certificate, a baptismal record may be accepted. Over half the states also require a statement from a doctor showing that the young worker is fit to work. Some states also ask for school records. And some require the consent of parents. Because these rules differ so much, it's a good idea to learn what your state's requirements are.

Most states have a specific person who issues employment certificates for each locality. This person is usually employed by the State Department of Labor or the State Department of Education. Your school counselor or someone in the school office can help you find out who issues certificates in your area.

Once you have received your work certificate, make sure you give it to your employer to keep on file.

37

COMPLETING TAX FORMS

It seems we are never finished with forms. You now need to become familiar with the forms used by your employer to deduct federal and state taxes from your paycheck. Yes, besides the social security tax, you also must pay federal income tax. And in many states, you also must pay a state income tax.

FEDERAL INCOME TAX

It is important that you understand why we have taxes and how our tax money is spent. We pay federal taxes to provide money for services we expect from our government. Federal tax money is spent for the following 13 categories:

National defense: Of each tax dollar spent by the government, 29 cents is used for national defense. This includes military assistance abroad, atomic energy, and support for the military services in this country. Over half the defense budget goes for the salaries and wages of people employed by the Department of Defense, including soldiers and sailors as well as research scientists.

International affairs: Of each federal dollar, 1.5 cents is set aside for foreign economic assistance, operation of embassies abroad, and foreign information activities.

Space research and technology: Nearly 1 cent of each government dollar is used for manned space flights and other space activities.

Agriculture and rural development: Of each government dollar, 2 cents is used to give income protection to farmers, to encourage greater farm productivity, and to help ensure enough food for people in this country and abroad.

Natural resources and environment: Although tax money has not been set aside for natural resources and environment concerns, the government gets money from offshore oil lands and timber sales to provide funds for pollution control, flood control, conservation projects, and for buying and maintaining of parklands.

Commerce and transportation: 5 cents of the tax dollar is spent on the development of the national transportation system. This includes highway construction, operation of federal airways, airport construction, shipbuilding, and subsidies to the Post Office Department.

Community development and housing: To help meet the nation's housing needs, the federal government makes grants and loans to state and local governments for community development. It also subsidizes low- and medium-income housing. This amounts to about 2 cents of every tax dollar.

Education and manpower: About 4 cents of the federal dollar is used to help elementary and secondary schools provide special programs in vocational education, special education, reading, and so forth. Help is also given to college students in the form of loans and grants.

Health: Through Medicare and Medicaid, the government helps pay the medical bills of elderly and poor people. In addition, the government provides funds for medical research, training in health occupations, con-

The federal government spends part of our tax money to make loans to state and local governments for housing. On what else does the federal government spend tax money? (Courtesy HUD Challenge)

struction of health facilities, and prevention and control of health problems. These programs amount to about 8 cents of the government dollar.

Veterans: About 5 cents of the federal dollar is spent to provide a variety of services and benefits to those who served in the Armed Forces.

General revenue sharing: About 2 cents of each federal dollar is shared with state and local governments for use as they see fit.

Net interest: Nearly 8 cents of each government dollar is used for interest payments on bonds and savings certificates held by the public.

General government: About 2 cents of each dollar is spent on general government programs, including collection of taxes and enforcement of federal laws.

All the services we have come to expect from our government are costly. The largest percentage of the money for these services is collected through federal income taxes.

Graduated Tax System

A main feature of the United States tax system is that each person pays according to his or her ability. This is called a *graduated*, or *progressive*, *tax system*. It means that the percentage that each taxpayer must contribute to the government increases as that person makes more money. Because of this feature, your tax as a beginning or part-time worker will be fairly low.

The federal income tax system operates on a pay-as-you-go basis. Therefore, your employer must withhold income tax from your paycheck in each pay period. The amount that is deducted varies from 14 to 70 percent. The percent, of course, depends on how much money you make. For most beginning workers, the amount is 14 percent.

One factor used to determine the amount of tax withheld in each pay period is the number of exemptions claimed by an employee. Each individual is allowed one exemption of $1,000. This means that the employee may earn $1,000 before having to pay any taxes. Persons 19 years old or younger and full-time students of any age are allowed to claim themselves as an exemption. One of their parents or a guardian may also claim them as an exemption, provided, of course, that the parent or guardian contributes more than half of what it costs to support the student. All young, beginning workers are allowed one exemption of $1,000. In most cases, a parent may also claim a $1,000 exemption if the young person still lives at home and depends upon the parent for most support.

Form W-4

When you first begin your job, you will need to fill out a federal form W-4, entitled "Employee's Withholding Certificate." A sample W-4 form, as completed by Gerald Wayne Moore, is shown below.

You will need to complete a W-4 form in the same way. Note that you print your full name, complete home address (number, street, post office box number, or rural route number), and city or town, state, and zip code. You then must print your social security number. (By now, you should know this number without having to look at your card.) Next, a check mark shows your marital status. You then fill in the number of exemptions you are claiming. For most of you, the number will be "1." If you are married and your spouse does not work, the number will be "2" (one exemption for you and one for your

spouse). If you have children, the number should include an exemption for you plus one for each child. If your spouse does not work, the number should include an exemption for you, your spouse, and each child.

In the next line, you may ask that your employer deduct more than is required. This is usually done by persons who are concerned that not enough money is being deducted. They are afraid they will owe the federal government additional tax money at the end of the year. For most of you, this will not be the case. Therefore, this line should be left blank. You then will need to write your signature. Be sure to include the date.

There is a special situation in which you can avoid having any federal tax deducted from your paycheck. If you did not pay any federal income tax last year and do not expect to make more than $3,300 this year, you should write "exempt" on the third line of the W-4 form. This form is especially useful for students who are working part time and do not expect to earn $3,300 for the year.

STATE INCOME TAX

Besides the federal income tax, which is deducted from an employee's paycheck, many states also collect a state income tax. The amount that is deducted from the paycheck varies from state to state. In most states that collect the tax, the

---

Form **W-4**	**Employee's Withholding Allowance Certificate**
Department of the Treasury Internal Revenue Service	This certificate is for income tax withholding purposes only. It will remain in effect until you change it. If you claim exemption from withholding, you will have to file a new certificate on or before April 30 of next year.

Type or print your full name GERALD WAYNE MOORE		Your social security number 480 - 32 - 9617
Home address (number and street or rural route) 207 "H" STREET, S.W.	**Marital Status**	☒ Single ☐ Married ☐ Married, but withhold at higher Single rate
City or town, State, and ZIP code HASTINGS, NEBRASKA 39261		NOTE: *If married, but legally separated, or spouse is a nonresident alien, check the single block.*

1 Total number of allowances you are claiming		*1*
2 Additional amount, if any, you want deducted from each pay (if your employer agrees)	$	
3 I claim exemption from withholding (see instructions). Enter "Exempt"		

Under the penalties of perjury, I certify that the number of withholding exemptions and allowances claimed on this certificate does not exceed the number to which I am entitled. If claiming exemption from withholding, I certify that I incurred no liability for Federal income tax for last year and that I anticipate that I will incur no liability for Federal income tax for this year.

Signature ▶ *Gerald Wayne Moore*   Date ▶ *January 12* , 19 _ _

Detach along this line

(Courtesy Internal Revenue Service)

amount is also graduated, or progressive, as in the federal system. In other words, the more money you make, the larger the percentage of your total paycheck that is withheld for state taxes.

Money that is collected from individual workers is sent to the state treasury to pay for many state government services. Some costs for public education in elementary and secondary schools are provided by state government. A large percentage of the cost of state colleges and universities and vocational or technical schools is provided by state tax money. Other services include state highway construction, welfare, housing, health, police and highway patrol, legal assistance, scholarships for students, and so on.

Because of the many differences among the states in how they collect tax money, no tax form is included here. Some states permit exemptions. But the amount that can be earned before state income tax is collected varies from state to state. Contact your school counselor or your State Department of Taxation for further information about state taxes.

38

GETTING ADDITIONAL FORMS, DOCUMENTS, AND INFORMATION

By now, you know that you may have to supply your employer with an employment certificate or a work permit. You know that you will need to provide a social security number. You also will need to complete an "Employee's Withholding Certificate." In addition, you probably also will need to complete a state income tax withholding form.

Now we're going to look at five additional documents or forms that you should know about: birth certificate; physical examination form; health certificate; special diploma, skill certificate, or license; and driver's license. We will also talk about another kind of document that can be

most important in helping you win a job: references from other people.

BIRTH CERTIFICATE

When you were born, one of your parents had to sign a document certifying your name, parentage, and date and place of birth. This information then was used to register your birth with the Vital Statistics Division of your State Department of Health. A Notification of Birth Registration, or *birth certificate*, then was mailed to your parents.

Your birth certificate is one of the most valuable documents you will ever have. It should

Local Record of Birth

MONROE COUNTY HEALTH DEPARTMENT
Bloomington, Indiana

THIS IS TO CERTIFY, That our records show................ **Sandra Leone Lynch**
Name of Child

was born in ....**Bloomington**............ , Indiana, on **February   9,   1971**
Month   Day   Year

Richard Lee Lynch   **Genevieve Ann Buechner**
Name of Father   Maiden Name of Mother

Iowa   **Wisconsin**
Birth Place of Father   Birth Place of Mother

Recorded locally in Book No.^Ch 50 Page No. ^24   **February 23, 1971**
Date Record Was Filed

Signed *George Williams M.D.*
County Health Officer

SEAL

Date   **April 5, 1971**

Figure 1

always be kept in a safe place. This document is used to prove your name, age, birthplace, and parentage for many purposes. It is used in registering for school and maintaining school records, applying for jobs, getting married, establishing your identity, getting a passport, and so on. You should always be able to find your birth certificate. A sample birth certificate is shown in Figure 1.

If you cannot find your birth certificate, write to the Vital Statistics Division of the State Department of Health in the state in which you were born. They usually can produce a copy of your birth certificate. When writing for a copy, be sure to include your full name given at birth, place of birth, parents' names, and date of birth. Sometimes the city or county government offices in the community in which you were born will also have a copy of your birth certificate. If you do not have a copy of your birth certificate, you should get one. You may not need it now, but you will soon need it for job applications.

PHYSICAL EXAMINATION REPORT

Many jobs require that you have a thorough physical examination before you begin working.

```
                  PHYSICIAN'S STATEMENT
                         FOR
                    EMPLOYEES OF
            MONTGOMERY COUNTY SCHOOL BOARD
          P. O. Box 29, Christiansburg, Va. 24073


    "As a condition to employment and requisite to continuation
    thereafter, every public school employee . . . . shall annually
    submit a signed statement by a licensed physician stating said
    employee appears free of communicable tuberculosis. Such cer-
    tificate is to be based on recorded results of those X rays, skin
    tests, and other examinations, singly or in combination, as
    deemed necessary by the physician and which have been performed
    within the twelve months' period immediately preceding the be-
    ginning of the school session."
                               —Code of Virginia, Section 22-249


       ┌─────────────────────────────────────────────────────┐
       │  Note to Physician: This statement shall be at the expense  │
       │  of the individual employee, except for school bus drivers  │
       │  and cafeteria workers.                                │
       └─────────────────────────────────────────────────────┘


    Name of employee _____
    School or department of employment _____

    In compliance with State law, on basis of examinations, I hereby
    certify that the above-named appears free of communicable
    tuberculosis, this date.

    (Signed) _____
    Address  _____
    Date     _____


    I am a licensed physician in _____ (State or District),
    United States.
```

Figure 2

Sometimes the company will pay for this examination, but usually you will be expected to have the examination at your own expense. Most companies have a physical examination form to be filled out by the examining doctor. Take this form to your doctor, have an examination, and ask the doctor to return the form to the company.

HEALTH CERTIFICATE

For some jobs, a health clearance form, or health certificate, is needed. A *health certificate* states that the individual has no serious contagious diseases, such as tuberculosis or venereal disease. Persons who work in hospitals, medical institutions, public schools, government offices, and libraries often must get a health certificate. The health certificate in Figure 2 certifies that the person is free of tuberculosis.

DIPLOMA, SKILL CERTIFICATE, OR LICENSE

For many occupations, one must be licensed or have special training or certification. Many professional occupations have this requirement, including nurses, doctors, teachers, and lawyers. Many other occupations also require a certificate, diploma, or license. Typical occupations include hair styling, plumbing, practical nursing, and taxicab driving, as well as many trade occupations. You should carefully investigate the requirements in your state for the occupation in which you wish to work. Find out whether a special license or certificate is needed in order to be employed legally in the occupation. Applications for certificates are shown in Figure 3.

As well as licenses, diplomas, or certificates that are required for specific occupations, many schools also issue diplomas or some type of certificate to show satisfactory performance in a special area. For example, many schools issue awards to those who can type 40 words a minute or take shorthand at 60 words a minute. Some schools issue a certificate to students who pass a unit on safety in trade or industrial arts classes. Many give awards for outstanding ability in local, district, or statewide competition among vocational youth organizations. These awards or certificates are important and can be used when applying for a job.

If you have received an award for outstanding performance in classroom or competitive activity, you should let potential employers know about it. For example, if you have a certificate showing that you have passed an in-school typing test at 60 words a minute, that would impress any employer who wants a clerk-typist or a secretary. Or perhaps you've won a national or local honor award in distributive education for winning a national contest in saleswork. This award would help impress any employer who is interested in hiring someone with selling skills.

Figure 3

DRIVER'S LICENSE

Many occupations require an employee to have a driver's license. Anyone over 18 years old can be employed in an occupation that involves driving a motor vehicle. Persons 16 and 17 years old cannot be employed in such occupations. However, they may be employed in jobs that require them to drive once in a while. Such an occupation might be a department store job that includes occasional home deliveries of merchandise. It would also include work in a drugstore that occasionally requires the delivery of prescriptions. Another example is work in a furniture store that occasionally requires one to drive to a customer's home and help unload furniture. If you want to get such a job, find out at once about your state's requirements for getting a driver's license.

In most states, one can get a driver's license at the age of 16. Some states require an individual to complete a program of instruction in driver's education before applying for a driver's license.

Requirements for a driver's license vary from state to state. Discuss your state's requirements for getting a driver's license with your school's driver education teacher or inquire directly at your local motor vehicle department office.

REFERENCES

You should consider one final aspect in the job of getting your job records together. You will need to list references from whom your potential employer can get information about you. A *reference* is a person who can provide information about your ability, responsibility, job performance, personality, or anything that is important to the job. It is your responsibility to name such references who are willing to provide information to your potential employer.

In making a list of references, consider the following types of people: former employers (if you have held a job for pay); ministers, rabbis, or

---

1776 West Road
Greenville
South Carolina 27382

July 13, 19—

Ms. Sadie Hawn
Good Hope High School
2781 Lore Avenue
Greenville, South Carolina 27382

Dear Ms. Hawn:

This is to request permission to use your name as a reference in my application for various jobs.

I will soon be graduating and am now in the process of finding a job. I hope to find employment in some aspect of business. I will be applying for jobs in retailing and hotels and motels.

If you prefer not to have your name used as a reference, please contact me at 983–6214. I thank you for your consideration and time in this matter.

Sincerely

Samuel J. Adams

Figure 4

priests; persons employed in various professions, such as physicians or teachers; your school counselor or vocational education teacher; persons for whom you have done a lot of baby-sitting, yard work, housecleaning, or any other type of job; close friends or neighbors of your parents who know your personality and abilities; or anyone else who is familiar with you and your abilities. You should not include anyone who is related to you or who is a close friend.

Before you give their names to a potential employer, be sure to ask your references whether or not they will mind giving information to a potential employer who might contact them. You may ask each person by telephone, in person, or in writing. Tell these people that you are planning to apply for a job and ask whether they would permit you to use their names as references. Tell them an employer may call or write to them about you. If they agree to do this for you, feel free to include their names on application forms.

You may not be able to contact each potential reference in person. In that case, write the person a letter. Figure 4 is a letter Samuel J. Adams wrote for that purpose.

Follow these guidelines in preparing a letter to a potential reference:

- Keep the letter short.
- In the first paragraph, state your reason for writing.
- Indicate in the second paragraph the types of jobs for which you are applying. The person should know the type of work in which you are interested in order to judge your abilities in that area.
- In the third paragraph, ask the person to contact you if he or she does not want to be named as a reference.
- If possible, type the letter with a clear, dark ribbon and on good-quality typing paper. Be sure there are no smudges or poorly erased corrections on the letter. Have the letter checked by your teacher or parents for correct spelling and grammar. You should type or write the letter on one side of the paper only.

Remember to be sure to follow up and thank your references for any support they give to your job application. Let the persons know the results of your application.

Getting It All Together

1. What are the six major purposes of the Social Security Act?

2. What are eight services of the federal government paid for through income taxes?

3. What are three uses for state income taxes?

4. List five occupations in or near your community for which you must be 18 years of age or older before being employed.

5. What are five types of people you should consider for references?

6. Why should you contact references before using their names?

7. Why should you contact references after they have answered questions from a potential employer?

UNIT

12

PREPARING TO GO JOB HUNTING

Your goals in this unit are given in the following list:

To identify local job opportunities by using school and community resources

To organize facts about yourself and to write a job resume

To write letters of job application

To groom yourself to increase the chances of getting a job in your chosen occupational area

You have examined your likes and dislikes, aptitudes, and skills. You have more or less decided on two or three occupational areas in which you would like to work. And you have gotten your records together. You now have a social security card, an employment certificate or a student work permit, if needed, and any other documents required in your community for job application.

You now should be ready to identify opportunities for employment. The employment may be part time, full time, or short term. You may be interested in a part-time job after school or on weekends. A short-term job might be good during summers or school vacations. Seasonal work, such as work in orchards, farm work, or shoveling snow might be available. Or you may be about to leave school and are ready for full-time employment.

In this unit, you will take a close look at some sources of information about job openings. You will study the kinds of information you should consider when you find out about a job opening.

How to put a summary of the facts about your life together in a resume will be discussed. This personal resume is a good method to present yourself to potential employers. It is a way of telling potential employers about you before you actually talk with them in a personal interview.

The whys and hows of writing letters of application for job openings are also discussed. And some information about how to groom and dress for successful job interviews is given.

Very soon you will begin to apply for job openings in your community or elsewhere. Knowledge about identifying job opportunities, writing job resumes and letters of job application, learning how to groom yourself to increase your chances of getting a job will better your chances for getting a job in your chosen occupational area.

39

IDENTIFYING LOCAL JOB OPPORTUNITIES

There are companies and individuals in your community who are interested in employing part-time or temporary workers. There are also companies and individuals who need full-time employees. There are likely to be companies and individuals interested in employing young people with interests and abilities similar to yours. It is now time for you to locate these companies and individuals.

Keep in mind that it may be somewhat difficult to find a job in your community. The chances of employment depend partly on the size of the community, the number of businesses or individuals who are hiring, and the number of young people looking for work at the same time as you.

If you are in a rural area or a small town, you may have to limit your search for a job to farm or orchard work, yard work, or work in a small business. This may be especially true if you are looking for part-time or seasonal employment. Of course, there will be more opportunities for different kinds of employment if you live in a city. However, even in a city, the number of people looking for jobs may prevent you from getting the one you most would like. So do not be too rigid about the type of work you will accept.

Do try to find a job in your area of interest. If that is not possible, consider accepting a job that is related to what you really would like to do. The experience you get while working will help you to find later employment. Plan to do well on this job. Take it seriously. Your employer will be helpful as a future job reference.

There probably is a job in your town or city for you. It is up to you to find it. To do so, you may need to use many school and community resources. Finding a job can be hard work. How-ever, if you are really interested in working and are willing to make the effort to find a job, your reward can be satisfying employment.

Many people in your school and community will have information about jobs. When first trying to locate a job, you should talk with teachers and counselors in your school. Throughout the school year, they are often in contact with people and companies looking for part-time or temporary employees. They also usually know about full-time openings. You should also check other sources, such as employment agencies and newspaper help-wanted ads.

When you get information about job openings from various sources, write on a card the information you need to apply for the job. Be sure to get such information as:

- The name of the company
- The address of the company
- The telephone number of the company
- The type of business
- The name and title of the person at the company to contact
- Any special information that you have learned about the job
- The name of the person who told you about the job

You should make up a card whenever you learn about an interesting job. Then, when you get ready to apply for a job, you will have all the information you need.

Here is an example of a card and the job information obtained from a school counselor:

```
Shell Oil Station
2101 South 13th Street
Milwaukee, Wisconsin
612-762-4310

Contact: Pat Litchfield, Owner

Type of business: Service station

Work about 20 hours a week after
school, $3.45 an hour. Apply in person
between 4 and 6 next Saturday after-
noon.

Information from J. R. Frank, school
counselor
```

IN-SCHOOL SOURCES FOR IDENTIFYING JOB OPPORTUNITIES

Within your school, there should be at least three of the following sources of information about local job opportunities:

- Guidance counselors
- Cooperative education or work-experience coordinators
- Vocational education teachers

Whenever you learn about an interesting job opening, write on a card the information you need to apply for the job. What information should you be sure to get? (Courtesy Adelphi University)

The Guidance Department

Nearly every school has at least one guidance counselor. Often, employers interested in part-time or temporary workers will call the school guidance office to get the names of available students. Business and industry persons are also in contact with guidance counselors when they have full-time openings. Most guidance counselors keep a list of companies and individuals who contact them. Therefore, your school's guidance counselor may be able to help you quickly locate an employer who wants someone with your interests and abilities.

Cooperative Education and Work-Experience Programs

Many schools now offer a combination school and work program, often called *cooperative education.* Many of you may be enrolled in a cooperative program or a similar type of program. In such programs, students go to school part time and work part time. Most of these students are enrolled in vocational education courses that are related to their jobs. The teacher of such a vocational education course also supervises the part-time employment of students. The teacher spends part of the day in the business or industrial community. This person, called a coordinator, is an excellent source of information about jobs in your community.

Some schools offer another type of cooperative education known as a *work-experience program* or work-study program. Whatever the program is called, its teacher or coordinator usually helps students find jobs. If you are not already enrolled in such a program, you should discuss your community's job opportunities with the program coordinator.

Most cooperative education programs are designed for students who are interested in specific occupational areas. For example, students interested in becoming office workers will be enrolled in a cooperative program in office education. Students interested in careers in marketing or other business occupations will be enrolled in a cooperative program in distributive education. Students interested in trade or industrial areas will be enrolled in a cooperative program in industrial training. Many schools offer similar programs for students interested in health occupations, agricultural occupations, or home economics.

The coordinators of the various cooperative education programs in your school should have up-to-date listings of job opportunities in their occupational areas. Contact the coordinator of the cooperative education program in the occupational area in which you wish to work. She or he probably will talk with you about enrolling in a cooperative education program. The coordinator also may help you find a job in your occupational area.

The Vocational Education Department

Nearly all schools have teachers who are concerned mostly with training young people for various jobs. These teachers are called *vocational education teachers.* They teach students in such subject areas as agriculture, business, distribution, home economics, health occupations, and trade and industrial occupations.

Many vocational education teachers will know about local job opportunities. They may keep a file of individuals and companies who are interested in employing students part time as well as full time. If you have enrolled in a vocational education course, talk with your teacher about locating employment in your subject area. If you are not enrolled in one of the vocational education courses, ask to speak with the director of vocational education in your school or ask your guidance counselor for help.

Other School Departments or Services

Your school also may have other departments or services to help you locate employment. This may include a part-time or temporary job as part of the program or service. Some of these will have special requirements about where you can work or how many hours you can work. Check with your guidance counselor or vocational education teacher to learn whether your school offers any of the following programs and to see whether you are qualified:

- Work study
- Work experience
- Neighborhood youth corps
- School job placement service
- Manpower development training program
- Work opportunity program
- Work exploratory career education program
- Work release program

OUTSIDE SOURCES FOR IDENTIFYING JOB OPPORTUNITIES

Your community will have many sources to help you locate employment. The help-wanted section of your local newspaper, your State Employment Service, private employment agencies, community social service organizations, employment offices of local businesses or industries, and your own friends or relatives are all good places to start your search for a job.

Newspaper Help-Wanted Section

Nearly every newspaper has a classified section that includes help-wanted advertisements. This is the section of the paper where employers list their job openings. Besides full-time jobs, the help-wanted section usually includes a list of part-time and temporary jobs. These advertisements often give a brief description of job requirements, as well as information about how to apply. Here are two such advertisements that recently appeared in the classifed section of a newspaper:

```
           CASHIER

Immediate, part-time em-
ployment; must have had
bookkeeping; experience;
excellent pay. Apply in
person between 4 and 6
p.m. Tuesday.

   BANTAM FOOD MARKET
   1701 Marguerita Road

    Equal Opportunity
         Employer
```

```
      SERVICE STATION
         ATTENDANT

Part time; must have ca-
reer interest and some
training in auto mechan-
ics. Phone 373-9217 to
arrange interview.

   BUD'S GAS STATION
   207 Knoxville Drive, SE
```

The people who work at the State Employment Service can give you employment tests or interest inventories. (Magnum Photo)

Both these jobs are appropriate for a student-worker. Note that both jobs require some special training. The job as a cashier requires bookkeeping. The job at the service station requires a career interest and some training in auto mechanics. You should also note that both advertisements give information about how to apply. If you wanted the job as a cashier, you would have to apply in person. If you wanted the job as a service station attendant, you would have to call to arrange for an interview.

Your newspaper has similar advertisements. Look for advertisements that describe jobs in which you are interested and for which you are qualified.

State Employment Service

In or near your community is an agency known as the *State Employment Service.* One main function of this government agency is to help people find employment. The people who work at the State Employment Service will know of job openings in your community. If necessary, they will give you employment tests or interest inventories. These tests or inventories should help you identify occupational areas for which you are qualified and those in which you might possibly be interested.

The State Employment Service is financed by public funds. There is no cost to you for using

its services. Many State Employment Services also have a Youth Opportunity Center, which helps 16- to 21-year-olds find employment. The State Employment Service is an excellent source of help for young people trying to find jobs.

Private Employment Agencies

Many communities also have *private employment agencies.* Private employment agencies differ from the State Employment Service in that they charge a fee for their services. Sometimes the fee is paid by the person seeking a job. This usually involves a registration fee, which entitles you to see the agency's list of job openings. If you accept a job from this listing, you usually must pay a certain percentage of your salary to the agency. Sometimes employers pay the fee charged by the private employment agency if they hire someone who was referred by the agency. If you plan to use a private employment agency in your job search, be sure you understand the financial arrangements before you accept any interviews or pay out any money.

Private employment agencies usually are listed in the classified section of the newspaper under the heading "Employment Agencies." Some agencies serve all occupational areas. Others specialize and locate jobs only in certain occupations, such as office workers, editors, salespeople, temporary laborers, and so on. Here is an example of a newspaper advertisement for an employment agency that helps find jobs in any occupational area:

```
      SERVICES UNLIMITED
      EMPLOYMENT AGENCY

      "Where the Jobs Are"
      A Most Reasonable Fee

           345-8801
       1512 Downtowner Rd.
           Franklin
```

Private employment agencies are also listed in the yellow pages of the telephone directory under the heading "Employment." The following advertisement was taken from the yellow pages of a telephone directory:

```
CAREER MANAGEMENT

Nationwide Personnel
System for Business
Men and Women

Executive — EDP — Sci-
entific — Technical —
Office — Commerical —
Administrative — Sales
   — Marketing

For information call
552-7575
204 N. Main St.
```

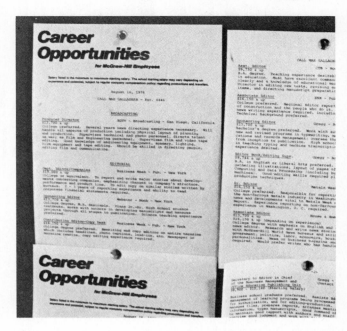

Many companies have bulletin boards outside their personnel offices that list job openings. (Dennis Purdy)

Community Social Service Organizations

In many communities, there are *social service organizations* that help young people locate part-time employment. The Young Men's Christian Association, the Young Women's Christian Association, and the Young Men's and Young Women's Hebrew Association often have sponsored job application classes for young people. They also have helped place young people in temporary or part-time jobs. The Urban League, the United Fund, the Alliance of Businessmen, the Alliance of Black Businesspersons, the Federation of Women's Clubs, and other local community groups have often helped young people locate employment by sponsoring a free employment service. By calling any of these organizations in your community, you can learn whether the organization does help young people find jobs.

Company Employment Offices

The employment offices of businesses and industries in your community provide information about job openings in their firms. Most business and industrial companies that employ many people have a separate employment office or personnel department. The people working in these departments usually know about immediate and near-future job openings for part-time, temporary, and full-time employees. They also can tell you about the qualifications needed for such jobs. Most companies list a separate telephone number for the employment office or personnel depart-

ment. Look in the telephone directory under the name of the company. By calling this number, you can contact someone who has appropriate job information.

Many companies also have bulletin boards outside their personnel offices. These list job openings in the company. Some companies also use billboards to list their openings. These billboards usually are located so that they can be seen by people who drive by. By regularly reading such bulletin boards and billboards, you can learn about job openings in many companies.

Friends and Relatives

Friends and relatives often know about job openings where they work. They also can give you valuable information about how to apply for jobs at local companies.

Many firms are especially interested in employing relatives of their present employees. Sometimes a clause in the union contract with management says that the children of present employees will get priority in hiring. Discuss these possibilities with your parents or guardians, your relatives, and friends.

CHAPTER 40

PREPARING A RÉSUMÉ

When you have found one or more jobs you would like to get, your next step is to prepare a résumé, or personal data sheet. A *résumé* is a summary of the facts about you that are important for the job you are seeking.

The main purpose of the résumé is to present a potential employer with all the facts about you that relate to the job you seek. The résumé should make the employer feel good about you because you have collected and organized all the important facts. This saves the employer from having to dig out the same facts.

Preparing your résumé is one of the most important parts of your job hunt. If it is done carefully and thoroughly, it will save time later when you apply for a job. A well-organized and complete résumé contains nearly all the information usually needed on employment application forms. If you have the résumé with you when you apply for a job, it will be easier to provide the information on the application form. You also should send a résumé with your letters of application, if such letters are needed to arrange job interviews.

It is important that your résumé be neat and well organized. It should be an advertisement of yourself to potential employers.

ORGANIZING FACTS ABOUT YOURSELF

A résumé should organize the important facts about you into seven categories:

1. Personal information
2. Position applying for
3. Education
4. Skills
5. Activities and interests
6. Work experience
7. References

Personal Information

The résumé should start with the following facts about you:

- Your full name
- Your complete address, including street number, street name, apartment number (if applicable), city, state, and ZIP code
- Your telephone number, including area code
- Your social security number

You may include other personal information, but it is optional:

- Your age
- Your height
- Your weight
- Your marital status

Position Applying For

The section on the position you are applying for should be specific enough so that the person reading your résumé can tell what type of job you want. Examples might be auto mechanic, bookkeeper, clerk-typist, salesclerk, cashier, bellhop, secretary, keypunch operator, repairer, waiter, or carpenter.

Education

In the education section, you should list all the schools you have attended, placing the last one first. List the dates of attendance at each school and indicate whether you graduated or received a diploma. If you have attended many schools, it is best to write a summary statement. For example:

```
                        RÉSUMÉ

                 GENEVIEVE ANN CARLSON
                 2072 Norris Drive, Apt. 18-E
                 Pine Bluff, Wisconsin 70652
                  Telephone: 612-723-1268
          Social Security Number: 497-62-8369
```

Figure 1

"Attended six different elementary and junior high schools in the Los Angeles, California, area." You might then give information about the high school you attended or are attending. If you have not graduated, state when you expect to do so.

You also should list any special courses or programs that especially qualify you for the job you seek. Finally, include any special awards or honors you received while in school.

Figures 2 and 3 show two examples of how this section might look on your résumé.

Skills

In the skills section, you should list skills that especially qualify you for the job you want. Also, list any machines that you can operate that might

be used on this job. For example, if you are applying for a job as a secretary, this section might appear as shown in Figure 4. If you are applying for a job in a restaurant, you might list your skills as shown in Figure 5.

Activities and Interests

For the activities and interests section, list all in-school and out-of-school activities in which you have participated. List your special interests and hobbies, too.

This is an important section, especially if you have not had much skill training in school or previous work experience. This section will give potential employers an idea about your participa-

```
EDUCATION

Attended the New Hampton Community High School, New Hampton,
Iowa, from August 19-- to present; currently enrolled in the
distributive education program; rank in the top 20 percent of
my class; anticipate graduating in June 19--.

Attended Roosevelt Junior High School, Charles City, Iowa,
from August 19-- to May 19--; received the eighth-grade diplo-
ma in May 19--.

Attended St. Mary's Catholic Grade School, Charles City, Iowa,
from August 19-- to May 19--.
```

Figure 2

```
EDUCATION

Attended Northside High School, Bloomington, Indiana, from
August 19-- to June 19--; completed several courses in graphic
arts and printing; graduated in June 19--.

Attended J. F. Kennedy Junior High School, Fort Wayne, Indiana,
from August 19-- to May 19--.

Attended several elementary schools while father was in mili-
tary service, from August 19-- to May 19--.
```

Figure 3

```
SKILLS

Typing: 50 words a minute
Shorthand: 80 words a minute
Filing
Operation of mimeograph machine, dictaphone, spirit dupli-
cating machine, rotary calculator, and ten-key adding ma-
chine
```

Figure 4

```
SKILLS

Cooking
Baking
Operation of cash register, adding machine, and grill
```

Figure 5

tion in school and community activities. It will also tell employers about your interests and hobbies. When considering whether to hire inexperienced workers, employers are interested in the applicants' interests and activities.

This section of your résumé might appear as shown in Figure 6.

Work Experience

If you have work experience, a section covering that should be added to your résumé. If you have not had previous work experience, leave this section out of your résumé.

Young people often forget to list two areas of work experience on their résumés that should be included: baby-sitting and paper routes. Although baby-sitting is not a regularly scheduled

work situation, it does show an employer that you can handle responsibility. It tells the employer that other people have trusted you and have confidence in you. You might indicate this aspect of your work experience as shown in Figure 7. If you have worked as a carrier for a newspaper, you might indicate this on your résumé as shown in Figure 8.

References

You already know about references, the people who know you well enough to recommend you for employment. Individuals whom you might ask to serve as references are present or former teachers; guidance counselors; former employers or supervisors; a priest, minister, or rabbi; friends or neighbors of your parents; or other individuals in your community who know your ability to perform on a job. You should list at least three persons who have agreed to serve as references for you. It is important to ask their permission before putting their names on the résumé. When you do list their names on the résumé, alphabet-ize them by last names. Be sure to put each individual's title with the name, such as Mr., Dr., Mrs., Miss, or Ms. Also, be sure to include their occupations and their work addresses.

Figure 9 is an example of how this section might look on your résumé.

Figure 6

```
ACTIVITIES AND INTERESTS

Enjoy participating in sports, especially bowling and tennis

Enjoy working with young children and am currently teaching
Sunday school

Participate in the following youth organizations at school:
Vocational Industrial Clubs of America (past historian, cur-
rently vice-president), Camera Club, and Student Government
Association

Participate in several church activities, sing in the choir,
member of the Methodist Youth Fellowship

Member of the school newspaper staff, play drums in the band

Enjoy stamp collecting, sewing, and playing bridge
```

Figure 7

```
WORK EXPERIENCE

For the past 3 years, I have been baby-sitting about three times
a week for a number of families in my neighborhood. Besides
taking care of children, I have helped prepare meals and clean
house.
```

Figure 8

```
WORK EXPERIENCE

Newspaper carrier for the Washington Post, June 19-- through
June 19--.
```

Figure 9

```
REFERENCES

Rev. Chris Gardner, pastor, First Christian Church, 2104 South
Clemson Drive, Chesapeake, Virginia 27036

Mr. Samuel Morgan, industrial arts teacher, Martin Luther
King High School, Norfolk, Virginia 24201

Mrs. Elizabeth Strelka, homemaker (neighbor), 436 Hilling-
ton Way, Madison, Wisconsin 95020
```

RÉSUMÉ

BILLIE MAY JONES
1317 Fifth Street, Apt. 218
Jackson, Mississippi 24612
Telephone: 213-729-8516 (Neighbor's)
Social Security Number: 513-78-2132

POSITION APPLYING FOR

Work in a zoo

EDUCATION

Attended Herbert Hoover High School, Jackson, Mississippi, from September 19—— to present; enrolled in agricultural education classes; anticipate graduating in June 19——.

Attended several elementary and junior high schools in Jackson, Mississippi, from August 19—— to May 19——.

SKILLS

Training in various aspects of the care of animals

ACTIVITIES AND INTERESTS

Enjoy all work with animals

Participate in the following youth organizations at school: Future Farmers of America (currently parliamentarian), Biology Club, Conservationist Club

Member of Shallow Creek 4-H Club and Christian Youth Fellowship

REFERENCES

Mr. Jim Cosby, agricultural education instructor, Herbert Hoover High School, Jackson, Mississippi 24612

Dr. Muriel Jackson, physician, Medical Clinic, 205 North Avenue, Jackson, Mississippi 24612

Mrs. Donna King, homemaker (neighbor), 319 Fifth Street, Jackson, Mississippi 24612

Figure 10

PUTTING THE FACTS TOGETHER

Once you have organized all this information about yourself, it is simple to write the résumé. To prepare the final copy of your résumé, follow these guidelines:

- Use a typewriter that has a good, clean ribbon to type the résumé.
- The résumé should be typed by a good typist. There must be no incorrectly typed or misspelled words on the résumé. All typing errors should be corrected neatly.
- Use good-quality bond paper. Avoid using mimeograph or duplicating paper or any paper that has lines printed on it.
- Arrange the résumé neatly on the page with a 1-inch border around the typing. (As the examples of résumés in this chapter are not on regular-size sheets of paper, the border is less than 1 inch.) It should be typed on only one side of the paper. If you need more space, use a second sheet of paper.
- Be certain there are no smudges or dirt on the final copy.
- After the résumé is typed, check the accuracy of all information one more time.

Finally, make several copies of your résumé. If the copies are of good quality, they can be given to more than one potential employer. But if you give the résumé to more than one employer, be sure the section entitled "position applying for" is appropriate for all of them. If it isn't, you will need to rewrite and retype your résumé to fit each position for which you apply.

The résumé shown in Figure 10 might serve as a model for you when you prepare yours. Note that Billie Jones has had no work experience, and so she has left that item off her résumé.

41

WRITING A LETTER OF APPLICATION

In most situations, once you have gathered your forms and completed your résumé, you are ready to contact potential employers. However, sometimes you may need to write a letter of application to the company before you can apply in person for the job. In nearly all such situations, you should write a brief letter of application and enclose a copy of your résumé to provide personal information and your qualifications.

It will be necessary to write to the company before you can apply for a job if:

- The company requests a letter of application.
- The company is located a great distance from your home.
- You want to ask about possible job openings but a personal contact is not yet appropriate.

THE COMPANY REQUESTS A LETTER OF APPLICATION

Companies often will place an advertisement in the help-wanted section of the newspaper asking applicants to write to the company. Sometimes the name of the company is not given. This type of advertising is called a blind ad, as shown:

```
        MAIL CLERK
Person  to  pick  up  and
deliver   mail.   General
clerical  duties,  includ-
ing   answering   routine
correspondence. 20 hours
a  week.  Write  Box  XY,
Kansas City 25173
```

Note that the company wants all applicants to write to a post office box. If you were interested in this position, you would have to write a letter of application.

Some companies ask for a letter of application in order to eliminate unqualified applicants. For example, the skills involved in carrying out the job duties may require an employee to write correctly. In the position described above, the employee must be able to answer correspondence that the company receives. Thus, the person must be able to write letters that are grammatically correct. To be sure that the person who is hired can write well, the company asks for a letter of application. It is important that anyone applying for this job know how to write a good letter of application.

Companies also may request a letter of application for clerical or typing positions. Here is an example of this type of newspaper advertisement:

```
Fast,   accurate   typist
for part-time employment.
Straight copy typing: at
your home or in our office.
Type  letter  to  Johnson
Printing Company,  North
Hamilton Drive,  Johnson
City
```

For clerical or typing positions, the company asks that the letter of application be typed in order to evaluate the accuracy of the typist before the person is hired.

Some Rules to Follow

When a company asks for a letter of application, follow these few rules:

- Keep the letter short. It is best to enclose a résumé to provide personal information and your qualifications.
- Indicate in the first paragraph your reason for writing. An example might be: "Please consider me as an applicant for the position of mail clerk as advertised in the Sunday edition of the *Kansas City Star*."
- Indicate in the second and third paragraphs the outstanding features of your résumé and why you are especially qualified for the position as advertised. This part of your letter should show that you are different from the other applicants. Avoid bragging, but do point out your qualifications. Figure 1 is an example of the second and third paragraphs that might be written in response to the blind ad for a mail clerk.
- The fourth and final paragraphs should be brief and should tell the reader how to contact you. This is the "action" part of the letter. It should encourage the employer to contact you for an interview. You also should include a statement thanking the employer for considering your application. Figure 2 shows an example.
- Your letter should be checked carefully for correct spelling, grammar, and style. Your teachers or parents can help you make sure that the letter is correct.
- The letter should be typed correctly on good-quality bond paper. There should be no smudges or poorly erased corrections on the letter. It should be proofread carefully after typing to be certain there are no errors.

Below is a help-wanted advertisement, and Figure 3 is a letter that might be written to respond to it.

```
            WANTED
Travel  agents  for  new
office  to  open  soon  in
Portsmouth. Outgoing, at-
tractive    personalities
needed. Write:

     P.O. Box 2119
     c/o this paper
```

Do not be too surprised or disappointed if you do not receive a reply to your letter of application. On the average, employers respond to about one out of every five such letters. The important thing is that you write a good letter that spells out your qualifications for the job.

THE COMPANY IS AT A GREAT DISTANCE

At some time in your life, you may need to write a letter of application to a company that is distant from your home. It is often necessary for people to change locations. Parents move, and spouses get transferred. You may graduate from school and decide to move somewhere else to work. It is

Figure 1

The enclosed résumé gives some details of my courses and activities at Radford High School. I have completed courses in typing and business English. I have received A's and B's in both courses. During my senior year, I will take typing and advanced English.

My résumé also details such experience as my serving on the school newspaper staff. Recently, I have been promoted to feature editor. I enjoy writing, and I feel that I do it well.

Figure 2

I am most interested in this job and would like to discuss my qualifications with you. Please call me at 816-951-1241 to arrange for an interview. Thank you for considering my application.

77 Locust Valley Road
Portsmouth, Delaware 21327
May 1, 19--

P.O. Box 2139
c/o Auburn Newspaper
2119 Oak Street
Portsmouth, Delaware 21327

To Whom It May Concern:

Please consider me an applicant for the travel agent position
you recently advertised in the Auburn newspaper.

I am most interested in this position because I enjoy talking
to and working with people. As you can see from the enclosed
résumé, I've enjoyed belonging to clubs and participating in
activities where I can be with people. I feel as though I get
along well with people, and have had special training in human
relations and communications in my high school distributive
education program.

You will note on the résumé that I have been working part time
at the Big Dime Variety Store for the past year. Since I will
be graduating next month, I am interested in locating full-
time employment. Your advertisement especially appealed to
me because of my interest in people and my interest in travel.

I hope to be able to discuss my qualifications with you. Please
call me at 302-723-8166 to arrange an interview. Thank you
for considering my application.

Sincerely,

Kelly C. Mason

Enclosure

Figure 3

a good idea to write ahead to companies in the city you are moving to and ask about employment opportunities.

The rules for writing this letter of application are basically the same as those for answering a company's request for a letter of application.

The main differences will be in the wording of the first paragraph. Remember that the first paragraph gives the reader your reason for writing the letter. Since your reason is the fact that you are moving to this city in the future, you should say this in your first paragraph. Examples of two possible first paragraphs are shown in Figures 4 and 5.

The rest of the letter would be much like the one written to a company that asks for a letter of application. The second and third paragraphs should describe your special qualifications and training for the job you want.

The fourth paragraph should tell the employer when you will be available for an interview and should request an interview. The paragraph also should thank the employer for considering your application. An example is shown in Figure 6.

Send a copy of your resume with the letter. The letter should be correctly and neatly typed on good paper, and it should be accurate in all details.

OTHER LETTERS OF APPLICATION

There are other situations in which you may need to write a letter of application. Sometimes a friend or relative may tell you about a job with a company and suggest that you write to its personnel manager. And some companies may be too small to have an employment office. You may need to write a letter of application to the manager or owners of the company because that is the only way to contact them.

Again, the basic principles of the letter of application are the same, regardless of the situation. The first paragraph should indicate who told you to write to this person or describe why you are writing. The second and third paragraphs should outline your qualifications. And the fourth paragraph should ask for an interview and thank the potential employer for considering your job application.

SOME WARNINGS

Letters of application should be written only when you cannot telephone the company or visit it in person. The letters should not be copied from textbooks. Rather, textbook letters should be used as guides. A letter of application has to reflect your own personality and way of communicating. The letter should be respectful but conversational. A resume should always be sent with the letter. Finally, the letter should be correctly written and neatly typed.

```
I recently have learned that my father is being transferred
and that we soon will move to Chicago. I am interested in locat-
ing a part-time job while completing my senior year of high
school and am hopeful that your company has a position avail-
able as a salesclerk.
```

Figure 4

```
In 2 months, I will graduate from high school and am planning
to move to Kingsport. I am interested in obtaining a position
with your company as a machinist.
```

Figure 5

```
I will be in Chicago on Tuesday and Wednesday, May 27 and 28.
Would it be possible to have an interview with you on either of
these two dates? I look forward to hearing from you. Thank you
for considering my application.
```

Figure 6

42

GROOMING FOR THE INTERVIEW

Probably no part of job hunting is as difficult to talk about as the area of grooming and appropriate dress. Years ago, the rules for job applicants were cut-and-dried. Women wore conservative dresses, hats, and gloves. Men wore suits, white shirts, and ties, and they were clean-shaven and short-haired. Today, however, a freer attitude exists. It is difficult to arrive at guidelines for grooming and dress that fit all job application situations.

Some companies are especially concerned about how their employees look. The people who hire new employees in these companies only interview applicants who look as they want their employees to look. For example, many employers will never consider a man with a beard or a woman who wears heavy makeup. You should find out what sort of grooming and dress are required or expected of employees in your chosen occupational area and in the company to which you apply.

There are several reasons why employers are particular about how a person looks when applying for a job. You should understand two of these reasons at this stage of your career.

First, many employers believe that how a person is groomed and dressed for the interview reflects that person's attitude. They see such things as a sign of how the person will behave on the job. First impressions are important. If you give a bad first impression because of inappropriate dress or careless grooming, you probably will not get the job. Potential employers will feel that if you don't care enough to clean up and dress for the interview, you probably won't care enough to do good work if hired. Whether you agree with this reasoning is not the point. The employer

doing the hiring has the right to choose whoever he or she wants to employ among equally qualified applicants. If the employer is interested only in neat-appearing employees, and if you want the job, you'd better be neat when you apply.

Second, many empoyers must care about how their employees look. Many companies make their money through day-to-day contacts with the public. They depend upon their employees to sell the firm's products and services. They cannot hire employees whose appearance might offend customers. These same employers are probably concerned about the image their firm presents to the public. They feel that this image is affected by how their employees look. They will not hire anyone who might give a bad impression. Whether or not you agree, many companies will not hire someone with inappropriate dress or grooming.

The major guideline that you should follow in preparing for a job interview is to have a clean body and to wear clothes like those worn by employees who work at the kind of job you seek. Such preparation is called grooming. *Grooming* is all those things that one can do to make one's body neat, clean, and pleasantly presentable. Some things about our appearance, such as height and physical traits, are beyond our control. But we do have control over our general physical condition, our cleanliness, the condition of our hair and skin, makeup, and oral hygiene.

YOUR PHYSICAL CONDITION

If you are in poor physical condition now, there is probably little you can do in the short time left before you apply for a job. However, now is a

Because many companies make their money through day-to-day contact with the public, they must care about how their employees look. (Courtesy United Airlines)

good time to think about your physical condition.

Weight Problems

You will need to consider your weight. The combination of a person's bone structure and height determines the correct basic weight. If you are overweight or underweight, you should do something about it. Unfortunately, people are often discriminated against on the basis of weight when applying for jobs. Weight problems often lead to additional medical problems, and so you should consult a physician who specializes in nutrition for help in reaching your best weight.

Proper Nutrition

In normal daily eating, it is important to choose correct foods to maintain a healthy body. Unfortunately, young people often neglect their nutrition. Heavy diets of soft drinks, hamburgers, pizza, spaghetti, and sweets eventually will cause some problems. While you are young, you probably can overcome the effects of an improper diet fairly easily. But as you grow older, the effects will begin to show. Three good meals a day will add greatly to your physical well-being.

The following is a brief description of the four food groups suggested by nutritionists at the United States Department of Agriculture as important for a balanced diet:

The milk group—includes milk, cheese, and ice cream, which provide calcium for bones and teeth, proteins, vitamins, and some carbohydrates. Everyone under 20 should drink a quart of milk a day; everyone over that age, at least a pint. Ice cream and cheese may be substituted for part of this requirement.

The meat group—includes beef, veal, lamb, pork, variety meats (such as liver, heart, and kidney), poultry and eggs, and fish and shellfish. The high protein value of this food group builds body tissues—muscle, blood, skin, and hair. In addition, meats provide necessary minerals and vitamins. You should have two or more servings of these foods each day.

The vegetable-fruit group—contains nearly all the vitamin C your body requires for strong gums and body tissues and more than half the vitamin A for growth, normal vision, and healthy, clear skin. Everyday you should eat four or more servings of fruits and vegetables. One of them should be a prime source of vitamin C, such as grapefruit, oranges, broccoli, or green peppers. For vitamin A, try dark green and deep yellow vegetables, apricots, cantaloupe, or mangoes.

The bread-cereal group—includes breads, cooked cereals, macaroni, spaghetti, noodles, and whole-grain, enriched, or restored rice. You should have a minimum of four servings of such energy foods each day because they offer a combination of worthwhile proteins, minerals, and vitamins that effectively balance the nutrients in the other three groups.

Proper Exercise

Another suggestion for maintaining or improving your physical condition is to exercise regularly. Unfortunately, most people get too little exercise. Automobiles have eliminated the need for walking or running. Thus, for most of us, exercise is no longer a "natural" thing. We have to work at it and include it into our daily routines.

You should set some time aside each day for a short workout. You can do this in the morning right after you wake up, after work, or before going to bed. For a daily routine, you will need to spend only 10 or 15 minutes on traditional exercises: touching the toes, pushups, situps, knee bends, lifting the legs, chinups, and so on. Consult one of the many available handbooks and exercise programs and begin a physical conditioning

To maintain or improve your physical condition, set some time aside each day for exercise. (Courtesy Bicycle Institute of America, Inc.)

program. You are sure to look better, feel better, and be healthier.

Sleep

Another part of your daily routine that greatly affects your physical condition is sleep. To do well in school or at work, you need enough sleep. During sleep, your body repairs damaged cells and grows new ones, and your mind relaxes from the day's work and tensions. Most people need 7 to 8 hours of sleep each night. Many require more, and a very few may need less.

CLEANLINESS

The physical condition of your body is the framework upon which you build your personal grooming program. However, if you want to be acceptable to a potential employer, and if you want to stay employed, you must give careful attention to keeping your body clean.

Today, there is a casual approach to grooming and dress. Worn-out shirts, patched blue jeans, and bib overalls are often worn to school and in the community. Fortunately, most people recognize that this is a style of dress and not sloppiness in dress. Your school and employer may permit casual dress (or they may not, depending on the type of work involved). But they will not be pleased if your body is basically dirty.

Daily Bathing and Deodorizing

People who are careless about body cleanliness often don't realize how offensive they can be to others. It is annoying to work with someone who smells bad. Sometimes a person is unaware of the fact, having become used to the odor. It is embarrassing to be told that you have body odor. But it is also embarrassing to tell someone that he or she has it. Thus, many persons with the problem may never be told.

Everyone should follow certain principles of body cleanliness. Most people need to shower or bathe each day. Everyone perspires, and this creates oil pockets that collect at pore openings in the skin. Frequent bathing removes these oil pockets and allows the skin to breathe.

A good soap that produces lots of lather should be used with the bath or shower. Particular care should be given to thoroughly cleaning parts of the body that perspire heavily. Fingernails and feet should be given special care. Stubborn dirt and odors underneath the fingernails and between the toes need to be removed. After you shower or bathe, apply a deodorant, if experience suggests you need one. Some people are allergic to ingredients in deodorants. You can determine which ones are effective and comfortable for you by experimenting. If you are allergic to all deodorants, you should see a dermatologist, a doctor who specializes in skin problems. The dermatologist usually can recommend a medicated soap that will delay bacterial growth and odor.

Some people like to use a body powder as well as a deodorant. These products also help prevent body odors. The powder is often sprinkled over the neck, back, stomach, and legs.

Hair Care

Another area of your body that needs special attention is your hair. At one time, the "rule" for young men was shortly cropped, neat, clean hair. Today, hair length is less important, as long as the hair is neat and clean. Nearly all employers will permit Afro-style haircuts. If you are a young man and have long hair, find out about the written and unwritten company policies about hair length. Do this before you apply for a job with the company. The company may not have a written policy about hair length, but the employer (or person conducting the job interview) may have an unwritten policy. If you are unwilling to cut your hair, be ready to accept the results: You may not be hired by that firm.

Regardless of the policy on hair length, you can assume that the company will want both male and female employees to have clean, neat hair. Consider your hair-care needs in these three areas: style, cleanliness, and dandruff.

Style.   Today, hairstyles, like clothes, are subject to fad and fashion. Generally, you should select a style that keeps your hair out of your eyes and face. The style should match your facial features, the shape of your face, and its size. Your best bet may be to see a professional hair stylist. These people are trained to analyze your facial features and then cut, shape, and style your hair to set those features off. Many barbers and beauticians are trained in hair styling and can advise you on a style.

Cleanliness.   Any hairstyle, of course, begins with hair that looks clean, smells clean, and is clean. Hair should be washed at least once a week, though many people do it more often. Young persons often wash their hair every day, especially those who have a short, full style. Choose a shampoo carefully. Many shampoos can harm your hair because they tend to dry it out. Dry hair often results in split ends and an ungroomed appearance. The advice of your hairdresser and some experimentation will help you find a shampoo that is effective for you.

Dandruff.   If you have dandruff, you have an additional hair problem. By all means, do something about it. Dandruff is unhealthy and unsightly. Use a shampoo that is especially developed to control dandruff. You may need to use it as often as twice a week, with a milder shampoo between dandruff treatments. You also should massage your scalp before shampooing or brush it with a stiff hairbrush. In severe cases, you may need to consult a dermatologist to get a prescription. Dandruff can be controlled, and it should be. It is annoying, both for the person who suffers from it and for the person who has to look at it.

At one time, the "rule" for young men was shortly cropped hair. Today hair length is less important, as long as the hair is neat and clean. (Courtesy Hellmuth)

Skin Care

A discussion of skin care for men and for women is considered separately.

Men.   For men, concern is mostly with shaving. In recent years, the wearing of facial hair for young men has become popular. Beards, sideburns, mustaches, or goatees are often worn. If you already have or are considering one of these styles, remember that on some people facial hair looks good but that on others it does not look so attractive.

When applying for a job, the general rule is always to be neat and clean. That rule includes skin care, which includes shaving. If you do have facial hair, be certain it is neat, clean, and well trimmed.

Some employers object to facial hair. Many object especially to full beards. Most employers probably will permit mustaches or sideburns. In any case, facial hair should be kept neatly trimmed and clean. Actually, growing and caring for facial hair may require more effort than shaving does. Beards, sideburns, and mustaches must be trimmed regularly, or they tend to irritate the skin. If left untrimmed, they look ragged, which results in a sloppy appearance.

If you are among the large percentage of young men who prefer to shave, do so daily. Without daily shaving, your face will seem to sprout "fuzz." This is unbecoming and gives a sloppy appearance. Many young men need to shave twice a day.

Many men finish their shave with an after-shave lotion, which soothes the face. However, do not apply so much lotion that those sitting or standing next to you can detect it. It is in poor taste to soak your face in cologne, and it may annoy those who have to smell it. Also, be careful about using talcum powder. Sometimes it tends to cake when you perspire.

Women.   For women, again the rule is one of neatness and cleanliness. All the makeup at a cosmetic counter in a department store cannot cover the dirt and skin oil that may be on your face. If you do use makeup, a good face cleanser must be used each morning and evening to clean the pores of your skin. Careless cleaning can cause serious skin problems.

The best guides for up-to-date developments in cosmetics and the application of makeup are fashion magazines or other periodicals. Beauty salons and department stores often employ cosmetic specialists, and they are also a good source of advice on face care. They can offer help on makeup or skin care, and their services are often free to customers who buy cosmetics.

Be careful when using makeup. Excessive cosmetics tend to make one look overdone and theatrical. Such an appearance rarely appeals to employers. And others may not enjoy working with you if you are vain or overly concerned with your appearance.

Skin Problems

At one time or another, we all have pimples or some other skin problem. This is an unfortunate fact of life for many young people. And it does not have a simple solution. Some experts think blemishes may be caused by eating certain foods, such as pastries, chocolates, fried foods, fats, sweets, or soft drinks. Others feel it may be caused by ineffective cleaning of the skin.

Some people have solved their problem by avoiding rich or fried foods and soft drinks. Some have used special medicated soaps or cleansers. These are good suggestions. You may need to experiment with them to clear up your complexion problems. Remember that greasy makeup or lotions often make matters worse. They should be used with care. If you have a problem with your skin, see a doctor or a dermatologist for advice or treatment.

Oral Hygiene

Although everyone has a mouth-odor problem once in a while, bad breath is usually as unnecessary as it is unpleasant. It is also a handicap if your job involves working with other people.

There are many causes of bad breath. Your physician or dentist usually can identify the source of the problem. Sometimes it is caused by decayed food between the teeth. Brushing your teeth carefully and regularly will correct most causes of bad breath and keep your teeth looking bright. Teeth should be brushed after you eat and before you go to bed. Use dental floss to help remove food particles from between your teeth and on your gums. Regular (twice a year) visits to the dentist for checkups and cleaning should also be part of your dental care. Generally, this will take care of bad breath.

Sometimes mouth odor is caused by poor digestion or intestinal illness. Infected tonsils also have been known to cause bad breath. If a regular program of dental care does not correct the problem, ask your doctor or dentist for advice.

Highly seasoned foods and certain types of drinks may also be the cause of unpleasant mouth odors. Especially noted for this are garlic, onions, highly spiced lunchmeats, colas, and alcohol.

There is much evidence about the medical dangers of tobacco. The general rule is, "Don't smoke." Smoking not only can harm your lungs and heart but also can cause oral hygiene problems. It sours the breath and often discolors the teeth. If you are a smoker, you have one more good reason to brush your teeth not only well but regularly.

43

DRESSING FOR THE INTERVIEW

As you know, the whole idea of what is appropriate dress for jobs has changed recently. Policies toward dress now are much more relaxed in nearly all occupations. Several years ago, women would never be seen at work wearing slacks, except perhaps in factories. Today, slacks and pants suits have become the style of dress for women in many occupations.

Men's clothing styles also have changed during recent years. The term that has been associated with occupations that required people to dress up is white collar. *White collar* refers to the fact that nearly all men in these occupations once wore white shirts with neckties. Today, in such white-collar occupational areas as retailing, banking, and clerical work, men often wear open-necked, tieless shirts or turtleneck shirts or sweaters. White shirts are the exception now rather than the rule. Bright-colored clothing and "mod" styles are now worn by both men and women.

In general, when deciding what to wear to a job interview, the main point to consider is the type of job for which you are applying. Jobs still are popularly classified into two categories: blue collar and white collar. *Blue-collar jobs* are involved with factory work, farm work, or work in trades such as plumbing, welding, and carpentry. *White-collar jobs* usually are involved with an office or selling occupation or one in which there is regular contact with the public.

When applying for a blue-collar job, you should dress like others employed in that occupation. And when applying for a job normally considered white collar, you should dress like other people employed in that occupation. Use common sense. Whatever the job—blue or white collar—make sure that you dress neatly and in moderate fashion.

BLUE-COLLAR OCCUPATIONS

Blue-collar jobs include factory work, service station work, farm work, construction, and other

In general, when deciding what to wear to a job interview, the main thing to consider is the type of job for which you are applying.

trades. Usually, workers in these occupations wear blue jeans or heavy slacks and shirts of a cotton-wool blend.

If you are applying for a job in a blue-collar occupation, wear a clean pair of slacks or blue jeans and a clean shirt. Both should be free of holes, and the collar, sleeves, and cuffs should be in good condition. In other words, the guideline is to be clean and neat.

WHITE-COLLAR OCCUPATIONS

Young people sometimes can locate part-time white-collar jobs as retail salespeople, grocery store workers, office clerks, and cashiers. Most workers in these occupations dress up. Many employers in these occupations do not permit employees to wear blue jeans.

It is usually safe to dress up when applying for any job. For example, a young woman applying for a job as salesperson in a department store should wear a conservative dress or pants suit with hose and dress shoes. A young man should wear a suit or a sports coat and dress slacks with shirt, tie, socks, and dress shoes. The clothing should be neat, clean, and well pressed. Do not wear too much jewelry that may call attention to yourself.

Most employers consider it inappropriate for job applicants to wear miniskirts, tight pants, or unbuttoned shirts. Check yourself carefully in the mirror and ask whether you look like a sensible and competent person. If you have any doubts about your appearance, change it. Try to dress like the person you would hire if you had

important work to get done. Once you have the job, you can relax more and can take note of what others wear to work. But for the job interview, show that you know how to dress carefully.

UNIFORMED OCCUPATIONS

Uniformed occupations include such jobs as nursing aides, assistants in beauty and barber shops, workers in short-order restaurants, waiters, and bus drivers. When applying for such jobs, it is probably best to dress as was recommended for white-collar jobs. Blue jeans should not be worn. You will probably never lose this type of job because you dressed up too much. However, you may lose it because you underdressed.

Regardless of the kind of job you apply for, it is important to wear clean, neat clothing that is appropriate for the job. Many people feel it is their right to wear what they want to wear when they want to wear it. They also feel it is their right to wear their hair in any style they choose and to do anything else with their appearance. Of course, this is a right. However, employers also have rights. One of those rights is to hire whomever they want from among equally qualified applicants. It is important that you realize this and that you understand the rights of employers.

Appearance is the largest part of the first impression you give in the job interview. And first impressions are often lasting, especially in competitive job situations. You owe it to yourself to make the best possible first impression by choosing your clothing carefully and paying careful attention to grooming.

Appearance is a large part of the first impression you give at an interview. Which of these applicants, do you think, will get the job even though each may be equally qualified?

Getting It All Together

1. What seven items of information should you record about a potential employer in order to apply for a job?

2. What are three departments in your school that might have information about jobs?

3. What are six sources of information outside your school where you can learn about jobs available in your community?

4. Why is a résumé important?

5. What are the seven categories around which a résumé is organized?

6. What are three situations in which it may be necessary to write a letter of application?

7. What three kinds of information should be in a letter of application?

8. Why is your appearance important when you apply for a job?

UNIT

GOING TO
GET THE JOB

Your goals in this unit are given in the following list:

To identify and describe a typical procedure used by a company in your community to choose new employees for a job in your area of occupational interest

To complete correctly typical job application forms

To discuss the reasons for employment tests and improve your performance on them

To succeed in getting a job in your chosen occupational area

So far, you have considered all the various aspects of applying for a job. In following the suggestions, you now have identified an occupational category in which you would like to work. You have gotten your records together, including your social security card and your birth certificate. You may have a driver's license. You are familiar with other records that you may need for job applications. You have completed a personal resume and have it ready to take with you on job interviews. Finally, you have given careful thought to how you will dress and present yourself for a job interview.

It is time to be concerned with the actual job interview and the various tasks you may need to complete on the day of the interview. Let's consider the procedures that are generally followed in arranging for job interviews. How to complete a company's application forms will be discussed. And some questions that are often asked in job interviews will be reviewed, as well as suggestions of how to follow up the interview.

The information in the following chapters is

important. Think about it. Talk it over with your friends, your teachers, and your parents. It deals with you and your part in the job interview. No one can help you when you face a job interviewer. At this point in the job of getting the job, you are on your own.

The chapters in this unit have been written to give you ideas and suggestions as you enter the final phase of getting the job. In reading this material, you have to decide what is best for you. And in talking with potential employers, you must decide what to say and how to say it. Your words and conversation must be natural. They must reflect your personality; they must reflect your training; and they must also reflect your thoughts and feelings.

Be natural on job interviews. Be real. Be yourself. The advice is useful only if it fits your needs. By now, you should have a pretty good idea of your values and what you want to do with your life. You control your future. You are in the driver's seat. Take the information seriously and apply it to yourself. Think about all of it. Then select those suggestions that fit **you**. Good luck, and happy hunting!

44

WHAT TO EXPECT BEFORE THE INTERVIEW

A job interview may be arranged in many ways, depending upon the situation and the type of job for which you are applying. Here are some examples of arrangements for job interviews:

Lora decided to apply for a job at a bakery. She stopped by the store to see when she could come in for an interview. The clerk told her that Mrs. Meyer, the manager, would see her in 2 days at 6 o'clock in the morning. It seems Mrs. Meyer helps her employees with the baking very early in the morning. She then wants to interview job applicants between 6 and 7 a.m., before she goes home. Lora now knows that she will be interviewed 2 days later at 6 a.m.

Ron Brown has decided that he would like to work at a short-order restaurant. He noticed in the paper that the Burger Haven will interview persons interested in short-order cooking, waiting on tables, and general cleanup from 2 to 4 p.m. on Tuesday. Ron knows that he must report for the job interview on Tuesday, any time between 2 and 4 o'clock in the afternoon. He can expect that there will be lots of persons at the Burger Haven at that time. The manager prefers to interview all applicants on one afternoon a week.

Chris Ball, the personnel manager at the Hall Manufacturing Company, prefers to schedule appointments for job interviews. Job applicants must first fill out an application form and leave it with a secretary at the company. When Chris has an opening for which an applicant is qualified, that person is called. Chris then schedules a specific day and time for the interview. Recently, Jo Topp received a call about an opening as a machinist. Jo will be interviewed for the position next Thursday at 10 a.m.

ARRANGING THE INTERVIEW

For some jobs, an interview will be arranged either by the employer or by the job applicant at a time both agree upon. Ordinarily, this is the best procedure for getting an interview. It generally ensures that you will get an interview when you arrive. The employer (or personnel manager or a representative) expects you and has set this time aside to talk with you. Therefore, if possible, try to arrange for a specific date and time for your job interview by calling or writing to the company.

Some companies, however, set certain periods for job interviews and will give them only during that time. For example, they prefer to interview all applicants between certain hours, such as from 9 a.m. to noon and from 2 to 4 p.m. Many of these companies will not make appointments. Instead, they ask all applicants to come during the specified hours. Call or write to the company to find out when you can be given an interview.

AT THE INTERVIEW

The person who interviews job applicants varies from firm to firm. In some companies, especially small businesses, the owner interviews all job applicants. In other firms, the manager may do it. A manager doesn't own the business. However, the *manager* is the person responsible for running the business. One of the manager's jobs is to interview and hire employees. In many large companies, a *personnel manager* (or *employment manager*) interviews job applicants. Personnel managers also have other duties, but interviewing and hiring employees are their main duties.

Interviewing procedures also vary. Some companies, especially those with a personnel or employment office, have a separate waiting room for job applicants. Usually, an assistant will explain how to apply for a job at that firm. The room often has tables and chairs where you may sit and wait for an interview. You will complete any necessary job application forms in this room.

Often, the assistant will give each applicant a job application form and then collect the form when the applicant has completed it. The assistant may also look the form over to be sure it is complete. In some companies, he or she also may give employment tests. The assistant may tell the applicant to be seated until a company representative is free to interview. Sometimes applicants are told that it is not necessary to be interviewed. Instead, they will be called if the company decides to employ them.

In this interviewing situation, where the company employs an assistant in a waiting room, you should always be polite. The assistant may be able to affect who gets an interview with someone who has direct responsibility for hiring employees. Upon arriving in the office, you should introduce yourself to the assistant and say why

Some companies, especially those with a personnel or employment office, have a separate "waiting room" for job applicants. (Fern Logan)

you are there. For example, a job applicant might say: "Good morning. I'm Janice Porter, and I'd like to apply for a job as a salesperson with your company. I've brought a résumé with me listing my qualifications."

It is important to realize that sometimes large companies have many applicants for only a few positions. And so it is important that the first impression you give be positive. You are strongly encouraged to dress appropriately, to take at least two résumés with you, and to show your best charm and manners with any person you meet in that firm. Politeness, good grooming, courtesy, and supplying the correct work records will strengthen the impression you make.

In some firms, it will not be necessary for you to meet an assistant or anyone other than the owner or manager of the firm. This is usually true of small construction companies; small, independently owned retail stores; small insurance or real estate offices; service stations; and so forth. You may not even be asked to fill out an application form or to take an employment test. Again, however, remember that there are probably many people applying for that job. Dress appropriately, be polite and courteous, and give the employer your personal résumé to make a good impression.

The importance of first impressions when applying for a job cannot be emphasized too much. Job interviewing and application procedures may vary a great deal from one firm to another. Some will require application forms, employment tests, physical examinations, and several interviews. Others may only require one short interview. In any event, your interest in the job and your positive first impression may be the deciding factors in your being hired over someone else.

THE APPLICATION FORM

Nearly every employer requires all job applicants to fill out a job application form. A *job application form* asks the job applicant for information similar to that in a personal résumé. The information helps the employer make decisions about hiring someone for a particular job. Since so many firms do require applicants to fill out an application form on the day of the interview, be sure to take two good pens and an eraser with you.

An application form is designed to meet the needs of a particular employer. Therefore, application forms vary from firm to firm. Some forms are long and take a considerable amount of time to complete. Others are short and can be completed in a few minutes.

Some companies use a brief "prescreening" form. This usually is a very short form. An applicant may only write her or his name, address, and a summary of prior work experience. If the employment interviewer feels the person applying for the job is a good candidate, a longer form must then be completed. Some companies prefer to have an applicant take the form home to complete and mail back to the company.

Application forms are used by companies for a variety of reasons. Some companies rely almost entirely on information shown on the application form as the basis for hiring or not hiring employees. They may hold a brief interview only to clear up questions about information contained on the application form.

Other companies may use the application form to indicate an applicant's ability for the job. A company may be interested in knowing whether or not an individual can follow directions. Some use the application form to determine how well an individual can understand questions and provide well-organized answers to them. The completed application form also gives some indication about a person's neatness, thoroughness, and spelling and writing abilities.

Other companies use the application form only to be sure they have basic information about the applicant: name, address, telephone number, social security number, age, and position applying for. Such application forms are usually very brief.

The sample application forms that follow were completed by Mark Roman. Note that Mark is applying for a job with the J. C. Penney Company. One form is brief and took only a few minutes to complete. The other form is longer and required Mark to think through some of the answers. Study the form in Figures 1, 2, 3, and 4 carefully.

Some Guidelines to Follow

There are several guidelines to follow when filling out application forms. Although the application forms themselves may vary, the following guidelines should help you complete all forms:

Read the entire form first. Read the entire form from start to finish before you begin to fill in any information on the form. Do not rush. Be sure to read all information. Think about your responses to the requests for information before you complete any item on the form.

Read the instructions. Read the instructions to determine whether you should print or write. Most companies prefer that you print the information. However, some may prefer that the form be completed in your handwriting. A few companies may require the form to be typed. Some companies, especially if they employ people for secretarial or typing positions, will let an applicant use a typewriter for this purpose. They may request that the applicant type the form at the time of the job application. Others will ask the applicant to type the form at home and return it to the office.

Provide accurate and complete information. Be sure that all information you provide is accurate and complete. It is important that you give accurate information about your home address, telephone number, social security number, and date of birth, as well as the addresses and telephone numbers of the people you are using as references. Again, this is another reason to take a copy of your personal résumé with you on all job interviews. Nearly all the information requested on job application forms will be in the résumé.

Be neat. Be as neat as possible in filling out all the blanks on the form. Try to avoid erasing or crossing out responses. If you really mess up the form, ask for another. Try to plan each response so that it fits into the space provided. Often that is difficult on some forms, but do as well as you can. You may have to write much smaller than usual.

Supply all information requested. If there is not an appropriate answer for you, write "N/A" to indicate "Not applicable." This means that the question does not apply to your situation. For you, there is no answer. Never leave a question blank or unanswered. The interviewer may feel you avoided the question. For example, if a question asks: "What were your job duties while serving in the military?" you would respond "N/A" if you have not served in the military.

Spell all words correctly. Be sure to spell all words correctly. Again, if you have your personal résumé with you, it should contain most words you will need for the application form. You might

APPLICATION FOR EMPLOYMENT
JCP-6300-1 (REV. 5/73) FRONT

JCPenney

PRINT IN INK

DATE OF APPLICATION: 1 / 1 / --

NAME	FIRST	M.I.	LAST	SOCIAL SECURITY NO.	TELEPHONE NO. (AREA CODE)
	MARK	E.	ROMAN	127 — 42 — 8248	(332) 6.2 - 1814

STREET ADDRESS	CITY	STATE	ZIP
22 MAIN STREET	SHAWSVILLE	MARYLAND	21738

DATE OF BIRTH*	HAVE YOU EVER BEEN EMPLOYED BY J.C. PENNEY CO?	IF "YES," WHERE?	WHEN?	WHY DID YOU LEAVE?
5 / 7 / --	☐ YES ☒ NO	/	/	/

NAME OF RELATIVE WITH PENNEY'S	LOCATION	POSITION	RELATIONSHIP
NOT APPLICABLE			

DESCRIBE YOUR GENERAL HEALTH	HAVE YOU EVER HAD A SERIOUS ILLNESS OR INJURY?	HAVE YOU EVER RECEIVED COMPENSATION FOR INJURIES?	HAVE YOU EVER HAD TUBERCULOSIS?
EXCELLENT	☐ YES ☒ NO	☐ YES ☒ NO	☐ YES ☒ NO

HAVE YOU EVER HAD A RUPTURE OR A HERNIA?	IF "YES," WHEN	WAS IT CORRECTED BY AN OPERATION?	DESCRIBE ANY PHYSICAL LIMITATIONS YOU FEEL SHOULD BE CONSIDERED IN JOB PLACEMENT
☐ YES ☒ NO	/ /	☐ YES ☒ NO	

WHAT TYPE OF WORK ARE YOU APPLYING FOR?	WHAT EXPERIENCE HAVE YOU HAD IN THIS TYPE OF WORK?	ARE YOU APPLYING FOR	DATE YOU CAN START
RETAIL SALESPERSON	PART-TIME RETAIL SALES PERSON IN THE BRADYS DEPARTMENT STORE LAST 2 YEARS OF HIGH SCHOOL	☒ FULL TIME ☐ PART TIME	8 / 1 / --

IF YOU ARE EMPLOYED AT PRESENT, WHY DO YOU WISH TO CHANGE?	HAVE YOU EVER BEEN CONVICTED OF A FELONY?	IF "YES," WHERE?	WHEN?
	☐ YES ☒ NO		/

DESCRIBE ANY BACKGROUND EXPERIENCE EDUCATION OR TRAINING WHICH YOU CONSIDER APPLICABLE TO THE POSITION FOR WHICH YOU ARE APPLYING.	NAMES AND LOCATIONS OF SCHOOLS ATTENDED	DATES ATTENDED FROM	TO
BUSINESS EDUCATION MAJOR AT HIGH SCHOOL; STUDENT IN DE COOPERATIVE PART-TIME PROGRAM (WORKED 2 YEARS AS PART-TIME RETAIL SALESPERSON); STUDIED GENERAL BUSINESS, RETAILING, BOOKKEEPING, AND SALESMANSHIP; MANAGER OF MIDDLETON HIGH BASKETBALL TEAM DURING SENIOR YEAR; WORKED AS STOCK CLERK FOR DALE'S VARIETY STORE DURING SUMMER OF 19--	HIGH SCHOOL: MIDDLETOWN HIGH SCHOOL, SHAWSVILLE, MARYLAND 21738	9 / --	6 / --
	COLLEGE	/	/
	OTHER (NAME OR TYPE)	/	/

*Federal law and a majority of state laws prohibit discrimination in employment because of age, sex, race, color, religion and national origin. The Age Discrimination in Employment Act of 1967 prohibit discrimination on the bais of age with respect to individuals who are at least 40 but less than 65 years of age.

APPLICATION FOR EMPLOYMENT
JCP-6300-1 (REV. 5/73) BACK

WORK HISTORY

EMPLOYED FROM MO./YR	TO MO./YR	EMPLOYER (START WITH LAST OR PRESENT EMPLOYER)	NATURE OF WORK DURING EACH EMPLOYMENT	EARNINGS STARTING	LEAVING	REASON FOR LEAVING
9 / --	6 / --	BRADY'S DEPARTMENT STORE CENTER STREET, SHAWSVILLE, MARYLAND, 21738	RETAIL SALESPERSON (DE COOPERATIVE PART-TIME PROGRAM); WORKED IN SEVERAL DIFFERENT DEPARTMENTS	$3.10 PER HOUR	$3.50 PER HOUR	PART-TIME POSITION ONLY
6 / --	9 / --	DALE'S VARIETY STORE 10th STREET, SHAWSVILLE, MARYLAND 21738	STOCK CLERK	$3.10 PER HOUR	$3.10 PER HOUR	SUMMER POSITION ONLY
/	/					

MAY WE CONTACT THE EMPLOYERS LISTED ABOVE? IF NOT, PLEASE NOTE THOSE YOU DON'T WISH US TO CONTACT.

I understand that; If employed, any misrepresentation of facts on this application is sufficient cause for dismissal. Classification as a regular associate depends upon successfully performing work assigned me during a trial period of up to 30 days and upon the further need of my continued employment by the company. The company in considering my application for employment may verify the information set forth on this application and obtain additional information relating to my background. I authorize all persons, schools, companies, corporations, credit bureaus and law enforcement agencies to supply any information concerning my background.

SIGNATURE AS SHOWN ON SOCIAL SECURITY CARD: *Mark E. Roman*

DO NOT WRITE BELOW THIS LINE

Figure 1(Courtesy J.C. Penney Co., Inc.)

PLEASE PRINT IN INK

				TODAY'S DATE
				7 / 1 / - -

PERSONAL DATA

LAST NAME	FIRST	M.I.	(PREFERRED NAME)	MAIDEN NAME
Roman	Mark	E.		

ADDRESS	NUMBER & STREET	CITY	STATE	ZIP	TELEPHONE NO. (AREA CODE)
22	Main Street	Shawsville	Maryland	21738	(332) 612-1814

SOCIAL SECURITY NO.	DATE OF BIRTH*	DO YOU HAVE A VALID DRIVER'S LICENSE?
127 — 42 — 8248	5/7 /--	☒ YES ☐ NO

POSITION OR GENERAL WORK AREA FOR WHICH YOU ARE APPLYING	EXPECTED STARTING SALARY	ARE YOU LEGALLY ELIGIBLE TO WORK IN THE USA?
Retail Salesperson	$ 3.10 PER Hour	☒ YES ☐ NO

TYPE OF EMPLOYMENT YOU ARE SEEKING	IF PART TIME, SPECIFY DAYS AND HOURS
☒ FULL TIME ☐ PART TIME ☐ 3 MONTHS OR LESS	

WHERE OR FROM WHOM DID YOU OBTAIN THIS APPLICATION?	HAVE YOU PREVIOUSLY APPLIED FOR A POSITION AT PENNEYS?	IF "YES", WHERE AND WHEN?
Personnel Assistant	NO	/ /

HAVE YOU EVER BEEN EMPLOYED BY THIS COMPANY?	IF "YES", WHERE?	TERMINATION DATE	LIST RELATIVES & ACQUAINTANCES IN OUR EMPLOY
☐ YES ☒ NO		/ /	NONE

WHAT PROMPTED YOU TO SEEK EMPLOYMENT WITH US?
LEARNED FROM WORK-EXPERIENCE COORDINATOR AND GUIDANCE COUNSELOR THAT J.C. PENNY WAS A GOOD COMPANY TO WORK FOR AND THAT THE COMPANY OFFERED OPPORTUNITIES FOR ADVANCEMENT. ALSO, SAW JOB ADVERTISEMENTS IN MY WORK AREA.

HAVE YOU EVER BEEN CONVICTED OF A FELONY?	IF "YES", EXPLAIN
NO	

LIST YOUR LAST THREE ADDRESSES — STARTING WITH THE MOST RECENT

DATES (MO. & YR.) FROM	TO	NUMBER & STREET	CITY	STATE	ZIP
9/2/--	5/7/--	22 MAIN STREET	SHAWSVILLE	MARYLAND	21738
/ /	/ /				
/ /	/ /				

HOW DO YOU SPEND YOUR LEISURE TIME (AVOCATIONS, HOBBIES, ETC.)
MEMBER OF YOUNG DEMOCRATS, MANAGED HIGH SCHOOL BASKETBALL TEAM DURING SENIOR YEAR, PLAY TENNIS, READ, MEMBER OF DECA

INDICATE THE GEOGRAPHICAL AREA IN WHICH YOU WOULD PREFER TO WORK (FIRST CHOICE)	SECOND CHOICE
SOUTH	EAST

WOULD YOU BE WILLING TO LIVE WHEREVER THE COMPANY MAY ASSIGN YOU TO WORK?	DO YOU HAVE OBJECTIONS TO A POSITION REQUIRING WORK OUTSIDE THE HOURS OF THE USUAL BUSINESS DAY?
☒ YES ☐ NO	☐ YES ☒ NO

LIST ANY PROFESSIONAL AND BUSINESS ORGANIZATIONS TO WHICH YOU BELONG
Deca

NAME OF PERSON TO CONTACT IN AN EMERGENCY	RELATIONSHIP
Edith J. Roman	Mother

ADDRESS	NUMBER & STREET	CITY	STATE	ZIP	TELEPHONE NO. (AREA CODE)
22	Main Street,	Shawsville	Maryland	21738	(332) 612-1814

*Federal Law and a Majority of State Laws Prohibit Discrimination in Employment Because of Age and Sex. (THE AGE DISCRIMINATION IN EMPLOYMENT ACT OF 1967 PROHIBITS DISCRIMINATION ON THE BASIS OF AGE WITH RESPECT TO INDIVIDUALS WHO ARE AT LEAST 40 BUT LESS THAN 65 YEARS OF AGE)

Figure 2(Courtesy J. C. Penney Co., Inc.)

EDUCATION AND TRAINING

| CIRCLE LAST YEAR COMPLETED ⇨ | GRADE, TRADE OR HIGH SCHOOL 1 2 3 4 5 6 7 8 9 10 11 (12) | TECHNICAL, BUSINESS, COLLEGE 1 2 3 4 5 | GRADUATE SCHOOL 1 2 3 4 | GRADE AVERAGE - LAST SCHOOL ATTENDED |

LIST EVERY HIGH SCHOOL, BUSINESS, TRADE SCHOOL OR COLLEGE ATTENDED	LOCATION CITY & STATE	DATE LAST ATTENDED	DATE YOU DID OR WILL GRADUATE	MAJOR	MINOR	DEGREE RECEIVED	CUM. AVG.
Middleton High School	Shawsville, Md.	6 /--	6 /--	Business Education			3.00
		/	/				
		/	/				
		/	/				
		/	/				

COURSES LIKED MOST: Retailing, General Business, Salesmanship

COURSES LIKED LEAST: Bookeeping

WHAT LANGUAGES DO YOU SPEAK OR WRITE FLUENTLY? None

ARE YOU CURRENTLY ENROLLED IN EVENING, CORRESPONDENCE OR OTHER TYPE COURSE STUDY? ☐ YES ☒ NO   IF "YES", EXPLAIN

EXTRACURRICULAR ACTIVITIES (INCLUDE OFFICES HELD, SCHOLARSHIPS, AWARDS, HONORS, ETC.)

MANAGER OF HIGHSCHOOL BASKETBALL TEAM, MEMBER OF DECA, MEMBER OF GLEE CLUB, WORKED ON HIGH SCHOOL NEWSPAPER

LIST ANY SPECIAL SKILLS & TRAINING
☒ TYPING   ☐ STENO   ☒ KEYPUNCH   ☒ BUSINESS MACHINES   ☒ SALES   ☒ OTHER (EXPLAIN)

40 WPM TYPING; LEARNED OPERATION OF KEYPUNCH AND BUSINESS MACHINES IN SCHOOL COURSES; STUDIED SALESMANSHIP IN SCHOOL COURSES; PRACTICAL EXPERIENCE IN ALL THREE AREAS AT PART TIME JOBS.

MILITARY SERVICE DATA

| HAVE YOU EVER BEEN IN THE ARMED FORCES? ☐ YES ☒ NO | IF "YES", WHAT BRANCH OF SERVICE? | DATE ENTERED / / | DATE SEPARATED/DISCHARGED / / | RANK WHEN SEPARATED/DISCHARGED |

DO THE CONDITIONS OF YOUR DISCHARGE REQUIRE YOU TO PARTICIPATE IN YEARLY TRAINING MANEUVERS? ☐ YES ☐ NO   IF "YES", WHEN WILL THIS OBLIGATION BE COMPLETED? / /   ARE YOU RECEIVING A PENSION OR DISABILITY INCOME? ☐ YES ☐ NO

PHYSICAL AND HEALTH DATA

| HAVE YOU EVER HAD A RUPTURE OR HERNIA? ☐ YES ☒ NO | PROBLEMS WITH YOUR FEET, BACK OR HEART? ☐ YES ☒ NO | ARE YOU CURRENTLY TAKING MEDICATION? ☐ YES ☒ NO | ARE YOU CURRENTLY UNDER A DOCTOR'S CARE? ☐ YES ☒ NO |

HAVE YOU EVER RECEIVED COMPENSATION FOR INJURIES? ☐ YES ☒ NO | WHEN DID YOU LAST VISIT A DOCTOR? 2/10 /-- | REASON GENERAL CHECKUP | DATE OF LAST PHYSICAL / / | PURPOSE | RESULT ☐ SATISFACTORY ☐ UNSATISFACTORY

If you have been confined in a hospital, sanitarium or mental institution during the last five (5) years, state conditions and dates of confinements. Describe any physical limitations you feel should be considered in job placement, also explain any affirmative replies to questions in this section.

FOR INTERNAL USE ONLY

NAME LAST	FIRST	M.I. OR MAIDEN	SOCIAL SECURITY NO. ___ — ___ — ___
ADDRESS NUMBER & STREET		DATE OF BIRTH / /	TELEPHONE NO. (A/C) ( )
CITY	STATE	ZIP MARITAL STATUS	NUMBER OF EXEMPTIONS
STARTING DATE / /	DEPARTMENT OR STORE NO. —	LOCATION	POSITION TITLE	POSITION CODE	SALARY $	P.R.L.

Figure 3

EMPLOYMENT EXPERIENCE — *Include part time — cover the last five years. Start with present or most recent job.*

DATES EMPLOYED	COMPANY NAME AND ADDRESS	POSITION HELD	SALARY	REASON FOR LEAVING
FROM 9/1/-- TO 6/30/--	COMPANY NAME BRADY'S DEPARTMENT STORE ADDRESS CENTER STREET, SHAWSVILLE MARYLAND 21758	1 RETAIL SALESPERSON (DE COOPERATIVE PART TIME PROGRAM) 2 3	INITIAL $3.10 PER HOUR FINAL $3.50 PER HOUR	PART-TIME POSITION ONLY
FROM 6/30/-- TO 9/10/--	COMPANY NAME DALE'S VARIETY STORE ADDRESS 10TH STREET, SHAWSVILLE MARYLAND 21758	1 STOCK CLERK 2 3	INITIAL $3.10 PER HOUR FINAL $3.10 PER HOUR	SUMMER POSITION ONLY
FROM / / TO / /	COMPANY NAME ADDRESS	1 2 3	INITIAL $ PER FINAL $ PER	

IF CURRENTLY EMPLOYED, MAY WE CONTACT YOUR EMPLOYER FOR A REFERENCE NOW?   ☐ YES   ☐ NO

Please use this space to elaborate on any background experience or other qualifications which you believe should be considered in evaluating your qualifications for employment.

_____

_____

_____

_____

_____

REFERENCES—*Do Not Include Relatives*—*List below the names of two persons who would be willing to answer a reference inquiry from our company in your behalf.*

NAME	ADDRESS	OCCUPATION
LOUIS ANDREWS	PEOPLE'S DRUGSTORE, ELMORE SHOPPING CENTER, SHAWSVILLE, MARYLAND 21932	DRUGSTORE MANAGER
SAM WETTSTEIN	MIDDLETOWN HIGH SCHOOL, SHAWSVILLE, MARYLAND 21758	DE INSTRUCTOR

I understand that : If employed, any misrepresentation of facts on this application is sufficient cause for dismissal. Classification as an associate depends upon successfully performing works assigned me and upon the further need of my continued employment by the company. The company in considering my application for employment may verify the information set forth on this application and obtain additional information relating to my background. I authorize all persons, schools, companies, corporations, credit bureaus and law enforcement agencies to supply any information concerning my background.

SIGNATURE AS SHOWN ON SOCIAL SECURITY CARD ▶ *Mark E. Roman*

DO NOT WRITE BELOW THIS LINE

TEST	MEDICAL	TYPING	STENO	OTHER

Figure 4

also ask the assistant for a dictionary if your résumé does not include a word you do not know how to spell. If you cannot find the correct spelling, try to use another word that has the same meaning as the one you don't know how to spell.

Give all education and employment dates. If the form asks for educational and employment history, be sure all dates and periods of education and employment are included on the form. Such words as "Still in school," "Military service," and "Have not worked" usually tell the potential employer your situation.

Sign the form if requested.   Be certain to sign the application form, if it so requests. Nearly all forms ask for the applicant's signature. Yet many job applicants fail to include their signatures on the employment forms.

Check the form.   As a final check, be sure to read over the completed application form for accuracy and completeness.

EMPLOYMENT TESTS

On the day of your job interview, besides filling out a job application form, you may also have to take an employment test. Some companies require all potential employees to take employment tests, while some require none. A few companies test potential employees only in certain job categories. For example, persons applying for jobs as typists are usually required to take a typing test. In any event, you should try to do as well as you can on the tests. However, keep in mind that an employment test is only one way the potential employer decides who to hire. Employers use many factors to determine who will get the job.

Employers give tests for several reasons. First, tests help the employer select only those applicants who are qualified for certain positions. Some jobs require a high degree of skill. For example, a secretarial position may require a person to take shorthand at 100 words per minute. If the applicant can take shorthand at only 60 words per minute, there is little point in considering the applicant for the position.

Employers also give an employment test to obtain additional information about possible jobs for the applicant. It is important to both you and your employer that you be placed in a job for which you are qualified. A job may be too difficult for you, but it also may be too easy. If a job is too

difficult, a person soon becomes frustrated and discouraged with the whole work environment. On the other hand, if the job is too easy, the resulting boredom and carelessness often cause a person to become unhappy and dissatisfied. Employment tests often can indicate the kind of job for which a person might best be suited.

A third reason for employment tests is to identify "promotable" individuals, those who have the talent and skills to advance within the company. Often, those who score high on employment tests are watched closely in the early stages of employment. If they show a good understanding and commitment to the work, they are considered for promotion.

Finally, employment tests are often used to help employers check on an applicant's job interest, general outlook on life, and likelihood of being satisfied with the job and the firm. Psychological tests are often given to new employees. Such tests are supposed to determine a person's general outlook on life and attitudes toward many aspects of society. The person's score on such tests is then compared with those of other employees in the firm. If the scores are similar, employers feel that the chances of the person's being happily employed in that firm are much greater. If the scores are quite different, many employers may feel that the applicant would not be very happy in that firm.

Different Kinds of Tests

There are many kinds of tests available for employment use. It is difficult to guess what kind of test you might be expected to complete when you apply for a job. However, a general list of the types of employment tests you may need to complete include the following:

Aptitude tests—measure your general aptitude for certain kinds of work, such as mechanical aptitude, potential for operating machinery, and so on
Skill tests—measure certain skills, such as shorthand, typewriting, haircutting, and so on
Interest tests—measure interest in certain kinds of occupations, such as your interest in working with the public as opposed to working outdoors, or your interest in selling things as opposed to fixing things
Academic tests—measure such things as understanding and use of mathematics, spelling, general information, and vocabulary

Get plenty of sleep the night before your scheduled interview, when you might be required to take an employment test.

Personality tests—measure certain personality traits, such as friendliness, persuasiveness, and so on

It is important that you try to do your best on employment tests. It is important that you get plenty of sleep the night before your scheduled interview, when you might be required to take an employment test. Many studies indicate that people do not do well on tests if they are sleepy, not feeling well, worried, or nervous. A good night's sleep usually helps you to avoid these negative feelings.

Also, be certain you understand what is expected of you in completing the test. If the directions are unclear, ask the person giving you the test to interpret them. Do not be afraid to ask questions if you do not understand any part of the test.

Try to relax while taking the test. If you understand the reason for the test, what to do on the test, and the directions, there should be little concern. People do have different abilities, skills, aptitudes, and interests. Although you may not do well in one area, you will excel in another.

45

FACING THE INTERVIEWER

Now that you have completed the job application form and have taken any employment tests that the company requires of applicants, it is time for the actual job interview. In most situations, an assistant will have given the interviewer your completed application form. If you took an employment test, the results will also be given to the interviewer. The assistant probably also will have given the interviewer your personal resume that you brought with you.

Some interviews can last for quite some time, perhaps as long as an hour or more. Others may only last a few minutes. The length of an interview can depend on many things. It may depend on company policy. For example, some companies may only interview for 10 or 15 minutes. It may depend on the job for which you are applying. Some companies may interview applicants for part-time jobs for only a few minutes. However, persons being interviewed for full-time jobs may spend an hour or more with the interviewer. It may also depend on the time available on the part of the interviewer and the amount of information the company has already gotten from you.

Job interviews can be divided into four parts:

1. The opening of the interview
2. Information-gathering by the employer
3. Information-gathering by the applicant
4. The close of the interview

THE OPENING OF THE INTERVIEW

In some situations, the assistant will introduce you to the person who will interview you for a job. The assistant will make a statement, such as, "Miss Harbor, this is John Jones, who is applying for a job as a bank teller." At that moment, Miss Harbor will probably extend her hand and ask you to be seated. By all means, shake hands and make an appropriate comment, such as, "I'm pleased to meet you." As soon as Miss Harbor has been seated, you should also sit.

In another situation, you may simply be asked to go into the interviewer's office. If so, take the lead and extend your hand to the interviewer and make some comment like, "Hello, I'm John Jones. I'm interested in a position with your bank as a teller." Note that this job applicant offered his hand for a handshake. And he told the interviewer why he was there and for which job he was applying. In either situation, you should speak clearly, smile, and offer your hand, avoiding a handshake that is too weak or too strong.

INFORMATION-GATHERING BY THE EMPLOYER

In most job interviews, the person doing the interviewing will take the lead and begin asking questions. Perhaps the four most frequent questions asked of job applicants in the first few minutes of the job interview are:

- In what kind of work are you interested?
- Why do you think you want to work for our company?
- Why do you think you are qualified for this kind of work?
- Tell me about yourself.

Be ready to answer the questions often asked by interviewers. (Courtesy Metropolitan Life)

You probably will be prepared to get through the first few minutes of any job interview if you have thought about your answers to these questions.

It is usually best to provide short, thoughtful responses to an interviewer's questions. Most employment people are very busy. They do not have time for long, drawn-out answers. On the other hand, it is generally not enough to respond only with a "yes" or a "no." You should prepare for the types of questions that you will be asked in job interviews. Perhaps your parents or a teacher can ask you typical interview questions and allow you to practice responding to them. Practice your answers to the following questions, which are often asked in job interviews:

- Tell me something about yourself.
- Tell me about your family.
- Do you spend a lot of time with friends?
- In what kinds of extracurricular activities do you participate?
- How do you like to spend your spare time?
- Do you plan to go to college? Trade or vocational school?
- What do you think you want to be doing in 5 years?

- What do you consider your major strengths? Weaknesses?
- Do you smoke? Take drugs? Drink?
- How do you get along with your parents? Sisters and brothers? Others in the house? Teachers in school?
- What things in life bother you the most?
- What subjects in school did you like best? Least?
- Did you attend school regularly? How many days did you miss last year? How many days were you late?
- What grades did you get in your school work? What grades did you get in your vocational classes (such as typing, shorthand, distributive education, auto mechanics, and so on)?
- How did you like school?
- Why do you think you want to work for this company?
- Are you looking for full-time or part-time work? Do you want regular or temporary employment?
- What kind of work do you think you want to do for this company?
- What salary do you expect?

- What kinds of jobs have you done? Have you ever baby-sat? Had a paper route?
- Do you have to help at home? Do you make your own bed? Help with dishes? Mow the lawn? Take out the garbage?
- What do you know about our company? What does our company manufacture? How did you get interested in our company?
- When can you begin work?
- How do your parents feel about your going to work?

Throughout the interview, try to give straightforward and honest answers. Never lie to an interviewer. Also, be aware that the interviewer may take notes in order to remember your answers. Try to be enthusiastic throughout the interview and give the interviewer your full attention. Look at the person during the interview. Be pleasant, even if the interviewer is not. You should not smoke, chew gum, or eat during an interview.

INFORMATION-GATHERING BY THE APPLICANT

You, too, have the right to ask questions during the interview. In fact, to be sure whether you want to accept the job if it is offered, you have a responsibility to get important information about the company. All employment interviewers expect job applicants to ask questions. Many times the interviewer will expect your questions and may provide information in the opening comments. However, you should prepare a list of questions that you want answered.

In asking questions of the interviewer, try to ask only meaningful ones. Silly or unimportant questions usually do not make a favorable impression. Do not ask questions just for the sake of asking questions. Carefully think out the things you would like to know about the company. Here is a list of questions that might be important to you in your future employment:

- What are the job duties?
- What are the qualifications: physically, emotionally, educationally?
- What are the working conditions?
- What is the pay and how is it computed (bonuses, commission, straight salary, hourly, and so on)? What is the amount of pay for overtime? How are raises determined?
- What type of clothing needs to be worn? Are there any special rules with respect to grooming?
- What are the opportunities for training for advanced positions or promotion?
- What are the fringe benefits (vacation, sick leave, insurance, retirement)?
- What are the hours of employment?
- Does the job involve working alone or with people? If with people, how do the people get along in that department now?

Try to be enthusiastic throughout your job interview and give the interviewer your full attention. (Courtesy Metropolitan Life)

• When will I know if I've been hired? What are my next steps?

You should consider asking each of these questions, as well as others that you can think of. It is perfectly acceptable to ask the employment interviewer to respond to any of these questions. But be courteous when you do so.

THE CLOSE OF THE INTERVIEW

The last part of the interview is the close. In most situations, the interviewer will indicate the close of the interview. The person will make a statement like, "You should be hearing from us within 10 days," or "I've thoroughly enjoyed talking with you." Such comments will be a clue to you that the interview is coming to a close. It is suggested that you stand, face the interviewer, smile, and thank the person for giving you the interview. If the interviewer has not indicated when you may hear about the job, it is all right for you to say, "When might I expect to hear from you about a job with your company?"

In most situations, the interviewer will extend a hand for a handshake. Do shake hands and express your appreciation for the interview. Also thank the assistant on your way out of the waiting room.

46

FOLLOWING UP
THE INTERVIEW

As you leave the company after a job interview, many thoughts will run through your mind. You may feel good about the interview and be confident that you will get a job with that company. You may feel bad about some part of the interview and realize that you should have been more prepared to respond to certain questions. You may not be sure you want to work for this company because of information you received from the interviewer. All these feelings are natural and are part of your personal evaluation of the job interview.

The first question, once the interview has been completed, is: What happens next? What will happen in your continuing efforts to get a job? There are four possibilities with respect to the job for which you just interviewed:

- The employer offered you a job, and you've decided to take it. The only decisions remaining are such things as the starting date, hours, and getting your forms completed. This is what you have hoped for. You are ready to go to work. Congratulations!
- You've decided that you really want the job, but you have a feeling that there is little hope of getting it. Perhaps the company does not have a position for which you are qualified at this time.
- You are offered a job, but you feel that the job is not really what you want at this time. You may have decided either that you do not want the job or that you need more time to study its requirements, your situation, or other factors.
- You really don't know where you stand with the company. Perhaps there were many people interviewing for the job and you couldn't tell from the interviewer just what your chances were.

In *following up the interview,* or finding out about your chances for employment with the company, you should evaluate the interview. How well do you think the interview went? From there, you should follow up the interview. This can be done by telephone, by writing a letter of appreciation, or by personally visiting the firm.

PERSONAL EVALUATION OF THE INTERVIEW

It is important that you thoroughly analyze the events that took place during the job interview. Were you prepared to fill out an application form? Did you do so neatly, clearly, and without errors? Did you have all the information needed on the form? Did you take a résumé with you? Were you polite? Did you do well on the employment tests? Were you prepared to take them? Did you learn from the tests? (Perhaps you need to practice in skill areas or refresh your knowledge in certain academic subjects.) How did you conduct yourself with the interviewer?

To help your evaluation, here are some factors often given as reasons why people are not hired. You are encouraged to analyze yourself and your performance during the job interview in terms of these factors:

- Poor personal appearance
- Overbearing, overaggressive, conceited; "superiority complex," "know it all"

- Inability to express oneself clearly—poor voice, diction, grammar
- Lack of planning for career, no purpose or goals
- Lack of interest and enthusiasm, passive, indifferent
- Lack of confidence and poise, nervousness, ill at ease
- Failure to participate in activities
- Overemphasis on money, interested only in best dollar offer
- Poor scholastic record, just got by
- Unwilling to start at the bottom, expects too much too soon
- Makes excuses, evasive, hedges on unfavorable factors in record
- Lack of tact
- Lack of maturity
- Lack of courtesy, ill-mannered
- Complaints about past employers
- Lack of social understanding
- Marked dislike for schoolwork
- Lack of vitality
- Fails to look at interviewer
- Limp handshake
- Indecision
- Sloppy application blank
- Merely shopping around
- Wants job only for short time
- Little sense of humor
- Lack of knowledge in field of specialization
- Parents make decisions for this person
- No interest in company or in industry
- Emphasis on who the person knows
- Unwillingness to go where sent
- Cynical
- Low moral standards
- Lazy
- Intolerant, strong prejudices
- Narrow interests
- No interest in community activities
- Inability to take criticism
- Does not appreciate the value of experience
- Late to interview without good reason
- Never heard of company
- Failure to express appreciation for interviewer's time
- Asks no questions about the job
- High-pressure type
- Indefinite responses to questions

It is important that you evaluate your job interview performance. Be honest with yourself. Be thorough. You want to improve your perfor-

It is important that you thoroughly analyze the events that took place during the interview. Remember to evaluate these events in terms of how well prepared you were. Does the evaluation of your performance tell you about any areas in which you might need to improve your skills?

mance in your next interview. There is no reason to become discouraged if you do not get the job. It is not unusual to have six to ten interviews before you get a job offer. And yet some people often do not try more than one interview. You should consider applying for several jobs. It is good to compare various companies. Often, a company that may have had little appeal to you in the early stages of your job search may have one of the best openings for you.

TELEPHONING THE COMPANY TO FOLLOW UP THE INTERVIEW

Often, a company's personnel department needs time to check on information concerning your application. The company will usually check with your references. They often contact the school you attended. They may check on your attendance record, your grades, or talk with your teachers or guidance counselor. They also may check with former employers about your personal characteristics and qualifications. Therefore, the person who interviewed you cannot tell you whether or not you have a job at the time of the interview. In most situations, it is acceptable for a job applicant to call the company a few days after the interview to ask whether the position has been filled.

If you really are interested in a position and want to be sure that the employment interviewer is keeping your application under consideration, it is proper for you to telephone the company about 5 to 7 days after your interview. For some people, this is difficult. They feel it is enough if the interviewer has said something like, "We'll call you in a few days." The applicant often will wait by the telephone for a call that never comes. Actually, most employment interviewers are very busy. They see many, many job applicants each day. It is difficult for them to remember everyone, much less keep in contact with them by telephone. A brief, polite telephone call will remind them of you.

In making a telephone call to the company, you should ask to speak with the person who interviewed you. Tell this person briefly and simply why you are calling. A short appropriate remark should be made, such as, "Ms. Wong, this is Herman Ross. I'm calling to ask about the waiter job I applied for last week." Note that Herman was brief, polite, and tactful in his call.

Avoid being a pest. Usually a call 5 to 7 days after the interview and perhaps another call a week after that should be enough. If you haven't received any encouragement after two follow-up telephone calls, look for another job. Also, the employment interviewer may make a statement such as, "Please don't call. If something opens up, we'll get in touch with you." If the interviewer says that, take the advice. Don't call again. Look elsewhere for employment.

WRITING THANK-YOU LETTERS

One final suggestion is that you send each employment interviewer a thank-you letter immediately after the interview. This will serve two purposes: (1) It sincerely thanks the person for considering you for a position with that company. (2) It tells the person of your interest in the company. Either you still want the job or you are no longer interested.

This letter should be short and to the point. As with other letters we discussed, it is important that they be neat, clean, and free of errors. This letter need not be typed.

It is probably best to think of the letter in three short paragraphs:

1. In paragraph one, state your reason for writing. An appropriate paragraph is shown in Figure 1.
2. In paragraph two, mention your interest in the job or tell the person that you are no longer interested. An appropriate comment for this paragraph is shown in Figure 2.
3. In paragraph three, you should again thank the person for the interview and ask to be contacted. An example is shown in Figure 3.

Figure 4 is an example of a letter that might be written if you were no longer interested in the job.

VISITING THE FIRM

In some instances, rather than calling or writing, you may want to visit the firm personally and ask

This is to thank you for considering me for a position as a cosmetologist in your beauty shop. I enjoyed visiting with you and the other persons in your shop during my interview yesterday.

Figure 1

I am most impressed with your shop and the people who work there. I am very interested in becoming a part of Beauty-Rama.

Figure 2

Again, thank you for your time and interest in me. I look forward to hearing from you.

Figure 3

```
                              55 Hudson Avenue
                              Morton, Illinois 83162
                              November 5, 19--


Mr. Richard Smith, Personnel Manager
Good Will Insurance Company
213 Hampton Street
Morton, Illinois 83162


Dear Mr. Smith:


This is to thank you for the time you spent with me yesterday.
I learned a great deal about your company. I feel the job in
your credit department would be most enjoyable and interesting.

However, I have decided to accept a position with another firm.
I therefore no longer wish to be considered for a position with
your company.

Best wishes in filling this position. Again, thank you for con-
sidering my application.


Sincerely,


Duane Frank
```

Figure 4

about the job. This is often best if the firm is very small or if you know the owner or manager. In either of these situations, a telephone call or a thank-you letter might seem inappropriate. For example, if you are applying at a small grocery store or service station in your neighborhood and you know the owners, it would probably be best for you simply to stop by and ask whether a decision has been made about the job. You might still want to write a thank-you letter after the job interview, but it is not a good idea to telephone regularly.

Getting It All Together

1. Why is giving a good first impression at a job interview so important?

2. Name four ways to improve your first impression.

3. Why is it important to complete an application form accurately, neatly, and completely?

4. What are four reasons why you might be given an employment test when applying for a job?

5. What are the four main parts of a job interview?

6. Why is it a good idea to evaluate your performance on the job application procedure after the interview?

7. Why should you go on several job interviews?

8. Why is it often necessary to follow up the job application with a telephone call several days after the interview?

9. Why is it important to send each employment interviewer a thank-you letter immediately after the interview?

COMMUNICATION AT WORK

SPEAKING AND LISTENING

Your goals in this unit are given in the following list:

To recognize the importance of effective speaking and listening

To recognize what elements contribute to effective speaking

To develop methods for improving your speaking

To improve your skill in listening by sharpening your use of some methods for effective listening: being prepared, searching for interest, being a critical judge, getting involved, controlling emotions, and overcoming roadblocks to listening

"I know you think that you understand what you thought you heard me say, but I'm afraid that what you do not realize is that I did not say what I really meant."

Perhaps you have seen or heard this statement before. Whoever made it was being funny. But the person summed up in one jumbled sentence the difficulties of communicating effectively. You must know what you want to communicate, express it clearly so that the other person can understand, and select a method of communicating that will be certain of reaching the other person.

Two elements essential to any communication, as the statement implies, are a speaker and a listener. Since there are many forms of communication besides speaking and listening, the two elements essential to any communication are usually identified as **sender** and **receiver**.

You cannot communicate in a vacuum. When Robinson Crusoe was first cast away on a deserted island, he lighted huge bonfires as a signal for help. There was nothing wrong with his choice of method of communication. In fact, it was the best method he could have selected under the circumstances. But his efforts at communication failed for a long time because there was no one else around to receive the message.

Communication requires a sender and a receiver. During your life, you will be both things many times. To a large extent, your ability to function as a sender and a receiver will determine your success in your career. Obviously some careers require greater communication skills than others, but all careers require some.

During your life, you will spend 70 percent of your waking time involved in the communication process as either a sender or a receiver. Seventy percent! Seven out of every 10 minutes that you are awake, you are either speaking, listening, reading, or writing.

How can your life be so involved in the communication process? Well, consider. You tell your parents what your plans are for the day. Your parents tell you what there is for breakfast or when they expect you home or what they expect you to do. On the way to and from school or work, you talk with your friends. You may discuss last night's television show, a new article of clothing, plans for the weekend. During the day, you talk or listen to teachers or bosses or strangers on a whole variety of topics: work for the day, instructions on how to do something, directions on how to get somewhere.

During the day, you also will probably read a book, or a newspaper, or a letter, or the instructions on how to put together a new bicycle. If you are looking at television, you still may have to read something: an address of where to send for a new record album, for example. Yes, even watching television, you are participating in the process of communication. You are participating as a listener, or a receiver.

VERBAL AND NONVERBAL COMMUNICATION

You send and receive messages on two levels. When you deal with words—reading, speaking, writing, listening—you are using *verbal communication.* When you smile, shrug, punch someone in the nose, you are using *nonverbal communication.*

Nonverbal communication tends to be more forceful. Verbal communication tends to be more precise. You can convey a much wider variety of meanings verbally than you can nonverbally. But both levels have their place. Often you will use the two levels of communication at the same time. When you are saying something pleasant, you will smile. When you are disagreeing, you will shake your head.

Verbal communication is further classified into two different types according to the way in which the words are conveyed: oral and written. *Oral communication* refers to speaking and listening. *Written communication* refers to writing and reading. Nonverbal communication is also called *body language* when the body is used as a form of communication.

COMMUNICATION AND YOUR CAREER

Deciding what career you want, learning the skills of a particular job, looking for and getting the job, and, finally, functioning successfully on the job are all phases of your life. In every phase, communication skills are important.

When learning about your future job, you will have to read and listen. Looking for a job will require you to read the job announcements and classified ads. In getting the job, you will have to tell an interviewer, both in writing and orally, about yourself and your background. Later, on the job, you will have to communicate with your co-workers,

bosses, and people who may eventually be working for you.

WHY SPEAKING IS IMPORTANT

You read that you spend 70 percent of your waking time involved in the communication process. Most of that time you are either speaking or listening.

Speaking well enough to function effectively does not mean you must be able to stand up and give a talk to several thousand people. But it does mean that you should have the ability to express yourself clearly so that one, or two, or sometimes several other persons can understand you.

LISTENING VERSUS HEARING

Hearing is the awareness of sounds, but *listening* is the process of making those sounds meaningful. Most people are very poor listeners. Research studies have shown that people usually forget 75 percent of what they hear during a 10-minute talk. Think about that. If you are an average listener, you remember only about 25 percent of conversations you hear.

In schools, at least 6 years are devoted to reading and writing. Some schools have special training in speaking, but few schools teach students how to listen. Listening training has mainly consisted of your teachers' and parents' saying "Pay attention!" or "Listen to what I'm saying!"

But there is more to listening training than that. Listening training also involves understanding why listening is important. Why it is important at home, at school, and at work. Listening training also means learning what to listen for and how to listen. There are many different types of listening, and becoming aware of them will enable you to be a better listener.

Can you become a better listener? Yes, you can. Listening, like the other verbal communication skills—reading, writing, and speaking—can be improved with training.

In this unit, you will learn some methods for becoming a more effective speaker. You will also learn how to improve your listening skills.

47

BASIC ELEMENTS OF EFFECTIVE SPEAKING

Pam looked at the clock. 7:30! She was late! Hurriedly she jumped out of bed and dressed. "Can't eat, can't eat. No time," she shouted as she raced through the kitchen, grabbed a piece of toast from her brother's plate, and dashed out the door. The slamming door cut short her brother's shout of protest and her mother's questioning "When are you . . . ?"

Pam practically ran to school, missed roll call in homeroom, and just made it into her history class. She barely had time to take a breath when the bell rang and her teacher called her name.

"Pam, it's your turn to give an oral report on the Civil War."

For a second, Pam was shaken, but then she remembered she had prepared an outline of the main points she wanted to cover. Using these notes, she spoke for about 10 minutes. When she sat down, her teacher praised her.

"Wow," Pam thought. "I'm glad I prepared those outline notes a couple of days ago."

At lunch, she, Sally, and Jeff sat together and chatted about things that interested them. They talked about a recent movie they had all seen, about the heavy workload, about how their part-time jobs were, and about other people they all knew. The talk was pleasant, and all too quickly the bell rang for them to return to classes.

During the afternoon, Pam took part in an interesting discussion on pacifism in a civics class.

Before leaving school, Pam met with her guidance counselor. They talked about how she was doing on her job and about plans for next year. Pam wanted to get more information about different careers, so she asked a lot of questions.

After the interview, Pam walked to her part-time job at the florist shop. On the way, an elderly woman asked her how to get to the town hall. Pam gave her careful directions. At the shop, she exchanged greetings with Ken, the owner, and then waited on customers. She tried to per-suade a young man to buy a dozen American Beauty roses for his girlfriend, but the man purchased a bouquet of forget-me-nots instead.

Later Jeff stopped in to walk home with her. Jeff had never met Ken, so Pam introduced them. On the way home, Jeff and Pam talked pleasantly for the most part but had a small argument over which movie to see on the weekend. When Pam arrived home, her mother scolded her about leaving so quickly that morning and not taking time to eat or to talk a minute or two with the family.

During her day, Pam took part in many conversations. She spoke to several people and in several different ways. She spoke for many different reasons and in many different situations. Pam adapted her manner of speaking to fit the reason for speaking and the situation. Sometimes she was successful. Sometimes she was not.

When she raced out of the house in the morning, she was not very polite to her brother or mother. At school, fortunately for her, she was prepared when she was called on to give her report in history class. At lunch, she had a good time just gossiping and exchanging pleasant information with friends. In the afternoon, she enjoyed a discussion. Later on she asked questions to learn about future careers. At the flower shop, she failed when she tried to persuade a customer to buy roses. She was, however, able to introduce Jeff to her boss. She had a not-very-serious argument with Jeff on the way home. When she finally arrived home, she paid the price for her impoliteness of the early morning.

In a typical day, you will find yourself in many different situations, just as Pam did. How effectively you speak in each of them will depend to some extent on your ability to identify the situation and respond in a suitable manner.

TWO KINDS OF SPEAKING

The kinds of speaking that you will do can be divided into two very broad groups, called formal and informal. Unless you become a politician, actor, educator, television personality, or similar public figure, you will not be called upon to speak formally very often during your working life. Most of the time you will be speaking informally. Knowing the difference between the two kinds of speaking will help you if you ever are called upon to speak formally. This knowledge can also help you avoid formality in situations that do not call for it. Furthermore, there are some common situations, such as job interviews, that require something in between formal and informal speaking.

Informal Speaking

Informal speaking is what you do most of the time in school, at work, or with friends and family. When speaking informally, you tend to use more slang words, talk in incomplete sentences, and use a lot of one-word exclamations—such as "yeah," "no," "maybe"—or two- or three-word phrases—such as "see ya," "take care," "keep the faith," "long time no see."

There are degrees of informality. Just how informal you are depends on the situation. You read about communicating up, down, and across. You probably are more informal—that is, use more slang words and expressions—when talking across with friends than you are when talking with parents, older people, or teachers. At least, you are if you value good communication.

When talking informally, you use body language a lot to reinforce your meaning or to add to it. You use a lot of expressions over and over again. With close friends or relatives, you may even talk your own brand of secret talk. That is, your words will have special meanings that are understood only by you and your listener. When talking informally, you probably use many shortcuts to speed up the exchange. If you used the same shortcuts in writing or formal speaking, you would make a bad impression and probably fail to communicate.

The degree of informality you use can range toward more formality as well as toward greater informality. When Pam took part in the classroom discussion, she probably spoke more formally than she did when chatting with her friends at lunch. She was probably more formal in talking with her boss and her guidance counselor than she was in talking to Jeff. But she was probably quite formal when introducing Jeff to her boss.

Although most of your everyday activities can be carried on by speaking informally, there are situations when you must speak more formally, although still not quite as formally as you would when making a public speech.

Formal Speaking

Giving a speech before an audience of several people is the major example of a situation in which you would use formal speaking. Giving a talk in a classroom would fall under this heading. Pam was in a formal speaking situation when called upon to report on the Civil War in her history class. Fortunately for her, she had taken the one most essential step toward being effective when giving a formal talk—she had been prepared.

When you speak in a formal situation, you should have prepared what you are going to talk about. Then you can either memorize it or use notes, as Pam did. When talking formally, you speak in complete sentences, your thoughts are organized, and you move logically from one point to another. It is not like chatting with a friend or two, where the conversation may jump back and forth all over the place and very often not go anywhere in particular. A formal talk should very definitely go somewhere.

Speeches are not the only examples of formal speaking. Radio and television announcers speak formally. People taking part in debates do also. To a lesser extent, those talking in a discussion group speak formally too. The important thing here is to be aware of what the situation calls for. If Pam spoke in a formal manner to her friends at lunch, they would begin to think she was trying to act stuck up or above them. But if she spoke to a large audience in the breezy slang she uses with her friends, people would think she was a very rude and poor speaker.

YOUR REASONS FOR SPEAKING

Whether you are in a formal or informal situation, it is important for you to know why you are speaking. In general, you can put your reasons for speaking under three broad headings: to inform, to persuade, and to entertain.

Former basketball star Kareem Abdul-Jabbar has to prepare what he plans to talk about in his position as radio jazz commentator and disk jockey. What kind of speaking do you think he practices in this job? (United Press International)

To Inform

Passing on information is probably the main reason you speak most of the time. Much of your everyday speech—at school, on the job, at home, or with friends—is aimed at passing on information. Do not forget that communication is a process requiring a receiver as well as a sender. Consequently, most conversations, at least on an informal level, involve the exchange of information, with those participating constantly changing roles from sender to receiver and back again. In the next unit, you will read more about your role as a listener. In this unit, however, you will be concentrating on your role as a speaker.

When Pam spoke to her history class, she was passing on information to them. She was also passing on information when she answered the woman who asked her how to get to the town

hall. When Pam talked with her guidance counselor, she became a receiver of information that the guidance counselor was able to give her. Later, when she introduced Jeff and Ken, she was passing on information to each of them about the other.

On the job, you may sometimes be asked to show a new worker how to do a certain task. In such a situation, you will be passing on the information you have acquired by working at the task. Your teachers spend most of their working days passing on information. Public speakers are usually attempting to pass on information, although, as you will read a little later on, politicians are often trying to do something besides inform their audiences.

When you pass on information, you are more effective when you get right to the point and leave out your opinions and jokes. When the woman asked Pam for directions to the town hall, she would not have appreciated Pam's views on how the town officials were running things. Neither would she have appreciated it if Pam had suggested by the tone or manner of her reply that the woman was dumb for not knowing how to get there. When you pass on information in such a way as to suggest you are superior for knowing it and the other person is inferior for not knowing it, you are not communicating well in passing on information.

To Persuade

You have no doubt often tried to get a friend or someone else to do something—play a game, go to the movie you want to see, help you with an assignment, lend you some money. At times, you have also undoubtedly tried to convince another person to accept an opinion of yours—tennis is more fun than swimming, city living is better than country living, a certain hockey team is better than another. Whatever the subject, you were speaking to persuade.

You will probably spend a lot of time trying to persuade people to see or do a thing your way. When you take part in a debate, you are trying to persuade people. If you run for public office, you will spend a great deal of time talking to persuade people to vote for you. Politicians, for example, are public speakers whose primary purpose is to persuade rather than to inform. It is possible, of course, to do both at the same time— that is, both inform and persuade your listener. In fact, the most effective speakers are those who can do this.

Here are four rules to help you become a more effective speaker. These rules will be useful for a variety of situations, but they are especially worth noting when you are trying to persuade someone.

1. Get the listener's attention.
2. Find out what the listener's needs and interests are.

Whether the situation is formal or informal, one of the main reasons for speaking is to pass on information. (Courtesy Adelphi University)

3.   Show how you can satisfy those needs.
4.   Ask for an appropriate reaction or approval.

Martha Adams and Gayle O'Connor both worked at the Worldwide Travel Agency. Martha did not know much about persuading people, but Gayle did. See what happened to each of them.

> One day Warren Slocum stopped in to get some information to help him decide where to take his vacation. He talked with Martha.
>
> "I'm interested in a vacation," Mr. Slocum began, and before he could say another word, Martha cut right in.
>
> "Hello, I'm Martha Adams. Let me tell you about our special to Hawaii. You can spend 9 days in Hawaii, see three islands, and get a total package deal for only $800. This includes meals and all hotel reservations."
>
> "Well, I don't know about Hawaii," Mr. Slocum said. "You see, I was thinking of Bermuda, because I . . ."
>
> "Oh," Martha said, cutting in again, "But Hawaii is just great this time of year. You would really like it in Hawaii. Here, let me show you these brochures."
>
> "I think maybe I'd better come back another time," Mr. Slocum said. "I just remembered that I have another appointment." He hurried out the door.

Martha was not very persuasive. She ignored Mr. Slocum's attempts to say what he wanted. She did not try to find out his needs and interests. In effect, she talked to herself. Gayle, her co-worker, handled things differently when Rosemarie Bunning, another customer, came in.

> "Good morning. My name is Gayle O'Connor. May I help you?"
>
> "Good morning. I've been thinking about taking a vacation."
>
> "You've come to the right place. We specialize in low-cost vacations here. And we should be able to help you stretch your vacation dollars."
>
> "Oh, great. My funds are pretty limited these days."
>
> "About how much money were you planning to spend for your vacation?"
>
> "I've got $1,000, and that's it!"
>
> "Well, for what you have to spend, the best vacation spot I can think of is Hawaii. How would you like to escape the winter for 9 days and have fun in the sand and surf of Hawaii?"
>
> "That does sound like fun, but how much would that cost?"
>
> "You can have 9 days in Hawaii, travel to three of the main islands, and be fed luxuriously for only $800. This price includes your round-trip

For what reason do you think Representative Bella Abzug is speaking? To inform, to persuade, or to entertain? (United Press International)

> air fare and all hotel accommodations too. Picture yourself getting a great suntan on those beaches near the sparkling blue sea. Then there is the excitement at night. And this is the best time of year to go."
>
> "It sounds almost too good to be true."
>
> "But it is true. And our Hawaiian vacation package seems to be just right for you. It is economical and includes all your major expenses. We have a special flight every 2 weeks. When were you thinking about leaving?"
>
> "I am planning my vacation for some time early next month."
>
> "Suppose I tentatively book you on the flight leaving on the 8th? If I book you now, you will be sure of getting space. There is only a small deposit, and if you cancel a week ahead, you will get your deposit back."
>
> "Sounds great. Let's do it."

Gayle's conversation with Ms. Bunning was effective. She achieved her goal—persuading Ms. Bunning to take a Hawaiian vacation. She did it by getting Ms. Bunning's attention, finding out what her needs were, showing how they could be satisfied, and getting final approval and action.

To Entertain

Quite often when you talk, you are trying neither to inform nor to persuade. You are talking just to entertain yourself and your listener. That does not mean you are being a stand-up comic or entertaining in any formal sense, like an actor. But talking is a pleasant, entertaining way to pass the time, and you spend a lot of time just chatting. Pam and her friends were entertaining each other during the lunch break at school.

Obviously when you are participating in bull sessions, passing on gossip, or just chatting, you are usually very informal. You do this kind of talking automatically, just as you walk. If you do not get what you want to say across, your listener will just drift away. If you cannot take part in this kind of talk with a friend, that person will probably not remain your friend very long. You do not study this kind of thing. You just do it. But it is good to remember that not all talk has to be for a specific purpose other than just plain fun.

SOME GUIDELINES FOR SPEAKING

Whether you are speaking in a formal or an informal situation and for whatever reason you are speaking, there are some basic guidelines you can follow to make you an effective speaker. These guidelines are given in the following sections.

Be Polite

Probably the most important thing is to be polite. If anyone has ever talked to you in an impolite way, you probably know how little communication gets done in this case. Your inclination is to be impolite and insulting right back. The subject is forgotten.

Always try to be courteous when talking. If you are angry, control your emotions. A good way to be courteous and polite is to put yourself in the other person's place. Try to make yourself feel what the other person feels. Putting yourself in another person's place in this sense helps you establish *empathy* for that person. When you are aware of how other people feel, you empathize with them. You make their needs your needs. Consider Tom Petronski, who had empathy for the youngsters he helped to teach.

Tom was a teacher's aide at Lincoln Elementary School. When he arrived at the school, he greeted the teacher, Nicole Sontay. As the students entered the classroom, he gave each one a warm hello, using their names. Tom thought of himself as a friend of the children. He considered their

interests and problems important. If a child had a question, Tom always stopped what he was doing to pay close attention. The children noticed Tom's politeness. In fact, they were learning how to speak more effectively just by being around him. Tom always considered other people's feelings, no matter what their ages. He responded to feedback from his listeners.

Be Factual

Unless you are speaking simply to entertain or pass the time, always talk to the point. Do not wander all over the place, as Jessica Burns did.

Jerry Higgins asked his boss, Jessica Burns, how long it would take to drive to his delivery spot on the other side of town. His boss responded "Well, Jerry, that depends on a number of factors. For example, the route you take will affect the amount of time it takes. Traffic is an important consideration too. Why, bad traffic can double the time it'll take! And weather conditions will affect the time too. But I'd say that the trip should take you somewhere between 20 and 25 minutes on the average."

Jessica Burns was not speaking effectively. She gave a very complex answer to a very simple question. When presenting simple factual information, don't make it more complex than it is. The fewer words you use, the better you will communicate.

Straying off the main point of what you want to say will also prevent you from being factual. Consider how Steve Franklin strayed off the main point.

Steve Franklin was a training supervisor for Dover, a large manufacturing company. One day he gave an orientation talk to a group of high school students who were recently hired for part-time work.

"The purpose of our meeting today," he began, "is to acquaint each of you with the policies and rules of the Dover Manufacturing Company. As a part-time employee, you will be expected to learn as much as possible about the company. Frankly, we should be able to offer some of you full-time jobs when you graduate from high school. That is, if business continues to go well. But who knows? The way the economy is going, we may end up with another Great Depression! Let me tell you, it was hard to get any kind of work back in those days! The whole country had it pretty bad then. Yes, that was the time when I started to work with the Dover Manufacturing Company. . . . But don't get me wrong. There are opportunities with Dover today. Let me explain some of our important policies to you. . . ."

Steve Franklin got sidetracked and strayed off the main point. His memories of the Great Depression may have been interesting. But they distracted attention from the main facts of his talk—acquainting the new employees with Dover's policies.

Effective speakers stick to one point at a time. Instead of trying to present many ideas at once, try to explain only one. Once you have accomplished this, you can move on to the next idea. It is much easier to hold one point in mind than several at once. By concentrating on only one point, you will be less inclined to get sidetracked, as Steve Franklin did. Many speech experts consider both normal conversation and formal speeches to be a series of one-point talks joined together.

Be Natural

Whether you are talking to a friend, work supervisor, teacher, or customer, speak and move in a way that feels natural and comfortable. Don't act the way Mary Jacobs did.

> Mary Jacobs tended to become very stiff when talking to her boss, Lois Meeker. Yet when talking to friends or customers, Mary was at ease and a much more effective speaker.

There may be many reasons why Mary is not as natural with her boss as she is with other people. She may not have much confidence in herself when talking to Ms. Meeker. She may feel shy. Chances are that Mary isn't aware of her behavior change with Ms. Meeker. If Mary were aware that she was not acting her natural self with her supervisor, she could begin to correct it.

When you talk with your boss (communicating up) at work, you will not talk in exactly the same manner that you would when talking to a close friend (communicating across). You should, however, strive to be yourself as much as you can in all situations.

To bring out the natural speaker in yourself, first evaluate your behavior. Consider how you normally speak when talking to friends or members of your family. Then think about how you speak when talking to your teachers or your work supervisor. Do you feel that your voice

Whether you're speaking to inform or persuade, you must be interesting. Do this by connecting your message to a need of the listener. (© 1980, Children's Television Workshop)

sounds much the same in both instances? If so, then you probably speak in a natural way most of the time. (Of course, your choice of words and phrases may and probably should be somewhat different.) Many people, however, freeze up when talking to certain people. Their voices become higher or lower. Their rate of speech may speed up or slow down. Their posture and movements may become stiff.

The best way to get rid of these unnatural speech characteristics is to relax. When your muscles are tense, you will have difficulty expressing yourself naturally. Awkward movements or gestures also are the result of tension. Taking a deep breath may help you relax. When people freeze up with tension, they begin holding their breath without realizing it. If you breathe in a normal manner, your muscles will be more relaxed, and you will be too.

Be Interesting

If you want to inform or persuade your listener (two of the primary purposes of speaking), you must be interesting. You can learn to catch your listener's attention and interest. One way to do this is to connect your message to a need of the listener, as Kristin Foss did.

Kristin Foss was a sales trainee for the Restfull Mattress Company. One day she was talking to a potential customer, Mr. Abner, about the Sleepeeze Mattress.

"If you want a good night's sleep, you can satisfy that need with the Sleepeeze Mattress. Its newly developed construction has been tested. So we can guarantee that you will wake up every morning more relaxed and more more rested than ever before."

Kristin's purpose was to persuade Mr. Abner to buy a mattress. She made her message interesting by tying it to Mr. Abner's need for sleep.

Some people buy bigger cars to satisfy their need to feel important. Others buy smaller cars to satisfy their need for economic security. By becoming aware of your listener's needs and relating your message to them, you will communicate more effectively. Applying this technique will almost surely guarantee that you get your listener's attention.

Your listener is a unique person. You should try to change your speech according to your listener's unique needs. After all, people are vitally interested in themselves.

You can become an effective speaker by practicing these four guidelines—be polite, be factual, be natural, and be interesting. The benefits will be the satisfaction of getting along with others and success in your career.

48

HINTS FOR BETTER LISTENING

Now that you've considered techniques for more effective speaking, let's focus on improving your listening attitudes and skills. You can make big improvements in your ability to understand others if you follow these rules:

- Be prepared
- Search for interest
- Be a critical judge
- Concentrate when listening
- Listen for names
- Get involved
- Control emotions
- Overcome listening roadblocks

BE PREPARED

When you go to class, you usually have to prepare for it. If you have a reading assignment, your teacher expects you to be prepared to discuss it.

Similarly your supervisor at work might want you to listen to a company orientation speech, which will inform you about company policies. You can prepare by reading about the company and thinking up questions before the orientation. The more you know about the speaker's topic—and the more you're aware that there is much more to know—the better prepared you are to listen.

SEARCH FOR INTEREST

Almost all people are guilty of being poor listeners when they find themselves having to listen to someone discussing something they're not interested in. You almost always can find something

that relates to your life, however, no matter how boring the topic. The trick is to be curious, to ask questions. Once you begin to search for interest, a boring speaker often becomes more interesting! Interest is catching. Consider the following:

Gerry was getting on-the-job training in the construction field. She was working with a journeyman electrician and learning about residential wiring. The problem was that Gerry was mainly interested in industrial wiring.

Gerry would not be an effective listener unless she considered such questions as "What wiring information is the electrician giving me that I can use later?" and "How is residential wiring like industrial wiring?" These questions are ways of finding areas of interest in the topic. If Gerry was a poor listener, she would decide that the topic of residential wiring was too dry and perhaps miss information that she could use later.

But Gerry had decided to make the best of the situation. She had a positive attitude about her job. She asked questions about what she heard. She followed the electrician's thinking and took in a lot of extra knowledge. Instead of spending months being bored, Gerry was able to enjoy the training period. She did so by searching for—and finding—points of interest.

BE A CRITICAL JUDGE

Some people listen without evaluating what they hear. Effective listening involves judging what others say. Consider what Paul's friend told him.

"I just know your new supervisor is going to be great," Paul's friend said. "Ann had her last semester and told me about her. Ann says that she is the greatest person to work for."

One hint for better listening is to concentrate on what is being said. This listener is concentrating effectively by fixing his eyes on the speaker and his ears on what the speaker is saying. (Courtesy United Nations)

But will the supervisor treat Paul exactly as she treated Ann? Will Paul react to the supervisor the same way Ann did?

A critical listener asks "How valid are the points the speaker is making?" "Is the speaker failing to consider something important?" As critical listeners, don't believe everything you hear.

CONCENTRATE WHEN LISTENING

When listening, concentrate on what is being said. By focusing your eyes on the speaker and your ears on what the speaker is saying, you can block out distractions. Sometimes you may try to look as though you're concentrating when actually you're daydreaming. You can improve your concentration skills by listening for relevant and irrelevant information and by putting facts with main ideas.

Listen for Relevant and Irrelevant Information

"Working in the sales field will be an exciting challenge for every trainee in this room," the sales manager began. "For one thing, there is no limit to the amount of money you can make. Your own drive and ambition will largely determine your success.

"My father had a lot of drive. Unfortunately he got sick. He was in and out of three or four hospitals. The doctors couldn't find out what was wrong with him. I don't know why the government gives so much money for medical research—doctors can't even find out what's wrong with my father. . . . Oh, let's see, where was I? Oh . . . yes . . . sales careers take plenty of drive and ambition. You have freedom to set your own hours. In sales, you are responsible for what you do or don't do."

Concentration is difficult when the speaker can't concentrate on the points to be made, as in the example just given. When this happens, the listener must become a critical judge and weed out the irrelevant from the relevant information. The part of the speech about the sales manager's invalid father is irrelevant information. *Irrelevant information* is a story or comment that has nothing to do with the main ideas that are being discussed.

Relevant information, however, supports one of the main ideas. The part of the sales manager's speech about the advantages of a sales career was relevant information. Those sales trainees who were good listeners sorted out the relevant and were not distracted by the irrelevant. The poor listeners were unable to do so. They left the conference room uncertain of what the sales manager's speech was all about.

Put Facts with Main Ideas

Listening involves putting together facts and understanding ideas. But too often you may spend so much time trying to memorize facts that you lose track of the main idea. Consider the following speech:

"As a telephone operator, you must remember that courtesy is very important," the orientation speaker said. "There are 5,000 telephone users in our area. We have over 2,000 business numbers. Our telephone equipment is the newest and best in the country. We have push-button dialing. We can even handle picture-phone calls with our equipment. Don't forget that the customer is always right. Your primary job is service to our telephone users."

It is easy here to become overwhelmed with facts and ignore the most important point of the speech—to be courteous to telephone users.

Speakers want listeners to remember and understand their ideas. Most people find that ideas are much easier to remember than facts. If you remember a speaker's ideas, chances are you'll remember at least some of the supporting facts. If, however, you forget a speaker's ideas, the supporting facts will be difficult to remember for long.

To be a good listener then, concentrate on the speaker's ideas, avoid distractions, and separate relevant from irrelevant information.

LISTEN FOR NAMES

Another skill you will have to develop as you gain experience in the world of work is remembering people's names. Listening for a person's name is always an important part of an introduction. Memory and listening are closely related. One way to fix a person's name in your mind is to repeat the name aloud. Some people want you to address them by their last names. Others prefer that you use their first names or nicknames. Hopefully they will also call you by the name you prefer.

Recalling people's names can be very important in many jobs, especially those that involve frequent contact with customers. Consider the following example:

"Ms. Frank," the automobile mechanic said. "Did you know your fan belt was almost worn through? Can we fix it for you?"

This automobile mechanic took the time and trouble to remember the customer's name. Most people appreciate being called by their names. The mechanic made a good impression on Ms. Frank by using her name.

Poor listeners miss names because they are not trying to remember them. Good listeners develop the habit of listening for important details. Sales clerks can make additional sales by remembering their clients' names. Such habits as not paying attention when being introduced to someone are not easy to overcome. Knowing your listening weaknesses, however, is the first step toward correcting them.

GET INVOLVED

"Randy, your training at this hospital is going to be very thorough. Do you have any questions so far?"

"No, Ms. Stitch," mutters Randy.

"One part of your job will involve delivering food to patients. You'll be expected to spend a little time making each patient comfortable. OK?"

"Uh . . . yes."

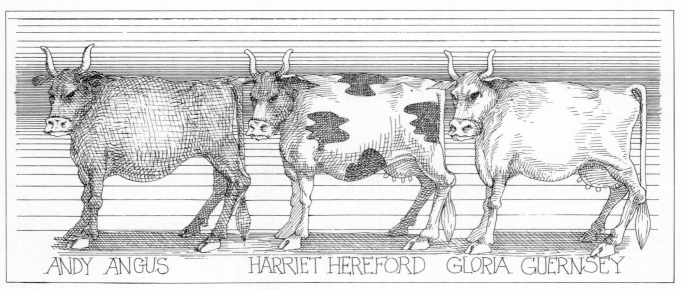

ANDY ANGUS   HARRIET HEREFORD   GLORIA GUERNSEY

In the world of work, listening for and remembering names is an important skill that all workers should attempt to develop. One way to fix a name in your mind is to repeat the name aloud.

"Now, another duty you will have involves keeping the patients clean and making their beds."

"Uh-huh."

"Well, Randy, how do you feel you're going to like working here?"

"Fine, Ms. Stitch."

How involved was Randy in that conversation? It sounded pretty much like a one-sided conversation. There are many possible reasons why Randy wasn't involved. Ms. Stitch's statement was somewhat disorganized and difficult to listen to. Randy might be shy and might feel that a new worker shouldn't talk too much.

Whatever the reason, Randy probably doesn't realize that speaking is an important part of the listening process! Had Randy been able to get involved, the conversation might have sounded like this:

"Randy, your training at this hospital is going to be very thorough. Do you have any questions so far?"

"Well, Ms. Stitch, I have been very impressed with the whole operation of the hospital. However, I do have one question . . ."

"Yes?"

"I want to make sure that I understand the procedure to follow when a patient has a heart attack. Could you go over it one more time?"

"I'm glad you asked that. It is very important that everyone know exactly what to do during a heart attack emergency. Seconds can mean the difference between life and death in such instances. The first thing you should do is . . ."

By asking that question, Randy was able to get Ms. Stitch to explain an important procedure more carefully. And the conversation had a two-way flow.

The basic difference between the first and second conversation is the extent of Randy's involvement. Active listening is giving full attention to what is being said—being fully involved with the speaker's ideas and information. In the second conversation, Randy was fully involved; he was an active listener.

Passive listening, not really being involved, is casual listening, similar to merely hearing. The passive listener does not pay attention to what is being said. In the first conversation, Randy was a passive listener. Normally a speaker would rather talk to an active listener. Such a person shows interest in the speaker's topic.

CONTROL EMOTIONS

Notice that this section is **not** saying "Never be emotional when listening." Life would be pretty dull if people never communicated their feelings. But people can become so emotional that they can't listen to what others are saying.

People often do not hear what they do not want to hear. They do not want to listen to statements that are likely to cause anxiety or other negative feelings.

Think of an incident in which you heard two people yelling at each other. How effectively do you think they were listening to each other? In a sense, your emotions act like hearing filters. Sometimes these emotional filters cause a lapse in listening, because you are hearing something you do not want to hear. "Tom, you could have done a better job" may be understood by Tom as "Tom, you could have done a better job, but what you're doing is OK. Don't worry about a thing."

Hold Back on Quick Conclusions

How can you listen effectively when your emotional filters are interfering? One solution is to withhold judgment. Wait until all the facts are in. Try not to tune out just because you've heard something you do not like. This is not easy.

Good listeners try to keep their emotions under control so that they can actually listen to what others are saying to them. How effectively do you think the people above are listening to each other?

Listening fully to someone requires practice. Consider the following example:

> Ms. Gonzalez, the senior reservations clerk at the airlines, had just noticed that Virginia Schaeffer was late to work again. She called Virginia into her office to discuss this problem.
>
> "Virginia, I've noticed that you have been arriving at work late on Tuesdays and Thursdays. What seems to be the problem?"
>
> "Oh, Ms. Gonzalez, I'm terribly sorry. I just don't know what to do."
>
> "Well, could you tell me a little more about it?"
>
> "Uh . . . it's my school."
>
> "What does your school have to do with your being late?"
>
> "Did you know that I just started my second semester?"
>
> "Yes . . ."
>
> "I had to take another class—on Tuesdays and Thursdays—and it doesn't get out until 2:00. And I'm supposed to be here at work then."
>
> "So, a change in your class schedule is causing the problem. Why didn't you come to me and discuss it?"
>
> "I . . . I guess I was afraid. I thought you might get mad at me, and I would lose my job."
>
> "Don't worry about that. Your work has been excellent. Let's figure out a way to change your working hours so you can attend your class and keep working here."
>
> "Oh, thank you very much, Ms. Gonzalez."

This discussion went quite well because Ms. Gonzalez listened to Virginia. Ms. Gonzalez could have been angry at Virginia for being late and not given her a chance to explain. But she did not prejudge Virginia. If she had not waited for the facts, the conversation would have been quite different. Reserving judgment is a good technique for effective listeners.

Try to Disprove Your Own Viewpoints

Another technique to help control your emotions while listening is to search for evidence that might prove your own viewpoints wrong. It is much easier to look for something wrong in what others say. It requires great effort to look for faulty ideas in your own conversation.

Root out Prejudice and Bias

Listen to yourself. Do you ever say one thing and do another? Do you tend to make oversimplified statements and generalizations?—for example,

"All customers are greedy and are looking for the cheapest deal they can get" or "The trouble with being a social service aide is that everyone wants to blame you for their troubles." Such statements are likely to be based on experience with only a few people. They hardly hold true for everyone. Effective listeners are able to spot faulty emotional ideas—their own and those of others.

Prejudice and bias prevent you from listening effectively. *Prejudice* is a prejudged reaction either for or against a person, group of persons, place, or thing. *Bias* is the distortion of facts because of personal feelings or attitudes. Any topic of discussion can be a biased one for the listener.

"What a dumb speech. I never did like mathematicians." In this statement, the listener shows a bias against mathematicians and maybe against the speaker.

How do you recognize biased speakers? They may make oversimplified statements, such as "The trouble with the world is. . . ." Or they may make rigid statements, such as "Everyone should go into the military service."

"Who does that guy think he is? A bigshot—just because he wears a gun and badge." In this comment, the listener shows prejudice against the police.

OVERCOME LISTENING ROADBLOCKS

Slang and accents, background noise, slow talking, and speaker status are some of the most common roadblocks to listening that you will encounter. When any one of these is present, you will have to work harder at listening.

Slang and Accents

Slang refers to a word or expression that is unacceptable in formal English. Young students often use slang words when talking to their friends. If students use a lot of slang on their jobs, how well do you think their supervisors will understand them?

"Wow, right on! Man, this place is far out" may not be listened to, or even understood, by an older supervisor. It's a good idea to avoid using slang at work.

When you hear someone using slang that is unfamiliar, you must cut through the unclear expressions. Don't let slang influence your listening ability. Try to listen to what people are really saying. Focus on their ideas, not their slang.

One way to achieve open communication and exchange of information is through effective listening. (Whitestone photo)

Accents are pronunciation patterns that are peculiar to different parts of the country. A Southern accent is a drawl in which some letters are slurred. A New England accent sounds like the speech of the late President John Kennedy. How do different accents affect your listening ability? Listen to people with accents and see how their accents affect your understanding.

Tour guides in national parks meet people from different parts of the United States. Their success as guides and their ability to communicate with the tourists depends in part on their ability to adjust to a variety of speech patterns and accents.

Background Noise

Sometimes people use background noise as an excuse for tuning out the speaker—"Oh, I couldn't hear what she said. It was too noisy at the office." Instead of focusing on the speaker, they focus on the distraction. Becoming aware that distractions can affect listening is an important step in becoming a good listener. Most background noise can be overcome by concentrating on the speaker. At times, you may have to move to quieter surroundings. You may have to shut a window or door to stop the noise. But background noise can be overcome.

Slow Talking

People are slow talkers. Most people speak between 120 and 180 words a minutes. They can, however, listen to much faster rates of speech—from 300 to 500 words per minute.

Thus, you have extra thinking time while listening to most speakers. It's possible to daydream for a moment and tune back in on the speaker without having missed anything. If this becomes too enjoyable, however, you can suddenly find the speaker far ahead of you.

It is during this free time that many listeners give in to their own internal distractions. The trick is to put the extra time to use. One good way to do so is to organize the speaker's topics mentally.

Speaker Status

Your impression of a person's status will determine how well you listen. An important person even may be able to change your attitudes. Not surprisingly you generally listen more carefully to speakers with high status. Perhaps you can think of times when you have strained to listen to a movie star or some other famous personality. You didn't want to miss a word.

Sometimes a person's status can have the opposite effect on your listening ability. Your listening can be poorer than usual with someone you believe to be of low status. When you become too concerned with the status of a person, be it high or low, your evaluation of the content of what is said may stop altogether. Your critical judgment is put to sleep, and you are left with thoughts like "If she says it's true, then it must be true!" or "Nothing **he** could say would be very important." or "I don't have time to listen to **her**."

The first step to take in overcoming this obstacle is to recognize that your impression of a speaker's status is a possible barrier to effective listening. The second step is simply to listen to this person just as you would to any person. If you can take both steps, status and role will not be roadblocks to effective listening for you.

Getting It All Together

1. Name the three basic reasons for speaking, and give two examples of each.

2. What are four guidelines to follow to be an effective speaker?

3. What are some roadblocks to effective listening?

4. Many people assume that if they are effective listeners, everyone else is, too. Is this a good attitude to have? Why or why not?

5. Agree or disagree: Speaking and listening are related skills—a person who's good at one is usually good at the other. Why?

15

READING

Your goals in this unit are given in the following list:

To recognize that you read for many purposes

To develop skill in using reading shortcuts, such as previewing and skimming

To discover ways to improve your reading speed and comprehension

Many people who say that they never read actually read a lot without realizing it. They read road signs, traffic signals, advertising signs and labels, price tags, and bus or train schedules. They read to get a driver's license and to bake a cake. You—and everybody else—do this kind of practical reading every day.

People also read for fun. In reading a good mystery, you're not so much interested in getting information as you are in being entertained.

People also read to learn. You probably read magazines and books for information on your favorite hobby or singing star. You read to learn more about something that interests you. Thus, the reading experience is an enjoyable one.

Reading on the job can be enjoyable too. If you're interested in your job, you will enjoy reading work-related information, and you will be a good reader without really trying.

Reading is the understanding of written or printed information. Like listening, reading is a communication skill. You receive information from other people when you read. Reading involves all types of thinking, including feeling, evaluating, and imagining.

The importance of reading to your job cannot be overstated. You will read a help-wanted ad to discover a job opening. You will read an application blank in order to fill it out. Once on the job, you will continue reading.

You may have an employer who is unable to give you as much direction and attention as your teacher does. If so, you will have to get a lot of information by yourself, often by reading. It is essential for you to be able to read effectively. You have to understand and remember what you have read if you are going to develop and advance on the job.

The desire to be a successful worker can make you want to read more. It did so with Rosa Mayfair.

Rosa was brought up in a family that believed women did not need education at all. At the age of 17, she married a man who shared her family's views on the role of women. Her marriage lasted 5 years and ended in divorce.

To support herself and her two children, Rosa got a full-time job as a waitress and enrolled in a computer school to become a keypunch operator. She enjoyed her hectic schedule. More important, she discovered abilities and talents she didn't know she had.

At every opportunity, Rosa read something on programming or computer technology. She couldn't read enough information involving her new career. Yet, in high school, Rosa had felt that reading wasn't really that important. After all, she was going to be a housewife!

Of course, reading is important no matter what you are going to be or to do for a living. You cannot know now just how important reading may end up being for you. A career you are considering may change quickly and require a lot of reading to keep up with the changes. You may find yourself in a career that you haven't considered yet at all—one that requires a lot of reading. This unit will give you a chance to look at your reading habits, skills, and attitudes.

49

SOME SHORTCUTS FOR EFFECTIVE READING

Before you buy something, you will usually look it over carefully. You know what you want it for. You want to make sure that it has what you need. Approach reading the same way. First know what you are reading for. What is your purpose? Are you reading for pleasure? Are you reading for specific information? The answers to those questions will determine whether you want to read very carefully or quickly. The answers will determine whether you want to read every word or just parts of the material.

If you are reading for pleasure, you will probably just begin at the beginning and go on through to the end or until you no longer feel any pleasure in reading. That is fine for fun reading. If you are reading to get information as part of your job, however, your approach will be different. You will have to read the material whether it brings you pleasure or not. But again, depending on what your needs are, you may not have to read every single word.

If you know what your specific needs are, you can use two devices to increase your reading efficiency and reduce the amount of unnecessary reading—previewing and skimming. *Previewing* is the process of looking at those parts of the reading material that summarize or outline what the material is about. *Skimming* is the process of glancing over reading material quickly and rather superficially.

PREVIEWING

Usually you can decide whether or not you have to take the time to read a book by previewing it briefly. Sometimes such a preview will give you all of the information you need. Other times it will tell you that you have to read the whole book, or just a section or a chapter of it. As you are reading the book later, you will find that the preview has given you more direction and speed.

The Title Is Descriptive

When previewing material, first consider the title. If you are looking for the wiring diagram of a Rainbow color television, for example, be sure that you have the right book in your hands. Does its title indicate in any way that the book actually describes a Rainbow color television?

You may be in the habit of browsing through and buying paperbacks and popular hard-cover books. Many of these titles serve more to attract attention than to give information. They often have little relationship to the book's actual content. Titles of manuals and educational materials that you will be using on the job, however, usually are informative, not just attention getters.

While previewing a book, keep your reading purpose in mind and think of specific questions that you hope the book will answer. In looking for a wiring diagram of a Rainbow color television, you have to ask, for example, "Where can I find a wiring diagram for a 21-inch portable Rainbow color television, Model 18703–42–0418, which was manufactured in 1979?"

The Preface or Foreword Tells You What to Expect

The preface or foreword can be an important source of information about the contents of the book. These two sections used to stand for the same thing, but present usage has given them different purposes. The *preface* contains the author's introductory remarks about his work. The *foreword*, however, now contains a statement about the book by someone other than the author. Both come before the actual text of the book begins. The preface or foreword may also tell you the main purposes of the book and whether it has been written for experts or beginners.

The Table of Contents Is an Outline

Next look at the table of contents. The *table of contents* is an outline of the book's main topics. It usually is a list of the chapter headings. The title indicates whether you've found the right book. The table of contents indicates which chapters will contain the information you need. If there is only one chapter on the wiring diagram of the

21-inch portable Rainbow color television, that is probably the only chapter you will have to read.

The Index Is a Guide

The index is a guide of great value, especially when you are looking for a particular item. The *index* lists the items discussed in the book and tells on what pages they can be found. There are basically two kinds of indexes—alphabetical and numerical. An alphabetical index lists the items or subjects discussed in the reading material in alphabetical order—from A to Z. A numerical index lists items in numerical order by their identifying number.

Most businesses use stock numbers to keep track of their products. You may have to use an alphabetical index to find a stock number. The stock number may also be the item's index number. It can be used to find such things as price,

An index lists the items discussed in a book and tells on what pages they can be found. Can you name the two types of indexes shown above?

original invoice, or where the item is located in the warehouse.

SKIMMING

Penny Peterson had been at her job with the Mayfair Moving Company for 3 months. Her work had been accurate, but Penny had a problem. She had to determine the prices and tariff regulations for each move. The rates and tariffs varied with the distance of the move.

In addition, special electronics equipment and household goods were shipped at different rates. Packing charges were based on an hourly rate for local moves. Yet, on interstate moves, an individual box rate was charged for packing.

Penny had various tariff books and rate sheets to help her determine pricing. But Penny was not a careful reader. She frequently had to correct prices because she used the wrong tariff book. Penny didn't know how to use the table of contents or index, so she often ended up doing a lot of unnecessary reading. On busy days, when there were a number of moves to check, she always fell behind.

A knowledge of simple previewing and skimming skills could have saved Penny time.

Looking for someone's number in the phone directory, searching for a word in the dictionary, finding a particular topic in an encyclopedia, and scanning a newspaper for interesting stories are all examples of skimming.

Have a Purpose

If you don't have a purpose in mind as you are skimming over material, you are wasting time. Your purpose can be as simple as looking for something interesting in a newspaper, or it can be as specific as looking for a particular speech given by Polonius in Shakespeare's play *Hamlet*. The point is that you must have a purpose, no matter how simple, as you skim.

Suppose you are working as a salesperson for a company called Natural Cosmetics. You have just returned from lunch and have an hour to kill before a 2:00 sales conference. Spotting a book entitled *The Soft Sell* on the receptionist's desk, you ask if you can borrow it. He replies that he's not through reading it, but that you're welcome to look at it for a few minutes.

Upon looking over the table of contents, you discover that only the fifth and eighth chapters interest you. You do not have to read the whole book, but there is not even enough time to read thoroughly those sections that interest you. So you decide to skim the two chapters for the main ideas.

Find the Topic Sentence

For the most part, you concentrate on the first sentence of every paragraph. This sentence often indicates the paragraph's content. When it does so, it is called the *topic sentence.*

Every so often you spot a paragraph that interests you, and you slow down your reading speed to take in the information fully. Other paragraphs discuss things you already know, so you skim over them. With these paragraphs, you don't read every sentence, but you do look for key words and phrases that tell what the author is saying. You do so just to make sure you don't miss anything. You keep your eyes moving from top to bottom, from left to right, without pausing or going back to reread anything.

Before you know it, the hour is up, and you have read all that you wanted to read in the entire book. When you return it to the receptionist, he says "It'll take me a couple of nights more to finish it, but you can have it when I'm done." You respond "Thanks, but I've already read it."

You read at different speeds, depending upon your purpose. You usually read slowly when you want to learn something new and quickly when you don't. Thus, you shift your reading speed from page to page, from paragraph to paragraph, and even from sentence to sentence. Just as varying road conditions determine the speed of a car, varying purposes determine the speed of your reading.

CHAPTER 50

HOW TO READ FASTER AND REMEMBER MORE

The essential differences between skimming over material and reading it thoroughly are speed of coverage and amount of information taken in. There are, however, many similarities between skimming and reading. With both, you read more than one word at a time and move at a constant pace from left to right down the page as you seek the main ideas. The sections that follow contain some techniques to help you read faster and remember more of what you read.

READ MORE THAN ONE WORD AT A TIME

As you read, do you say each word to yourself? Sounding out words silently as you read them is called *subvocalization*. This slows your reading speed to one word at a time. Obvious subvocalizers move their lips and tongues when they read. Other subvocalizers keep their lips and tongues still but make a slight movement of the muscles in their throat. To find out if you subvocalize, place your fingers on your vocal cords and read. If you feel movement, you are subvocalizing.

One technique to help you to stop subvocalizing is to hum a tune silently while reading. It is hard to subvocalize and hum at the same time!

Another exercise to help you to stop subvocalizing is to tap your feet while reading. This activity will help to distract you just enough from reading along with yourself. Only conscious and persistent attention to the problem of subvocalizing can stop it.

Do you move your head from side to side as you read? You only have to move your eyes. Your eyes move faster over words than your head does. By moving your head, you are slowing your reading down.

Vertical Field of Vision

other subjects. But he also knows that he's an excellent note-taker, and he knows how to concentrate when he studies. So he uses study skills to improve his English performance. He tries. He does not simply give up about making some achievement in English. Of course, he may never become the greatest writer in the world; he may not even succeed in pulling his grade up very far. But his effort will still pay off. It will produce far more successes than if he pretends that he had no difficulty.

Lateral Field of Vision

Reading involves using both the lateral and the vertical fields of vision. The lateral field of vision is the number of words in a line you can read at a single glance. The vertical field of vision is the number of lines you can see above and below the line you are focused on.

If you read whole phrases at a time, you increase your reading speed and effectiveness. Slow readers see only one word at a time. If you focus your eyes on only one word at a time, you reduce your reading speed. Furthermore, single-word reading focuses your attention on isolated words instead of on whole ideas. Try to read several words at a glance.

Read for thoughts, ideas, information—none of which can be expressed in a single word. The more words you can take in at a single glance, the more meaning you will get from them, and the better you will understand what you read.

Your *lateral field of vision*—the amount of a line you can read in a single glance—takes in from three to five words. Consider this with the fact that you can make as many as four eye contacts with the page in 1 second! In other words, it is possible to read 20 words per second—1,200 words per minute! Of course, this is an ideal reading speed. Most people read at much slower speeds—between 200 and 300 words per minute. But with practice, you can increase your lateral field of vision.

Reading also involves your *vertical field of vision*—that is, seeing one or two lines above and below the line you are focused on. Your vertical field of vision takes in from two to three words or phrases above and below the point at which your eyes are fixed. Reading involves using both lateral and vertical fields of vision.

DO NOT REREAD

Are you in the habit of rereading words and sentences? Many people find themselves going back over what they have already read or pausing at a word. They may believe that rereading is going to improve their comprehension. Actually, however, rereading can decrease comprehension by preventing the person from going on to the next sentence, which will probably explain away the confusion.

Read at a steady pace to avoid the problems caused by rereading. Also remember to keep your eyes moving from left to right while reading. In this way, you will avoid reading words over again. Of course, there will be times, when you are studying something intensively or memorizing something, when you will have to reread. But that is not the case with most reading.

READ FOR MEANING

Many ads for sales representatives are for nonsalaried jobs. The pay on such jobs consists only of commissions, which are a percentage of the amount the customer pays for a product sold. Thus, nothing sold, nothing earned. Some nonsalaried sales jobs for experienced salespeople are excellent jobs. But many such jobs for beginners are not good jobs at all.

A good reader is able to detect come-on ads for nonsalaried, straight-commission jobs that make such promises as "Earn up to $1,000 your first week," "Work your own hours," "Unlimited earnings potential," or "Move into management if you qualify." The ability to read for meaning can save you time and gas spent chasing such worthless job offers.

Good readers are able to figure out the meaning of what they read. They let the writer speak without imposing their own beliefs and desires onto what the writer is saying. When you are able to understand what you read, you generally remember it. Four ways that will help you to read for meaning and to remember more are to concentrate, to form pictures, to form patterns, and to increase your vocabulary.

Concentrate

You can remember anything as long as you want to. If you are looking for a job as a short-order cook, for example, it is easy for you to remember the salary and benefits stated in an ad. The key to remembering what you read is concentration. *Concentration* requires focusing your thoughts in a particular direction. Don't let your mind wander when you are reading. Think about the subject, not about something that happened in school or what you are going to do when you put the book down.

Concentration largely involves awareness of thoughts—the ability to know what you are thinking about at any given moment. It is difficult for many people to know when their minds are wandering from what they are reading. When someone asks you what you are thinking about, how often do you say "Oh, nothing at all"? Your mind is never empty, however. You are always thinking about something, often several things at once.

When you are aware of your thoughts, you can catch your mind wandering, eliminate the distracting thoughts, and focus on what you are reading.

Form Pictures

By forming a picture in your mind, you can better understand what you are reading. Assume that you are working in a sports shop and that a customer returns a fishing reel. When the customer complains that it doesn't work, you examine the reel and see that the spool is freewheeling. You pick up the owner's manual and turn to

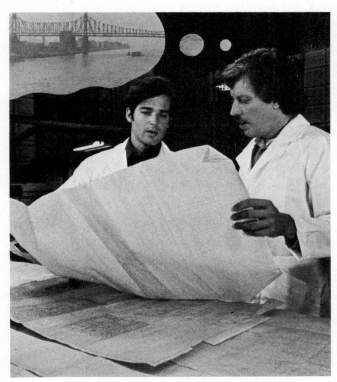

Form mental pictures to help you read for meaning. This method helps when reading something complicated such as the blueprint that the men above are reading. (Courtesy National Tool, Die and Precision Machining Association)

the section headed "Free-Spool Clutch," where you read the following:

> The small lever attached to the right side plate of your reel and extending out to the edge of the plate itself is the free-spool lever. It enables you to "shift gears"—that is, to engage or disengage the spool. A little experimenting will quickly teach you the correct shifting motion for your reel.

You look at the reel and try to form a picture in your mind of what you just read. Forming a picture is easy with the reel in front of you. If you read the description again tomorrow, however, you will have the same picture in mind, even without the reel. Forming mental pictures while you read makes you a better reader.

Form Patterns

Another procedure in reading for meaning is to try to distinguish the main ideas from the details. When you are able to see the organization of the details surrounding the main ideas, you have grasped the pattern of the author's writing. When you can recognize the details in their relationship to the main ideas, you will have become a skillful reader. You will be able to outline mentally what you have read.

You should also try to relate what you already know to what you are reading. In other words, after you have read a piece of writing, you should try to fit it in with your own knowledge and experience on the subject. In this way, you can make your reading experience more personal. When a piece of writing has personal meaning for you, you will remember what you've read.

Increase Vocabulary

Most trades and professions develop their own *jargon*—that is, words that refer to products and operations peculiar to a specific business or field. In some jobs, it may seem that you have met up with a foreign language.

Suppose that you have a job as a carpenter's helper. You show up for work at 9:00 and find a note from the carpenter explaining that he will return shortly. He has also left some instructions:

1. Put a pound of galvanized tenpenny nails in your apron pocket and go to the west wing and help Amy get the joists in place.
2. Count the bundles of shakes that have been delivered.
3. Start gathering defective studs and cut them down to size to be used for the fire wall.

When you are new on the job, you will hear words that are either new to you or used in a new way. Sometimes you will not have time to look up the new word in a dictionary. Or you may be embarrassed to ask what the word means.

You will often be able to understand a new word, however, if you look for clues to its meaning. These clues are contained in the sentence that the word appears in or in preceding and following sentences. When you arrive at a definition this way, you are finding meaning from *context*—that is, the sentences or paragraph that surround a word and that may help to reveal what the word means.

One of the clues may be a restatement of the idea or the use of a *synonym*—that is, another word meaning the same thing. For example, you would probably be able to interpret the meaning of "studs" from the following sentence: "We will

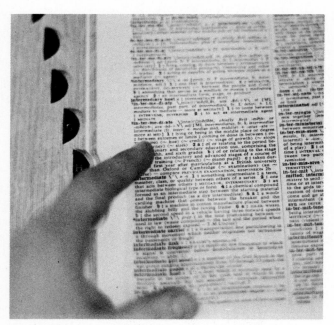

Increasing your vocabulary will help you to read for meaning. The best way to confirm the meaning of a word is to check it in a dictionary. Using a dictionary is part of your vocabulary growth. (Marsha Cohen)

have to use some other 2 × 4s on the fire wall, so we can use these studs somewhere else." From its context, you know that a stud is a 2 × 4 used in the wall of a building.

Look at another example. Anthony is reading a passage in his cookbook on soups: "Be sure to season the soup well, or it will be bland. Nothing is worse than a tasteless soup." From the context, Anthony discovers that "bland" and "tasteless" are synonymous.

Sometimes you will be able to understand a word because an *antonym*—that is, a word that has the opposite meaning—is used in context with it. For example, you are told that the kitchen cabinet doors have a mahogany veneer, but that the doors for the bar in the den are solid oak. You guess from this context that a "veneer" is a surface finish.

Don't let unfamiliar words slip by. Use them as opportunities to increase your vocabulary. The best way to confirm the meaning of a word is to check it in a dictionary. Using a dictionary is part of your vocabulary growth. Your job performance will be enhanced with the word knowledge you gain.

If, for some reason, you cannot use a dictionary or figure out the meaning from the context, do not hesitate to ask what the word means. Better to be a little embarrassed at first than to make a serious mistake because of misunderstanding a word. Besides, when you are word-conscious, you show that you are interested in what you read and in what you do.

The techniques suggested for reading effectively will be helpful only if you use them. If you work at making good reading a habit, you are sure to notice a marked improvement in your reading ability. In addition, you will receive an extra dividend in the form of career growth.

Getting It All Together

1. What is the difference between previewing and skimming?

2. What are some actions that may slow your reading and reduce your comprehension?

3. Name five items you read every day other than books.

4. What benefits can you think of that would result from being a more effective reader?

5. Agree or disagree: Not enough time in school is devoted to teaching reading. Why?

16

WRITING

Your goals in this unit are given in the following list:

To realize that almost any job requires some writing

To understand that writing requires knowing your readers, your purpose, and your subject, as well as spelling and grammar

To become aware of your self-identity as it is expressed in your writing

To become sensitive to your readers' needs and interests

Writing can take many forms—novels, poems, essays, memoirs, plays, newspaper and magazine articles. In the business world, there are also annual reports, ads, press releases, memos, and letters. On many jobs, much of the work, such as filling out orders and invoices, requires writing. The purpose of this unit is to show you the importance of written communication. You will discover that your personality shows in your writing. You will also learn a few basic techniques for improving your writing on the job.

You have probably heard people say "Where I'll be working, I won't have to write on the job" or "I want a job where I don't have to do much writing." It is true that some jobs, such as many in manufacturing and construction, require less writing than business and office occupations. So why bother with learning how to write?

Most jobs do require some writing. Truck drivers, for example, have to fill out trip reports, delivery receipts, accident reports, and maintenance reports. You can't assume that you won't have to write on your job.

In your personal life, you will probably meet up with many situations in which you will have to write. You will be able to handle such situations more effectively if you can write acceptably. You may have to write a letter complaining about an appliance that did not work, or a store that did not sell you what it promised. Writing lists of things to do or buy often helps you organize your thinking. You will learn that writing is an important tool at work and away from work.

In this unit, you will learn why it is necessary to be prepared before you actually begin writing. Who will your readers be? For what purpose are you writing to them? Do you know enough about the subject on which you are writing? When you can answer these questions with a "Yes," then you are on your way to preparing yourself to write.

Learning how to express yourself in writing and how to write clearly are the next steps to becoming an effective writer. In this unit, you will also be given some guidelines that will help you to master these steps.

51

BE PREPARED TO WRITE

Writing always involves three elements—the reader, the writer's purpose, and the subject matter. Before beginning to write anything, it's a good idea to consider each element with some care, in order to give your message a good chance to get through clearly.

KNOW YOUR READERS

Writing is like throwing a dart. You can't hit the target if you don't have a clear view of what you are aiming at. In writing, having a clear view of the target means knowing your readers. You have to consider your readers' ages, backgrounds, and reasons for reading your writing. What do they already know? What don't they know?

The answers to these questions will give your writing more focus. There is nothing more difficult than writing for a vaguely defined audience or a wide variety of people—people of different ages and backgrounds, people with different reasons for reading your writing.

When you think about your readers, ask yourself questions about them. Who are they? How many readers will you have? If there are several, what are their common interests? If there is only one reader, what is that person's main interest? Is the reader your boss, a fellow employee, or a customer?

Suppose that you need a piece of pipe. Because you live out in the country, you have decided to order it by mail. In order to describe the particular pipe you need, you have to organize your thoughts. You could draw a picture and put in some measurements to get your message

When writing, you must have a clear view of your readers. This means knowing your readers' ages, backgrounds, interests, and reasons for reading your writing. (Courtesy Salt River Project)

across. If you are an effective writer, however, you will be able to describe what you want accurately by drawing pictures with words. You will be able to do so partly because you will be able to figure out the reader's viewpoint and determine what the reader has to know.

Just as you have to keep your reader in mind if you want to buy something, you have to do the same thing if you want to sell something. Stephanie Frazer wants to sell a case of oil. Read a copy of the letter Stephanie plans to send to see if she knows her reader.

Dear Ms. Miller:

We sell large quantities of high-grade oil at very competitive prices. For example, you could buy 30-weight oil from us at 99 cents a can. This is detergent-type oil, packed 24 cans to the case. The price represents a 40 percent saving compared to what you are presently paying for this type of oil. If you purchase in larger quantities, we can quote even lower prices.

We would appreciate serving you.

Very truly yours,
Stephanie Frazer

Stephanie does know her reader. She knows that she can save her customer at least 40 percent of what she is paying for oil. She has Ms. Miller's interest in mind and doesn't present her with irrelevant information.

KNOW YOUR PURPOSE

At work, the purpose for your writing will frequently be determined by your assignment. Most writing that you do on the job will be to inform, request, confirm, or persuade. The following sentence fragments illustrate different purposes:

"Jack, I just wanted to let you know . . ." (Inform)

"I would greatly appreciate it if you could . . ." (Request)

"This note will confirm our agreement . . ." (Confirm)

"Therefore, the project will fulfill two very pressing needs . . ." (Persuade)

Companies use up tons of paper every year conducting their business correspondence. They do so to keep people informed of ongoing developments, to request certain actions, to confirm agreements in case of future dissent, and to persuade people to agree with a plan or buy a product.

KNOW YOUR SUBJECT

You cannot write about a subject unless you know something about it. There is nothing more

Knowing your subject means getting all the information about it before you begin to write. Then you'll be able to select only the material you need to prepare a clear and informative report when you're ready to write.

frustrating than trying to write about something you yourself don't understand thoroughly. You have experienced this frustration if you have ever taken an essay test unprepared! The more job experience you acquire, the more you will know about certain subjects and the more able you will be to write about them.

Before you begin to write on any topic, try to get all the information you can on it. The most effective writers know much more about their subjects than they put down on paper. What they write is often just the tip of the iceberg of their knowledge.

KNOW SPELLING AND GRAMMAR

You can know your readers, your purpose, and your subject yet still fail to write so that you can be easily understood. It is equally important to know how to spell and to use words properly. If you do not spell correctly or use the right grammar, people will not be able to understand what you have tried to say in your writing. Consider the following two examples:

Bethann Kroll was head lifeguard for the summer at the town beach. She was a good swimmer and

Some embarrassing situations can arise if you don't know how to spell. If you are not sure of how a word is spelled, look up the word in a dictionary.

enjoyed her job. But she sometimes had trouble controlling the other lifeguards. One day the beach manager complained to her that not one lifeguard was on a guard platform. Bethann was shocked to see that all the guard towers were indeed empty. She found two guards walking on the beach, two more patrolling in the rowboats, and another taking a lunch break. Bethann knew that at least one person should always be on the platform of one of the guard towers to be able to see and be seen. She typed the following notice for the bulletin board:

```
ALL LIFEGUARDS MUST NOT LEAVE THEIR
PLATFORMS DURING DUTY HOURS. TWO MAY
BE ON THE BEACH OR IN ROWBOATS, AND
ONE MAY BE TAKING A BRAKE AND BUY SODA.
```

Bethann's problems did not end with the posting of this notice. They became worse. Soon some of the lifeguards were complaining that they did not know where they were supposed to be. Others refused to take turns rowing the boat or patrolling the beach. Her notice was so poorly written that the lifeguards did not know if she meant that all of them must be on the platforms all the time. Those who did not like patrolling used the notice as an excuse to avoid it. Furthermore, Bethann did not stimulate much confidence in her leadership ability by misspelling a word like "break." Bethann's poor use of words and her misspelling could very well cost her her job as head lifeguard.

Grant, an excellent photographer, felt that he would never have to worry about such dull stuff as spelling and grammar. "In this field, who needs it?" Grant thought. When he decided to go into business for himself, he found that he had to write business letters in order to get jobs to work on. After much struggle, he produced the following letter:

```
Dear Sir:
My name is Grant Field, Im a commersal
photographer with much expereince.
I know that whichever you're needs, Im
more then capible of doing it. I do
color, black & white, and transpar-
encies. Im sure that no other photo-
graphers cant do as good as me for the
same prise. So if you ever really need
great pictures you wont be sorry.
Sinserly,

Grant Field
```

Well, not too many people are going to call on Grant Field to do photographic work for them. He may be an excellent photographer, but he will have a tough time getting the chance to convince anyone if he must rely on such poorly written letters filled with misspellings and bad grammar.

To write effectively, then, you must have a basic knowledge of spelling and grammar. The way you use language determines not only whether you will be understood but also what other people think of you and of the quality of your work.

52

EXPRESSING YOURSELF IN WRITING

"Why do I have to write at all?" You might answer, "I write because I want to communicate with someone else." But why not tell the person your message? When do you communicate by speaking and when by writing? Think for a minute about how much time you spent yesterday communicating by speaking and how much by writing.

The average person spends about three times as much time speaking as writing. If you spend more than the average amount of time writing, what does this say about you and your personality? What kinds of jobs do people who enjoy writing have? What if you spend less time writing than most other people? What does this say about your personality?

Speaking is easier for most people than writing. For some, the opposite is true. How sociable you are probably affects how you communicate with others. When you speak, you exchange ideas. When you write, you present ideas.

Imagine that the end of the school year is 2 weeks away and that you are planning to quit your part-time job. Your employer, however, assumes that you will work through the summer. Will you write your employer a letter of resignation? Or will you tell your employer that you are planning to leave? Your personality will affect your decision.

Your personality affects not only your decision to communicate through writing or speaking but also what you say. Usually you are not present when someone reads what you have written. You are not there to explain further what you meant to say or to receive feedback from the reader. Compare the written pictures presented by Mr. Brown and Ms. Epstein in the following example:

The Brown and Epstein Real Estate Firm was renting summer cabins at a large lake. Both Mr. Brown and Ms. Epstein were writing short descriptions of the cabins for prospective renters.

Mr. Brown wrote:

```
This cabin is made of solid oak. It
has 1,200 square feet of living space
and a 400 square-foot porch. The bath
is equipped with modern plumbing. You
will really like this cabin.
```

Ms. Epstein's description said:

```
The cabin is well constructed, made of
solid oak. For your vacation enjoy-
ment, it is located near a large moun-
tain lake where the fishing is great.
The cabin is very spacious, with 1,200
square feet of living space. In addi-
ion, there is an enclosed porch that
surrounds the cabin. You will have
plenty of room for your family's
recreation. Modern plumbing has re-
cently been installed. This cabin,
located in the natural wonder of the
Big Tree Forest, will give your family
the ideal summer experience.
```

Could you picture the cabin in Mr. Brown's description? A prospective renter would see a more favorable picture of the cabin in Ms. Epstein's description. Her description of the cabin is more interesting and has more personality in it than Mr. Brown's. You can tell that she herself believes that renting the cabin is a good idea. Your attitudes are reflected in your written words.

EXPRESS A POSITIVE SELF-IDENTITY

Your self-identity—the way you feel about yourself—can change as you grow and mature. You communicate your self-identity in the way you dress, act, and speak. "But," you may be asking yourself, "what does my self-identity have to do with what I write?" Compare the following letters of resignation written by Pat and Theo to answer that question:

Dear Ms. Mager:
I am very sorry, but I am going to have to quit. I'm sure you won't have any problem replacing me. I'm sorry that I was late so often during my employment here. I hope that it will not affect what you say to my future employer. Thank you for giving me a chance. I hope that my leaving won't cause you any inconvenience.
Sincerely yours,

Pat Zimmerman

Dear Ms. Mager:
I have certainly enjoyed my work at the XYZ Company. It has been a pleasure working with you.

Because there are more opportunities for advancement at the ABC Company, I have accepted a new position there. Please accept my resignation, effective May 30.

Thank you for the kind consideration that you have shown me during the past year. My work experience has been both pleasant and worthwhile.
Sincerely yours,

Theo Walsh

Which letter reflected a negative self-identity? If you were Ms. Mager, which person would you recommend more highly?

Theo's confident and positive self-identity clearly showed in his letter. Your self-identity is revealed in most things you write. A sloppy, ill-thought-out message reflects you. A neat, well-organized message also reflects you.

GET YOUR READERS INTERESTED

Knowing what catches a reader's fancy and what misses a reader's interests is invaluable knowledge for the writer. You can either interest or bore your readers. No matter what you're writing—a letter, a memo, or a telegram—you must keep your readers in mind. You must understand how your writing affects the readers' behavior and thinking.

Understanding this is particularly important when you are writing to get your readers to do something. If you are writing to persuade, it's a good idea to ask yourself "How does the reader benefit or gain from what I am asking?" Most people are interested in things that benefit them, so persuasive writing necessarily stresses what is positive for the reader. Consider how you would have written the memo that Willie Mae Berla was working on in the following example:

Willie Mae Berla worked for a large company that promoted sports and entertainment shows—Mid-South Sports Action, Inc. She was working on a memo about a new health plan for company employees. But she was not quite sure just how to make the health plan appeal to the employees.

The purpose of the memo was twofold—to inform employees about the health plan and to persuade them to accept it. Obviously the best way to write such a memo was to stress the benefits of the health plan.

Ms. Berla decided to review the positive aspects of the plan from the employees' viewpoint. The plan would mean greater security for the employees. All hospital and doctors' bills would be paid in case of an accident or illness. The company was willing to pay for most of the insurance costs. The average employee would have to pay only $10 a month.

Ms. Berla's final draft of the memo read this way:

TO: ALL EMPLOYEES
FROM: WILLIE MAE BERLA
SUBJECT: A NEW HEALTH PLAN
                    January 5, 19—
Exciting news! No more need to worry about hospital or doctors' bills. You and your family can feel secure in knowing that all your health care needs will be provided for when you join our company's new health plan.

Best of all, this health plan will be very inexpensive. Mid-South Sports Action will pay for most of the premium, leaving the average employee with only $10 a month to pay.

To find out more, attend our office meeting next Thursday, at 11:30 a.m.

To get and retain your readers' interest, you must keep them in mind when you are writing.

Choose a Tone and Style to Appeal to Your Readers

The style and tone of Ms. Berla's memorandum was designed to make the readers interested in a new health plan. The current trend in writing memos or informal reports is to be relaxed. Stiff or formal writing is not very popular today. There is, however, no clear-cut rule about when to be informal and when to be formal in business correspondence. Tone and style are largely determined by company executives and vary greatly from one office to the next.

Some writers think they are being formal by writing in the third person instead of in the first person:

"The order was requested by the sales representative" instead of "I requested the order."

"It is the opinion of this interviewer" instead of "My opinion is."

"It is recommended that" instead of "We recommend that."

Avoid using the third person (he, she, they) or such constructions as "It is recommended." Use instead the more direct first person "I recommend" or, if you really do mean you and some other people, "We recommend." Queen Victoria

of England would say "We" when referring to herself. Anyone else who does so sounds a little silly and very pompous. In fact, even she did.

If you are writing to convey the action of a group, it is proper to say "It is recommended." In general, though, stick with the first person "I" if you are writing about your own requests, recommendations, needs, and so on. Never strain to be formal. It is much better to be clear and direct. Courtesy, proper spelling, and proper grammar create formality enough for virtually every writing situation.

Emphasize Subjects That Appeal to Your Readers

Appealing to your readers' interests involves them in your writing. When writing, think about what aspect of the subject will interest your readers. Money and profits? Status? Security?

The more personal your writing is, the better. A customer would rather receive a note saying "Ms. Current: Your package is ready for delivery. You may contact me at 666–5300" than "Dear Customer: Your order is ready. Contact the below number to have it delivered."

Remember that certain facts and information are important to your reader. Consider the telephone message that Bernard wrote for his supervisor, Karen Michele.

Some man called. He said that it was pretty important to talk with you and mentioned something about one of his salespeople.

Look what happens when Bernard remembers details and names.

Kevin Sheldon called you at 2:30 to talk about one of his salespeople, Corrie McMillan. He said that it was very important that you call him as soon as possible. His number is 321–7000.

Bernard's second telephone message was not only more personal but also a lot more informative to his supervisor than the first version of the message. Although a relatively minor form of writing, phone messages can be made more interesting. In any event, they must contain all the essential information.

CONSIDER YOUR READERS' FEELINGS

Kay and Dick worked as dental assistants. Their job included sending out personal notices reminding patients of their 6-month checkups. They worded their notices quite differently, however.

Dr. A. J. KEMP
111 Main Street
Centreville, Illinois 62206

Dear Ms. Mayo:
Your 6-month dental appointment has been scheduled by this office for April 15, at 8 a.m. Please be on time.

Sincerely,

Kay Cahill

Dr. A. J. KEMP
111 Main Street
Centreville, Illinois 62206

Dear Mr. Kaiser:
Just a reminder to let you know that your 6-month dental checkup is due. Please call our office for an appointment that is convenient for you. We're looking forward to seeing you again.

Sincerely,

Dick Oakley

There's a good chance that Ms. Mayo will become annoyed over the note Kay composed. Who can blame her? The appointment was set without regard for Ms. Mayo's own schedule. Furthermore, the note, through implication, criticized her for possibly being late. The way Dick phrased his note, however, showed respect for the reader.

Although Kay didn't intend to criticize Ms. Mayo, some writers do criticize their readers intentionally. The result is almost always a very negative one. Generally people react to criticism by becoming defensive and seeing the criticism as an insult. Some people may act as though they don't mind and try to ignore their own hurt feelings. Remembering that people don't like to be criticized can help your writing. Consider the following letter written to the plumbers' union by Joe Kneller, a plumber's apprentice, and the union's response:

Dear Union Representative:
I have been using carbolic acid for cleaning our pipes. It works real good. Please tell me if this is OK.
Very truly yours,

Joe Kneller

Dear Mr. Kneller:
Do not use carbolic acid as a cleansing agent for pipes. Carbolic acid is a purging agent. It is incompatible with pipe material and results in corrosion and rapid deterioration.
We are surprised that a member of the profession would ask such a question. Your question shows a serious lack of knowledge about your job. We suggest that you spend more time learning about your trade.
Sincerely,

The Plumber's Union

Do you think the union's reply is going to have a positive effect on Joe Kneller? If anything, it will stop Joe from asking questions and learning about his profession!

When writing, think of your readers' feelings as well as trying to interest them in what you are saying. These considerations are important even when writing brief and casual notes.

CHOOSE THE BEST WORDS TO GET YOUR MESSAGE ACROSS

The average person's vocabulary is approximately 30,000 words. The words you select from your vocabulary reflect your character.

Short and Long Words

Here are two sentences written by two different people:

> The nocturnal shipment was expedited in a perfunctory manner.

> The evening shipment was handled routinely.

The meanings of these two sentences are really the same, but they do reveal two different characters. The writer of the first sentence apparently is the kind of person who thinks big words impress people. In fact, this writer must care more about impressing people than about being understood, for the sentence must be read twice—and with a dictionary at hand!

Good writers use uncommon words—words not in most people's speaking vocabulary—only when simpler words won't say the same thing. If you have a choice between two words, pick the simpler and more familiar one.

Abstract and Concrete Words

The fewer the number of abstract words and the greater the number of concrete words, the clearer the writing. *Abstract words* refer to ideas, concepts, or generalizations. They are not easily understood. Examples of abstract words are socialism, democracy, and independence. There is often more than one meaning to an abstract word. Consider the word "beauty." To some people, "beauty" means good looks. To others, it is a certain charm. When you write with abstract words, you run the risk that your reader may come away with a different meaning from the one you intended.

Concrete words refer to a particular event or tangible object. They are not general. Examples of concrete words include paper clip, golf ball, necklace, the American Civil War, and snow. Most concrete words are easily understood.

Many words fall somewhere between abstract and concrete. For example, the word "transportation" is more abstract than concrete. The word "car" is fairly concrete. And "1974 blue Ford station wagon" is very concrete. To illustrate further, read the following police reports, which move from the abstract to the concrete:

> The suspect escaped using what is thought to be his own transportation.

> The suspect escaped in a car.

> The suspect escaped in a station wagon.

> The suspect escaped in a 1974 blue Ford station wagon.

When writing on the job, be as concrete as possible so that no one will misunderstand you.

The more ways you know of saying something, the more accurately you will be able to express your thoughts and feelings. If you work at it, you can learn many new words every day and use them effectively. When you learn a new word, one way to transfer it to your active vocabulary is to use it in your writing. Consult a dictionary whenever you come across a new word. Correct word usage can go a long way toward portraying you in a favorable manner.

Jargon

As you read in Chapter 50, most trades and professions develop their own *jargon*. Within a particular business, jargon makes for more efficient communication among employees (otherwise these new words never would have been created). If jargon is used with people outside the business, however, a communication breakdown can result. Consider the following example:

> Joyce worked in a warehouse shipping department. Recently she had received a number of letters from confused customers, all of whom had purchased a particular 10-speed bike through the company catalog. Joyce decided to check the catalog. The ordering instructions simply said:
>   SPEED-O 10-speed Bicycle, model # 053570. Specify size (from 15- to 20-inch) and color choice (brown, green, or red). Price $99.50 plus appropriate state tax, if any. (KD).
>   As Joyce read the instructions, she realized that the customer complaints centered on one problem—having to assemble the bike. Apparently the customers didn't expect the bike to arrive unassembled.

What does the word "artist" suggest to you? Does the word bring to mind the illustration shown here? Or does it suggest a different picture? Look up the denotation, or explicit meaning, of "artist" in the dictionary and compare it with your connotation of "artist." (Courtesy U.S. Department of Labor)

Joyce knew that KD meant "knocked down" (that is, unassembled), but she put herself in the customers' shoes. She saw that warehouse jargon was inappropriate for the catalog because "outsiders" wouldn't understand what KD stood for. Thanks to Joyce, the next issue of the catalog contained the word "unassembled."

As you enter a new profession or trade, you will meet up with jargon. It is important for you to learn the meanings of such words and be able to use them. But it is also important for you to remember when to use them. In writing to a customer or some other outsider, you will have to replace the jargon with words that will be meaningful to that person.

Shades of Meaning

People put personal meanings on words, based on their past experiences. The meaning a word suggests, or implies, is known as its *connotation*. The explicit, or standard, meaning of a word is its *denotation*. The workers who dispose of your trash might resent it if you called them garbage collectors. But if you call them sanitation workers, they will feel that you have some idea of the complexity and importance of their work.

Imagine an ad for clothing that reads "Too fat to fit? Then come to Barry's for the outfit that's made for you!" Generally people are very sensitive about their body shape and size. Words like "fat," "skinny," "hairy," "bony," and "chunky" have strong emotional impact on the reader.

As a writer, you must be careful to choose words that won't offend your readers. Effective writing essentially is effective word choice. You can't choose your words effectively if you don't keep the readers' feelings and interests in mind. If you do, your writing will reflect a positive image of you and will have a positive effect on your readers.

Getting It All Together

1. What are two ways that your self-identity affects your writing? Describe each way briefly.

2. What is the difference between the connotation of a word and the denotation of a word?

3. Why is being able to express yourself in writing important both on the job and off the job? Give examples from your own life.

4. What's the difference between abstract words and concrete words? Which are usually easier to understand?

5. Why is it important to have a basic knowledge of grammar and spelling?

6. Can you name at least one situation in which each of the following individuals would need to be able to write effectively:

a nurse	a secretary	a teacher
a police officer	a job applicant	a carpenter
a parent	a consumer	a salesperson

WORKING AT HUMAN RELATIONS

17

THE NEED FOR HUMAN RELATIONS

Your goals in this unit are given in the following list:

To become familiar with the idea of human relations

To recognize how human relations affects your career

To develop key concepts for using knowledge about yourself in human relations

To develop key concepts for using your understanding of others in human relations

Human relations may sound like a heavy phrase to you. But if you think it's just something for teachers to talk about in the classroom—or that it doesn't have much to do with your everyday life—you are mistaken. Human relations is what your everyday life is all about.

Think about it for a minute. What does human relations really involve? Do you realize that you are having human relations right now?

That's right. As you read this page, you are taking part in one form of human relations—communication. You are receiving a message that the writer has delivered. True, the action of the writer took place some time ago, whereas your action is taking place now. Still, writer and reader are both involved in human relations. And that is an interesting point to keep in mind: An act that has taken place at an earlier time can affect human relations in the present.

Take another example. On your way to school or work today, you probably were involved in human relations. Saying hello to your friend or your teacher or the bus driver is another form of communication. And all forms of communication are human relations. Whether you write, read, speak, or use sign language, you are having human relations.

But communication is not the whole story. You relate to people in other ways too. You relate to them in how you dress, in how you take care of your body,

in how you view your work and yourself. Furthermore, **what** you communicate—even more than **how** you communicate—affects the quality of your human relations. The "what" is made up of your feelings about others and how you relate to them.

You may have human relations problems if you are not aware of exactly what you are communicating or how you are relating to other people. This does not mean that you should be self-conscious in your dealings with other people. You want to be comfortable and natural so people believe you enjoy spending time with them.

But you should be aware of the effect you have on others. People who bore others by talking too much or by talking only about themselves are obviously unaware of the impression they are making. Good human relations requires that you care about others and that you have enough self-awareness to judge your effect on other people.

In this crowded, complex world, you are relating to other people all the time. So it is only common sense to develop good human relations that will produce the effects you want. Many people feel that effective human relations depends on common sense. There is truth in that. And common sense can be learned, and developed, and sharpened.

Your goal in this unit is to develop and sharpen your common-sense approach to human relations.

CHAPTER 53

YOU ARE NOT ALONE

Getting along with people may not be the only important thing in life. But whatever life is all about, you will enjoy it more if you do get along with people. That is because human beings are social animals. In today's world, you have to depend on other people from birth on. How others react to you and how you react to them will affect how you will succeed in every area of your life.

This dependence on others is particularly strong in the pursuit of a career. Few occupations today can be followed in isolation. And even careers that are solitary—such as writing or painting—require the individual to make contacts with others more or less regularly. In most careers, of course, contact with others is an everyday occurrence.

People would all like to think that success can be achieved by skill or hard work alone. They do not want to believe that someone can get ahead simply by being well liked. Well, many factors play a part in a person's success. Someone who works hard and has talent probably will be a success to some degree, whether or not he or she has good human relations. And someone with little or no skills and lazy habits may enjoy considerable success just by being charming and by having good human relations.

However, successful people in either category are rare.

There are more people in the world today than ever before. How you get along with others can affect almost every area of your life. (Marsha Cohen)

285

Most people fall somewhere between these two extremes. That is, they do not have enough talent to ensure success in spite of getting along poorly with other people. Nor are they charmers who can succeed in a career without real technical skills and human relations skills.

GETTING ALONG AND GOING ALONG

You probably have heard the old saying "To get along, you must go along." This suggests that to succeed you must do what the majority wants or what the boss wants, no matter what your own feelings and moral code demand. This is not true. It presents a false picture of human relations.

You will hear many such sayings in life. Ignore them. They block good human relations by making you think in worn-out, simpleminded ways. Each situation and each person are a little different. You must draw upon your past experiences to deal with each new situation and person. Compare new situations and persons with those you've known in the past. It is important that you look to see what is different in them. Then you can respond and handle the new situation.

Old sayings aside, it is possible to disagree without being disagreeable. You **can** succeed without going along, without denying your personal code. But to do so, you must be prepared in both areas of your career: You must develop good technical skills **and** the ability to handle human relations.

Successful People

Many successful people seem to have outstanding personalities. That is, they are good at human relations. There is something about them that makes you like them for their own sake.

In other words, they appear to get along well with others. But not all famous or successful people are sweet and kind. Many of them do things that offend others, as newspapers and television report almost daily. Some successful people even seem to have bad human relations, though these are few. They must have exceptional talent to get away with it. In such cases, people respect their talent but dislike their personalities at the same time.

Many famous sports figures and show business celebrities seem to go out of their way to offend. And they get away with poor human relations, up to a point. But there is a certain

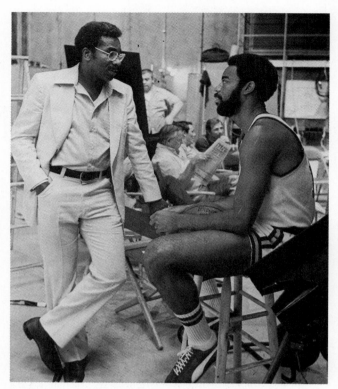

Basketball star Walt Frazier is an example of a public figure who is good at human relations. There is something about him that makes him liked by others. (© 1980, Children's Television Workshop)

amount of acting in what they do. Their irritating ways are something of a put-on. They know that their actions will get them publicity and recognition. And they have ability and skill to back them up.

Even so, they have to be careful. In fact, they are fully aware of how to handle human relations. They know just how to play the game in order to be successful. You might say that such people fully understand the important relationship between technical skills and human relations. They get along by making it a point **not** to go along.

Winning and Human Relations

That you can get along without going along can be seen clearly in the career of Muhammad Ali:

Muhammad Ali proved his talent as a boxer again and again. And while he fought for money inside the ring, he fought for his beliefs outside it. He refused to fight in a war he did not support—the

Vietnam War. As a result, he was sentenced to jail. His title as heavyweight champion of the world—which he had fought hard for and had won fairly in the ring—was taken away from him.

But Ali continued to fight. He fought his jail sentence in the courts and won. Yet his beliefs cost him a lot. He was not allowed to box during some of the best years of his life. Even so, he returned to the ring and won his title back.

Muhammad Ali's success was based on more than his unusual talent and skill as a boxer. He also understood human relations. He knew how to handle people with his words and thoughts as well as with his fists. And he never seemed to forget that he had to deal with people outside the ring as well as in it. He added human relations skills to his talent, and his success followed.

TURNING PEOPLE OFF

One way to see the importance of good human relations is to think of people you would rather not be with. In asking yourself why you feel as you do, you will see how much is involved in human relations. Other people's talk, dress, mannerisms, and attitudes may bother you. In the same way, your human relations may be spoiled by a habit of yours that you are unaware of but that annoys others. Sometimes a very small habit can turn someone off.

To get an idea of how many factors affect human relations, read the advice column in your local newspaper, such as "Dear Abby" or "Ann Landers." Most of the letters in these columns deal with poor human relations. People are bothered by bad human relations. They want advice about how to deal with friends, relatives, and co-workers who annoy them. Their problems range from how people dress or talk to how they behave.

Human relations involves communication. And communicating is more than making yourself understood. You have to make the person you are talking with want to listen and understand. And if you have an annoying habit of some kind, you may turn the other person off. For instance, how do you feel about someone who says "you know" or "understand" or "say" or "like" or "man" after every phrase? Or how do you feel about someone who is never on time? Such habits can be seen in others around you. If

Letters in the advice columns of local newspapers often deal with problems of human relations.

DEAR CINDY—

What do you think of this? After my mother came home from the hospital, we didn't discuss her operation with anyone outside the family. But a few days later, it seemed that everyone knew all about it. I finally traced the story to our doctor's assistant. My next door neighbor had the same experience with him. How can I make sure that my medical matters are kept "confidential" in the future?

ANNOYED

DEAR CINDY—

My problem is the man who works at the shop with me. He is always "borrowing" money from me——and he never pays me back! When I remind him about it, he laughs it off. I'd like to talk to the boss about it, but this man has been around longer than I have and I'm afraid I'll look like a troublemaker. Would you tell the boss or try to ignore it?

OUT OF MONEY

DEAR CINDY—

Alice, who shares my office, seemed nice enough when she was hired. But the last few weeks she's stayed out longer and longer at lunch. She also gets in later than I do in the morning. So far, I've been doing more than my share of the work and covering up—— I don't like to make a fuss——but I'm getting sick of it. Should I tell my boss about it, or wait until she wakes up and notices it herself? I guess Alice wouldn't be fired for being late. I don't want that on my conscience.

HAD IT

someone annoys you, try to figure out what the trouble is. In this way, you can improve your own skill at human relations.

HUMAN RELATIONS AND YOUR CAREER

What does all this have to do with being successful in your career? Well, as you have seen, the ability to do the job is usually not enough to ensure success. Often, in fact, a career requires that there be no separation between human relations skills and job skills. Both are needed all the time. Salespeople, for example, must have good human relations skills. If they cannot deal with people, they cannot do their job. The skills needed for success as a salesperson are almost entirely human relations skills.

There are many jobs in which dealing with people is important. In such cases, the importance of human relations skills is clear. Receptionists usually must have typing skills as well as other clerical skills. Often they must operate a switchboard. But no receptionist is successful without an ability to deal with people. This is true no matter how well developed the other skills are.

Teachers, bus drivers, police officers—those whose jobs put them into frequent contact with people—must have good human relations skills. OK, you may say. That point is obvious. But what about the thousands of jobs in which you do not have to meet people?

All Jobs Involve People

Few, if any, jobs have no contact with people. There may be exceptions. But even the night guard in an office building has contact with people. If the contact is not with the general public, it is with fellow workers and supervisors. You're going to be a plumber? Well, you will have to deal with customers. And you may work with a helper or partner. The same is true if you are to be a television or appliance repairer.

A truck driver? Although separated physically within the cab of the truck, you still will have to deal with people. And not all human relations is carried out by talking. In fact, an understanding of human relations will help you be a safer driver. For example, a person whose car begins to skid on an icy road will often react by slamming on the brakes, thus dangerously aggravating the situation. Recognizing such

Ability to do the job is usually not enough to ensure success. The ability to deal with people is also important. (Courtesy New York City Transit Authority)

tendencies—both in yourself and in others—can help you to avoid accidents.

When you are aware that certain things annoy you, you can try to avoid them or prepare yourself to deal calmly with them. In that way, you are not likely to meet them unexpectedly or to become angry if you do. A calm driver is a safer driver than an angry one. Understanding yourself is part of good human relations. In this sense, all careers involve human relations.

Even Lunch Breaks Matter

"Enough of this," you might think. "I'm not going to do any of these things. I'm working on an assembly line. I know my job. It has no contact with people. Well, just a little with the people on either side of me. We just sit there and do our job. We don't have to be experts."

But does a job on an assembly line offer no contact with people? What about coffee breaks, lunch hour, getting to work, and going home? You can avoid people during these periods, but you will not be very happy if you do. And you probably will not be promoted to supervisor or to other responsible positions. Such positions require you to make contact with people, and your unwillingness to do so would make you a poor candidate for promotion.

YOU ARE INVOLVED

Say, for the sake of the discussion, that you do not care about being promoted. You are an extreme case, and you do not even join other workers during breaks. Are you then free of the need to consider human relations? Unless you are shut off in a room by yourself and can get to and from that room without seeing anyone, the answer is no.

Suppose, for example, that you are working on an assembly line doing your thing. The worker next to you keeps coughing in your direction. You have a human relations problem that you must deal with. And if **you** are doing the coughing, your neighbor will quickly draw you into a human relations situation.

Perhaps the worker next to you chews gum and keeps cracking it. That can be irritating. Or maybe the worker near you doesn't take baths regularly or has bad breath. That could make you and others on the job uncomfortable.

Human relations is an important part of all jobs. And everything you do or don't do affects your human relations. If you do not bathe regularly, if you are late, if you are unpleasant to be around, you will have poor human relations.

So getting along with people—human relations—is important for success in your career, whatever it is. Knowing the importance of good human relations is one thing. Knowing how to practice good human relations is something else. In the following chapters, you will discover some guides to help you improve your human relations.

CHAPTER 54

KEYS TO UNDERSTANDING YOURSELF

To have good human relations, you must understand people. And the first person you must understand is yourself. You must be aware of yourself. Being aware of yourself does not mean being self-conscious or being selfish. A self-conscious or selfish person usually has poor human relations. If you are self-conscious or selfish, you may be too busy thinking only about yourself to relate well to other people. Being aware of yourself is a different thing, as this case shows:

> Peter was self-conscious without being truly aware of himself. He was quite handsome, and, when he was at ease, he had a nice smile and a good speaking voice. But unfortunately for Peter, he was seldom at ease among other people. He was too busy thinking about himself and wondering how he looked to others.
>
> "Is my shirt in? How's my hair? Did I say that word right? Should I have stood up? Should I sit down?" All these questions and more would be running through Peter's head all the time. His face would freeze, and his voice would become strained. If he had been aware of his many good points and less self-conscious about what kind of an impression he was making, he would easily have made a very good impression. As it was, he didn't.

When you lack a self-identity—that is, you do not understand yourself—you tend to be impatient, lazy, and restless. You are unable to stick to anything for long. You are, in fact, a self-conscious person who is too busy trying to find out about yourself to pay much attention to others. You cannot build good human relations if you are like this.

LIKING YOURSELF LEADS TO LIKING OTHERS

A self-identity is important also because you must know yourself in order to develop a sense of purpose. Out of your values and your sense of purpose, you develop your self-esteem, or sense of worth. That means a liking and a respect for yourself.

Now you may have been told many times that it is conceited or somehow bad to like yourself. This is not true. It is good—it is

A healthy liking for yourself means looking at yourself fairly, without exaggerating your good points—or your bad ones.

STAYING ALIVE

BEING FREE OF ANXIETY

BEING LOVED

BEING ADMIRED AND RESPECTED

REALIZING YOUR POTENTIAL

All our actions stem from five basic needs. These needs can be arranged in the order in which people seek to satisfy them.

essential—for you to like yourself. In fact, you first must like yourself before you can begin liking others. And although you can have polite relations with someone you do not care for, it is easier to have good relations when you do care for people. If you do not care for yourself, if you have no self-esteem, you will have poor human relations because you will not be able to care about anyone else.

First of all, then, you need a healthy liking for yourself. That does not mean you should stand admiring yourself in front of a mirror for hours on end. It means a healthy liking in which you can see both your good points and your bad points without false humility or pride.

If you are able to look at yourself without ignoring or enlarging either your good or your bad points, you probably have the self-confidence to deal easily with other people. Think about that for a moment. Knowing other people is important. But the most important thing is to know yourself first. With that knowledge, you will have the strength to deal with all kinds of people in all kinds of situations. Self-knowledge is the basis for good human relations.

ALL PEOPLE HAVE NEEDS

To understand yourself—and others—it is helpful to know that all people have certain needs and

that, in general, they spend their lives fulfilling these needs.

Human needs have been classified into five general types. Experts on how people behave say that these needs can be arranged in the order in which people seek to satisfy them. Your needs and the order in which you meet them are

1. Keeping alive
2. Being free of fear and anxiety
3. Being loved
4. Being admired and respected (in your own eyes and others')
5. Realizing your potential

The basic motivation for all your actions stems from these five general needs. Sometimes you are striving to satisfy more than one need at a time. But you must always satisfy the first need before you can go on to the second, and so on. A closer look at these five human needs follows.

Keeping Alive

If you cannot keep yourself alive, obviously you cannot satisfy any other needs. Keeping yourself alive requires eating and breathing and taking care of your body functions. Some of these things, such as breathing, you do automatically, or without conscious effort. You are forced to do other things by demands your body makes, although you can control the demands to some extent. You can put off eating when you first feel hunger—at least for a while. But you will have to eat sometime in order to stay alive.

Being Free of Fear and Anxiety

Once you have done what is necessary to keep alive, you want to make your life as safe and as comfortable as possible. You dress to keep warm and dry. You try to avoid obvious physical dangers. The unknown can threaten you, and so you try to organize your life. You set up daily routines and habits. You try to change people or situations that make you feel insecure, and you surround yourself with people and situations that make you feel safe.

Being Loved

You meet your need for love and affection in many ways. Research shows that babies who are raised without care and love may develop into normal adults physically, but their human relations will suffer because they have not learned how to give or get affection. Children learn from their families and friends how to behave in order to get love. Later, as adults, they still seek love through marriage. You never outgrow the need to have others treat you with affection, care, and love.

The decision to love somebody else is not simply a sexual attraction. It is a commitment to another person. You hope to share happy moments together. But when there are sad moments and disappointments, you stand by the ones you love. This need to give and receive love makes you join clubs and groups, ties you to your family, and makes you seek out and please friends. You want to feel that you belong.

Being Admired and Respected

Once you feel that you belong, that people like you, you then want them to respect you. You want to earn their admiration as well as their love. You need admiration and attention. They build your self-confidence. In school, you seek the approval of your teachers by doing well. On the job, you try to please your bosses or supervisors so that they will show approval. This ties in with

your need to stay alive, because a boss's approval often takes the form of a pay raise, which will buy food, shelter, and so on.

Realizing Your Potential

All people have a sense of what they can do and achieve in life. When your other needs are taken care of, you can think of what you are capable of doing. But you do more than just think about it. You try to fulfill yourself by doing what you know you can. If you do not fulfill yourself in this way, you become frustrated.

Self-realization in this sense does not simply mean becoming rich or famous or powerful. Those things may be involved too. But a person who earns a living by growing flowers may be happier and more fulfilled than one who is rich and powerful. Fulfillment depends upon how you feel about what you are doing. If you know you can do more, the need for self-fulfillment will make you try to do so. Until you have explored your full potential, you will not feel fulfilled.

To satisfy this final need, you first must have a realistic idea of your potential. Most people do. But consider whether you underestimate or overestimate your potential. If you underestimate yourself, you will be satisfied too easily and will make excuses for yourself. You will avoid challenges and will never learn all you are capable of. If you overestimate yourself, you will feel frustrated because you cannot achieve what you think you can. People who always fail to reach their goals should try to set more realistic goals.

Your idea of what you can achieve will change through life. It can change as the result of reevaluation. At one time, you may have thought that earning good grades was not very important. Then you realized that your school record could help you get the job you wanted. You reevaluated what was important, and you saw that you could get higher grades with just a little effort.

Your evaluation of yourself can also change as a result of recognition, as Don's did:

> Don always got high grades in math, but he never seemed to do well in English class. One day, he was asked to read one of his papers out loud to the class. He was praised by the teacher and by his classmates for work well done. Don had never thought of himself as a good writer. But from that day on, Don realized that he had the potential to improve upon his writing skills, and he saw that the effort would pay off. Until then, he had avoided thinking about any career that included

writing. Now Don's potential was greater because others had recognized a talent he had overlooked in himself.

Your idea of what you can do may also change as a result of actual achievement. You may set an early goal to become a supervisor in the factory where you work. After becoming a supervisor, you may realize that you have the ability to be a general manager. Thus, you begin to work to achieve that position.

Needs and Human Relations

When you know yourself and what motivates you, you are better able to get along with others. On a simple level, you may know that when you are hungry, you tend to become annoyed. With that understanding, you would be wise to avoid situations in which you might be dealing with people on sensitive matters when you are hungry. Many people in business prefer to talk about things like contract negotiations either at lunch or just after lunch.

As your needs are met, you will become more relaxed and agreeable. When they are not met, you may become tense and disagreeable. Your disposition, or mood, influences your human relations. You can't help it. But you can and must control it. Why? Because how you conduct your human relations will affect your success in meeting your other needs.

In short, meeting your needs makes it easy to maintain good human relations. And good human relations makes it easier to meet your needs. This cycle is further proof of what you learned in the first chapter: People are social animals, and no one works alone.

THREE ASPECTS OF CHARACTER

Do you realize that there are three aspects to your character? These have been created and shaped by your experiences. In any given situation, one or another of these aspects might be strongest. In some people, one part may be stronger than the other two. But it is best when all three are balanced.

For simplicity, experts have labeled these three aspects of character the "adult," the "parent," and the "child." When these ordinary words are used in this way, they relate only slightly to what is usually meant by an adult, a parent, or a child. But your character aspects are similar to

Experts say that a parent, an adult, and a child can be found in each of us.

these three different groups. At some time, and to some degree, the adult, parent, and child aspects come out.

The Parent in You

The parent part of your character is made up of the rules and teachings that you absorbed at an early age. Since you got most of these ideas from your parents and since you use them as a parent does toward a small child, "parent" is an appropriate term to describe this particular aspect of your character.

As the parent, you may try to give orders or be overbearing or act intimidating. This part of your character makes you critical of others. It is the parent acting in you who unthinkingly says that something is good or bad. Your prejudices are found in your parent self. Some things in your parent self are good. They are automatic and stem from common sense. They can be lifesaving commands, such as "Don't play with a loaded gun!"

When this aspect of character is in command of a human relations situation, you act mostly in an unthinking manner. You rely on the basic ideas you learned when you were young, without testing to see whether they suit the occasion.

The Child in You

If the parent part of your character is where you store preconceived thoughts and ideas, the child section is where you store your emotions. And when the child takes control, you act out these emotions. This can be good when your feelings are happy. It is not so good when you have sad or angry or mean feelings.

Also, as the term suggests, the child self wants someone else to take control and say what to do. It even wants to be criticized. When the child aspect of your character takes control, you want to follow others rather than to lead or be active. But the child self is not all negative or passive. It also carries the urge to be creative.

The Adult in You

The adult is the questioning aspect of your character. When the adult is in control, you do not respond only with a preconceived idea or with emotion. Instead, you consider all the facts before you. You sift through the responses available in the child self and in the parent self. You then pick the right response. If you are dealing with a loaded gun, the right response is the parental command, "Don't play with a loaded gun!" The child response is not so good: "Let's shoot it to hear the bang!"

The adult self represents a thinking response to a situation rather than the more automatic responses of the child self or the parent self. After thinking the situation over, you may call upon the child self or the parent self to respond. You may even use a combination of the two if the adult self is in control.

When to Be What

Good human relations usually will result if you develop the adult self and let this aspect of character control you. Certainly, in most situations, it is best to think before you act.

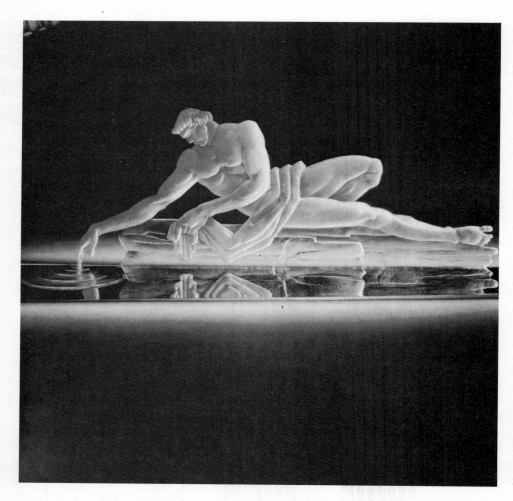

It is possible to spend too much time examining yourself. Narcissus, a character from Greek mythology, became so concerned with himself that he lost interest in everything and everybody else. He spent all his time staring at his own reflection in a pond. (Courtesy Steuben Glass)

Sometimes, though, the automatic reaction of the child self or the parent self is more suitable. If you always take time to think, you may get a reputation for being cold or distant. If you are like that, or even if people think you are, it will be difficult to develop warm, easy human relations with others.

Although most people react automatically much of the time, their reactions are not always the most suitable ones. You should consider yourself lucky if your automatic response is usually the right one. If it isn't, you can work to correct it. By identifying the different aspects of yourself, you can usually tell if an undesirable part is too strong. Once you learn that, you can correct it. All people react with different aspects of their characters from time to time. There is no harm in that. But sometimes that reaction is useful, and sometimes it isn't.

Human relations problems develop when you act or react in one way only. If you have had to put up with a bossy person who is always acting out the parent self, you know how unpleasant it is to deal with such a person. On the other hand, dealing with persons who can only play the child, who always want support, is also annoying.

If you wonder whether one aspect of your character is too strong, ask yourself this ques- tion: "What behavior do I find most annoying in other people?" Then think about the answer. It is often true—though not always—that the behavior trait you find most annoying in others is one you yourself exhibit.

TOO MUCH SELF-EXAMINATION

Remember that you can become too self-conscious in trying to become more self-aware. Think about yourself from time to time and evaluate what you do. This is especially important after you have made an error or failed to accomplish a goal. But do not spend too much time on yourself. Today there are many experts studying people and how they behave, and many television commercials, advertisements, and other pressures to be a certain way. It's possible to think about and examine yourself too much.

There is an ancient myth about a young man named Narcissus who became so interested in examining himself that he lost interest in everything and everybody else. All he did was stare at his own reflection in a pond. Those who fall in love with themselves as Narcissus did will not be able to meet their human needs because they will fail at human relations.

CHAPTER 55

KEYS TO UNDERSTANDING OTHERS

Everyone is different from everyone else. But most people have the same basic ingredients. How these ingredients are mixed in each person makes that person an individual. Almost all people have two arms, two legs, one mouth, two eyes, two ears, and so on. But the size, weight, length, color, and shape of these physical traits are different from person to person.

Just as a person's physical appearance is made up of the same basic ingredients, so is each person's personality—the nonphysical traits that make one an individual. When you learn about yourself, you learn something about others as well. Everyone has the same five needs you learned about in the last chapter. And everyone must satisfy these needs in the same general order. That is, first people want to stay alive, then to be free of fear and anxiety, then to be loved, then to be respected, and then to realize their potential.

No two people are alike, but many of the ingredients are the same. (United Nations/R. Grunbaum/ARA)

Knowing that everyone has these needs will help you to understand others. And understanding leads to good human relations. Usually, however, you cannot know which need a person might be responding to. If you are starving, your need for food is obvious. But if you are only hungry, you may postpone satisfying this basic need to meet another need. If you are on a diet and trying not to eat much, you will resent anyone who forces food on you. That person is not practicing good human relations.

It is difficult—sometimes impossible—to pinpoint exactly which need a person is trying to satisfy at any moment. Everyone's approach to fulfilling needs is a mixture of experience and heredity. Out of this mix, people develop the three aspects of character: the parent self, the child self, and the adult self.

All people have these three parts in them. The parent self contains the rules and beliefs received at an early age. The child self responds automatically with emotion or creativity and wants someone else to make decisions. The adult self looks for the reality of each situation, asks questions, and responds.

How these functions are carried out is different for each individual. No two people—not even identical twins—will have exactly the same mix of experience and heredity. Thus, the three aspects of personality will be different in each person. And how these aspects combine will be different from one person to another. Some individuals will have a strong parent self, others will have a strong adult self, and still others will have a strong child self.

How is all this important in human relations? The more you know about people, the better you can get along with them. If you have no idea of what makes another person tick, you cannot relate well. And one of the most important things that you can know about anyone is that no two people are alike.

NO TWO PEOPLE ARE ALIKE

Knowing that no two people are alike may seem obvious and of little use. But this knowledge is actually very helpful in maintaining good human relations. If you know this and follow it, you will not make the mistake of treating everyone in the same way.

This mistake is often made by people who are visiting in a foreign country. They do not always realize that everybody is not like the people back home. Addressing someone by his or her first name—a gesture that would be considered friendly in one country—is often taken as rude and overly familiar in a country with more formal traditions. Knowing that everyone is different will keep you from thinking that everyone will behave as you do, or that everyone will react as you do.

You **will** find some people who behave as you do. These people probably will become your friends. But even your closest friends will see some things differently than you do. To maintain your friendship, you must recognize and accept this, or make allowances for it. In fact, the closer you are to a person, the more you must be aware of your differences. Assume that you have differences, and look for them. Otherwise, you may find yourself in the spot that Roger and Janet did:

> Roger and Janet had been friends since childhood. The two seemed to think alike in everything. For Janet's birthday, Roger wanted to give her a special gift. Roger loved chess and he knew Janet did. He decided the perfect gift for Janet would be a new chess set. He was sure Janet would be thrilled with it. But when Janet opened the present, she just stared and then she mumbled, "Thank you. It's very nice."
>
> "You don't really like it," Roger said.
>
> "Oh, I do," Janet replied. "It's just that I was surprised. You know I've been working all year carving my own chess set out of wood."
>
> "But," said Roger. "I thought you'd be even happier with a real chess set from a store."
>
> Janet and Roger made the best of it. They kept playing chess together. And by the time Janet had her next birthday, the two friends knew each other better than before. They were aware of their differences as well as their similarities. Roger now understood that Janet liked something she could make for herself. This time, Roger went out and got his friend a new jackknife and a boxful of carving wood.

People **are** different. And if you are not aware that differences exist, you may have bad human relations. But if you learn to respect and appreciate other people's differences, you will find many friendships to enjoy.

EVERYBODY WANTS TO FEEL LIKE SOMEBODY

For successful human relations, then, you must recognize that other people are different, and you

One key to understanding others is to recognize that everybody wants to feel like somebody. (Courtesy United Nations/MB/b)

must respect their differences. It's natural to feel that what is different from you is somehow not as good, or may even be bad.

After all, you know yourself better than you know others. But just as you excuse and explain your own actions, you must realize that others have good reasons for their actions too. You must respect their right to be different, just as you expect them to let you do things your own way.

No one likes it when somebody shows that he or she does not respect them. Lack of respect makes a person feel like a nobody. Here is a safe guide to follow in dealing with people: Everybody wants to feel like somebody.

Test it on yourself. Think of some time when you felt put down. Maybe a classmate laughed at you for asking a "silly" question. Perhaps a clerk in a store ignored you but took care of a customer who came in after you did. Or maybe someone with authority ordered you to do something in a harsh tone of voice.

How did you feel in such situations? Like a nobody? Were you comfortable? Did you enjoy

it? Did you want to have much to do with the person who put you down?

Probably you would not want to see someone who put you down and made you feel like a nobody—except, perhaps, to get even. Well, assume that others feel the same way. Unless you want to annoy people and make them want to get even, try to show that you respect their right to be different.

Think about the five basic human needs talked about earlier. Three of them—being loved, being respected, and realizing your potential— are included in the idea that everybody wants to feel like somebody. The only people you are likely to meet who do not have this general need or feeling are those who have not yet satisfied the first two needs. That is, someone who is starving will not be too concerned about feeling like somebody. Food will be more important. And someone who is filled with fear and anxiety over physical safety will not care much about it either.

Usually, however, the people you deal with have satisfied these two basic needs to some extent. They will want to feel like somebody. Your success at human relations will be affected by how well you make other people feel like somebody and how well you avoid making them feel like nobody.

This rule applies to all the people you meet, not just to those who have authority. Often it may seem harder to show respect for those who **do** have authority, but they too have the need to feel like somebody. In school or on the job, you can let your teachers or supervisors know that you think they are somebody without polishing apples or buttering them up. It is simply a matter of respect, or treating others as you would like to be treated. Bill overlooked that fact and risked hurting someone's feelings:

Bill did not intend to seem rude. He just did not see any reason to be friendly with his boss, Ms. Rowbotham. After all, the boss **was** somebody. She did not need to be reminded of that by the newest employee. He was also a little in awe of her.

One day Ms. Rowbotham joined Bill and some other workers during a coffee break. When she started to tell a joke, Bill got up to get another soda. He just walked away. He didn't think he was being rude. He told himself that someone as important as Ms. Rowbotham would not even notice that he had left.

But Ms. Rowbotham **did** notice it. She said nothing about it, of course, but she wondered why Bill was so rude to her.

Fortunately for Bill, an older worker, Olivia, talked to him.

"Ms. Rowbotham's a good person," Olivia told him. "You ought to try to get to know her. It seems that every time she comes around, you either move or clam up. She's going to think you don't like her."

"She's the boss," Bill said. "What does she care about what I think?"

Bill forgot that everybody—even bosses—wants to feel like somebody. And he did not realize that every person can make someone else feel like a nobody by showing that she or he doesn't respect that person. And Bill made one more mistake: He failed to consider the whole person.

THE WHOLE PERSON MUST BE CONSIDERED

Bill saw Ms. Rowbotham simply as the boss. He did not think of her as a human being with the same needs as everyone else. When you begin to put people into boxes and react to them on only one level, you are heading toward poor human relations.

People are not just bosses, or teachers, or parents, or brothers, or sisters, or co-workers. They are many other things as well. People play many roles in life, and these roles affect each other. Besides, as you have learned, people are different kinds of persons at different times, depending on which aspect of their character (parent, child, or adult) is strongest.

Bernice was an electrician's helper for a large construction company. Raoul, the electrician she worked with, was usually fair and pleasant. Lately, though, he was edgy and angry much of the time. He shouted at Bernice for no real reason. Often he criticized her for being slow or careless, even though she wasn't.

This was hard for Bernice to take. She began to think that she was no good at her job. She began to dislike Raoul and even to argue with him. Then Bernice learned that Raoul's child was very ill. She understood that he was a father as well as an electrician. She knew that Raoul's behavior was a result of worrying about his child.

Bernice decided to understand Raoul's problem and his moods. When the child got well, Raoul became his old self again. He even showed his appreciation to Bernice by telling the boss how helpful she had been.

If Bernice had not taken the whole person into consideration in dealing with Raoul, she might have caused a serious break in their relationship. Instead, she practiced good human relations. Here's another example:

Walter worked in one division of a large company. His good friend Louise worked in another division. Walter received a promotion and was transferred into Louise's division. Louise had the senior position, and part of Walter's new job was to assist her.

Walter looked forward to working with his friend. But things did not go well. Although there was plenty of work, Louise tried to do it all. She worked during breaks and lunch hours, and she stayed late. She did not give Walter much to do. That made him uncomfortable. Sometimes when Louise was out of the office, the boss gave Walter some work. When Louise learned this, she acted angry and did not talk to Walter for a while.

Walter was bothered by his friend's odd behavior, and he thought of asking for another transfer. But he stayed, and slowly he began to see what the problem was. Louise had no outside interests. Her job was her whole life. As a result, she felt threatened when someone helped her with her work.

By learning about the whole person, Walter was able to understand Louise and to make allowances when she was irritable or silent. He knew that Louise's anger was not directed at him. And he was able to help her feel more secure by stressing her good personal qualities.

Walter learned another lesson that helped him to have good human relations. He learned that although people's reasons may not always be obvious, their actions usually stem from a desire to satisfy one of their needs.

PEOPLE ACT AS THEY DO BECAUSE OF NEEDS

Sometimes when you try to fulfill your basic needs, you are aware of it. On a simple level, when you are thirsty, you take a drink of water. If you fear loneliness and have a need for companionship, you look up a friend. At other times, though, you may not be aware of what need you are trying to satisfy.

Knowing that people are trying to satisfy one need or another can help you to maintain good human relations. Like Bernice and Walter, you will not be quick to get angry with another's behavior if you understand why the person is doing it. By understanding others, you can solve your own human relations problems. Here's an example:

Betty and Alice were salespeople in a large department store. When there was no work to do, they would chat for a while. Unfortunately, Alice

often bragged: She did the best, she had the best, she was the best—on and on and on.

This can be very annoying. But Betty was wise and had a good sense of human relations. She reasoned that Alice needed recognition and approval. So Betty went out of her way to say something nice to Alice near the start of each day. By doing this, she helped to satisfy Alice's need for approval. As a result, Alice did not feel the need to brag so much, and Betty had solved her human relations problem.

It is not always easy to figure out what need is motivating someone. Often it is impossible. Sometimes it isn't necessary to know. However, knowing what motivates a person is another key you can use to help understand others and thus have good human relations.

REVIEWING THE KEYS

To review, the following four keys can help you understand people:

- No two people are alike.
- Everybody wants to feel like somebody.
- The whole person must be considered.
- People act as they do because of needs.

It takes practice and patience to have good human relations all the time. Sometimes you will have poor human relations. You will lose your temper. You will feel hurt or sad. You will decide someone is just not worth bothering with. But most of the time it is not practical or useful to lose your temper. These keys can help you to build good human relations by making you consider what other people want and need.

Getting It All Together

1. Why is good human relations important to you?

2. Why must you understand people to have good human relations?

3. How does knowing yourself help you have good human relations?

4. What labels have been given to three aspects of our character? What do they signify?

5. What five basic needs do all people have?

6. What are the four keys you can use to help you understand other people and improve your relations with them?

7. Collect five advertisements from newspapers or magazines, and list five commercials on television or radio that are aimed at convincing people to buy the advertised product in order to satisfy some basic need. Determine which needs these examples focus on. Do you think the ads are effective? Why or why not?

18

COMMUNICATING FOR GOOD HUMAN RELATIONS

Your goals in this unit are given in the following list:

To become aware of the connection between human relations and communications

To recognize two common ways in which poor communications can hinder good human relations

To identify abstractions that can hinder good communications

To develop your ability to communicate with all kinds of people in different situations

To recognize four common roadblocks to good communications and human relations

To recognize the need to consider the source of information

You are always sending and receiving messages. Sometimes you do this consciously. That is, you are aware of sending or receiving messages. You know you are trying to communicate. Often, though, you send and receive messages unconsciously. That is, you are not aware of what you are doing. You do not know that you are sending a message to those around you or that a message is coming in. Human relations is sending and receiving messages—knowingly or unknowingly.

"Aha!" you say. "You're talking about communications." That's true, but in a very broad sense. Communications and human relations **are** almost the same thing—you can't have one without the other. But have you ever heard the statement "The whole is greater than the sum of its parts"? That statement is true in this case. Human relations **is** communications, but it is also much more.

Certainly you cannot have human relations without some form of communication. And if human relations is to be helpful and productive for both parties, there must be good communication between the sender and the receiver. It's possible that two people could be in a room together and make no effort to communicate. They could just be there and

concentrate on whatever task they each have to do, ignoring each other. This would be an unusual situation. But even so, there probably are some communication and human relations, however poor.

Any movement that one makes—or any noise, such as coughing or clearing one's throat—will give a message to the other person in the room. The message may have no real meaning as such, but the person receiving it may react. That person may express annoyance or leave the room suddenly.

In fact, that is what probably will happen if the two people in the room make no conscious effort to communicate and get to know one another. The absence of an effort to make contact sends a message, an unfriendly one. As the old saying goes, "Silence cannot be misquoted, but it can be misinterpreted." In other words, even when you do not communicate, you are sending a message. You are telling someone something.

It is human nature to reach out and communicate with others. If that effort is not made, you wonder why, or you take it as a sign of hostility or, at least, dislike. Thus, communication is basic to human relations. In this unit, you will learn to develop effective communications and good human relations.

56

SAYING WHAT YOU MEAN

There are two forms of communication—verbal and nonverbal. As a general rule, you could say that when you are verbal—when you write or speak—you communicate consciously, or knowingly. Nonverbal communication also can be conscious. When you shake hands, pat someone on the back, frown, smile, or hit someone, you are communicating on a nonverbal level in a conscious, knowing way.

Sometimes, though, you may frown without being aware of it, or you may smile or laugh without thinking. Then you are communicating unconsciously, or unknowingly. How you hold your body communicates something. If your shoulders droop, and your head hangs, and you shuffle along, you are telling people that you do not think much of yourself or that you are sad. At least, that is what most people would read into your body postures. You might not intend to send any message. If you do not say "Good morning" or "Hi" or some such thing to your co-workers when you get to work, you still are sending a message. In this case, your message is that you are unfriendly and do not want to bother with people. An unconscious message can be just as clear as a conscious one.

Knowingly or unknowingly, you are always sending and receiving messages when other people are around. Those who know this probably will work to maintain a straight, alert posture most of the time so that a positive message goes out, even when they are not thinking about it. Such people will develop an attitude and appearance that sends a friendly, pleasant message, especially when no conscious effort is being made to communicate.

FALSE MESSAGES

When communication is unconscious, or unknowing, a person may send a false message, as Clyde did:

Clyde was an employee of a large airline company. His job was to check passengers in at the loading gate. He liked his work. He enjoyed meeting people. He liked solving problems that came up. There was only one thing, although Clyde was not aware of it. He frowned a lot. He frowned when he was thinking. Sometimes he frowned because he was involved with a tough question.

The message that the passengers got was that Clyde did not like what he was doing, that he didn't like them, and that he didn't like to solve problems. "What a sourpuss," they thought. When the supervisor checked to see that the employees were doing their work properly, she thought the same thing. "What a sourpuss."

Fortunately for Clyde, the personnel department at his company was interested in solving problems, not firing employees. When they asked him why he did not like his work, Clyde was surprised. He said he **did** like it, and then **they** were surprised. "Well, you sure don't look it," they said.

With a little help, Clyde learned to relax the muscles in his face and to smile more on the job. At first, this was difficult. Clyde had to concentrate on it so that his nonverbal communication would not send a false message. But after a while, he smiled automatically—he stopped frowning—and he did not have to think about this particular nonverbal communication. He could let it happen unconsciously. Clyde stopped sending a false message.

Remember that you communicate in many different ways, knowingly and unknowingly. When people are around, you always communicate—that is, relate—in one way or another. Sometimes when you communicate unknowingly, you send a false message. Keep that in mind when you receive messages too: The sender may not know that the message being sent is false.

TWO COMMON PROBLEMS

Here are two ideas to be aware of in order to communicate effectively:

- Sometimes more than one message is sent at a time, and the messages may contradict each other. (Sometimes, of course, the messages support each other.)
- Sometimes, even when communication is conscious, a false message may be sent. (Or the receiver may get a false message.) In this case, the message is garbled, or confused, by either the sender or the receiver.

A closer look at these two communication problems follows.

More Than One Message

Perhaps you've watched parents trying to reason with a small child who has just tried to cross a busy street alone because other children are on the other side. "You don't want to get hit by a car, do you?" the parents may say. "N-o-o-o," the child replies, all the time looking across the street and obviously wanting to go there, cars or not. The child answers no, but nonverbal messages make it clear that a different message is being sent: "I want to cross the street."

The child is sending two messages at the same time. One is verbal ("No, I don't want to get hit by a car"). The other is nonverbal ("I want to cross the street"). One message says one thing, while the other says the opposite. It's like shaking your head when you say yes, and nodding your head when you say no.

Sometimes people are aware when they do this. Often they are not. People who like to be coaxed often will send two contradictory messages. "No, I don't want to play the guitar—I'm not very good, and no one wants to listen," a person may say. But the tone of voice carries an opposite message: "I'd love to play—please keep asking me."

Sometimes a message is sent even though no conscious effort is made to communicate. Can you read the message being sent here?

Watch out too for contradictory messages when people tell you too many times not to make a fuss about their birthday. If you don't, they're often hurt.

This kind of behavior is immature. It is important for good human relations to say exactly what you mean and to take others seriously when they say something. People will not enjoy being with you if they cannot be certain whether you mean one thing or exactly the opposite.

Garbled Messages

When you communicate and are not aware of it, you sometimes will send a false message, as Clyde did. But sometimes when you consciously try to communicate, you still may send a false message. Or—just as bad—the receiver may get a false message. How does this happen?

You are not likely to garble your message when communicating on a simple level. "How do I get to the post office?" "Go two blocks east on Main Street and turn left on Green Street. It's the first building on your right." The sender and receiver had no problems here. Both related in a direct, meaningful way.

However, people do not always communicate on this simple, concrete level. In fact, much of the time they communicate on a higher, more *abstract* level—that is, what they talk about does not really exist outside their minds. One cannot point to the postal system as one can to the post office building.

If one moves from talking about **where** the post office building is to **how** the postal system is run, the message becomes more abstract. The more abstract a message is, the more likely it is to be garbled by the sender or the receiver. That is, when one cannot refer to something physical (the post office building), the sender and receiver may have different abstract mental pictures (the postal system).

"I don't think that the postal system is run well. There is too much waste."

"What's the matter with you? You got something against postal workers?"

Something went wrong in that conversation. The first speaker could clarify the message by stating exactly what may be wrong with the postal system. Or the second speaker could ask, "Do you mean that postal workers are at fault?" Messages become garbled when people are not careful about the words they use and when they talk in general or abstract terms.

For effective communications and good human relations, it is worthwhile to consider words and how people use them. You will study abstractions and generalizations. An understanding of these two kinds of communication can help you in your human relations.

Abstractions. In their haste to get a point across, people often tend to be sloppy speakers and thinkers. This can result in ineffective communication and poor human relations. People often fool themselves by confusing words with things. This is most often the case with abstractions. As a simple example, take the word "dog." You may think this is a simple word that everyone can understand. Actually, "dog" is an abstraction: Two people may take it to mean two entirely different things.

Because of your experiences, for example, the word "dog" may make you think of a friendly, tail-wagging pet. But if you one day meet a mean, unfriendly dog and try to pet it, you may learn a painful, but useful, lesson: There is no such thing as "a" dog in the real world. "Dog" is a handy label for a certain kind of animal. But some dogs are small and hairless and others are large and shaggy. Some dogs are noisy and nervous and others are quiet and stately. Some dogs are timid. Others are aggressive. It's a mistake to think all such animals are the same. They are not.

Be careful not to confuse words with things. Avoid using abstract words as though they refer to only one thing that actually exists. A good way to guard against this is to try always to think of the *referent* of the word that you are using—that is, the thing in the real world that the word refers to. The referent is the thing you can see, feel, touch, and describe in detail. If there is no single referent for a word—it can mean many things—then it is an abstraction. Be careful with abstractions. They are necessary and useful, but they can be confusing.

As you have seen, "dog" is a useful abstraction. But it is only an abstraction. It does not have a single, specific referent. Every dog is different from every other dog. It can be confusing to ignore this fact. The words "my dog, Fritz," on the other hand, are specific. They refer to only one dog.

Generalizations. Generalizations can be useful tools—language shortcuts you might call them. But generalizations, like abstractions, can also result in confusion. A *generalization* lumps together several words, things, or ideas and makes

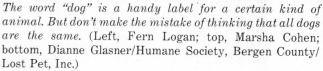

The word "dog" is a handy label for a certain kind of animal. But don't make the mistake of thinking that all dogs are the same. (Left, Fern Logan; top, Marsha Cohen; bottom, Dianne Glasner/Humane Society, Bergen County/ Lost Pet, Inc.)

a statement about all of them without considering the individual characteristics of each. Generalizations usually begin with or include such words as "all" or "every." Generalizations can result in confusion because they tell only part of the story but seem to be saying a lot. Consider the generalizations in this example:

"I'll never learn this job," Frank moaned. "**Everything** I do is wrong. **All I ever** do is make

mistakes." In a moment of discouragement, Frank is making some wild generalizations about himself and his new job in a cosmetics plant. He has been working there for only 2 days—not enough time to make a statement like "I'll never learn this job."

During his first 2 days, Frank has done several things right. So it is untrue for him to say, "**Everything** I do is wrong. **All I ever** do is make mistakes." Frank is a better worker than he thinks. But his thinking is sloppy and lazy. If he continues to think this way, his generalizations will affect his attitude and his relations with others. He even may convince everyone that he can't do his job.

Frank is generalizing in a negative way about himself. But it is also possible to generalize in a positive way. "This job is a snap. I know **everything** about it. I **never** make mistakes." Positive generalizations are as dangerous as negative ones. Both may lead to confusion and sloppy thinking.

When you think about yourself or other people, abstractions and generalizations can be dangerous. You have to remember that they do not refer to something specific in the real world. Consider, for example, what might happen if you believed this generalization: "All bosses are bad and out to get me." At best, you would have an unhappy working life. Probably you would look for one job after another. No doubt some bosses are bad and do take advantage of workers. But a lot do not. Generalizations will not help you to figure out how you feel about **your** job or **your** boss.

Don't make positive generalizations either. They are no more helpful than are negative ones.

"All young people are irresponsible." Why is the picture shown here a good example of how people can fool themselves with such statements? (Courtesy New York Botanical Gardens)

"All jobs are great" is as silly as "All jobs are awful." Later on you will read about how to have good human relations by not generalizing about co-workers and the other people you meet.

57

IT TAKES ALL KINDS

To have good human relations, you must be able to communicate with all kinds of people. You must be able to communicate not only with members of your family and close friends, but also with co-workers, acquaintances, strangers, people your own age, people younger, people older, enemies and loved ones, people you work for, and people who work for you.

Communication attitudes may be classified into three groups, depending on the receiver of the message. One attitude is used to talk with a younger sister or brother (communicating down). Another attitude is used to talk with a close friend of the same age (communicating across). And still another attitude is used to talk with a supervisor, teacher, or older person (communicating up).

Be careful when using these categories. They are based on generalizations. You do not always treat everybody in one category the same way. Your attitude depends on the situation. You talk differently with a stranger your own age than you do with a friend your own age. The category is only a guide to help you choose the most productive attitude for good human relations. Of course, you will base your communications on respect for the other person.

Being able to put people into one of these three groups will help you establish good communications. But remember that everyone is different. No two people are alike. For that matter, people do not always behave in the same way, or react the same, or think the same way.

YOUR MANY ROLES

To maintain good human relations and have effective communication, you must be aware that every individual can and does play many roles

during a lifetime—or even during a single day. If you recognize the different roles you and others play, and if you deal with them effectively, then you are likely to have good human relations.

Even though people behave differently at different times, the situation is far from hopeless. You can learn to deal skillfully with people and maintain effective communications and good human relations. In fact, you have read about three useful tools already.

THREE BASIC ASPECTS OF CHARACTER

Recall the three basic aspects of character that all people share: the parent self, the adult self, and the child self. These terms, remember, are for convenience only. They do not mean a real parent, a real adult, or a real child. In a general way, these three aspects share some characteristics of parents, adults, and children. But only in a general way. A real child has all three aspects of character, just as a real adult does.

Although everyone shares these aspects of character, they differ in each person and are mixed differently in each person. Recall that the parent self is made up of the rules and teachings you learn at an early age. When you use the parent self, you do not have to think much. You just react with whatever built-in rule or saying you have. The parent self usually wants to tell others what to do.

The child self is made up of your emotions. It is your creative, spontaneous side, and it wants others to make decisions. The child self wants to be told what to do.

Both the parent self and the child self tend to deal in abstractions and generalizations. The parent self reacts on the basis of generalizations that were learned from real parents or from people who controlled you when you were young. The child self reacts with generalizations based on a mental or emotional image of yourself. This image is usually not very accurate.

The adult self causes you to examine and question each new situation. Then you decide upon the appropriate response. It could be based on one aspect or on a mixture of two or three.

CONTROLLING YOUR RESPONSES

Although this chapter is about communicating with others, you first have to know yourself. When you know something about yourself, you know something about others. Then you can see when someone is letting the child self take control, and you can respond appropriately. Or, you might tell yourself, "Oh, oh. I'm letting my parent self come on too strong in this situation. I'd better cool it."

Being Bossy

When your parent self is in control, you tend to be bossy. You want to tell others what to do and what not to do. Words like "should" or "must" are often used. Here is an example:

Cecilia had a strong parent self. In many ways, that was good. It made her a good bank teller. She was punctual, accurate, careful, and dependable. All these traits were part of her parent self. She was such a good teller that the bank manager, Ms. Friend, promoted her to chief teller.

Now it might seem that having a strong parent self is the best thing for a boss to have. Not so. For Cecilia, it was the worst thing. She could not resist giving orders in direct, sharp terms.

"Benjamin, do it this way!"

"Rita, you must keep your cash record in this drawer."

"Matsuo, you should not talk to the customers so much."

Cecilia felt that everyone should do things her way. She had been a good teller. Now she was boss, and the other tellers must recognize this. It was for their own good.

Actually, Benjamin, Rita, and Matsuo didn't recognize this at all. They did not think that what Cecilia was doing was for their own good. They decided she just wanted to be bossy and make a name for herself with Ms. Friend. They began to dislike Cecilia. They did less work, and they gave her a hard time.

An effective supervisor knows that asking—not ordering—usually gets the best results. (Courtesy Metropolitan Life)

Fortunately for Cecilia, Ms. Friend saw what was going on. She talked to Cecilia about her human relations. Ms. Friend was able to show Cecilia that people do not like to be ordered about. They would rather be shown.

"Gee," Cecilia said. "I thought that when I became a boss, I should just order people to do things."

"No," Ms. Friend said. "To get the most work, a boss **asks** people to do things. A boss rarely orders. Not good bosses, anyway."

Wanting to Be Ordered Around

Cecilia learned the lesson. She got her parent self under control and used her adult self more. If one of the tellers had wanted to play the child to Cecilia's parent self, communication between them might have been smoother, but it would not have been more productive.

Say, for example, that Benjamin's attitude at work was controlled by his child self. He would always want Cecilia to tell him what to do. He might even work below his level on purpose so that Cecilia would order him about, correct him, and criticize him.

This would create a different problem for Cecilia. She could be trapped into spending all her time making sure that Benjamin did the work right. She could handle this too by controlling her parent self. She would try to use her adult self to deal with Benjamin. Rather than telling him how to do things, she would encourage him to think and to use his adult self as well.

You should try to use your adult self in dealing with others who do so. That will ensure effective communication and good human relations. Most other kinds of interaction are not productive, and they may often result in anger or hostility.

Heading for a Clash

If two persons come on with their parent selves and both try to give orders, there will be a clash. This is true whether both are equals at work or whether one is in a superior position. If they trade opinions that both agree with, there will not be a clash. But if they trade opinions that both do not agree with, there will be a clash. Here is an example:

> Calvin and Jane worked together in the shipping room of a large factory. They had to cooperate to make sure that the packages contained the right materials and were sent to the right places. They were good workers. But they both let themselves be controlled by strong parent selves. They each held opinions about everything. And their opinions did not often agree.
>
> "You should type all the labels before putting them on the boxes," Calvin said.
>
> "You should put the labels on as you type them," Janet said.
>
> "You should fill the easy orders first," Calvin said.
>
> "You should fill the hard orders first," Janet said.
>
> "Television is great. I watch it all the time," Calvin said.
>
> "Television is terrible. I never watch it," Janet said.
>
> "Everyone should vote for Mr. X," Calvin said.
>
> "Everyone should vote for Ms. Y," Janet said.

Calvin and Janet never took the time to examine what they were saying or hearing. They soon disliked each other a lot and could not work well together. As a result, customers' orders were not made up or were sent to the wrong places or contained the wrong materials. Soon Jane and Calvin were both fired. If they had learned about themselves and had tried to control the parent aspects of their characters, they might still be working happily.

WHEN THE BOSS IS BOSSY

Sometimes your boss or supervisor will play the parent strongly with you. That can be difficult and unpleasant. No one likes to be ordered about all the time or treated like a child. But if your boss behaves like that, what can you—one of the workers—do about it?

First, you can realize that the boss is acting out the parent self—giving orders, being strict, treating others like children. When your boss acts that way toward you, don't blame yourself or feel bad. You should not think you are always doing things wrong or behaving like a child. The boss's behavior is not under your control. You do not have to feel guilty or defensive when you have done nothing wrong. Knowing what the real problem is will help you deal with it effectively.

The second thing you can do is react to the boss with your adult self. Show that you can do the work without constant direction. When needless commands are given, try to point out calmly that the work is being done and will be done when it should be. Usually people will respond to your adult self with their adult self. If the boss does not do so, at least she or he probably will be a less strong parent type over a period of time.

If you respond to the boss with your child self and show that you want and need constant direction and orders, you will strengthen the parent in your boss. And if you respond to the boss's parent self with your parent self, you

When two people react with their parent selves, the result will probably be a clash. (Philip Teuscher)

probably will provoke a clash and solve nothing. The third thing you can do, then, is to avoid responding with your child or parent self.

BUILDING EFFECTIVE COMMUNICATION

The most effective communications and the best human relations develop when people use their adult selves. You cannot expect everyone to do this, of course, but you can work to develop the adult aspect of your own character.

It is not so hard. You can examine yourself and your values. A strong adult self has a system of values for making decisions and relating to people. You can learn the mechanics of making wise decisions. All these factors strengthen your adult self and thus build good human relations.

Here are some other things you can do:

- Learn to recognize the child aspect of your character. There are times when you will want to let the child self take over. It is the fun-loving, emotional side of you. It wants to be taken care of—everyone does, from time to time. It wants to be reassured. And it likes to daydream and fantasize. There's nothing wrong with any of this—in its place. At work, though, there are few occasions when the child self is appropriate. There's no place in work for temper tantrums, sulking, or avoiding responsibility. Learn to recognize your child self and control it.
- Learn to recognize the parent aspect of your character. Coming on strong with your parent self in any situation is not very productive. And sometimes such behavior causes clashes. Probably your parent self has a lot of good, solid information and ideas to guide your behavior. But these ideas should be considered by your adult self before you use them.
- Learn to recognize when others are letting their child self or parent self control their actions. If the child aspect comes out, you know that the person needs reassurance, help, or just a kind word. If the parent aspect shows up, you usually can blunt or change it by reacting with your adult self.

Silence is often an excellent tool for maintaining good human relations when you are com-

You should learn to recognize the child part of yourself and to control it.

municating. Take a few seconds, whenever necessary, to sort things out before responding. Those few seconds of silence often can do more to build good human relations than anything you might say or do. "Count ten before you act" is good advice. But while you count, think about the information you are receiving and consider what your response might be. Remember to let your adult self make this decision. Then act on it.

SUMMING UP

Maintaining good human relations calls for your full attention. Even if you only communicate with close friends and relatives, you will have problems from time to time. But you must communicate with all kinds of people—those you know and those you do not know at all. At work, you must often cooperate with others and get them to cooperate with you. Depending on the situation, you and your co-workers will act differently at different times. Appreciate the differences and look for them. You now have some tools for dealing with your own behavior and that of others. If you want to, you can maintain good human relations with effective communications.

58

COMMUNICATION ROADBLOCKS

You have learned that communication can be hindered when people let their parent self or their child self control their relations with others. If you do not use your adult self to stop, think, and consider what is going on in a communication process, you may run into roadblocks.

What form can these roadblocks take? How can you recognize them and deal with them effectively? There are certain common roadblocks to good communication that you will meet often. In fact, the ancient Greeks knew about them. And way back in the Middle Ages, scholars gave them a name: logical fallacies.

Logical fallacy is just another way of saying communication roadblock—but it's more exact. It could be called a false argument, or faulty logic, or poor thinking. Whatever you call it, it results in poor human relations.

Some people use logical fallacies on purpose to make a point or to win an argument when they have no reasons to support their statements. Other people use them without knowing it. Everyone is tempted to use them at one time or another. But logical fallacies mess up communication and weaken human relations. By learning about such communication roadblocks, you can recognize them when others use them and keep from using them yourself.

THE PERSONAL ATTACK

If you call someone insulting names, you will be communicating, but you certainly will not build good human relations. You will communicate dislike. Although that may be necessary sometimes, most of the time it is not. However, there

A logical fallacy may result from a false argument, faulty logic, or poor thinking. But in any case, the result is a roadblock to good communications—and also to good human relations.

are verbal personal attacks that are not as obvious as an outright insult, and they also stop effective communication. Here's an example:

"Say, Frank," said Al, one of the workers in the S&W TV Repair Shop, "Carmen has figured out a pretty good way to check these old color sets. You ought to have her show you."

"I don't think I'll bother," Frank said. "Anyone who wears the dumb clothes that Carmen does couldn't have any good ideas."

Did you notice what Frank did? He set up a roadblock to communication. Carmen's idea might not be good. But it might be excellent. Al thinks it is. Yet Frank ignores the idea. He doesn't even consider it. He just makes a personal attack on Carmen. He does not like the clothes she wears, and so he does not like any of her ideas. Since there is no connection between what Carmen wears and how she repairs television sets, Frank's reaction is foolish. Yet people do this sort of thing often. They ignore the topic or argument at hand and instead attack the person who puts it forward.

Sometimes people do this on purpose. Lawyers, for example, may use the personal attack as a tool of their trade. One famous lawyer put it this way: "When I have a strong legal case, I argue the law. When I have a lot of good facts, I argue the facts. When I have no case at all, I abuse my opponent."

Personal evaluations are sometimes important, of course. When deciding whether to vote for one candidate or another, you should consider facts about their personal characters. That is not a logical fallacy. Perhaps the health of the candidates is a factor: Are they strong enough and well enough to serve? But people who said that President Roosevelt's policies were wrong be-

cause he was handicapped were building roadblocks, just as Frank did.

There is a Latin name for this kind of logical fallacy that creates roadblocks to communication: *ad hominem.* It means "to the man" (or woman) and describes arguments that are aimed at a person instead of at an issue. You can dazzle your friends by calling their arguments *ad hominem* when they set up this kind of roadblock. The important thing, however, is to recognize it when others use it and to avoid it yourself.

SO ARE YOU

"So are you" is another dandy roadblock to communication. Everyone has used it. When you were children, you used it almost automatically: "You're a liar!" "You are too!" You are most likely to set up this roadblock to effective communication when you are criticized or when your work is corrected. It is a way of defending yourself—you throw the criticism back at the other person. Here's how it works:

> "Charles, I think you'd make fewer typing errors if you did not try to go so fast," Alice said, trying to help her friend.
> "I notice you never remember to cover your typewriter when you leave at night," Charles replied.

The conversation ends in a roadblock. Alice may have had a good point. Charles would not know until he tried it. But Charles didn't even want to listen to it. Instead he found something about Alice to criticize. Of course she should cover her typewriter at night. But that has nothing to do with her suggestion about typing too fast.

Sometimes when someone says, "You're a liar!" it is logical to reply, "And you are too!" If both of you are already communicating on that level, what can you lose? But when you make an unrelated counterattack instead of responding to the issue, you are putting up a roadblock and damaging your human relations. Here's another example:

> "Say, Marty. The inspectors said that the last few joints you welded were not as smooth as they should be. You know the company wants those welds nearly perfect."
> "Oh yeah? Well I think the company should provide more parking spaces for the workers."

Another logical fallacy—attacking the person rather than the issue. Learn to recognize such communication roadblocks when others use them and to avoid them yourself.

Some people defend themselves by throwing the criticism back at the other person. Such conversations usually end in a roadblock.

Marty jumped from welded joints to parking spaces without a second's thought. He tried to defend himself by attacking someone else. He would have been better off trying to find out how he could improve his work instead of playing "so are you."

APPEALING TO GREAT FIGURES

It is perfectly proper to quote experts to support a position you take or to turn to them for guidance. If, however, you do this in situations that do not warrant it, or if you do it in place of your own thinking, you are building roadblocks to communication and understanding.

Examples of this practice can be found on the television set. Thousands of commercials use this device to get people to buy their products. The message in the commercials is that because a certain well-known person uses the product, you should too. Such commercials are acting as a parent. If you believe them, you are letting your child aspect control you.

"Famous football players drive Blank cars!" the commercial says, showing a famous player driving one. The suggestion is that famous football players know a lot about automobiles. The truth is that most famous players don't know any more about cars than most other people do.

Cars, cosmetics, soap, and clothes are all sold by this technique. A famous person uses such and such a product—you should use it too. "Doctors recommend . . ." or "Nine out of ten dentists say . . ."—these are appeals to authority to convince you to do something. Before being influenced by such appeals, consider them with your adult self.

If your doctor, after examining you, tells you to do something or to take a certain medicine for a specific reason, do it. But if an advertisement or a friend tells you to try Hogwash Mouthwash because doctors recommend it or because Stella Starlet uses it, forget it.

You will run into this communication roadblock many times. Friends, relatives, and co-workers will all use it now and then to convince you of something. You probably use it yourself. In Latin, this kind of fallacy is called *ad verecundiam.* It refers to an appeal "to revered authority." The fallacy comes in when the authority is respected for something that is not related to the subject at hand. (What do football players know about cars?)

Don't hesitate to raise questions when someone mentions an authority to back up a position. Examine the facts and decide whether the quoted authority knows anything about the field and is up to date. You can hinder your communications and human relations by blindly following authorities—especially when they are out of date. Janice learned that the hard way:

Janice was a darkroom technician at Modern Photos, Inc. She made excellent prints from the negatives she was given. Many people brought their negatives to the company because she did quality work. But there was one problem. Janice was slow. She was so slow, in fact, that the company did not earn a profit when she made the prints. And they could not keep up with the demand.

The company manager, Neal, tried to learn what the problem was. He wanted Janice to work faster without losing the quality of her work. He felt it could be done.

Neal quickly found out what the problem was. Janice insisted on washing all prints for 12 hours. She had been taught by an excellent photographer many years ago that it was very important to get all the chemicals off the picture.

"Look," Neal said to her. "With the new kinds of photographic paper we use today, you don't have to wash the prints that much, In fact, you only have to wash them for about 4 minutes. You can make your prints faster and still keep the same quality."

*How do you recognize authority? Don't hesitate to raise
questions when an authority is used to back up a product.*
(© 1980, Children's Television Workshop)

"Are you sure?" Janice asked. And she quoted what the famous photographer had told her: "If you do not wash them the proper length of time, they will turn dark."

Fortunately Janice decided to run a few tests, despite what her out-of-date authority had told her. She discovered that Neal was right and that she could shorten her work time in other ways as well.

Appealing to authority is fine. Make sure, though, that you also consider the facts of the situation at hand.

OVERGENERALIZING

"Just because I say I like sea bathing," the senior Oliver Wendell Holmes once said, "that doesn't mean I want to be pickled in brine." He probably said that after having run into one of the most common and biggest communication roadblocks: overgeneralizing. You *overgeneralize* when you take one or two facts—or maybe just a part of a fact—and jump to conclusions. This habit also weakens communications and human relations, and it can destroy your ability to listen.

Overgeneralizing is probably the biggest roadblock to listening well. You listen to just a little of what someone is saying, and it sounds like something you've heard before. Thus you immediately classify the speaker as "one of those." That person is a liberal, or a conservative, or a teacher, or whatever. You "know" what the speaker is going to say, so you stop listening. You have labeled the person in your mind on the basis of the generalization. In fact, the speaker may go on to say something quite different from what you expect, but you won't hear it. Here's an example:

> "Jules, when you type this report, . . ." Mindy started to say, but that is all Jules heard. He knew Mindy. She was like all office managers. She was always giving needless directions. Jules had typed hundreds of these reports. He knew what to do. "Sure, fine. Yes, I understand," he said when Mindy finished talking.
>
> He typed the report quickly and accurately, as he always did, and sent it to Mindy. Soon she was standing angrily beside his desk.
>
> "Didn't you hear a word I said?" she demanded. "I told you this was a special report, to triple-space it, and also to put 3-inch margins at the top and bottom. You typed it just like all the other reports."

Jules overgeneralized. It is all too easy to do that when one is in a familiar setting. Unfortunately, though, the habit makes people poor listeners, which—as in Jules' case—can result in doing the wrong thing at work. He "knew" all about typing reports. They were all double-spaced to him.

Resist the urge to jump to conclusions. Listen. Wait. Hear all the facts. Your generalizations may be appropriate most of the time. That is the problem. Most of the time is not all of the time.

Be on your guard against this type of communication roadblock when listening to people who are trying to convince you to do something. Such people often will take one small fact and blow it up into a very wide generalization:

"If you do not vote for me, the Communists will take over the country."

"If boys wear long hair, the country will fall apart."

"You can't trust anybody over 30."

"If teenagers are given the vote, they will legalize marijuana."

Generalizations may be appropriate some of the time. But some of the time is not all of the time. It's always best to be on your guard.

When you hear people making generalized statements like those above, your mind should pick up a warning. Beware of the kind of thinking—or lack of thinking—that jumps from one small fact to a sweeping and unproved conclusion. At the same time, be careful not to read more than is intended into what someone is saying.

The fallacy of overgeneralization also has a Latin name: *secundum quid*, which means "according to something." Throw it into a conversation the next time someone sets up the over-generalization roadblock. Don't fall into the *secundum quid* fallacy. Don't be taken in by it.

SUMMING UP

These are just a few of the roadblocks to effective communication and good human relations that you will meet. There are many others, but these are the most common. If you learn to recognize and avoid them, you will increase your potential worth and ability.

59

CONSIDER THE SOURCE

One of the biggest communication problems you face today is sorting out the huge amount of information that cries for your attention. Television stations broadcast information all day long. Books, magazines, and newspapers pour off the presses in a large, unending stream. Parents, teachers, friends, co-workers, and bosses all seek your attention and feed information to you.

Handling this steady flow of information is difficult. You shut a lot of it out in self-protection. But in protecting yourself, you must be sure not to shut out needed information. It's important to consider where the information comes from—that is, its source. That will help you to decide how reliable it is and whether to shut it out.

At no time in your life will you receive more new information than when you are starting out on a new career. Then a confusing amount of information reaches you over a period of a few days or a few weeks. You must sort it out, accept some, reject some, act on some, and avoid acting on some. How do you do this? What guides are there for you to use?

You face a big communication problem every day, sorting out all the demands on your attention.

SOURCES OF INFORMATION AT WORK

At work, you may have three major sources of information: your supervisor (or supervisors), labor organizations—if they exist in your place of work—and co-workers. Most information will come to you in a verbal way—that is, it will be spoken. But on many jobs, it will be written as well.

Written information, of course, is usually more reliable and easier to handle. You can study it at your own speed. You can think over what it tells you. You can refer back to it.

The sources of written information on the job usually will be your company or a labor organization. Written information can be passed on in several ways. It may appear as a notice on the bulletin board. Most companies have bulletin boards on which they post notices of interest to employees. And bulletin boards are also used by labor organizations to give information to union members.

As a rule, you can consider the information communicated on these bulletin boards to be reliable. In fact, you should check bulletin boards at work regularly. Many companies let employees use bulletin boards to communicate with one another as well. Notices of cars for sale or houses for rent can be found there. Usually these notices are reliable also, but use more caution when

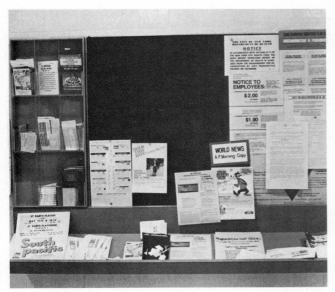

Written information can be passed on in several ways. Most companies have bulletin boards on which they post notices of interest to employees. (Marsha Cohen)

acting on them. A person would be foolish to buy a used car without checking it first, even though a co-worker advertised it for sale on the company bulletin board.

Neither your company nor a union will back up messages other than their own on the bulletin board. Usually you can assume that notices posted by co-workers will be more reliable than those that strangers put in newspapers. Anyone who takes advantage of the bulletin board to sell worthless articles to co-workers will not get along very well at work. But even though bulletin board messages at work may be more reliable than other types of messages outside of work, you still must be careful.

Other forms of written communication from the company could include a brochure that lists all the policies, rules, regulations, benefits, history, and other information you should know about the company. In addition, the company may include printed notices with your paycheck from time to time. You may receive a letter or a memorandum about something that affects only you. Many companies put out newsletters as well.

A labor organization will use similar written communications to give you information. Unions also often publish newsletters.

All this written information from your company and labor organization is useful and, for the most part, reliable. But remember that a company and a union will have different points of view

sometimes. Consider their points of view when interpreting the messages.

"PUT IT IN WRITING"

You may have heard someone say, "Put it in writing" when someone else made a wild promise. The purpose in saying this is usually to show disbelief. People are more willing to believe something that is put in writing than something that is only spoken, because the written statement can later serve as proof, or evidence. If everyone had to put everything in writing, people would be more careful about what they say. Although such a situation might strengthen communications, it also would slow things down. It is not practical to put everything in writing.

And so people talk a lot. In fact, you probably get much more information from talking than from writing. You will receive information from your boss and from a union orally. It is reliable too, but not quite as reliable as the written word. With verbal information, there is a greater danger that you will misunderstand or forget some part of it. And there is a greater danger that your company or union officials will not say exactly what they intend to say. Basically, though, you can rely on the information you receive from these people. Of course, you should examine it with the adult aspect of your character to see how their particular point of view may color it.

KEEP AN OPEN MIND

On the job, you also will receive a lot of oral information from your co-workers. You must be most careful when evaluating this information.

Long-time employees will try to be helpful, for the most part. They almost always will have certain feelings, complaints, or opinions that they have developed over the years. Without thinking about it too much, they will try to make their opinions yours. Don't let them. Listen to everyone, but keep an open mind. Consider all the information you receive from all sources, and then make up your own mind about work conditions, other workers, the union, the boss, and everything else.

Long-time workers can give you hints about getting along on your new job. But be especially careful about acting on their advice when they talk about personalities. Don't let them prejudice

Consider all the information you receive before you form an opinion.

you against other workers, supervisors, or the company. Make up your own mind about people as you gain experience on the job. Marilyn and Arlene learned to do that:

When Marilyn went to work at the fish hatchery, Mildred, an older employee, made an effort to welcome her. That was friendly of Mildred. Unfortunately, though, one reason Mildred did so was because she had no other friends among the workers. She had annoyed everyone else by her bragging and laziness.

Now she tried to prejudice Marilyn against all the other workers. Marilyn was bright enough not to let this happen. She was friendly to Mildred. She thanked her for her help. But she also made a point of talking to and getting to know other employees. She made up her own mind about everyone.

When Arlene began working as a nursing assistant at Maryville Hospital, two or three older employees kept telling her how bad Donald, the supervisor, was. "You better watch him—he'll report you for anything," they said. "If you are 1 second late, you'll be in trouble. He's mean."

This information on the first few days on the job from "helpful," "friendly" co-workers began to make Arlene feel uneasy around Donald. That made it hard for her to learn her new job, which

made her more uneasy. After about a week, during which Arlene did rather poorly, another nursing assistant, Theresa, talked to her.

"Donald asked me to talk to you," Theresa said. "He thought you were getting too uptight and it would bother you more if he talked to you. Listen, Donald's a good supervisor. He's fair. I've seen a few people around here talking to you quite a bit. Don't let them scare you. You watch them awhile and watch Donald. Then make up your own mind."

Arlene did that. She began to see that the workers who complained about Donald and said he was tough were among the slower workers. The ones who complained the most did the least work. They were often late and took extra time at breaks during the day. She saw that Donald had to keep after them all the time. Arlene soon realized that if Donald was hard on the complainers, it was their own fault. She decided to make up her own mind about people in the future.

THE GRAPEVINE

The word for informal, oral communication among people is *grapevine.* Why "grapevine"? What does this way of spreading information have to do with a real vine on which grapes grow? Well, the use of "grapevine" to mean the informal spread of information began during the Civil War. "A dispatch by grapevine telegraph" was the passing of information or rumors by secret or unusual means rather than over the regular telegraph wires. Perhaps a grapevine was necessary because the telegraph wires had been cut or because the sender was afraid the message would get into enemy hands. Of course, the messages actually were carried by messenger or by word of mouth.

This early grapevine did not work very well. Messages often were garbled. They sometimes became distorted, hard to understand, or unclear. The grapevine moved messages when there was no other way available, but it often messed them up. This informal, word-of-mouth procedure spreads messages quickly, but it also distorts them.

Today it's common for someone to say they "heard it on the grapevine." The grapevine is probably the source of most news and information you get in the world of work. But you must be careful when handling information that comes to you by the grapevine. The information may seem clear, but often it can be distorted, blown up, or completely wrong.

The use of the word "grapevine" to mean informal, oral communication began during the Civil War. If telegraph wires were cut, information was passed from one person to another by word of mouth.

One kind of message that the grapevine specializes in is the rumor. You know about rumors: They usually are untrue or exaggerated versions of a small truth. It is not easy to ignore rumors because they often are about things that interest you. You may want to believe them. You certainly want to listen to them. In fact, you enjoy them. You have to struggle to reject them or demand proof that they are true.

Another characteristic of rumors is that they are ambiguous—that is, they are not clear. They can be understood in different ways by different people. This ambiguity increases as a rumor is spread from person to person.

To establish good communications and human relations as you begin your career, keep yourself open to all sources of information. Don't let one source crowd out the others. Listen to them all and weigh them. Then form your own opinions upon which to base your actions.

SUMMING UP

As you weigh information that comes to you, always consider the source. Whether the source is a company official, a union official, or a co-worker, you can assume that the information will reflect the interests and point of view of the source. There's nothing wrong with that as long as you recognize it. When you pass on information, you color it according to how you see it. The "unvarnished truth" does not exist. But reality does exist, and some information will reflect reality more carefully and accurately than other information will.

Written information is more easily dealt with and, generally, more reliable than oral information. Most information you receive on a day-to-day basis at work will be oral. Rumors are not passed along in written form. Be slow to accept unwritten information. Always try to verify it either by actual observations of your own or by seeking further information from other sources.

Getting It All Together

1. What two common problems are you likely to meet when you communicate?

2. Why must you be careful when dealing with abstract terms?

3. What can happen if two people let their parent aspect come on too strong?

4. What are four common roadblocks to effective communication and good human relations?

5. How can overgeneralizing weaken good communications?

6. Why is it important to consider the source of information you receive?

7. What are three major sources of information at work?

8. How does the grapevine work, and how reliable is it as a source of information?

HUMAN RELATIONS AND CAREER SATISFACTION

Your goals in this unit are given in the following list:

To demonstrate how needs, motivation, and the will to work are related

To identify several factors that influence morale and job satisfaction

To recognize the differences between positive and negative attitudes

To identify several characteristics of effective leadership

You are aware that you have to develop good human relations skills to succeed in any career. You also know that relating to other people is not simple: Every individual is a complex mixture of different value systems, different outlooks, and different reactions.

Although there are no quick, easy rules that ensure that you will always have ideal human relations (you will not), you have learned some basic concepts that can help guide your behavior and reaction to others. These concepts, discussed in Unit 17, are no two people are alike, everybody likes to feel like somebody, the whole person must be considered, and people act as they do because of needs. The basic needs that all people share are keeping alive (food, drink, shelter), being free of fear and anxiety, being loved, being admired and respected, and realizing your potential.

These concepts can help you to understand yourself and others and to anticipate problems so that you can avoid them. Your motivation stems from your desire to satisfy your basic needs. Everyone's does. How you view these needs will determine how highly you are motivated. For most people, the basic needs

of keeping alive and being safe are satisfied fairly easily. The needs for love, respect, and self-realization are met less easily. As a result, much of people's motivation stems from their efforts to fulfill these needs.

Some people are highly motivated. Their need for love, respect, or self-realization is strong. They may try to meet many of these needs outside of work. But careers make up such an important part of most people's lives that they generally will try to satisfy these needs through their work.

Sometimes people's strong needs cause them to set very high career goals. When they do not achieve these goals, they become frustrated and tense. Poor human relations results. Such a situation may cause them to work even harder. Or they may stop and take time to rethink things. They may decide that their goal is beyond their abilities. If so, they try to set other goals. They are happiest, and they have the best human relations, when their goals and their achievements match. In this unit, you will learn what is involved in achieving the greatest amount of need satisfaction in a successful career.

CHAPTER 60

THE WILL TO WORK

Your will to work depends upon your motivation. The greater your motivation, the greater, in general, your will to work. You probably have heard people say of hard workers, "They are highly motivated." Motivation differs from person to person, but all people are motivated by the desire to satisfy their basic needs.

People try to satisfy their different needs at different times and in different ways. For some people, the needs for esteem and self-realization can be met only by getting lots and lots of money. Other people have a greater need for affection, and so they will give up money and make other sacrifices for the sake of having friends. Still others desire power in order to satisfy their need for self-realization.

You can be a more efficient worker and have better human relations when you know what motivates you and when you understand what motivates others.

UNDERSTANDING THE MOTIVATION OF OTHERS

For good human relations, it helps to know what motivates other people in any given situation. Knowing this can often help you understand another person's behavior. And when you understand that, you are less likely to be annoyed by it or to cause that person to be annoyed. In short, you can improve your human relations.

If you were the manager of a plant, you might not care about the workers' motivation as long as they had the will to work. Well, that might be OK up to a point. But suppose that, by not understanding their motivation, you took steps that weakened or destroyed it. You would be destroying their will to work as well. And you

would not be an effective manager. Consider this case:

Doug owned a small construction company that built new homes. He employed four workers. When the crew was first hired, they all worked hard and willingly. They showed that they enjoyed their work, and they did a lot of it. Doug never tried to learn what motivated them. He was happy enough that they worked so hard. He assumed they were all motivated by the desire to earn money.

Many workers are motivated by pride in their work. (Philip Teuscher)

324

Business went well. Everyone who bought one of Doug's houses was pleased. The construction was excellent. Doug had no trouble selling all the houses he could build because word of their high quality spread.

Then Doug had what he thought was a brilliant idea: If he could build more houses, he would make a lot more money. Doug told his workers that he would pay bonuses whenever they could do more work than usual in a day. The bonuses would be individual so the workers would compete for them. Those who worked hardest would get the most money.

For a few weeks, the plan seemed to work. More work was done. Then something began to happen. First the crew seemed to get less friendly and to enjoy their work less. Then the quality of their work dropped. Doug offered more bonuses, but things got worse. Then one worker quit, and another one threatened to.

Finally Doug realized that his workers had not been motivated only by money. They wanted fair pay, of course. But before Doug introduced the elements of competition and speed, the workers had enjoyed each other and had taken pride in doing quality work. Not knowing what motivated them, Doug had destroyed their will to work with his mistaken notion that money alone was their motivation.

Now you will not own a company, or even be a supervisor, right away. Still, it is important for you to know that people have different motivations for working. Knowing this can help you build and maintain good human relations. If you know that one of your co-workers takes pride in the work itself, you are not likely to offend that person by talking as if only money mattered. And if another co-worker is interested only in money, you won't waste time talking about the work itself with that person.

UNDERSTANDING YOUR OWN MOTIVATION

Knowing about your own motivation is important too. Surprisingly, your own motives are not always clear. They depend on your values and the goals you set for yourself—after, of course, you have satisfied your basic needs.

Some people are not very highly motivated. They are happy simply to earn a decent living in order to have food, clothes, and a roof over their heads. There's nothing wrong with that. They do

their work well enough to keep their jobs, and they are unlikely to become bored. They know that they are working to meet their needs.

Other people are highly motivated. They try to get increasingly important jobs or to do increasingly better work. Such people are said to have *aspirations*—that is, strong desires to achieve. In a way, they have high hopes. One aspires to be the president of the union or the supervisor or the division manager. One hopes to do the best job that has ever been done.

Young persons just starting out on their careers generally have high aspirations. Older workers either have attained their goals or have had to settle for something less than what they had first hoped for. Some people set unrealistic goals and later suffer because they do not reach them. It is important to spend some time deciding who you are and what your values are. In this way, you can set realistic goals.

After you have reached your goals and satisfied your aspirations, you still can get satisfaction from doing your job well. This satisfaction will do much to help you avoid the boredom that many workers face in their later years. The more realistically you have chosen your goals and identified your aspirations, the less likely you are to become bored at your work.

OUTSIDE MOTIVATION

The likelihood of becoming bored with your work is real, even under the best conditions. A good protection against boredom on the job is a full, satisfying life away from the job. Hobbies and other interests that provide outside motivation are important for rounding out your life.

Many people are strongly motivated at work by their outside interests. They are willing to work hard to earn money or time off so they can spend it on hobbies outside of work. There is nothing wrong with that. No one said that a person should live only to work. In fact, the more sensible course is to work in order to live an interesting life.

For some people, a job is less important than a hobby. Agnes, for example, was very interested in skin diving and surfing. So she took jobs as a waiter at resorts where she could follow these hobbies. She would work in the north during the summer and then move south in the winter. Benji followed a similar plan. He liked to ski. He used his skills as a carpenter to find jobs at ski resorts, and he moved around with the ski season. People like Agnes and Benji are highly motivated too, but their motivation comes from outside their work.

CLUES FOR JUDGING MOTIVATION

Although it often may seem difficult to understand your own motivations, much less the motivations of others, some understanding of what motivates others will help you to maintain good human relations. People seem to follow patterns that can serve as hints about their motivation. Be careful using these clues. Remember that gener-

Some people are motivated by their outside interests. They work hard to earn money or time off so that they can enjoy leisure-time activities. There is nothing wrong with that. (Philip Teuscher)

alizations can be misleading. With that in mind, consider the following motivation patterns.

Finished-Job Pattern

People who have a finished-job pattern are motivated by the desire to finish a job for its own sake. They work hard to achieve a feeling of accomplishment. They could be satisfying a basic need for esteem or for self-realization—an outside observer can only guess which one.

But the important point here is that, for such people, the sense of accomplishment that comes from doing a job well is more important than money. Doug's construction workers had this motivation. That's why they built such good houses. If Doug had recognized the pattern, he would not have thought that bonuses would generate more work.

Friendship Pattern

People who make every effort to be liked by others and to be surrounded by friends are said to display the friendship pattern. Such people probably are fulfilling their basic needs for affection and recognition. They have a problem, though, in balancing their need for friends against their other values.

For example, many workers may compromise some of their principles and even their self-respect for the sake of remaining friendly with their co-workers. They may keep their mouths shut in order to avoid problems.

Such people run a risk: To keep from rocking the boat, they may never get it away from the shore. Sometimes it is necessary to take a stand. That can be difficult if you are ruled by the need to be liked.

Perfection Pattern

People who are more interested in the technical aspects of a job rather than in their co-workers or in finishing the job show the perfection pattern of behavior. Such people value excellence and devote themselves to achieving it. They usually strive for professional growth and mastery of the job. These things mean more to them than money, friendship, or the final completion of the job. And once the job **is** completed, these

People may be motivated by the desire to be liked, the love of power, the satisfaction of finishing a job, or a regard for excellence. Look for patterns of behavior that can serve as hints. Understanding what motivates others will help you to maintain good human relations.

people will push on to the next job and will try to do it perfectly too.

Power Pattern

Some people are motivated by power above all else. Such people often make excellent leaders and will usually perform best in a situation when their role as a leader is emphasized. A possible problem with such people, however, is that they may choose to retain control at the expense of performance.

Combined Patterns

Some people may follow two or more of these motivation patterns, but usually one pattern will rule a person's life. You can use the pattern as a clue to understanding the motivation of others. But remember that it is dangerous to generalize, particularly when dealing with people. Remember too that people's needs—and thus their motivations—may change from time to time. Do not expect one pattern to rule in every situation.

EVERYONE HAS MOTIVATION

Everyone is motivated in some way or another by one thing or another. If you hear someone say that another person has no motivation at all and just doesn't care about work, don't believe it. The person may not be motivated to do a particular job. But that person does have other motivations.

It is difficult to say why people are motivated to satisfy one need rather than another. On the most basic level, people are motivated to satisfy their most pressing need first. If they are very hungry, they will be motivated to eat. If they are very tired, they will be motivated to sleep. And when they try to satisfy their higher-level needs, they seem to follow the same pattern. That is, they are motivated by the need they feel most strongly. And that need is usually the one they have not satisfied much.

For example, a person who has never had to worry about money usually will not be strongly motivated by a desire to earn money and security. Instead, the need for affection might be stronger, especially if the person had been given little affection early in life.

So people satisfy their higher-level needs in the same way they do their basic needs: The strongest need gets their attention first. By knowing which needs you feel most strongly, you can become aware of your motivation pattern and build better human relations.

RELATING MOTIVATION TO YOUR CAREER

To make the right career choice, you should be aware of your needs and understand your motivation. People do not perform well on the job if their motivation does not relate to their careers. Your will to work depends upon your motivation, which must relate in some way to your career.

A tired donkey may get up for a carrot—but not right after a feast. People, too, are usually motivated to satisfy their most pressing needs first.

Motivation may be indirect—as in the case of a person who works hard to support an outside hobby—but there is a connection. Without this connection between motivation and career, there is little will to work, no great success, and poor human relations.

61

JOB SATISFACTION AND MORALE

What is job satisfaction and what does it have to do with morale? Well, they go together. They feed each other. If you enjoy your work, you will have high morale. But if you have low morale, you are not likely to enjoy your work.

Satisfaction comes from having a sense of doing a worthwhile job and doing it well. All people like to feel that they are somebody and that what they do is important. A problem that some workers face is that their jobs seem unimportant to them. They cannot see how what they do connects to the final product, and they do not feel that they are doing something worthwhile. Such workers derive little job satisfaction, no matter how well motivated they are. Their morale is low.

Morale grows out of job satisfaction. Morale displays itself in a willingness to perform even the less pleasant tasks that are a part of every job. High morale reflects cheerfulness and confidence. Where there is high morale, there should be good human relations. Where morale is low, human relations will probably suffer.

MOTIVATION AFFECTS MORALE

Without motivation you will have little job satisfaction. Your morale will be poor. This will hold true no matter how high your pay is or how pleasant your surroundings are. Does this mean that job satisfaction and morale depend completely upon your own motivation? Happily, they do not.

Although it is true that you must be motivated in order to have job satisfaction and high morale, these things will not automatically follow high motivation. Other factors strongly influence how you feel and the amount of satisfaction you get from your work.

Two major influences affect your job satisfaction and morale: your own motivation—what you bring to the job—and your job environment. You read about motivation in the last chapter. Now you will look at environmental factors that are important to your sense of job satisfaction.

JOB FACTORS ALSO AFFECT MORALE

Your pay, your physical surroundings, your co-workers, your supervisors, and company policies all affect your morale.

Your Pay

Pay is important to you for many reasons. First of all, of course, you need a certain amount of money simply to live. You must buy food, clothes, and shelter. You also will want money to buy some of life's pleasures—a nice car, an evening at the movies, dinner out, and so on.

These are good, practical reasons why your pay is important to you. But it is important in another way too. Pay is a measure of your success and status in society. To some extent, the higher your pay, the greater your success.

For all these reasons, your salary has a direct effect on your morale. Your primary motivation may not be to make money, but if you do not get enough of it, your morale will be affected.

Your Physical Surroundings

Your physical surroundings on the job can also affect your morale. If you work in a dirty, crowded, dark, poorly ventilated place, your morale will suffer no matter how well motivated you are. There are some things you can expect your company to do to protect your safety and health. Many of these same things affect your morale. Tell your supervisor about conditions that keep you from performing well, such as poor lighting or uncomfortable temperatures.

Your Co-Workers

Your morale also can be affected by the people with whom you work. For this reason, good human relations is important on the job. Sometimes, of course, there is little you can do to change an unpleasant co-worker into a pleasant one. But few people are unpleasant all the time. And, as you have learned, you can improve your own human relations to make friends or at least acceptable companions out of most co-workers.

Your Supervisors

Another factor on the job that can influence your morale is the type of supervision you receive. If your supervisor overuses the parent aspect of character and always orders you about, your morale will suffer. In the same way, your morale will suffer if the supervisor always ignores you, or never praises what you do, or always criticizes.

Company Policies

Company policies, plus the benefits you receive in addition to pay, will affect your morale. The extent of the effect depends on how bad or how good the policies are. This is true of all external conditions that affect your morale. For most workers, external conditions will neither be very bad nor exceptionally good. Most companies will do all they can to make external conditions as favorable as possible.

For your peace of mind—and to improve your relations with others—realize that you are not the only one responsible for your morale. It

Pay can be a measure of success and status in society and has a direct effect on morale. (Marsha Cohen)

can be, and probably will be, affected by external conditions.

NORMAL HIGHS AND LOWS

Another thing you should know about the state of your morale is that it will change. Changes in morale may not relate directly to anything— neither to external conditions of the job nor to internal conditions of your motivation. This is normal.

Psychologists who study morale changes have determined that most people swing through a cycle during their working lives. When they first start to work, they tend to have very high morale. They look forward to their new life and to the opportunities it presents. After about a year, this enthusiasm weakens, and so does their morale.

After around 2 years on the same job, a worker's morale is likely to be fairly low in comparison to what it was at first. How low it goes depends upon one's motivation, as well as upon external conditions at work. But regardless of all these factors, morale tends to slump after about the third year. Many workers change jobs after 3 or 4 years.

If you experience this slump in morale, do not despair. There does not seem to be any real reason for it. Studies of workers have shown that after about 5 years, morale and interest begin to pick up again—even though job conditions and pay are not much different from what they were during the low period.

This change in morale happens because, after 5 years on the job, workers will tend to change some of their goals. Consciously or not, they try to evaluate what they want. If necessary, they may lower their goals as a realistic adjustment to their lives and careers. In addition, after 5 years, workers have learned their jobs well enough to enjoy a strong feeling of confidence. They have learned how to get along with their co-workers—even with those few who create problems—and they feel accepted.

WHEN MORALE IS LOW

Be prepared for your morale sometimes being low. At such times, be especially careful about your human relations. When your morale is low, you are likely to be annoyed easily, to be rude to people, and even to be unfriendly. At such times,

In contrast to the sweatshops of the past, most working conditions today show that employers recognize the importance of physical surroundings to an employee's morale. (Top, courtesy Brown Bros.; bottom, Oscar Mayer)

you must control yourself when dealing with others, especially with your co-workers and your supervisors.

If your morale does sink, try to find out why as quickly and objectively as you can. Some guidelines follow.

Check Yourself First

First, consider whether your own motivation—or lack of it—could be the reason for your low

An important thing to know about your morale is that it will change. (Marsha Cohen)

morale. Many workers are quick to blame the company when things do not go right. Consider that possibility, but don't kid yourself. If the fault is your own, but you think changing jobs will correct it, you will be disappointed. And your career will probably go nowhere. Louis was a case in point:

> Louis had had three different jobs in 4 years, and he was about to change jobs again. He was unhappy. He had never felt any job satisfaction, and his morale was low. He blamed this on the companies he had worked for. He felt that no one understood him. And so Louis moved from company to company. He was always employed as a shipping clerk.
>
> Louis did not particularly want to be a shipping clerk. He had drifted into it. Now it was the only thing he knew how to do. But Louis really felt he should be running things. Because he did not value his job, he never bothered to learn the company procedures and policies affecting it. He figured it did not matter how he did the work. When supervisors tried to tell Louis how the company wanted the work done, he would say, "Yeah," and promptly forget it.
>
> Louis was annoyed much of the time because his supervisors always seemed to be picking on him. As a result, his morale stayed low. He kept changing jobs, hoping to find a supervisor who would not pick on him. Fortunately, Louis began to realize that his problem stemmed from within himself—he lacked motivation. That discovery

helped him to turn his life around. He began to work harder because he was motivated to get a better job—not one that only paid his way, but one that satisfied him.

If you suffer from low morale and are not getting any satisfaction out of your job, look at yourself realistically. Ask yourself two basic questions: Are you doing what you really want to do? Are your expectations too high? Try to answer these questions objectively. Many companies have personnel officials who are trained to help you straighten things out. You can also seek outside advice.

Check Your Job Environment Second

If you know that you are not just in a down period and you feel that the problem does not lie within you, take steps to identify external factors that may keep you from having job satisfaction.

Your first step is to talk with your immediate supervisor. At this time, your human relations skills will be important. You may feel annoyed and unhappy, but you should try to discuss things calmly. Above all, avoid making complaints about your co-workers, supervisors, or the company. This is a good way to end a conversation, not to start one. At this point, you want to start a conversation in order to discover what the problems are and how to solve them.

If something is bothering you on the job, it is better to bring it into the open and talk about it than to bottle it up. If you try to hide your problems, they will grow inside you. Your morale may sink lower, and you probably will become even less effective in your human relations.

When something weakens your morale, the best way to face the problem is to level with your supervisor. Ask him or her to set time aside for a talk. It is more productive to approach the supervisor this way, with some warning, than to rush in with your problem at a time when you are being emotional.

When you do meet with the supervisor, describe the problem as clearly and honestly as you can. Avoid the communication roadblocks—personal attacks, appeals to great figures, generalizations, and so on. Stick with the facts as you see them. Consider this example:

Millicent Scott developed a morale problem. She worked as a legal secretary for five lawyers. She liked her work and was good at it. For a long time, her morale was high, and she got much satisfaction from her work. Then one of the lawyers was replaced by a new person, Gale Ming.

Many workers are too quick to complain when things do not go right. The wise employee first checks his or her own motivation—or lack of it.

Gale's approach bothered Millicent. She began to feel dumb and inefficient because Gale would give her detailed instructions for every job. Gale would also say such things as, "Do you think I can have this back by 5 o'clock?"

That question particularly annoyed Millicent, because it was asked at 9 o'clock in the morning. Millicent knew that she did her work fast. She resented Gale's suggesting that she could not finish the job in time. Millicent's morale went down, and she began to think about finding another job.

But there were many good things about her job, and so Millicent decided to tell Gale what was bothering her. She asked Gale for some time to talk, and she resolved not to become emotional. She would try to tell Gale what the job meant to her and how she felt about it.

Millicent was wise. She began by telling Gale how much she liked her job. She said that one main reason she liked it was that she felt confident and able to do it well, and that the other lawyers seemed to agree. She liked to have responsibility. She then asked Gale whether she was doing anything wrong.

"Why, no," Gale said. "Your work is really excellent."

Millicent then asked why Gale gave so many directions, even on the most routine jobs.

"I didn't realize I was doing that," Gale answered. "I guess it's because I'm new here and I want to do everything right."

"I sometimes feel you don't think I will get your work done," Millicent said.

"What on earth gives you that idea?" Gale asked.

"Well, whenever you give me something—no matter how early in the day—you always ask whether I can finish it by 5 o'clock."

"That's just my way of apologizing for giving you so much work," Gale explained. "I certainly don't mean to suggest that you are at fault. Quite the opposite—you're very helpful to me. I'm sorry that those useless expressions have bothered you, and I'll try to avoid them from now on. Thanks for letting me know how you feel."

Millicent felt much better after the talk. Her morale shot back up. She realized that Gale did respect her. A straightforward conversation is often the best way to solve such problems.

The Formal Approach

If an informal approach does not work, you can take other steps to correct working conditions that affect you in a negative way. As you know, most companies have grievance procedures to handle complaints and problems of employees. They provide a formal course of action you can take to solve problems at work. The procedures usually require your complaint to be in writing, and they often will involve a hearing before company representatives. If there is a union, its representatives may also be involved.

Grievance procedures are used to correct serious, obvious offenses. They are used when the company or its representative violates a work contract, a fair labor law, or health and safety standards. Formal grievance procedures are not used to deal with minor problems that develop in the daily give-and-take of a worker's life, no matter how badly they may affect your morale. You can solve these problems on your own, as Millicent did, by effective human relations.

The Last Resort

Only as a last resort should you quit and find another job. But be careful. If you are mistaken about the cause of your problem—if it is in you, not in the job—you will take your problem with you to the new job. Even if your problem is caused by the job environment, it is often best to try to solve it where you are. Remember that few

Most companies have grievance procedures to handle complaints and problems of employees. These procedures usually require a complaint to be in writing and they often involve a hearing before company representatives.

jobs are perfect—all have their problems. Quitting a job is the **last** resort, the solution when all else fails.

CHAPTER 62

YOUR ATTITUDE SHOWS

Dulcie thought of herself as clever. She saw herself as an individual. She did her own thing. Work was a necessary evil to her. If she didn't make it at one job, she would at another, she thought. So why worry? She did not think in terms of a lifelong, satisfying career. She thought in terms of a day-to-day existence, working only as necessary.

Dulcie's first job was in a bank. She wore her granny gowns and carpenter coveralls to work. They were "her." She sometimes wore her bathing suit under a halter top with short shorts. She considered herself a night person—which made getting up in the morning a drag. She was often late for work.

Dulcie did not let her job interfere with the really important activities in her life. If there was a rock concert, a super beach party, or any other type of happening, she would call in sick and take the time off. The next day she would brag to her co-workers about the far-out time she had had.

At the end of her probationary period, Dulcie was out of a job. At first, she enjoyed the freedom of being unemployed. But after a few weeks, she began to wonder why she was having trouble finding another job. Something seemed wrong.

What was wrong with Dulcie? A lot of things. But they can all be summed up in one word: attitude.

A STATE OF MIND

Attitude is your state of mind. It is your feelings about things. Your attitude is reflected in your behavior. It affects how you carry yourself, how you talk, and how you do your work. Your attitude reflects all the other things you have been reading about: motivation, morale, values, self-knowledge, goals.

Your attitude shows how you put all these things together and present them to the world. It is what's out front. And the world will judge you pretty much on the attitude you present. Bruce found that out:

Bruce could be a good electrician. He had taken a course in school and did well. He looked forward to the day he would become a licensed electrician and could go into business for himself. In fact, he spent so much time looking forward to it that he did not think much about his present job as an apprentice. He showed no initiative and had no interest in his work or his co-workers. Bruce felt he was a natural electrician, and so he did not bother much with routine things now. This job was just something to get through.

Bruce did exactly what he was told—no more, no less. Every day he had to be told again to do the same things. When the head electrician tried to talk to him, Bruce just said that he did not intend to spend his life working for that company. But he spent less time there than he had expected. He was fired after a few weeks. Though he may have been a good electrician, his attitude was poor.

Now Bruce may have had no intention of remaining an apprentice electrician all his life. It was all very good that he had ambition and plans. But his attitude hurt him. He concentrated so hard on the future that his attitude toward the present was poor. Although it is good to plan for the future, you cannot ignore the reality of the present. And your attitude will be judged and evaluated in the present, not the future.

Your attitude determines whether you will have good human relations or poor, ineffective human relations. It determines how well you will succeed on a job. If you project a poor attitude, an indifferent attitude, or a negative attitude, you will have problems in dealing with others.

You may think it doesn't matter if you're late to work. But remember, the world will judge your attitude in terms of your behavior.

CHANGING YOUR ATTITUDE

If attitude is your state of mind—how you feel about things—what can you do if you do not like a situation or a person you must deal with? After all, Dulcie's and Bruce's attitudes only reflected how they really felt about things. What could they have done about that?

Well, they could have realized two things: First, that if they did not change their basic attitudes, they probably would have unsatisfying careers. Second, that they could have exercised some willpower in order that they might project a different attitude.

The world will evaluate your attitude in terms of your behavior. Often it is necessary to behave differently than you really want to at a given moment. But if you do not do so, human relations problems may result. Sometimes it suits your purpose to behave differently than you'd like.

You may say, "Well, if I behave differently from how I feel, isn't that somehow dishonest or not telling it like it is?" Not at all. In the first place, honesty or dishonesty is not involved. It is more a matter of your acting with grace under pressure.

You might argue that the only "honest" behavior when you are feeling out of sorts is to let everyone know it, to be surly or rude. But it is ridiculous to claim that it is dishonest to behave pleasantly toward others when you feel bad. It is as silly as saying that you are a dishonest football player if you continue to play with a painful, but minor, injury. You are not showing how you really feel, but you are displaying a positive attitude.

If you had a serious injury, though, you could not play football. You would be foolish to try. It is the same thing with your attitude. You can and should work to project a positive attitude, one that will balance your downs, or negative feelings. At the same time, you can work to change negative feelings so that you will be happier.

YOU HAVE SEVERAL ATTITUDES

An attitude is not fixed forever in concrete. Nor do you have just one attitude. You have many attitudes, at different levels, and they change often. You have one attitude toward cars, another toward school, and so on. You like some people better than others, and your attitude shows it.

A Basic Theme

Together these attitudes reflect your essential character. How you feel about something at different times will be determined by your basic values, by your sense of identity, by your goals, and by how you feel you can achieve them. The basic theme that will run through all your attitudes can be characterized as either positive or negative. It's to your advantage in life to develop a positive attitude. After all, your attitude will pretty much determine what you get out of life and how you will be treated.

Look at the two following cases:

Carla had a negative attitude toward school when she was there. She felt it was a waste of time. She got nothing out of it. Because of her negative attitude, she did not try very hard. She ignored her assignments. She rarely read her textbooks. She never listened to the teachers. Not surprisingly, she got little in return. That strengthened her negative attitude and her belief that school was a waste of time.

Sylvia, on the other hand, was a naturally positive person. School was not her favorite pastime, but she had to go, and so she decided to get all she could from it. Sylvia had a positive attitude. She listened. She read. She thought about things. Sure enough, she got something for her effort—just as she had expected. Her experience strengthened her positive attitude.

Carla and Sylvia were experiencing a *self-fulfilling prophecy*—that is, they each got what they had expected out of school. The self-fulfilling prophecy affects much of one's life. People get what they deserve, most of the time. And that is why a positive attitude is important.

YOUR ATTITUDE IS CONTAGIOUS

An important thing about your attitude is that it will spread. It is contagious. If you display a positive attitude, you will find that you usually are surrounded by other people with positive attitudes. The same applies if you have a negative attitude—you'll be surrounded by negative people much of the time.

There is no magic involved in this. It is how things work, and it is easy to understand. Consider the case of Tim:

Every morning Tim's boss came into the office looking sour and angry. He ignored Tim. He then would work until the coffee break, when he sometimes would come out and talk with one or two other workers. Tim was upset by this behavior. He felt that the boss was ignoring him on purpose. But he did not try to speak with his boss. Tim thought it was the boss's place to speak first.

The company had a policy that supervisors were to evaluate the performance of all employees once a year. Tim's boss gave him high ratings for the quality of his work, but low ones for his attitude. When Tim questioned this, the boss said he was standoffish, and unfriendly.

Tim was surprised and somewhat resentful. When he asked for some examples, the boss said, "Well, when I come in in the morning, you never say anything. Also, when I join the other workers for a coffee break, you never join in."

Tim left the meeting with mixed feelings. But he decided to try to change. His attitude had been that the boss should speak first. Now he was determined to be more outgoing, and his attitude reflected it. He made a point of greeting the boss each morning. To his surprise, it seemed to change his own mood as well. Most workdays became more pleasant.

A pleasant, positive attitude usually will pay off for you. If you give someone else a lift during the day, he or she probably will respond to you the same way.

BEHAVIOR CLUES TO ATTITUDE

As you have already read, others will interpret your attitude in terms of your behavior. If you are always late for work, your supervisor is going to decide that you do not have the right attitude. If you complain a lot, do not show initiative, and seem sour all the time, people are going to say that you have a negative attitude.

Remember that you are always communicating when you are with other people. Based on what you communicate, people will decide whether you have a positive attitude or a negative one. Sometimes what they decide may be different from what you feel. Remember that you can send false messages without realizing it.

There are several common behavioral clues that people use to classify attitudes. It is worth your while to learn the characteristics associated with a positive attitude. If you have a positive attitude, you probably display them naturally. But if you have bad periods or have to force

A negative attitude is contagious.

you. Here are some characteristics of a positive attitude:

- Willingness to change
- Willingness to see the other side
- Not complaining or making excuses
- Pleasant, friendly expression
- Readiness to accept responsibility for errors
- Not critical of others
- Many interests
- Respect for others

IT TAKES AN EFFORT

Although most people tend to have a positive attitude, you cannot take that attitude for granted. When you face problems and have difficult times, it is all too easy to develop a negative attitude toward life. That is when you must be on guard. If you often find yourself showing a negative attitude, it is time to take stock and use your willpower. Study the list of positive characteristics and try to behave as they suggest. A positive attitude will build good human relations and earn you a satisfying career.

yourself to overcome a negative attitude, knowing the positive behavior characteristics can help

When you face problems, it is all too easy to develop a negative attitude. At such times you must be especially on guard.

63

LEADERSHIP SKILLS

Not everyone will become president of a company or general manager or even supervisor. Some people do not want to be leaders. In some careers, managing or leading other people is not a factor. And, of course, if everyone were a leader, who would follow?

You are just beginning a career and the possibility of leadership seems a long way off. However, this is the time to start developing leadership skills. If you do step into a managerial position someday, you cannot expect to learn leadership skills overnight. And when you need the skills is not the time to be learning them. Those who become managers get their skills as they go along. They improve their skills after

becoming managers. So now, when you are starting out on your career, is a good time to begin learning what leadership involves.

WHO NEEDS LEADERSHIP SKILLS?

There are other good reasons for thinking about leadership skills at this point. Even though you will not all become leaders in your careers, many of you will need leadership skills outside your careers. You may be asked to take over the leadership of a fund-raising committee for a club or for your church or synagogue. You may advise a scouting troop, coach a Little League team, or

You learn a lot about leadership from the people who lead you.

serve as chairperson on the local school board. All people find themselves in a leadership position at some point in their life. Human relationships demand it from time to time.

Knowing leadership skills at this point can also help you to be a better worker. By knowing the skills, you will understand better what your supervisor is trying to do. You will learn by watching the strengths and weaknesses of other leaders, and you may even offer helpful advice to your own supervisor. Leadership skills, then, are really only human relations skills used in a specific way.

CAN ANYBODY LEAD?

You may think that being a supervisor is easy. Who needs human relations skills for that? Supervisors, after all, have the power of their position. People do what they're told or they get fired. Anybody can give orders.

Well, it may seem that way. But that is **not** what it's like. Sure, some managers get by just by ordering people about: "Do this . . . Do that . . . Don't do the other thing . . . ." Actually, this kind of person does not last long as a supervisor and is not likely to be productive.

Bossing people around is not leading them. You can get only so far trying to boss people. Ask yourself whether you like being bossed around. Not much, probably, unless you let the child aspect of character rule your life. In that case, you might like having a strong, bossy parent type around. But probably, like most people, you would rather be led than bossed.

Leaders get more out of people than bosses do. Consider Carl and Cathy in the next example. Which one would you make your best effort for?

"Hey you," Carl shouted. "Finish that report this afternoon!"

"I'm working on one report, and the department needs another one this afternoon," Cathy said. "Could you try to get this one done? If you need any help, let me know, and I'll see what I can do."

Well, you might finish the report for Carl. But you probably would resent his attitude and be inclined to do just an average job. You would not feel like doing anything extra for Carl. With Cathy, though, you would be more willing to help. Her attitude would encourage you to join her effort to get all the work out.

TWO WAYS TO LEAD

Several years ago, a psychologist named Douglas McGregor studied how businesses were run. He identified two basic ways in which management related to workers. He called these two different approaches to managing people Theory X and Theory Y. Perhaps after reading about them, you will find some more revealing names for these theories.

Theory X

Theory X is the traditional management approach. Management, McGregor said, had based its approach to workers on this philosophy for many years. Writing in the 1950s, McGregor said that Theory X was based upon the following assumptions:

- The average person does not like work and will avoid it whenever possible.
- Because people dislike work, they must be forced to do the work necessary to achieve the company's goals. Thus, people must be controlled closely, directed completely, and threatened with punishment for failure to produce.

The Theory X approach to leadership assumes that people dislike work and must be forced to do the work necessary to achieve the company's goals.

- The average person likes to be directed, wants to avoid responsibility, lacks ambition, and seeks security above all else.

What do you think of the Theory X approach to management? What would conditions be like in a place that manages people on the basis of these assumptions? Would you like to work in such a place? Do you think the assumptions are true for you? In general? Does the average person dislike work?

McGregor pointed out that the assumptions of Theory X management were not based upon careful scientific study of human behavior. A few people, way back when industry was beginning its growth, may have said to each other, "Most of the other people are lazy. We'll have to force them to work in our factories." Or maybe they themselves did not like work and assumed that no one else did either. Or maybe the work was so demanding and unpleasant that no one did like it.

Work conditions were certainly different then. After all, not so very long ago workers were expected to work 12 hours a day, 6 days a week. They had no benefits as people today know them, and there was not much concern for workers' safety, comfort, or happiness.

Anyway, the Theory X assumptions were never closely examined, and over the years, the myth developed that people had to be forced to work. Some people let the parent aspect of their character take charge, and they felt they had to order everyone else around.

As you can imagine, places that do operate today on Theory X assumptions are not the most pleasant places to work. They use the stick—force—to prod workers along. Sometimes there is a carrot on the end of the stick—a pay raise. But mostly, in companies operating on Theory X assumptions, there is the stick: strict rules, close supervision, quick penalties, little freedom, and no real responsibility.

Theory Y

Today many companies try to base their approach to managing workers on what McGregor called Theory Y principles. According to McGregor, Theory Y is based on a realistic view of how people behave and why they do what they do. Theory Y takes into account that motivation must come from within and that workers who have objectives and goals will have the motivation to work.

The Theory Y approach recognizes that the best results are not achieved through force. People actually work hardest when they are reaching for a goal to which they are committed. Meeting a goal can be a reward in itself.

Theory Y is therefore based on the following principles:

- Work is as natural for people as play or rest.
- People will work to achieve an objective to which they are committed without external controls or threats of punishment.
- People feel that reaching a goal to which they are committed is a reward in itself.
- The average worker, under proper conditions, will not only accept but also seek responsibility.
- Most people have the ability to use their imagination and creativity to solve company problems.
- Most modern jobs do not seriously challenge the ability of the average worker.

What do you think of management based on Theory Y assumptions? What would conditions be like in a company that manages people on the basis of Theory Y assumptions? Would you like to work in such a place? Do you think the assumptions are true for you? For other people? Do you think most people will work for goals they set themselves?

Although most companies today follow management procedures based on Theory Y assumptions, they generally concentrate on the first four.

The last two assumptions are difficult to act on, especially in large companies employing hundreds of people. In addition, the last assumption deals with a characteristic of jobs that cannot really be changed.

Management knows that some jobs can be deathly boring. This is especially true of jobs on assembly lines. Many assembly-line production procedures were developed during World War II, when there was a shortage of trained workers. Industries broke jobs down into a lot of simple steps so that new workers could learn quickly and join the assembly line with little or no training. Workers could be replaced easily if they were called off to join the war effort or if they left for other reasons.

During the war, goods were needed badly, and production was the main concern. Today there has been a small trend in the other direction, toward making jobs a little more complex and demanding. Instead of just standing and turning one or two screws all day, workers are given the chance to complete a whole unit by themselves in some automobile factories. The intent, of course, is to motivate workers by stimulating their interest.

QUALIFICATIONS FOR A LEADER

You may think that the main qualifications for a leader are technical skills, a grasp of one's field, and superior knowledge. All of these are essential qualifications, but without basic human relations skills, a qualified person could still fail.

The best leaders are those who combine the ability to motivate people with technical skills or knowledge of their field. In fact, some persons with inferior technical skills have made it as leaders on the strength of their human relations skills. They surround themselves with people who have more technical expertise than they do, and they mold these experts into a team of willing workers.

At one time, it was believed that good leaders were born, not made. Leadership was thought to be inherited or bred into a person. Experience today shows that this is not the case. Almost anyone can develop into an effective leader. Good leaders are those people who have developed their human relations skills for getting along with others. Those skills are the same ones that you have to know and use.

Leaders, of course, have a somewhat special point of view. Their basic aim is to get other

The best leaders are those who combine technical skills or knowledge of their field with the ability to motivate people. (Courtesy United Nations/Jerry Frank)

people to do things. To be successful, they must develop the following human relations traits.

- Leaders do not let their feelings control them. When they are angry or annoyed, they do not explode. If they are frustrated, they do not sulk.
- Leaders tend to be more democratic than dictatorial. That is, they encourage those around them to participate in setting goals, assuming responsibility, and making decisions. They do not order people around.
- Leaders set realistic goals. This grows out of the trait above. If more people are involved in setting goals, the goals are more likely to be realistic. A rough definition of a realistic goal is one that is challenging but not impossible to achieve. Good leaders know that.
- Leaders are able to examine themselves and correct mistakes in their methods or their thinking.
- Leaders are able to build group loyalty by seeing that workers are rewarded for their good work, both in deeds and in words. Effective leaders do not try to take all the credit for a job well done.

As you can see, all these traits are designed to make people feel needed and respected. Being able to do that is the essence of good human relations at any level.

Getting It All Together

1. What basic factors contribute to a person's motivation?

2. Why is motivation important?

3. What are the two basic sources of morale and job satisfaction?

4. Is it possible for someone to like a job and feel strong motivation but still have low morale? Explain.

5. Why is having a positive attitude important?

6. Explain the difference between Theory X and Theory Y assumptions of managers.

7. What are some of the traits of a good leader?

8. Explain what is meant by a "self-fulfilling prophecy." Can you give an example?

20

HUMAN RELATIONS IN A "TOSSED SALAD"

Your goals in this unit are given in the following list:

To develop an awareness of the many different groups that make up this country

To understand and recognize biases and stereotypes that hurt human relations

To develop a positive approach to working with members of different groups

To develop skills for dealing with biases and stereotypes

You live in a pluralistic society. Perhaps you have read something like that before, or maybe you have heard someone say it. What does it mean? Well, the root word is "plural"—more than one. A *pluralistic society* is a society in which many different ethnic, religious, racial, or cultural groups live side by side.

The United States is a unique country. There is not another one like it anywhere, and there never was. As a citizen of the United States, you are participating in the greatest ongoing social experiment ever tried. Part of the experiment—a large part—is to see whether people can govern themselves. This is democracy.

Another part of the experiment has been to open the country to everyone. The result has been that people from all over the world came to this country over the years. Some came long ago. Others came more recently. Perhaps your parents or your grandparents came to the United States to join the experiment. That people came—not **when** they came—is the important thing.

Anyway, the result is a unique country. No other country has such a great mix of people from different backgrounds, different races, different religions. Most people who came to this country did so of their own free will. Some left countries they no longer liked.

Others were looking for a chance to make their fortunes. Still others came so that they could practice their religion freely. But some of the first people to come were kidnapped in Africa and brought here by force. Given the chance, they might have come on their own. However, they were not given that chance. They were brought as bond servants and slaves.

In time, some black people won their freedom, but they still suffered from race discrimination. Even 100 years after slavery was declared illegal, many white people refused to admit black people into schools, jobs, and communities. Recently the federal government began to pass laws forbidding discrimination. Black people, whose ancestors first came here more than 300 years ago, are finally becoming a part of the democratic experiment.

The many different people that make up the United States today share—with the exception of one group—the experience of having come here from someplace else. That group, of course, is made up of native Americans, whom Columbus mistakenly called Indians. They were here already. This is their native land. Most native Americans were killed by those invading the land. Their descendents are only now enjoying the rights that others take for granted.

For a long time, this country has been called the melting pot. Americans were proud of that label. People from throughout the world could come here, according to the melting pot idea, and mix into the society so that everyone would be alike—just Americans.

But many people who came here did not want to drop everything that made them different. They did not want to blend into a faceless whole. They had many traditions that they wanted to keep alive. In addition, some people could not really blend in because of physical differences. The idea began to grow, slowly, that there really was no need for everyone to fit into the same mold. Differences are good. They make the country more interesting.

It also was recognized, slowly, that there is no single best way for everyone to act, to be, or to look. So the melting pot has become more of a tossed salad: People are all mixed in here together, but they are all keeping their separate identities.

Well, having so many groups of people believing in different things, doing things in different ways, and looking different has created some confusion, and some problems. A weakness that most people share is a tendency to fear that which is different from them in any way. Of course, like all fears, this one goes away when people get to know and understand the differences. Sometimes, unfortunately, people do not take the time to understand.

It is no surprise that there are problems in this experiment. When many different kinds of people try to get along together, problems are bound to result. Think of your own family. You are all basically the same, right? But even the best of families have misunderstandings, arguments, fights—in other words, problems. If, within your own family, you have to make an effort to get along, think of how much effort is needed in a society that includes all kinds of people.

What does all of this have to do with you and your career? Everything. As you pursue your career, you will be dealing with many of the different kinds of people who make up this country. How well you can do this will determine how successful you are in the long run. In this unit, you will read about the many groups that make up this society and the special problems they have met. And you will learn about some of the laws and human relations skills that help people to work successfully in this pluralistic society.

64

SO, WHO'S OUT THERE?

During your working life, you are likely to meet and have to deal with many people who belong to different groups from the one (or ones) you do. Yes, a person can belong to more than one group at a time. Everyone does, in fact.

GROUPS YOU BELONG TO

To begin with, you belong to one of the two major groups into which human beings fall: female and male. In addition, you are a member of some *ethnic group*—that is, people who share a specific culture or language, such as Italian, Spanish, Irish, and so on. Finally, you might belong to a religious group, a social group, a professional group, or a group that engages in a certain sport or hobby.

Where you live has something to do with the groups you are associated with. Northerners, Southerners, Midwesterners, mountain people, coastal people, city dwellers, country people—all these groups have some things in common. They share things that set them apart from others. Your economic status—how much money you have—is one of the most powerful factors controlling what groups you belong to.

You are also in a particular age group. And you can be grouped according to your physical characteristics. You may be tall, short, stocky, or skinny. Perhaps you are left-handed. If so, you are a member of a special minority, and you are reminded of it every time you turn a doorknob.

During your life, you will move from one group to another. You grow older. You may lose or gain weight. Your hair may fall out. The important thing to remember, however, is that although you are part of several groups, you still are, and always will be, a unique individual.

It is easy enough to remember that about yourself. You know very well that you are an individual. You know exactly how you are like others in the groups you belong to, and you know how you differ from them. You probably are especially conscious of how you differ. You may get annoyed when an adult pegs you as "one of those teenagers." In the same way, a middle-aged person dislikes it when a young person says, "You can't trust anyone over 30."

DISCRIMINATION

Groups are good things to have. It's nice to belong to one. Everyone likes to have a sense of belonging, and being part of a special group gives people that feeling. But there is a danger here. Because people like the feeling of belonging to a special group, they begin to think their group is better, if not the best. Other groups, they decide, are not as good. They begin to think that groups that are different must somehow be bad or inferior. This feeling is strengthened by a natural fear of what is different.

Different? Yes. Bad? Inferior? Something to fear? No. Communications and human relations are destroyed when one group of people treats another group as bad. The poor treatment of one group by another group is called *discrimination*. Discrimination becomes particularly bad when one group has more members or controls the power in a community. Such a group (the majority) often uses its power to hurt the smaller or the less powerful group (the minority). The majority may voice a lot of reasons for discriminating against the minority. But such actions really are based on a fear of what is different and a desire to keep the minority from getting any power.

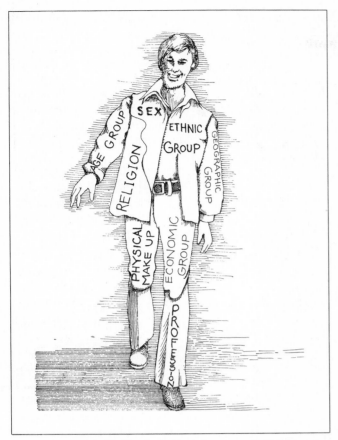

As a complete individual, you are the sum of all the groups you belong to.

Minority Groups

The government identifies four minority groups: blacks, Spanish-speaking people, native Americans, and Orientals. In general, these people have suffered more from discrimination than any of the other groups that make up this country.

Besides these minority groups, the law recognizes several groups as deserving or requiring some form of protection against discrimination. These groups are called *protected classes,* and they include ethnic groups, women, old people, and religious groups. Handicapped people make up yet another group for whom special efforts are made to avoid discrimination.

Discrimination in Employment

In the world of work, discrimination has had particularly bad results. Persons who belong to minority groups have found it difficult to get good jobs and satisfying careers because the majority wanted to keep the best jobs for themselves.

Today it is against the law to practice this form of discrimination in the United States. As you read earlier, this country is an experiment. An experiment involves making mistakes and correcting them. The law says that you cannot be denied a job because of your race, color, creed, or sex.

Some people have become discouraged with this country's experiment. They have grown up in poverty because their parents could not find jobs. The new laws against discrimination can't change the past, but they can change the future. You may find that discrimination still exists in the job market. That is not surprising. Discrimination is tough to wipe out. It is not a United States invention. The sad truth is that discrimination exists throughout the world. But these new laws are an attempt to correct the situation here.

Some persons—those who are in the majority—may fear these laws in the belief that it gives minority groups an unfair edge in the job market. But these laws are intended only to eliminate the unfair edge that the majority has enjoyed in the past. They provide for honest competition in the job market. Persons with the right skills and attitude need never fear honest competition.

In the long run, the laws against discrimination in employment protect all workers. As long as there is discrimination, there will be a pool of cheap labor, and so all wages will be kept down.

Extent of Job Discrimination

You can see that job discrimination is a large human relations problem from the number of complaints that have been filed with the Equal Employment Opportunity Commission (EEOC). The EEOC is a federal commission charged by law to investigate and correct discriminatory practices found in companies with more than 15 employees. Not all cases of discrimination are reported to the EEOC, and not all businesses are under its jurisdiction. Yet a 1975 report showed that 107,846 charges were filed with the EEOC in a single year. That's a lot.

A breakdown of these charges shows that nearly 54,000 were made because of race discrimination. There were nearly 34,000 charges of discrimination because of sex. More than 12,000 charges concerned discrimination because of a person's national origin. And there were 2,200 charges of religious discrimination. The other charges were made for miscellaneous reasons.

Forms of Discrimination

How are minority groups discriminated against? Well, the EEOC report said that race discrimination usually took the following forms: discharge, terms and conditions of employment, hiring and promotion, wages, and retaliation—in that order of frequency. People of minority groups had to have more qualifications and do more to be hired or promoted. They were hired last and fired first. And they were paid less for the same work.

Discrimination based on sex usually took the following forms, in order of frequency: wages, terms and conditions of employment, discharge, promotion, hiring, and job classification. Women were paid less for doing the same work as men. They were denied jobs and promotions because of their sex.

In addition to federal laws, several states have their own laws prohibiting discrimination.

IDENTIFYING DISCRIMINATORY PRACTICES

Because there are laws against discriminatory practices, officials upholding the laws, together with the courts, have had to establish some guidelines for defining discrimination. It is worth knowing what some of these guidelines are. Knowing them may help you in filing a complaint if you are ever a victim. And whether you are a member of a minority group or not, knowing these standards can help you improve your human relations.

Many people act in a discriminatory way toward others simply because they do not stop to think. They have been raised to believe certain things or think in certain ways. These beliefs are found in the parent aspect of their characters. When they let their parent aspect control their relations with minority groups, they are likely to create human relations problems.

By thinking about the standards given below and applying them to your personal situations, you can avoid some human relations problems. The standards were set up to guide companies in dealing with employees.

Differential Treatment

If you treat someone differently than you treat everyone else just because that person is from another group, then you are practicing discrimination. An example of this type of discrimination would be a company that keeps four inefficient, ineffective workers while firing a handicapped person whose job record is no worse.

Some company rules have had discriminatory effects because not all potential employees have had the same advantages. Such rules, in effect, give majority workers the advantage. In one such incident, the courts ruled that a high school diploma could not be required of all job

Sexual discrimination has caused women to demonstrate for their rights. (Courtesy United Nations/ARA)

applicants because this had the effect of screening out minority-group applicants. In this particular state, fewer minority members had the chance to finish high school. Also, at one time, this company had not required workers to have a high school diploma, and workers who were hired without one were able to do the job just as well as those who had a diploma. The company had added the requirement in order to keep minority members out, and so the requirement was ruled discriminatory.

Indirect Discrimination

Sometimes discrimination is practiced in indirect ways. One example occurred when a black manager was fired because she performed less well after being demoted. An investigation showed that the manager had been demoted for racial reasons. Since her work became poor because of the demotion, and since the demotion was discriminatory, firing her for poor work was found to be—at least in part—discriminatory too.

To put people into lower positions because of the groups they belong to and then to blame them for their behavior in response to this action is a particularly harsh form of discrimination.

Blaming Minority Groups for the Bias

It is considered discrimination if a company fires a minority-group member on the grounds that he or she cannot get along with the majority group. This most often happens in cases of race discrimination, but it also occurs because of sex, age, or handicaps. It puts minority members in a trap. First they are treated differently because they belong to a minority group. Then they are blamed because they "need" special treatment. Such circular reasoning is damaging to everyone.

Forced Action

It is also considered discriminatory when a worker is forced into an unwise action because she or he is a member of a minority group. For example, if other workers constantly insult you because of your sex, age, religion, or ethnic group, you may get angry enough to quit your job. Where this happens, the courts have found that the company was guilty of discriminatory discharge because it allowed the work atmosphere to become difficult and painful for the minority-group member. Even though the worker actually resigned from the job, the company was found to be at fault for allowing discrimination to force that action.

CHAPTER 65

PEOPLE DON'T FIT INTO PIGEONHOLES

There is nothing more convenient than being able to put a label on a person. It makes life very simple. "Oh, there's so-and-so. She's a such-and-such." So-and-so has been neatly labeled and put into a pigeonhole. Now you know **all** about her. You have stereotyped her.

In Unit 18, you learned about generalizations and how dangerous they can be. A stereotype is a generalization in one of its most dangerous forms. Stereotypes do more to hinder human relations than any other form of generalization.

Here's how a *stereotype* works. People consider only one or two facts about an entire group of people and apply them to each individual. Often, in this country, this is done on the basis of sex or skin color. But it also happens because of family background, age, religion, or handicaps. People who use stereotypes consider all those who fit into any group as identical. One group member is just like every other member.

As you know, however, **no** two people are identical. So it is always unfair to apply stereotypes to individuals. Stereotypes are usually harmless enough when they are flattering ("Dog owners are friendly" or "People who wear bright clothes are lively"). But trouble arises when stereotypes are unflattering or harmful. Unfortunately, many stereotypes are just that.

STEREOTYPES, BIASES, PREJUDICES

A bad thing about using a stereotype in thinking about people is that it will strengthen your bias. A *bias* is an unthinking opinion about something or somebody. Remember that people like the sense of belonging to one group and tend to fear different groups that they do not understand. Also, to make their group seem superior, they might try to belittle all groups that are different. In this way, they develop biases.

A person with many strong biases is said to be *prejudiced*, which means to "**pre**-judge." Prejudiced people judge others without considering all the facts. They jump to conclusions without thinking at all.

Unwilling Groupings

A funny thing about groups is that although most people want to belong to them, they do not want to be judged only by what groups they belong to. Also, people are sometimes grouped or stereotyped in ways that they would rather not be. "She's a redhead. You know what tempers they have." In fact, this person might be very sweet and even-tempered. But that doesn't cross the mind of a person who has a stereotype of redheads. To that person, **all redheads have bad tempers.**

At one time, people thought that all left-handed individuals were evil. That was a tough stereotype to fight against. "Blondes have more fun." (A lot of hair dye has been sold to people who think in stereotypes.) "You can't trust a skinny person." "Fat people are more jolly." Ho hum.

As you read earlier, all generalizations are loose and imperfect. Stereotypes are **very** loose and imperfect. They simply do not exist in the real world. Therefore, it is impossible to take one

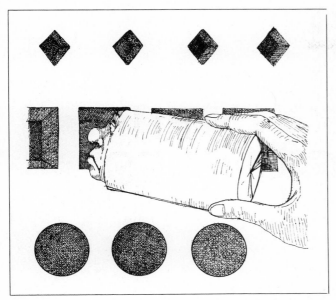

Stereotyping can be dangerous. People simply don't fit into pigeonholes.

fact about a group of people and apply it to all the people in that group. Everyone is different. A thinking person will enjoy the differences.

Unconscious Biases

Everyone has biases. You like some people. You dislike others. You may even dislike whole groups of people. But you should always wait before classifying people into groups until after you have met them and seen them function. You may not like people who brag and talk loudly all the time. Or you may not like practical jokers. Such opinions are logical and not bad in themselves. They become bad when you allow them to

determine your bias—especially if the bias is based on some meaningless stereotype.

You must use your human relations skills to overcome unreasonable biases. As you establish your values and self-identity, you will learn to recognize biases that have been absorbed in your parent aspect. The following story shows how widespread unconscious biases may be:

A father and his son were in an automobile accident. The father was killed immediately. The son, critically injured, was rushed to a nearby hospital. The doctor entering the operating room, looked at the boy, and said, "I can't operate on him. He's my son."

People who were told this story were asked, "How can this be?" Most suggested that the father had not really been killed or that the man killed was the stepfather, whereas the doctor was the real father of the boy. Few people gave the right answer: "The doctor is the boy's mother."

The belief that certain jobs are for men only is a strong illustration of how deep some biases go. Even the names of many jobs reflect this kind of bias: foreman, chairman, cameraman.

Some people hold stereotypes of other people so firmly in the parent aspect of their characters that they must work hard to control their biases. If they are not careful, their bias comes out automatically. When that happens, their human relations will be destroyed. In a way, they cut off their nose to spite their face.

Women—who make up a large part of the work force—suffer from many forms of obvious and not-so-obvious bias among men. Here is how a male supervisor may show bias in his comments to a female worker compared with what he says to a male worker:

Supervisor Dealing with Male Worker	*Supervisor Dealing with Female Worker*
This is Mr. Parker.	Here's my new girl, Jane.
Have a nice weekend.	Take it easy, sweetheart.
What's your work experience?	Are you married?
Would you like to move up to a higher position in the office?	You wouldn't want to move up because you would feel uncomfortable working with all those men.
You've been late a few times. Try to get here on time in the future.	You'd better cut out the dates, Jane, if you can't get here on time.

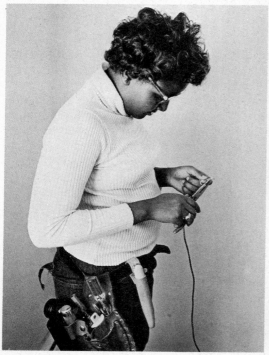

The belief that certain jobs are for men only and other jobs are for women only illustrates the limitations that bias sets up. (Top left, courtesy United Nations/Y. Nagata/ARA; top right, Bethlehem Steel Corp.; bottom left, U.S. Department of Labor; bottom right, IBM.)

A Woman's Place . . .

Bias against women in most societies is something that has been developed over the centuries. It is so strong that women as well as men sometimes accept the stereotype that women are supposed to be the servants of men. As a result, one should examine biases against women very carefully, since they are so widespread and are accepted so automatically.

More than 38 million women work outside of their homes. They make up some 49 percent of the work force. (Top left, courtesy United Nations/Y. Nagata/ARA; top right, © 1980, Children's Television Workshop; bottom, United Nations/ Guthrie)

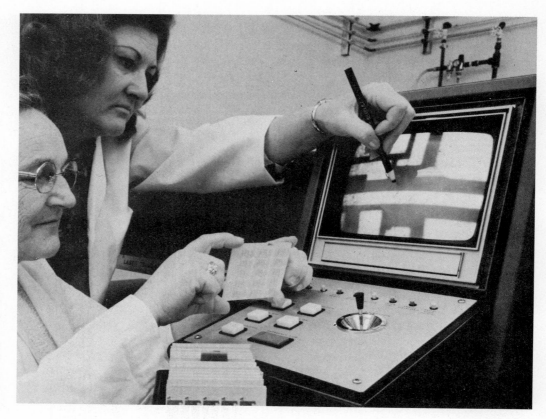

Not only are huge numbers of women working, but they work for the same reasons men do: money, self-satisfaction, and fulfillment. (Courtesy TRW)

Take that old saying "A woman's place is in the home." This statement reflects a standard stereotype of women and a bias against their being anyplace else. Human relations problems enter in when the bias against women's being anyplace else crops up.

There is nothing wrong with being a homemaker. It is a good, honorable life for anyone, male or female. In fact, the argument could be made that raising children and keeping a family together is one of the most challenging, necessary, and interesting things a person can do. On the open job market, the skills demanded for this work would range up in the middle-management level, at least. But to suggest that women should be found nowhere but in the home is discriminatory and biased.

A person thinking of women in terms of a homemaker stereotype overlooks many obvious facts. More than 38 million women work outside of their homes. They make up some 49 percent of the work force—which is nearly half. No one can look at those figures and then seriously suggest that a woman's place is only in the home. Not only are large numbers of women working, but they

work for the same reasons that men do: money, self-satisfaction, and fulfillment.

DEALING WITH STEREOTYPES

Denying that you have any biases or stereotypes is not the best way to handle them. Rather, become aware of them and do not let them get between you and the individuals you meet and must relate to. To help you maintain good human relations when dealing with members of groups different from yours, remember the following:

- People like to be treated as individuals. They become offended when they are treated as though they were just part of a group.
- Stereotypes do not exist in the real world. Applying the general to the individual usually doesn't work.
- Do not fear what is different. Get to know and to understand people who are different from you. Be tolerant of other people's differences and cultures. Try to learn to appreciate them. Treat others with respect.

CHAPTER 66
FACING BIAS IN THE WORK WORLD

In almost any career you choose, you will have to work with other people. Two basic factors influence your relationships with them: your background (identity, values, and ethnic, racial, and religious groups) and the background of others. In some situations, you may belong to the minority group. In others, you may belong to the majority. In both cases, you must operate within the framework of your background.

How you get along with others will affect your job performance. If you allow differences that exist among people to influence your relations and judgments, you will not succeed very well. This is true whether you are a member of a minority group or not. Any bias that keeps you from seeing the individual will affect your potential and your self-concept. This often will result in poor job performance.

People are different. When they work in groups—which is essential in most careers—there will be tensions. The situation may never be perfect. Recognize that. Accept it. Bias is a fact that will be around for some time to come. The point is not to let it affect your on-the-job relationships. This is important to remember whether you are the victim of bias or the one who displays it.

PUBLIC RELATIONS TOWARD MINORITY GROUPS

You will be working with members of different minority groups at some time in your life. When working with a member of a minority group, try to understand each person as an individual. Do not try to solve all the problems of the world.

Try to wipe all labels, good or bad, from your mind. Say to yourself, "Here is another individual, a human being. This person has the same basic needs I have and probably has similar goals." Evaluate the person on the basis of your day-to-day experiences. You may decide that the person has bad work habits or is annoying in other ways, and you may not want to become friendly. That's OK if you think so because of daily evaluation and not because of bias. In such a situation, you can develop a good working relationship even if you never become close friends.

Bending Over Backward Isn't Necessary

You do not have to become good friends. No one asks that. Some people make the mistake of thinking they must bend over backward to be nice to members of every minority group. They think they should not see anything wrong or unpleasant in such individuals. That, of course, is silly. People who play this game are as guilty of prejudice as those who think minority-group members are all bad. They still are treating the minority individuals differently, rather than treating everyone the same.

Maude is a case in point:

Maude was an excellent supervisor at a factory that made sporting equipment. Mark was a new worker under her. Maude was white and very conscious that Mark was black and that black people have been discriminated against. She was determined to be more than fair in this regard.

Maude went out of her way to welcome Mark and make him feel at ease. This was Mark's

Bias distorts. (Philip Teuscher)

first job, and he was eager to learn. Because he was new, he had much to learn. But he began to find it difficult to learn. Whenever he slowed down or had a problem, Maude would hurry over and help. She would try to make things easier for him by doing some of the work herself. Or she would not ask him to do as much as she asked some other workers to do. She would correct Mark's mistakes without telling him what he should do differently.

Finally Mark had to speak to Maude. "Look," he said, "I appreciate all the help and what you are doing for me, but you have got to let me make it on my own, just like any other worker. I don't want to be treated any differently."

That opened Maude's eyes. In trying to help Mark, she had treated him differently. After their talk, she reacted to Mark and his mistakes just as she did to everyone else. Soon he was one of the top producers. Then Maude could begin treating him differently again—as a top producer.

Maude was trying too hard to avoid any bias she may have had. As the story shows, that can be as unproductive as being biased. She was not giving Mark a fair chance to prove whether or not he was a good worker. If he had turned out to be a poor worker, she should not have given him special treatment because of his skin color any more than she should have held that against him.

Unintended Displays of Bias Also Destroy Good Relations

An out-and-out display of bias is so obvious and so likely to trigger an immediate and unwanted response that most people are careful to control it. But less obvious forms of bias can also destroy good relations on the job. This is true whether the bias is displayed in a negative way or through well-meaning efforts to make allowances, as Maude did.

Many phrases that people use unthinkingly when they talk to minority-group members reflect bias and can be annoying to the receiver:

"Oh, I thought all you people liked . . ."
"How do you people feel about . . ."
"Gee, you did a good job for a . . ."
"That comes natural for you . . ."

Ethnic or racial humor—jokes whose points revolve around supposed characteristics of a particular group—can be especially offensive. When people of different backgrounds get to know each other well, they may use this kind of humor on each other to show their trust and respect. But using such humor in general situations is very unkind.

Women are particular victims of a continuing, unthinking bias on the part of men. Many men think that women like to be flirted with. These men think it is OK to call women pet names or use terms of endearment to them. The stereotype of women as weak and helpless, or scatterbrained and vain, dies hard for some. Natalie experienced this type of bias:

Natalie and two other women worked in an office with several men. The men would playfully put their arms around the women. Sometimes the men called them "dear," even in business conversations. Naturally, all this annoyed the women.

"I'm sure that most of them don't mean anything by this, although, with some, I'm not so sure," Natalie said. "Anyway, I feel that there is no reason—at any time—for the men to put their hands on us. We don't encourage them. Perhaps we haven't properly discouraged them. But we did not feel it necessary to make a scene over such a supposedly innocent gesture as a touch on the shoulder or an arm around the waist," she explained. But the women were always faced with the problem of putting up with this innocent (but biased) gesture or being accused of making a scene over nothing.

"I hate to cause embarrassment," Natalie said. "But it makes me angry. These men would never treat other men that way. The only reason they do it is because we're women. They don't feel any real respect for us as co-workers and as their equals. The only way they feel they can deal with us is by teasing."

Many women also do not get the respect all workers deserve from employers. Some bosses ask women to run errands that they would never expect from men, such as making coffee, buying gifts, and planning staff parties. In staff meetings, women are often expected to take the notes, but they are also likely to be left out of the final decision-making process.

Everyone Hates to Be Patronized

If you are a member of a minority group, you may feel especially angry when people *patronize* you—that is, treat you as a child and give you special handling. Everyone hates to be patronized, and with good reason. It is very offensive.

In the example earlier, Maude was patronizing Mark by doing his work for him and not letting him learn from his mistakes. People with foreign accents are often patronized. Some well-meaning but uninformed people will talk with them in a loud voice or use very simple expressions that are almost baby talk. Just because people speak with an accent is no reason to suppose they are hard of hearing or unintelligent. Rosa met up with this type of patronizing:

Rosa spoke with an Italian accent. When she began working on a new job, the supervisor talked very slowly and loudly. Then the supervisor had a good idea. She called in Roberto, who spoke Italian, to help explain things to Rosa. Rosa politely pointed out that she had spoken English since she was a girl and had a high school diploma. She did not need an interpreter, nor was she hard of hearing.

Glenn was the victim of another type of patronizing attitude, but he did not have an accent:

Glenn spoke English perfectly. He held a college degree. Both he and his parents were born in the United States. His grandparents came from Japan. Glenn was as American as a person can be. Yet, because he looked Oriental, thoughtless people often said stupid things to him. A question he particularly hated was, "Gee, do you ever miss your country?" Glenn learned to reply, "I really couldn't say. I've never left it."

Avoiding the outright expression of bias is fairly easy. But you must guard against the unconscious patronizing attitude that can destroy good public relations on the job.

PUBLIC RELATIONS FOR A MEMBER OF A MINORITY GROUP

Perhaps the hardest thing to avoid if you are a member of a minority group is becoming defensive. *Defensive* people are always protecting themselves. They overreact. They act as though they really needed to defend themselves from an

Everyone hates to be patronized—and with good reason.
(Philip Teuscher)

attack or criticism. Remember that any attack or criticism based on bias is unjustified. The first thing to do is to ignore it.

If a prejudiced person continues to be offensive or if you cannot ignore the problem, try to correct the person as calmly and as clearly as you can. Avoid reacting by insulting the prejudiced person. That may make you feel good for the moment, but it will settle nothing in the long run. It will just add to the friction and lack of communication between you.

If you continue to suffer from prejudicial attitudes on the job, talk with your supervisor about it. Try to state your case as unemotionally as possible. Ask for a good-faith effort to solve the problem. Look for a solution, not for revenge.

If the problem continues, notify your supervisor in writing. Again show your willingness to try to solve the problem. Putting the matter into writing will provide proof that you have made an honest, sincere effort to have the situation corrected. Then if the problem continues, file a formal grievance with your company. Most companies have grievance procedures for such situations as this.

If your company does not have formal grievance procedures or fails to solve the problem, you still have some choices open. You can seek advice and help from a local civil rights agency. You can quit your job and look for work elsewhere. Or you can try to live with the problem. Quitting your job should be your last resort. Local civil rights organizations can help explain your rights and help you to protect them under the law. These organizations will be able to tell you what state and federal agencies can help.

Here is how it works if you file a charge of discrimination with the EEOC or with a state or city agency:

First you will be interviewed about your complaint to determine whether it is against the law. If the commission or agency thinks your case has merit, it will try to settle the case. You may be compensated for what you have lost—pay or a job. If the case cannot be settled, court action may be necessary. Some state agencies will handle the case for you. In other states, or if the commission handles the case, you may have to get your own lawyer. Keep in mind that a company cannot legally fire you or in any way punish you for making a charge against it.

Being on the receiving end of remarks and actions that grow out of bias is not easy. It takes skill at human relations to handle such situations and correct the problems. It is not fair, but members of minority groups sometimes have to work harder than others to maintain good human relations. Today, though, members of minority groups do have some help from federal and state laws.

BIAS IS UNTHINKING

People whose physical characteristics put them into special groups experience the most obvious forms of bias. But people can show bias toward anyone who is different for any reason. Persons with religious beliefs that are different from the majority—such as the Amish, Jews, or Quakers—have been victims of prejudice. So have people from different countries—such as China, Ireland, or Italy.

People who speak another language are also often victims. Workers from such countries as Cuba, Mexico, or Puerto Rico who speak Spanish or English with an accent are sometimes victims in this regard.

Why the ability to speak two languages is not appreciated by biased people is one of the many mysteries surrounding bias. It shows how unthinking bias is.

That bias is unthinking can be seen in the experiences of people who have suffered discrimination after coming to this country. They then have suffered discrimination when they returned to their original countries because they were here. That happened to Luisa:

When Luisa was young, her parents brought her to the United States from Puerto Rico. At first, she had difficulty in school because she spoke only Spanish. She had the usual troubles that members of minority groups have. Other kids picked on her. They made fun of her and showed her she did not belong.

Well, Luisa learned to speak English and more or less adjusted to life here. But shortly after she graduated from high school, her parents moved back to Puerto Rico, taking Luisa with them. "Well," Luisa thought, "at least I will belong again."

Poor Luisa. In Puerto Rico, she found that many people considered her an outsider—someone from "the States." Some made fun of her accent, which had changed while she had lived in New York. Others made fun of how she dressed and did things. When she was in New York, many people made her feel she was an outsider because she was from Puerto Rico. Back in Puerto Rico, many people made her feel she was an outsider because she had lived in New York.

The truth, of course, is that Luisa was just an individual. She had her share of abilities and her share of failings. She would have preferred to have been judged on the basis of those.

Discrimination is unthinking. It hurts everyone. Your best chance for success in any field is to forget stereotypes and deal with individuals.

Getting It All Together

1. In what ways does everyone belong to more than one group at the same time?

2. What are some advantages of belonging to a group? What are some dangers?

3. Under the law, which groups are classified as minorities and which as protected classes?

4. What are three guidelines for avoiding the use of stereotypes?

5. What are some mistakes people make in trying to avoid prejudice?

6. What are some things a minority-group member can do to maintain good human relations when being discriminated against?

GROWING ON THE JOB

UNIT

21

YOU'RE HIRED! NOW WHAT?

Your goals in this unit are given in the following list:

To develop a positive program for starting your career right, using these five general rules as guidelines: accept and resolve your fears; learn about your company; learn how your job fits in; develop goals; and consider your appearance

To recognize that things can go wrong and to be able to identify problems that can cause trouble in your career

To recognize and understand the difference between formal and informal ways of solving job-related problems, from both your point of view and the company's

To develop a program for job advancement that recognizes the characteristics needed for success

In the process of getting a job, you have gained and used many skills. Besides technical skills needed to do the job, you have used life-adjustment skills such as establishing values and recognizing your self-identity, making decisions, communicating, and developing good human relations. Now you will use these same skills to keep your job and to progress in your career.

During your years in school, you have used and improved skills that will help you on the job. You have used skills such as being punctual, following directions, and obeying rules. While school and work may seem similar on the surface, they are basically different.

One major difference is that schools are set up to serve students. The school system revolves around you (although it may not seem to at times). But in the world of work, you are no longer the center of the system. You are just one part of it—an important part, but only a part.

Teachers often change the classroom activities and try to make lessons interesting so that students don't get bored. But there will be no teacher on the job to make your work easier. You will find many routine things that must be done. And no one will try to keep you from getting bored. That will be up to you.

The move from school to a career is a major change in your life. You'll be asked to adjust to a new environment and to meet and get along with new people. There will be new rules to obey and a new job to learn.

A good attitude when making the change from school to a career is important. In the next units you will learn about a positive plan that is based on five general rules. It can help you start your career off on the right foot.

There may be problems along the way as you move from school to a career. But showing a good attitude and following a positive plan are the qualities needed to succeed and advance.

67

STARTING YOUR CAREER RIGHT

Few things equal the thrill of getting your first paying job. You have arrived. The problems of job hunting are over. The difficult interviews are behind you. It is all easy sailing from now on.

These are natural thoughts and feelings to have. You earned them. Enjoy them. They will last from the time your employer speaks those thrilling words "You're hired!" until the morning you report for work—or at least until the night before. Then all the doubts and worries begin. "Will I be able to do the job?" "Will the other workers like me?" "Will I look stupid?"

When such thoughts begin, you at first try to fight them. You think of all the things you learned in school, at home, and at play. You may decide that these don't add up to much. You may begin thinking that you really don't know the first thing about anything, especially the new job you have just been hired to do. Then you may panic and want to call the whole thing off. Or you may take an "I don't care what happens" attitude.

Such reactions—panic, quitting before you start, or an "I don't care" attitude—are not the answer. The first thing to do is to recognize that your doubts and fears are natural. Everyone has them—or at least everyone who wants to do a good job. In fact, without such feelings you probably could not do the job or care whether you do it well. Experience shows that people must care how well they do in order to perform well on the job.

You must try to strike a balance. Accept the butterflies in your stomach. But don't let natural fears and worries stop you. Some people become so unsure of themselves that they freeze up. They become unable to do the simplest things because they let their fears take over. The first rule presented in this chapter will help you to handle your fears and worries.

ACCEPT AND RESOLVE YOUR FEARS

Your first day on the job will be affected by the type of company you have joined and its size. If it is small and informal, you probably will be thrown almost at once into the water, so to speak, and expected to swim. At large companies, the first day may be used to *orient* you, to make you feel "at home." During orientation, many people will give you important information about the company and about your place in it. You will learn what to expect from the company and what will be expected from you.

Whether your company is large or small, remember that the people who hired you want you to succeed. They are not in business to make you fail. They have interviewed several people to find a new worker, and they have hired *you*. They want you to succeed as much as you do. That is why large companies will use your first working day to tell you about the company. And even in small businesses, people will take time to help you adjust. The supervisor, boss, or owner will show you around. He or she will expect you to have questions and to be a bit confused at first.

You can also count on your fellow workers for some help. The tradition of "testing" new workers by giving them a hard time or by playing jokes on them is not generally practiced today. Personnel managers in large companies frown upon such things for good reasons. If older workers have time to put new workers through a trial, they must not be working as hard as they

Most people have fears their first day on the job. Your supervisor, expecting this, will try to help you get a good start by showing you around and introducing you to other employees.

should. Safety is also a factor. Most modern plants have safety programs that do not allow for pranks. In small companies, usually all the employees are too busy to test a new worker. Most are probably looking to the new worker to take some of the work load from them.

But that does not mean you will be accepted right away by your fellow workers. You must prove yourself to them just as you must to your bosses. Realize, though, that most of your new associates will be rooting for you and will help in any way they can. Rule one in your positive program for adjusting to your job during the difficult first weeks follows:

1. Accept and resolve your fears. Recognize that new-job jitters are natural. Do not let them stop you. Realize that everyone wants you to succeed.

LEARN ABOUT YOUR COMPANY

One of the fastest ways to adjust to a new job is to learn all you can about your company. Those of you who are alert probably learned as much as you could even before asking for a job. That

knowledge might have given you an edge in getting the job. Given two people with equal skills, an employer will hire the one who shows some interest in and knowledge of the company. Once you are on the job, build on that knowledge and increase it.

If you have joined a small operation, learning about your new company is fairly simple. If you have been hired by a large company, the task may seem more difficult because there is more to learn. Yet in fact, it may be easier. Large companies often will give you a printed booklet that has the information you need to know.

Look and Read

Such a booklet might present a brief history of the company. It almost certainly will contain company rules and regulations. Most booklets also list the benefits you can expect to receive. A typical booklet includes information on the following subjects:

Absences, address change, bonuses, cafeteria, call-back pay, call-in pay, clothes—work, credit union, dependents' hospitalization, drinking, drugs, educational assistance plan, fire, first aid station, funeral leave, gambling, guards, hospitalization and surgical insurance, hours of work, housekeeping, hygiene, injuries, jury duty, lateness, life insurance, lockers, lost and found, meals, outings, overtime, paid holidays, parking, payday, periodicals, probation, promotions, recreation programs, safety equipment, safety program, savings plans, scholarships, shift premiums, showers, sick pay, smoking, solicitation, telephones, time cards, "United Fund," vacation plan, visitors, weekend pay, workmen's compensation

Another good source of information—especially about your benefits and rights—is the employee contract, if there is one. If the workers have a union, there is probably a written contract between the company and the union. Get a copy of it, and read it.

Listen and Hear

In smaller companies, there may be less formal information for you to learn. You may get most of it from talking with your boss and fellow workers. But don't make the mistake of thinking you already know all there is to know about your job and your company, just because your company is small. Consider Ron, who made that mistake:

Ron got a job working at a local service station. That was great for him. He had had a driver's license for one year, and he loved cars. He had often hung around a station where a friend worked.

Ron thought he knew everything there was to know about his job. When Joan Sullivan, the manager, tried to tell him some things, Ron didn't pay much attention. He just kept assuring her that he knew what he was doing.

During his second week on the job, Ron was working alone one evening because of an illness in the manager's family. A customer walked in with a broken fan belt and asked for a new one. There were many fan belts in the station, but Ron did not know which was the right kind for the customer's car. Also, he didn't know what price to charge. But he was too embarrassed to admit this to the customer. Instead, he said the manager had told him not to sell anything but gas and oil when he was working alone.

The customer became angry and thought it ridiculous that a worker in a service station could not sell spare parts. He learned where Joan Sullivan lived and made a complaint.

Ron no longer works at the service station. If he had not felt that he knew so much and had

listened, perhaps the manager would have overlooked his mistake.

Ask Questions

Listen carefully when your boss or supervisor tells you things during the first few weeks. The amount of new information may be great. You probably will not be able to remember it all. But don't let that worry you. If you forget or if you don't know something, ask questions. Never be afraid to ask questions when you have doubts. Ask your boss. Ask your fellow workers. If you have trouble remembering, make notes, and study them after work.

Some people are afraid to ask questions. They think that will make them seem dumb. That isn't true. In fact, if you ask questions that have occurred to you after a week on the job, the supervisor will probably be pleased that you show such interest. However, you should not bother others all the time with a lot of questions. Instead, make a list of your questions, and ask them when others can spare a moment. If a question is urgent, of course, you should ask it at once.

One way to learn about your company is to read all the information the company gives you. (Courtesy Celanese Corporation)

Your questions should deal mostly with job performance. If you always ask about what benefits you can expect or when you can quit working or how little you can get by with, then you may have problems. Your superiors may dislike such an attitude.

Also, use your common sense to find answers for simple questions without bothering others. The following case illustrates a bad question that has an obvious or pointless answer.

Frank got a job training to be a reporter for a newspaper. Now, reporters are supposed to ask questions, but they should know what kinds of questions to ask. Once when Frank was making a telephone check with the police station to see if anything was happening, the desk officer told him that the only thing going on then was a brush fire.

"How do you know it's a brush fire?" Frank shot back, showing a talent for asking the needless question.

The general rule is this: "When in doubt, ask." But like most rules in life, it must be changed slightly to meet your situation. Consider whether you need the answer or whether the answer is obvious. Then ask, if necessary. Thus you will be following rule two:

2. Learn all you can about your company as quickly as you can. Read company booklets and union contracts, listen to supervisors, talk with fellow workers, and ask questions.

LEARN HOW YOUR JOB FITS IN

The next rule is to learn how your job fits in. As you gain general information about your company, you will become more and more aware of how you and your job fit into it.

Whether your company makes automobiles, television sets, or clothespins, you should learn exactly how your job contributes to the finished product. It may be obvious. It may not be. If your company offers a service (as a hotel does, or a laundry), you should develop a clear picture of what you do toward providing that service.

Knowing how you fit in is important for several reasons. For example, it helps create job satisfaction. If your job is joining some wires together on an assembly line all day long, you may become bored and dissatisfied. But if you know how important these wires are in making a color television work, you will be interested in what you are doing.

Your Job Is Important

Any job, by itself, may not seem important. Thinking that your job is not important could lead you to think that being late or taking a day off will not matter much. But if you know how important your job is in the overall operation, you will be less likely to be late or to take days off when the mood hits you.

Most personnel managers or supervisors probably would say that their biggest problems with new workers are *tardiness* (being late) and *absenteeism* (not coming to work). If you think your job is unimportant, you may also think it doesn't matter much whether or not you are there or on time. But if you are aware that others will be unable to do their work unless your job is done, you will see the importance of what you do.

Everything Fits Together

Andy has the job of joining those wires together at a television manufacturing company. "Oh, what difference could those silly wires make?" he asks himself one beautiful morning. "None. I think I'll go to the beach today."

Andy goes to the beach, and the wires do not get joined. Edith, the next person on the assembly line, has the job of putting joined wires into a box. She gets to work on time but finds no one there to join the wires. She has to wait until a replacement is found for Andy. Edith doesn't like that. She, like the other workers, is paid on the basis of how many units she completes in a day. She loses money while waiting for someone to replace Andy.

The supervisor, Mrs. Day, is upset. Her workers are supposed to finish a certain number of units each day. Today, the group will not meet its goal, and so Mrs. Day will be paid less. The company has an order for a certain number of finished television sets which must be ready by the end of the month. Now, it may not have the full number of sets ready. The whole order could be lost. When Andy returns from his day on the beach, he will not be very popular with his fellow workers or his bosses.

Even if another worker does not depend on what you do, your absence can be costly to the company. Perhaps you operate a large drill press, or a sorting machine, or a stamper. When you do not report for work, the machine does nothing. Perhaps the company paid several thousand dollars for the machine. Unless it produces a certain amount of work each day, the company loses money. Consider the following case:

How does this worker's job fit in with providing the services his company offers? (above, courtesy Burger King Corporation; below, Marsha Cohen)

Julie works at a large plant that operates twenty-four hours a day. To do this, the plant has three shifts of workers. Each shift works eight hours. Julie operates a sorting machine on the shift from four in the afternoon to midnight. She likes this shift because she's left with time during the day to go fishing, her favorite recreation. Julie usually does a little fishing during the afternoon, before reporting for work. But she often loses track of the time and is five, ten, or even more minutes late for work.

What Julie overlooks is that the sorting machine must be kept running all the time. When she is late, Nat—the person she relieves—must work until she arrives. Then Nat has to stay a few minutes longer to tell Julie what work is being done.

Up to a point, Nat doesn't mind when Julie is late. The company pays him overtime wages for any amount of time he works beyond his regular eight-hour shift. But sometimes he wants to do something after work. Also, he gets tired after being at the sorting machine for eight hours. So Nat is becoming angry at Julie for being late so often.

The company doesn't like Julie's lateness because it has to pay overtime rates for work that should be done at regular rates. Not being aware of how her job fits in, Julie is quickly reaching the point where she won't fit in at all.

Rule three in adjusting to a new job follows:

3. Become aware of exactly how your job fits into the overall operation of the company.

DEVELOP GOALS

Knowing how your job fits into the overall operation of the company will lead you to develop good work habits. It also will help you take the next step in adjusting to your work. As a new employee, you probably have less responsibility than workers with experience. That's to be expected. Through training and time on the job, you can earn more responsibility. But some people never see beyond the job they are doing. Others see where they might do better and set about earning a better job.

Probably when you applied for the job in the first place, you had an idea of what you wanted to do later. Employers like to find people who have a plan and will work for their own advancement. They do not like people who come looking for a job without knowing what they want.

A personnel manager at a large manufacturing plant once said that setting a goal is the most important thing a worker can do. "First you get the job," the manager said. "Then you prove yourself, and then you aim at the next higher job."

You can be ambitious without being pushy. If you are a new worker with a know-it-all attitude and a belief that you can do the boss's job, you may not be very popular. But if you are a new worker with a quiet ambition to learn and a confident belief in your ability to advance, others will enjoy working with you.

Those in charge like workers who show that they want to advance. This is not surprising. A worker who is interested in advancing is usually a good producer. This kind of worker reports for work every day on time, is willing and available to work overtime when necessary, and tries to get the greatest output from the equipment. In short, such a worker is eager to make a valuable contribution to the company in order to realize personal career goals and to earn more money and prestige.

On the other hand, a worker with no plan or goal is likely to develop bad habits, to be less productive, and to do poor work. That is not surprising, either. If all you can see in life is getting up, going to the same old job, and coming home, you are not likely to take great interest in your work. You are more likely to look around for something other than work to add interest to your life.

Outside interests are, of course, healthy. You should develop skills and hobbies that are not related to your job. But you should not forget that your work takes up a third of your day. It doesn't make sense to write that third off as an unpleasant, but necessary, period to be gotten through with the least amount of physical or mental effort.

Your first job might be that of janitor or clean-up person in a large factory. While doing it, you can learn about other jobs in the factory and what is required for successful performance. Then you can prepare a plan to get one of them.

Knowing your company and understanding how your job fits in will help you to develop specific goals.

These goals should be both short-term and far-reaching. A short-term goal might be getting the next-better job. A long-term goal might be to become a supervisor or a general manager, or even to start your own company. You can have daily goals to finish a certain amount of work and monthly goals to learn or increase certain skills. Goals can and will change. The important thing is to have some goals and to avoid drifting aimlessly when starting on your career. Goals increase your value and thus your income and prestige.

Here is the fourth rule for adjusting to a new job:

4. Develop specific goals, both long-range and short-range.

CONSIDER YOUR APPEARANCE

Finally, and always, you should recognize the importance of appearance. You might argue that "appearances" mean nothing—that acts or thoughts or words are what count. True enough, up to a point. But appearances obviously affect how people see us. And if you extend the meaning of appearance to include good grooming and hygiene (health practices), it becomes even more important on the job and during the period of adjusting to it.

A long-range career goal might be to start your own company.

The importance of appearance can be seen in the number of television commercials dealing with some aspect of the subject. In fact, there are so many that a creature from outer space might think that human beings are totally self-conscious.

We do put a lot of emphasis on appearance. Even those who wear strange or unusual clothes and have messy hair to protest the stress on appearance are actually admitting its importance. In fact, such people are using their appearance to make a point.

Be Reasonably Presentable

Today, workers in all sorts of jobs can be more casual about their clothes than in times past. Women wear pants suits as often as they wear dresses now. (Just a few years ago, many offices would not allow women to work in anything but dresses.) The same relaxed attitude applies to men with beards or long hair. Some companies let workers wear jeans to work. The key is to learn what is acceptable in the company you work for. In some jobs the only rule now seems to be, as one personnel manager put it, "Be reasonably presentable." This manager added, "We see nothing wrong with long hair or a classy style. But at least, you should look good. Appearances create impressions."

Some jobs require the wearing of a uniform. Municipal employees such as police officers, fire fighters, and sanitation workers wear uniforms for obvious reasons. Police officers and fire fighters must be recognized instantly and easily. Sanitation workers wear uniforms that are designed to protect them and keep their own clothes clean. Workers in a chemical plant might wear smocks or coveralls to protect themselves and their street clothes. Construction workers wear hard hats and safety shoes, which are a kind of uniform. You can see that in many occupations, what you wear is easily determined. You need not be greatly concerned about what to put on each day.

Practice Good Personal Hygiene

An important part of appearance is personal hygiene, or health practices. You might get by with dirty fingernails or dirty hair. But your co-workers will protest if you let yourself develop bad breath or an unpleasant body odor because you do not wash or change your clothes regularly.

This seems simple enough, and most of us learned to take care of our bodies as children. You will, however, become uncomfortably aware of this problem if you have to work closely with someone who is careless about personal hygiene. If you do not think such situations can arise, look at the advice columns in your local newspaper. Invariably, there are letters from people asking for advice in dealing with a co-worker who has a personal hygiene problem.

The number and kind of television commercials that sell deodorants, toothpaste, or soap should make you conscious of the need for cleanliness and a presentable appearance. A good washing with soap and hot water daily, regular teeth cleaning, and a daily change of clothes should become your habit.

The fifth rule of your positive program to start your job right follows:

5.   Be conscious of your appearance.

68

WHEN THINGS GO WRONG AT WORK

It would be nice to think that once students graduate from school and find jobs, all their troubles will be over. Nice, but unrealistic.

Throughout life you will meet problems, and you will have to deal with them. Things can and do go wrong. However, if you realize that problems may arise from time to time, you can handle them better when they do. You will not be completely surprised, as you would be if you ignored their possibility.

Problems that affect your work may grow out of professional or work-related activities. They may stem from personal feelings—your image of yourself, your work, and the people with whom you deal.

When problems do arise at work, you will deal with them from your own point of view, naturally. And the company will deal with them from its point of view. Your aim and the company's may be the same—to solve the problem. But the methods used may differ. And the final solution from the company's point of view may not be a solution from your point of view: The company can simply dismiss you.

However, dismissal is used to solve problems only in extreme cases and only after all other solutions have been tried. Companies do not want to fire people. If they fire many, they get a bad image and cannot hire good workers. And if they fire people often, they destroy the morale of the remaining workers. Whenever companies fire a worker, they must train a new worker to do the job. It is usually more economical to solve the problem in some other way, and most companies try hard to find a fair solution that keeps the worker on the job.

Some things that you may see as a problem may not be a problem from the company's point of view. You may not like something about your work, but the company can ignore it. So problems may or may not exist, depending on the point of view. Solutions may be good or bad, also depending on the point of view. In practice, employees and employers must try to see each other's side. They must solve problems in a way that pleases both sides, or avoid problems altogether. Let's look at some situations that can exist and see what you and the company can do about them.

FROM YOUR POINT OF VIEW

From your point of view, performance on the job can be affected by two general kinds of problems: (1) personal problems and (2) job-related problems. Your success in dealing with problems will affect your success in your career. Sometimes a problem may be only an annoyance, and the best solution is to ignore it. At other times the problem may be so serious that you cannot do your job well.

Personal Problems

In general, personal problems can be divided into outside problems and inside problems, depending on where they begin. But no matter where they come from, problems may have a carry-over effect. What happens at work may affect your life away from work. When you have a bad day on the job, you may be in a bad mood all evening. When you have a good day at work, you may be in a good mood all evening.

Many things that happen to you off the job will affect your work. If you solve a personal problem, you will be cheerful, lively, friendly, and "up." But if you cannot deal with a personal problem, you will be unhappy, lifeless, unfriendly, and "down."

When you feel good, it shows in your work. You do more work, and you do it better. And when you feel bad, that shows, too. You do less work, and you do it poorly.

Outside problems.   If you have a problem outside of work, it's best to leave it there. You may not be able to fight a bad mood that comes from outside problems, but you must do your best on the job. Do not bring outside problems to your work by talking about them with everyone and looking for sympathy. Your employer will not like it if you tell other workers your troubles and make it hard for them—and you—to do good work.

Co-workers and bosses will be sorry that you have an outside problem. But they also will expect you to solve it in some way soon. People will feel sorry for the young parent who comes to work tired because "the baby kept me up all night"—up to a point. But other workers probably have similar problems and have solved them.

Sympathy will wear thin in a few days if the young parent fails to do a fair share of the work.

Most companies will make allowances for some outside problems. If there is a serious illness in the family or if a close relative dies, a worker usually can take some time off. Often a union contract will state that a worker may take a certain number of days off when there is a death in the family. And even when there is no union agreement, there usually is an informal understanding about such events.

Except in the case of a serious illness or death, workers are expected to solve outside personal problems in a way that does not affect their work. Workers who cannot solve outside personal problems or keep them away from work will soon have job-related problems as well. Such workers usually get themselves fired and build up a poor work record that makes it hard to find a new job. (Employers do check work records when hiring a new worker.)

One outside problem that can affect a worker is getting into debt in a bad way. Chapter 77 explains the garnishment law, which allows people to collect money you owe by taking it out of your pay.

Whatever your problems are—broken friendships, troubles with a landlord, debts, a car that is always breaking down—solve them quickly, and keep them away from your work.

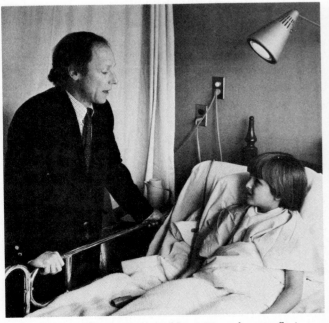

Bringing outside personal problems to work can affect your job performance. (Philip Teuscher)

Inside problems.   Personal problems on the job usually stem from poor human relations. For example, you and a co-worker may not get along. Or a co-worker may have a habit you don't like, such as wanting the windows open when you want them closed.

Usually such problems are minor. At least, their causes are minor. But sometimes workers let them become major. That should not happen. By understanding yourself and others, you usually can handle such problems before they become important. You can learn to apply human relations skills and insights.

Job-Related Problems

Some problems stem from circumstances or conditions directly related to the performance of your job. They can involve human relations as well as personal matters. There is overlap. Difficulty in getting along with your supervisor is both a personal human relations problem and a job-related problem. The same could be true of any difficulty in getting along with a co-worker if your relationship is directly related to the tasks you are performing. Many tasks require the close cooperation of two or more workers. If the workers do not get along, a job-related problem usually results, as in the example below:

Hank, an administrative assistant to the plant manager, and Laura, who was in charge of the duplicating services, did not get along. Whenever Hank had to have copies of correspondence made for the plant manager, Laura seemed to be busy with other work. She would make the copies finally, but it always took a long time. Also, if Hank brought the correspondence late in the afternoon, Laura would never work beyond quitting time to make the copies he needed. If the plant manager needed the copies that day, Hank would have to stay to make them himself.

The bad feelings between Hank and Laura caused inefficiency. Even if Laura had a good reason to dislike Hank, who did happen to be very bossy, she should not have let it affect how she did her job. She should have remembered that the copies of the letters were for the plant manager and for the company.

Job-related problems can be caused by physical surroundings, too. If the lighting is poor, you could have problems doing your work. But even if you could do it well enough, you may rightly wonder whether the poor lighting will affect your

sight. Or perhaps the ventilation system is not very good. Even if it were not a health hazard, it could cause you to work poorly. Suppose your working environment is dirty, noisy, or cramped. For physical problems like these, most workers can call upon a federal law for help. (See the information on the Occupational Safety and Health Act in Chapter 71.)

Job-related problems also can be caused by your supervisor's actions or by unreasonable demands from the company. Here's an example:

Ken liked his job as a switchboard operator—at first. But Mildred, the chief supervisor, was always finding fault with him. After a while, he began to dislike his job, and he lost interest in trying to do his best.

Mildred always seemed to be standing behind Ken when he took calls asking for information. She complained about how he handled the calls: He was not fast enough, or he was too fast. He sounded too impersonal, or he was too friendly. Nothing Ken did was right. He had a serious job-related problem.

Informal solutions.   Usually, you first should try to find an informal solution to a job-related problem. This could be something as simple as weighing your approach and trying to change, if that seems wise.

If you have a problem with a co-worker, you could try sitting down and talking things over to clear the air. You might suggest that the two of you talk with your supervisor.

If you have a problem with your supervisor, talking it over might still be the easiest way to solve it. Without getting upset, explain what is bothering you, and suggest a solution. If that doesn't work, suggest that you and your supervisor talk with someone else who has authority.

Some companies have a suggestion box. Employees can use it to make complaints or suggestions in an informal way. Usually, you do not have to sign the suggestions you drop into the box.

Formal solutions.   If an informal approach does not solve your job-related problem, you might try a formal solution. Most large companies have specific steps that you can take. These are called *grievance procedures.*

Every union contract has a section that outlines grievance procedures and the employees' right to use them. Unions consider such procedures to be one of the most important ways of protecting workers' rights.

Grievance procedures can be followed when there is something about your working environment that is unsafe or unhealthy. You can use them if you think that your work load is unfair, or if you are being punished for no reason, or if your supervisor makes unreasonable demands.

A grievance committee is set up to handle complaints. It includes one or more employees, one or more members of management, and, often, someone from outside the company who will be fair. In some companies, especially those with unions, the employees elect fellow workers to the grievance committee.

In the first step of a grievance procedure, a worker takes his or her problem to the employee representatives on the grievance committee. They probably will try to settle the matter in an informal way. They may meet with everyone concerned to talk the problem over.

If nothing is settled by talking, the committee may ask the worker to present the problem in writing. The committee then may hold a formal hearing so that both sides can present their stories. After getting the facts—either in writing or orally—the full grievance committee will make a decision. Usually, either side may then appeal the decision. The matter may be brought up with higher levels of management or, finally, with the courts.

In later chapters you will read about several federal laws that protect the rights of workers. Each law has formal procedures to follow if your rights are violated.

Uncomfortable working conditions can be a source of job-related problems. (Marsha Cohen)

FROM THE COMPANY'S POINT OF VIEW

When workers do not do their work, the company has a problem. If a worker always comes to work late, or often fails to come in, or comes in and does not do much, the company must do something about it.

All companies want to make a profit. If they fail to make money, they go out of business. Company leaders or owners figure out how much it will cost to produce a product or provide a service. To do so, they include the amount they must pay workers. That amount is determined by how much work the workers are expected to do. If the workers do not produce what is expected for what they are paid, the company will lose money. It is important that workers provide the company with a full day's work for the wage agreed upon.

Many of you will work for government agencies or for nonprofit organizations. The YWHA and the YMCA are two examples of nonprofit organizations. While these organizations do not exist to make a profit, they do have to perform services. In the examples of the YWHA and YMCA, the services offered may be a summer camp or year-round educational, cultural, and recreational programs. The organizations owe it to the taxpayers or to contributors to perform the services for the least amount of money. It is as important for them to receive a full day's work for a full day's pay as it is for profit-making companies.

Informal Solutions

For many reasons, companies tend to go easy on workers who do not produce as expected. Once a worker has been trained, it is hard to find a good replacement. And whenever a replacement is made, production drops until the new worker learns the job. Training new workers is costly. Therefore, a company will usually do all it can to help a worker who is having problems that lower productivity.

One major personal problem that causes problems for a company is alcoholism. A worker who goes to work drunk will be fired eventually. But companies usually try to help problem drinkers who lose many days of work because of drunkenness or hangovers. Some companies sponsor groups like Alcoholics Anonymous. Others send workers to special camps or rest homes to be cured. Others provide counseling and medical help.

Some companies also have special services for workers who have gone into debt or who have other personal problems. They provide counseling and technical advice. Some companies offer day-care nurseries for workers with young children. Others help organize car pools or provide buses to solve transportation problems.

Recognizing the value of efficient, well-trained workers, nearly all companies will try to give workers several chances when they break rules or fail to do what is expected. But serious offenses—such as assault, stealing, or lying—must be dealt with at once.

Apart from such serious offenses, most companies will try to talk with workers and help solve problems in an informal way. If that fails, the company will use formal procedures to deal with workers who must be corrected in some way.

Formal Solutions

Formal procedures protect both the company and its employees. They provide the company with a series of steps to follow that can lead to the firing or other punishment of employees who deserve it. Procedures also ensure that employees get a fair hearing. That is, employees are not punished for nothing. They are told what is wrong and are given a chance to present their side, or to make corrections, or to appeal.

When a serious problem arises—say one worker hits another—dismissal follows at once. But in other cases firing a worker is the last resort. Other actions can be taken first—pay or other benefits may be withheld. Formal disciplinary procedures usually involve four steps:

1. A verbal warning
2. An official written warning
3. Suspension without pay for one to five days
4. Dismissal

In practice, more than one verbal warning is given before the next step is taken. Usually the supervisor, or whoever gives the warning, will make a note of it for future reference. Consider the following example:

> Ted was often late for work. He would be late by 30 minutes or more. His supervisor, Chris, warned him about it after a month. Ted promised to do better, and for the next week or so, he did.
> But then he began coming in late again. And each day he came in later and later. Chris again

warned Ted verbally. In fact, Chris warned him three different times in informal talks. Each time, Ted promised to do better. And each time, he did better for a while and then went back to coming in late.

Finally, Chris had to make an official written warning. It became part of Ted's personnel record. He had to sign it and return it to show that he had read it. This did the trick for about two weeks, but then Ted began being late again.

Chris discussed this problem with the department head and with the personnel office. He showed that Ted had been warned verbally many times. The written warning was shown.

Ted was invited to talk about his problem with the department head. He said he was sorry and that he had a problem waking up in the morning. He lived alone, and alarm clocks did not wake him up. Ted promised once more to do better, but after a few days he began being late again. Chris suspended Ted for three days without pay. But that did not solve the problem, either. Finally, Ted was fired.

Results of formal procedures. If you are laid off because of cutbacks in work or employees, that does not make a bad mark on your record. It is nothing to be ashamed of. But if you are fired for failing to do what was expected, the results can be serious. When you apply for another job, you must state where you worked before. The new company will check to see what the old company thought of your work. If you made a bad impression, it will not help you get the new job.

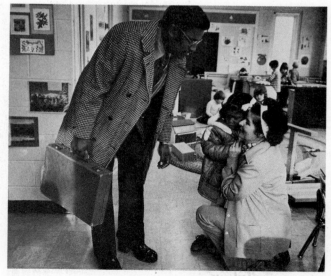

Some companies offer the benefit of day-care nurseries for employees with young children. (Philip Teuscher)

DID YOU MAKE THE RIGHT CHOICE?

Finding a new job because you have to can be a difficult problem. But sometimes you may *want* to change your job. You may want one that offers more pay and benefits. Or you may decide that your first career choice was a mistake, as Priscilla did:

All through high school, Priscilla was sure she wanted to be a carpenter. She took all the woodworking classes offered. She took a part-time job as a carpenter's helper during the summer. And she joined a work-experience program. After graduation, she began to work full time as a carpenter's apprentice building new houses.

After a year or so, Priscilla began to wonder about her choice. She enjoyed the physical labor and liked to watch a house take shape as a result of her work. But something was missing. Priscilla began to feel that once she had mastered all the skills, she would become bored with the job.

While in school, Priscilla had been so sure that she wanted to be a carpenter that she had not thought much about other careers. She didn't consider the results of aptitude tests that measured her interests. Now, in order to learn what might satisfy her, Priscilla checked her high school records.

She decided to enroll in a vocational course in the evenings so that she could become an architect. Her school records showed that she had the interest and ability to do this type of work. She decided that building houses was not enough. She wanted to design them.

Priscilla did not quit her apprenticeship program. It provided both experience and money, which she used to pay for further schooling. She moved slowly toward making the change in her career after deciding that her first choice was not the best one.

You Can Change Your Decision

Making a career choice is not easy. Before deciding, you should try to get all the facts about yourself and consider all available choices. Even then, though, you might make a choice that you later want to change. There's nothing wrong with that. A career choice does not lock you into a particular job for life. People change careers for many reasons and at different times in their life. It is not uncommon for someone to make a change and start a whole new career at age thirty or forty, as Joel did:

Joel was a lawyer in a large city. Like all lawyers, he had spent many years and much money to get his training. And he was successful. But in time, Joel became less and less happy about his job. He no longer liked living and working in large cities. He began to want to work with his hands. In his forties, Joel decided to move to a small town in the country and learn how to run a small poultry farm. Although Joel had a lot to learn, he was very satisfied with his career change.

You Should Think Before Changing

Joel's case is unusual. While many people make changes, they seldom make such drastic ones. Still, you should not be afraid to make a change if you are unhappy in what you are doing.

Before making a change, give your present career a fair and thorough trial. You once had good reasons to choose the job. Review those reasons carefully, along with your reasons for leaving the job. Before jumping into another job, be sure your reasons are good.

Among the wrong reasons for changing a career is the fact that some parts of the job have become boring. Remember that every career has some boring parts. Anything can become boring when you become too familiar with it. Changing jobs only offers short-term relief. After you learn the new job, you may face the same problem. Be aware of this possibility, and accept it. Often you can avoid boredom by finding ways to grow and improve yourself on the job. Boredom sets in when people stop wanting to grow. Before changing jobs, be sure that you are not blaming the job for something you can correct.

If, after a fair test, you still feel that your career is not the best one for you, do not be afraid to admit your mistake. Then make your move carefully, after reviewing yourself and other possible careers. Career decision making is a process, not a once-in-a-lifetime step. You should continue to analyze and weigh your decision whenever you learn new things about yourself or about your career.

All decisions bring results. And though you cannot take back decisions you have made, you can change the results by making new, different decisions.

Sometimes it is not possible to change a career. Perhaps you really do not want to, even though you feel your job is dull at times. Having an interesting and fulfilling life outside of work will help you deal with the boring parts of your job.

CHAPTER 69

PLANNING FOR ADVANCEMENT

Your advancement toward a possible promotion or a pay raise begins on the first day of your job. Don't tighten up. Your bosses will not be looking at you through a magnifying glass to discover every sign of promise. And don't act as though you know everything and want to be president.

You should, however, try to make a good impression from the day you start. How the impression you make adds up over the days, weeks, months, and years will help decide how often you are rewarded in terms of money and increased responsibility.

WHAT IS ADVANCEMENT?

What is advancement? What makes up a promotion or a reward? Obvious answers might include higher pay, more important jobs, and greater responsibilities.

How do you earn or achieve such rewards? The usual way is by doing a good job, by making yourself valuable. To some degree, you may earn them simply by building up years of experience on the job.

In many jobs—especially those covered by union contracts—pay increases are given more or less automatically. A person begins at the minimum starting salary and then receives annual salary increases until reaching the maximum in a certain number of years. Once the maximum is reached, further annual raises may be given for special merit or for increased experience.

Some companies give a cost-of-living pay increase. When the cost of living goes up, employees' wages are raised by the same percentage. This usually is done where a union contract requires it. Strictly speaking, this cannot be considered a raise in pay. Although you are taking home a few more dollars, your buying power stays the same.

More Is Involved Than Pay

Higher pay is only one reason to want another job. Perhaps the other job has better hours. Or it may have more responsibility or offer a better chance for further promotion. Do not be quick to turn down the offer of a new job with your company simply because it does not pay more money. Look to see what else it offers, as in the case below:

Tony enjoyed his work in the machine shop and looked forward to becoming supervisor. He did his work well. The bosses seemed to like him, and he had already received two pay raises. One day, the supervisor asked Tony if he would be willing to take on the responsibility of checking in new supplies when they came. Carmen, who had been doing this, was leaving the company.

Tony knew that Carmen did not receive any extra pay for doing this work. He also knew that sometimes, when supplies came in the afternoon, Carmen had to work late. Tony decided to pass this offer by and wait for a real promotion.

Jan, another worker, took on the responsibility. About a year later, a new position as assistant supervisor was created, and Jan got the job. Tony was annoyed by this and asked why he wasn't given the job.

"Well, you and Jan are both good workers," he was told. "The only real difference was Jan's willingness to take on responsibility. It gave us a chance to see what Jan could do on the kind of tasks a supervisor has."

Advancement means more than just additional pay. Advancement also means more important jobs and greater responsibilities.

By thinking only in terms of dollars and cents, Tony lost his chance for a promotion. He should have realized that the added responsibility would have given him a chance to show he could handle different kinds of tasks.

You Should Avoid Exploitation

It is possible, of course, that some companies may try to exploit you—that is, have you do more work involving greater responsibility without increasing your salary. Workers become aware of exploitation quickly and usually will warn each other of it. Be aware that exploitation can happen, but, as a general rule, be ready to give your company the benefit of the doubt at first. Accept the opportunity to assume more responsibility.

WHEN ARE YOU READY FOR A RAISE OR A PROMOTION?

If your company has a policy of raising employees' pay every year, you will know when you will receive a raise and about how much it will be. But what about companies that have no such policy? How do you know when you are ready for a promotion?

Usually, most people tend to feel they deserve a raise or a promotion long before they actually receive it. It is always difficult to judge one's own abilities and accomplishments. Before looking for a raise or a promotion, try to determine whether you have mastered your present job.

Questions To Ask Yourself

To decide whether you have mastered your present job, ask yourself these questions:

- Have I learned all aspects of my job thoroughly? (It takes several months—often as long as a year—to learn most worthwhile jobs completely.)
- How does the amount of work I do compare with what others do?
- How does the quality of my work compare with the work of others?
- Is my work free of errors? Do I make many mistakes? Do I keep making the same mistakes?
- How much supervision do I need? Can I do my job without a lot of directions?

Before you can expect a promotion, you must be able to answer these questions positively. Only by doing the best possible job in your present position can you reasonably expect either a raise or a promotion.

Even when you have mastered all the technical skills of your present job, you cannot expect an automatic promotion or even a raise. Usually only a certain number of promotions are possible, and only a limited amount of money is available for pay raises. And there are more people who want promotions and raises than there are jobs or money. Several people probably will have the same level of technical skill. In such situations, time on the job—*seniority*—may be the deciding factor.

Seniority

In many occupations, seniority decides who will get raises, rewards, or promotions. Most unions want pay raises or other rewards to be based on how long someone has worked for the company. Even in companies that do not have unions, however, seniority counts a lot for promotions and pay hikes.

When the seniority rule is in effect and a better job opens up, employees who have been with the company longest usually have the first chance to fill it. Sometimes the company will post a notice of the vacancy on the bulletin board. Then employees "bid" on it. The qualified person with the most seniority will receive it.

Seniority also may be used to decide which shift someone will work. New employees may have to start working on a less-desirable shift and then move to a better one only after gaining some years of service.

Seniority has good and bad points. As you get older, you tend to see the good points. When you are young and starting out, the bad points are more obvious. Seniority systems favor older employees, since they usually have worked longer. If you are young and ambitious, you may find it hard to wait for seniority to reward your efforts. You might do well to avoid jobs in which rewards depend on seniority. But if you want security and more regular pay increases and can wait for promotion, seniority is a good system for you.

BECOME A VALUABLE EMPLOYEE

Technical skills and seniority are important for advancement. But they are not the whole story. To make yourself a valuable employee, you must consider what else your employer may expect. Below is a list of questions dealing with the major things an employer looks for:

- Are you always on time for work?
- Do you go to work regularly?
- Do you always give notice as soon as possible when you know you will be absent or late?
- Are you familiar with company rules and regulations, and do you follow them?
- Do you take care of company equipment?
- Do you show loyalty to the company and respect for the people you work with?
- Do you show initiative?
- Do you have a pleasant personality?

Besides technical skills, these are the things that an employer looks for in employees. If you can honestly answer yes to the questions, you almost certainly will earn higher pay and more important jobs. Now look at some ways to become a valuable employee.

Punctuality

In the first chapter you learned how knowing about the company and the part you play in it helps you to be on time. Punctuality is important. When employees report to work late, their co-workers may have to work late, or equipment may stand idle, or the department may be unable to complete its work.

Everyone is late for work at one time or another because of unexpected and unavoidable developments. Employers expect this and are willing to put up with it. But workers who are often late—say several times a month—are not likely to get promotions and may not even keep their jobs.

There is no excuse for being late to work over and over. From the employer's point of view, the workers have agreed to the conditions of work by taking the job. And one major condition is to be on the job at a certain time. If some outside problem makes it hard to be on time, a worker should solve the problem or give up the job. Consider the following case:

Shelley Sanser works at a real estate office to support herself and her young child, Dion. She is studying to earn a real estate license so that she can be a full-time salesperson. She is the office manager now. She has to open the office at 8:30 in the morning.

This is a problem for Shelley. Dion, who is just five years old, goes to nursery school while Shelley is at work. The nursery school does not begin until 9 in the morning, and no one is there until 8:45. The school is near the office, and so Shelley can leave Dion there at 8:45. By hurrying, she can get to the office in five minutes. So Shelley opens the office twenty minutes later than she should.

Shelley feels that being late does not matter much because no one comes to the office much before 9 o'clock. And she takes a short lunch break to make up the twenty minutes.

This plan worked well for a while. But one morning Alex Hedden, the owner of the real estate agency, was waiting at the office when Shelley arrived. He didn't look happy. Several important clients had tried to reach the office shortly after 8:30 recently. One client, who had wanted to leave an important message about selling a big piece of property she owned, came to the office twice and found it locked. She decided to ask another agency to handle her sale. Alex was annoyed.

Shelley explained what she had been doing and why. When Alex calmed down, he said he was sorry about Shelley's problem. But he had his own troubles. He wanted the office opened at 8:30 so that people could call or stop by before they had to be at work at 9 a.m. Many of his best customers left messages during that half hour. He told Shelley that he could not change the hours and that if she could not be on time, he would have to find someone who could.

Shelley liked her job. It paid well and promised more money when she became a licensed real estate agent. She promised Alex that she would solve her problem. Fortunately, she had met the parent of another child who lived near the nursery school. She arranged to leave Dion at the other child's house before 8:30 so he could be taken to school later, and so she was able to open the office on time.

Shelley's excuse was better than most, but it still was not acceptable at work. Cars that keep breaking down, buses that are always late, traffic jams, poor alarm clocks—none of these is an acceptable excuse for being late often. Employers expect employees to solve such problems. Usually the solution is simple: Get up sooner, and start to work earlier.

It is especially important to develop the habit of promptness when you are new on the job. That is when you are making your strongest impression. You are expected to show your best personal habits. Everyone understands that your job skills must be developed, but your personal habits are set. If you come in late a few times when you should be showing your best, people will wonder what to expect from you when you have time to relax.

Being late for work continually may indicate a greater problem. Although you may not have admitted it to yourself, you may fear or dislike your job. You may not be trying to be late, but something always "seems to come up." Look closely at yourself and the job if this is happening to you.

If you are late often, the boss will look closely at you. And whether it is true or not, your habitual lateness will be taken to mean that you do not care about what you are doing. When promotions are handed out, they will go to those who show that they do care.

Evaluation Areas	Very Good (3 points)	Good (2 points)	Fair (1 point)	Poor (0)
Have learned aspects of job thoroughly				
Amount of work compared with others				
Quality of work compared with others				
Work is free from errors				
Clean in personal appearance				
Attitude towards work				
Job knowledge				
Follows instructions well				
Works well with co-workers				
Possesses resourcefulness				
Total points earned				

Are you ready for a raise or a promotion? Find out by completing this form on a separate sheet of paper. If you can answer most of the questions and/or evaluation areas listed above with a "Very Good" or a "Good," you may be ready for a move upward. Add up the points you have assigned yourself in each column. Then compare your totals with the totals of your friends. Do you think your boss would rate you the same way you rated yourself?

Absenteeism

An absent employee creates the same problems that a late one does. Sometimes it is necessary to miss work. If you have a cold or are coming down with the flu, staying home is a good idea. By taking care of yourself, you will get better sooner and therefore miss fewer days of work. Also, by staying home you do not spread germs to your co-workers. Some people go to work even when they are ill. Though their intentions are good, they may make themselves sicker or make others ill.

If you do have to miss a day or more of work, call and let your supervisor know as soon as possible. Your absence may make it necessary to hire a substitute or to double up on work. Otherwise, some work may not be done. Your supervisor needs time to make these arrangements. If you do not call in, your absence will cause your supervisor and co-workers to wonder about you. They will be concerned. It is only polite to let them know as soon as you can why you must be absent.

Dependability

Being dependable means not being late and not being absent without good reason. It means letting the company know when you will be absent or late. And it also means doing the work that you are supposed to do. If you go to work but then do not do the job, you are not dependable. And if you are not dependable, you will not earn a promotion. Consider this case:

Carl worked in a large accounting firm that did bookkeeping for many clients. Carl was punctual. He was always at the office on time and was even a little early. He was seldom absent from work. And when he was, he called in promptly. Carl often stayed late at the office, and almost every night and weekend he took home a bulging briefcase of work to be done.

Carl seemed to be an ideal employee, headed for bigger and better things. There was only one problem. Carl never got much work done. Other accountants always had to help him finish work for a client. His work load was the smallest.

Carl's work habits were bad. When he arrived in the morning, he would chat with everyone willing. Next, he would get coffee. Then he would sharpen pencils and straighten the papers on his desk. He would then skim a newspaper until it was time for his midmorning break. After the break, and during the afternoon, it was more of the same. Carl chatted, daydreamed, and put-

tered about. At the end of the day, he would scoop all his unfinished work into his briefcase and take it home, being sure to tell everyone he was going to work at home. At home the briefcase remained unopened.

Carl put in his time in the office, but he did little. He was not dependable, and so he was never promoted.

Following Rules

It sometimes seems that the many rules and regulations in life are meant to annoy us. There are so many rules, and the reasons for them are not always clear. Not knowing the reason for a rule makes it harder to obey it. But that is no reason to ignore rules. Try to find the reason behind a particular rule.

It may be that in industry there are some unnecessary rules that seem to serve no purpose. However, if you are interested in getting promoted and rewarded, a good personal rule to follow is to obey all the company rules.

Many rules in industry are designed to promote safety. Such rules might deal with clothing, or with hair length and style. Some might concern habits such as smoking. Others might cover how tools and equipment are to be used.

The "no smoking" rule where explosives are handled has an obvious purpose. No one will argue with it. The reason for a rule that says hair must be short or covered with a net may be less obvious. But there is a good reason for not having long, free-flowing hair if you work around moving machinery—it can get caught in the machinery.

The following case shows how rules can be important:

Charlie was offered a promotion at a large chemical plant that made penicillin, eyedrops, and other medicines. He was told, though, that he would have to shave off his beard and moustache or wear a face mask at his new job.

Charlie was angry about this. First of all, his beard was handsome and had taken a long time to grow. He wasn't willing to cut if off or squash it under a stupid mask. Second, he felt that the company had no right to tell him how he should look.

The company really did not care how Charlie looked. But it did care about the safety of its workers and the purity of its products. It could not afford to have workers getting pulled into moving machinery or to have long hair or dandruff dropping into its medicines. And so, the rule for this department was to shave or to wear a face mask and keep the head covered.

Charlie did not like the rules. He didn't bother to find out the reasons behind them. That was his right. But the company did not promote Charlie. That was their right.

Not following rules can prevent you from winning promotions. In extreme cases it can get you fired.

Care of Equipment

Taking care of equipment is one of your job skills. You must use company equipment and tools properly in order to do a good job. Whatever equipment you are trusted to use—whether it is a typewriter or a 5-ton-truck—treat it with respect. This is another aspect of responsibility that the company looks for when giving rewards or promotions.

Loyalty

Loyalty includes all the things you have read about so far, since they reflect your attitude toward your company. If you misuse your company's equipment, you are not being loyal. Neither are you loyal if you ignore the rules and regulations, if you are irresponsible and undependable, and if you shirk your duties and are often late or absent.

Loyalty is all these things and more. It is identifying closely with your company, making its goals your goals, seeing things its way. Loyalty also includes such obvious responsibilities as not giving away confidential information about your company or downgrading it when talking with co-workers, friends, or strangers.

Loyalty is believing in your company and defending it, if necessary. It is being proud of what you do and where you work.

Of course, loyalty is a two-way street. Your company owes you its loyalty as well. If your company breaks its own rules, if it tells you one thing and does another, or if it plays favorites, fires without cause, and breaks promises, it is not being loyal to you. You would do well to leave such a company.

One display of loyalty is a willingness to work a little later when an important job needs to be finished. If your company takes advantage of such willingness on your part and never rewards you or, worse, refuses to pay you overtime, you would have reason to refuse the extra work without pay. At such a company, rewards are few. And promotions, if given, are probably meaningless in terms of increased earning power or increased stature.

Initiative

Initiative is simply the ability and willingness to look beyond your immediate job, when there is time, to see how you can make yourself valuable to the company. Here's an example:

Gerry Gillespie worked at a supermarket. He did whatever he was told to do willingly and cheerfully. But he never showed initiative. Every day he would have to be told what specific tasks to do. Otherwise, he did not do anything. The manager, Mrs. Ryan, might ask Gerry to unpack twenty cases of coffee, mark the cans, and place them on display.

Gerry would do just that—unpack the cases, mark the cans, and display them on the counters. Then he would return to the stockroom and read a magazine. Finally, Mrs. Ryan asked Gerry why he was not working much of the time. Gerry was unconcerned. "I do what I'm told to do," he said.

"Look, Gerry," Mrs. Ryan said. "There is a lot of other work to be done in the market. If you can't see what has to be done and have to be told everything, I'm afraid you are not of much value to us. We need someone with initiative."

Domingo Perez, another stockperson in the supermarket, was different. After a few days on the job he did not need to be told to do every task. He knew what needed to be done, and he had the initiative to do it. When he saw that the supply of cans on the shelves was getting low, he would unpack the cases and fill the shelves. When the stockroom became dirty, he would get a broom and sweep. And when a promotion to head stock-clerk came up, it was given to Domingo.

Initiative is not only finding additional things to do on the job. It is also taking responsibility to learn another job. When you learn how to do the jobs of other workers, you become a more valued employee.

Use good judgment in learning other jobs. Do not make a pest of yourself with your co-workers. Do not give the impression that you are trying to steal their jobs.

Emergency situations often bring an opportunity to show good judgment and initiative. Domingo did just that at the supermarket one day:

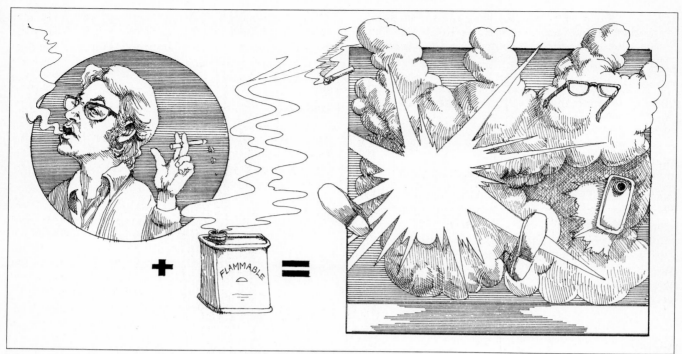

There are always reasons for company rules and regulations. Most times, the rules are designed for your safety on the job.

One Saturday evening the manager of the meat department was called home because of a sudden illness. Mrs. Ryan had already left work for the evening. Individual department managers were responsible for closing their departments.

At closing time, Domingo noticed that no one had taken the meat from the display counters and put it in the refrigerator for the night. If it were left out all weekend, it would spoil.

Domingo used his initiative and judgment. He took the time to put all the meat into the refrigerator. He worked an hour late to do it.

On Monday morning, the meat manager was back at work. When she learned that Domingo had put the meat away, she was thankful. In her own crisis, she had forgotten some of her responsibilities. She told Domingo that she would not forget his thoughtfulness.

Domingo had made a good friend of the meat department manager, who praised him to Mrs. Ryan. When the position of assistant store manager opened up, Domingo was at the head of the line for the promotion.

Personal Characteristics

Your personal characteristics—how you deal with people and what they think of you—will always be considered before you are promoted. You must apply human relations skills—not only to be able to enjoy your work, but also to earn promotions.

Skill on the job is important. Equally important is your skill at getting along with your co-workers and your supervisors.

CAN YOU HANDLE A PROMOTION?

The ability to perform your present job is a first requirement for being promoted to a more important job. To ensure success at a higher-level job, though, you should have a good idea of what it requires before you accept it.

Many companies have job descriptions for their various positions. These are written down and can be obtained from the personnel office. They can give you a good idea of what qualifications and skills each job requires. They outline the responsibilities and what the jobholder is expected to do.

Organizational charts also contain information about higher positions. They are most helpful to those interested in administration. They show the lines of responsibility within a company.

You can see, at a glance, who reports to whom and who is in charge of what department.

No one, of course, is expected to work at peak efficiency when promoted to a new job. It is recognized that a certain amount of time is needed for a person to learn a job and adjust to it. A probationary period is often allowed for this breaking in and learning.

If you have studied a job description or taken other steps to learn about the new job, you will be more at ease when you begin working. Thus, you will be able to learn what else is necessary quickly.

Some companies provide in-service training to help workers learn higher-level jobs. Some rotate workers through different jobs. Others provide time for the person new to the position to work with a veteran in it before taking over completely.

CONTINUE YOUR EDUCATION

Another good way to help your upward climb is to continue taking formal courses. These can be in your field or in subjects that will help you in your field. You could take a course in welding if you operate a grinder and wish to be promoted to welder. You could take a course in office management if you are a clerk and want to move up to manager. You could take a course in public speaking if you are a salesperson and want to improve your sales techniques.

What courses you take will depend, of course, on what is offered in your area. Check the colleges, universities, trade schools, or business schools. Perhaps your local public school system has adult classes in the evening. If a college or university is not near enough for you to attend classes, check to see whether they offer extension divisions. Sometimes you can take courses over television, particularly on public television channels. Some schools offer correspondence courses that you can complete at home.

Be sure to check any school carefully before signing a contract or paying out money. Private schools, especially, should be looked at closely. They are in business to make money. While most of them are honest and provide the training they advertise, some are dishonest and provide poor training. Try to talk to people who have attended the private schools.

No matter what field you are in, the chances are good that you will be able to find some kind of formal training that will help you advance. If it happens that you cannot find additional formal training, you still can learn on your own. Get books from the library on your chosen career. Subscribe to trade magazines. In many fields, associations have been formed that help keep members informed about developments. If there is an association in your area, join it.

CHANGING COMPANIES

Changing companies is one way for people to get higher pay or better jobs. But change with care. Many factors should be considered before you leave a company.

Do not make a change simply because the hourly pay rate might be a little higher at the new company. Consider the fringe benefits. They may be worth more where you are. Consider the chance of promotion. The new company may be paying more because it offers little chance of advancing. Consider the working conditions and atmosphere. If you are in a good working environment with a friendly atmosphere, making a change for a few extra dollars may not prove to be worth it. It's better to be happy at work, than to earn a few extra dollars.

Another important factor to consider before making a change is seniority. You have what is known as *equity* in your job. This is just another way of saying that you have time invested in your job. At the new company you will have the lowest seniority.

When the economy is weak and jobs are scarce, you must be especially careful about changing jobs. The rule "last hired, first fired" is followed nearly everywhere. So, if you were to move to a new company and the economy turned bad and forced the company to cut jobs, you probably would be one of the first to go.

For all these reasons, changing companies for higher pay or a better job is a risky business. Sometimes it may be the only way to get more money or a better job. If so, do not ignore it as an avenue for advancement. But be sure to look into all the factors and to weigh them carefully.

Never change companies just because you are tired of what you are doing. All jobs get tiring at times. Never change in a fit of anger to "get even." Most decisions made when people are angry turn out to be unwise ones. And never give up your present job until you know you have the new one.

Most people seek promotion and want to climb to the next highest job on the career ladder. But not everyone wants to be promoted over and over again. For some people, the job satisfaction of their present position is reward enough. (Marsha Cohen)

ADVANCEMENT IS NOT FOR EVERYONE

Too often this society stresses the idea that you must always aim for a bigger, better, and more important job. Otherwise, you may be considered a failure. That idea, of course, is nonsense.

Not everyone wants to be promoted over and over. Many people find a job in which they are happy and are content to stay in it for life, drawing the maximum pay and benefits from it. Such people are usually happy and well adjusted. They know what they want, recognize it when they have it, and stay with it.

Not everyone can get to be "the boss." If all people thought they should be boss, many would be unhappy throughout most of their working careers. The so-called "boss" or managerial positions are not necessarily better than any other positions. A person who might be an excellent worker and get a great deal of satisfaction out of doing a certain job would be foolish to try to get promoted simply because that was "the thing to do."

The happiest workers are the ones who have developed their skills and know that they are doing the best they can. They are rewarded with daily satisfaction and have a sense of accomplishment. The job they are doing really matters. It could be sweeping the streets, or building a house, or sewing an outfit, or typing a letter. Skilled workers take pride in their work. Any job done skillfully is a job that deserves respect. As a skilled, competent worker, you will be aware of your own worth, and you will enjoy the feeling of freedom and independence. You will enjoy being your own "boss" in a meaningful way. Here is an example:

Isaac Hardy was an excellent teacher. He really enjoyed being in the classroom and working with students. He showed this, and the students responded. They liked his classes and learned a lot from him. The school board was aware that Isaac was a good teacher. When they needed a school principal, they promoted him as a reward for good work.

Isaac took the promotion because "it was the thing to do." He did not think about it too much one way or the other, except to be pleased at the recognition for good work. But after a few months, he realized that he wasn't as happy as when he had been teaching. He did the work satisfactorily, but he did not like spending all his time in an office doing paperwork and handling administrative details. He missed the classroom and contact with students.

Isaac was smart enough to realize that he was happier as a teacher. He asked for his old job back. The board let him have it. They realized that promotions are not always the best rewards. And they knew that good teachers are worth a lot and should be kept in the classroom.

Today, skilled workers like Isaac are often given recognition and pay that is equal to that of persons in managerial positions.

JOB SATISFACTION IS ITS OWN REWARD

All people want promotions and higher pay because these increase their self-esteem by showing that they are important and wanted. A salary or wages also satisfy the basic needs for food, clothing, and shelter.

As long as you earn enough to satisfy comfortably the basic needs, the way you satisfy your higher needs depends to some extent on how you feel about yourself and your job. You may need constant reassurance from others that you are doing well. If so, promotions and pay raises will mean more to you.

On the other hand, you may need only the sense of satisfaction that comes from doing your job well. In this case, promotion will not be as great a need as long as you are paid well.

The point is that all people are different. You should not try for bigger and better jobs all the time simply because "it is the thing to do."

Have a plan to advance beyond your entry-level job. After that, keep in mind that the main thing is job satisfaction. Find out what suits you. Do it well. Stick to it.

Getting It All Together

1. What are some of the normal feelings and emotions people have when starting on new careers? What is the best way to handle them?

2. What are five good rules to follow when starting out on your career?

3. What is the purpose of having grievance procedures? How do they work?

4. What are the formal steps a company usually follows when disciplining an employee?

5. What is the seniority system? What are some advantages of it. What are some disadvantages?

6. What are some of the characteristics a worker must show in order to be rewarded or promoted?

7. Is promotion always a good thing? Why or why not?

8. What do you think are the most important things you can get from your career?

UNIT

22

WAGES, RIGHTS, AND UNIONS

Your goals in this unit are given in the following list:

To know the minimum wage to which you are entitled

To understand regular time worked and overtime worked

To know how to tell whether your work conditions meet minimum safety and health standards

To be able to develop a list of pros and cons to help you decide what to do about joining a union

To outline a plan of action to take if your work rights are violated

Not too many years ago—people your grandparents' age remember it—it was not unusual for a person to work 5½ and even 6 days a week. A working day could be 12 hours long. That would mean that you would report for work at 7 o'clock in the morning. You would work until 7 o'clock in the evening. You might have an hour lunch break, but more likely it would be half an hour.

Your first reaction might be: "Oh wow! Think of the overtime. I'd be rich." Well, you wouldn't be rich. It didn't work that way. There was no such thing as overtime. It was just straight time. And the hourly rate of pay was not very good. In fact, it was just a few cents. It was often so small that wages were not even based on hours. Workers were paid by the day. They would be paid something like $1.20 for a 12-hour day. Think about that: one dollar and twenty cents for a long day's work.

Prices were low back then, of course. One dollar and twenty cents could buy a lot more than it can today, but not that much more. And your 12-hour day did not begin until you were actually on the job working.

If you were a coal miner and had to spend 15 or

30 minutes traveling deep into the earth, you did that on your own time. You went down into the pit on your own time—before 7 a.m. At 7 a.m. you had to be at the head of the tunnel—pick in hand and swinging. The same thing happened at the end of the day. At 7 p.m. you stopped working. You walked out of the tunnel and then cleaned up on your own time. If you were fast, you might be on your way home before 8 o'clock at night.

In those days, women and men often worked side by side, but women got much lower pay. And there were no laws saying you had to be 14 or 16 or 18 before you could work. Children, 8, 9, and 10, went into the factories and down into the mines alongside their parents. They worked the same hours, though they were paid less. They couldn't do as much work. The hours were long and the pay low.

Workers were abused a great deal in those days, and so they organized in unions to fight for their rights. As a result, laws were passed to protect working people. You benefit from those laws today. Some of those laws resulted in discrimination against racial minorities and women. Where that happened, the laws have been or are being changed.

CHAPTER 70

A DAY'S WORK A DAY'S PAY

One federal law of major interest to you as a worker is called the Fair Labor Standards Act (FLSA). It sets minimum wages, establishes rules for overtime pay, prohibits the employment of persons under a certain age, and requires equal pay for equal work.

MINIMUM WAGES

The Fair Labor Standards Act says that a company must pay you at least a certain amount for each hour of work. The company may pay you more than the minimum wage set by law. But, it is illegal for a company to pay you less.

Beginning in 1980, the basic wage for most workers covered by the law was set at $3.10 an hour. For most workers the basic wage was $3.10 an hour in 1980 and will become $3.35 an hour in 1981. Many workers, of course, receive more than the minimum. Many start at the minimum and then receive raises as they gain experience and skill. Many union contracts call for workers to start at rates higher than the minimum.

While the Fair Labor Standards Act covers most workers in this country, it does not cover all workers. Workers not covered by its minimum-wage provisions include, for example, administrators, executives, and salespersons. These people receive salaries or commissions instead of wages.

Salaries, Wages, and Commissions

What's the difference between salaries and wages? Generally, if a person is paid a fixed sum per week, per month, or per year, the earnings are called a *salary*. If the person is paid by the hour, the earnings are called *wages*. Wages can also mean money earned doing piecework. As a worker doing piecework you would be paid a certain amount for each item you produce. You might be making boxes, or pieces of jewelry, or parts of a radio.

Commissions are different. They are a percentage of a sale. As a salesperson you might receive a commission of, say, 5 percent of your sales. Thus, if you sold $5,000 worth of goods or products in a week, your pay would be $250 (5 percent of $5,000) for the week.

Work-Experience Programs

Workers might not be covered by the minimum wage laws if they are in a work-experience program. The company you worked for in such a program could pay you less than the minimum wage under certain conditions. Most companies probably will pay the minimum wage, but they do not have to if you are a student-learner in a vocational training program. A *vocational training program* is one in which part-time, on-the-job training is given along with classroom teaching of technical knowledge and theory. If a company wants to pay a student-learner a lower rate, it must apply for permission. Permission is not granted if:

- The job does not require a skill that takes some time to learn.
- The student-learner will replace another worker.

- The needs of the community or industry are not great enough for that particular type of worker.
- The number of student-learners makes up more than a small part of the company's working force.
- The company is seriously violating provisions of the Fair Labor Standards Act.

OVERTIME PAY

Besides setting a minimum wage for workers, the Fair Labor Standards Act says that if you work more than 40 hours in a week (*overtime*), you must be paid at a higher rate for the additional hours worked.

Again there are exceptions. Some workers who must be given a minimum wage do not automatically earn overtime under the provisions of the FLSA. Workers not covered by the overtime provisions include those on railroads, news editors, some farm workers, and employees of motion-picture theaters. Because of the nature of their work, these people may work more than 40 hours in a week without the extra hours counting as overtime. In most cases, the companies do pay overtime anyway, or provide for *compensatory time off*: The workers get extra time off when they work more than a certain number of hours in a week.

On the other hand, some workers who might not be covered by the minimum-wage provisions of the law can still earn overtime pay.

How Do You Figure Overtime Pay?

In general, you must receive overtime pay for every hour you work over 40 hours in a week. Many workers, of course, are covered by union contracts or by other agreements that set the basic workweek at less than 40 hours—say, at $37\frac{1}{2}$ or 35 hours. For any time worked over that amount, workers earn overtime pay. Some workers have contracts or agreements that say they must be paid overtime if they work more than 8 hours in a day. Thus, if you work 9 hours on one day, you receive overtime for the extra hour, even if you did not work more than 40 hours in that week (or whatever the basic workweek is set at).

Overtime pay must be not less than $1\frac{1}{2}$ times your regular rate of pay. Your regular rate of pay, if you are covered by the FLSA, must be at least the minimum of $3.10 an hour. It can be more, of course. If you are getting the minimum rate of $3.10 an hour and your workweek is 40

The idea of "working time" has changed over the years. Coal miners, for example, were not considered to be working until they were actually at the wall digging out coal. Today, the time it takes miners to enter, leave, and clean up is considered working time for the purpose of figuring pay and overtime. (Courtesy National Coal Association)

hours, here is how you would determine your overtime pay: Say you work 45 hours one week. You are entitled to 1½ times $3.10 for each hour over 40 that you work. In this case, it is 5 hours. Your base pay for the week is $124.00 for the first 40 hours worked. Your overtime rate is $4.65 an hour (1½ times $3.10). You worked 5 hours of overtime, and so your overtime pay is $23.25. Your total pay for the week is $147.25 ($124.00 regular pay plus $23.25 overtime).

Workers who earn a weekly salary instead of an hourly rate are not covered by the minimum-wage provisions. But these workers are entitled to overtime pay. To figure their overtime pay, you must determine their effective hourly rate of pay. You can find the hourly rate simply by dividing their weekly salary by the number of regular hours they work each week, which by law cannot exceed 40. Thus, workers paid $124.00 for a 40-hour week have a regular hourly pay rate of $3.10 ($124.00 divided by 40 hours). Their overtime rate if $4.65 (1½ times $3.10) for each hour worked over 40.

It is sometimes possible to take compensatory time off instead of money when you work overtime. This time off must be at the time-and-a-half ratio. Thus, instead of a day's overtime pay, you would be entitled to take 1½ days off.

It is worth noting that if you voluntarily work more than your shift or regular day, your company must pay you for overtime even if it did not ask you to do the extra work. This is true as long as your supervisor knows or has reason to know that you are continuing to work. The rules say that it is the duty of management to see that work is not performed if it does not want the work done. The company cannot accept your extra labor without paying for it. Furthermore, if the company has a rule against unauthorized overtime, it has the power to enforce such a rule and must try to do so.

When Are You Working?

It is important to know what are considered working hours in order to determine when overtime pay has been earned. Consider the coal miners mentioned earlier. At one time they were not thought to be working until they had entered the mines and were actually at the wall digging out coal. Today, they are considered to be working just as soon as they enter the mines. The time it takes them to leave the mine and clean up is also considered working hours for the purpose of figuring pay and overtime.

As you can see, the concept of what is "working time" has changed. Today, ordinary travel from home to work and back again is not considered working time. But if you have a job that requires special preparations, the time taken to make those preparations is considered working time.

Court rulings have had a lot to do with defining working hours. At one time, the U.S. Supreme Court ruled that working time was all time spent in "physical or mental exertion" controlled or required by the company. Since then, the Court has ruled that there need be *no* exertion at all during time counted as hours worked:

> A stenographer who reads a book while waiting for dictation, a messenger who works a crossword puzzle while awaiting assignments, a fireman who plays checkers while waiting for alarms and a factory worker who talks to his fellow employees while waiting for machinery to be repaired are all working during their periods of inactivity.

In short, the Court has ruled as follows:

> The work week ordinarily includes all time during which an employee is necessarily required to be on the employer's premises, on duty, or at a prescribed work place.

That seems clear enough. If you have to be at your place of work during certain hours, those hours are to be considered hours worked. But what about time out for meals, or coffee breaks, or rest breaks? Is such time considered working time?

Generally speaking, a break long enough for a meal would not be counted as working time. But rest breaks up to about 20 minutes are considered part of your hours worked. The general rule of the Court is as follows:

> Periods during which an employee is completely relieved from duty and which are long enough to enable him to use the time effectively for his own purposes are not hours worked. He is not completely relieved from duty and cannot use the time effectively for his own purposes *unless* he is definitely told in advance that he may leave the job and that he will not have to commence work until a definitely specified hour has arrived. Whether the time is long enough to enable him to use the time effectively for his own purposes depends upon all of the facts and circumstances of the case.

Thirty minutes or more is considered long enough for a meal, and this time can be used as a

Among other things, the Fair Labor Standards Act (FLSA) sets the minimum hourly wage your employer must pay you. In many companies, workers punch a time clock to show when they arrive and leave work. What other points does the FLSA cover? (Philip Teuscher)

measure. Rest periods of from 5 to 20 minutes must be counted as time worked. Workers need rest periods in order to do their jobs efficiently throughout the day. And so it makes sense for the company to consider rest periods part of the time worked.

If you must receive medical attention while at work, the time you spend waiting for it or receiving it is counted as time worked. That is, your supervisor cannot take an hour off your time worked because it takes an hour for the company nurse to treat a cut.

What Is a Workweek?

You have read a bit about the 40-hour workweek in terms of determining overtime pay. The law says you must receive overtime pay after you have worked 40 hours in a week. So, what is a workweek?

Well, it may be the calendar week—from Sunday to Saturday—and in most cases it is. But because some people must work weekends and are off in the middle of the week, another definition of workweek is needed for purposes of applying the Fair Labor Standards Act with regard to overtime. Under the law, *workweek* means "a period of 168 hours during seven consecutive 24-hour periods. The work week may begin any day of the week or any hour as established by the employer."

For most people, the workweek is the same as the calendar week. They put in their 40 or less hours from Monday to Friday. Some people, however, work different "weeks." If you worked

from Thursday to Monday, for example, your workweek would be from Thursday to Wednesday. Whatever the workweek is, a company cannot change it around to avoid paying overtime. It cannot tell you as a Thursday to Monday worker that you are not entitled to overtime pay because you work only a few days in each calendar week.

Another thing that your company cannot do is average the time you worked over two or more workweeks to avoid paying you overtime. Say you worked 42 hours one week and then only 38 the next week. The company cannot add your two weeks of work together (80 hours) and then divide the hours worked by 2 to say you worked only 40 hours each week. It must pay you 2 hours' overtime pay for the extra work in the 42-hour week. This is true even if you are paid only every two weeks, or once a month. It is true regardless of when payday is.

Are You Paid to Study?

As a student in a work-experience program, you will not be paid for time spent in the classroom, even though what you learn there will make you a more valuable employee. For example, suppose you are in a work-experience program and work part time as a salesperson. Although you spend part of the day in school and improve your ability to handle customers, as a student-learner you will not be paid for time in the classroom.

In some cases, however, a worker is paid for attending classes or lectures. Suppose that you are a full-time secretary. Your boss instructs you to take a course in shorthand and provides time during the day for you to take it. The time you are using to take the course must be counted as working time. Suppose, however, you decide on your own to take such a course and do so after working hours. The time you spend taking the course cannot be counted as hours worked, even though the course will make you a more valuable employee.

Somewhat different rules apply to people in apprenticeship programs. Usually such programs require classroom work. The company employing the apprentices does not need to count time spent in the classroom as working time, as long as federal standards for such programs are met.

WHEN YOU HAVE A COMPLAINT

If you find that you have not been paid basic wages or overtime pay that you have earned, you can sue for back pay plus an additional sum for attorney or court costs and damages. *Damages* are losses you suffered because of not having received the pay due you. Perhaps you would have put your pay in the bank, where it would have earned interest. Loss of that interest is a damage to you. To claim back pay, you usually must file for it within two years.

If you ever have a complaint or questions about your basic wage or overtime pay, contact the nearest office of the Wage, Hour and Public Contracts Division of the U.S. Department of Labor. You will find the offices listed in your telephone directory. (Don't forget to look under "U" for "United States." Then look under that general heading for "Labor Department," and then for "Wage, Hour & Public Contracts.") It is against the law for a company to fire a worker for filing a complaint or for taking part in any procedure under the Fair Labor Standards Act. Further information about the law's provision on equal pay for equal work is included in Chapter 73.

Even if you do not have a complaint, you should know who administers the FLSA. Changes are often made in the law. The minimum wage could change. The definition of overtime could change. You can get information about the latest changes from your local office of the Wage, Hour and Public Contracts Division.

FEDERAL AND STATE LAWS

A lot is said about federal laws because they cover persons in all states. However, many states also have their own laws about working condi-

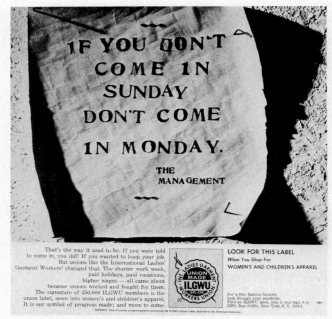

The concept of a 40-hour workweek did not always exist. What was a typical workweek before the FLSA?

tions, child labor, and so forth. Some state laws are the same as the federal laws. Others may have stricter standards or may not require as much. It can be confusing.

As a rule, the federal law usually takes precedence over state law (its force is stronger and greater). Most federal laws, however, say that state laws may cover the same area and that if they do, whichever laws are stricter or have higher requirements will take precedence.

A FINAL WORD

In this chapter you have read about many things that workers deal with daily on the job. There seems to be a law or regulation everywhere you turn. If one of them doesn't apply to your life— the minimum wage, for instance—why should you know about it?

Actually, all the topics in this chapter have a lot to do with you. All workers have to answer the questions "What's a day's work?" and "What's a day's pay?" No matter what your job is, or what career you plan to explore, you work some amount of time for some amount of pay. Whether you work part time or full time or overtime, you work sometime. And whether you earn a wage or a salary or overtime pay, you earn something. By knowing what is expected of you (time) and what you can expect in return (pay), you will be able to make good career decisions.

71

YOUR RIGHTS TO SAFE CONDITIONS AT WORK

As you read in Unit 21, you have the final responsibility for avoiding accidents and ill health. The company you work for, though, has a legal responsibility to do all it can to make your working conditions safe and healthy.

As part of its efforts to keep you safe, your company probably has a safety program. If so, the program was one of the first things you learned about when you were new on the job.

Some occupations, obviously, are more dangerous than others. If you are a deep-sea diver, you do not need to be told that your job is dangerous. You know that a mistake can be fatal. You follow every safety procedure. You do not become careless about safety even after years of diving. If you work in a steel mill, you also remain safety-conscious. Persons in dangerous occupations are always alert. They have to be.

IDENTIFYING DANGEROUS OCCUPATIONS

Dangerous occupations are not always easy to spot. Remaining alert is more difficult when the danger is less obvious. Is there any way of knowing whether your occupation is considered dangerous? Yes. The U.S. Department of Labor keeps records of job-related accidents. So does the National Safety Council in Chicago, Illinois.

The Department of Labor uses the *injury frequency rate* to measure how dangerous an occupation is. This is a rating scale. A record is kept of all job accidents in each industry. The more injuries an industry has, the higher the injury frequency rate.

Occupational injuries and illnesses occur at a rate of 9.2 per 100 full-time workers; on the aver-

age, 1 out of every 11 workers is injured or made ill while on the job. Or, in terms of hours of exposure on the job, one injury or illness is recorded for every 21,700 hours worked. These figures represent an average for all industries. Some "high-risk" industries have a higher than average rate. Other industries have lower injury and illness rates.

What is the injury frequency rate for your job? It is important to know if there is a low or a high risk of injury where you work. (Courtesy Jones & Laughlin Steel Corporation)

Industry	Injury Frequency Rate (per 100 Full-Time Workers)
Meat packaging	34.7
Sawmill	34.5
Mobile home	32.0
Travel trailers & campers	30.3
Truck trailers	29.3
Steel foundries	28.4

Try to discover the injury frequency rate for your occupation. Check at the library for publications of the Department of Labor or the National Safety Council that have the statistics.

In its drive to make all industries safer, the Department of Labor has identified five industries that have a high risk of injury. Their injury frequency rates are double the national average, as shown above:

OSHA

Do you think much about the Williams-Steiger Occupational Safety and Health Act of 1970? No? How about OSHA? No, again? That's not surprising. But as you enter the working world, you should learn something about the Williams-Steiger Occupational Safety and Health Act of 1970. It is a federal law that affects your daily safety on the job.

OSHA stands either for the act itself or for the Occupational Safety and Health Administration, which is the governmental body that sees that the law is obeyed.

The law requires your employer to maintain clean, healthy, safe conditions. It also requires something from you. You must, for example, comply with occupational safety and health standards and all rules, regulations, and orders issued under the act. If you are a heavy-construction worker and refuse to wear a hard hat, you will be blamed if you are injured by a falling object. If you do not wear protective eyeglasses on a job that requires them and your eye is injured, the fault is yours.

To help you fulfill your responsibilities as seen by OSHA, here is a handy checklist:

- Read the OSHA posters at your jobsite.
- Know and follow OSHA standards that apply to your work.
- Follow all your employer's safety and health standards and rules.
- Wear or use prescribed protective equipment for your work.
- Report all dangerous conditions at work to your supervisor.

- Report any job-related injuries or illnesses to your supervisor, and seek treatment right away.
- Cooperate with OSHA officials when they conduct inspections.
- Use your rights under the law responsibly.

OSHA covers about five million places of work. Obviously, OSHA inspectors cannot visit all of them regularly. Some industries have not been visited at all. There are so many that it would take an army of inspectors to check them all to make sure conditions are safe. So OSHA officials have established a system of priorities for checking workplaces.

Three Priorities

When there is a major or fatal accident, OSHA inspectors try at once to learn what was wrong and prevent it from happening again by setting new safety procedures. Correcting conditions that result in serious accidents is OSHA's first priority.

OSHA's second priority is to deal with valid employee complaints. When an employee complains about unsafe conditions, OSHA inspectors visit the company. As an employee you have a right—even a duty—to report unsafe conditions to OSHA if your company refuses to correct them. The procedure to follow in reporting a health or safety hazard is given later in this chapter.

OSHA's third priority for inspections and corrections is to deal with what officials have called "target industries" and "target health hazards." *Target industries* are those identified as having high injury frequency rates. *Target health hazards* include materials, chemicals, or substances that are dangerous to your health.

The National Institute for Occupational Safety and Health, which is part of OSHA, has identified more than 15,000 *toxic*, or poisonous, substances found in industrial processes. That's a lot. Most workers, however, are not likely to have much or anything to do with such substances. Even so, some dangerous substances should be studied.

job safety and health protection

The Occupational Safety and Health Act of 1970 provides job safety and health protection for workers through the promotion of safe and healthful working conditions throughout the Nation. Requirements of the Act include the following:

Employers: Each employer shall furnish to each of his employees employment and a place of employment free from recognized hazards that are causing or are likely to cause death or serious harm to his employees; and shall comply with occupational safety and health standards issued under the Act.

Employees: Each employee shall comply with all occupational safety and health standards, rules, regulations and orders issued under the Act that apply to his own actions and conduct on the job.

The Occupational Safety and Health Administration (OSHA) of the Department of Labor has the primary responsibility for administering the Act. OSHA issues occupational safety and health standards, and its Compliance Safety and Health Officers conduct jobsite inspections to ensure compliance with the Act.

Inspection: The Act requires that a representative of the employer and a representative authorized by the employees be given an opportunity to accompany the OSHA inspector for the purpose of aiding the inspection.

Where there is no authorized employee representative, the OSHA Compliance Officer must consult with a reasonable number of employees concerning safety and health conditions in the workplace.

Complaint: Employees or their representatives have the right to file a complaint with the nearest OSHA office requesting an inspection if they believe unsafe or unhealthful conditions exist in their workplace. OSHA will withhold, on request, names of employees complaining.

The Act provides that employees may not be discharged or discriminated against in any way for filing safety and health complaints or otherwise exercising their rights under the Act.

An employee who believes he has been discriminated against may file a complaint with the nearest OSHA office within 30 days of the alleged discrimination.

GPO 892-171

Citation: If upon inspection OSHA believes an employer has violated the Act, a citation alleging such violations will be issued to the employer. Each citation will specify a time period within which the alleged violation must be corrected.

The OSHA citation must be prominently displayed at or near the place of alleged violation for three days, or until it is corrected, whichever is later, to warn employees of dangers that may exist there.

Proposed Penalty: The Act provides for mandatory penalties against employers of up to $1,000 for each serious violation and for optional penalties of up to $1,000 for each nonserious violation. Penalties of up to $1,000 per day may be proposed for failure to correct violations within the proposed time period. Also, any employer who willfully or repeatedly violates the Act may be assessed penalties of up to $10,000 for each such violation.

Criminal penalties are also provided for in the Act. Any willful violation resulting in death of an employee, upon conviction, is punishable by a fine of not more than $10,000 or by imprisonment for not more that six months, or by both. Conviction of an employer after a first conviction doubles these maximum penalties.

Voluntary Activity: While providing penalties for violations, the Act also encourages efforts by labor and management, before an OSHA inspection, to reduce injuries and illnesses arising out of employment.

The Department of Labor encourages employers and employees to reduce workplace hazards voluntarily and to develop and improve safety and health programs in all workplaces and industries.

Such cooperative action would initially focus on the identification and elimination of hazards that could cause death, injury, or illness to employees and supervisors. There are many public and private organizations that can provide information and assistance in this effort, if requested.

More Information: Additional information and copies of the Act, specific OSHA safety and health standards, and other applicable regulations may be obtained from the nearest OSHA Regional Office in the following locations:

Atlanta, Georgia
Boston, Massachusetts
Chicago, Illinois
Dallas, Texas
Denver, Colorado
Kansas City, Missouri
New York, New York
Philadelphia, Pennsylvania
San Francisco, California
Seattle, Washington

Telephone numbers for these offices, and additional Area Office locations, are listed in the telephone directory under the United States Department of Labor in the United States Government listing.

Washington, D. C.
1975
OSHA 2203

John T. Dunlop

John T. Dunlop
Secretary of Labor

U. S. Department of Labor
Occupational Safety and Health Administration

The Occupational Safety and Health Act (OSHA) requires your employer to maintain clean, healthy, and safe working conditions. It also requires you to comply with the OSHA health standards and with all rules, regulations, and orders issued under the act.

Five Common Industrial Poisons

Five toxic substances are used or are present a great deal in many different industries. As a result, many workers will come into contact with them. You should know what these common toxic substances are, where they might be found, and how they can be dangerous. You need such information to protect yourself.

The five toxic substances most common in industry are asbestos, lead, cotton dust, silica, and carbon monoxide. Let's take a brief look at them to learn what damage they can do and where they are likely to be found.

Asbestos. The term *asbestos* is a general one used to describe several "fibrous mineral silicates." "Fibrous" means stringlike. "Silicates" are a common part of rocks or sand. Asbestos can be white, grayish, or greenish. It can come in a mass or appear as long, silky fibers. Asbestos is highly heat-resistant, which makes it good protection against fire. That is probably how you have seen it used or have heard of it. Asbestos is also used for insulation, for brake and clutch linings on cars, for building materials, as a filter, and in plastics.

If you breathe in a lot of asbestos material, it can build up in your lungs and make it difficult to breathe. Workers who handle products with asbestos must be careful when they are cutting or doing other operations that cause it to fill the air.

Good ventilation is necessary where asbestos is used. Air filtration masks that purify the air must be worn where there is a lot of asbestos in the air.

Lead. You can find lead in more industries than you might think of. It is used to make printing type and plumbing fixtures, telephone and power cables, and radiation shields.

When lead is mixed with another metal, it forms what is called an *alloy*. Solder is a lead alloy. A lot of solder is used in electrical and electronic industries.

Lead compounds are used to make paint. And lead is found in car batteries and ammunition. Lead gets around, as you can see.

Lead can cause serious illness and even death. You can breathe it. You can absorb it through your skin. You can eat it. If you get enough of it in your body, it will attack your stomach, intestines, blood, and central nervous system.

As with asbestos, good ventilation is essential where lead is used. Furthermore, the work

To protect yourself against injury, find out if your job involves working with toxic, or poisonous, substances. In this photograph, a laboratory assistant wears protective clothing with a self-contained air system to protect him against toxic substances in the air (Courtesy E.I. du Pont de Nemours and Company)

area should be wet or cleaned by vacuum every day to get rid of lead dust. Personal hygiene is important for workers exposed to lead a lot. They should wash themselves and their clothes thoroughly. Protective clothing should be worn instead of street clothes. Workers should never take food and beverages into work areas where lead is used.

Cotton dust. Wherever there is cotton, there is cotton dust. Workers are most likely to be exposed to cotton dust in the textile mills where cloth is made. It gathers on the machines, which must be cleaned often. When they are cleaned, cotton dust can escape into the air.

No one knows exactly how cotton dust affects the body. But it is known that a person breathing cotton dust for a long period (say 10 or more years) will get a lung disease called *byssinosis*. It causes coughing, difficulty of breathing, and a tightness in the chest. These conditions can get worse and worse and can lead to other lung illnesses as well.

Proper ventilation is the key to controlling cotton dust. Machinery can be enclosed, and the cotton can be treated to reduce the amount of dust that gets into the air.

Silica.   A substance found in many minerals, silica is used a lot for metal-casting operations. It is used in ceramics (plates, dishes, bowls), decorative material, insulation, building materials, and glass. It is found in many industrial facilities, including mining centers, mineral processing plants, and plants that make abrasive soap or glass or pottery.

Again, problems are caused by breathing in the silica dust. Its name is used for the disabling lung disease it causes: *silicosis.* Persons suffering from silicosis have difficulty breathing. The condition can lead to tuberculosis.

Some industries solve the silica problem by finding other, harmless substances to use in its place. Where it is used, the ventilation should be good, machines should be covered as much as possible, and the area should be kept clean and wetted down. Operations requiring the use of silica should be separated from other operations.

Carbon monoxide.   The exhaust gas of automobiles contains carbon monoxide. This toxic substance is given off by any gasoline-powered engine. In fact, it is produced whenever wood, gas, coal, oil, or gasoline is burned. Obviously, carbon monoxide can be found nearly everywhere. It is colorless, almost odorless, tasteless, and nonirritating. That makes its presence hard to detect. And that makes it dangerous.

If you breathe carbon monoxide into your body, it enters your bloodstream and displaces the oxygen. When that happens, suffocation and death result. Unlike some of the other toxic substances, carbon monoxide does not build up in the blood. You have to breathe in quite a lot of it to get sick, and your body gets rid of smaller amounts of the poison after you stop breathing it in.

As with the other substances, good ventilation is essential in eliminating carbon monoxide. Many industries use systems that detect the gas when it is in the air and automatically sound an alarm.

If you have any doubts about any substance where you work, and you fear that there may be some danger to your health, write to the National Institute for Occupational Safety and Health (NIOSH) at the Department of Health and Human Services in Washington, DC. NIOSH

What toxic substances do you think are bothering these workers in an auto shop? How might these conditions effect their job performance? What should be done to make their work conditions safer?

publishes a list of all known toxic substances every year. This publication also tells you at what levels of concentration each substance becomes dangerous.

Nonhazardous Jobs

If you are in a job with definite or obvious health and safety hazards, laws such as OSHA help protect you. But what about an ordinary job? Say you work in an office or store where there are no obvious hazards. Would the law be of concern to you then also? The answer is yes.

Under the law all employers must provide decent, clean places in which to work. Lighting must be good enough in an office so that eyesight is protected. The ventilating system must keep odors from building up. And all work areas must be kept clean.

Work Facilities and Conveniences

Here are some other things you should know about your place of work. Note, of course, that if you have a job that takes you outside, some of the items probably will not apply.

Drinking water.   Your company should supply you with water that you can drink while at work. If this is provided through a water fountain, the fountain must be one from which you can drink without fear of picking up germs. The water nozzle should be adjusted so that water does not fall back on top of it. There should be a guard over the nozzle so that a person's mouth cannot come into contact with it. The water should drain well. If water is supplied from a faucet, cups must be provided. If paper cups are used, they must be kept in a clean container, and a wastebasket must be provided for used cups.

Toilet facilities.   The place where you work must provide toilet facilities for workers. There must be separate facilities for men and women (except for single-use rooms that can be locked from inside). For 15 or fewer workers, one toilet is enough. Two toilets must be supplied for 16 to 35 workers; three for 36 to 55; four for 56 to 80; five for 81 to 110; six for 111 to 150; and one additional fixture for every 40 over 150.

If there is more than one toilet in a room, the toilets must be separated by partitions to ensure privacy. Each toilet room must have a holder with toilet paper.

Hot water and soap.   Your company must have a room where you can wash up. There must be at least one sink for every ten people. Each must have hot and cold running water and hand soap, and there should be individual hand towels (paper or cloth) or warm-air blowers for drying your hands. Some industries—those in which workers face particularly dirty conditions—must provide showers.

Clean work areas.   The law says that "all places of employment shall be kept clean to the extent that the nature of the work allows." Floors should be kept as dry as possible. They must not have nails that stick out, splinters, loose boards, holes, or openings. Clean containers must be provided for waste, and, where necessary, they must be emptied each working day. Your work area must be kept free of insects, mice, and rats.

Exits.   The building where you work should have exits placed so that you and your fellow workers can escape promptly if there is a fire or other emergency. These exits should take you directly to a street or to an open area that allows you to reach a public street safely. They should be marked with lighted signs in bright colors, with the word "exit" in letters at least 6 inches high. If you are in a room with more than 50 workers, the exit doors should swing outward in the direction you will be traveling to escape.

Lunchrooms.   Your company does not have to provide a lunchroom. If it does, however, the room must be clean and sanitary. Food must be unspoiled and wholesome. Covered receptacles must be provided for waste food. Whether there is a lunchroom or not, you are not allowed to bring food or drink into the toilet rooms or any area where there might be poisonous material.

Protection from noise.   Probably one of the greatest single occupational hazards is noise. Millions of workers have suffered hearing loss of varying degrees from noise during working hours. If your job generates noise above a certain level, your company must provide protection, usually in the form of ear protectors. If you think the noise on your job is above a level that requires protection, and you do not have it, talk to your supervisor. If you are then unsatisfied, contact an OSHA representative.

These are just a few of the general work facilities and conveniences covered by OSHA to make your on-the-job experience safe. The law takes up to 31 pages of fine print. The rules and regulations implementing OSHA cover 326 pages. The governmental body—OSHA—puts out many publications telling about the law, the regulations, and your rights and responsibilities under the OSHA law.

Filing a Complaint

If you are doing your part to make your job safe, but you think that a hazardous condition exists and your supervisor has done nothing about it, you can ask OSHA to send an inspector to investigate. You would address such a request to the OSHA area director who covers the place where you work. If you do not find the address of an area office in your telephone directory, check at your local post office.

A request for an inspection must be in writing. It must be specific. You must identify the hazard and tell how it affects you. When seeking information, asking for an inspection, or filing a complaint, you can request that your name be withheld from your company.

The OSHA protects you even if your job does not involve obvious health and safety hazards. For example, under OSHA all employers must provide for their workers drinking water, toilet facilities, and clean work areas. What are the requirements of OSHA if your employer provides a lunchroom? (Top left, right, center, and bottom right—Fern Logan; bottom left, United Nations, Y. Nagata/ARA)

CHAPTER **72**

YOUR RIGHTS TO ORGANIZE

One of your most important job rights is the right to join a union in order to bargain collectively for higher pay, job security, and better working conditions. The right to join carries with it the right not to join, of course. At one time or another, most workers in America will be faced with the question of whether or not to join a union.

The decision might be determined by the choice of a career. In some careers it is necessary to join a union. If you want to be a sailor on a merchant vessel of the United States, you will need to join one of the sailors' unions. To be a worker at one of the large automobile manufacturing companies, you would have to join a union. You could begin work without being a union member, but you would have to join within a certain number of days in order to continue working.

On the other hand, you would not need to join a union to be an automobile mechanic or a body repair worker. You could work in these careers at companies that do not have unions or do not require union membership. Many kinds of office workers have a choice of whether to join a union or not.

Teachers can join a labor organization. The same is true of salesclerks in department stores. Most steelworkers and coal miners must join unions. Truck drivers working for large companies must join. However, drivers working for themselves or small companies are not required to join a union.

Until well into the 1960s, less than half the workers in the United States were in organized unions. Since then, efforts to organize more workers have increased. Today labor organizations exist in nearly all occupations in both the *public* and *private* sectors. Everyone is employed in either of these two sectors. Anyone who works

for any level of government is said to work in the public sector. Everyone else—those who work for businesses, industries, and stores—is employed in the private sector. Public school teachers, police officers, and fire fighters work in the public sector. They are public employees. Car salespersons, textile workers, and teachers in private schools work in the private sector.

Originally, blue-collar workers—the people in the factories and in the mines—were the only ones organized into unions. Unions of white-collar workers—people in the offices and the salesrooms—are common today. At first, unions were considered necessary only for nonprofessional workers. But today there are many labor organizations made up of professional workers.

Just what is a labor union? Basically, it is an organization of workers who have joined together to increase their income and to improve their working conditions. Some unions are built around crafts or professions. There are unions for carpenters, for electricians, for plumbers, for teachers, and for fire fighters. Other unions are built around industries, such as the United Mine Workers or the United Auto Workers.

WHY UNIONS?

Several factors led workers to organize themselves into unions. Increased mechanization had the effect of lowering the need for skilled craft workers, thus reducing their bargaining power as individuals. The benefits of science and invention resulted in increased profits for business but little improvement for labor. With new machines, industry produced more with fewer workers. Technological progress resulted in the rise of large corporations. In many cases, this destroyed the personal relations that had existed between

Labor organizations exist in nearly all occupations in the public and private sectors. Government employees such as mail carriers (left) work in the public sector. All other employees, such as the truck driver (right), work in the private sector. (Left, courtesy United States Postal Service; right, courtesy United Parcel Service)

employee and employer in which a worker could effectively bargain as an individual to get a good salary.

At one time, there was almost a family relationship between employer and employee. If you were a boss, you would know everyone in your shop. You would call your employees by their first names, and you would know their families. You would swap jokes and stories and perhaps some food with each other. In short, there was a friendly human relationship between employer and employee. But that soon changed. No such relation existed between the great coal magnates and the thousands of miners who worked for them. Very few mine workers ever met their boss. The great coal companies, which employed tens of thousands, could easily fire any particular miner. But the miners and their families could not survive without the companies.

By joining together, workers gained strength to equal the strength of the companies. Companies might be able to do without the service of one worker. But they could not do without the services of large numbers of workers. The most effective weapon that organized workers have is the strike. This is accepted as a legal tool to use to obtain higher wages or other rights, provided certain conditions are met. It took many years for the workers to win the right to strike. They did not get it until the early part of this century.

Today your rights to join a union, to bargain with your employer for better working condi-tions or higher wages, and to strike are all protected by law. The law not only gives you the right to bargain. It also requires your employer to bargain with you in good faith.

The history of labor unions has not been entirely favorable. As some unions became powerful, criminal elements moved in to take them over. They frightened workers into joining and paying high dues. In some cases it seemed that workers were being squeezed between big business and big unions.

Not all companies are willing to deal with an individual worker's complaint. Check with your personnel office if your supervisor is unable or unwilling to answer your questions about your rights.

If you need outside help, the law that protects your rights to organize and strike is the National Labor Relations Act of 1935 (NLRA). Originally, the law sought only to help individual workers deal with large companies that hired them. Eventually, the law was amended to curb the abuses of powerful unions. The law now protects the individual worker from the growing power of the union as well as from the power of the company.

MAJOR PROTECTIONS

Below, in outline form, are some of the major protections provided by the national labor relations laws.

Regulations Covering the Conduct of Unions

1. A union may not raise its dues or fees, or levy a special assessment, unless the action is approved by a majority membership vote in a secret ballot.
2. A union may not limit your right as a member to bring suit in court or to contact your congressional representative.
3. Other than for nonpayment of dues, a union may not punish you without first putting its charges against you in writing, giving you time to prepare your defense, and providing you with a fair hearing.
4. National unions must elect officers by secret ballot at least every five years. Local unions must elect officers by secret ballot at least every three years.
5. A union may not use money from dues or assessments to promote the candidacy of any person running for a union office.
6. The union must provide safeguards ensuring a fair election, including the placement of an observer at the polls, which any candidate has the right to request.
7. A union may not lend a union officer or employee more than $2,000, and it may not pay the fine of any officer or employee who has been convicted of willful violation of the NLRA.
8. If you are a union officer, you must file annually with the Secretary of Labor a complete report on your financial dealings related to the union.
9. Elected union officials guilty of serious misconduct may be removed by a secret ballot vote of the membership.
10. Embezzlement of union funds by a union officer or employee is a federal offense.
11. Any person convicted of a serious crime may not hold any union position other than a clerical or custodial one for a period of five years following conviction.

Rights of Union Members

1. You may express views at union meetings.
2. You may obtain a copy of the labor contract affecting you.
3. You may examine books and records of the union if you can show just cause.
4. You may refuse to cross a union picket line at another company if the union is on an authorized strike against that company.

Regulations Governing the Conduct of Companies

1. An employer may not contribute any money to aid in the election of any person running for union office.
2. Payments by an employer to a union officer are prohibited if they are in the nature of bribery or blackmail.

One of your rights as a union member is to attend and express your views at union meetings. (Courtesy 1199 News)

3. An employer must file annual reports with the Secretary of Labor concerning various types of financial transactions with a union, its officers, or its members.
4. The employer, in most cases, cannot finance, encourage, or participate in a suit against a union by a member. Nor can the employer take part in a member's communicating with a congressional representative.

In an effort to limit work stoppages in key industries, the federal government can:

1. Seek an injunction (court order) halting for a total of 80 days any strike or lockout that endangers national health and safety
2. Poll workers on their employer's final offer before allowing a strike to be called

Basically the law gives workers the right to organize, which means to vote to join a union or to form one. A vote must be by secret ballot.

Companies cannot stop you from joining a union. Neither can unions force you to join. Either of these actions would be considered an unfair labor practice.

Under the law, workers, as represented by their union, may bargain collectively on wages, hours, and other working conditions and benefits. The National Labor Relations Board has the responsibility for enforcing the law. The board can only act, however, when it is formally requested to do so. You, your employer, or the union may petition the board by filing charges of unfair labor practices. If you have a complaint, contact the nearest office of the National Labor Relations Board. You can get the address from your local post office or telephone directory.

YOU AND A UNION

There are four basic situations in which you are most likely to find yourself in relation to unions. You may be working at a company where there is

The National Labor Relations Act protects individual workers from the abuses of powerful unions as well as from the power of large companies. Your rights as a union member are covered under this act.

Agreement made this.. day of.., 19.........,

between the undersigned Producer and..., Actor.

1. AGREEMENT OF EMPLOYMENT. The Producer engages the Actor to render services in the part (or understudy)

of.."

in the play now called "...
and the Actor hereby accepts such employment upon the following terms:

2. OPENING DATE. The date of the first public performance shall be the...................day of.........................., 19.........,
or not later than fourteen (14) days thereafter.

Employment hereunder shall begin on the date of beginning of rehearsals, which date shall not be earlier than four (4) weeks [five (5) weeks in the case of musicals] prior to the date of the first public performance herein agreed upon.

3. ORGANIZATION POINT. It is agreed between the Actor and the Producer that the organization point of the Company shall be one of the following: (Please Circle One)

NEW YORK CITY, TORONTO, CHICAGO, SAN-FRANCISCO, LOS ANGELES
If no choice is made, the Organization Point shall be New York City.

4. COMPENSATION.

(A) The Producer agrees to pay the Actor each week before noon on Friday the sum of..................................

Dollars ($..............................) for employment at the Organization Point.

(B) The Producer further agrees to pay the Actor each week before noon on Friday the sum of...........................

Dollars ($..............................) for employment outside the Organization Point, of which $.......................... shall be for out-of-town expenses and paid by separate check.

No reduction of this salary shall be binding on the Actor without the written consent of Equity.

5. EQUITY RULES.

(A) The Producer recognizes Actors' Equity Association ("Equity") as the exclusive bargaining representative for the Actor for the purpose of collective bargaining and the administration of matters within the scope of this Agreement.

(B) Both the Producer and the Actor agree that each and every provision including the Arbitration Rule contained in the Basic Agreement between Equity and The League of New York Theatres and Producers, Inc. and the Agreement and Rules Governing Employment under the Production Contract is and becomes a part of this Agreement, as though set forth herein at length; that they have read said Rules and admit actual notice and knowledge of same; that each and every term of said Rules is of the essence of the contractual relationship between them and that said Rules may not be waived or modified without the written consent of Equity. Nothing herein shall be construed contrary to the Basic Agreement.

6. SECURITY. It is of the essence of this contract and a condition precedent to the engagement of the Actor that the Producer shall file and shall at all times maintain with Actors' Equity Association security satisfactory to Equity as required by its existing Security Agreement and Rules.

7. AUTHORIZATION. The Actor hereby assigns to Equity from any wages earned or to be earned under this contract such amount for dues, initiation fees, and periodic assessments as may be certified to the Producer by the Association to be due from him. The Actor authorizes and directs the Producer to deduct such amounts from his weekly salary and to remit same to the Association. This assignment, authorization and direction shall be effective and irrevocable for the term of the Actor's employment contract, or one year, whichever is shorter.

8. INDIVIDUAL SIGNATURE REQUIRED. The Producer agrees that execution of this Contract binds not only the producing company, but the individual signator to this Contract as well as any person under whose authority this Contract is executed.

(PRODUCER MUST SIGN FIRST)

Producing Company...

Employer's Registration Number
for Unemployment Insurance

Individual Signature..

Actor...

OBLIGATION FOR ACTORS' FUND: See Rule 5.

Social Security No...

WHITE COPIES FOR ACTOR, PRODUCER AND AGENT, IF ANY.
PALE BLUE COPY MUST BE FILED WITH EQUITY BY PRODUCER IMMEDIATELY UPON EXECUTION.
DARK BLUE COPY MUST BE FILED WITH EQUITY BY ACTOR IMMEDIATELY UPON EXECUTION.

no union and no interest in forming one. You may be working at a company where there is no union, but there is interest and action toward forming one. You may be employed at a company where there is a union, but you are not required to join. Or you may be at a company where there is a union, and as a condition of your employment you must join the union.

In the first and last situations, you do not need to make a choice. As a student-learner, you probably will not have a choice, anyway. But as a full-time worker, you will face a choice in the second and third situations. What you do, of course, depends on the specific circumstances and your own background and wishes, your values, and your lifestyle.

Generally speaking, if you are working at a company where there is an active union, the pressure will be great on you to join even if it is not required. The major argument will be that the union benefits all workers, and so all workers should support the union.

In some plants it is possible for a worker to not join a union but still have to pay dues or some assessment. Persons whose religious beliefs might prohibit their joining a union take this route. Where a strong union exists, you will probably need a strong personal reason (such as a religious belief) to avoid joining.

In the situation in which there is no union, but some workers are trying to start one, you probably will face a more difficult decision. In such a situation, you must take a hard look at what the company is providing now and what the persons advocating the union say it will get for you. Compare your job, wages, and benefits with those of workers in other companies. Consider what responsibilities and costs (dues, assessments) the union will impose.

Problem Solving and Decision Making Regarding Unions

Use this four-step process for making a decision about whether or not to join a union:

1. *Analyze the situation.* What is your pay now? What benefits do you receive? How are your working conditions? What about job security? Is there a good pension plan? What are the chances for promotions and raises? What is your company's reputation for dealing with workers? How does your situation compare with that of other workers in the area, both union workers and nonunion workers? What does the union have to offer? What will membership in it require? What is the union's reputation?

2. *Look for solutions.* You could join a union to improve your working conditions through collective bargaining.

    You might not join a union because your present situation is satisfactory to you.

3. *Consider the outcomes.* If you choose not to join a union, you might face pressure, even anger, from your co-workers. You would lose the opportunity to bargain collectively. You could have problems maintaining informal relations with management. (Once a formal working contract is signed, managers who had been relaxed about employee behavior in many areas might begin to demand that the letter of the contract be followed.) If you do join a union, you will be able to bargain collectively. You will have the responsibility to support strikes and respect picket lines. You will have to pay dues, initiation fees, and assessments. (Many unions charge new members a special initiation fee to join. Some unions assess members a fee to help other members on strike.)

4. *Pick the best alternative.* This listing does not cover all the factors that you might have to consider in a real situation. It is a made-up guide that simply suggests some of the aspects you should explore. The point is to think about your options when faced with a choice. You cannot assume that the leaders of the union have your welfare at heart any more than the owners of the company do. People operate businesses to make money first of all. They provide jobs and pay what they must only insofar as the businesses are profitable. In the same spirit people become professional union organizers and officials to earn a living. If they can earn their living by helping you, fine—just as company owners are willing to help you if they can make a profit doing it.

    There is good and bad on both sides. Few choices in life are clear-cut and easy to make. That's what makes deciding such a difficult task most of the time.

Choosing between Unions

The choice of whether or not to join or help organize a union can be more difficult if more than one union wants to represent you. In order for any union to represent the workers, it must be *recognized.* That means you and your co-workers must vote in secret ballot for it to represent you. This is true whether only one union or two are seeking recognition. Once you have voted for a union, it is known as your *bargaining agent* or *representative.*

Some bitter fights have occurred when two different unions have tried to represent the same workers. In such a situation, you must decide not only whether you want to join a union at all but also which one to join. You would use the four steps in decision making, but in this situation you would also add questions about the merits of each union.

A fifth situation that could occur is one in which there is an elected bargaining agent, but another organization is trying to replace it. Under the National Labor Relations Act, workers have the right to vote to change their bargaining agent. Suppose another union is trying to replace the existing union. This is not likely to happen if the existing union is strong and is doing a good job of representing the workers. If it does happen, you will have to weigh the merits of both unions in order to vote in your best interest.

A sixth situation that can arise is one in which a move is made to get rid of the union.

Under the law, workers can vote to not have any bargaining agent by throwing out a union that has been representing them. This has happened when workers decided that the union was collecting their dues but not really doing them much good.

SPEAKING THE LANGUAGE

You will hear and use many special words and phrases when you talk or read about labor organizations. You must be familiar with the language in order to make the best decisions about your participation. Below are some of the more commonly used terms:

Arbitration: A method of settling labor disputes whereby the two parties involved agree on the choice of an impartial chairperson who decides the issue at hand.

Blacklist: An employer's method of industrial warfare. It lists workers who cause trouble or agitate other workers to make them strike. The list is circulated among employers. Its use is considered an unfair labor practice.

Boycott: An organized attempt by the unions to keep the products of a named manufacturer from being sold or purchased. The word comes from the name of the first victim, Captain Boycott (1880). When the pressure is brought directly against the person or manufacturer toward whom the boycott is directed, the boycott is *primary.* When a third party pressures the employer or manufacturer—for example, if the employees of one company are forbidden to make articles used by a manufacturer against whom the boycott is aimed—the boycott is *secondary.*

Casual Worker: A temporary worker who has no seniority rights and does not belong to a labor union.

Checkoff: The deduction of labor union dues from the pay of the employee. The employer sends it directly to the union.

Closed Shop: A place of employment in which only union members may work and in which only union members are employed.

Collective Bargaining: The settlement of labor disputes by discussions between the union leaders and employers.

Company Union: A labor union that is made up only of workers within a single company. It

There are many questions to consider before deciding whether or not to join a union. Use the four-step decision-making process to help you decide whether or not you should join a union. What are the four steps in that process?

usually is not connected with any other union and often implies control by the company.

Conciliation: A method of settling labor disputes by which a third party is appointed who suggests various ways to settle a dispute. The third party has no authority to force the sides to agree.

Craft Union: A labor union made up of skilled workers from one trade or of skilled workers from a few trades that are closely linked.

Featherbedding: A labor union practice designed to provide easy jobs. Union rules demand that more employees be assigned to a given task than are needed or that full wages be paid for unnecessary jobs.

General Strike: Stoppage of work in all industries throughout a region or nation.

Guild: An association of persons who are engaged in some common work and who have united together for mutual aid and protection. The medieval guild was the forerunner of the labor union.

Industrial Union: A labor organization that takes members from an entire industry. It is also called a *vertical union.* (An example is the United Mine Workers.)

Injunction: A court order commanding a person or persons to perform or not perform certain actions.

Living Wage: A salary that is large enough to allow the worker to support a family, to educate children, and to save enough for support in case of an emergency or illness and for use in old age.

Lockout: The result when an employer keeps employees out of the plant.

Maintenance-of-Union Clause: An agreement or arrangement between an employer and a union by which employees who are members of a union at the time the agreement is made must either remain members until the agreement expires or be discharged.

Mediation: A formal procedure for settling disputes that involves the use of a commission or board to which interested parties air their differences.

Open Shop: A company in which workers do not need to belong to a union.

Picketing: A device used by labor whereby the members of a union seek to persuade outsiders not to have dealings with the firm in conflict. Workers march, with or without signs, near their company.

Profit Sharing: A policy adopted by some corporations whereby the workers receive, besides their regular wages, a share in the profits of the corporation for which they work.

Scab: A person who works under conditions not approved by labor unions; a person who works while other employees are on strike.

Seniority List: A list of employees which indicates the length of service of each employee. It is a basis for wage increase, promotion, and retirement.

Strike: A temporary stoppage of work to force an employer to give in to the demands of the employees.

Sweatshop: A place of employment which makes people work for very long hours and for low wages.

Union Label: A tag attached to merchandise or manufactured goods which indicates that the product was produced by union members.

Union Shop: An industry in which all employees must belong to a union. Nonunion members are hired on the promise that they will join a union within 30 days.

Vertical Union: A union made up of all the employees of an entire industry. (It is also called an *industrial union.*)

LABOR RELATIONS LAWS

National Labor Relations Act of 1935 (also known as the Wagner Act). This was the first major piece of legislation regulating the relationship between workers and employers. It affirms labor's right to organize and bargain collectively.

Labor-Management Relations Act of 1947 (better known as the Taft-Hartley Labor Act). This amended the National Labor Relations Act of 1935. It set more controls on union functions. Among other things, it outlawed secondary boycotts and closed shops. It gave government the power to impose an 80-day "cooling-off" period if a potential strike threatened national health or safety.

Labor Reform Act of 1959 (also known as the Landrum-Griffin Act). This act further amended the labor relations laws to tighten control over unions. It prohibited unions from raising union dues without a vote of the members, for example.

73

YOUR RIGHTS TO EQUAL CAREER OPPORTUNITIES

Not so long ago, most people tended to think of some careers as being for men only and other careers for women only. Women would not apply for jobs as carpenters. If they did, they would not be hired simply because they were women. No one would ask whether or not they could do the work. It was just assumed that this type of work could not be done by women.

To a lesser extent some careers were considered "off bounds" for men and suitable only for women. Some jobs considered "women's jobs" were flight attendants, switchboard operators, and receptionists.

With this false distinction between different careers, everyone suffered. Everyone's career choice was unnecessarily limited. There were always some jobs, of course, that both men and women were considered capable of doing. Both might stand at the looms in a textile mill. Both might work as file clerks. Often women were paid less money when they did the same work as men. That's *discrimination* by sex.

People used a lot of shallow excuses to explain this practice. "Women can't work as hard or as long," they said. "Men must be paid more because they have families to support," they said. "Women are supported by their husbands."

These excuses were just that—excuses. Rather empty ones. The real reason was economics—money. Employers were interested in only one thing: keeping a cheap source of labor available. It was always unfair. Today it is illegal.

Men also suffered from this kind of wage discrimination, although on the surface they did not seem to. But as long as employers had women as a cheap source of labor, they could use that excuse to keep men's wages down. Men were paid more than women, but not that much more.

Having a supply of cheap labor tends to keep everyone's wages down.

Women were not the only workers short-changed in this way. Members of racial and ethnic minorities suffered the same kind of treatment. Members of minority groups had trouble getting any kind of work. As a result, they were forced to work whenever and wherever they could. This usually meant lower pay and the worst jobs. For industry, this kind of racial or ethnic discrimination was a dollar-and-cents thing. Industry could exploit prejudice to get pools of cheap labor.

Today, companies must not only treat all people equally—regardless of color or race or sex—in hiring. They also must continue to treat people equally after they have been hired. This means that workers must be paid equal pay for equal work. It also means that they must all be considered equally for promotions and benefits and work assignments.

TITLE VII

Title VII of the Civil Rights Act of 1964 is the federal law that protects your right to equal career opportunities. As with all federal laws, this one applies to most workers in the country, although not all workers are covered by it. In general, if you work for a company that has 15 or more employees, you are covered by Title VII.

Title VII is enforced by the Equal Employment Opportunity Commission (EEOC). If any of your job rights as protected by Title VII are violated, you should contact the EEOC.

The false distinctions between so-called "men's jobs" and "women's jobs" are slowly

Today, women have the legal right to work in jobs that were once generally considered to be for men only. (Courtesy Con Edison)

disappearing. No longer do newspapers run "help wanted" advertisements under separate headings for men and women. Men are becoming flight attendants, and women are becoming carpenters.

EQUAL PAY FOR EQUAL WORK

The Equal Pay Act of 1963 amends the Fair Labor Standards Act. It prohibits specifically the practice of paying women less money than men for doing the same work. This was one of the most serious abuses of job rights in the past. If you are a woman and have reason to suspect that male co-workers are paid more for the same work, you may file a complaint with the Wage, Hour and Public Contracts Division of the Labor Department, the same division that enforces the minimum wage law.

It was during a period of national emergency that the unfair practice of paying women less money for doing the same work as men became a public issue. During World War II many women were hired to fill the jobs left by men who entered the armed services. Women became welders in the shipyards, electricians in the airplane factories, plumbers, painters, and so on.

They did all the things that women were not supposed to be able to do.

Because the new workers were women, the companies hiring them paid them less. At that time there was a government agency called the War Labor Board. The board's responsibility was to see to it that labor was treated fairly and that labor and management got together to produce the goods needed for the war.

Soon the board began to receive complaints from women who were not being paid as much as men had been for the same work. The board ruled consistently that women must be paid the same rate for doing the same job.

Keep in mind, though, that in order for the War Labor Board—or any board—to have made such a ruling, someone had to raise the issue. The same is true today. The laws are on the books. It is up to you to see that they are working. To do this, you must be aware of them and know what your rights are and how you can register a complaint if your rights are violated. An unused law is no law at all.

Before making a complaint, however, check to see that you have your facts right. Is your claim valid? Learn whether the company can explain its actions. Read the job descriptions and other company information about hiring and promotion practices. You always, of course, should try to get company action through proper procedures before going outside the company.

Do not fear that if you complain your company will reduce everyone else's pay to your level as a means of making all pay rates equal. That is certainly illegal. A company can equalize pay rates between women and men by increasing the lower rate—never by lowering the higher rate.

Do not make the mistake of interpreting the law to mean that all workers must be paid at exactly the same rate. Obviously other factors are involved. Your rate of pay can be based on your previous experience or your length of service. Naturally, the rate of pay can be different for different kinds of jobs.

The law says only that the same factors must be used to determine the pay rate of all employees. Equal pay means equal overtime pay, vacation pay, holiday pay, and fringe benefits. Everyone must be treated the same way in all these areas.

Equal Work

"Equal pay for equal work" is easy enough to say. But it is not always so easy to define. What exactly is equal work? Here, again, the National War Labor Board established the basic policy during World War II. The board ignored minor differences in job content when applying the equal pay for equal work rule.

Generally, the law recognizes only the actual job requirements and performance in applying equal pay standards. Job classifications or titles are not used because they can be too vague or simply fail to reflect the job.

For example, one person may be called a custodian and another a janitor. But whatever these workers are called, they must be paid the same rate if they perform the same duties. On the other hand, not all clerks need be given the same rate of pay. The title "clerk" can be applied to a large number of employees doing a wide variety of work. All clerks could not automatically expect equal pay.

Job differences as well as titles are taken into account. Retail clerks may sell different kinds of merchandise, but the basic skills required to sell are similar. Thus, male and female retail clerks usually would have to be paid the same rate.

For equal pay standards to apply, three basic tests must be met. The jobs must require (1) equal skill, (2) equal effort, and (3) equal responsibility. The Wage, Hour and Public Contracts Division has given examples of what these terms mean, as described in the following sections.

The Equal Pay Act gives women the legal right to be paid the same money as men for doing the same work. (Top, courtesy United Nations, YN/PAS; bottom, Pratt)

Equal Skill

Both men and women may be classified as typists. Both spend two-thirds of their time typing or doing related activities such as proofreading and filing. The other third of their working day is spent doing different tasks. Perhaps one employee runs a calculator, and the other runs a copying machine. Their pay rates must be the same *unless* running a calculator requires more skills and can command a higher rate than running the other machine. In such cases, employers must allow all employees equal opportunity to learn to use the same machines.

Equal Effort

Two people employed as checkers in a supermarket spend part of their time on other duties. One carries out heavy packages and replaces stock, which requires lifting heavy items. The other does work that requires dexterity, such as rearranging displays of food items. The difference in their efforts does not justify different pay scales under the law. Doing something every now and then that requires extra physical or mental effort is not enough to support a finding of unequal effort which would justify paying separate rates.

However, a worker on the end of the assembly line who lifts the finished product off and puts it on a platform for shipping is entitled to a higher pay rate if he or she does this regularly.

Equal Responsibility

Situations often occur in which one employee in a group performing jobs that are equal must assume supervisory duties. Perhaps the regular supervisor is ill or on vacation or taking a business trip. A person acting as supervisor can be paid at a higher rate than others. The same is true, say, of a salesclerk who has the additional responsibility of approving checks for cashing. Such responsibility merits extra pay even if everything else the worker does is the same as the tasks of the other salesclerks. In both cases, of course, it would be illegal if only men were given the opportunity to do the more demanding work.

Additional minor responsibility does not allow an employer to set up a different pay scale. For example, a company may give a man in the office the responsibility for turning off the lights and locking up. This alone does not justify a higher rate of pay in terms of this law. The company could, of course, pay the man anything it wanted. But if it paid the man more than it paid a woman doing similar office work, the woman would have a case for getting her wages increased. The company could not then reduce the man's wage to bring about equality.

DISCRIMINATION BECAUSE OF AGE

If you think of age discrimination at all, you probably think of it in terms of companies not hiring young workers. Rightly so, from your point of view. But the law's concern is with older people. It has little bearing for you right now. But some day you might need to know there is a law protecting older people's job rights. It is unlawful for a company not to hire someone because the person is over 40 years of age.

Believe it or not, it often is harder for older people (over 40) to get work than for young people just starting out. You may find that hard to believe because personnel managers may have told you many times that they are looking for someone with more experience. But it is true. And the day may come when the age discrimination law will protect you.

UNIONS MUST RESPECT RIGHTS

Rights given to you under the law cannot be violated by a labor organization. It is illegal for a company not to hire you because of race, sex, color, religion, or national origin. It is also illegal for a union to refuse membership for these reasons. Often union membership is necessary to hold a job. Thus, a person denied membership is in effect denied a job. Labor organizations are bound by the same rules and regulations affecting companies.

If you are unable to get the company to answer a claim by following formal procedures, contact the U.S. Equal Employment Opportunity Commission (1800 G Street, N.W., Washington, DC 20506). In matters regarding equal pay, contact the Wage, Hour and Public Contracts Division of the Employment Standards Administration (U.S. Department of Labor, Washington, DC. 20210). For faster response, contact field officers first. They are listed in your telephone directory.

All workers whose jobs require equal skill, effort, and responsibility, should receive equal pay regardless of sex or regardless of any small differences in job duties. (Philip Teuscher)

Getting It All Together

1. Why should you learn about federal labor laws?

2. What are some major federal laws that affect your career?

3. When must overtime be paid, and what is the rate for workers covered under federal law?

4. Why have workers formed labor unions?

5. What are some disadvantages of belonging to a union?

6. What does the Occupational Safety and Health Act do?

7. What can you do if you believe your working conditions are unsafe?

8. What does the Equal Employment Opportunity Commission do?

YOUR PAY: WHAT'S ADDED, WHAT'S TAKEN, WHAT'S LEFT

Your goals in this unit are given in the following list:

To identify four or more basic fringe benefits most workers receive

To identify the two basic types of pension plans and know the advantages and disadvantages of each

To be aware of the benefits of the Social Security Act and its cost to you

To be able to determine how much is deducted from your pay for social security and federal income tax

To identify involuntary deductions that can be taken from your pay

Jack had every reason to be happy. He was working on his first job. His pay was $150 a week—$600 a month. Jack figured out that his rent, food, clothes, and other items would cost about $400 a month. "Great," he thought. "I'll be able to buy a car!"

Jack bought a good secondhand car. Since he did not have enough cash, he arranged to pay $150 a month for it. "No problem," he thought. But when Jack received his first pay envelope, it did not contain $150. It contained only $134.87. Jack was shocked. He raced to his supervisor, who told him to look at his pay stub. It showed a record of his pay and what happened to it.

The heading "Earnings" showed that Jack did indeed make $150 for the week. But there was another heading: "Deductions." Under it were things like "W/H Tax," "FICA," and "Disab. Ins." Jack saw that $16.35 was taken out for "W/H Tax." Another $8.78 was deducted under "FICA."

The supervisor explained that "W/H Tax" was the amount deducted for income tax payments. "FICA" was the amount taken out for social security.

smaller amounts were taken out for disability insurance and for a pension plan.

In figuring how much cash he would have, Jack had thought only of his total earnings. He should have thought about "take-home" pay instead. *Take-home pay* is the amount you have left after deductions for taxes and benefits such as insurance and a pension have been made.

You will never see it on the best-seller list, but a paycheck stub or a pay envelope is one of the most widely read items. It carries much important information for you as a worker. It tells you just how much actual cash you will have in hand at the end of the pay period. It shows your *gross*, or *total*, *earnings*. It tells you what deductions have been made and how much they are.

Your paycheck stub will not tell you everything, though, as you will learn in this unit. For example, it will not tell you how many paid holidays you can get. In this unit you will also learn about workers' benefits and what they mean in terms of deductions from your paycheck.

CHAPTER 74

FRINGE BENEFITS

Fringe benefits are an important part of your earnings. These vary from company to company and often can decide whether you will turn down one job and accept another. If the pay and hours are similar for both jobs, fringe benefits could make one job more attractive than another.

As the term suggests, *fringe benefits* are something you receive besides regular wages or a salary. They may be in the form of a cash payment. More often, they are in the form of a service or free time or an insurance plan.

Although fringe benefits do not bring you hard cash, you should not overlook their very real monetary value. Lower wages with greater benefits may be a better deal than higher wages and fewer benefits. But not always. You must decide what the final value of fringe benefits is and whether it outweighs your need to have hard cash right away.

Labor unions seek more and greater fringe benefits as well as higher pay for their members. Fringe benefits make up an important part of all contracts between labor and management. In labor negotiations, fringe benefits are often an important issue. Let's look at them closely.

PAID TIME OFF

Paid time off is a traditional fringe benefit. This time can take the form of paid holidays or paid vacations. Many companies give workers certain paid holidays such as New Year's Day, Washington's Birthday, Memorial Day, Independence Day, Thanksgiving, and Christmas. If you must work on one of these legal holidays, your company may pay you extra or give you some other time off.

Besides these regular holidays, a company may give you Good Friday, the day before or after Christmas, Yom Kippur, or some other special day. In some companies, workers can take a day off on the anniversary of the date on which they started to work.

Usually a company will have a rule that you must work a certain number of days or hours in a week before being eligible for a paid holiday in that week.

Vacation Plans

Every company has its own plan for giving paid vacations. Length of service is usually the factor that determines how much vacation time you will get. The more time you are working for a company, the more vacation time you will receive. A typical plan might be like this:

One week. Employees who are hired on or before April 15 of the year in which the vacation is taken and who have worked for 6 months prior to vacation are given 1 week of vacation at the base rate of pay. (*Base rate of pay* is regular pay. It does not include overtime pay.)

Two weeks. Employees who are hired on or before January 15 of the year in which the vacation is taken and who have worked 8 months prior to vacation are given 2 weeks of vacation at the base rate of pay.

Three weeks. Employees who will have worked 5 years prior to the year in which the vacation is taken are given 3 weeks of vacation at the base rate of pay.

In addition to the regular paid holidays, such as Christmas and Thanksgiving, a company may give employees additional paid holidays, such as Passover, Good Friday, or Chanukah. (Religious News Service Photo)

Four weeks.   Employees who will have worked 15 years prior to the year in which the vacation is taken are given 4 weeks of vacation at the base rate of pay.

Five weeks.   Employees who will have worked 25 years prior to the year in which the vacation is taken are given 5 weeks of vacation at the base rate of pay.

Other Forms of Paid Time Off

Other forms of paid time off include funeral leave, maternity leave, and sick leave. *Funeral leave* may be up to 3 days for the death of a member of your immediate family (a parent, grandparent, child, grandchild, spouse, brother or sister, including in-laws, foster-, step-, or half-relations).

Maternity leave is given to a woman employee who wants to return to work after her child is born. Company policies differ regarding this. Check to see what your company does.

Most companies grant *sick leave* according to the length of time you have been with them. Almost all companies require a waiting period. That is, if you were out for only one or two days, you would be eligible for sick pay but not for sick leave. Sick leave is granted only for longer illnesses. Some companies will continue to pay a worker who is sick for several months. Again, company policies differ. Check yours to see how many weeks are allowed for sick leave and whether you will receive full pay or half pay.

INSURANCE BENEFITS

Insurance plans—life, health, medical—paid for in full or in part by companies form another important group of fringe benefits.

Some companies provide their workers with completely paid-up life insurance that is equal to double their annual pay. The cost of such life insurance could be two or three hundred dollars. Other companies might pay part of the insurance cost so that their workers can get life insurance at a relatively low rate. Almost all companies offer some form of life insurance at low group rates.

Similar plans apply to insurance to cover medical costs, dental costs, or hospitalization. These are all important to you. The cost of such insurance could be as high as several hundred dollars a year. If your company provides any of this insurance at no cost, it is an important fringe benefit for you.

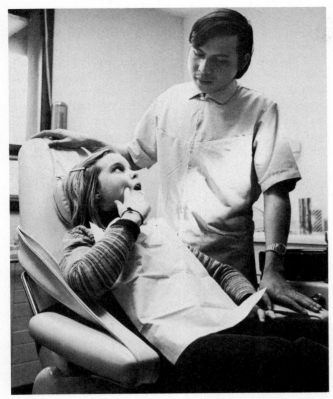

An important fringe benefit that some companies provide is insurance to cover dental costs. The insurance may also apply to the employee's family. (Philip Teuscher)

Medical and hospitalization insurance plans cover you for any injury or illness. Worker's compensation insurance pays for job-related medical costs. Since this is required by law, it is not, strictly speaking, a fringe benefit. But some companies provide more coverage than the law requires. Check to see what your company provides to a worker who suffers a job-related injury or illness.

OTHER BENEFITS

Of the many other kinds of fringe benefits, some of the common ones include:

- Being allowed to buy company products at a discount
- Being allowed to buy other products in company or related stores at a discount
- Being allowed to use company athletic equipment and exercise rooms
- Being allowed to form clubs, athletic teams, and drama groups with the company as sponsor

These are just a few of the many benefits workers may be given. There are others. Some benefits are determined by the kind of company you work for or by its location.

Many companies provide educational assistance as a fringe benefit. Some employers will pay all or part of your tuition for job-related courses taken in night school or at a college or university.

Profit sharing is a fringe benefit if it is not considered part of your regular earnings. In such a plan, employees share company profits. Some companies pay their employees annual bonuses, usually near the end of the calendar year. The size of these bonuses often is determined, too, by how much profit the company earned for the year.

Another type of fringe benefit is being allowed to buy company stock, usually at a price below the market price. This means that you are given the first chance to buy stock in the company you work for at a price below what an outsider would pay. You thus become a part owner of your company. Of course, if it is a big company with a lot of stock, your share will be relatively small. Stock in a profitable company is well worth having. The stock can increase in value. It also can pay an annual dividend, or a share of the profits for the year.

Some fringe benefits may not have monetary value but still may be important. For instance, the company may arrange to have your paycheck deposited in a checking or savings account for you. It may provide attractive rooms for coffee and lunch breaks.

Make it your business to learn what your company offers. Decide how important each benefit is. You usually would not take or leave a job just because of fringe benefits. But if all other things are equal, fringe benefits may make a difference. Also, if benefits are available, you need to know about them so that you can use them. As you develop on your job and become a full-time worker, your interest in fringe benefits will grow.

YOUR PENSION

Pensions may not be a big concern for you right now, since you are just beginning your career. Pensions are payments for older people who no longer work, and that is a long way off for you.

Still, though pensions are a long way off, you should not ignore them completely. It is never too early to begin saving and planning for your future. Besides, the kinds of pension plans available may help you to decide which job to take now.

Suppose you must choose between two jobs at different companies. Both jobs are the same from your point of view. The pay is the same, the hours are the same, and both locations are good. But one job offers a pension plan, while the other does not. You would be wise to take the job with the pension plan.

Now suppose that both companies have pension plans which pay the same amount to workers after they retire at age 65. But in one pension plan the workers must make a weekly contribution from their pay. In the other plan, the company pays, and workers do not lose any pay.

At first glance, you might think that the better plan is the one to which workers do not contribute. It might be. But, in fact, it may not be a good plan. A lot depends on how clearly workers' rights are spelled out in each plan and how firm they are.

If you contribute nothing to a pension plan, you could end up receiving nothing. If your company pays for the plan, it could end it at any time. If you contribute to your pension plan, you own part of it. Even if the company goes bankrupt, you still would receive the amount of money you paid in, as well as interest earned on it.

Another advantage of contributing to your pension plan is that you will be able to take your money with you if you change jobs. It is a form of saving. On the other hand, if you had been working at a company where you did not contribute to the pension plan, you would have nothing to take with you if you left. That might make you think twice before taking another job—even a better one. This is especially true if you have

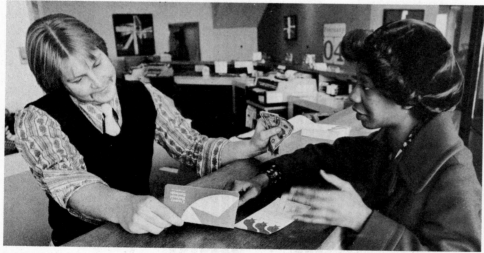

Pensions and retirement may seem far from your thoughts right now. But early planning for your retirement through some form of savings (above) may enable you to do the things that you find satisfying when you retire (below). (Philip Teuscher)

built up a few years of service and have increased the value of your pension plan. If you then leave your job for another one, you cannot transfer this value to another pension plan.

Today social security provides income for those who no longer work, and so pensions are not as important as they once were. But they still have a lot of value for most people. Although the amount of money people receive under social security has been increasing over the years, it is still not enough for most of them to meet all their needs.

Generally, pension plans allow workers to receive half pay when they retire. The best plans provide for half pay by themselves. But many plans give just a certain amount of money so that the retired person's social security and pension *together* add up to half pay.

Sixty-five has been the traditional age of retirement. But as with social security, some pension plans provide for earlier retirement—sometimes as early as age 50. Some pension plans provide for retirement after a certain number of years of employment, such as 20, regardless of age. The pension plans of the armed services do this. The pension plans of many municipal workers also provide for retirement after 20 years. Police officers, fire fighters, and sanitation workers are municipal workers who may have such plans.

Some pension plans are based on the age of the worker and the time worked. A person can retire at a certain age (say 65) or after a certain number of years on the job (say 20), whichever comes first.

Many companies require that you work a certain number of years before you can collect a pension. A standard requirement is that you must work for the company at least five years before you can be covered by a pension plan.

Many pension plans are set up as a result of negotiations with unions. In such cases, the pension plans are part of the labor contract that the company signs with the union.

Federal laws control and regulate pension plans to some extent. Their intent is to prevent workers from losing their pensions. Still, you must look out for yourself. Keep in mind that there are two basic types of pension plans: contributory (in which you pay some of your own money) and noncontributory (in which the company pays for everything). Know what rights you have under the pension plan at your company.

You can set up your own personal pension plan through a bank or an insurance company. In such a plan, you save money and deduct the amount of your savings from your income. You do not pay taxes on those savings until you retire. Even though retirement may seem a long way off, you should take steps now to prepare for it.

75

SOCIAL SECURITY: YOUR GUARANTEED PENSION

"Social security?" Bill thought. "That's like a pension, isn't it? That's for old people. You have to be 65 years old in order to get social security. It helps out when you're unable to work because of your age. But I'm young. I just started working. I have other things to think about. Social security can wait."

Well, in general Bill's right. Social security primarily helps you when you are older—when you have to retire. But there *are* benefits for people who are *under* 65. And you *do* begin making social security payments as soon as you start working. In fact, you have to get a social security number when you begin to work. Perhaps you have already filled out the necessary forms and have your social security number tucked away somewhere. Maybe you thought this was just one of the thousands of bits of red tape you went through in order to get a job.

This bit of red tape, however, represents an important change in the status of workers in the United States. At one time, most people had to worry about what would happen to them when they no longer could work because of age. Few companies, however, had pension plans for ordinary workers.

People were expected to save money for their old age. Salaries, however, were so low that most people could only feed, clothe, and house themselves and their families with the money they earned. For most workers, saving for old age was only a dream.

In the past, people were expected to support older members of their families who could no longer work. That obviously made it more difficult for the young generation to save funds for their own old age. It was something of a vicious circle. Often, families were unable to take care of parents who could no longer work. In such cases, the state or local communities provided minimum food and shelter in homes for the poor. It was grim, depressing, and hard. It was the common fate of many workers.

THE DEVELOPMENT OF SOCIAL SECURITY

Today, nearly all workers have some degree of protection for themselves and their families if they become unable to work because of age, disability, or death. In a kind of three-way partnership, you and your company contribute to a government-operated trust fund from which you will be paid monthly benefits when you can no longer work.

This program of social security was established by federal law in 1935, during the time called the Great Depression. Social security is run by the Social Security Administration.

At first, social security only provided benefits for workers who retired at age 65. This helped families when the breadwinner could no longer work but was still alive. But there was no help for families if the main worker died. The survivors received nothing.

In 1939, the social security law was changed so that survivors could be paid the worker's benefits if the worker died. Another important change made that year provided for payments to certain dependents as well as to the retired worker. That is, if a retired worker still had young children at home, social security provided a little more money to help support them.

In 1954 another important change was made in the law. Disability insurance was added. Thus,

In the earlier, agricultural society of the United States, most people produced for themselves the products they wanted and needed. But today, loss of earning power is serious because we rely on buying goods and services from other people. Thus the need for social insurance programs, as a protection against loss of income, is essential. (Editorial Photocolor Archives)

today, if you become disabled and are unable to work, you will receive monthly payments. You will receive these payments regardless of your age.

Still another important change was made in the social security program in 1965. That year medical insurance protection was provided for people 65 and over. Called Medicare, the insurance plan was designed to help older people pay their hospital bills. The law was changed further in 1973 to include people under 65 who have been receiving disability checks for two or more years.

Since the beginning of the social security program, the amount of money paid to people has more than doubled. At first, the amount of money workers received was determined by the amount they earned before retirement. The amount received never changed. As a result, many old people found that their monthly social security checks bought less and less food, clothing, or shelter when prices rose. Now social security benefits are tied into how much it costs to live. When you are qualified to receive payments, they will increase as the cost of living increases.

TO BECOME ELIGIBLE

To become eligible for social security benefits on your own (not as a survivor or dependent), you must have worked a certain number of months, and you must have earned a certain amount of money. You receive credit for one-quarter of a year's work whenever you earn $50 or more in a three-month calendar quarter. Once you have

credit for ten years of work, you are fully covered. You keep this coverage even if you never work again. Of course, if you work only ten years, your monthly payments will not be very large when you receive them at age 62 or 65.

Once you have earned social security protection, it is yours even if you change jobs, if you move from one community to another, or if you move from one state to another. Wherever your contributions come from, your social security number identifies them as yours, and computers keep a record of them throughout your working life.

TO GET YOUR NUMBER

A social security number is one of the records you should have before going to a job interview. If you have not yet gotten a social security number, do so at once. It is easy to get one. You do not need to have a job. You need only to write to, call, or visit the nearest Social Security Administration office.

To find the office, look in the telephone directory under the letter "U" for "United States Government." All federal agencies and offices are listed alphabetically under the main heading "United States Government." The number for the Social Security Administration may be in a special box labeled "frequently called numbers" at the head of the list of federal numbers. If it is not, look down the list to "H" for Health and Human Services." That is the department in which

During the great depression of the 1930s, many people lost their jobs. Without money, people stood in bread lines to get food for their families. This led to the passage of the Social Security Act of 1935 to protect families against loss of income of the breadwinner. (The Bettmann Archive, Inc.)

the Social Security Administration operates. You will find its number and address here.

One Number for Life

Tell the Social Security Administration representative that you want a social security number. The representative will give you or send you a simple application to fill out. Fill it out, and return it. In a few days you will receive a double card marked with your number. That number will be yours for the rest of your life. Put one half of the card in a safe place. Carry the other half with you.

It is helpful to memorize your social security number. You will use the number many times when filling out forms in school, on the job, and elsewhere throughout life. Your social security number is also used to keep a record of your income tax.

If You Lose Your Card

If you ever lose your social security card, let the Social Security Administration office know. The office will give you a new card with the same number on it. If you change your name, you must also let the office know so that you can get a new card with your new name but the same number. Do not use your new name to apply for a new card, because then you would have two numbers. Your future benefits could be endangered. You do *not* need to notify the Social Security Admin-

istration when you change your address or change your job.

TO USE YOUR NUMBER

You must show your social security card to your employer when you begin work. Most employers will ask to see it. If for some reason your employer does not ask for your number, be sure to bring it up. As soon as you are working in a job covered by social security, you should begin receiving credit toward future benefits.

To receive this credit, you and your company must make payments to the trust fund. Whenever you are paid, your check stub or pay envelope should show the amount of money deducted for social security. At the end of each calendar year, your company must give you a statement called a "W-2 form." It shows how much money you earned during the year, how much money was taken out for taxes, and how much money was taken out for social security. (For more information on W-2 forms, see Chapter 76.)

If your company does not deduct money for social security, or if you do not get a statement of the total amount deducted at the end of the year, contact the nearest Social Security Administration office.

HOW MUCH IS DEDUCTED

Sue had just begun working as a dental technician. She visited her local Social Security Admin-

Social security offices will answer your questions about social security, supply information about various programs and benefits, and help you to apply for benefits. There are more than 850 social security offices throughout the country. (Left, Social Security Administration; right, courtesy Internal Revenue Service)

istration office and talked with Ms. Eleanor Lopez, the manager. "How do I know if they are taking the right amount out of my pay?" Sue asked. "I mean, how much is taken out each week? Is it the same for everyone?"

"Good questions," Ms. Lopez replied. "To answer your last question first, yes and no. The same *percentage* is taken out of everyone's pay. Therefore, the more you make, the more you contribute—and the more you get back when you retire."

The Amount Is Changing

Ms. Lopez explained that the percentage taken out has been changing and will continue to change at least until 1987. In 1977, workers paid 5.85 percent of their earning into social security. In 1980, workers paid 6.13 percent. By 1987, they will pay 7.15 percent.

"You will pay this percentage of your earnings only up to a specific amount each year. When the rate taken is 6.65 percent, the most a worker pays in any one year is $1,975.05. As the rate increases, so does the earnings limit taxed. Your employer must match the amount you pay into the fund."

What FICA Is

Joe, an electrician's helper, knew all about social security payments and other deductions. So when

he received his first paycheck, he carefully examined the stub that carried this information. He saw that money had been taken out for something called FICA, but there was nothing for social security. This concerned him, and he went to see his supervisor.

"Excuse me, Mr. Sancour," he said. "I think there has been a mistake on my deductions."

"Oh?" Mr. Sancour answered. "In what way?"

"Well, look here," Joe said. "There's nothing taken out for social security. You did take out money for something called FICA, which I don't understand."

Mr. Sancour smiled. "That confuses a lot of people, Joe," he said. "Typical government style. Everyone expects to see the social security deduction listed under letters such as 'SS.' But instead the deduction is listed under 'FICA.'"

"Huh?" Joe asked. "What for?"

"Well, it makes sense. At least to the government," Mr. Sancour explained. "*FICA* stands for Federal Insurance Contributions Act. That's the law under which the federal government takes your contribution and the amount the company adds to it. The money is put into the trust fund for your social security benefits."

"So the amount shown deducted under FICA is my social security payment?" Joe asked, to make sure he had it right.

"Yes," Mr. Sancour said. "And it is listed that way on the W-2 form I give you at the end of the year and on all income tax forms."

HOW MUCH YOU GET BACK

"What I'd like to know is how much money I'm going to get back when I'm 65," Kay, a salesperson, said. "Do we all get the same amount?" She was calling Mr. Jackson at the local social security office.

"No. It depends on how much you make," Mr. Jackson told her. "But there is a minimum amount and a maximum amount. The amount of your monthly benefits will depend on your average earnings over a period of years."

He said it is not possible to figure exactly what Kay, a new worker, will be receiving. Kay's salary will change during the years she works. But if she were to work the maximum number of years at the maximum salary covered, she could receive over $400 a month when she retires at 65. If she has dependents—people she must support—she could receive more than $700 a month. The amount of the payment depends on the amount earned as well as on the number of dependents.

No Double Payments

"Suppose I get married and my husband and I both work. I guess we will both be paying in," Kay said. "Do we get double benefits? And if I become a widow, do I get widow's benefits plus those benefits I earned in my own right?"

"Yes, you both pay in. But your benefits do not double," Mr. Jackson said. "You would be entitled to benefits either on your own earnings record or on your husband's, whichever gives you the larger amount. The same thing is true if you are a widow. You would not get double benefits. But you would receive benefits for any dependent children you might have."

Benefits for Widowers

Art, a carpenter, called his local social security office and asked a slightly different question. "If a widow gets benefits for herself and for dependent children when her working husband dies, do I get the same benefits if my working wife dies?"

"No," Ms. Greenberg said. "The man, a widower, would not receive any benefits that his wife earned—either for himself or for his dependent children—unless he can prove that the entire family had been dependent on her earnings."

"That doesn't seem fair," Art complained.

Medicare Benefits

"A lot of people agree with you, Art," Ms. Greenberg said. "There are cases in court right now. The law may soon be changed."

"I hope so," Art said. "And can you tell me just what Medicare is about?"

"It is a form of hospital insurance," Ms. Greenberg said. "When you are 65 and are receiving monthly payments, you also will be covered by Medicare. Any hospital bills you have will be paid under this program."

Earlier Retirement

"By the way, Art," Ms. Greenberg said. "You do not have to be 65 to retire and collect benefits. You can retire at say, 62. But if you retire earlier, the amount of your monthly payments will be smaller. If you work after age 65, your benefits can be higher. Also, you would not be covered by Medicare if you retire before 65—except if you were disabled."

Benefits for Widows or Children

Beside the benefits noted above, if you are a widow and your husband was covered by social security, you will receive monthly benefits for children you must support—your dependents. You receive these payments even if you continue to work.

Disability Payments

You can begin receiving social security benefits before age 65 if you become disabled and cannot work. Even if you became disabled before you reached age 24, you would receive payments if you had worked for 1½ years during the 3 years before becoming disabled. It is important to have an idea of how much money you will get under social security when you retire or how much money your survivors will receive if you die. Knowing this can help you make good decisions about joining pension plans, saving money, and buying life insurance.

HOW TO FILE FOR BENEFITS

When you retire, you need to show some simple proofs to the nearest social security office. You need your social security number, a birth certificate or other record of your age, and your most recent W-2 form or tax return form. If you are applying for disability payments, you must have proof of the disability. If you are the surviving spouse of a worker who has died, and you are

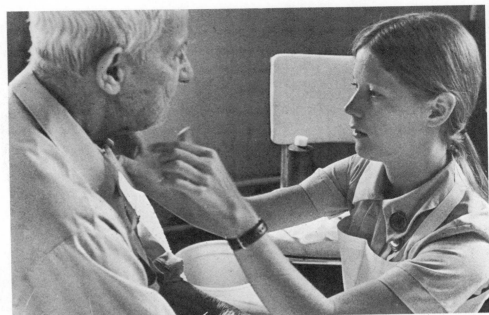

Social security benefits are available to those who become disabled before the age of 62. (Courtesy Visiting Nurse Service of New York)

eligible for survivors' benefits, you must submit proof of the worker's death.

JOBS NOT COVERED

While most jobs in this country are now covered by social security, a few are not. It is possible that your job could be one of these, or it may have special provisions. Social security does not cover you if you are under 21 and work for your parents, or if you work in the private home of your employer. Baby-sitting is an example of such a job. If you work on a farm or have a job that brings a large part of your income from tips, you come under special provisions. Check with the local office of the Social Security Administration for information on rules for these jobs.

CHAPTER 76

PAYING YOUR INCOME TAX

Throughout your working life, you will have to pay a tax on your earnings to the federal government. This is called an *income tax.* The government makes it relatively easy for you to pay your income tax by requiring the company you work for to take it out of your paycheck. This is known as *tax withholding.*

You should know the amount of your withholding tax. It makes up most of the difference between your *earned pay* (the total amount of money you have earned by your work) and your *take-home pay,* or *net pay* (the amount of money you have left to spend after taxes have been withheld). Generally, withholding taxes are the federal income tax and your social security contribution. In some areas, state and city taxes may be withheld, too.

Other amounts may also be deducted from your pay—payments for a pension plan, or for group medical insurance, or for a savings plan. These additional deductions are voluntary. You can start and stop them whenever you wish.

You cannot stop or start tax withholding. Your company must take out a certain amount. The minimum amount and the maximum amount are set by law. Within these limits, you do have some control over the amount withheld for your federal income tax (but not for your social security payment).

WHAT IS TAXED?

Not all your income is taxed. Another important term you should understand is *gross income.* This is *all* the money you make. It includes all your wages or salary as well as any other income—

from a second job, tips, or interest on savings. If you win a gambling bet, for example, the winnings are counted as part of your gross income for the year in which you won the bet. Just about any money you receive is considered part of your gross income for tax purposes. One of the few exceptions is scholarship assistance.

Gross income is the starting point for determining how much income tax you owe. You do not need to pay a tax on your gross income, however. You are allowed to subtract certain amounts from it. You are taxed on the remainder, which is called your *taxable income.*

EXEMPTIONS

The tax you owe is withheld automatically, but you do have something to say about how much is withheld, within limits. Two factors determine the amount withheld from your pay: (1) how much you earn and (2) how many *exemptions* you claim.

When figuring your tax, you can deduct $1,000 from your gross earnings for every exemption you claim. The exemption is an allowance for every dependent you support. Everyone is entitled to claim one exemption—for herself or himself. This is called a *personal exemption.*

The more exemptions you claim, the less tax you owe, and the less money will be taken out of your pay each pay period. On the other hand, the fewer exemptions you claim—and you do not need to claim any for withholding purposes—the more money will be taken out of your pay.

It would not be legal to claim more exemptions than you really have. But many people claim fewer exemptions for withholding purposes. As a

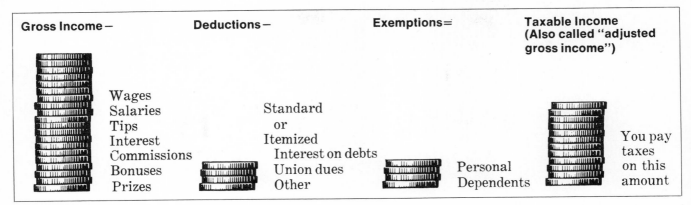

Gross Income —	Deductions —	Exemptions =	Taxable Income (Also called "adjusted gross income")
Wages Salaries Tips Interest Commissions Bonuses Prizes	Standard or Itemized Interest on debts Union dues Other	Personal Dependents	You pay taxes on this amount

Taxable income is your gross income minus deductions and exemptions.

result, more money is taken out of their pay during the year than they will owe for taxes at the end of the year.

Some people claim fewer exemptions to be sure that enough money is taken out during the year. If enough money is not taken out of your pay, you will have to make up the difference when you file your tax return. You would be in trouble if you claimed more exemptions for withholding than you were entitled to. At the end of the year you would owe quite a lot of taxes.

Some people claim fewer exemptions as a form of saving money. At the end of the year they get back the extra money they have paid to the government. They feel that the refund check is something of a bonus. Actually this is not true. They do not get any interest on their refund money, as they would if they put it in a bank. Nor can they get the money if they need it before they file a tax return.

Should You Claim Exemptions?

If you are single and do not support any relatives, your choice is limited. You can either claim one exemption or none. If you claim none, the amount withheld is based on your gross income as if it were your taxable income. When you file your income tax return, you then would claim the one exemption allowed you. The $1,000 would be deducted from your gross income, and your tax would be based on the rest (taxable income). You would owe less than you had paid, and therefore you would receive a refund check.

You have more choices if you are married. If your spouse does not work, you can claim one exemption for him or her as well as one for

yourself. Thus you can claim two exemptions. If you both work, each of you can claim one exemption, but not two. One person could still claim two exemptions, but the other person then would not be able to claim any. Some married couples who work have made the mistake of claiming both themselves and each other. The result has been that they have owed a large sum of unpaid taxes at the end of the year.

A worker supporting minor children can claim an exemption of $1,000 for each child. Thus a worker with two children and a spouse who is not working could claim four exemptions (one for each person). With four exemptions, the worker deducts $4,000 from his or her gross income (4 × $1000). If the worker's gross income was $15,000, the taxable income would be $11,000 ($15,000 − $4,000).

If you are under 19, or if you are a full-time student and are supported by your family, your parents can claim you as an exemption whether you earn more than $1,000 or not. But once you turn 19 and are no longer a full-time student, your parents cannot claim an exemption for you if you earn more than $1,000. Even if your parents claim you as a dependent, as they would while you are in school, you can still claim your own personal exemption of $1,000 if you are working and must file an income tax return.

To determine exactly how much money should be withheld for your rate of pay and number of exemptions, check with the tables that the government provides for the use of your employer. These tables are easy to read, and your employer should let you see them. If you are not allowed access to them at your place of work, you can get them from the Internal Revenue Service or from the post office.

Form W-4

Employee's Withholding Allowance Certificate

Department of the Treasury
Internal Revenue Service

This certificate is for income tax withholding purposes only. It will remain in effect until you change it. If you claim exemption from withholding, you will have to file a new certificate on or before April 30 of next year.

Type or print your full name
MARIA J SANCHEZ

Your social security number
123-45-6789

Home address (number and street or rural route)
300 W. 75ᵗʰ STREET, 2B

City or town, State, and ZIP code
NEW YORK, NY 10023

Marital Status

☒ Single ☐ Married
☐ Married, but withhold at higher Single rate
NOTE: *If married, but legally separated, or spouse is a nonresident alien, check the single block.*

1 Total number of allowances you are claiming . . . . | 1
2 Additional amount, if any, you want deducted from each pay (if your employer agrees) . . . . $
3 I claim exemption from withholding (see instructions). Enter "Exempt" . . . .

Under the penalties of perjury, I certify that the number of withholding exemptions and allowances claimed on this certificate does not exceed the number to which I am entitled. If claiming exemption from withholding, I certify that I incurred no liability for Federal income tax for last year and that I anticipate that I will incur no liability for Federal income tax for this year.

Signature ▶ *Maria J. Sanchez*   Date ▶ 12/12   19--

Detach along this line

1 Control number   222   2 Employer's State number

3 Employer's name, address, and ZIP code
XYZ BROADCASTING COMPANY
800 THIRD AVENUE
NEW YORK, NY 10022

4 Subtotal Correction Void
☐ ☐ ☐

5 Employer's identification number
10-1112131

6 Advance EIC payment   7

8 Employee's social security number
123-45-6789

9 Federal income tax withheld
1,288.90

10 Wages, tips, other compensation
8,145,76

11 FICA tax withheld
388.01

12 Total FICA wages
8,084.22

13 Employee's name (first, middle, last, and address
MARIA J. SANCHEZ
300 W. 75ᵗʰ STREET, 2B
NEW YORK, NY 10023

14 Pension plan coverage? Yes/No
NO

15

16 FICA tips

18 State income tax withheld
207.07

19 State wages, tips, etc.
8,145 76

20 Name of state
NEW YORK

21 Local income tax withheld
45.14

22 Local wages, tips, etc.
8,145.76

23 Name of locality
NEW YORK City

Copy 1 For State, City, or Local Tax Department
Employee's and employer's copy compared. ☐

Wage and Tax Statement 19--

On a W-4, or Employee's Withholding Allowance Certificate, you tell your employer whether you are single or married and how many exemptions you are claiming. What does a W-2 form show you?

FORM W-4

When you begin working, your boss should give you a W-4 form to fill out. The full name of this important form is "Employee's Withholding Allowance Certificate." But everyone refers to it as the W-4. The W-4, the W-2, and the 1040 or 1040A are the basic forms you use when figuring your income tax. The W-4 form tells your employer whether you are single or married and how many exemptions you are claiming. You fill out a W-4 form whenever you start a new job or whenever the number of your exemptions changes (through marriage, divorce, birth, or death).

If you work two jobs, you fill out a W-4 at each job. In such a situation, do not claim the same exemptions twice—not even your personal exemption. If you claim all your exemptions at one job, you cannot claim any at a second job.

FORM W-2

Your W-2 form is very important. Your employer must give you this filled-out form before January 31 each year. It will show you the total amount of money you earned during the year, the total amount of money withheld for income tax, and the total amount of money withheld for social security.

You should be given at least two copies of this form. You must send one copy in with your federal income tax form. You keep the second copy for your own records. In some states, your employer may give you a third copy of the W-2 form. This is for state or local taxes. You should have a W-2 form from every company you worked for during the year.

FILING A TAX RETURN

The law requires you to file an income tax return for any year in which you earned more than $3,300. An *income tax return* is a statement of your earnings and taxes owed. The government supplies the forms you must use.

As a practical matter, you will want to file a return for any year in which you had income tax withheld from your pay, even if you do not owe any tax. If you do not owe any tax, the money withheld from your pay will be returned. This will not happen automatically. You *must* file an income tax form to get this money back. You have until April 15 to file an income tax return for the previous year.

What Form You Should File

The simplest form the government supplies for you to use is called "Short Form 1040A." Many people use this because it is easy to fill out.

You can use the short form if all your earned income came from wages, salaries, and tips, and if you did not have more than $400 in unearned income (that is, from dividends or interest). *Earned income* is all the money you received for working or performing a service. *Unearned income* is money you receive in the form of interest on a savings account, or in the form of dividends for stocks or bonds you own.

The short form is easy to use. It has a place to show the amount you earned and the amount withheld for taxes. A tax table helps you figure out how much you owe.

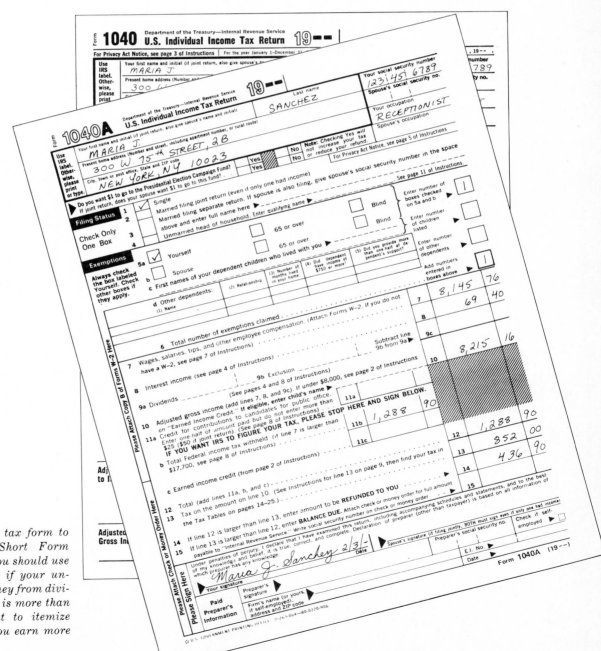

The easiest income tax form to complete is the Short Form 1040A. However, you should use the long form 1040 if your unearned income (money from dividends and interest) is more than $400, if you want to itemize deductions, or if you earn more than $10,000.

If the amount of tax you owe for the year is greater than the amount withheld during the year, you must send the difference in when you file your return. If the amount you owe is less than the amount withheld, you can ask that a refund be sent to you, or you can have this money applied to next year's tax.

What You Can Deduct

You are allowed to deduct from your taxable income the amount you spend for certain things. You can deduct money spent for some kinds of taxes and for interest on loans. You can deduct money given to charity. You can deduct some of the money you spent for medical expenses. These are just some of the more common deductions that people take. There are others.

If you are using the long form (form 1040), you must list every deduction that you claim. The long form provides you with space to do this. The law is quite clear about what items you can deduct, and the 1040 form lists most of them.

In claiming deductions, you must be able to prove that you spent the money as you say you did. Such proof usually would be in the form of a receipt showing that you paid interest or a tax, or that you gave money to charity.

Adjusted Gross Income

Adjusted gross income is another phrase you should be aware of when preparing an income tax return, although you are not likely to use it when you are first starting to work, except in one instance. Here's what it means:

Your gross income is *all* the money you receive in a year. It is the base from which your taxable income is figured. Although you must declare all money received, you are allowed to eliminate certain kinds of income for tax purposes. That is, you can adjust your gross income by deducting any money you received for sick pay, for business expenses, or for moving expenses. Sick pay was discussed earlier. Business expenses include money spent for supplies or for anything else you need to run your business. Moving expenses might be encountered early in your career. If you must move to be near your job, and your company pays the cost, you must declare the payment as part of your income. But then you can deduct that payment from your gross income.

Where To Get Forms

The Internal Revenue Service (IRS) is the government branch that collects income taxes. It mails either the regular 1040 or the short form (1040A) to taxpayers. If it is your first year as a worker, however, you might not receive a tax form. In that case, go to the nearest post office to pick up the form you need. Do the same thing if the IRS sends you the short form and you have decided to use the long form.

FILLING OUT FORMS

When filling out any income tax form, you can round off to the nearest dollar. That means you do not need to bother adding up cents. If an item is $150.49, for example, you can drop the 49 cents. If it is $150.51 you can make it $151. In short, everything from 1 cent to 49 cents can be dropped. Everything from 50 cents to 99 cents can be made a full dollar. If you round off numbers throughout the form, you will find that the total amounts come out even.

Where To Get Help

The Internal Revenue Service has offices in most cities. The people working for the IRS in those offices are there to help you. If you have any trouble filling out a form or any question about your income tax, go see them, or call them on the phone. If you are not near an IRS office, you will find a toll-free number to call in your telephone directory. Remember to look under the letter "U" first for "United States Government."

Despite what you may have heard, the income tax forms are not difficult to fill out, especially the 1040 and the 1040A (short form). Read the forms carefully, and use your common sense.

When To Send Forms

You must attach a copy of your W-2 to the form you return to the IRS. Remember that your employer should have mailed you your W-2 forms before the end of January. If you have not received the forms by that time, you should ask where they are. If you have not received a W-2 in time to make the deadline for filing your return (April 15), file a return with the IRS anyway. Include a statement explaining how you determined any tax withheld for which you claim credit.

If you have any trouble filling out your income tax forms, you can get help from the Internal Revenue Office nearest you. (Courtesy Internal Revenue Service)

You should keep copies of the tax returns you send to the IRS. You may later need to check on mistakes. Also, they will help you prepare a return the following year.

If April 15 falls on a Saturday, a Sunday, or a holiday, you have until the first day that is not a weekend or a holiday to file. Otherwise, the deadline is midnight on April 15. If you have your tax return in the mail before midnight on April 15, you are on time. If not, you are late, and you could be required to pay a penalty.

If your return shows that you owe money, you must send the money in with the return, unless it is less than a dollar, in which case you can forget it. Do not send cash through the mail. Pay by check or by money order, and write your social security number on your payment. Do this even though the number is already on your return.

Send your return in at least a day or two early, if at all possible. The government does not consider the tax paid until the check (if that is what you use) is paid by the bank. You can go to an office of the Internal Revenue Service (see the telephone directory for its location) and pay in cash. If you do this, you will be given a receipt to show that you paid. Save it! Mistakes do happen, and if the Internal Revenue Service has no record of your payment, you must be able to prove that you made it.

Where To Send Forms

You can get a list showing you where to send your returns wherever income tax forms are available. Persons in different states send their returns to different places. You do not send them to Washington, DC.

Before mailing in your form, check it to make sure that your arithmetic is correct. Also make sure that you have signed the form, and that your name, address, and social security number are correct. If you do make an error, you can get forms from the Internal Revenue Service to make corrections.

Your employer should post information about income tax on bulletin boards where you can easily see it, especially when there are changes in the law. Your employer should also let you know where to get other forms and additional information about taxes.

77

DEBTS, DUES, AND OTHER DEDUCTIONS: HANDLING WHAT'S LEFT

You control deductions from your pay, except for taxes and one other item: an involuntary deduction that occurs when your wages have been *garnisheed*. What happens when your wages are garnisheed? What does that unpleasant-sounding word mean?

GARNISHMENT

Garnishment is a procedure through which a person or a firm can arrange to have money you owe deducted from your pay.

Obviously, you will not experience garnishment unless you allow yourself to get very much in debt or if you ignore a legal debt. In either of those cases, your creditor—the person to whom you owe money—can go to court and get a court order. This court order will tell your employer to withhold a certain amount of money from your pay each week and to pay it to the creditor.

Federal law limits the amount of money that can be withheld from anyone's paycheck in this way. The amount that can be garnisheed cannot be more than 25 percent of your *disposable earnings* (the amount of your take-home pay, or the money left after all deductions required by law have been made).

There are some exceptions to this 25-percent limit. It does not apply to court orders that involve support for dependents, such as a child, or debts due to state or federal taxes.

If a person has less than $60 a week in disposable income, then those earnings cannot be garnisheed.

The law prohibits a company from firing an employee simply because his or her wage has been garnisheed for one debt. But it does not protect a person whose wage is garnisheed for more than one debt, even if all the money is owed to the same creditor. Such an employee can be fired. It would not be worth the company's time to keep all the necessary garnishment records. A company probably would not want to keep such an employee. Indebtedness resulting in garnishment indicates a serious problem on the part of the employee.

If you are a person in debt, you can agree to have some of your wages "assigned" to meet a debt. The company then deducts the money automatically until the debt is paid. This has the same effect as garnishment, but since you take the step on your own, it does not appear to be as bad as garnishment.

CHECKOFF

There are many voluntary deductions that might be taken from your pay. Union dues are often deducted. Many companies agree to deduct these dues automatically. When this is done, the deduction is called a *checkoff*. Unions like the checkoff and try to have it written into their contracts. It is an easy way to collect the dues, and it helps keep the union strong.

If the checkoff is written into a contract between labor and management, and if you are required to be a member of the union, your control of this deduction is limited. In such a situation, it is an involuntary deduction.

SAVINGS AND INSURANCE

If you pay part of the premiums for the life, health, or medical insurance offered by your company, that amount will be deducted from your paycheck. You can decide how much of each kind of insurance you want and how much you are willing to pay.

You might want to join a company savings plan, if your company has one. Under such a plan, money is deducted from your pay and deposited into a savings account. The account could be either in a local bank or in a company *credit union*. Many companies have credit unions. They operate like banks, but they lend money to employees at a lower rate of interest, and they pay higher rates of interest on savings than banks do.

In some companies, you can have money deducted to buy United States savings bonds or stock in the company.

KEEP RECORDS

Not all the deductions described above will be taken out every pay period. Some might be taken out once a month, while others will be withheld every other week. You need to know how much will be taken out and when so that you can know how much cash you will have in hand for each pay period.

You can change or end most voluntary deductions whenever you want. An exception, as noted, might be union dues at a company where union membership is a condition of employment.

Your check stub or pay envelope should give you a complete record of every amount that is deducted from your pay. It should also show why the money was deducted. Your W-2 form will, at the end of each year, show how much money you earned and how much was deducted for taxes and social security. But it will *not* show how much was deducted for other things.

It is a good idea to keep your paycheck stubs or pay envelopes for a year or two. In this way, you will have a record of how much you paid for each item. Also, if you are in a savings plan, you should receive periodic statements of your savings and interest. And if you are in a savings bond program, you will receive the bonds when they are paid for.

HANDLING WHAT'S LEFT

Now that you have learned about the various deductions from your paycheck, you can see why it is important to think of your net pay rather than your gross pay. Your net pay is what you will have left to spend. And there will be something left for you to spend after all the deductions have been made. You should try to use this remaining money wisely. That's the way to get the most for your money. Job satisfaction and fulfillment are important, but the main reason many people work is to earn money. It makes sense to try to get the most out of what you earn.

Budgets

Setting up a budget is the first step toward using your money wisely. A budget does not need to be elaborate. Simply make a list of your expenses on a weekly, biweekly, or monthly basis. Basic items would be food, clothes, shelter (rent), and transportation. These are expenses you will have to meet.

After subtracting these expenses from your net pay, you can decide what to do with what's left. You probably will want to spend some money on entertainment for yourself: books, movies, concerts, whatever.

Name	Pay Period Ending	Gross	Hosp.	Union	C. Union	FICA	W/H	NET
D.R. Public	8/22	150.00	2.95	2.50	5.25	8.78	16.35	124.17

Your check stub or pay envelope should give you a complete record of all money that has been deducted from your pay. It should also show you why the money was deducted.

Budgets and Saving

It's a good idea not to spend all the money you have left after paying necessary expenses. Put a little away each payday. It is true that because of social security and pensions you probably will not need to worry as much about old age as your grandparents did. But money saved can make the difference between just getting by after you retire and being able to take trips and do other interesting things.

But forget about retirement for a moment. There are many good reasons for budgeting and saving. When you want to make a major purchase, you will need a large sum of money. The more you have, the less you will have to borrow, and the less interest you will have to pay. By budgeting—putting aside a small amount each payday until you have enough to make the purchase—you can save money.

It is also good to have money put aside for emergencies. Again, you do not need to worry as much as your grandparents did about having money for hospital and doctor bills or for when you might be out of work because of illness or other reasons. As you have read, many federal and state programs will help protect you in emergencies. Unfortunately, though, money available under state and federal programs is not always enough to cover your needs in an emergency. Having some money put aside will help in such situations.

Banks

The easiest way to save, of course, is through a company credit union or a company savings bond program. That way you can have a certain amount deducted from your pay. Since you never get the money, you are not tempted to spend it. Saving becomes automatic.

The same is true about borrowing. If your company has a credit union or some other plan for borrowing money, you will find it is the simplest way to borrow. Again, you repay the money automatically.

Another reason for using company credit unions to save or borrow is that the interest rates are usually more favorable to you. You may, however, work at a company that does not provide such services. In that case, you will have to deal with banks. At some time in your life you probably will deal with a bank for making a major purchase, such as buying a house, that you cannot arrange through a company credit union.

Everyone should know something about banks.

The first thing to know about banks is that they are not all alike. There are basically two kinds of banks: savings banks and commercial banks.

Although savings banks and commercial banks are becoming more alike, they do not pay the same amount of interest on savings accounts. Savings banks tend to pay a higher interest. Do not assume that all banks offer the same interest rate. When you want to open a savings account, learn what interest is paid at several banks. Also, some banks pay interest from the day of deposit to the day of withdrawal. Others do not. Some *compound* the interest—that is, they pay interest on the interest. Others pay interest only on the deposit. Shop around.

It is easy to open a savings account. You simply fill out some forms (requiring your name, address, and signature) and make your deposit. Usually a minimum deposit is required, but it is only a few dollars.

Shop around when borrowing money. Some banks charge a higher rate of interest than others. Companies other than banks also loan money. But be careful when borrowing. Look closely at the interest rate that will be charged. Learn exactly how much you will have to repay.

Checking Accounts

You already know that it is important to keep records. Records can help you spend your money wisely and can protect you. A checking account is a good thing to have. It gives you an almost automatic record of what you spend.

It makes sense to use checks to pay your bills. With checks, you always have a record of payment and are less likely to pay twice. If the company you owe money to loses its records—and that happens—you will have your own record to prove you paid.

Using checks is often safer than paying by cash. You probably will pay many bills by mail, and it is not safe to send cash through the mail. A check is better. You could, of course, pay by money order, but that means a trip to the post office or a bank each time you want to pay a bill.

You get a double record when you use checks. First, you have the stub that you make out each time you write a check. This has the same information that is on the check. Second, after the check has been cashed, you will get the canceled check back. Keep canceled checks. They show that the people or companies you sent them

There are many good reasons for budgeting and saving.
What other reasons can you think of?

to have received them and cashed them.

Just as banks and interest rates differ, so do checking accounts. Some banks charge for each check. Others do not charge anything. Some banks, where state law allows, pay interest on money in a checking account if you maintain a set balance.

Some banks require you to maintain a minimum balance in your checking account. Others let you drop below a minimum balance but charge you a fee for checks when you do. Some have no minimum-balance requirement.

Savings banks in some states may offer checking accounts. But some people do business with two banks. They have a checking account in a commercial bank and a savings account in a savings bank, where the interest is higher. Since dealing with two banks may be inconvenient, some people keep both their checking and savings accounts in a commercial bank, even though commercial banks may pay less interest. The laws about interest rates and banking services change often, and you should look around carefully when setting up a checking account.

A Final Benefit

Savings and checking accounts help you use your money wisely and provide you with needed records. They also have another important benefit: They provide you with a *credit reference.* That is, they show you are trustworthy and pay your debts. Credit references are important when you want to arrange a loan for an automobile or get a mortgage for a house. When you apply for such loans, the bank or other lending institution will ask for credit references. Savings and checking accounts are two of the best you can have. They show that you can handle money wisely.

To some extent, you are following your career in order to earn money for what you need. The information in this chapter will make it easier for you to use your money wisely. As a result, you can be free of money problems and can use your energy at work to develop your talents and interests. You will not have to wonder—as some people do—why you are working in the first place. When you make your money work for you, you will be happy to work for it.

Getting It All Together

1. What are some fringe benefits that most workers enjoy?

2. What are two basic kinds of pension plans, and what are their advantages and disadvantages?

3. What major benefits do workers receive under social security?

4. How much must you contribute to social security each year?

5. What payroll deductions are required by law?

6. What payroll deductions can you choose to take?

7. Who must file an income tax return?

8. What are some basic differences between commercial banks and savings banks?

24

DEALING WITH LAYOFFS AND INJURIES

Your goals in this unit are given in the following list:

To be prepared for a course of positive action if you lose your job

To be able to develop a program of action if you are injured or disabled on the job

To understand worker's compensation

To know where to go for job-related help and information

The beginning of your career is a time for happiness and confidence. It is not a time for sad thoughts—especially about losing your proudly won position.

The realities of life are such, though, that many of you at different times in your careers may face the prospects of losing a job.

Even if you never lose your job, you may lose days of work because of an accident or injury. You may even be disabled on the job and have to stop working.

It is important for you to begin your career with positive thoughts of advancement and security through improved skills and experience. At the same time, you should be aware of the possibility of becoming jobless so that you will know what to do if it happens to you. Consider the following three cases:

Jonathan never imagined that he might one day lose his job. He was a very good bookkeeper. In five years he had been given several raises and had even been promoted to office manager. His future looked bright. But one day that future turned dark. The company was sold to another, larger one. The two office staffs were combined, and many people in Jonathan's company lost their jobs. Jonathan was one of them.

Jonathan panicked. He collected his last paycheck and then went home to worry. He did not know what he would

do when the money was gone. He did not know where to turn for help. Jonathan did not have a plan of action for seeking a new job. He wasted many weeks deciding what to do.

Lori worked in the same office as Jonathan. She had been there almost as long as he and had also been successful in her job. But Lori had made it a point to learn what she could and should do if she suddenly lost her job. If Lori loses her job, she will be ready to act.

George was hurt badly one day while working in the mill. He was taken to the hospital. The doctor told George that he probably would have to stay in the hospital for several weeks.

"I can't afford it," George said. The thought of losing his pay besides having large hospital bills was almost worse than the pain he felt.

"Well, you have a sick leave plan at your company," the doctor said.

"Oh, that's right," George said. "I guess I'll get my pay. But I still won't be able to afford to pay you and the hospital."

"Haven't you heard about worker's compensation?" the doctor asked.

"No," George said. "I'll have to look into it."

In this unit you will learn about worker's compensation and unemployment insurance. And you will learn where to get help when you are out of work.

WHEN YOU LOSE YOUR JOB

Losing your job and being out of work are hard to take. The older you are, the harder it is. But it is not easy at any age. For a long time—from about World War II on—this country has enjoyed steady and increasing employment. There have been only a few times when many people lost their jobs and were out of work for a while. Usually this happened at different locations. A mine might shut down. A certain kind of business might fail. It was not a national situation.

In the early and mid-1970s, however, the job situation changed for the worse. More people throughout the nation became unemployed during this period than during any other time since the Great Depression before World War II.

Being unemployed may mean moving to another place to find work. It may mean giving up something that you are used to, such as your automobile. The first three things most people cut back on when they lose their jobs are gasoline, food, and utilities such as heating, gas, and electricity.

It is important that you do not feel hopeless or useless if you lose a job. If you lose the job through some fault of your own, work to correct that fault while looking for another job. If you lose your job through no fault of your own, its loss does not reflect on your ability. Keep that thought firmly in mind.

A lost job can mean that you have to begin over in another career. The younger you are, the easier it will be to change careers. Always keep the possibility of change in mind. Change may be for the best. Do not try to keep your line of work or career if all opportunities for it have passed. A person who continues to make buggy whips long after the last buggy has been junked is not facing the facts.

It May Be Your Fault

There are several reasons why you might lose your job. You can control some situations. Others you can do nothing about. One basic reason why you might lose a job is that you do not do it well. But if you have prepared for your career, have chosen your first position wisely, and have been carefully selected by the company, this situation should not occur.

Of course, you will not know everything about your new job the first day you start. You will have a lot to learn. That is expected. But as long as you are willing and able to learn, you will not need to fear losing your job because you cannot perform. You will be given a period of probation during which you will be expected to learn the job.

Companies do not want workers to fail. That is why personnel managers interview prospective employees. They are making a choice, just as you are. And they, too, want to make the right choice.

Another basic reason why you might be dismissed is that you have a poor attitude. You might be a good worker and do your job well, but a poor work attitude will count against you. If you are rude, or unclean, or always late, you will not last long on any job. You must be able to get along with your co-workers and supervisors.

It May Not Be Your Fault

Your ability to do the job and your attitude are two factors you can control. However, you could lose your position for reasons that are outside your control. For example, you could lose your job if:

436

- Your company shuts down or reduces its work force because business is bad.
- Your company adopts new processes or procedures that bypass your job.
- Your company moves to another part of the country.
- Your company is sold.

Although you cannot control situations like these, there are some things you can do if they happen. If your company is changing its processes, you might learn the new processes. If your job is being eliminated, you might learn a new job in the company. If your company decides to move to another part of the country, you might be given the choice of moving with it.

Except in rare cases, the loss of a job should not come as a complete surprise. There almost always are signs. An employer usually will let you know if your work is not satisfactory. It is more difficult, of course, if you are unaware of your own faults. There are usually signs when a company is in trouble and may close. There are also signs that indicate a company might be moving or changing its methods of operation. Don't bury your head in the sand and ignore such signs. Being prepared is half the battle. Usually, the only question is "When?" You might see a change coming within the next month or year, but the exact date may be unknown.

NOTICE AND SEVERANCE PAY

Whatever the reason for an employee's dismissal, all reputable companies will give at least two weeks' *notice.* That is, your supervisor will tell you two weeks in advance that you will no longer have a job. Some companies will give you two weeks' pay and let you go right away. The reason for giving notice is the same: It gives you a chance to look around and find another job before your pay has ended.

If a company closes, moves, or eliminates jobs, the custom is to give workers *severance pay.* The amount of severance pay depends on

You can sometimes lose your job for reasons beyond your control. But be aware of early warnings. Don't bury your head in the sand and ignore the signs that tell you what's happening.

how long a worker has worked. The formula might be to give a worker a week's pay for every year worked. Thus a worker with 10 years of service would receive at least 10 weeks of pay after his or her job ended. In addition, the company would probably pay the traditional two weeks' severance pay.

If your company has a union and uses a negotiated contract, the contract most likely specifies what notice must be given, the amount of severance pay, and under what conditions an individual might be fired. For instance, most contracts say that after a probationary period a worker can be fired only for "cause." This means that your supervisor must have a good reason for letting you go, such as poor work or bad habits. The supervisor must be able to prove the reason. Most unions regard the rule of showing cause as one of the most important clauses in their contracts. It was one of the first things unions wanted when they began to gain strength. They were eager to stop abuses in which workers were fired for no good reason. If your company has a contract, you should be aware of its terms regarding dismissals and severance pay.

HAVE A PLAN OF ACTION

If you lose your job, the first thing to do is take inventory. Look around. Ask questions. What are the job opportunities in your field? Are there any jobs in your present location? Are there jobs available elsewhere?

If there are no jobs available in your area, you may want to decide to move. If jobs are not available anywhere, or if you do not want to move, you may have to decide to look for work in another field.

If you decide to change careers, take stock of your talents, training, and experience. Look for a related career in which your background and training will be useful. Pick one you think you would like.

Look for training opportunities. This could mean going back to school or joining a new apprenticeship program.

USE ALL SOURCES OF HELP

In finding your first job, you probably used either the ads in the newspapers or a state or private employment agency. Use these sources again when you are unemployed. If you do use an employment agency to help you find a job, learn what the agency's fee will be. Sometimes the employment agency will charge the fee to your new employer. Sometimes you, the worker, must pay the fee. If you must pay the fee, find out how much it will be and how it must be paid. Most fees are figured on a percentage of the wage for the new job. You can pay the fee a little at a time over a period of weeks.

Check on several employment agencies before you use them. If possible, use agencies that have helped people you know. Most agencies are honest and will be helpful. But there are always a few that may be either dishonest or so poorly run that they are useless.

Pay nothing to any employment agency until you actually have a permanent job. If an agency insists on some payment in advance, that is a sure sign that it cannot be trusted. You should not deal with such an agency.

If you must sign any agreement with an employment agency, read it carefully. Make sure it says that you owe nothing unless you get a job and keep the job for a certain time. You do not want to pay for finding a job that turns out to be temporary.

Spread the Word

Do not overlook one of the most important sources of help in finding another job: friends and

If you lose your job, have a plan of action and make use of all sources of help. (Marsha Cohen)

relatives. Some people, through a mistaken sense of pride, try not to let anyone know they are out of work and looking for a job. Nonsense! Tell the world. Spread the word. You are looking for work. Possibly a friend, relative, or neighbor will be able to steer you toward the perfect job. The more people who know you are hunting for a job, the more help you are likely to receive.

Investigate Federal Training Programs

There are many federally operated programs that train workers to enter new fields when jobs in their original fields are eliminated. You can get information about these and other federal programs from your state employment office, from the state department of education, or from your local division of vocational-adult education, which is operated by the public school system.

The Comprehensive Employment and Training Act (CETA) is a major federal law that authorizes programs to help people train for new jobs. CETA programs are administered by states, large cities, and counties. They are designed to develop job opportunites through training and education. CETA also helps people get and keep jobs for which they are trained. Check the Manpower Administration of the U.S. Department of Labor in Washington, DC, for general information about CETA.

Another important source of help is your state employment service.

UNEMPLOYMENT INSURANCE

Severance pay is not the only cushion you will have if you lose your job through no fault of your own. Under programs run by the states, *unemployment insurance* provides an unemployed worker with a weekly sum of money for a certain length of time. The amount of money and the length of time vary from state to state. Eligibility requirements also differ. In general, a worker receives about half the average weekly wage earned while working. The payments continue for at least 26 weeks. When jobs are scarce and unemployment is high, most states increase the number of weeks that a worker may collect benefits.

In some states not all workers are eligible for unemployment benefits. For example, agricultural workers, household workers, people who work for state or local governments, or teachers. Check your own situation to see if you are eligible for unemployment insurance.

Sometimes you can transfer your unemployment benefits from one state to another if you feel you must move to find work. But you must be able to show that your move from one state to another will improve your chances of getting a job.

Penalties

In most cases, you receive unemployment benefits regardless of the reason you lost your job. The only time you are not eligible for these benefits is when you lose the job through your own fault. To collect benefits, you must have worked for a certain length of time. To keep receiving the payments, you must be available for, and seeking, work. If you refuse a suitable job offer, you can lose your benefits. Here's an example:

> Julie Cox was an accountant. When her company went out of business, she began to collect unemployment payments. Then she was offered another job for which she was qualified. However, since the job was over 10 miles from her home, she turned it down. She did not like to travel that far every day. As a result, Julie was penalized. Her unemployment payments stopped for a penalty period of four weeks. Then she had to apply for payments again and wait two more weeks before she started getting them. She had trouble paying her rent and buying food.

Penalties range from suspensions of a few weeks to complete loss of payments.

Most states have a waiting period between the time you apply for benefits and the date when payments begin coming. It could be a month. It could be 10 weeks. Again, it depends on the state you are in.

All states impose penalties on persons who voluntarily quit their jobs. Such persons may have to wait longer before they become eligible for unemployment benefits. Or, they may not be eligible for benefits at all.

Filing for Benefits

To apply for unemployment benefits, go to your local unemployment insurance office at the state employment security agency. You will find it listed in the phone directory under your state labor department.

You must file a claim for unemployment insurance benefits and register for work with the employment service. You must continue to report to the office on a fixed schedule (usually every week). The state employment service will help you find another job. It will arrange interviews for you and explore all career possibilities. If you do not report to the employment office, or if you refuse to accept help in finding another job, you will be penalized. If you are penalized or denied benefits unjustly, you can demand a hearing. Again, procedures vary from one state to another.

This program of unemployment insurance is covered by federal and state funds and by a special tax that your employer must pay.

SUMMING UP

Being unemployed is frightening. But you can do many things to soften the blow and return to gainful employment. To review, you can:

1. Be sure that you get severance pay due you.
2. File for your unemployment benefits.
3. Begin a positive program of job hunting:
    a. Assess all your experience, training, and talents.
    b. Identify other careers that your background qualifies you for.
    c. Use all sources of help (want ads, employment agencies, friends).
    d. Check state and federal programs to help you retrain if necessary.

Many people who have lost their jobs unexpectedly take time to reevaluate their lives. No matter how carefully you have planned and trained, you may find that you made a mistake in choosing your career. Discovering and admitting this can be one blessing in losing a job. Being unemployed is a good time to rethink things. If it happens to you, take advantage of it. Remember that every ending can be the start of something new.

CHAPTER 79

WHEN YOU ARE INJURED ON THE JOB

The first duty of all workers is to avoid injury. You should follow your company's safety program to protect yourself and your co-workers. But even in the best situation, you might be injured while performing your job. Injuries are more likely to occur in hazardous jobs, but they can happen on any job—as Carla found out:

Carla was a key-punch operator in a modern, well-run office. The lighting was perfect, the ventilation was good, and the office was kept neat and clean. The equipment was in good repair, and the furniture was modern, without sharp edges or wooden splinters. You could not think of a safer place to work. Yet Carla suffered a job-related accident.

One day she wanted to move a filing cabinet, and she tried to do it alone. Carla wrenched her back. She was unable to work for several weeks.

KNOW WHAT TO DO

Learn what facilities your company has for taking care of an injured worker. Large manufacturing companies are likely to have a first aid station or a dispensary. Usually, a nurse will be on duty, and sometimes there is a doctor. When workers are injured, they are treated first by the company nurse or doctor.

Smaller companies may not have their own nurse or doctor. They should, however, have a standard procedure to follow when a worker is injured. Telephone numbers of the fire department, the rescue squad, an ambulance service, and the police should be posted so that the supervisor or another worker can find them quickly. Find out where these telephone numbers are listed. Usually, the company will rely on a particular doctor and make arrangements with a nearby hospital.

The first thing you should do when injured is seek aid. After the emergency has passed and the injury has been taken care of, you should report what happened to your supervisor as soon as possible. Most companies will have forms that must be filled out. These forms will ask for information about how and why the accident happened. These forms will also ask what kind of injuries were suffered.

WORKER'S COMPENSATION

If you are injured on the job, or if you get a disease related to your job, you are entitled to be paid for the time you are unable to work as a result. Equally important, your doctor and hospital bills will be paid. You receive this money or compensation under state laws known as *worker's compensation*. These laws are important to you. Before they were passed, workers who were injured on the job and were unable to work as a result suffered severe financial problems.

Compensation Laws Are Needed

Before the industrial revolution, compensation laws were not needed. The relationship between an employer and an employee was usually personal. A craftmaster would have one or two apprentices. Often they lived together. If an apprentice was injured, public opinion forced the employer to help the victim.

With the rise of the large factories, this personal relationship ended. Workers handling

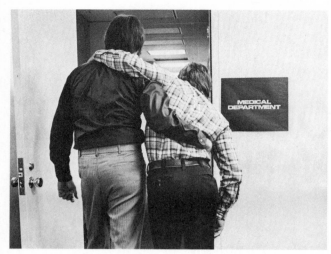

Learn what facilities your company has for taking care of an injured worker. (Marsha Cohen)

new and more dangerous equipment often had little training. Factory owners were not immediately involved. Even supervisors were often untrained. Common law determined whether an injured worker was entitled to compensation. Under common law, the employer had to meet five simple tests to avoid paying for the injuries. That is, employers only had to show that they had:

1. Provided a reasonably safe workplace
2. Provided reasonably safe tools and other equipment
3. Used reasonable care in selecting employees
4. Enforced reasonable safety rules
5. Provided reasonable instructions about the dangers of the job

Employers could show rather easily that they had met these five requirements. Furthermore, three important defenses could be used in court if a worker tried to sue. Employers could argue that:

1. They were not liable because the injury was caused by the carelessness of another worker or workers.
2. They were not liable because the worker had caused the injury through carelessness. This is known as *contributory negligence.*
3. They were not liable because the worker accepted all the obvious risks when taking the job.

In about 40 percent of all industrial accidents, both the worker and the employer are at fault. In another 30 percent, the worker is mostly at fault. Thus, 70 percent of all workers disabled on the job could not win compensation under the common law. Injured workers, needing money to pay doctor bills and feed their families, would settle for small sums of money.

Courts Uphold Laws

The first worker's compensation laws were passed in this country during the early part of the twentieth century. The very first law was passed by the federal government in 1908 for its own employees. Within a few years, states passed similar laws, not only for state employees but also for employees who worked in private industries.

At first, the laws were declared unconstitutional. The courts said that the states could not force coverage on employers and employees. They also said that employers could not be forced to pay without being personally at fault. But in 1917, the U.S. Supreme Court ruled that states may enact worker's compensation laws as part of their power to provide for the public health, safety, and welfare.

Compensation Laws Vary

The compensation laws vary from state to state. But they all have the same underlying principles. Under such laws, it is no longer necessary for a worker to prove that the employer was at fault. The employer gives up the right to use the common law to avoid paying an injured worker. The worker gives up the right to sue for unlimited amounts of money and instead accepts a specific amount.

Under the laws, your medical bills will be paid if you are injured on the job. If your injuries cause you to lose work, you will receive payments that are less than your regular wage. If you are disabled permanently, you will receive payments for the rest of your life. And if you are killed on the job, your family will receive certain benefits.

Occupational Diseases May Be Covered

In addition to injuries caused by accidents, the laws in most states cover *occupational diseases.*

The definition of an occupational disease varies from state to state—you should learn what your state law says. Occupational diseases could include lung diseases, or cancer, or other ailments caused by conditions at work.

One reason that most new workers are required to take physical examinations is to make sure that they do not have such a disease before they begin working. Thus, they cannot claim later that they got the disease on the job.

Laws Vary on How to Qualify

In order for you to qualify for payments under compensation laws, your injuries must be caused by something that is related to your employment. The trend, however, is to award benefits even if the relationship between the injury and the job is slight. In some states, laws allow for payments of benefits for injuries that are not job-related at all. Such coverage is voluntary for both the worker and the employer. Usually, both must contribute toward paying the necessary insurance premiums.

As a general rule, you will receive benefits even if the injury was your own fault, as long as it happened while you were working. In some states, you lose benefits or receive reduced ones if you violate safety rules or ignore an order. If your injury results from intentional misconduct, you can lose your benefits. And you lose benefits if you injure yourself deliberately or while you are intoxicated.

Medical expenses will be paid immediately, but compensation for lost pay usually will not be paid until several days have passed. This discourages workers from taking time off from work because of minor injuries.

There Are Two Basic Kinds of Laws

There are two basic kinds of state compensation laws: *compulsory* and *elective.* Most states have the compulsory laws. This means that your employer must take part in the plan and must pay specific compensation. A few states have elective laws. This means that your employer can elect, or choose, to provide coverage under the law. But if an employer does not provide coverage, common law cannot be used as a defense in court. Most employers elect to participate in compensation programs. If the law is elective, you also have the

In order to qualify for payments under Workers' Compensation Law, your injuries must be caused by something that is related to your job.

option of not being covered by it. But there is rarely a good reason not to accept coverage.

Some Jobs Are Not Covered

Some jobs are not covered by compensation laws, and the occupations differ from state to state. Usually, the jobs not covered are in agriculture, domestic service, and casual employment. In some states, nonhazardous occupations are not covered. At first, only hazardous occupations were covered by the compensation laws. Now the trend is to extend coverage. Often the law lets employers choose to cover jobs that are not specifically listed. If employers do not choose coverage, however, they do not lose their right to use the common law as a defense in court.

Since the occupations covered vary from state to state, it is important that you know what the law says in your state. In about one-fourth of the states, the law applies mainly to hazardous jobs. In many states, the law applies only to companies that have more than a certain number of workers. For example, in South Carolina a company is not covered by worker's compensation laws unless it has 15 employees. Georgia law sets the limit at 10 employees, while Nevada and Oklahoma set it at 2. Many states do not base exemptions on the number of employees, and so a firm with only one employee would be covered.

Minors are covered by the compensation laws, even if they are under age and working illegally. In such cases, most states impose penalties on the employer.

Certain Amounts Are Paid

The amount of money you can receive under compensation laws is usually set at a percentage of your normal weekly wage. As noted, you usually must wait for a period of several days before receiving a payment.

Medical expenses must be paid immediately, however, and half the states place no limits on the amount that can be paid. These benefits can be for hospital fees, for surgical or doctors' fees, and for the cost of necessary medical treatment. Benefits also can include the cost of rehabilitation and the cost of artificial limbs.

Most compensation acts require your employer to supply adequate medical, surgical, and hospital services if you are injured. Under the law, most employers select the physician who will treat you, although in some states you have the right to choose your physician.

Companies obey the compensation laws by buying accident insurance. The amount paid by the company depends on the size of the payroll and the number of accidents that occur. The more accidents, the more the company pays for insurance. When a worker is injured, payments come from the insurance company. The cost of the insurance is included in the price the company charges for its products or services. In this way, the cost of industrial accidents is part of the cost of operating a business. As such, the cost a company pays for insurance is passed on to consumers who use the products or services.

You Should Check Your State's Laws

Make an effort to find out about compensation laws in your state. The director of your state labor department or the industrial commission can provide information. Look in your telephone directory under the heading of your state for the telephone number and address of the nearest office.

80

WHEN YOU NEED HELP

If laws and regulations are to protect you, and if your job rights are to mean something, you must know what to do when the laws are ignored or your rights are violated. At such times, your greatest aid is an everyday object that you have used hundreds of times for hundreds of ordinary reasons: the telephone book.

TELEPHONE BOOK

This simple tool is in nearly every home. It can be found in public telephone booths, in the post offices, and in other public buildings. It usually is the first tool you use when you need to contact a state or federal official. In the telephone book you can find a telephone number to call or an address to which to write.

As you know, using the telephone book is simple. When you want to call a friend but do not know the number, you look up his or her last name. And if you want to write a letter to a friend but do not know the address, you can also get this information from the book. Most people who have telephones are listed in the telephone book. The listings are alphabetical by last name. Some people ask that their numbers not be listed. In such cases, you will have to learn the numbers and addresses for yourself—the telephone company will not give out the information.

Calling for Assistance

If your friend lives outside the area covered by the telephone directory, you then need to call for information. Each telephone book covers only a certain area, usually a city or a group of neigh-

boring towns. If you do not know the exact listing for a government agency in your area, or if the agency is in another area, call for assistance.

When calling to get a number outside your area, you need to know the area code of the location you want to call. At the front of all telephone books, there is a map of the United States that shows the area codes. When a state has more than one area code, you need to know the name of the city and its location within the state. You can determine this from a regular map. If you dial the wrong code and get a wrong number, the operator usually will be able to tell you the right code. To get the right operator for information, dial the area code and 555-1212.

To get information about a local number, you need dial only 411. (Sometimes you have to dial 1 before the 411.) Every telephone directory begins with instructions about how to get information and how to dial the operator for assistance.

Reaching Government Offices

Trying to reach a state or federal government office can be more complicated than trying to reach your friend whose last name you know. However, if you remember how the state and federal government agencies are listed, it is still simple enough.

First, all state agencies are listed under the name of the state, in its proper alphabetical position. If your state is Kansas, say, you will find state offices listed in the "K" section. There probably would be many listings under "Kansas," because many businesses will use the name of the state. When several entries have the same last name or principal name, the other names are used to decide each entry's position. Thus "Kansas Light and Power Company" would come before "Kansas, State of," because "L" comes before "S." But "Kansas Terminal Company" would come after.

In most directories, the state listings have a large heading such as "Kansas, State of." A notice such as "End of Kansas, State of" will follow all the state agencies listed.

The various departments and agencies are arranged alphabetically under the state heading. There is often a box labeled "frequently called numbers" at the head of the list.

If you want, say, the state employment service, you first would look for the listing of state offices under the name of your state. Then you would look through state listings for "Labor Department," because the employment service is in the labor department. Under "Labor Department" you will find "Employment Service" and the number. The address might be under the major heading "Labor Department," or it might be under "Employment Service," depending on whether or not all labor department offices are in the same building.

Finding federal departments and agencies is just as simple. You look in the section under the letter "U." The "U" is for "United States," and all government agencies are listed alphabetically under that heading. Generally, you need to know in which major department the agency you want is located. For wage, hour, and public contracts, you would look under "Labor Department." For information on your income tax, you would look under "Internal Revenue Service."

Since all the names (listings) are entered alphabetically, you may think that a telephone book does not need an index, or that an index would be of little use. But the index is very useful. It is located near the front of the book, along with other useful information.

There probably also will be a box of "emergency numbers" at the beginning of your telephone book. Included here are the numbers for your local police and fire departments.

Checking the Yellow Pages

The Yellow Pages, a section at the back of the telephone directory also offer much help. If you are out of work and looking for a job, you can quickly find the names of businesses and industries, listed alphabetically by the products they

make or by the services they sell. The Yellow Pages are a handy guide if a city directory is not available. (A city directory lists every home and business, usually with additional information about individuals such as their occupation. It may or may not carry telephone numbers.)

In the Yellow Pages you can also find the names, addresses, and telephone numbers of employment agencies, should you need the services of one.

UNITED STATES GOVERNMENT MANUAL

A second publication that you should know about is the United States Government Manual. You should be able to find one in most libraries, among the reference books. This is a valuable reference book for anyone who has to deal with the federal government. Today, that includes most of us, for many federal laws affect us directly.

Sometimes it is simple to find out which government agency to contact with regard to a particular need or problem. Sometimes it is difficult. When you have trouble, in most instances the U.S. Government Manual will provide you with the necessary information to solve your problems. Not only does this manual give the names, addresses, and telephone numbers of the many government agencies. It also describes the purposes and programs of many agencies. Most of the addresses listed are in Washington, DC. But when an agency or department has regional offices, all the addresses are given.

The U.S. Government Manual is updated every year. It has an easy-to-use index in the back. There is a table of contents in the front and a thumb index on the back cover.

If you think your company or labor union has done something unfair that affects you, get a copy of the manual, and look in the subject index under "Labor." There you will find the listing "Unfair Practices." Turning to the page number shown, you will find the heading "National Labor Relations Board." The main address in Washington, DC, will be given, along with main telephone numbers and the names of board members and key staff members.

In the manual, you can also read about the National Labor Relations Act and the duties of the board. There is a brief description of how to file charges and how to appeal rulings. You will find, in addition, a listing of all the field offices of the National Labor Relations Board, the offices'

The United States Government Manual is a valuable reference book for anyone who wants to contact a government agency for a particular need or problem. (Marsha Cohen)

addresses and telephone numbers, and the name of the chief official in each office.

A special section in the front of the manual can help you if you are not sure of which person you should call for your particular problem. This section, called "Guide to Government Information," tells you about other government publications that can help. It also tells you about the Freedom of Information Act, which says that information held by federal agencies must be made available to the public. (The entire act is printed in an appendix to the manual.)

Also in the "Guide to Government Information," and more closely directed to your needs, is a complete list of federal information centers throughout the country. Their addresses and toll-free numbers are given.

The U.S. Government Manual, like the telephone directory, is not a book you would want to sit down and read for enjoyment. But if you have a question about your job and want to get it answered, the manual will direct you to a source of help.

WHEN YOU ARE STUMPED

If all else fails, try contacting your elected officials—state senators and representatives or United States senators and representatives. Most officials are listed in local telephone directo-

ries. If they are not, you can get their numbers by calling information.

WHAT IS WORK?

You are about to finish this program of study. You may be ending a semester of school. Perhaps you are already working part-time or are ready to start working full-time. In any case, pause now and ask yourself this question: "What is work?"

You may think the answer is obvious. "Work is a chore, or a task, or an assignment to be done to earn money." True enough. But this definition of work does not go far enough. It reflects only the need to work for money to buy food, clothes, and shelter.

It's true that most people work because they must. But even if people did not need to work, most of them would anyway. As you have read, people also satisfy psychological needs through work. They gain recognition, find fulfillment, and get satisfaction from work. Work helps them to define their lives. It gives them a purpose. People who cannot work often become bored and restless. They want something to do. So work is more than doing a task for pay. Your work will fill the major portion of your adult life. It will, to a large extent, shape your life.

For your life to be satisfying, your work must be satisfying. And for work to be satisfying, you must enjoy it, you must know you are capable of doing it, and you must do it willingly. Even the most glamorous job can become a grating chore if it is done reluctantly.

How can you be sure of finding a satisfying job? There is no guarantee that you will. But you can learn many things that will increase your chances of building a satisfying career. That is what you have been doing in this course.

You learned about yourself and your values, the kind of lifestyle you want, and what your interests and abilities are. Use this information in the decision-making process to choose a career that fits your values, abilities, and interests.

Getting along well with others is essential in all careers for a full, satisfying life. Practice and develop the communicating and human relations skills you have read about. Use the practical information you have learned to find a job and to grow on the job. Take advantage of all the help that is available to make your career happy and successful.

What is work? To a large extent it is what you make it.

UNIT 24

Getting It All Together

1. Why do you think it is important to have a plan to follow when you are unemployed?

2. What steps might you take in seeking another job?

3. What is unemployment insurance?

4. What must you do to receive unemployment payments?

5. What is worker's compensation? How does it differ from unemployment insurance?

6. Other than accidental injury, what is covered by worker's compensation laws?

7. Under what conditions might you lose benefits even if your job is covered by worker's compensation?

INDEX